33809370

WHERE IT'S AT

in Teaching Consumer Behavior

CONSUMER BEHAVIOR

Buying, Having, and Being, Second Edition

MICHAEL R. SOLOMON, Rutgers University

Michael Solomon's fascination with consumer research and his love of being a consumer energizes *CONSUMER BEHAVIOR, Second Edition,* and is the key to the first edition's phenemonal success. He celebrates the diversity and interdisciplinary nature of the field, communicating his enthusiasm through an engaging, jargon-free writing style which students can really relate to.

Solomon's approach to consumer behavior is both open-minded and balanced. By covering the macro side including the disciplines of anthropology and sociology and the micro side, or psychology of consumer behavior — and by synthesizing theory and research with real-world applications — Solomon firmly establishes *CONSUMER BEHAVIOR, Second Edition,* as the realistic way to teach this course.

NEW To This Edition

- New and Exclusive! "The Simmons Connection" exercises and accompanying data disk using actual data from the Simmons Market Research Bureau

- New and Exclusive! "CNN Video Connections" — end-of-chapter features coordinated with video segments, on hot topics such as "sensory advertising"

- All-new chapter opening vignettes

- New "cutting-edge" topics such as semiotics, postmodernism, hyperreality, advertising resonance, and more

- New overview of consumer behavior research methods

- New chapter devoted exclusively to lifestyles includes newest lifestyle research (Ch.13)

- New Appendix of Sources of Secondary Consumer Data

- New Appendix on Careers in Consumer Research

WHERE IT'S AT

Relevant! Real! Refreshing!

Solomon Brings Consumer Behavior to Life By Focusing on Relevant Consumer Experiences

In all-new chapter opening vignettes and all through the text Solomon captures student interest with fascinating stories of consumers' experiences. He involves students in the material by making it easy for them to relate what they are learning to their own behavior. His engaging writing style, which is free of jargon and complicated models, is another major plus!

Solomon Attracts and Keeps Students' Attention with an Extensive Art Program

The second edition now makes even better use of illustrations and full-color ads, many from around the world, to demonstrate and reinforce concepts by showing students their real-world applications.

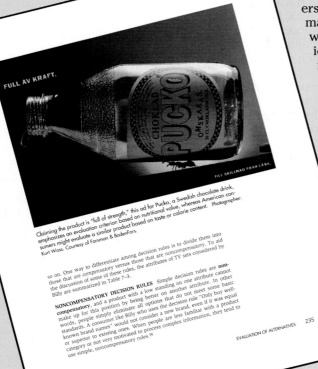

Claiming the product is "full of strength," this ad for Pucko, a Swedish chocolate drink, emphasizes an evaluation criterion based on nutritional value, whereas American consumers might evaluate a similar product based on taste or calorie content. Photographer: Kurt Wass. Courtesy of Forsman & BodenFors.

so on. One way to differentiate among decision rules is to divide them into those that are *compensatory* versus those that are *noncompensatory*. To aid the discussion of some of these rules, the attributes of TV sets considered by Billy are summarized in Table 7–3.

NONCOMPENSATORY DECISION RULES Simple decision rules are **noncompensatory**, and a product with a low standing on one attribute cannot make up for this position by being better on another attribute. In other words, people simply eliminate all options that do not meet some basic standards. A consumer like Billy who uses the decision rule "Only buy well-known brand names" would not consider a new brand, even if it was equal or superior to existing ones. When people are less familiar with a product category or not very motivated to process complex information, they tend to use simple, noncompensatory rules.[36]

EVALUATION OF ALTERNATIVES 235

Balanced! Unified!

Solomon Provides a Balanced, Unified Overview of the Entire Field

A new overview of consumer behavior research methods in Chapter 1 reviews both exploratory and conclusive techniques covering subjects ranging from auto driving to lab experiments.

Solomon Stresses Current Research on Consumers in the Marketplace

State-of-the-art research includes multidisciplinary citations from social psychology and cultural anthropology in addition to the marketing and consumer behavior literature.

Solomon Integrates The "Cutting-Edge" Topics Marketers Work With and Are Influenced By

Includes concepts and topics from many perspectives which have enriched the field of consumer behavior and which students need to know about as marketing majors, such as: semiotics, postmodernism, hyperreality, advertising resonance, constructive processing, age cohorts, and more!

will exhibit **sex-typed traits**, or characteristics that are stereotypically associated with one sex or the other. A consumer's subjective feelings about his or her sexuality are crucial as well. Unlike maleness and femaleness, masculinity and femininity are not biological characteristics. A behavior considered masculine in one culture may not be viewed as such in another. For example, the norm in the United States is that males should be "strong" and repress tender feelings ("real men don't eat quiche"), and male friends avoid touching each other (except in "safe" situations such as on the football field). In some Latin and European cultures, however, it is common for men to hug one another. Each society determines what "real" men and women should and should not do. The Bijan ad shown here interprets the contrasting ways in which women are viewed in different cultures.

SEX-TYPED PRODUCTS   Many products (other than quiche) also are sex-typed; they take on masculine or feminine attributes, and consumers often associate them with one sex or another.⁹⁰ The car, for example, has long been thought of as a masculine product. The sextyping of products is often

This ad for Bijan illustrates how sex roles identities are culturally bound by contrasting the expectations of how women should be in two different countries. *Courtesy of Bijan. Photographer Jim Koch.*

302   CHAPTER 9 • PERSONALITY, SELF-CONCEPT, AND SEX ROLES

Solomon's Expanded Focus on the Self Enhances Students' Understanding of Themselves — And Others

An expanded chapter (Ch.9) on "Personality, Self-Concept, and Sex Roles," an innovation in consumer behavior texts, provides a framework for understanding one's self, and how self-concept relates to consumption. The information on sex roles is updated with new and expanded coverage of gender differences in information processing, and gay and lesbian consumers. This chapter also includes an entire section on body image!

Solomon Stresses Relevance and Reality With a Unique New Chapter on Lifestyles!

The second edition offers a totally new chapter devoted exclusively to lifestyles (Ch. 13). Covered are: new lifestyle research, the growth of materialism in the United States and Europe (including psychographic segmentation in Eastern Europe), exporting Western culture to other countries such as China and France, and emerging lifestyle trends.

WHERE IT'S AT in Teaching Consumer Behavior

NEW! EXCLUSIVE!

"CNN Video Connection"

A unique, exclusive agreement between Allyn & Bacon and Cable News Network now allows us to offer specially edited videos to accompany specific text material. Each chapter of *CONSUMER BEHAVIOR, Second Edition*, now features a CNN video segment that directly illustrates marketing strategy and consumer behavior principles. These brief video segments (3-6 minutes) provide dynamic visual reinforcement.

Each video segment relates directly to an end-of-chapter feature, "CNN Connection," that illustrates text material and poses intriguing questions. Michael Solomon introduces each video segment to get students thinking.

A complete CNN Video User's Guide is included in the Instructor's Manual.

Hot topics include:

◆ The Museum of Modern Mythology (Ch. 1)

◆ Sensory Marketing (Ch. 2)

◆ The Weight-Loss Wars (Ch. 5)

◆ American Culture Around the World (Ch. 13)

◆ Compulsive Shopping (Ch. 17)

AT THE CUTTING EDGE

NEW! EXCLUSIVE!

"Simmons Connection"

Students Use Real Data From the Simmons Market Research Bureau

The "Simmons Connection," a new and exclusive feature to this second edition, allows students to analyze the same data used by marketing professionals to study the actual consumption patterns of different consumer segments.

An accompanying disk, found in the back of the Annotated Instructor's Edition, contains real data from the Simmons Market Research Bureau's comprehensive American household panel of over 20,000 consumers. Data files have been specially selected to accompany end-of-chapter exercises for 11 chapters.

In the end-of-chapter exercises, called "Simmons Connections," students are asked to examine

relative consumption patterns for specific segments (such as owners of motorcycles) and to draw conclusions about how marketing strategies can be tailored to target each segment's purchasing behavior. A description of these exercises and guidelines for the implementation appear in the Instructor's Section of the Annotated Instructor's Edition.

NEW! EXCLUSIVE!

WHERE IT'S AT

in Teaching Consumer Behavior

Solomon Highlights International and Multicultural Topics

- **Multicultural Dimensions** boxes, now in every chapter, examine issues related to global marketing and marketing across cultures.
- **Chapter 14** covers ethnic and religious groups in depth. In addition, the text includes many global and multicultural examples of current research on values and lifestyle segmentation, plus segments throughout on international consumer behavior.

Solomon Brings The Real World of Marketing Into The Classroom

Thought-provoking boxes in every chapter provide numerous examples of specific real-world applications of consumer behavior concepts.

- **Marketing Opportunity** boxes illustrate the potential of consumer behavior research to strengthen marketing strategy.
- **Marketing Pitfall** boxes address issues of ethics and public policy by examining marketing mistakes and ethically suspect activities.
  - **Chapter 17** includes updated material on the "dark side" of consumer behavior, such as compulsive shopping; how cultural changes will affect the future of consumer behavior; and the fascinating interrelationships between marketing activities and our perception of reality.

FIGURE 17–1 Projective Drawing to Study the Motivations Underlying the Giving of Self-Gifts Source: Based on David G. Mick, Michelle DeMoss, and Ronald J. Faber, "Latent Motivations and Meanings of Self-Gifts: Implications for Retail Management," Research Report, Center for Retailing Education and Research, University of Florida, 1990.

Figure 17–1 is available as Transparency 48.

Holiday Rituals
On holidays consumers step back from their everyday lives and perform ritualistic behaviors unique to those times.[37] Holiday occasions are filled with ritual artifacts and scripts and are increasingly cast as a time for giving gifts by enterprising marketers. Holidays also often mean big business to hotels, restaurants, travel agents, and so on. The marketing of Christmas products alone is worth about $37 billion a year.

MARKETING OPPORTUNITY

In addition to established holidays, new occasions are invented to capitalize on the need for cards and other ritual artifacts that will then have to be acquired. More than 120 million adults buy at least one greeting card in a year.[38] These cultural events often originate with the greeting card industry, which conveniently stimulates demand for more of its products. Some recently invented holidays include Secretaries' Day and Grandparents' Day.

VALENTINE'S DAY On Valentine's Day, standards regarding sex and love are relaxed or altered as people express feelings that may be hidden during

596 CHAPTER 17 • CONSUMER BEHAVIOR AND CULTURAL PROCESSES: EMERGING ISSUES

AT THE CUTTING EDGE

Outstanding Pedagogy Captures Student Attention and Builds Understanding

All-New Chapter Opening Vignettes
These graphic examples introducing chapter concepts are presented as stories about real people to whom students can relate.

Chapter Summaries
Useful for reviewing the material, they give quick overviews of the chapter material.

Key Terms
Highlighted in the text and noted for review, each term is also defined in a Glossary at the end of the text.

Consumer Behavior Challenge
Located at the end of each chapter, the *Consumer Behavior Challenge* sections provide a focus both for class discussions and for student projects. The projects are engrossing activities that will involve students in learning first-hand about consumer behavior.

Notes
Each chapter ends with an extensive bibliography of additional up-to-date references to both major journals and the popular press.

WHERE IT'S AT in Teaching Consumer Behavior

The Fully Integrated Teaching Package Starts with the Annotated Instructor's Edition.

Teaching Is Easier, More Interesting with the Annotated Instructor's Edition (AIE).
And the Simmons Connection Data Disk Is Packaged Right Inside!

Simmons Connection Instructor's Manual

Found at the beginning of the Annotated Instructor's Edition, the Manual provides easy-to-follow instructions for accessing the data disk along with a walk-through of a sample Simmons Connection exercise. The user-friendly exercises are designed to increase student involvement in the learning process. Solutions for the exercises also appear in the Manual.

Annotations Appearing in the Margins Throughout the Text Section of the AIE Help You Maximize Lecture Quality. These Blue Annotations Do Not Appear in the Student Text.

Teaching Hints These provide more information on important points, suggestions for class discussion and additional reference material on the topic.

Research Reports Summaries of recent consumer behavior research findings you can use to enrich your lectures.

Additional Examples Additional illustrations you can use to help enhance your students' comprehension of a specific topic.

Cross-Cultural Examples Illustrations of how differing cultural practices can affect consumer decisions and behavior.

International Examples Adds a contemporary dimension to your teaching by showing students how consumers behave throughout the world.

CNN Connections Helps you make the most effective use of each video by reminding you that the CNN Connections box at the end of the chapter directly corresponds to an accompanying video.

Simmons Connections Appear with Simmons Connection segments to point out the integrated Simmons Data Disk included at the back of the Annotated Instructor's Edition.

Buying, Having, and Being Indicates which articles from *Buying, Having, and Being: The Washington Post Consumer Behavior Companion, Second Edition* were specifically selected to complement the material in each chapter.

Transparency Indicates where a text figure or additional illustration is available as a color transparency acetate.

AT THE CUTTING EDGE

The Most Comprehensive Supplements Package Available for Consumer Behavior!

Instructor's Manual With CNN Video Users Guide & Transparency Masters

by Lewis Hershey and Pamela Kiecker, Texas Tech University
The Manual contains lecture outlines, teaching suggestions, suggested answers for the Consumer Behavior Challenge sections, notes for the transparency package, the CNN Video User's Guide, and an updated set of over 100 Transparency Masters that complement the text.

The CNN Video User's Guide contains a summary of the videos, preview questions with suggested answers, discussion questions with suggested answers, and project suggestions related to the video material.

CNN Videos

Keyed to the CNN Connection box at the end of each chapter, the tape contains one video segment per chapter — 17 segments in all. See page *IS-iv* for details.

Test Bank

by M. Frances Estep, Pace University
Contains more than 1500 questions — completely revised for this edition! Includes a mixture of multiple-choice, true-false, matching, and essay questions.

Computerized Test Bank

Easy to use and flexible — for IBM and compatibles.

Transparency Package

Includes both figures from the text plus many additional examples of advertising from outside the text. Many are in full-color.

Buying, Having, and Being: The Washington Post Consumer Behavior Companion, Second Edition

Washington Post Writers Group Edited by Michael R. Solomon, Rutgers University
This selection of lively and diverse articles from *The Washington Post* offers students a variety of perspectives on many of today's most controversial issues in consumer behavior. Available packaged with Solomon's *CONSUMER BEHAVIOR, Second Edition* at a special Value-Pack price.

MICHAEL R. SOLOMON

Rutgers University

SECOND EDITION

Annotated Instructor's Edition

Consumer

Behavior

Buying, Having, and Being

Allyn and Bacon
Boston
London
Toronto
Sydney
Tokyo
Singapore

Editor-in-Chief, Business: Rich Wohl
Senior Series Editor: Suzy Spivey
Senior Developmental Editor: Judith S. Fifer
Editorial Assistant: Karen Joseph
Text Designer: Melinda Grosser, for *silk*
Editorial-Production Services: Sylvia Dovner, Technical Texts
Editorial-Production Administrator: Elaine Ober
Electronic Manuscript Manager: Andrew Walker
Electronic Page Layout: Gayle A. Robertson
Manufacturing Buyer: Megan Cochran
Prepress Buyer: Linda Cox
Cover Coordinator: Linda K. Dickinson

Copyright © 1994, 1992 by Allyn and Bacon
A Division of Paramount Publishing
160 Gould Street
Needham Heights, Massachusetts 02194

In regard to the software disk accompanying this text, the publisher assumes no responsibility for damages, errors, or omissions,
without any limitation, which may result from the use of the program or the text.

ISBN 0-205-15370-4

Printed in the United States of America

10 9 8 7 6 5 4 3 2 1   96 95 94 93

Brief Contents

INSTRUCTOR'S SECTION

Introduction to
the Annotated
Instructor's Edition

I was motivated to write the first edition of this book for two reasons. First, I was puzzled by the complaint I heard from students and colleagues that the consumer behavior course was among the most boring and unrewarding in the marketing curriculum. As a consumer researcher—and a consumer!—I had a great deal of trouble understanding this. *Everyone* can relate to consumer experiences, whether these involve agonizing over a new pair of shoes, choosing a new CD, selecting a college, or getting married. To me, consumer behavior is the "juice" in marketing; it reflects the dynamic, intriguing aspects of the (at times inscrutable) marketplace.

Furthermore, while some researchers tend to see the field as somehow "removed" from the day-to-day practice of marketing, I view the study of consumers as absolutely essential to sound marketing decisions. If you don't understand people, how can you possibly hope to satisfy their needs? Consumer behavior is fascinating, and we owe it to our students to share with them the excitement experienced by those of us who do research and teach in the field.

Second, I was frustrated by the failure of many existing texts to adequately reflect and celebrate the diversity and interdisciplinary nature of the field of consumer behavior. Our literature has been enriched by work emanating from many perspectives, from cognitive psychology to semiotics. I felt strongly that our students should benefit from these perspectives, so I set about to integrate them with traditional approaches. I found it helpful to develop the "wheel of consumer behavior" as a pedagogical device to underscore the complex—and often inseparable—intersections between the individual consumer and his or her social realities.

The feedback I received from reviewers, colleagues, and students on the attempt to ground consumer behavior in the daily lives of students has been quite positive. Indeed, many colleagues have commented to me that the topics I included were what they *really* talked about in class anyway! I have been extremely gratified by this response, and I've incorporated many constructive suggestions into the second edition. I'd like to take this opportunity to enumerate some of the changes and refinements in this new version:

Major Themes

Current Research on Consumers in the Marketplace

As in the first edition, the second edition of this book stresses the complex and interdependent relationships between marketing stimuli and the day-to-day social lives of consumers. Discussion of consumer behavior phenomena is multidisciplinary and includes state-of-the-art research citations from social psychology, sociology, cultural anthropology, and other related disciplines in addition to the marketing and consumer behavior literature. Brand new chapter opening vignettes in this edition present scenarios based on the experiences of consumers in realistic situations that arouse students' interest and foster identification.

Global and Multicultural Consumer Behavior

Consumer behavior phenomena transcend the focus found in many competing texts on the American experience. Examples of research on values, lifestyle segmentation, and so on from around the world are included in the text (in addition to several segments devoted exclusively to international consumer behavior). In addition, each chapter features a box called "Multicultural Dimensions," which highlights a relevant aspect of consumer behavior that affects some ethnic or nationality segment. The book also contains a large number of advertisements from around the world.

Ethics and Consumer Behavior

Unlike many texts that present largely uncritical accounts of ways marketers try to persuade consumers, this text also highlights some negative effects of the marketing process on consumers. For example, the section on body image discusses consumers' motivations to engage in unhealthy behaviors such as binge eating. Every chapter contains special features called "Marketing Pitfalls," which discuss dangerous or ethically suspect marketing practices. In addition, the book features a major section on the "dark side" of consumer behavior in Chapter 17 that includes discussions of compulsive shopping, gambling, shoplifting, and vandalism.

Consumer Behavior and Marketing Strategy

The majority of our students who take this course will seek to use the knowledge they have gleaned about consumers to improve their performance as marketers. I have tried very hard to ground seemingly abstract, "ivory tower" concepts in reality—to show how consumer behavior constructs are used (and misused) in the real, rough-and-tumble world of marketing. Numerous applications examples are provided to underscore the connections between consumer behavior research and marketing practice. Additional examples are provided for your benefit in the annotated margin notes throughout the

Annotated Instructor's Edition. Finally, each chapter contains special features labeled "Marketing Opportunity" that highlight some real-world application of a consumer behavior construct.

New Features

Integrated Videos: The CNN Connection

Each chapter features a video segment with material from CNN that directly illustrates a topic in the text. The video package reflects Allyn and Bacon's exclusive arrangement with CNN for use of CNN's business programs and material. These videos are intentionally designed to be *brief* (3–6 minutes) supplements that provide visual reinforcement for lectures. This brevity responds to the requests from many instructors for relevant, *integrated* video material that does not sacrifice valuable class time. Each video segment is accompanied by an end-of-chapter feature, CNN Connection, that presents a short case derived from a CNN news story and a still photo from the actual video. Each video segment is introduced by me. The complete CNN Video User's Guide included in the *Instructor's Manual* provides a summary of each segment, additional Discussion Questions with suggested answers, and Suggested Projects that allow student to follow-up on the video material on their own.

The Simmons Connection

This new feature allows students to analyze the same data used by marketing professionals to study the actual consumption patterns of different consumer segments. An accompanying disk provided with the Annotated Instructor's Edition contains real data from the Simmons Market Research Bureau's comprehensive American household panel of over 20,000 consumers. Portions of these data, made available through an exclusive agreement between Simmons and Allyn and Bacon, are excerpted on the disk to correspond to exercises for eleven chapters. These end-of-chapter exercises are described in the text in the Simmons Connection feature. Students are asked to examine relative consumption patterns for relevant segments (e.g., gender or ethnic groups) and to draw conclusions about how marketing strategies should be targeted to the purchase behavior of these segments. A description of these exercises and guidelines for their implementation appear in the Instructor's Section of the Annotated Instructor's Edition.

Buying, Having, and Being: The Washington Post Consumer Behavior Companion, Second Edition

A student supplement, *Buying, Having, and Being: The Washington Post Consumer Behavior Companion*, Second Edition, is a collection of articles from the Style and Business sections of *The Washington Post*. These articles provide students with readings that broaden their understanding of the many connections between textual material and the real world. To aid their in use, reference to specific relevant readings are provided in the Annotated Instructor's Edition. These references also appear in the Table of Contents of the student's edition to indicate the set of readings that is appropriate to each chapter. The *Consumer Behavior Companion* is available at half price when ordered and shrinkwrapped with the student text.

Appendix I: Sources of Secondary Consumer Data

This feature provides a listing of secondary data compiled by private and government agencies. It allows students to get a start in accessing aggregate data that will be valuable to them for reports as well as for future reference when they embark on marketing careers.

Appendix II: Careers in Consumer Research

Students are often unaware of the many possibilities available to them in the field of consumer research. This new feature provides an overview of possible career paths, and it also includes some suggested references for further exploration.

Chapter Openers

Each chapter is kicked off with a new opening vignette that chronicles a consumer situation from the point of view of the end consumer. These are designed to be relevant and engaging to students, allowing them to see how their daily lives are affected by marketers and consumer behavior phenomena.

Expanded Art Program

The second edition contains numerous color ads and photos, many of them new to this edition, to illustrate important points and hold the student's interest.

Up-to-Date References

This new edition continues in the tradition of the first edition by including up-to-the-minute reference citations. Numerous citations from 1992 and 1993 have been added from both the academic and popular press to keep the material fresh and relevant.

Using the AIE

Types of Annotations

Each chapter contains a large number of margin notes to help instructors in maximizing lecture quality. The various types of annotations are as follows.

- *Teaching Hints* provide suggestions for class discussion and/or point the instructor to additional reference material on the topic in the research literature.

- *Research Reports* provide a summary of recent consumer behavior research findings that can be referred to in lectures.

- *Additional Examples* give the instructor one or several other illustrations of how marketers have addressed the relevant consumer behavior topic.
- *Cross-Cultural Examples* provide illustrations of how the phenomenon being discussed has been addressed by marketers targeting ethnic groups of consumers in the United States.
- *International Examples* provide illustrations of how the phenomenon being discussed has been addressed by marketers outside of the United States.
- *CNN Connection* annotations remind the instructor that the CNN Connection feature at the end of each chapter directly corresponds to an accompanying video that expands on the contents of the feature.
- *Simmons Connection* annotations refer the instructor to the Simmons Data Disk that is found inside the back cover of the Annotated Instructor's Edition.
- *Buying, Having, and Being* annotations refer the instructor to the readings in *Buying, Having, and Being: The Washington Post Consumer Behavior Companion*, Second Edition, selected to correspond to each chapter.
- *Transparency* annotations refer the instructor to supplementary acetates provided to reinforce points made in the text.

Major Updates and Changes from the First Edition

Chapter 1 provides an introduction to the field of consumer behavior. It provides updated information on the process of target marketing and emphasizes the importance of defining distinct and usable consumer segments. Updates include a new focus on segmenting strategies of fashion magazines, as well as discussions of such segments as the military market and the disabled. The section detailing the impact of marketing on consumers contains more information on ethical issues and social responsibility, including added emphasis on consumerism and public policy. In addition, a new section has been added to provide students with an overview of consumer behavior research methods. This section reviews both exploratory and conclusive techniques used by consumer researchers, covering subjects ranging from autodriving to lab experiments.

Chapter 2 covers perception. Updated material on corporate identity campaigns and on trademark protection is included. The discussion of marketing symbolism and semiotics has been expanded to include postmodernism and hyperreality.

Chapter 3 covers motivation and consumer involvement. New information is included on strategies to increase consumer involvement, with a new Multicultural Dimensions box featuring a consumer situation in Eastern Europe.

In *Chapter 4*, the discussion of learning and memory has been sharpened. In particular, distinctions among types of reinforcement have been clarified (e.g., negative reinforcement versus punishment). New research on the role of memory in consumers' receptivity toward pioneering brands and novel advertising executions is covered, as is emerging work on autobiographical memories.

In *Chapter 5*, the treatment of attitudes has been reorganized. The chapter now begins by showing the relevance of attitude research to social marketing and then goes on to focus on how attitude formation is influenced by the hierarchy of effects.

Chapter 6 expands upon the current usage of such promotional strategies as celebrity endorsements and infomercials. Fear appeals are illustrated by a discussion of the marketing of guns to women. The section on the literary construction of persuasive communications is expanded, with the inclusion of new work on the effects of advertising resonance.

The section on the consumer as a decision maker has been reorganized to accommodate instructors' suggestions. Chapter 7 begins with a focus on individual consumer decision making, while Chapter 8 expands this discussion to include the many decisions that are made jointly or by families. *Chapter 7* includes updated material on procedural learning, while *Chapter 8* features a more detailed treatment of demographic variables related to household composition (including the growing singles market) and an updated discussion of the family life cycle.

The first edition featured an entire chapter that was devoted to the self, personality, and sex roles, and this innovation is further refined in the new *Chapter 9*. Updated information on gender differences in information processing is included, as is an expanded treatment of both gay and lesbian consumers.

Chapter 10, which focuses on situational factors and purchasing activities, has been reorganized. It now begins with antecedent states (e.g., usage context and time pressure), continues with a focus on the purchase environment—including the shopping environment and sales interactions—and concludes with such postpurchase issues as consumer satisfaction and product recycling.

Chapter 11 illustrates the power of reference groups with a new focus on bikers. The section on word-of-mouth now includes a discussion of consumer boycotts. Expanded coverage is given to market mavens and surrogate consumers.

Chapter 12, which focused on social class, has now been significantly expanded to include a more general treatment of economic influences on consumer behavior. Special emphasis is given to the effect of consumer confidence on discretionary spending.

Chapter 13 is a new chapter devoted exclusively to lifestyles. In addition to new lifestyle research (including psychographic segmentation in Eastern Europe), the chapter discusses the growth of materialism in the United States and Europe. It also covers the issue of exporting Western culture to other countries such as China and France. The chapter also reviews emerging lifestyle trends.

In *Chapter 14*, the treatment of ethnic and religious groups is updated to include current demographic trends. In particular, Hispanic-American segments are more precisely defined.

Chapter 15 expands the previous coverage of age cohorts and geographic segmentation. In particular, students will find new material on the somewhat cynical outlook of "Baby Busters" (or "Generation X") highly relevant. More information is also included on the college student market, as well as on market applications of geodemography (e.g., PRIZM).

The final two chapters of the text have been entirely redone. *Chapter 16* examines how consumer culture is created by marketers, and how the products that emanate from the marketing system diffuse throughout society and are adopted by consumers. This discussion considers how cultural values help to determine the acceptance or rejection of a product and how this dynamic varies across cultures. This emphasis on cultural factors also includes expanded discussions of popular culture versus high culture, the marketing concept as applied to entertainment and aesthetic products, and the fashion system.

Chapter 17 concludes with a focus on how our everyday lives as consumers are affected by marketing and cultural variables. It begins by considering how cultural changes will affect the future of consumer behavior. It includes such topics as sacred and profane consumer behavior, myths and rituals, and offers updated material on the "dark side" of consumer behavior (e.g., compulsive shopping). The chapter concludes with new material bearing on the fascinating interrelationships between marketing activities and our perceptions of mundane reality.

Supplements

The following supplements are available to text adopters.

- *Instructor's Manual* by Professor Pamela Kiecker of Texas Tech University and Professor Lewis Hershey. The *Manual* contains lecture outlines, teaching suggestions for the Consumer Behavior Challenge sections in the text, notes for the transparency package, additional transparency masters created for the text by Professor Hershey, and the CNN Video User's Guide created by Professor Michael R. Solomon.

- *Test Bank* by Professor M. Frances Estep of Pace University. The *Test Bank* contains more than 1600 questions, all rewritten for this edition. Items include multiple-choice, true–false, matching, and short essay questions, all page-referenced to the text.

- *Computerized Test Bank* using the Allyn and Bacon Test Manager system, for use with IBM or IBM-compatible PCs. The Allyn and Bacon Test Manager allows you to create your own customized tests from the questions in the test bank, to edit the questions, and to add your own questions.

- *Transparencies*, including both figures from the text and many additional advertising examples from outside the text. Many of these are in full color.

- *Buying, Having, and Being: The Washington Post Consumer Behavior Companion*, Second Edition. A collection of articles from the Style and Business sections of *The Washington Post* chosen to complement the material presented in each chapter. The articles are annotated in the Annotated Instructor's Edition, and are also noted in the Table of Contents of the student version for students' benefit.

- *CNN Video* segments that are the subject of the CNN Connection feature at the end of every chapter. All segments were selected by the author, who introduces each CNN Connection on the tape. A CNN Video User's Guide, containing a summary of the videos, preview questions with suggested answers, discussion questions with suggested answers, and project suggestions related to the video material, is included in the *Instructor's Manual.*

- *The Simmons Connection Data Disk* containing actual data provided by the Simmons Market Research Bureau to accompany the interactive exercises, written by Basil Englis of Rutgers University, in the Simmons Connections features. The data disk is provided bound into the back of the Annotated Instructor's Edition. Students can access the data on an IBM-compatible PC, using Lotus, Excel, or Quattro. A manual is provided in the Instructor's Section of the Annotated Instructor's Edition to aid in the use of the Simmons Data Disk and the Simmons Connection exercises. A special introduction in the student text provides information to students on how to load and use the disk in order to complete the Simmons Connection exercises.

Acknowledgments

I am grateful for the many helpful comments on how to improve the first and second editions that were provided by my peer reviewers. Special thanks go to:

Ishmael Akkah, Wayne State University

Laurel Anderson, Arizona State University–West

Sharon Beatty, University of Alabama at Tuscaloosa

James Cagley, University of Tulsa

Douglas Allen Cords, California State University, Fresno

Bettina Cornwell, Memphis State University

M. Frances Estep, Pace University

S.J. Garner, Eastern Kentucky University

Ronald Goldsmith, The Florida State University

Cathy Goodwin, University of Manitoba

Ronald Hill, Villanova University

Nathan Himelstein, Essex County College

Carol Kaufman, Rutgers University–Camden

Robert Kleine, Arizona State University

James Leigh, Texas A&M University

Brian Lofman, Central Connecticut State University

Patricia Manninen, North Shore Community College

Lee Meadow, Salisbury State University

Alan Miller, Tennessee State University

Bruce Newman, DePaul University

A. Nancy Panos Schmitt, Westminster College of Salt Lake City

Carol Scott, University of California–Los Angeles

Gail Tom, California State University, Sacramento

Melissa Martin Young, University of Utah

Mary Zimmer, University of Georgia

George Zinkhan, University of Houston

Extra special thanks are also due to the preparers of the supplements: Lewis Hershey and Pamela Kiecker of Texas Tech University for preparation of the *Instructor's Manual;* M. Frances Estep of Pace University for completely revising the *Test Bank;* and Lewis Hershey for the transparency masters. Additional thanks go to my colleague Basil Englis of Rutgers University for preparation of the Simmons Connection database exercises and their accompanying student and instructor materials.

Several practical data-oriented exercises have been designed for selected chapters in the text. These exercises are designed to give students some hands-on experience with the sort of data that marketers use to better understand the behavior of consumers. Each exercise is keyed to examples and concepts covered in the chapter in which it appears. There is also a computer disk that contains real market data. In order to "solve" the various problems posed in these exercises, you will need to access the data contained on the disk. The exercises and data file are "user-friendly" and will increase your involvement in the learning process. Most of the exercises relate directly to the opening vignette of the chapter in which they are assigned. You may wish to reread the vignette before you begin working on an exercise.

The data come from a widely used *syndicated* data service: The Simmons Study of Media & Markets. This very extensive study includes data on 800 product and service categories. A panel of 22,406 adult Americans provides the data that make up the Simmons database. The real value of this database is that it allows marketers to look at patterns of buying behavior as a function of a wide array of consumer characteristics, including demographics (age, education, income, race, and so on) and psychographics (attitudes, self-concept, buying style, and so on).

The Simmons Study of Media & Markets is conducted annually and the results are tabulated into 34 separate volumes that are offered as Simmons products. Additional tabulations are prepared on a custom basis for individual clients. Simmons also conducts studies of special groups: For example, CompPro is a study of computer professionals, STARS focuses on teens between twelve and nineteen years old, and KIDS focuses on those younger than twelve. For the exercises in your text, Simmons has extracted portions of its 1992 database and provided summary data in the form of spreadsheets that contain the critical information needed to work on each exercise. Although Simmons provides a great deal of information at the *brand level,* for most of the exercises the data have been aggregated to the product category level.

In order to use the data from the Simmons disk, you will need access either to a DOS or Macintosh computer *and* a standard spreadsheet program such as Lotus, Excel, Quattro, or comparable program. The files are saved on the disk in what is called a "WKS" format, which is a generic format for spreadsheets. This means that any standard spreadsheet program should have no problem reading the information from the disk. Since the disk itself is already a DOS disk, DOS users can access the files with no prior translation. If you are using your own computer and the computer has a hard drive, then you should first copy all of the files from the floppy disk onto the computer's hard drive.

If you are using a Macintosh computer, you will need to run a utility program called "Apple File Exchange," which is an Apple Computer system program that is currently bundled with all Macintosh computers. All system 6.0.5 and up users have received this program. If you do not have this program, you can obtain it either through your local Macintosh Users Group or directly through Apple. The following instructions apply whether you are copying the files onto another floppy (in Macintosh format) or onto a hard drive (only the destination changes). In order to translate the files, first open the Apple File Exchange icon. Then insert the Simmons disk into your floppy drive. The dialog box will show the Simmons files on the right-hand portion of the screen. Select all of the Simmons data files and click on the "Translate" button. The next dialog box will ask how you want the files translated—just select the format that matches your spreadsheet program.

A total of 14 files are on the data disk. Some files are titled "Chap#" to indicate the chapter in which you will find related Simmons exercises. The other three files, labeled "Self," "Style," and "Media," are general reference files that may come in handy for several of the exercises. You should open several of the files and browse through them to familiarize yourself with the kinds of information they contain. Note that it will be much easier to browse through spreadsheets if you learn how to have the spreadsheet program keep the row and column labels visible on the screen. Although the method for doing this varies from program to program, most have this capability.

The example below will help you understand the data you will find in the spreadsheet files. Like the actual Simmons data files on your disk, this sample spreadsheet contains a cross-tabulation of data: columns by rows. Each bit of data is entered in a cell, which is the intersection of a row and a column. In the sample, three magazines (columns) are broken down by the gender of the reader (rows). For each row item, the Simmons spreadsheet files contain three pieces of information. The first is the actual number of respondents that fit the characteristics defined by variables given in the column and row labels. In the sample, the cell at the intersection of the TOTAL row and the TOTAL column shows the total number of respondents, which is 22,406. At the intersection of TOTAL row and *American Health* column, the cell shows a value of 633, which means that of the entire sample, 633 respondents reported that they are readers of *American Health*.

The second entry for each row variable in a Simmons spreadsheet file is identified by a row label of (000). This number is a projection based on the raw count and the total U.S. population. It lets marketers immediately project the Simmons sample values onto the total U.S population and thereby estimate total potential market size. In the sample given here, if the Simmons panel were projected onto all U.S. consumers there would be 2,770,000 readers of *American Health* magazine.

The last entry for each row variable—Index—is extremely valuable for marketers because it tells them whether a particular consumer group is more or less likely than all members of a particular "universe" of consumers to consume a particular product (or product category). For example, if we are interested in magazine preferences, we would consider all adult magazine readers as our universe. Each Simmons file identifies the universe of consumers that form the basis for these index values.

	B	C	D	E	F	G
13				MAGAZINES	MAGAZINES	
14				-Total	-Total	MAGAZINES
15				Audience:	Audience:	-Total
16				AMERICAN	AMERICAN	Audience:
17	ROW	CELL	TOTAL	HEALTH	PHOTO	AUDUBON
18						
19	TOTAL	#RESP	22406	633	246	452
20		(000)	184117	2770	875	1416
21		INDEX	100	100	100	100
22						
23	SEX:MALE	#RESP	11499	260	185	261
24		(000)	88034	811	662	777
25		INDEX	100	61	156	114
25						
27	SEX:FEMALE	#RESP	10907	373	61	191
28		(000)	96083	1959	214	639
29		INDEX	100	135	46	87

For any variable defined in the row labels—say, gender of reader—an index value of 100 means that a particular group of consumers was no more or less likely to be a reader of *American Health* than the total universe (all adults). In the sample, if you look at the intersection of Male and *American Health,* you will see an index value of 61, which means that adult males are 39% less likely (100 – 61) than all adults to read this magazine. In contrast, females are 35% more likely (135 – 100) to read *American Health.* Notice how the index values for male and female readers differ for *American Health* (higher female readership) and *American Photo* (higher male readership). By comparison, the difference in preference for *Audubon* magazine by gender is not nearly so extreme. The index values are computed using the projected population values.

Because the index values are a direct comparison of a market segment's behavior with a relevant universe of consumers, they provide extremely useful information for marketers. The index values are a particularly useful tool in defining market segments whose tastes, preferences, and past consumption behavior are particularly well-suited for a particular product or product category.

The following table lists the Simmons data files and identifies the column and row variables in each file.

File Name	Columns	Rows
Chap1	*Subset of Magazines:* Seventeen Mademoiselle Harper's Bazaar Ladies' Home Journal Vogue Elle	*Subset of Demographics:* Age Education Occupation Sex
Chap4	*Credit Cards Used:* Last 12 months Last 30 days Number of times used	*Subset of Buying Style:* Ad believer Cautious Economy minded Experimenter Impulsive Planner
Chap5	*Environmental Issues:* 17 environmental issues Willingness to pay more taxes	*Subset of Demographics:* Age Education Occupation *Buying Style:* Ecologist
Chap6	*Single Products:* Disposable diapers Disposable plates Tobacco (all) Veal Weed killer Fur jackets/coats—real Fur jackets/coats—synthetic	*Environmental Issues* (all) *Buying Style:* Ecologist *Demographics:* Age
Chap8	*Shopping Influence—Male:* Automobiles Household furnishings Food shopping	*Demographics:* Size of household Number of employed adults Education Age *Psychographics:* Broadminded Creative

File Name	Columns	Rows
		Dominating
		Efficient
Chap9	Health-Care Products:	Self-Concept (all)
	Contact lenses	
	Diet control	
	Doctor's visits (general check-ups)	
	Hearing aids	
	Travel:	
	Health or resort spa	
Chap11	Motorcycles:	Demographics:
	Most recent bought	Age (18–34 year olds only)
	(new/used)	Income (HH)
	Make	Education— < HS, HS
	Engine size—less than	grad, < college grad,
	399 cc, 400–1000 cc,	college grad
	more than 1000 cc	Marital status
	Sports, Leisure:	
	Motorcycling	
Chap12	Malt Beverages & Wines:	Demographics:
	Wine by the case	Index of Social Position
	Distilled Spirits:	HHI— > $40,000
	Spirits by the case	Occupation
	Travel:	
	Passports	
	Theme parks	
	Coffee, Tea:	
	Espresso/Cappuccino	
	Int'l flavored instant	
Chap13	Distilled Spirits:	Demographics:
	Jack Daniels	Occupation
	Absolut Vodka	Income
	The Glenlivet Single-Malt Scotch	Index of Social Position
	Malt Beverages & Wine:	
	Champagne (aggregated all brands)	
	Malt liquor	
	New Autos:	
	BMWs (aggregate all models)	
	Trans Ams/Camaros	
	Mini-vans (aggregate all brands)	
Chap14	Tobacco:	Race:
	Cigarettes	Black, white, Asian
	Cigars	Spanish/Hispanic
	Malt Beverages & Wine:	Demographics:
	Malt liquor	Locality type
	Dry beer	Geographic region
	General Foods:	
	Rice/rice dishes	
	Pets:	
	Cat/dog ownership	
Chap17	Travel:	Buying Style (all)
	Theme parks	Self-Concept (all)
	Books, Discs, etc.:	
	Digital audio tape	
	Surround sound decoder	
	Cellular, car or portable phone	

continued

File Name	Columns	Rows
	Laser disc player	
	Interactive computer services	
	Banking:	
	Home banking by computer	
Media	*Magazines:*	*Demographics:*
	A random set of magazines	*
Style	*Buying Style* (all)	*
Self	*Self-Concept* (all)	*

*The three general reference files all use the same set of demographic variables: Age, Sex, HHI, Education, Race, and Marital Status.

Chapter 1 Data File: Magazine Readers

Although the data file contains information about education and occupation, it is really age of the reader that discriminates among the various magazines listed in the exercise. The following table of index values is taken from the data file for Chapter 1.

Age	Elle	Harper's Bazaar	Ladies' Home Journal	Mademoiselle	Seven- teen	Vogue
18–24	292	247	45	286	376	282
25–34	115	75	96	115	53	113
35–44	95	92	119	87	118	79
45–54	50	93	118	58	60	68

These readership figures by age of reader show that 18–24 year olds are more likely to read *Elle, Harper's Bazaar, Mademoiselle, Seventeen,* and *Vogue* than the average reader. Readership drops off with increasing age for all of the magazines except *Ladies' Home Journal,* which is more popular with 35–54 year olds.

Because there is such a strong preference among 18–24 year olds, it is difficult to use the other demographic measures of education and occupation. Many of these readers have not yet completed their education and/or begun to work in their eventual careers.

The breakdown by sex of reader shows that these are magazines that are far more likely to appeal to (and be read by) women as compared to men.

Note: Instructors can set up the discussion by asking students to consider how marketers might use this sort of information to better understand the interests and habits of consumers.

Chapter 4 Data File: Credit Card Users

Since the question for this exercise is framed in terms of heavy versus light credit card users, students have some flexibility in how they may define these groups. However, the sharpest differences should emerge when comparing heavy users (more than 20 occasions per month) with the lightest users (1 to 5 occasions per month).

A comparison of index values of heavy and light users shows that Cautious, Experimenter, and Impulsive buying styles are the most different between these two user groups. For all three, heavy credit card users have higher index values.

Buying Style	More Than 20 Times/Month	1–5 Times/Month	Difference
Cautious	118	105	13
Experimenter	105	87	18
Impulsive	117	102	15

Most students will find it easy to understand why Experimenter, and Impulsive buying styles would be associated with heavy credit card use. But, the higher value for the Cautious buying style consumers is less straightforward. The discussion can focus on the fact that planned purchases can be transacted as readily with credit cards as can impulsive purchases.

Buying style can also be used to discuss the rewarding and punishing aspects of credit cards. Although Impulsive and Cautious buyers are more likely to be heavy credit card users, the Impulsive group may find it punishing when they receive the month-end bill while the Cautious group may not (since they know what to expect).

Note: This exercise can be expanded by having students relate these buying styles to demographic characteristics. They can use the reference file titled "Style" to do this.

Chapter 5 Data File: Green Marketing

Note: Since the exercises for Chapters 5 and 6 both focus on the Green Movement, students can be encouraged to use the data from both files for these exercises.

A good way to set up this exercise is to start a discussion before students work on the exercise. Ask students to give their own perceptions of consumers who are environmentally conscious—older versus younger consumers, males versus females, and so on. Many students will assume that younger consumers are more sensitive to environmental issues, but the Simmons data show that concern about the environment is greater among older consumers—the middle of the life cycle seems to be the low point for concern over the environment.

Age Group	Index Value Averaged Across Environmental Issues (Agree Columns)
18–24	93
25–34	88
35–44	97
45–54	101
55–64	112
64 +	117

Educational level is generally unrelated to environmental attitudes. All educational groups show index values that are very close to the population norm of 100.

Note: By averaging the index values for the environmental attitude items, students can easily compare the various demographic categories. They should use the columns that reflect agreement with statements supporting the tenets of the Green Movement.

Chapter 6 Data File: Politically Sensitive Products

The focus of this exercise is on attitude–behavior consistency. Do supporters of the Green Movement exhibit consumption behavior that is consistent with their attitudes? A positive answer to this question should be reflected in lower index values for "politically sensitive" products among adherents of the Green Movement.

And, indeed, the index values for those who agree that products that pollute the environment should be banned are higher for products such as disposable diapers than the index values for those who disagree that such products ought to be banned. The same pattern is found for disposable plates and weed killers.

In contrast, consumption of real fur coats in not different between these groups. But, environmentally minded consumers are much more likely to use synthetic fur coats.

Age by itself does not provide a very useful demographic breakdown for these products. The instructor may use this idea to introduce the notion that some consumption patterns are heavily influenced by one's position in the family life cycle.

Note: Students can refer back to the data in the Chapter 5 file and consider demographic patterns that relate to these consumer groups. This exercise can also be expanded by encouraging students to examine tobacco products. While these may not be environmental polluters in the narrow sense, they are increasingly viewed as harmful products for the user and for others in the immediate environment. Generally, ecologically minded consumers are less likely to use tobacco products—except for the "roll-your-own" and pipe categories.

Chapter 8 Data File: Gender-Based Purchasing Decisions

Note: This file contains a breakdown of male-influence questions into four categories of influence—"a lot," "some," "a little," and "none." For the most part, the discussion can focus on the columns giving the data for respondents saying that males have "a lot" of influence.

It is no surprise that male influence is highest for automobile purchases and lowest for food purchases. And, there are some interesting patterns in these data. For example, the instructor can point out that as family size increases beyond two people, male influence on food purchases declines, while male influence increases for automobiles and furnishings. These findings may indicate an increased separation of roles as consumers become parents.

The patterns of male influence are not very different as a function of educational level.

Male influence remains high for automobiles and home furnishings for the psychographic breakdown by self-concept items. However, male influence is higher for food products among creative and broadminded consumers.

The data can also be discussed in terms of the characteristics of the product categories—automobiles and home furnishings are durable, high ticket items while food products are relatively inexpensive and an unsatisfactory purchase is not as difficult to remedy. Males have traditionally occupied the role of "bread-winner" and so should be expected to exert greater influence for high-ticket products. This can lead to a discussion of how (or if) these patterns of influence are changing in today's American families. Students can also consider the patterns of influence that might be found in other cultures.

Chapter 9 Data File: Consumers' Self-Concepts

Although there are only five product categories, it may be helpful to suggest that students average the index values across products to make it easier to compare the different "self-concept" groups. The top half of the file shows the data for respondents who "agree" that each self-concept item is characteristic of themselves. The bottom half shows the data for respondents who "disagree" with each item. So, for example, someone who disagrees with the item Intelligent is really saying that they view themselves as Not Intelligent.

Note: Hearing aids are a more age-related product than the other products listed in the data file. Students should be encouraged to compare their conclusions when this product is included in the set with their conclusions when they do not include hearing aids.

One way to generate a self-concept profile is to look at the average index values. Respondents who characterize themselves as Amicable (112), Refined (111), and Not Reserved (112) are all more than 10% more likely that all adults to use these products. (Hearing aids were omitted from these computations.)

On the other hand, respondents who display a somewhat negative self-concept by their responses to the following items are also much less likely than average to use the products listed in this file: Not Efficient (88), Not Intelligent (69), Not Kind (71), Not Self-Assured (87), Not Sociable (70), and Not Trustworthy (65).

To the extent that self-concept may be affected by how one feels about one's physical attractiveness, it is somewhat surprising that the index values are as low as they are for the "negative" self-concept items. To the extent that products which enhance physical appearance have a positive effect on self-concept, this group may represent a particularly important market for such products. The class can discuss how they would approach marketing to consumers with poor self-concepts.

Chapter 11 Data File: Motorcycle Ownership

In order to profile motorcycle preferences among the 18–34 year olds, students can compute percentages for each brand by using the raw count for each brand in the rows for 18–34 year olds against the raw count at the top of each brand column.

These percentages show that 18–34 year olds are the largest market segments for Suzuki (54%) and Kawasaki (48%), followed by Yamaha (44%), Harley-Davidson (40%), and Honda (39%). Only 25% of BMW owners are in this age group.

By looking at the index values under the Harley-Davidson column students can discover that a peak in ownership occurs for those who have had three years of college, but not higher. And, the index values for higher income groups support the general notion of a RUB subculture. Although the raw counts are small for some of these groups, they may nonetheless represent a lucrative opportunity for motorcycle producers. As the text points out, the motorcycles that appeal to RUBs are premium bikes, and there are a full range of accessories and apparel items that also appeal to this emerging biker subculture. Therefore, the overall expenditure level per consumer will be quite high.

The index values show that single adults are more likely than married motorcyclists to own large motorcycles.

Marital Status	Engine Size		
	Less than 300 cc	400–999 cc	More than 1000 cc
Single	98	96	115
Married	116	109	95

Chapter 12 Data File: Index of Social Position

There are several approaches that students can take in working on this exercise. Although the questions are framed in terms of social class (as defined by Simmons' Index of Social Position), the data file for this exercise also contains a separate breakdown by occupation. Students may elect to compare consumer groups with similar occupational status but who do not necessarily share the same educational level.

The sample solution ahown in the following table adheres closely to the questions in the exercise. One way for students to assess income versus social class influences is to compare the top two (or three) social class categories against the high-income group. In terms of income, the top two social class categories are most comparable to the greater than $40,000.00 household income group. However, since income and social class are imperfectly correlated, the group defined in terms of income alone is a more heterogeneous group of consumers (it includes a range of educational level and occupation).

	Wine by the Case	Spirits by the Case	Ski Resorts	Theme Parks	Passports	Espresso	Instant Coffee
Class I	153	66	191	223	120	96	104
Class II	142	88	165	180	102	116	108
Class III	121	96	131	126	119	107	117
More than $40,000	127	100	136	141	119	108	117
Class I	153	66	191	223	120	96	104
Class V	64	107	61	49	68	85	85
Difference	89	−41	130	174	52	11	19

The bottom portion of the table directly compares the top-most and bottom-most class categories. Wine by the Case, Ski Resorts, and Passports most sharply differentiate between these groups of consumers. The coffee products, Theme Parks, and Distilled Spirits by the Case are least distinctive. One explanation is that although both groups can afford to purchase alcoholic beverages by the case, their social class acts much like a taste culture in determining differential preferences. For example, one group may find it more acceptable to serve white wine than Jack Daniels bourbon.

Passports and Ski Resorts can similarly be explained in terms of taste differences. However, in both cases (foreign travel and skiing) the consumption activity is very high cost. So, the differences between the groups may as readily be explained by income differences as by subcultural taste differences.

Chapter 13 Data File: Patterns of Consumption

It is clear that Jackie's preferences are more consistent with the current role that both occupy. Although the vignette at the beginning of the chapter does not provide a great deal of demographic detail, there are several inferences that students can

	Jack Daniels	Absolut Vodka	Glenlivet Scotch	Imported Champagne	Malt Liquor	BMW 325	BMW	Camaro	Mini-Vans
Professional	70	108	236	200	72	118	164	89	148
Class II	94	108	206	172	69	150	134	88	142
$60,000–$75,000	125	137	192	139	94	132	125	123	172
$75,000–$100,000	71	80	414	167	59	145	220	109	138
College Graduate	103	118	261	195	76	200	175	77	145

make. First, since they are both just starting out, they probably fall into Class II of the index of social position (they are minor/lesser professionals at this stage of their careers) and as Washington lawyers they should be in the $60,000–$100,000 range for income. They are professionals who graduated college. As the following table shows, there are some notable patterns of consumption that are associated with these characteristics.

The discussion can focus on how the joint consumption of a particular group of product (e.g., Glenlivet Scotch and BMW cars) can serve to define a lifestyle or other social group—in this case perhaps, an occupational group.

Chapter 14 Data File: Cultural Buying Patterns

The sharpest distinctions are between African-American and Hispanic consumers in the Malt Liquor and Cigarette categories. Students should also note the large difference for cat and dog ownership, which is higher among Hispanic consumers than for either African-Americans or Asians. The following table gives the index values for these product categories.

	Smoke Cigarettes	Smoke Cigars	Malt Liquor	Dry Beer	Rice Dishes	Syrup	Cats	Dogs
Hispanic	88	104	74	110	96	90	90	74
African-American	124	96	283	114	97	96	46	55
Asian	63	0	87	109	109	73	54	53
White	98	104	76	98	100	101	108	107

Students should be encouraged to discuss the origins for these differences. For example, those of Asian origin may find it difficult to view a dog as a pet if they came from a culture in which dogs are food animals. How many American consumers would consider a cow as a pet? Similarly, the class can consider the extent to which a preference for Malt Liquor is a culturally based preference and the extent to which it has been shaped by marketers' efforts to market these products to the African-American community. (Note the controversy that has arisen over such practices in the areas of alcoholic beverages and tobacco products.)

The scope of this exercise can be expanded by asking students to consider regional consumption differences. This can lead to a discussion of the regional sub-cultures of America. (The Simmons file gives a breakdown by region as well as size of community.)

Chapter 17 Data File: High-Technology Buying Behavior

For this exercise, innovators can be defined according to their higher-than-average consumption of the group of "high-technology" products listed in the data file. An easy way to develop the profile is to average the index values across product categories. Students should consider high and low cutoffs that are 10 percent above/below the average index value of 100.

High index values for this group of products are associated with the following self-concept dimensions: Affable (115), Creative (114), Demanding (120), Daring (111), Efficient (113), Egocentric (113), Intelligent (112), Sophisticated (116) [note that this list is not exhaustive]; and with Impulsive (112), Style Conscious (111), and Ecologist (117) buying styles.

Students should be encouraged to use the Self and Style reference files to isolate the demographic characteristics of these consumers. Several of the self-concept items (affable, creative, demanding, efficient, intelligent, sophisticated, egocentric) show higher index values (average = 115) among higher-income consumers (more than $75,000.00 household income), and among highly educated consumers (more than 3 years of college: average index value = 110) and those in a technical occupation (average index value = 113).

They can also use the Media file to identify magazines that would be good print vehicles for publicity and advertising campaigns.

MICHAEL R. SOLOMON

Rutgers University

SECOND EDITION

Consumer

Behavior

Buying, Having, and Being

Allyn and Bacon
Boston
London
Toronto
Sydney
Tokyo
Singapore

Editor-in-Chief, Business: Rich Wohl
Senior Series Editor: Suzy Spivey
Senior Developmental Editor: Judith S. Fifer
Editorial Assistant: Karen Joseph
Text Designer: Melinda Grosser, for *silk*
Editorial-Production Services: Sylvia Dovner, Technical Texts
Editorial-Production Administrator: Elaine Ober
Electronic Manuscript Manager: Andrew Walker
Electronic Page Layout: Gayle A. Robertson
Manufacturing Buyer: Megan Cochran
Prepress Buyer: Linda Cox
Cover Coordinator: Linda K. Dickinson

Copyright © 1994, 1992 by Allyn and Bacon
A Division of Paramount Publishing
160 Gould Street
Needham Heights, Massachusetts 02194

Chapter Opening Photo Credits: *Chapter 1, p. 2,* © David E. Dempster; *Chapter 2, p. 46,* Oliverio Toscani for BENETTON; *Chapter 3, p. 78,* 1992 © Dingo Women's National Consumer Magazine Ad/Acme Boot Company; *Chapter 4, p. 108,* Courtesy of First Interstate Bank; *Chapter 5, p. 144,* Courtesy of General Motors do Brazil Ltda; *Chapter 6, p. 178,* Courtesy of Saga Furs of Scandinavia; *Chapter 7, p. 214,* Courtesy of CNA Insurance Companies, Advertisement by Frank C. Nahser, Inc./Advertising 1990, Photography by Tony D'Orio; *Chapter 8, p. 250,* © Bob Daemmrich/ Stock Boston, *Chapter 9, p. 286,* Reprinted by permission of Allure Magazine, Copyright 1990 by The Conde Nast Publications Inc.; *Chapter 10, p. 324,* © 1991 Paul Barton/The Stock Market; *Chapter 11, p. 362,* Courtesy of Harley-Davidson Motor Company; *Chapter 12, p. 400,* Courtesy of Jaguar Cars Inc.; *Chapter 13, p. 436,* © Laima Druska/Stock Boston; *Chapter 14, p. 466,* Photo courtesy of Mattel, Inc.; *Chapter 15, p. 498,* Courtesy of General Media Incorporated, ©1991; *Chapter 16, p. 534,* Photo by Mario Ruiz; *Chapter 17, p. 582,* © Greg Davis/Sygma.

Library of Congress Cataloging-in-Publication Data
Solomon, Michael R.
    Consumer behavior : buying, having, and being / Michael R. Solomon.
        p.   cm.
    Includes bibliographical references and index.
    ISBN 0-205-14995-2
    1. Consumer behavior.   I. Title.
HF5415.32.S6 1993
658.8'342—dc20
                                                            93-36506
                                                            CIP

Printed in the United States of America

10 9 8 7 6 5 4 3 2 1   96 95 94 93

To Gail,
Amanda, Zachary, and Alexandra—
Still my favorite consumers!

About the Author

Michael R. Solomon is Associate Professor and Chairman of the Department of Marketing in the School of Business at Rutgers University, New Brunswick, New Jersey. He also holds a graduate appointment in the Department of Psychology at Rutgers. Prior to joining Rutgers in 1987, Professor Solomon was on the faculty of the Graduate School of Business Administration at New York University, where he also served as Associate Director of NYU's Institute of Retail Management. Professor Solomon earned B.A. degrees in Psychology and Sociology at Brandeis University and an M.A. and a Ph.D. in Social Psychology at The University of North Carolina at Chapel Hill.

Professor Solomon's primary research interests include consumer behavior and lifestyle issues, the symbolic aspects of products, the psychology of fashion and image, and services marketing. He has published many articles on these and related topics in academic journals. He is an Editorial Board Member of the *Journal of Consumer Research*, the *Journal of Retailing*, and *Psychology & Marketing*.

Professor Solomon received the first Cutty Sark Men's Fashion Award in 1981 for his research on the psychological aspects of clothing. He is the editor of *The Psychology of Fashion* and co-editor of *The Service Encounter: Managing Employee/Customer Interaction in Services Businesses*, both published in 1985 by Lexington Books.

Professor Solomon is also a frequent contributor to mass media. His feature articles have appeared in *Psychology Today, Gentleman's Quarterly,* and *Savvy*. He has been quoted in numerous national magazines and newspapers, including *Allure, Elle, Glamour, Mademoiselle, Mirabella, Newsweek, The New York Times Magazine, Self, USA Today,* and *The Wall*

Street Journal. He has been a guest on "The Today Show," "Good Morning America," CNBC, Whittle Communications' Channel One, "Newsweek on the Air," "Inside Edition," and National Public Radio.

Professor Solomon has provided input to a variety of organizations on issues related to consumer behavior. He has been a consultant to such companies as the Celanese Corporation, Levi Strauss & Company, Johnson & Johnson, Kayser-Roth, and Hakuhodo Advertising (Tokyo). He is also in demand as a speaker to many business groups on consumer behavior and marketing topics. He lives with his wife Gail and their three children in New Jersey.

Brief Contents

Contents

SECTION I
The Consumer in a
Marketing Content   1

CHAPTER 1
An Introduction to
Consumer Behavior   3

Buying, Having, and Being

1. Anthropology, Inc.: The Scientists of Culture Help Business Discern Corporate Rites and Wrongs, Elizabeth Corcoran 2. Goodbye, Book of Dreams: Sears' Catalogue Epitomized—and Drove—A Consumer Century, Paul Farhi 3. Consummate Consumer—Don't Just Hang Up: Putting the Kibosh on Phone Solicitation, Don Oldenburg 4. Wheels—The Buyers' Choices: When Consumers Speak, Market Researchers Listen, Jay Mathews

Buying, Having, and Being: The Washington Post Consumer Behavior Companion, Second Edition, is a separate reader available to accompany your text. Your instructor can order it by calling Allyn & Bacon at 1-800-233-1360 and ordering 0-205-15374-7 for your book-store to carry.

Buying, Having, and Being

12. Consummate Consumer—Reading the Market: Hooked on Phonics and Its Lure of Literacy, David Streitfeld 13. Multiple Brand Names Confuse Consumers, Don Colburn 14. A Troll Down Marketing Lane: In N.Y., Hot New Products at Licensing '92, Paula Span 15. Homing in on Growing Nostalgia: Antique-Looking Products Popular at Trade Show, William F. Powers 16. Packaging Unfiltered Nostalgia: Liggett Seeks to Revive Chesterfield With a Puff of the Past, Jay Mathews

---

Buying, Having, and Being

17. Trends—Socially Correct Marketing: Many Firms Are Coming up with 'Big Cause' Ads, Don Oldenburg 18. Players at Risk for Sexual Diseases: Lifestyle, 'Immortality View' Make Pro Athletes Highly Vulnerable, Robin Herman

---

Buying, Having, and Being

19. Gone West: When Clint Eastwood Gets into the Act of Selling Furniture, America's Family Rooms Won't Be Far Behind, Julia Koncius 20. Shoe Giant Nike Steps on Sports World's Toes, Christine Brennan 21. They're Wacky, They're Zany, They're an Ad? Bell Atlantic Tests Blend of Sitcom, Infomercial, Paul Farhi

---

Buying, Having, and Being

27. Women—How You Doin'?: Their Level of Self-Esteem, Barbara Mathias 28. Selling Women Short: Why Are New Movies Turning to the World's Oldest Profession? Rita Kempley 29. June Cleaver, Call your Agent: On Daytime TV Ads, It's Stereotypes of '50s Women! And You're Soaking in Them!, Paul Farhi 30. Students Give it Their Best Shot: Photos Capture Their Personalities, Sari Horwitz 31. Clothes Make the Man . . . Uh, Woman: On Paris's Fashion Runways, Male Models Wear the Skirts, Sharon Waxman 32. Did Fashion Throw Women a Curve? Industry Denies It Helped Spur Implants, Cathy Horyn

---

Buying, Having, and Being

33. A Shopper's Nightmare: The Sales Clerks Who Can Make or Break Your Day, Kara Swisher 34. Running Rings Around the Competition: Saturn Dealers Court 'Be-Back' Customers, Cut Haggling—And Increase Car Sales, Warren Brown 35. Clues on Queues: What's in Our Minds About Those Lines? Malcolm Gladwell 36. Shopping Smart to Save the Earth: At Supermarket, the Environmentally Correct Hunt for Products, Bill Miller 37. Giving Customers What They Want: While Some Retailers Are Sliding Into Bankruptcy, Others Are Going to the Bank, Kara Swisher

SECTION IV
The Consumer as a Group Member   361

. . . .

CHAPTER 10
Purchase and Postpurchase   325

CHAPTER 11
Group Influence and Opinion Leadership   363

Buying, Having, and Being

38. Charging Up Madison Avenue: As Clinton's Era Dawns, Advertising Draws on His Symbols, Themes, and Images, Paul Farhi 39. Focus—Dangerous Dips: Teens' Fast Ride Down Smokeless Tobacco Road, Laura Blumenfeld 40. Weapon Wear in Style: Many in Area See Gun T-Shirts as Disturbing Trend Among Teens, Sari Horwitz, Avis Thomas-Lester 41. Children—The Eyes Have It: Wearing Glasses Without Making a Spectacle, Gigi Anders

CHAPTER 12

Social Class and Economic Influences 401

Buying, Having, and Being

42. Economy Puts a Downside on the Belief in Upward Mobility, Barbara Vobejda 43. Recession Picking the Pocket of Childhood: Hard Times Causing High Anxiety Among Youngsters, Experts Say, Evelyn Hsu 44. Consummate Consumer—The New Frugality: Rethinking the Value of One's Dignity, Don Oldenburg

CHAPTER 13

Lifestyles 437

Buying, Having, and Being

45. Targeting the Gay Market: Companies Spending More of

Preface

I wrote this book because I'm fascinated by the everyday activities of people. The field of consumer behavior is, to me, the study of how our world is influenced by the action of marketers. Since I'm a consumer myself, I have a selfish interest in learning more about how this process works—and so do you.

In many courses, students are merely passive observers, learning about topics that affect them only indirectly, if at all. Not everyone is a plasma physicist, a medieval French scholar, or even an industrial marketer. We are, however, all consumers. As a result, many of the topics dealt with in this book are of both professional and personal relevance to the reader, whether he or she is a student, professor, or marketing practitioner. Nearly everyone can relate to the trials and tribulations associated with last-minute shopping, primping for a big night out, agonizing over an expensive purchase decision, fantasizing about a week in the Caribbean, celebrating a holiday, or commemorating a landmark event such as graduation, getting a driver's license, or (dreaming about) winning the lottery.

Beyond Canned Peas: Buying, Having, and Being

As the book's subtitle suggests, my version of this field goes beyond the act of buying to having and being as well. Consumer behavior is more than *buying* a can of peas; it also embraces the study of how *having* (or not having) things affects our lives and how our possessions influence the way we feel about ourselves and about each other—the state of *being*.

In addition to understanding why people buy things, we also try to appreciate how products, services, and consumption activities contribute to the broader social world we experience. Whether shopping, cooking, cleaning, playing basketball, hanging out at the beach, or even looking at ourselves in the mirror, our lives are touched by the marketing system. And, as if these experiences were not complex enough, the task of understanding the consumer multiplies geometrically when a multicultural perspective is taken. This book not only probes the psyche of the American consumer, but also attempts wherever possible to consider the many other consumers around the world whose diverse experiences with buying, having, and being are equally valid and vital to understand. In addition to the numerous non-American examples of marketing and consumer practices that appear throughout the book, each chapter contains a box called "Multicultural Dimensions" that highlights cultural differences in consumer behavior. I developed the model of consumer behavior that appears at the beginning of each text section to underscore the complex—and often inseparable—interrelationships between the individual consumer and his or her social realities.

The Relevance of Consumer Research

The field of consumer behavior is young, dynamic, and in flux. It is constantly being cross-fertilized by perspectives from many different disciplines. I have tried to express the field's staggering diversity in these pages. Consumer researchers represent virtually every social science discipline, plus a few from the physical sciences and the arts for good measure. This "melting pot" has created a healthy "stew" of research perspectives, viewpoints regarding appropriate research methods, and even deeply held beliefs about what are and what are not appropriate issues for consumer researchers to study in the first place.

Several unique features in the book will help you to experience the potential of consumer research. The CNN Connection at the end of each chapter provides a visual, real-world tie-in to relevant topics currently reported in the news. Related video segments showing the CNN news stories are also available. Similarly, vivid examples from articles that have appeared in one of the country's best newspapers are available in *Buying, Having, and Being: The Washington Post Consumer Behavior Companion,* Second Edition. These have been selected to complement what you read in the text. In addition, the exercises described in the Simmons Connection features (and contained on the Simmons Data Disk made available to your instructor) will allow you to "play with" real data from the Simmons Market Research Bureau that illuminates some of the consumption activities described in the text. These data are the same findings used by many actual marketing organizations to develop their consumer targeting and communications strategies, so you'll be "reading from the same page" as many of the important decision makers in the field of marketing. Finally, I hope this course will inspire you to consider the field of consumer research as a career. If that's the case, you'll find the career information presented in the Appendix helpful. Appendix II, Careers in Consumer Research, provides an overview of possible career paths, and it also includes some suggested references for further exploration.

Consumers and Marketing Strategy

The book also emphasizes the importance of understanding consumers in formulating marketing strategy. Many (if not most) of the fundamental concepts in marketing are based on the practitioner's ability to know people. After all, if we don't understand why people behave as they do, how can we identify their needs? If we can't identify their needs, how can we satisfy those needs? If we can't satisfy people's needs, we don't have a marketing concept, so we might as well fold our tents and go home! To illustrate the potential of consumer research to inform marketing strategy, the text contains numerous examples of specific applications of consumer behavior concepts by marketing practitioners and of "windows of opportunity" where such concepts could be used (perhaps by alert strategists after taking this course!). Many of these possibilities are highlighted in special features called "Marketing Opportunities."

The Good, the Bad, and the Ugly

This strategic focus is, however, tempered by an important qualification: Unlike some contemporary treatments of consumer behavior, this book does not assume that *everything* marketers do is in the best interests of consumers or of their environment. Likewise, as consumers, we do many things that are not positive either. People are plagued by addictions, status envy, ethnocentrism, racism, sexism, and other "isms," and regrettably, there are times when marketing activities—deliberately or not—encourage or exploit these human flaws. This book deals with the totality of consumer behavior, warts and all. Marketing mistakes or ethically suspect activities are also highlighted in special features labeled "Marketing Pitfalls."

On the other hand, marketers have helped to create many wonderful (or at least unusual) things, such as holidays, comic books, the music industry, "pet rocks," and the many stylistic options available to us in the domains of clothing, home design, the arts, cuisine, and so on. I have also taken pains to acknowledge the sizable impact of marketing on popular culture. Indeed, the final section of this book reflects very recent work in the field that scrutinizes, criticizes, and sometimes celebrates consumers in their everyday worlds. I hope you will enjoy reading about such wonderful things as much as I enjoyed writing about them.

Acknowledgments

I am grateful for the many helpful comments on how to improve the first and second editions that were provided by my peer reviewers. Special thanks go to the following people.

Ishmael Akkah, Wayne State University
Laurel Anderson, Arizona State University–West
Sharon Beatty, University of Alabama at Tuscaloosa
James Cagley, University of Tulsa
Douglas Allen Cords, California State University, Fresno
Bettina Cornwell, Memphis State University
M. Frances Estep, Pace University
S.J. Garner, Eastern Kentucky University
Ronald Goldsmith, The Florida State University

Cathy Goodwin, University of Manitoba
Ronald Hill, Villanova University
Nathan Himelstein, Essex County College
Carol Kaufman, Rutgers University–Camden
Robert Kleine, Arizona State University
James Leigh, Texas A&M University
Brian Lofman, Central Connecticut State University
Patricia Manninen, North Shore Community College
Lee Meadow, Salisbury State University
Alan Miller, Tennessee State University
Bruce Newman, DePaul University
A. Nancy Panos Schmitt, Westminster College of Salt Lake City
Carol Scott, University of California–Los Angeles
Gail Tom, California State University, Sacramento
Melissa Martin Young, University of Utah
Mary Zimmer, University of Georgia
George Zinkhan, University of Houston

Extra special thanks are also due to the preparers of the supplements: Lewis Hershey and Pamela Kiecker of Texas Tech University for preparation of the *Instructor's Manual;* M. Frances Estep of Pace University for completely revising the *Test Bank;* and Lewis Hershey for the transparency masters. Additional thanks go to my colleague Basil Englis of Rutgers University for preparation of the Simmons Connection database exercises and their accompanying student and instructor materials.

I have been tremendously impressed by the competence and professionalism of the people at Allyn and Bacon, who have so ably guided me through the dangerous shoals of writing and revising a textbook. Ellen Mann first got me "hooked" on writing, and she and Jerry Higgins continue to contribute unflagging support. Other special thanks go to Sylvia Dovner, Sandi Kirshner, Elaine Ober, and particularly to both the ever-patient and thorough Judy Fifer and to bluesman Bill Barke (whose bark is worse than his bite). Finally, I am most indebted to the good sense, bubbly enthusiasm, and Southern charm of my editor, Suzy Spivey, for helping me through this project.

My friends and colleagues at Rutgers have been fantastic since this project began. Without their support and tolerance, I would never have been able to sustain the "illusion" that I was still an active department chairman during this time. I would also like to thank Sakae Hata for her helpful advice, and Carol Gibson for her assistance throughout. I am particularly indebted to Basil Englis for his intellectual and emotional support—he personifies my image of what a good colleague and friend should be.

Other colleagues around the country have also been wonderfully supportive of my efforts to include "cutting edge" research in the book. Despite the inevitable risk of leaving out some people, my thanks go to Laurel Anderson, Eric Arnould, Gary Bamossy, Sharon Beatty, Russ Belk, Jim Bettman, Cindy Clark, John Deighton, Ron Goldsmith, Ron Hill, Steve Hoch, Morris Holbrook, Jack Jacoby, Jerry Kernan, Sid Levy, David Mick, Marsha Richins, Dennis Rook, John Schouten, John Sherry, Ruth Smith, Alladi Venkatesh, and Melanie Wallendorf for their helpful comments and contributions to the second edition.

Also, I am grateful to my students, who have been a prime source of inspiration, examples, and feedback. The satisfaction I have garnered from teaching them about consumer behavior motivated me to write a book I felt they would like to read.

Last but not least, I would like to thank my family and friends for sticking by me during this revision—they know who they are, since their names pop up in chapter vignettes throughout the book. My apologies for "distorting" their characters in the name of poetic license! My gratitude and love goes out to my parents, Jackie and Henry, and my in-laws, Marilyn and Philip (with one l). My super children, Amanda, Zachary, and Alexandra, always made the sun shine on gray days. Finally, thanks above all to Gail, my wonderful wife, friend and partner: I still do it all for you.

Ancillary Materials Available for Instructors

The following supplements are available with this text:

- Annotated Instructor's Edition (including the Simmons Connection Data Disk)
- Instructor's Manual, including transparency masters and CNN Video User's Guide
- Test Bank and Computerized Test Bank
- Transparencies
- *Buying, Having, and Being: The Washington Post Consumer Behavior Companion*, Second Edition
- CNN Video

Simmons
Connection Exercises:
Student Introduction
and Instructions

Several practical data-oriented exercises have been designed for selected chapters in the text. These exercises are designed to give students some hands-on experience with the sort of data that marketers use to better understand the behavior of consumers. Each exercise is keyed to examples and concepts covered in the chapter in which it appears. There is also a computer disk that contains real market data. In order to "solve" the various problems posed in these exercises, you will need to access the data contained on the disk. The exercises and data file are "user-friendly" and will increase your involvement in the learning process. Most of the exercises relate directly to the opening vignette of the chapter in which they are assigned. You may wish to reread the vignette before you begin working on an exercise.

The data come from a widely used *syndicated* data service: The Simmons Study of Media & Markets. This very extensive study includes data on 800 product and service categories. A panel of 22,406 adult Americans provides the data that make up the Simmons database. The real value of this database is that it allows marketers to look at patterns of buying behavior as a function of a wide array of consumer characteristics, including demographics (age, education, income, race, and so on) and psychographics (attitudes, self-concept, buying style, and so on).

The Simmons Study of Media & Markets is conducted annually and the results are tabulated into 34 separate volumes that are offered as Simmons products. Additional tabulations are prepared on a custom basis for individual clients. Simmons also conducts studies of special groups: For example, CompPro is a study of computer professionals, STARS focuses on teens between twelve and nineteen years old, and KIDS focuses on those younger than twelve. For the exercises in your text, Simmons has extracted portions of its 1992 database and provided summary data in the form of spreadsheets that contain the critical information needed to work on each exercise. Although Simmons provides a great deal of information at the *brand level,* for most of the exercises the data have been aggregated to the product category level.

In order to use the data from the Simmons disk, you will need access either to a DOS or Macintosh computer *and* a standard spreadsheet program such as Lotus, Excel, Quattro, or comparable program. The files are saved on the disk in what is called a "WKS" format, which is a generic format for spreadsheets. This means that any standard spreadsheet program should have no problem reading the information from the disk. Since the disk itself is already a DOS disk, DOS users can access the files with no prior translation. If you are using your own computer and the computer has a hard drive, then you should first copy all of the files from the floppy disk onto the computer's hard drive.

If you are using a Macintosh computer, you will need to run a utility program called "Apple File Exchange," which is an Apple Computer system program that is currently bundled with all Macintosh computers. All system 6.0.5 and up users have received this program. If you do not have this program, you can obtain it either through your local Macintosh Users Group or directly through Apple. The following instructions apply whether you are copying the files onto another floppy (in Macintosh format) or onto a hard drive (only the destination changes). In order to translate the files, first open the Apple File Exchange icon. Then insert the Simmons disk into your floppy drive. The dialog box will show the Simmons files on the right-hand portion of the screen. Select all of the Simmons data files and click on the "Translate" button. The next dialog box will ask how you want the files translated—just select the format that matches your spreadsheet program.

A total of 14 files are on the data disk. Some files are titled "Chap#" to indicate the chapter in which you will find related Simmons exercises. The other three files, labeled "Self," "Style," and "Media," are general reference files that may come in handy for several of the exercises. You should open several of the files and browse through them to familiarize yourself with the kinds of information they contain. Note that it will be much easier to browse through spreadsheets if you learn how to have the spreadsheet program keep the row and column labels visible on the screen. Although the method for doing this varies from program to program, most have this capability.

The example on page xxv will help you understand the data you will find in the spreadsheet files. Like the actual Simmons data files on your disk, this sample spreadsheet contains a cross-tabulation of data: columns by rows. Each bit of data is entered in a cell, which is the intersection of a row and a column. In the sample, three magazines (columns) are broken down by the gender of the reader (rows). For each row item, the Simmons spreadsheet files contain three pieces of information. The first is the actual number of respondents that fit the characteristics defined by variables given in the column and row labels. In the sample, the cell at the intersection of the TOTAL row and the TOTAL column shows the total number of respondents, which is 22,406. At the intersection of TOTAL row and *American Health* column, the cell shows a value of 633, which means that of the entire sample, 633 respondents reported that they are readers of *American Health.*

The second entry for each row variable in a Simmons spreadsheet file is identified by a row label of (000). This number is a projection based on the raw count and the total U.S. population. It lets marketers immediately project the Simmons sample values onto the total U.S population and thereby estimate total potential market size. In the sample given here, if the

	B	C	D	E	F	G
13				MAGAZINES	MAGAZINES	
14				-Total	-Total	MAGAZINES
15				Audience:	Audience:	-Total
16				AMERICAN	AMERICAN	Audience:
17	ROW	CELL	TOTAL	HEALTH	PHOTO	AUDUBON
18						
19	TOTAL	#RESP	22406	633	246	452
20		(000)	184117	2770	875	1416
21		INDEX	100	100	100	100
22						
23	SEX:MALE	#RESP	11499	260	185	261
24		(000)	88034	811	662	777
25		INDEX	100	61	156	114
25						
27	SEX:FEMALE	#RESP	10907	373	61	191
28		(000)	96083	1959	214	639
29		INDEX	100	135	46	87

Simmons panel were projected onto all U.S. consumers there would be 2,770,000 readers of *American Health* magazine.

The last entry for each row variable—Index—is extremely valuable for marketers because it tells them whether a particular consumer group is more or less likely than all members of a particular "universe" of consumers to consume a particular product (or product category). For example, if we are interested in magazine preferences, we would consider all adult magazine readers as our universe. Each Simmons file identifies the universe of consumers that form the basis for these index values.

For any variable defined in the row labels—say, gender of reader—an index value of 100 means that a particular group of consumers was no more or less likely to be a reader of *American Health* than the total universe (all adults). In the sample, if you look at the intersection of Male and *American Health,* you will see an index value of 61, which means that adult males are 39% less likely (100 – 61) than all adults to read this magazine. In contrast, females are 35% more likely (135 – 100) to read *American Health.* Notice how the index values for male and female readers differ for *American Health* (higher female readership) and *American Photo* (higher male readership). By comparison, the difference in preference for *Audubon* magazine by gender is not nearly so extreme. The index values are computed using the projected population values.

Because the index values are a direct comparison of a market segment's behavior with a relevant universe of consumers, they provide extremely useful information for marketers. The index values are a particularly useful tool in defining market segments whose tastes, preferences, and past consumption behavior are particularly well-suited for a particular product or product category.

The table on pages xxvi and xxvii lists the Simmons data files and identifies the column and row variables in each file.

File Name	Columns	Rows
Chap1	*Subset of Magazines:* Seventeen Mademoiselle Harper's Bazaar Ladies' Home Journal Vogue Elle	*Subset of Demographics:* Age Education Occupation Sex
Chap4	*Credit Cards Used:* Last 12 months Last 30 days Number of times used	*Subset of Buying Style:* Ad believer Cautious Economy minded Experimenter Impulsive Planner
Chap5	*Environmental Issues:* 17 environmental issues Willingness to pay more taxes	*Subset of Demographics:* Age Education Occupation *Buying Style:* Ecologist
Chap6	*Single Products:* Disposable diapers Disposable plates Tobacco (all) Veal Weed killer Fur jackets/coats—real Fur jackets/coats—synthetic	*Environmental Issues* (all) *Buying Style:* Ecologist *Demographics:* Age
Chap8	*Shopping Influence—Male:* Automobiles Household furnishings Food shopping	*Demographics:* Size of household Number of employed adults Education Age *Psychographics:* Broadminded Creative Dominating Efficient
Chap9	*Health-Care Products:* Contact lenses Diet control Doctor's visits (general check-ups) Hearing aids *Travel:* Health or resort spa	*Self-Concept* (all)
Chap11	*Motorcycles:* Most recent bought (new/used) Make Engine size—less than 399 cc, 400–1000 cc, more than 1000 cc	*Demographics:* Age (18–34 year olds only) Income (HH) Education— < HS, HS grad, < college grad, college grad Marital status

File Name	Columns	Rows
	Sports, Leisure: Motorcycling	

Chap12	*Malt Beverages & Wines:*
	    Wine by the case
	Distilled Spirits:
	    Spirits by the case
	Travel:
	    Passports
	    Theme parks
	Coffee, Tea:
	    Espresso/Cappuccino
	    International flavored instant
		Demographics:
		    Index of Social Position
		HHI— > $40,000
		    Occupation

Chap13	*Distilled Spirits:*
	    Jack Daniels
	    Absolut Vodka
	    The Glenlivet Single-Malt Scotch
	Malt Beverages & Wine:
	    Champagne (aggregated, all brands)
	    Malt liquor
	New Autos:
	    BMWs (aggregated, all models)
	    Trans Ams/Camaros
	    Mini-vans (aggregated, all brands)
		Demographics:
		    Occupation
		    Income
		    Index of Social Position

Chap14	*Tobacco:*
	    Cigarettes
	    Cigars
	Malt Beverages & Wine:
	    Malt liquor
	    Dry beer
	General Foods:
	    Rice/rice dishes
	Pets:
	    Cat/dog ownership
		Race:
		    Black, white, Asian
		    Spanish/Hispanic
		Demographics:
		    Locality type
		    Geographic region

Chap17	*Travel:*
	    Theme parks
	Books, Discs, etc.:
	    Digital audio tape
	    Surround sound decoder
	    Cellular, car or
	        portable phone
	    Laser disc player
	    Interactive computer services
	Banking:
	    Home banking by computer
		Buying Style (all)
		Self-Concept (all)

Media	*Magazines:*
	    A random set of magazines
		Demographics:
		    *

Style	*Buying Style* (all)	*
Self	*Self-Concept* (all)	*

*The three general reference files all use the same set of demographic variables: Age, Sex, HHI, Education, Race, and Marital Status.

I. The Consumer in
a Marketing Context

II. The Consumer
as an Individual

III. The Consumer as
a Decision Maker

IV. The Consumer as
a Group Member

V. The Consumer
and Culture

1. An Introduction to Consumer Behavior

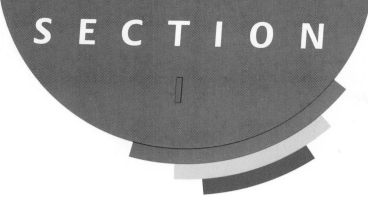

SECTION

1

The Consumer

in a Marketing

Context

This introductory section provides an overview of the field of consumer behavior. Chapter 1 looks at how the field of marketing is influenced by the actions of consumers and also at how we as consumers are influenced by marketers. It describes the discipline of consumer behavior and some of the different approaches to understanding what makes consumers tick. The chapter also provides a bit of a "refresher course" on marketing research as it briefly summarizes some of the many and varied techniques that are available to scientists who study consumers in the marketplace, in their homes, and in the laboratory.

CHAPTER 1

An Introduction

to Consumer

Behavior

Buying, Having, and Being: Selections 1–4 from *Buying, Having, and Being: The Washington Post Consumer Behavior Companion*, Second Edition, accompany this chapter.

Ellen is killing time before her Operations Research class by browsing in the college bookstore. Between studying for her O.R. and Finance exams, she realizes she hasn't looked through a magazine in weeks. Enough of the serious stuff, she decides. It's time for some *really* educational reading.

The magazine section is filled with what looks like a hundred different selections, from *Fortune* to *Better Homes and Gardens*. Ellen is a dedicated *Seventeen* reader, but as she scans the many titles looking for it, she is struck by the different "types" of glamorous models featured on the covers of most of the women's magazines. She thinks maybe it's time to expand her horizons a bit. After all, she's a college junior now—time to listen to her sorority sisters and remake her somewhat innocent image.

Looking over the many choices, Ellen considers buying a copy of *Vogue*. No, that still seems a bit too old and stodgy for her, even though she knows from her Consumer Behavior class that the magazine is trying hard to reposition itself as a more "with it" alternative to *Elle* and *Glamour*. *Cosmopolitan* is full of pictures of slightly older working women in revealing dresses. Well, she's not quite ready to go that far! *Harper's Bazaar* and *Mirabella* look like magazines her mother (a stylish "mature" woman) would read, and she can look at *Family Circle* and *Ladies' Home Journal* anytime she visits her Aunt Elaine and the kids in the suburbs—as if she'd want to read about endless diets and home decorating ideas.

Finally, Ellen is intrigued by a copy of *Mademoiselle*—the cover model has a new, short hairstyle that she's been thinking about trying for herself. As Ellen flips through the pages, her attention is caught by the many ads showing cute clothes, and she catches a whiff of that new perfume her friend Judy just bought. Yeah, this magazine is just what the doctor ordered to help create the New Ellen. Judy and the rest of the girls will be proud of her . . . .

Consumer Behavior: People In The Marketplace

This book is about everyday people like Ellen. It concerns the products and services they buy and use, and the ways these fit into their lives. This introductory chapter briefly describes some important aspects of the field of consumer behavior, including the topics studied, who studies them, and some different ways these issues are approached by consumer researchers.

For now, though, let's return to one "typical" consumer: Ellen, the business major. This brief story allows us to highlight some aspects of consumer behavior that will be covered in the rest of the book.

- As a consumer, Ellen can be described and compared to other individuals in a number of ways. For some purposes, marketers might find it useful to categorize Ellen in terms of her age, sex, income, or occupation. These are some examples of descriptive characteristics of a population, or *demographics*. In other cases, marketers would rather know something about Ellen's interests in clothing or music, or the way she spends her leisure time. This sort of information comes under the category of *psychographics*, which refers to aspects of a person's lifestyle and personality. Knowledge of consumer characteristics plays an extremely important role in many marketing applications, such as defining the market for a product, or deciding upon the appropriate techniques to employ when targeting a certain group of consumers.

- Ellen's purchase decisions are heavily influenced by the opinions and behaviors of her friends. A lot of product information, as well as recommendations to use or avoid particular brands, is transmitted by conversations among people rather than by way of television commercials, magazines, billboards, and so on. The bonds among Ellen's group are cemented by the common products they use. There is also pressure on each group member to buy things that will meet with the group's approval, and often a price to pay in the form of group rejection or embarrassment when one does not conform to others' conceptions of what is good or bad, "in" or "out."

- As a member of a large society, such as the United States, people share certain *cultural values*, or strongly held beliefs about the way the world should be structured. Other values are shared by members of *subcultures*, or smaller groups within the culture, such as Hispanics, teens, Midwesterners, or even "Valley Girls" and "Hell's Angels." The people who matter to Ellen—her *reference group*—value the idea that women in their early twenties should be innovative, style-conscious, independent, and daring (at least a little). While many marketers focus on aging "baby boomers" (consumers between thirty and fifty years old), some are recognizing that "twentysomethings" are a valuable, overlooked market. For example, women in their twenties are more likely to splurge on luxury products like designer lipstick. Compared to their older sisters, they are also more influenced by brand names, and they tend to regard shopping as entertainment.[1]

- When examining magazines, Ellen was exposed to many competing "brands." Many magazines did not capture her attention at all, while others were noticed and rejected because they did not fit the "image" with which she identified or to which she aspired. The use of *market segmentation strategies* means targeting a brand only to specific groups of consumers rather than to everybody—even if it means that other consumers will not be interested or may even deliberately avoid that brand.

- Brands often have clearly defined images or "personalities" created by product advertising, packaging, branding, and other marketing strategies that focus on *positioning* a product a certain way. The purchase of a magazine in particular is very much a lifestyle statement: It says a lot about what a person is interested in and what she is not interested in, as well as something about the type of person she would like to be and would not like to be. People often choose a product because they find its "image" desirable or because they feel its "personality" somehow corresponds to their own. Moreover, a consumer may believe that by buying and using the product or service, its desirable qualities will somehow "rub off" onto him or her.

- When a product succeeds in satisfying a consumer's specific needs or desires, as *Seventeen* did for Ellen, it may be rewarded with many years of high *brand loyalty,* or a bond between product and consumer that is very difficult for competitors to break. Often a change in one's life situation or self-concept is required to weaken this bond and thus create opportunities for competitors. Brand loyalty can also be affected when a brand's image is altered, or *repositioned,* as *Vogue* is now attempting to do (e.g., the magazine recently devoted an entire issue to fashion items that could be bought for under $500, a radical contrast to its usual emphasis on pricey *haute couture*).

- Consumers' evaluations of products are affected by physical factors and *perceptual cues,* such as the shape and color of a package, as well as more subtle factors, like the *symbolism* used in a brand name, in an advertisement, or even in the choice of a cover model for a magazine. These judgments are affected by—and often reflect—how a society feels that people should define themselves at that point in time. For example, Ellen's choice of a new hairstyle says something about the type of image women like her want to project in the mid-1990s.

If asked, Ellen might not even be able to say exactly why she considered some magazines and rejected others. Many product meanings are hidden below the surface of the packaging and advertising, and this book will discuss some of the methods used by marketers and social scientists to discover or apply these meanings.

MULTICULTURAL ● DIMENSIONS

The "Cosmo Girl" is an image that is carefully cultivated by the editors of *Cosmopolitan*. The magazine is read by 2.7 million Americans each month. The American "Cosmo Girl," as described by editor Helen Gurley Brown, expects to get married, but is not in any hurry. She may wait until her late thirties to have children. Sex is ". . . very important, but not on the first date." She bought at least one long black skirt with a slit this year, owns many pairs of shoes, and wears big jewelry.

While the American Cosmo Girl is well-defined, the magazine also publishes 25 international editions, most of which are separate entities with their own editorial staffs. In some cases local cultures conflict with the Cosmo Girl's liberated image. Latin American editors, for instance, face problems created by a more macho society that often has a double sexual standard for men and women. Advertisers are sometimes reluctant to buy into a magazine they see as "perverted," and some parts of the magazine are censored. In countries such as Hong Kong, the American image fits well, since women are expected to be more independent and ambitious. New Cosmo girls are on the drawing board for Russia, Poland, Hungary, and India.[2]

What Is Consumer Behavior?

Consumer behavior covers a lot of ground: It is the study of the *processes involved when individuals or groups select, purchase, use, or dispose of products, services, ideas, or experiences to satisfy needs and desires.* Consumers take many forms, ranging from an eight-year-old child begging her mother for Gummy Bears to an executive in a large corporation deciding on a multi-million-dollar computer system. The objects that are consumed can include anything from canned peas, a massage, democracy, or rap music, to other people (e.g., the images of rock stars). Needs and desires to be satisfied range from hunger and thirst to love, status, or even spiritual fulfillment.

THE PROCESS In its early stages of development, the field was often referred to as *buyer behavior,* reflecting an emphasis on the interaction between consumers and producers at the time of purchase. Marketers now recognize that consumer behavior is an ongoing process, not merely what happens at the moment a consumer hands over money or a credit card and in turn receives some good or service.

The **exchange,** in which two or more organizations or people give and receive something of value, is an integral part of marketing.[3] While exchange remains an important part of consumer behavior, the expanded view emphasizes the entire consumption process, which includes the issues that influence the consumer before, during, and after a purchase. Figure 1–1 illustrates some of the issues that are addressed during each stage of the consumption process.

FIGURE 1–1 Some Issues That Arise During Stages in the Consumption Process

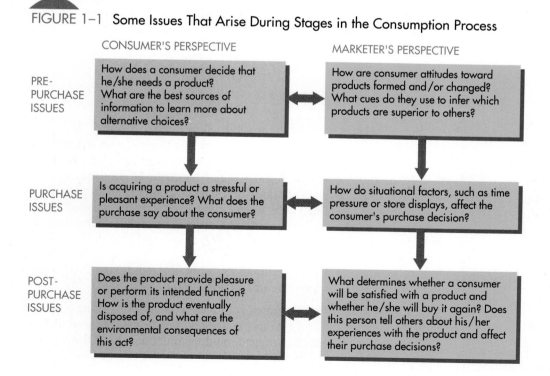

CONSUMER'S PERSPECTIVE

MARKETER'S PERSPECTIVE

PRE-PURCHASE ISSUES
How does a consumer decide that he/she needs a product? What are the best sources of information to learn more about alternative choices?

How are consumer attitudes toward products formed and/or changed? What cues do they use to infer which products are superior to others?

PURCHASE ISSUES
Is acquiring a product a stressful or pleasant experience? What does the purchase say about the consumer?

How do situational factors, such as time pressure or store displays, affect the consumer's purchase decision?

POST-PURCHASE ISSUES
Does the product provide pleasure or perform its intended function? How is the product eventually disposed of, and what are the environmental consequences of this act?

What determines whether a consumer will be satisfied with a product and whether he/she will buy it again? Does this person tell others about his/her experiences with the product and affect their purchase decisions?

THE CONSUMERS A consumer is generally thought of as a person who identifies a need or desire, makes a purchase, and then disposes of the product during the three stages in the consumption process. In many cases, however, different people may be involved in the process. The *purchaser* and *user* of a product might not be the same person, as when a parent picks out clothes for a teenager (and makes selections that can result in "fashion suicide" in the view of the teen). In other cases, another person may act as an *influencer,* providing recommendations for or against certain products without actually buying or using them. For example, a friend, rather than a parent, accompanying a teen on a shopping trip, might actually pick out the clothes that the teen decides to purchase.

Finally, consumers may be organizations or groups, in which one person may make the decisions involved in purchasing products that will be used by many, as when a purchasing agent orders the company's office supplies. In other organizational situations, purchase decisions may be made by a large group of people—for example, company accountants, designers, engineers, sales personnel, and others—all of whom will have a say in the various stages of the consumption process.

CONSUMERS AS ROLE PLAYERS The perspective of *role theory,* which this book emphasizes, takes the view that much of consumer behavior resembles actions in a play.[4] As in a play, each consumer has lines, props, costumes, and so on, and makes relevant consumption decisions. Since people act out many different roles, they sometimes alter their consumption decisions depending on the particular "play" they are in at the time. The criteria that they use to evaluate products and services in one of their roles may be quite different from those used in another role. In the Carrier Furnaces ad shown here, the consumer is shown in two of his roles: engineer by day and homeowner by night.

Consumers' Impact on Marketing Strategy

The field of consumer behavior as defined in this book covers many topics. Why should managers, advertisers, and other professionals learn about this field? Very simply, understanding consumer behavior is good business. An elementary marketing concept states that organizations exist to satisfy consumers' wants and needs. These wants and needs can be satisfied only to the extent that marketers *understand* the people or organizations that will use the products and services they are trying to sell and that they do so better than their competitors.

The following are a few examples of marketing strategies that resulted from studies focused on understanding consumers.

- Schick devised an ad for its razors with a woman gently stroking a man's face after a study of consumer perceptions of rival brands showed that Gillette ads featuring men in rugged, outdoor situations made them feel like "lone wolves," rather than people who like to be touched.[5]

This ad for Carrier Furnaces highlights the fact that consumers use different criteria to evaluate products, depending on the role they are playing at the time.   Courtesy of Carrier Corporation, subsidiary of United Technologies Corporation.

- A woman in a group of consumers who were gathered to talk about tooth care observed that tartar felt "like a wall" on her teeth. This imagery was used in ads for Colgate Tartar Control, in which room-sized teeth were shown covered by walls of tartar.[6]

- American Express redirected its advertising emphasis away from over-achievers after its consumer research indicated that people were intimidated by its approach. One subject, asked to pretend that he was an American Express card come to life, sneered, "You're not really my type—you can't keep up." Later ads instead featured people in laid-back situations, such as spontaneous vacations.[7]

- A Danish firm wanted to introduce a new cigarette brand targeted to blue-collar American males. Unfamiliar with American consumers, it sent researchers to interview men in Arkansas, where the brand was to be test marketed. In-depth interviews found that many potential customers felt sexually frustrated and powerless and that they responded to these deep feelings by getting together with their buddies and smoking cigarettes. The company used an ad depicting a brash confident smoker and challenged these frustrated men to "Make your move."[8]

Additional Example: The Young & Rubicam agency hired anthropologists to accompany letter carriers on their routes for its client, the U.S. Postal Service. It was discovered that many people view the carriers as friends and derive great satisfaction from seeing them each day. The resulting ad campaign featured individual mail carriers.

- Researchers for a manufacturer of Swiss chocolate found that many chocolate lovers hide secret "stashes" around their houses. One respondent confessed to hiding candy bars inside her lingerie drawer. The result was an ad campaign theme of "The True Confessions of Chocaholics."[9]

Consumer response is the ultimate test of whether or not a marketing strategy will succeed. Thus, knowledge about consumers is incorporated into virtually every facet of a successful marketing plan. Data about consumers helps marketers to define the market and to identify threats and opportunities in their own and different countries that will affect consumers' receptivity to the product.

Targeted Marketing: Listening to Consumers

A **targeted marketing strategy** defines both a market and the tactics used to reach that market. To appreciate the centrality of consumer behavior data in this vital process, consider the steps a company might go through after it decides to produce and market a new product.[10]

1. Define the relevant market. In this step, the market is broadly defined in terms of *product form*, or category, such as toothpaste, diet soda, or cigarettes.
2. Analyze the characteristics and also the wants of potential customers. In this analysis, the company utilizes both demographic and psychographic information.
3. Identify bases for segmenting the market. For the company, this process involves the identification of characteristics that could isolate smaller markets existing within the larger market.
4. Define and describe market segments. After identifying appropriate bases for segmentation, the company develops *market segment profiles* for the different groups by describing their unique characteristics and desires. The Whittle Communications ad shown here highlights some of the consumer characteristics used in defining market segment profiles.
5. Analyze competitors' positions. Within each segment of interest, the company wants to know how consumers perceive the brands that are already available. It identifies the **determinant attributes** of these brands, or product features that influence the consumers' choices.
6. Evaluate market segments. The cost of developing a new product to meet the needs of each segment is considered as well as the revenue potential if these needs are met.
7. Select market segments. On the basis of its analysis of the segments it has identified, the company decides which segment(s) to target.
8. Finalize the marketing mix. After selecting a target market, the company now decides upon the specific **marketing mix,** or the combination of variables over which marketers have control and which are usually known as the "Four P's": product, place (where the product is sold), price, and promotion. Careful decisions must be made about the new brand's position and how its image will be communicated in terms of pricing, naming, packaging, advertising, and so on.

are also "at the mercy" of marketers, since we rely on them to sell us products that are safe and perform as promised, to tell us the truth about what they are selling, and to price and distribute these products fairly.

Popular Culture

Popular culture, consisting of the music, movies, sports, books, celebrities, and other forms of entertainment consumed by the mass market, is both a product of and inspiration for marketers. Our lives are also affected in more far-reaching ways, ranging from how we acknowledge cultural events such as marriage, death, or holidays to how we view social issues such as air pollution, gambling, and addictions. The Super Bowl, Christmas shopping, presidential elections, the Teenage Mutant Ninja Turtles, newspaper recycling, and cigarette smoking are all examples of products and activities that touch many of our lives.

Marketing's role in the creation and communication of popular culture is especially emphasized in this book. This cultural influence is hard to overlook, although many people do not seem to realize how much their views of the world around them—their movie and musical heroes, the latest fashions in clothing, food and decorating choices, and even the physical features that they find attractive or ugly in men and women—are affected by members of marketing systems.

For example, consider the *product icons* that marketers use to create an identity for their products. Various mythical creatures and personalities—from the Pillsbury Doughboy to the Jolly Green Giant—have been at one time or another central figures in popular culture. In fact, it is likely that more consumers could recognize such characters than could identify past presidents, business leaders, or artists.

Marketing Ethics

In business, conflicts often arise between the goal to succeed in the marketplace and the desire to conduct business honestly and maximize the well-being of consumers by providing them with safe and effective products and services. Although many would argue that by the time people reach college, graduate school, or actually are employed by companies it is a little late to start teaching ethics, many universities and corporations are focusing very intently on teaching and reinforcing ethical behavior.

PRESCRIBING ETHICAL STANDARDS OF CONDUCT In addition, professional organizations often devise a *code of ethics* for their members. For example, the American Marketing Association's Code of Ethics provides guidelines for conduct in many areas of marketing practice, some of which are as follows.[14]

- Disclosure of all substantial risks associated with a product or service.
- Identification of added features that will increase the cost.
- Avoidance of false or misleading advertising.
- Rejection of high-pressure or misleading sales tactics.
- Prohibition of selling or fund raising under the guise of conducting market research.

SOCIALLY RESPONSIBLE BEHAVIOR Whether intentionally or not, some marketers do violate their bond of trust with consumers. In some cases, these actions are actually illegal, as when a manufacturer deliberately mislabels the contents of a package or a retailer adopts a "bait-and-switch" selling strategy whereby consumers are lured into the store with promises of inexpensive products with the sole intent of getting them to switch to higher-priced goods.

In other cases, marketing practices have detrimental effects on society even though they are not explicitly illegal. Some companies erect billboards for alcohol and tobacco products in low-income neighborhoods characterized by excessive abuse of these products, while others sponsor commercials depicting groups of people in an unfavorable light to get the attention of a target market (e.g., many people have complained that Coors' "Swedish bikini team" campaign demeans women in an attempt to appeal to young male beer drinkers).

Marketers' Responses to Unethical or Dangerous Situations. A pivotal situation in ethical behavior is what actions a marketer takes once the company is aware of a problem. In 1987 the Chrysler Corporation was involved in a scandal when the company was accused of resetting the odometers of supposedly new cars that had actually been driven by managers prior to sale. The company only admitted the practice after some managers tried to get out of paying speeding tickets by claiming that their speedometers didn't work because the cable was disconnected![15]

In contrast, Procter & Gamble voluntarily withdrew its Rely tampons from the market following reports of women who had suffered toxic shock syndrome (TSS). Although scientists did not claim a causal link between the usage of Rely and the onset of TSS, the company agreed with the Food & Drug Administration to undertake extensive advertising notifying women of the symptoms of TSS and asking them to return their boxes of Rely for a refund. The company took a $75 million loss and sacrificed an unusually successful new product that had already captured about one-quarter of the billion-dollar sanitary product market.[16]

Industry is increasingly coming to realize that ethical behavior is also good business in the long run, since the trust and satisfaction of consumers translates into years of loyalty from customers whose needs have been met. However, many problems remain. Throughout this book, ethical issues related to the practice of marketing are highlighted. Special boxes called "Marketing Pitfalls" feature questionable practices by marketers or the possible adverse effects on consumers of certain marketing strategies.

Public Policy and Consumerism

Concern for the welfare of consumers has been an issue since at least the beginning of this century. Partly as a result of consumers' efforts, many federal agencies have been established to oversee consumer-related activities. These include the Department of Agriculture, the Federal Trade Commission, the Food and Drug Administration, the Securities and Exchange Commission, and the Environmental Protection Agency.

After Upton Sinclair's 1905 book *The Jungle* exposed the awful conditions in the Chicago meat-packing industry, Congress was prompted to pass important pieces of legislation—the Pure Food and Drug Act in 1906 and the Federal Meat Inspection Act a year later—to protect consumers. A summary of some important consumer legislation since that time appears in Table 1–3.

THE AGE OF CONSUMERISM President John F. Kennedy ushered in the modern era of consumerism with his declaration of consumer rights in 1962. These include the right to safety, the right to be informed, the right to redress, and the right to choice. The 1960s and 1970s were a time of consumer activism as consumers began to organize to demand better-quality products (and to boycott companies that did not provide them). These

TABLE 1–3 Sampler of Federal Legislation Intended to Enhance Consumers' Welfare

Year	Act	Purpose
1951	Fur Products Labeling Act	Regulates the branding, advertising, and shipment of fur products.
1953	Flammable Fabrics Act	Prohibits the transportation of flammable fabrics across state lines.
1958	National Traffic and Safety Act	Creates safety standards for cars and tires.
1958	Automobile Information Disclosure Act	Requires automobile manufacturers to post suggested retail prices on new cars.
1966	Fair Packaging and Labeling Act	Regulates packaging and labeling of consumer products. (Manufacturers must provide information about package contents and origin.)
1966	Child Protection Act	Prohibits sale of dangerous toys and other items.
1967	Federal Cigarette Labeling and Advertising Act	Requires cigarette packages to carry a warning label from the Surgeon General
1968	Truth-in-Lending Act	Requires lenders to divulge the true costs of a credit transaction.
1969	National Environmental Policy Act	Established a national environmental policy and created the Council on Environmental Quality to monitor the effects of products on the environment.
1972	Consumer Product Safety Act	Established the Consumer Product Safety Commission to identify unsafe products, establish safety standards, recall defective products, and ban dangerous products.
1975	Consumer Goods Pricing Act	Bans the use of price maintenance agreements among manufacturers and resellers.
1975	Magnuson–Moss Warranty-Improvement Act	Creates disclosure standards for consumer product warranties and allows the Federal Trade Commission to set policy regarding unfair or deceptive practices.

movements were prompted by the publication of such books as Rachel Carson's *Silent Spring* in 1962, which attacked the irresponsible use of pesticides, and Ralph Nader's *Unsafe at Any Speed* in 1965, which exposed safety defects in General Motors' Corvair automobile. Consumers themselves continue to have a vigorous interest in consumer-related issues, ranging from environmental concerns, such as pollution caused by oil spills, toxic waste, and so on, to excessive violence and sex on television.

CONSUMER RESEARCH AND CONSUMER WELFARE The field of consumer behavior can play an important role in making our lives as consumers better.[17] Many researchers play a role in formulating or evaluating public policies such as ensuring that products are labeled accurately, that people can comprehend important information presented in advertising, or that children are not exploited by program-length toy commercials masquerading as television shows. Many of these ethical and health issues will be raised in later chapters. In addition, the final chapter (Chapter 17) also considers the flip side of the exploitation of consumers by marketers by discussing the "dark side" of consumer behavior, which occurs in situations where consumers abuse or misuse products.

Consumer Behavior as a Field of Study

Although people have certainly been consumers for a long time, it is only recently that consumption per se has been the object of formal study. In fact, while many business schools now *require* that marketing majors take a consumer behavior course, most colleges did not even offer such a course until the 1970s. Much of the impetus for the attention now being given to consumer behavior was the realization by many business people that the consumer really *is* the boss.

Interdisciplinary Influences

Consumer behavior is a very young field, and as it grows, it is being influenced by many different perspectives. Indeed, it is hard to think of a field that is more interdisciplinary. People with training in a very wide range of fields—from psychophysiology to literature—can now be found doing consumer research. Consumer researchers are employed by universities, manufacturers, museums, advertising agencies, and governments. Several professional groups, such as the Association for Consumer Research, have been formed since the mid-1970s. A summary of career opportunities in consumer behavior can be found in Appendix II.

To gain an idea of the diversity of interests of people who do consumer research, consider the list of professional associations that sponsor the field's major journal, the *Journal of Consumer Research:* American Home

Economics Association, American Statistical Association, Association for Consumer Research, Society for Consumer Psychology, International Communication Association, American Sociological Association, The Institute of Management Sciences, American Anthropological Association, American Marketing Association, Society for Personality and Social Psychology, American Association for Public Opinion Research, and American Economic Association.

LEVELS OF ANALYSIS: THE BLIND MEN AND THE ELEPHANT You might remember a children's story about the blind men and the elephant. The gist of the story is that each man touched a different part of the animal, and as a result, the descriptions each gave of the elephant were quite different. This analogy applies to consumer research as well. For example, a similar consumer phenomenon can be studied in different ways and at different levels depending on the training and interests of the researchers studying it.

Figure 1–2 provides a glimpse at some of the disciplines working in the field and the level at which each approaches research issues. These diverse disciplines can be roughly characterized in terms of their focus on *micro* versus *macro* consumer behavior. The fields closer to the top of the pyramid concentrate upon the individual consumer (micro issues), while those toward the base are more interested in the *aggregate* activities that occur

MICRO CONSUMER BEHAVIOR INDIVIDUAL FOCUS

Experimental Psychology
Clinical Psychology
Developmental Psychology
Human Ecology
Microeconomics
Social Psychology
Sociology
Macroeconomics
Semiotics/Literary Criticism
Demography
History
Cultural Anthropology

MACRO CONSUMER BEHAVIOR SOCIAL FOCUS

FIGURE 1–2 **The Pyramid of Consumer Behavior**

among larger groups of people, such as consumption patterns shared by members of a culture or subculture (macro issues).

To demonstrate that the same marketing issue can be explored at different levels, Table 1–4 lists research issues that might be of interest to each contributing discipline and provides examples of how these might be applied in the marketing of women's magazines.

The Issue of Strategic Focus

Many people regard the field of consumer behavior as an *applied social science*. Accordingly, the value of the knowledge generated should be evalu-

TABLE 1–4 Interdisciplinary Research Issues in Consumer Behavior

Disciplinary Focus	Magazine Usage Sample Research Issues for
Experimental psychology: Product role in perception, learning, and memory processes	How specific aspects of magazines, such as their design or layout, are recognized and interpreted; which parts of a magazine are most likely to be read
Clinical psychology: Product role in psychological adjustment	How magazines affect readers' body images (e.g., do thin models make the average woman feel overweight?)
Microeconomics/Human Ecology: Product role in allocation of individual or family resources	Factors influencing the amount of money spent on magazines in a household
Social psychology: Product role in the behavior of individuals as members of social groups	Ways that ads in a magazine affect readers' attitudes toward the products depicted; how peer pressure influences a person's readership decisions.
Sociology: Product role in the social institutions and group relationships	Pattern by which preference for one magazine nature of spreads through a social group (e.g., a sorority)
Macroeconomics: Product role in consumers'relationswith the marketplace	Effects of the price of fashion magazines and expense of items advertised during periods of high unemployment
Semiotics/literary criticism: Product role in the verbal and visual communication of meaning	Ways in which underlying messages communicated by models and ads in a magazine are interpreted
Demography: Product role in the measurable characteristics of a population	Effects of age, income, and marital status of a magazine's readers
History: Product role in societal changes over time	Ways in which our culture's depictions of "femininity" in magazines have changed over time
Cultural anthropology: Product role in a society's beliefs and practices	Ways in which fashions and models in a magazine affect readers' definitions of masculine versus feminine behavior (e.g., the role of working women, sexual taboos)

ated in terms of its ability to improve the effectiveness of marketing practice. Recently, though, some researchers have argued that consumer behavior should not have a strategic focus at all or be a servant to business. It should instead focus on the understanding of consumption for its own sake, rather than because the knowledge can be applied by marketers.[18]

This rather extreme view is probably not held by most consumer researchers, but it has encouraged many to expand the scope of their work beyond the field's traditional focus on the purchase of consumer goods such as food, appliances, cars, and so on.

This more critical view of consumer research has also led the field to recognize that not all consumer behavior and/or marketing activity is necessarily beneficial to individuals or to society. As a result, current consumer research is likely to include attention to the "dark side" of consumer behavior, such as addiction, prostitution, homelessness, shoplifting, or environmental waste. This activity builds upon the earlier work of researchers who have studied consumer issues related to public policy, ethics, and consumerism.

The Issue of Two Perspectives on Consumer Research

One general way to classify consumer research is in terms of the fundamental assumptions the researchers make about what they are studying and how to study it. This set of beliefs is known as a **paradigm.** Like other fields of study, consumer behavior is dominated by a paradigm, but some believe it is in the middle of a *paradigm shift,* which occurs when a competing paradigm challenges the dominant set of assumptions.

The basic set of assumptions underlying the dominant paradigm at this point in time is called **positivism,** or *modernism.* This perspective has significantly influenced Western art and science since the late sixteenth century. It emphasizes the notion that human reason is supreme and that there is a single, objective truth that can be discovered by science. Positivism encourages us to stress the function of objects, to celebrate technology, and to regard the world as a rational, ordered place with a clearly defined past, present, and future.

The emerging **interpretivism,** or *postmodernism,* paradigm questions these assumptions. The proponents of this perspective argue that there is too much emphasis on science and technology in our society and that the ordered, rational view of consumers denies the complex social and cultural world in which we live. Others feel that positivism puts too much emphasis on material well-being and that its logical outlook is dominated by an ideology that stresses the homogeneous views of a culture dominated by white males.

Interpretivists instead stress the importance of symbolic, subjective meaning and the idea that meaning is in the mind of the person—that is, we each construct our own meanings based on our unique and shared cultural experiences, so there are no single right or wrong answers. In this view, the world in which we live is composed of a *pastiche,* or mixture of images.[19] The value placed on products because they help us to create order in our lives is replaced by an appreciation of consumption as a set of diverse expe-

Teaching Hint: The *positivist* and *interpretive* terms are very broad, and each encompasses many diverse viewpoints. The positivist school includes such approaches as logical positivism, modern empiricism, and objectivism. The interpretive paradigm includes subjective, naturalistic, qualitative, and humanistic approaches and is sometimes also referred to as "post-positivism." See Laurel A. Hudson and Julie L. Ozanne, "Alternative Ways of Seeking Knowledge in Consumer Research," *Journal of Consumer Research* 14 (March 1988): 508–21, for a more complete discussion of these approaches.

Teaching Hint: Aspects of postmodernism may be confusing to students. However, some of them have probably been exposed to some of these ideas in other areas of their curriculum. For example, many have probably been introduced to deconstructionism in literature courses, to the mixing of styles in architecture or art, or to feminist ideology. To help them understand these concepts, consider discussing them in the context of consumers' changing lifestyles—that is, compare the relatively focused, restricted roles played by consumers in the 1950s to today's consumers, who "try on" many different styles and roles and who have access to a staggering assortment of niche magazines, food types, and so on.

Research Report: The interpretive research paradigm differs in many important ways from the traditional scientific method. Some major differences include reliance on the researcher as a source of data, the development of *grounded theory* (i.e., the substantive theory emerges from the data), the use of *emergent design* (i.e., the methodology is modified as the study progresses), and the negotiation of outcomes (i.e., respondents participate in the interpretation of their behaviors).   For a more complete description, see Yvonna S. Lincoln and Egon G. Guba, *Naturalistic Inquiry* (Beverly Hills, Calif.: Sage, 1985).

Teaching Hint: Both the positivist and interpretive approaches to consumer research focus primarily on *describing* the social condition, rather than trying to change it. The student with an interest in consumerism or public policy should be referred to critical theory, a third approach that adopts a social change orientation. A stimulating class discussion can be led around the question of what consumer researchers can or should do to help consumers and policymakers function in the market-place.   For an excellent overview of critical theory, see Jeff B. Murray and Julie L. Oz- anne, "The Critical Imagination: Emancipatory Interests in Consumer Research," *Journal of Consumer Research* 18 (September 1991): 192–44.

TABLE 1–5 Positivist Versus Interpretivist Approaches to Consumer Behavior

Assumptions	Positivist Approach	Interpretivist Approach
Nature of reality	Objective, tangible	Socially constructed
	Single	Multiple
Goal	Prediction	Understanding
Knowledge generated	Time free	Time bound
	Context independent	Context dependent
View of causality	Real causes exist	Multiple, simultaneous shaping events
Research relationship	Separation between researcher and subject	Interactive, cooperative with researcher being part of phenomenon under study

Source: Adapted from Laurel A. Hudson and Julie L. Ozanne, "Alternative Ways of Seeking Knowledge in Consumer Research," *Journal of Consumer Research* 14 (March 1988): 508–21, 509. Reprinted with the permission of the University of Chicago Press.

riences. The major differences between these two perspectives on consumer research are summarized in Table 1–5.

An Overview of Consumer Behavior Research Methods

There is no single right way or wrong way to conduct consumer behavior research. Because the field is composed of researchers from so many different disciplines, the researcher's "toolbox" is filled with a variety of approaches and techniques. The choice will depend on both the researcher's theoretical orientation and the nature of the problem. For example, is the researcher's goal to *understand* current behavior for its own sake or to *predict* consumers' future behavior? Is the researcher interested in testing a hypothetical model or in looking for findings that can be incorporated in, to a marketing strategy?

The first step in designing the research is defining the general problem to be addressed and specific objectives to be pursued. The problem may be to explore some consumer phenomenon that is of scientific or public policy interest, such as how consumers process nutritional information on product packages. In such a case, the objective might be identifying how perceptual and cognitive issues relate to consumers' processing of packaging information rather than determining how these dynamics affect the fortunes of any one brand.

On the other hand, the research problem may be directly related to a marketing manager's desire to improve the performance of a particular brand in the marketplace. In this case, the researcher will address such issues as which version of three different packaging alternatives best communicates the desired image for the product, or how packaging alternatives affect consumers' purchase behavior in the supermarket.

The researcher's next step is to identify the specific components of the research task. These include the characteristics of the consumer population of interest and the environmental context of the problem (e.g., a brand's performance relative to the prominence of nutritional information on the package or a brand's performance history when prior packaging changes were made). Depending on the researcher's theoretical foundation and assumptions of the problem, the same research components can be approached in radically different ways. One useful way to classify the approaches to consumer behavior research relies on the distinctions between exploratory and conclusive research.

Exploratory research is designed to provide insights into a problem where the phenomenon is not yet well-defined. The research process is relatively flexible and unstructured and may involve the in-depth probing of relatively few consumers. Due to emphasis on the subjective rather than objective nature of the research process, this book groups interpretive (or post-positivist) research methods under the rubric of exploratory research. This type of research is often used as a precursor to the design of conclusive research.

Conclusive research is designed to test specific hypotheses. The information needed is clearly defined, and the sample consumer population is intended to be representative of some larger group. The findings in this type of research are often used as input to decision making.

A summary of the methods and techniques used in these approaches to consumer behavior research is given in Figure 1–3.* Although there are exceptions, many researchers equate qualitative methods with exploratory research and quantitative methods with conclusive research.

Exploratory Research

Exploratory research is performed to learn more about consumer behavior issues, to generate ideas for future, more rigorous studies, or to test a researcher's initial hunches about some phenomenon. It is not usually done to "explain" anything or to provide immediately actionable results to management, but rather to get a better sense of what further work needs to be done. Since the researchers are not concerned that results will be generalizable to large groups of consumers, at this stage they usually have the "luxury" of being able to do more in-depth work with small numbers of consumers to really understand why these individuals feel or act the way they do. Exploratory research often consists of a "grab bag" of innovative methods that

---

*The remainder of this section provides an overview of a wide variety of research methods and techniques used to study consumer behavior[20]; it is not intended to provide the detailed information to be found in a marketing research textbook.

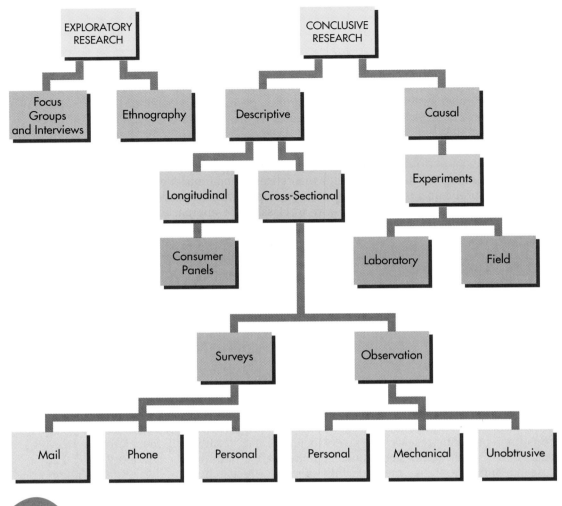

FIGURE 1–3 Alternate Approaches to Consumer Behavior Research

Figure 1–3 is available as Transparency 1.

are used to understand the marketplace from the consumer's point of view. The researcher's experience and personal interpretation of the findings often are a crucial facet of the analysis.

FOCUS GROUPS Of all exploratory research techniques, focus groups are the most widely used.[21] It has been estimated that approximately 140,000 such groups are held each year in the United States alone. **Focus groups** help to gather information from group interaction that is *focused* on a series of topics introduced by a discussion leader or moderator. Each participant is encouraged to express his or her views and to react to the views of others. The group typically consists of five to nine people who have been screened on some basis, often to represent demographic characteristics of the target market of interest.

Advantages and Disadvantages of Focus Groups. Compared to an individual interview, the group setting may stimulate participants by allowing them to feed off of comments made by others. Group interplay makes meaningful comments more likely. It also allows the researcher access to useful data with little direct input.

In some situations the security of being in a group may also encourage more candor, especially if other group members share some important characteristic. For example, one project used groups of overweight women to explore their reactions to clothing and shopping. Amongst themselves, members had a tendency to bitterly refer to themselves as "fat ladies." They felt ignored by the rest of society (especially by merchants). This insight allowed the client to develop a strategy that stressed the special attention paid to this group.[22]

Another advantage is that groups representing specific, desired characteristics can be assembled. The client can obtain feedback from representatives of a distinct segment, and can elicit responses from multiple segments. General Motors regularly conducts focus groups among *both* consumers and dealers to identify desirable car features possessed by competitors. These results led them to model their air filter covers after Mazda's, and to follow the example of Saab in putting fuses in the glove box.[23]

One drawback to focus groups is that, while they are easy to conduct, they are not often based in natural settings. As a result, there is always some uncertainty about the accuracy of responses.[24] Another problem is that individual decision-making processes are not always the same as group processes. For example, the degree to which people accept risk as members of a group tends to differ from when they make a decision alone. Group judgments tend to be polarized (i.e., more extreme) than individual judgments, and under some circumstances, this factor leads to riskier decisions by groups. (This increased tolerance of risk is known as the "risky shift phenomenon.")

PROJECTIVE TECHNIQUES

A projective stimulus is often used in conjunction with individual interviews, although focus group moderators may also use one to stimulate group discussion as well. Projective tests involve the presentation of an ambiguous, unstructured object, activity, or person to which the consumer responds in some way (e.g., explaining the object, telling a story about it, drawing a picture of it, etc.). Projectives are used when it is believed that a consumer will not or cannot respond meaningfully to direct questioning.

Projective techniques allow consumers to respond to neutral situations, where presumably their own feelings are not at issue and they are freer to respond openly. These techniques assume that a person's responses can then be inferred to reflect back to his or her own deep-seated feelings about an issue. Because there are no right or wrong answers, it is hoped that consumers will project their own unconscious feelings into their answers.

Teaching Hint: The term *projection* was first used by Sigmund Freud to refer to an ego defense mechanism similar to rationalization or repression. The ego masters threats to the self by distorting reality and attributing anxiety about these threats to the outside world. The basic assumption is that the individual will interpret material to be consistent with his or her value system. See Harold H. Kassarjian, "Personality and Consumer Behavior: A Review," *Journal of Marketing Research* 8 (November 1971): 409–18.

Research Report: While projective test results are often interpreted subjectively by the researcher, in a few applications response baselines have been established. Some researchers attempt to organize comments so that they can be generalized a bit more. For example, a matrix might be constructed based on respondents' descriptions of the images they have of three types of people: (1) a user of a particular product, (2) a lapsed user of the product, and (3) a nonuser of the product. Responses of a number of participants can then be aggregated to pinpoint any consistencies that might emerge. See Wendy Gordon and Roy Langmaid, *Qualitative Market Research* (Hants, England: Gower, 1988).

Additional Example: A milk company was concerned about its poor reputation. Its sales force reported that the reasons for this problem were that the milk was seen as being low in butterfat and unclean. However, in a balloon test it was discovered that parents disliked the milk because their children were exerting pressure on them to buy brands of milk advertised on children's television programs. See Harold Kassarjian, "Personality and Consumer Behavior: A Review," *Journal of Marketing Research* 8 (November 1971): 409–18.

An early application of projective research illustrates the value of these procedures.[25] When Saran Wrap was introduced in the 1950s, consumers developed strong negative attitudes toward it because it was very difficult to handle. Depth interviews revealed that this product attribute per se was not responsible for the negative effect.

At that time, women did not have an acceptable outlet to express their dislike of housekeeping. Their frustration with the product was a symbolic reflection of their frustration with the role of homemaker. This deep-seated feeling would not have been expressed in a straightforward interview. Acting on these findings, the product was made less clingy, and its non-kitchen uses were stressed in advertising.

Pictorial Projectives. Consumers enjoy working with pictures, and a number of projective techniques involve the use of pictorial stimuli. Some techniques are simply useful devices to stimulate associations by presenting a consumer in a situation and assessing reactions to it.

Bubble drawings depict a person in a commonplace situation (e.g., in a supermarket or driving a car) and require respondents to provide a caption. Alternatively, a consumer in the drawing might be shown confronting a new situation (e.g., a new product or a change in product packaging), and the respondent is asked to fill in the consumer's comments in the bubble. In either case the responses are interpreted as the respondent's own feelings or doubts about the situation depicted. The bubble drawing in Figure 1–4 allows the respondent to voice concerns about trying a new product by imagining what the woman in the picture is saying.

FIGURE 1–4 A Bubble Drawing Projective Instrument: The respondent is asked to supply the shopper's comments. Source: Wendy Gordon and Roy Langmaid, *Qualitative Market Research* (Hants, England: Gower, 1988), 104. By permission of Gower Publishing Group.

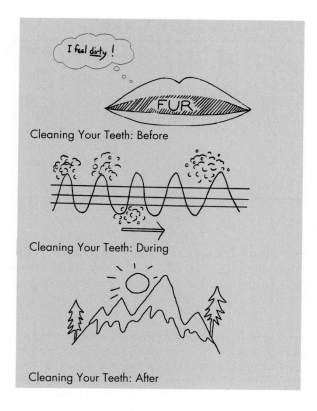

FIGURE 1–5 A consumer's psychodrawing of the act of toothbrushing   Source: Wendy Gordon and Roy Langmaid, *Qualitative Market Research* (Hants, England: Gower, 1988), 104. By permission of Gower Publishing Group.

One study employed a set of drawings specifically designed to assess underlying dimensions of grooming behaviors and rituals.[26] By responding to pictures of people engaged in various activities (e.g., applying make-up), respondents projected their own priorities and fantasies. Some of the resultant grooming themes included the magical and healing qualities attributed to cosmetics (e.g., restoration of youth), their linkage to sexual fortune, the use of grooming products to exhibit maturity and social capability, and the performance of "secret identities" (e.g., homosexual behavior).

Psychodrawing allows the respondent to express his or her perceptions of products or usage situations in a pictorial format. In Figure 1–5, a consumer has projected feelings before, after, and during toothbrushing. In a variation of this technique, an ad agency asked fifty consumers to sketch pictures of people who were likely to buy two brands of cake mixes. As seen in Figure 1–6, many subjects drew Pillsbury users as grandmotherly types, while Duncan Hines customers were younger and more dynamic.[27]

Autodriving uses visual and verbal recordings of consumers themselves as projectives. For example, a family might be photographed as it goes about such evening rituals as preparing for dinner. These photographs are then shown to family members on a later occasion, and they are asked to talk about the pictures. These interviews can shed light on underlying family dynamics (e.g., how are meal preparation tasks divided up among family members?) or attitudes regarding the use of different food products or appli-

FIGURE 1–6 Con-
sumers' Sketches of
Typical Cake-Mix
Users Source: Annetta
Miller and Dody
Tsiantar, "Psyching Out
Consumers," *Newsweek*
(February 27, 1989):
46–47. By permission
of McCann–Ericson
(Research Department).

Who Baked the Cake?

ances. As one example, here is how a full-time housewife who is in charge of meal preparation responded when she was "autodriven" by being shown a picture of her eight-year-old daughter removing stems from spinach (note how her ambivalence about her housewife role starts to come to the surface):

> I was Betty Crocker Homemaker of Tomorrow in high school, embarrassingly so. I think I'm a good cook and I enjoy it . . . . Sometimes I don't want to do it, but most of the time I do enjoy it . . . . I didn't like that image of myself . . . . Sometimes I wish I wasn't so domestic. But it's my nature and I'm real happy doing it . . . . Every so often I wonder if it would have suited me, I know it wouldn't have, but I sort of wish I had the personality where I could have stayed with my career and not chosen to stay home with the kids although I wouldn't have been happy doing that.[28]

Verbal Projectives. In addition to pictures, researchers also rely on a variety of verbal exercises to allow subjects to project their feelings about products. With a *sentence completion* technique, for example, the respondent is given a sentence and asked to fill in the missing word(s). In keeping with the intent of projection, the sentences are phrased in the third person. Sentence completion has the advantage of being focused and yielding concise answers. For this reason, it is especially useful in large groups, since it can be administered to more than one person at a time and responses across people can be easily compared. Commonly used examples include "The average person considers television _____" and "Most people feel that men who use cologne _____." Some versions supply a short story and ask people to describe how it ends.

One study employing this technique found that men and women view automobiles differently. When asked to complete the sentence "When you first get a car, . . ." women tended to supply responses like "you would go for a ride," while men responded "you check the engine," "you polish it," and so on. These results imply that women see a car as something to use, while for men it is an object to protect and be responsible for.

With a *stereotype* technique, respondents are given a description of a typical family or person and are asked to supply related information. For

Additional Example: A related technique is to ask cunsumers to write an obituary for a product. People then are forced to describe the product in human terms, highlighting its memorable qualities.

example, a description of a successful executive might be followed by the request to describe the contents of his wallet. By assessing which credit cards appear there, the researcher can determine which are associated with this social type.

In one of the classic demonstrations of this approach, women in the 1940s were asked to describe two housewives based on their shopping lists.[29] The only difference between the lists was that one included regular coffee, while the other instead specified instant coffee. The "instant coffee house-wife" was described as lazy and a poor planner. This response revealed the concern of women (at that time) for buying time-saving products that would lead their husbands to think they were poor homemakers.

These findings were incorporated directly into marketing strategy. Advertisements for instant coffee were subsequently executed in family settings with the husband's approval clearly communicated. Obviously, this concern would not be present in today's society, where quickness is considered a virtue rather than a vice. Indeed, by 1970 researchers were unable to repeat these findings in a replication study.[30]

INTERPRETIVE STUDIES   Interpretive studies attempt to generate a "thick description" of the experiences of one or a few people. The emphasis is on getting a lot of in-depth information from relatively few people rather than generalizable, descriptive information from a lot of people. No attempt is made to generalize the experiences to others, although the interpretations of each informant can certainly be compared and contrasted to others' explanations.

In interpretive studies, the researcher is considered a part of the interpretive process because his or her own beliefs and background influence what is being studied. Because of the interpretivist belief that consumer behavior cannot be studied apart from the natural context in which it occurs, researchers tend to prefer to travel to the site of consumption activities, rather than bring consumers into a laboratory setting. A consumer's responses in the laboratory cannot be compared to what he or she tells friends or family.

Although relatively new to consumer behavior research, interpretive studies are gaining popularity. They are being applied to topics ranging from the construction of shopping environments (e.g., the mixing of architectural styles, store types, and varieties of ethnic foods in a mall) to the rise of the "body culture" in our society, where consumers alter their bodies through dieting, exercise, and surgery to make unique statements about themselves. Some techniques for collecting data in interpretive studies have been around since the early days of consumer behavior, some are now being borrowed from other fields such as anthropology and literary criticism, and still others are under development.

Ethnography.   The methodology for studying consumers in their natural "habitats" is derived from techniques used by anthropologists when studying foreign cultures. A common strategy is *participant observation,* in which the researcher is immersed in the host culture. Although the researcher does not "go native," the aim is to try to understand the people on their own terms. This in-depth study of a specific group's behaviors, social rules, and beliefs is called **ethnography.** Research is usually done in a natural setting, and is reported in the form of a very detailed *case study.*

The ethnographic approach has come to the forefront of the consumer behavior research largely as the result of a recent project called the Consumer Behavior Odyssey, in which a team of marketing professors traveled across the United States in a recreational vehicle to interact with consumers in a wide variety of natural settings, ranging from swap meets and festivals to convents and museums.[31] The project yielded enormous quantities of field notes, still photos, and videotapes that documented interviews with many diverse types of consumers. The Odyssey was one of the first systematic attempts by consumer researchers to study consumers in their real environments rather than in controlled or laboratory settings.

More recently, a major advertising agency borrowed a page from anthropologists by going "undercover" in a typical American small town. The Chicago office of the Foote Cone & Belding Agency decided to learn more about the increasing desire of consumers to return to a simpler life, so it chose a small Illinois town that it code-named "Laskerville" as the site of its project (the project is named after one of the agency's founders, Albert Lasker). On several occasions agency researchers have visited the town, talking with local residents, reading local newspapers, and attending town functions (even funerals) to determine what issues are important to the consumers. No tape recorders or notes have been allowed, and the town's identity remains a closely guarded secret—even the agency's CEO doesn't know its real name. The agency's goal in monitoring Laskerville is to gain insight into what makes Middle America "tick."[32]

MARKETING PITFALL

The potential invasion of privacy by market researchers is an issue for researchers who go "underground" to study consumers in their natural environments. A California couple sued Nissan, charging that the company had planted a "spy" from Tokyo in their home. The researcher's assignment was to study the living and car purchasing patterns of U.S. consumers, and he allegedly rented a room in the couple's home while he observed the behavior of the plaintiffs and their neighbors. The suit was eventually dropped.[33]

Conclusive Research

Conclusive research is generally a goal-oriented process in which the researcher wants to make some definitive statements about relationships among variables. Since conclusive research aims to provide decision makers with actionable information, the emphasis is on descriptive information that is generalizable beyond the sample and quantifiable for comparison across individuals.

In obtaining generalizable data, this research perspective assumes that while there may be some individual variations or effects due to chance, the differences will "wash out" if enough different subjects are studied. In obtaining quantifiable data, the aim is to maximize the reliability of the results and make it more likely that the same effect will be observed in future studies. The goal is not to predict the behavior of any one person, but rather to predict the typical or average response of people who share certain characteristics.

The methods for collecting data require little interpretation on the part of the researcher, who is expected to remain an impartial observer. The responses elicited from the studied consumers can be physiological (e.g., eye movements measured in eye-tracking studies to determine what parts of commercials capture the consumers' attention), verbal (e.g., responses to questions about commercials the consumers have seen), or behavioral (e.g., purchase volume after the consumers have been exposed to a special price promotion).

Not surprisingly, conclusive inquiry can be further divided into two types: descriptive and causal. The major goal of descriptive research is to describe something without necessarily explaining the reason for the phenomenon. Causal research, in contrast, is performed to obtain evidence of cause-and-effect relationships.

Descriptive Research. Descriptive consumer research is usually done to identify the characteristics of a consumer segment or one or more products in the marketplace. For example, a brand manager for a soft drink might want to know the profile of the "heavy user" of her product as compared with people who drink her competitors' products. Or, this manager might want to track the public's consumption of diet versus regular soft drinks over time. In addition, she might want to know whether changes in promotional expenditures for the brand are associated with a change in the brand's sales.

A *longitudinal design* tracks the responses of the same sample of subjects over time. Market researchers often rely on *panel studies,* where a sample of respondents (usually drawn from consumer households) that is statistically representative of a larger market agrees to provide information about purchases on a regular basis. Participants respond to detailed questionnaires about their purchasing habits, media usage, and so on. A sample page from one such survey is shown in Figure 1–7.

A *cross-sectional design* is the most widely used in marketing research. This format involves the collection of information from one or more groups of respondents at only one point in time. Specific types of surveys that are used in cross-sectional designs will be discussed at a later point.

Causal Research. Causal research attempts to understand cause-and-effect relationships. Marketers often want to know what variables, called *independent variables,* cause a phenomenon and what variables, called *dependent variables*, are affected when the independent variables are changed. To be able to rule out alternative explanations, they must carefully design *experiments* that test prespecified relationships among variables.

For example, while a brand manager may find from descriptive research that sales tend to rise when the brand is promoted more heavily, he or she

Research Report: Some consumer researchers have also adapted research methods from the discipline of history to explain causes for change over time. For a discussion of these techniques, see Ruth Ann Smith and David S. Lux, "Historical Method in Consumer Research: Developing Causal Explanations of Change," *Journal of Consumer Research* 19 (March 1993): 595–610.

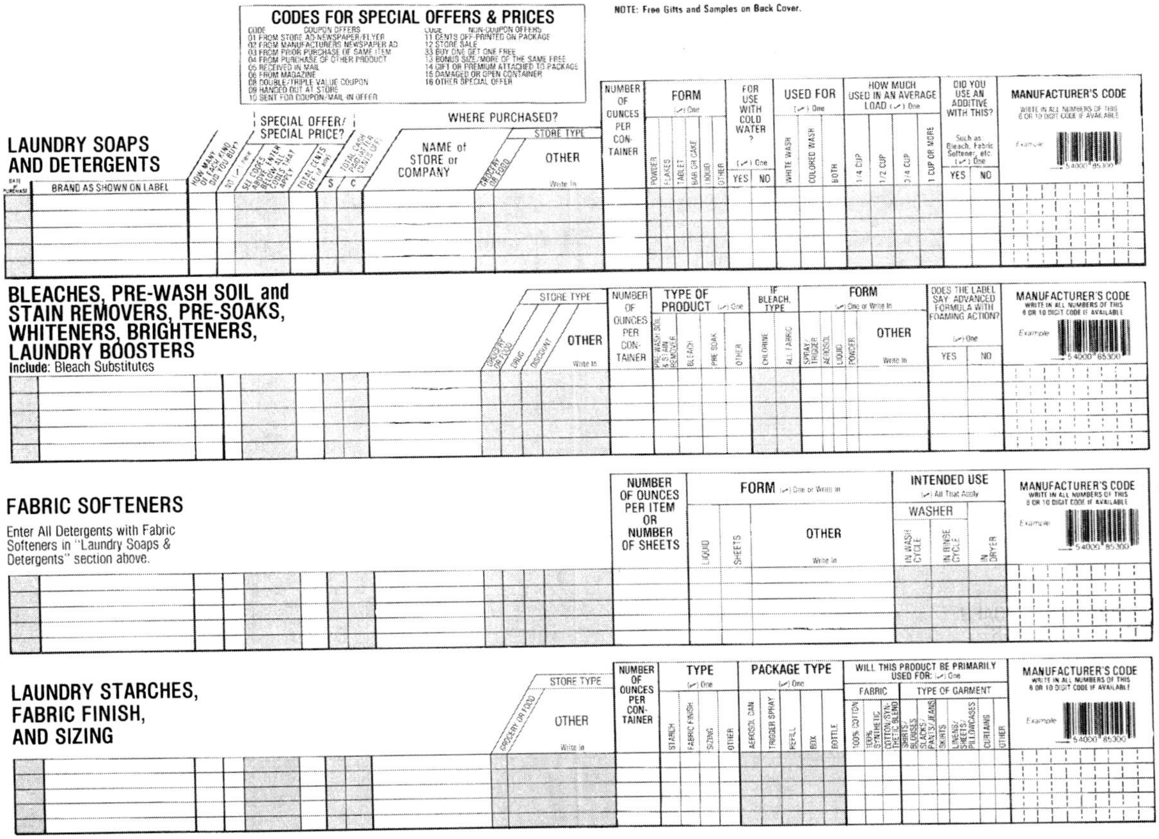

FIGURE 1–7 A Page from a Typical Survey Form: This page illustrates the detailed information syndicated services collect from consumer panelists regarding their purchase patterns.

cannot be sure that the extra promotional effort is really the *cause* of the sales rise. Some third factor may be at work that is affecting sales at the same time (e.g., people naturally buy more during the Christmas shopping season, so the product may sell more simply because people are out in the stores looking harder for things to buy).

Causal studies may be performed in laboratories or in carefully controlled field settings, such as stores, restaurants, or homes. In either case, the researcher must be able not only to manipulate the independent variables that are under study but to hold constant other factors. If a change in the dependent variable is observed after only the independent variable(s) has been manipulated, the researcher can be more confident in concluding that the independent variable(s) in fact exerts a causal (rather than merely correlational) relationship with the dependent variable(s).

For example, a manufacturer might want to assess whether a package change for one of its products (an independent variable) will increase sales (a dependent variable). With the cooperation of a store chain, it might select some outlets that are matched in terms of location, customer demographics, and so on. One set of stores might feature the product with the new package, while another set would continue to sell the product in its old package. Management could then compare sales of the brand between the two sets of stores. If sales rose significantly in stores carrying the new package, researchers could conclude with a reasonable degree of confidence that the new package did, in fact, exert a causal effect on sales.

Types of Data

The actual data collected by consumer researchers can be divided into two general categories: primary data and secondary data. Very simply, *primary data* is any information that is collected specifically for the purposes of the present study. *Secondary data,* on the other hand, is information that already exists in some form; it has been originally collected for another purpose but may be very useful to the present research.

PRIMARY DATA Primary data, which is collected by the researcher, can take many forms. Exploratory research designs often rely upon qualitative methods like those already discussed. Conclusive research designs involve either experimentation (in the laboratory or field), surveys, or observational techniques.*

Obtaining Survey Data. Most surveys consist of some type of questionnaire, where a respondent is presented with a set of statements and is asked to respond to them. These questionnaires can take many forms, but the most widely-used is a **Likert scale.** The respondent simply checks or circles a number that indicates how much he or she agrees or disagrees with a statement:

Sears is a fun place to shop.

Disagree   1   2   3   4   5   Agree

A **semantic-differential scale** is also popular. This survey tool consists of a series of bipolar adjectives (e.g., good/bad, pretty/ugly) that anchor either end of a set of numbers; the respondent evaluates a concept along the various dimensions:

The atmosphere at Sears is

Cold   1   2   3   4   5   Warm

Another measuring device is a **rank-order scale,** where the respondent

---

*This section will very briefly review some survey and observational methods; experimental designs are beyond the scope of this book.

is asked to rank products or stores in order of preference according to some criterion:

In terms of stores that are fun places to shop, please rank the following from 1 to 4.

_____ J.C. Penney

_____ KMart

_____ Sears

_____ Wal-Mart

Essentially, a researcher who wants to administer a survey to a large number of consumers has three choices: Use the telephone, use the mail, or interview people in person.

- Mail surveys usually consist of a one-shot questionnaire that is sent to a sample of consumers, often with some *incentive* to return the survey (the incentive may be a dollar bill attached to the survey or the promise to donate money to the respondent's favorite charity). Alternatively, a consumer may belong to a panel like those described earlier and receive a packet of materials in the mail on a regular basis. Mail surveys are relatively easy to administer and offer a high degree of anonymity to respondents. On the down side, the researcher has little flexibility in the types of questions asked, and little control over the circumstances under which the questionnaire is answered (or, for that matter, who actually answers it).

- Telephone surveys usually consist of a short phone conversation where an interviewer reads a series of brief questions. Technological developments have made computer-assisted telephone interviewing much more common; the interviewer reads questions from a CRT screen and the respondent's answers are recorded directly into the computer. While telephone interviewing can yield data from large numbers of consumers very quickly, researchers are limited in that the respondent can't be asked to react to any visual stimuli. Furthermore, the proliferation of *telemarketing*, where business solicitations are made over the phone, has eroded the willingness of many consumers to participate in phone surveys.

- Personal interviews can be conducted in the respondent's home, although this practice has declined markedly in recent years due to escalating costs and security concerns. More typically, the researcher conducts a "mall-intercept" study, where participants are recruited in shopping malls or other public areas and asked to respond to a survey. The advantage of being able to tailor the interview based on the respon- ses obtained (e.g., the researcher can *probe,* or ask further questions, to follow up on what a person has said) may not materialize because respondents are often reluctant to answer questions of a personal nature in a face-to-face context.

Obtaining Observational Research Data. Observational research situations are those in which the researcher wishes to record some aspect of consumer behavior without actually intervening in any way or manipulating the situation. Observational research data can be very useful as a way to corroborate respondents' own reports of what they do. For example, when mothers were interviewed in focus groups, they claimed they bought a fruit snack made by General Mills because of its "wholesomeness." When researchers hung around supermarkets and observed mothers shopping with their children, however, a different story emerged: Children tended to beg their mothers for different food items, and mothers did not appear to care which brand they bought. In other words, the desire to buy wholesome food was relevant to the category of fruit snacks, but did not translate into the motivation to buy a specific brand.[34]

- When *personal observation* is employed, the behavior of people is simply recorded. For example, a researcher might observe customers in a store, noting what questions they ask of salespeople and how they handle the product.

- *Mechanical observation* relies on devices to record behavior. Turnstiles in stores are used to track how many people have visited the establishment over a certain period. The widespread use of the UPC (Universal Product Code) on products has fostered the growth of scanning technology, where consumers' purchases can be recorded to track buying patterns. In another use of this technology, marketers can tailor their promotions to the specific needs of consumers (e.g., by issuing diaper coupons to consumers who have purchased baby food). Another widespread application of mechanical observation is the meter method used by A.C. Nielsen to record consumers' television watching. The data obtained from metering devices is used to determine who is watching which shows; these television ratings are how the networks determine how much they will charge advertisers for commercials (and which shows eventually get canceled or renewed).

- *Unobtrusive measures* are methods of data collection that do not require direct human responses. These techniques are sometimes called *trace analysis* because they rely on the physical traces, or evidence, of past behavior. They are often used when the researcher suspects that people will probably distort their responses, either because they may not be able to accurately recall their behavior or perhaps they want to portray themselves in a more favorable light. For example, instead of asking a person to report on the products that are currently in his or her home, the researcher might actually go to the house and perform a "pantry check," recording the products that are actually on the person's shelves. One innovative research method, called *garbology*, involves sifting through people's garbage (after it has been collected and anonymously labeled) to determine product usage. This unobtrusive technique is especially useful when the individual might be reluctant to report his or her usage truthfully, as may be the case for such sensitive products as liquor or contraceptives.[35]

SECONDARY DATA Secondary data is not directly collected by the researcher. It is usually in the form of published data and is usually available from many sources. These sources of secondary data can range from a company's sales history (*internal data* is generated by the organization

Research Report: Another example of an unobtrusive technique is provided by a study of magazine readership that measured exposure to specific pages by placing small glue spots on each page. Researchers could then record which seals had been broken to determine what sections had been skipped over. See David A. Aaker and George S. Day, *Marketing Research,* 4th ed. (New York: John Wiley & Sons, 1990).

Research Report: One classic study gauged the relative popularity of different exhibits in a museum by measuring the frequency with which floor tiles around them had to be replaced: the greater the erosion, the more people walking through. A survey of cars consigned to junkyards determined that the usage life of American-made cars (regardless of how many times the car had changed hands) averaged 10.56 years, much longer than had been thought. See J. Webb Eugene, Donald T. Campbell, Richard D. Schwartz, and Lee Sechrest, *Unobtrusive Measures: Nonreactive Research in the Social Sciences* (Chicago: Rand McNally, 1966); R.A. Gould and P.B. Potter, "Use-Lives of Automobiles in America: A Preliminary Archaeological View," in *Toward an Ethnoarchaeology of Modern America,* ed. R.A. Gould (Providence, R.I.: Brown University, Department of Anthropology, Research Papers in Anthropology, 1984), 4.

itself) to such government sources as the U.S. Census Bureau (*external data* is information obtained from a source other than the organization). Secondary data is often helpful in understanding a problem (and interpreting primary data) by placing it in a broader context. Many general business sources of secondary data are available (usually for a fee). These range from business directories and computerized data bases to syndicated services such as VALS, Simmons, and the Yankelovich Monitor that track the purchases, attitudes. and lifestyles of different consumer segments. A list of sources of secondary data is provided in Appendix I.

MARKETING PITFALL

The growing use of sophisticated demographic data bases is not sitting well with many consumers, who are concerned about possible violations of privacy. After receiving 30,000 complaints, Lotus Development Corporation killed plans to sell its *MarketPlace: Households* software data base, which contained demographic information on 80 million households. At around the same time, New England Telephone & Telegraph canceled plans to sell a list of 4.7 million of its customers, and Blockbuster Entertainment Corporation denied its intent to sell information detailing customers' video rental habits.[36]

Plan of the Book

This book covers many facets of consumer behavior, and many of the research perspectives briefly described in this chapter will be highlighted in later chapters. The plan of the book is simple: It goes from micro to macro. Think of the book as a sort of photograph album of consumer behavior: Each chapter provides a "snapshot" of consumers, but the lens used to take each picture gets successively wider.

The book begins with issues related to the individual consumer and expands its focus until it eventually considers the behaviors of large groups of people in their social settings. The topics to be covered correspond to the wheel of consumer behavior presented in Figure 1–8.

Section II, "The Consumer as an Individual," considers the consumer at his or her most micro level. It examines how the individual receives information from his or her immediate environment and how this material is learned, stored in memory, and used to form and modify individual attitudes. Section III, "The Consumer as a Decision Maker," explores the ways in which consumers use the information they have acquired to make decisions about consumption activities. Section IV, "The Consumer as a Social Being," expands the focus further by considering how the consumer functions as a part of a larger social structure. This structure includes the influence of social groups to which the consumer belongs, social class, and lifestyle, as well as the effects of the person's ethnic group, age group, and place of residence.

Finally, Section V, "The Consumer and Culture," completes the picture as it examines marketing's impact on mass culture. These effects include the relationship of marketing to the expression of cultural values, how products and services are related to rituals and cultural myths, and the interface between marketing efforts and the creation of art, music, and other forms of popular culture that are so much a part of our daily lives.

FIGURE 1–8 The Wheel of Consumer Behavior

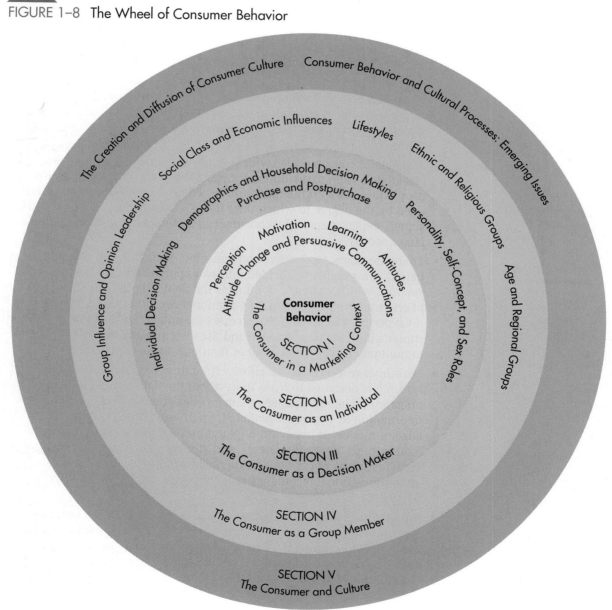

Chapter Summary

- *Consumer behavior* is the study of the processes involved when individuals or groups select, purchase, use, or dispose of products, services, ideas, or experiences to satisfy needs and desires.

- A consumer may purchase, use, and/or dispose of a product, but these functions may be performed by different people. In addition, consumers may be thought of as role players who need different products to help them play their various parts.

- *Market segmentation* is an important aspect of consumer behavior. Consumers can be segmented along many dimensions, including product usage, demographics (the objective aspects of a population, such as age and sex), and psychographics (psychological and lifestyle characteristics).

- Marketing activities exert an enormous impact on individuals. Consumer behavior is relevant to our understanding of both public policy issues (e.g., ethical marketing practices) and of the dynamics of popular culture.

- The field of consumer behavior is interdisciplinary; it is composed of researchers from many different fields who share an interest in how people interact with the marketplace. These disciplines can be categorized by the degree to which their focus is micro (the individual consumer) versus macro (the consumer as a member of groups or of the larger society).

- There are many perspectives on consumer behavior, but research orientations can roughly be divided into two approaches. The *positivist perspective,* which currently dominates the field, emphasizes the objectivity of science and the consumer as a rational decision maker. The *interpretivist perspective,* in contrast, stresses the subjective meaning of the consumer's individual experience and the idea that any behavior is subject to multiple interpretations rather than one single explanation.

- Consumer research can be either exploratory or conclusive. *Exploratory research* is designed to learn more about the nature of a problem or phenomenon, while *conclusive research* is designed to obtain actionable information or to test predictions (hypotheses) based on prior knowledge or models of behavior. Exploratory methods include the use of focus groups, depth interviews, and ethnography. Conclusive methods include the use of controlled experiments, surveys, consumer panels, and observational techniques ranging from scanning technology to garbology.

- *Primary data* refers to information that is collected for the purposes of a specific observational or experimental research study, while secondary data refers to existing information that may be adapted to the current study. *Secondary data* sources include computerized data bases, the U.S. Census, and many syndicated studies conducted by companies and made available to clients for a fee.

Key Terms

conclusive research, p. 23

consumer behavior, p. 7

determinant attributes, p. 10

ethnography, p. 30

exchange, p. 7

exploratory research, p. 23

focus groups, p. 24

interpretivism, p. 21

Likert scale, p. 33

marketing mix, p. 10

paradigm, p. 21

positivism, p. 21

projective techniques, p. 25

rank-order scale, p. 33

semantic-differential scale, p. 33

targeted marketing strategy, p. 10

Consumer Behavior Challenge

1. This chapter states that people play different roles and that their consumption behaviors may differ depending on the particular role they are playing. State whether you agree or disagree with this perspective, giving examples from your personal life.

2. Some researchers believe that the field of consumer behavior should be a pure, rather than an applied, science. That isresearch issues should be framed in terms of their scientific interest rather than their applicability to immediate marketing problems. Give your views on this issue.

3. Name some products or services that are widely used by your social group. State whether you agree or disagree with the notion that these products help to form the group bonds, supporting your argument with examples from your list of products used by the group.

4. Although demographic information on large numbers of consumers is used in many marketing contexts, some people believe that the sale of data on customers' incomes, buying habits, and so on constitutes an invasion of privacy and should be stopped. Comment on this issue from both a consumer's and a marketer's point of view.

5. List the three stages in the consumption process. Describe the issues that you considered in each of these stages when you made a recent important purchase.

6. State the differences between the positivist and interpretivist approaches to consumer research. For each type of inquiry, give examples of product dimensions that would be more usefully explored using that type of research over the other.

7. What aspects of consumer behavior are likely to be of interest to a financial planner? To a university administrator? To a graphic arts designer? To a social worker in a government agency? To a nursing instructor?

8. Critics of targeted marketing strategies argue that this practice is discriminatory and unfair, especially if such a strategy encourages a group of people to buy a product that may be injurious to them or that they cannot afford. On the other hand, The Association of National Advertisers argues that banning targeted marketing constitutes censorship and is thus a violation of the First Amendment. What are your views regarding

both sides of this issue?

9. Select a product and brand that you use frequently, and make a list of what you consider to be the brand's determinant attributes. Without revealing your list, ask a friend who is approximately the same age but of the opposite sex to make a similar list for the same product (although the brand may be different). Compare and contrast the identified attributes and report your findings.

10. Collect ads for five different brands of the same product. Report on the segmentation variables, target markets, and emphasized product attributes in each ad.

CNN Connection

CNN. A video segment is available to accompany this CNN Connection.

The Museum of Modern Mythology

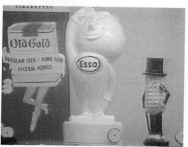

What reasonably alert consumer living in our society would not recognize the likes of Ronald McDonald, the Jolly Green Giant, or Mr. Peanut? It is hard to ignore the enormous impact marketers have on the daily lives of consumers. Many of our most favorite (and despised!) imaginary characters were created by advertisers who hope to embody a product's characteristics in a mythical figure, whether portrayed by an actor or in animated form. The successful creation of a product icon allows a brand to take on a "life of its own."

Marketing creations are appreciated by some scholars for their social significance. As this chapter observed, the marketing system is highly interconnected with other spheres of our daily lives and our culture. The Museum of Modern Mythology in San Francisco is devoted entirely to collecting video, print, and plastic figures of such "national treasures" as Colonel Sanders (Kentucky Fried Chicken) and Charlie the Tuna.

People enjoy these exhibits because they bring back childhood memories (e.g., many older people fondly remember the Philip Morris messenger boy). At the same time, popular culture researchers find value in these artifacts because they reflect aspects of family life and political and social issues at different times in our society. For example, the Museum displays ethnic and racial characters that many would consider offensive today, such as the original version of Aunt Jemima (depicted as a slave "mammy") or the Frito Bandito, a stereotype that was retired by Frito-Lay after Hispanic groups protested its use. The existence of this museum, as well as other collections such as the artifacts housed in The Museum of American History in Washington, D.C., reminds us that consumer behavior cannot be understood apart from the rich social and cultural context in which it occurs.

SIMMONS Connection

Data File: Magazine Readers

Ellen usually reads *Seventeen* magazine, but today she has decided to read *Mademoiselle* instead. As you will discover in later chapters, there are a great many potential reasons why she may have made this particular choice or decided that she needed a change in the first place. But as Ellen perused the magazine covers, she clearly had some very specific reactions to each. And, she had some definite ideas about how readers of, say, *Harper's Bazaar* are different from readers of *Ladies' Home Journal*.

As we saw in this chapter, marketers often use general characteristics of a population—demographics—to define their target markets. If they are successful, then their products appeal to just those types of consumers that the marketers had in mind in the first place. As a consumer, Ellen has her own intuitive sense of the demographic characteristics that define the readers of various magazines. But, how accurate are Ellen's perceptions?

First, consider that Ellen herself usually reads *Seventeen*, but today chose *Mademoiselle*. On the basis of the demographic information provided in the Simmons file titled "Chap1," do these magazines appeal to the same "type" of reader? If not, what are the primary differences between the two groups?

Notes

1. Joanne Lipman, "Women in Their 20s Seem to Be Ignored," Wall Street Journal (June 9, 1992): B8.
2. Suzanne Cassidy, "Defining the Cosmo Girl: Check Out the Passport," New York Times (October 12, 1992): D8.
3. William F. Schoell and Joseph P. Guiltinan, Marketing: Contemporary Concepts and Practices, 4th ed. (Boston: Allyn & Bacon, 1990).
4. Erving Goffman, The Presentation of Self in Everyday Life (Garden City, N.Y.: Doubleday, 1959); George H. Mead, Mind, Self, and Society (Chicago: University of Chicago Press, 1934); Michael R. Solomon, "The Role of Products as Social Stimuli: A Symbolic Interactionism Perspective," Journal of Consumer Research 10 (December 1983): 319–29.
5. Ronald Alsop, "Agencies Scrutinize Their Ads for Psychological Symbolism," Wall Street Journal (June 11, 1987): 27.
6. Jeffrey F. Durgee, "On Cezanne, Hot Buttons, and Interpreting Consumer Storytelling," Journal of Consumer Marketing 5 (Fall 1988): 47–51.
7. Bernice Kanner, "Mind Games," Marketing Insights (Spring 1989)9: 50.
8. Joshua Levine, "Desperately Seeking Jeepness," Forbes (May 15, 1989): 134; Anthony Ramirez, "New Cigarettes Raising Issue of Target Market," New York Times (February 18, 1990): 28; Howard Schlossberg, "Segmenting Becomes Constitutional Issue,"Marketing News (April 16, 1990): 1.
9. Annetta Miller, "You Are What You Buy," Newsweek (June 4, 1990)2: 59.
10. These steps are adapted from a discussion of targeted marketing strategy in Schoell and Guiltinan, Marketing.
11. Cyndee Miller, "Military Market Considered Strong Despite Troop Cuts," Marketing News (August 3, 1992)2: 1; Eben Shapiro, "Consumers in the Military Require Precision Marketing," New York Times (May 26, 1992): D10.
12. Elizabeth Roberts, "This Ad's For You," Newsweek (February 24, 1992): 40.
13. Jolie Solomon, "Putting the 'Con' in Consumer," Newsweek (October 26, 1992): 49.
14. American Marketing Association, Code of Ethics, rev. ed. (Chicago: American Marketing Association, 1985).
15. "Dear Chrysler: Outsiders' Advice on Handling the Odometer Charge," Wall Street Journal (June 26, 1987): 19.
16. Larry Edwards, "The Decision Was Easy," Advertising Age (August 26, 1987)2: 106.
17. For consumer research and discussions related to public policy issues, see Paul N. Bloom and Stephen A. Greyser, "The Maturing of Consumerism," Harvard Business Review (November–December 1981): 130–39; George S. Day,

Assessing the Effect of Information Disclosure Requirements," Journal of Marketing (April 1976): 42–52; Dennis E. Garrett, "The Effectiveness of Marketing Policy Boycotts: Environmental Opposition to Marketing," Journal of Marketing 51 (January 1987): 44–53; Michael Houston and Michael Rothschild, "Policy-Related Experiments on Information Provision: A Normative Model and Explication," Journal of Marketing Research 17 (November 1980): 432–49; Jacob Jacoby, Wayne D. Hoyer, and David A. Sheluga, Misperception of Televised Communications (New York: American Association of Advertising Agencies, 1980); Gene R. Lacznizk and Patrick E. Murphy, Marketing Ethics: Guidelines for Managers (Lexington, Mass.: Lexington Books, 1985), 117–23; Lynn Phillips and Bobby Calder, "Evaluating Consumer Protection Laws: Promising Methods," Journal of Consumer Affairs 14 (Summer 1980): 9–36; Donald P. Robin and Eric Reidenbach, "Social Responsibility, Ethics, and Marketing Strategy: Closing the Gap Between Concept and Application," Journal of Marketing 51 (January 1987): 44–58; Howard Schutz and Marianne Casey, "Consumer Perceptions of Advertising as Misleading," Journal of Consumer Affairs 15 (Winter 1981): 340–57; Darlene Brannigan Smith and Paul N. Bloom, "Is Consumerism Dead or Alive? Some New Evidence," in Advances in Consumer Research 11, ed. Thomas C. Kinnear (Provo, Utah: Association for Consumer Research, 1984), 369–73.

18. Morris B. Holbrook, "The Consumer Researcher Visits Radio City: Dancing in the Dark," in Advances in Consumer Research 12, eds. Elizabeth C. Hirschman and Morris B. Holbrook (Provo, Utah: Association for Consumer Research, 1985), 28–31.
19. Alladi Venkatesh, "Postmodernism, Poststructuralism and Marketing," paper presented at the American Marketing Association Winter Theory Conference, San Antonio, February 1992; see also A. Fuat Firat, "Postmodern Culture, Marketing and the Consumer," in Marketing Theory and Application, eds. T. Childers et al. (Chicago: American Marketing Association, 1991), 237–42; A. Fuat Firat and Alladi Venkatesh, "The Making of Postmodern Consumption," in Consumption and Marketing: Macro Dimensions, eds. Russell W. Belk and Nikhilesh Dholakia (Boston: PWS-Kent, 1993).
20. Some of the material in this section is adapted from Naresh K. Malhotra, Marketing Research: An Applied Orientation (Englewood Cliffs, N.J.: Prentice Hall, 1993). The reader is encouraged to consult this or the other excellent textbooks currently available for further information on the field of marketing research.

21. Bobby J. Calder, "Focus Groups and the Nature of Qualitative Marketing Research," *Journal of Marketing Research* 14 (1977): 353–64.

22. Judith Langer, "Getting to Know the Consumer Through Qualitative Research," *Management Review* (April 1987): 42–46.

23. David Kiley, "At Long Last, Detroit Gives Consumers the Right of Way," *Adweek* (June 6, 1988): 26–27.

24. Nicholas G. Calo, "Focus Group Data Can Be Used Immediately—But Be Careful," *Marketing News* (October 24, 1988): 24.

25. David A. Aaker and George S. Day, *Marketing Research*, 4th ed. (New York: John Wiley & Sons, 1990).

26. Dennis W. Rook and Sidney J. Levy, "Psychosocial Themes in Consumer Grooming Rituals," in *Advances in Consumer Research* 10, eds. R. Bagozzi and A. Tybout (Provo, Utah: Association for Consumer Research, 1983), 328–33.

27. Annetta Miller and Dody Tsiantar, "Psyching Out Consumers," *Newsweek* (February 27, 1989)2: 46.

28. Quoted in Deborah D. Heisley and Sidney J. Levy, "Autodriving: A Photoelicitation Technique," *Journal of Consumer Research* 18 (December 1991): 257–72.

29. Mason Haire, "Projective Techniques in Marketing Research," *Journal of Marketing* 14 (April 1950): 649–50.

30. Frederick E. Webster, Jr., and Fredrick Von Pechmann, "A Replication of the 'Shopping List' Study," *Journal of Marketing* 34 (April 1970): 61–63.

31. Russell W. Belk, Melanie Wallendorf, and John F. Sherry, Jr., "The Sacred and the Profane in Consumer Behavior: Theodicy on the Odyssey," *Journal of Consumer Research* 16 (June 1989): 1–38.

32. Carrie Goerne, "Researchers Go Undercover to Learn About 'Laskerville'," *Marketing News* (May 11, 1992): 11.

33. Gary Levin, "Anthropologists in Adland: Researchers Now Studying Cultural Meanings of Brands," *Advertising Age* (February 24, 1992)2: 3.

34. Roberts, "This Ad's For You."

35. Joseph A. Cote, James McCullough, and Michael D. Reilly, "Effects of Unanticipated Situations on Behavior-Intention Differences: A Garbology Analysis," *Journal of Consumer Research* 12 (September 1985): 188–94.

36. Alan Radding, "Consumer Worry Halts Data Bases," *Advertising Age* (February 11, 1991): 28.

II. The Consumer as an Individual

III. The Consumer as a Decision Maker

IV. The Consumer as a Group Member

V. The Consumer and Culture

2. Perception

3. Motivation

4. Learning

5. Attitudes

6. Attitude Change and Persuasive Communications

SECTION

II

The Consumer as

an Individual

In this section, we focus on the internal dynamics of consumers. While "no man is an island," each of us is to some degree a self-contained receptor for information from the outside world. We are constantly confronted with advertising messages, products, other people persuading us to buy, and reflections of ourselves. Each chapter in this section will consider a different aspect of the consumer that is invisible to others: sensations, memories, and attitudes.

Chapter 2 describes the process of perception, where information from the outside world about products and other people is absorbed by the individual and interpreted. Chapter 3 discusses our reasons or motivations for absorbing this information, and how particular needs influence the way we think about products. Chapter 4 focuses on the ways this information is mentally stored and how it adds to our existing knowledge about the world as it is learned.

Chapters 5 and 6 discuss how attitudes—our evaluations of all these products, ad messages, and so on—are formed and (sometimes) changed by marketers. When all of these "internal" parts are put together, the unique role of each individual consumer as a self-contained agent in the marketplace will be clear.

CHAPTER 2

Perception

Buying, Having, and Being: Selections 5–9 from *Buying, Having, and Being: The Washington Post Consumer Behavior Companion*, Second Edition, accompany this chapter.

I t's two o'clock in the morning, and Gail is pulling an all-nighter for her Accounting exam. As her energy starts to lag, she knows she needs some "munchies" as soon as possible. Even though it's cold and rainy, she walks five blocks to an all-night convenience store. She immediately heads for the junk food aisle, ignoring the numerous magazines and novelties that beckon for her attention.

As soon as she's standing in the aisle, Gail knows that only one remedy will do: Chocolate! Her gaze falls on the selection of candy bars displayed at eye level. A new one catches her attention because the brown and gold label seems to say that it's filled with rich dark chocolate, not light milk chocolate. When she picks it up, its heavy "feel" convinces her that it will be hearty enough to satisfy her appetite. She also notices that its name—Lindt—is European, which confirms her hunch that it will indeed deliver a rich, sophisticated "chocolate fix."

Anticipating how good it will taste, she decides to take two—it could be a long night . . . .

Introduction

We live in a world overflowing with sensations. Wherever we turn, we are bombarded by a symphony of colors, sounds, and odors. Some of the "notes" in this symphony occur naturally, such as the loud barking of a dog, the shades of the evening sky, or the heady smell of a rosebush. Others come from people; the person sitting next to you in class might sport tinted blonde hair, bright pink pants, and enough perfume to make your eyes water.

Marketers certainly contribute to this commotion. Consumers are never far from advertisements, product packages, radio and television commercials, and billboards that clamor for their attention. Each of us copes with this bombardment by paying attention to some stimuli and tuning out others. When we do make a decision on a purchase, such as a candy bar, we are responding not only to these influences but to our interpretations of them.

This chapter focuses on the process of perception, in which sensations are absorbed by the consumer and used to interpret the surrounding world. After discussing the stages of this process, the chapter examines how the five senses of sight, smell, sound, touch, and taste affect consumers. It also highlights some interesting ways in which marketers develop products and communications that appeal to the senses.

The chapter emphasizes that the way in which a marketing stimulus is presented plays a role in determining whether the consumer will make sense of it or even notice it in the first place. The techniques and marketing practices that make messages more likely to be noticed are discussed, as is the topic of subliminal persuasion, which includes techniques designed to influence consumers through images and sounds of which they are not aware. Finally, the chapter discusses the process of interpretation, in which the stimuli that are noticed by the consumer are organized and assigned meaning.

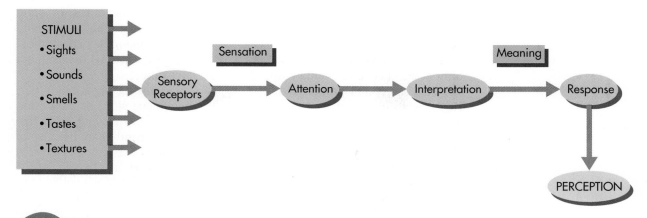

FIGURE 2–1   An Overview of the Perceptual Process

The Perceptual Process

Figure 2–1 is available as Transparency 2.

As you sit in a lecture, you might find your attention shifting. One minute you are concentrating on the instructor's words, and in the next, you catch yourself daydreaming about the upcoming weekend before you realize that you are missing some important points and tune back into the lecture.

Like computers, people undergo stages of information processing in which stimuli are input and stored. Unlike computers, though, we do not passively process whatever information happens to be present. In the first place, only a very small number of the stimuli in our environment are ever noticed. Of these, an even smaller amount are attended to. And the stimuli that do enter consciousness might not be processed objectively. The meaning of a stimulus is interpreted by the individual, who is influenced by his or her unique biases, needs, and experiences. The stages involved in selecting and interpreting stimuli are illustrated in Figure 2–1, which provides an overview of the perceptual process.

From Sensation to Perception

Sensation is the immediate response of our sensory receptors (e.g., eyes, ears, nose, mouth, fingers) to such basic stimuli as light, color, and sound. **Perception** is the process by which these stimuli are selected, organized, and interpreted. Like a computer, we process raw data (sensation). However, the study of perception focuses on what we add to or take away from these sensations as we assign meaning to them.

The subjective nature of perception is demonstrated by a controversial advertisement developed for Benetton by a French agency and shown at the beginning of this chapter. Because a black man and a white man were handcuffed together, the ad was the target of many complaints about racism after it appeared in magazines and on billboards around the United States, even though the company has a reputation for promoting racial tolerance. People interpreted it to depict a black man who had been arrested by a white man.[1] Even though both men are dressed the same, people's prior assumptions distorted the ad's meaning.

The Benetton ad referred to here is available as Transparency 3.

Such interpretations or assumptions stem from the **schemas,** or organized collections of beliefs and feelings, that a person has. That is, we tend to group in our memories the objects we see as having similar characteristics, and the schema to which an object is assigned is a crucial determinant of how we choose to evaluate this object at a later time.

The perceptual process is illustrated by Gail's craving for a candy bar. Her needs dictated that she would find a convenience store at 2:00 a.m., and her goal of locating a quick energy "fix" led her to tune out other distractions, like magazines. She selected the category of candy bars because of the associations she had with chocolate, and the candy bar she selected was in her field of vision. She used package information, such as the color of the wrapping, the weight of the bar, and the European name, to infer characteristics of the product (even though she had never tried it). Gail thus accessed a small portion of the raw data available and processed it to be consistent with her needs. These expectations are largely affected by a consumer's cultural background. For example, many Europeans are "chocolate purists" who would not bother to make a choice between milk and dark chocolate and certainly would not be impressed by a European name on the package!

Stages in the Perceptual Process

Gail's perceptual process can be broken down into the following stages.[2]

1. *Primitive categorization*, in which the basic characteristics of a stimulus are isolated: Gail needs a pick-me-up and chooses chocolate.
2. *Cue check*, in which the characteristics are analyzed in preparation for the selection of a schema: Gail has her own unique schemas or categories for different types of candy bars, such as "creamy milk chocolate" or "rich dark chocolate with a 'kick' to it." Gail uses certain cues, such as the color of the label, to decide in which schema a particular candy bar belongs.

M A R K E T I N G   P I T F A L L

A misunderstanding stemming from a marketer's promotional campaign illustrates what can happen when the categorization process goes awry. Sample bottles of Sunlight dishwashing liquid, which contains 10 percent lemon juice, were mailed to consumers. Almost 80 people were treated at poison centers after drinking some of the detergent.[3] These individuals apparently assumed that the product was actually lemon juice, since many of the packaging cues resembled Minute Maid frozen lemon juice. Among the characteristics of the Sunlight stimulus used during the cue check stage in the perceptual process was the yellow bottle with a prominent picture of a lemon. During confirmation check, a juice schema was selected instead of a dishwashing liquid schema. Consumers found out their mistake the hard way following confirmation completion.[4]

3. *Confirmation check*, in which the schema is selected: Gail decides that the new candy bar most likely falls into her "European dark chocolate" schema.
4. *Confirmation completion*, in which a decision is made as to what the stimulus is: Gail decides her choice is a good candy bar and then reinforces this judgment by considering the label and the "substantial" feel of the bar.

Sensory Systems

External stimuli, or *sensory inputs*, can be received on a number of channels. We may see a billboard, hear a jingle, feel the softness of a cashmere sweater, taste a new flavor of ice cream, or smell a leather jacket.

The inputs picked up by our five senses constitute the raw data that generates many types of responses. For example, sensory data emanating from the external environment (e.g., hearing a song on the radio) can generate internal sensory experiences when the song on the radio triggers a young man's memory of his first dance and brings to mind the *smell* of his date's perfume or the *feel* of her hair on his cheek.

Sensory inputs evoke *historic imagery*, in which events that actually occurred are recalled. *Fantasy imagery* is the result when an entirely new, imaginary experience is the response to sensory data. These responses are an important part of *hedonic consumption*, or the multisensory, fantasy, and emotional aspects of consumers' interactions with products[5]. The data that we receive from our sensory systems determine how we respond to products.

Additional Example: A California company called Subjective Technologies is marketing a sensor system that allows human movements to trigger the playing of sounds and images. For example, an athletic shoe store could simulate the feeling of being at Wimbledon, surrounded by crowd noise. When a customer enters the "court," a video image and sound of a ball being hit would emanate from a corner. The consumer could "return" the ball by going to a diagonal corner and raising a hand. The system can also be adapted to simulate different parts of the world so that travel agents could transport potential clients to distant locales without ever leaving the travel agency. See Cyndee Miller, "Interactive Marketing Hits Surrealistic High," *Marketing News* (November 25, 1991): 6.

MARKETING OPPORTUNITY

Although we usually trust our sensory receptors to give us an accurate picture of the external environment, new technology is making the linkage between our senses and reality more questionable. Computer-simulated environments, known as *virtual reality*, allow surgeons to "cut into" a person without actually drawing blood or an architect to see a building design from different perspectives. This technology, which creates a three-dimensional perceptual environment that the viewer experiences as being virtually real, is already being adapted to more everyday pursuits. The Battletech Center in Chicago features an interactive video game that lets players compete against each other in a simulated 31st century war.[6] Enterprising business people will no doubt continue to find new ways to adapt this technology for consumers' entertainment—perhaps by developing "virtual catalogs" that allow a person to browse through a store without ever leaving his or her armchair.

Marketers rely heavily on visual elements in advertising, store design, and packaging. Meanings are communicated on the visual channel through a product's size, styling, brightness, and distinctiveness from competitors. Color is one of the most potent aspects of visual communication.

COLOR IN THE MARKETPLACE Colors are rich in symbolic value and cultural meanings. For example, the display of red, white, and blue evokes feelings of patriotism for both Americans and French people. Such powerful cultural meanings make color a central aspect of many marketing strategies. Color choices are made carefully with regard to packaging, advertising, and even store decor.

The expectations created by colors can actually affect consumers' experience of products. For example, when the background color on Barrelhead Sugar-Free Root Beer was changed from blue to beige, consumers said it tasted more like old-fashioned root beer served in a frosty mug.[7]

Package Design: Telling a Book by Its Cover. The choice of color is frequently a key issue in package design. These choices used to be made casually. For example, the familiar Campbell's soup can was produced in red and white because a company executive liked the football uniforms at Cornell University! Now, however, color is a serious business, and companies frequently employ consultants to assist in these decisions.

Some color combinations come to be so strongly associated with a corporation that they become known as the company's *trade dress,* and the company may even be granted exclusive use of these colors. For example, Eastman Kodak has successfully protected its trade dress of yellow, black, and red in court. As a rule, however, trade dress protection is granted only when consumers might be confused about what they are buying because of similar coloration of a competitor's packages.[8]

The U.S. Supreme Court recently refused trademark protection for the pastel blue used by Equal, the sugar substitute. The NutraSweet Company had sued the makers of its chief rival, Sweet 'n Low, after they used a similar color for a new product called Sweet One. The justices let stand a ruling by an appeals court that said "The essential purpose of trademark law is to prevent confusion, not to bar new entrants into the market."[9]

Since the number of competing brands has proliferated for many types of products, the color of a package can be a crucial spur to sales. When RJR Nabisco introduced a version of Teddy Grahams (a children's product) for adults, restrained packaging colors were used to reinforce the idea that the new product was for grown-ups. However, after finding that sales were alarmingly low, the company undertook a crash redesign program. One major change was to make the box a bright yellow. This color implied that the product was intended to be a "fun" snack, rather than a "serious" graham cracker. Sales picked up dramatically after the changes.[10]

THE COLOR INDUSTRY In a given year, certain colors appear to be "hot" and to show up over and over in clothing, home furnishings, cars, and so

Additional Example: Some product designers believe that lower-income consumers prefer simple colors—those that can be described in two words, such as "grass green" or "sky blue"—and that these people find complex colors dirty or dull. In contrast, higher-income people are thought to like complex colors such as "gray-green with a hint of blue. Forest green and burgundy are the colors preferred by the wealthiest 3 percent of Americans. See Bernice Kanner, "Color Schemes," *New York* (April 3, 1989)2: 22.

International Example: An instant coffee container was redesigned in Switzerland with diagonal strips of mauve. The package won an award for design, but sales dropped off significantly. Consumers simply did not associate the color mauve with coffee. See Maryon Tysoe,"What's Wrong with Blue Potatoes?" *Psychology Today* (December 1985)2: 6.

Additional Example: Black is associated with power and may even have an impact on people who wear it. Teams in both the National Football League and the National Hockey League who wear black uniforms are among the most aggressive; they consistently rank near the top of their leagues in penalties during the season. See Mark G. Frank and Thomas Gilovich, "The Dark Side of Self- and Social Perception: Black Uniforms and Aggression in Professional Sports," *Journal of Personality and Social Psychology* 54 (1988)1: 74–85.

on. These favored colors tend to disappear as fast as they come, to be replaced by another set of "hot" colors the next year or season.

The color choices of many consumers are affected by these trends. One simple reason is that consumers' choices are largely limited by the colors available in the stores they patronize. Few people, however, realize the extent to which these "hot" colors result from deliberate choices made by a small group of people. Several trade groups and consulting firms engage in the practice of *color forecasting*, in which a set of experts attempts to estimate what colors will best reflect a season in one year, five years, and sometimes even ten years. For example, DuPont recently offered a forecast of colors that will be preferred by car buyers over the next 3–5 years. While white (currently the most popular color for cars) will remain strong, the report predicts deep green will gain in popularity, as will turquoise/aqua, yellow, and purple.[11]

Smell

Odors can stir emotions or create a calming feeling. They can invoke memories or relieve stress. Some of our responses to scents result from early associations with other experiences. As one marketer noted, an example ". . . is a baby-powder scent that is frequently used in fragrances because the smell connotes comfort, warmth, and gratification."[12]

Consumers' love of fragrances has contributed to a very large industry. Americans alone spend well over $3 billion a year on women's perfume. Because this market is extremely competitive (about thirty to forty new scents are introduced each year) and expensive (it costs an average of $50 million to introduce a new fragrance), manufacturers are scrambling to find new ways to expand the use of scents and odors in our daily lives.[13]

Home fragrance products, consisting primarily of potpourri, room sprays and atomizers, drawer liners, sachets, and scented candles, bring in about $250 million annually.[14] Morton Salt is even trying to position its product as

International Example: While the British prefer avocado bathrooms, the French tend to use blue in their decorating schemes. See Maryon Tysoe, "What's Wrong with Blue Potatoes?" *Psychology Today* (December 1985)2: 6.

Teaching Hint: Fragrances can be classified into various types: floral, woodsy, green, citrusy, spicy, oriental. Experts create fragrances by combining a number of individual scents—as many as 200–300 ingredients. Like color, our perception of fragrance has three components, known as the top, middle, and bottom notes. Top notes, perceived with the first sniff, provide only a fleeting sensation, middle notes carry the aromatic theme, and bottom notes retain the character of the fragrance. See Cynthia Morris, "The Mystery of Fragrance," *Essence* (May 1988)3: 71.

MULTICULTURAL DIMENSIONS

Fragrances play an obvious role in interpersonal attraction and feelings about our immediate environments, and other effects that they may have on consumers are now beginning to be explored. An industry group known as the Fragrance Research Fund, for example, supports research on what it has called "aromachology."

A large Japanese construction company was recently granted a patent on a computerized system for "environmental fragrancing." The system delivers fragrances to large buildings through the ventilation ducts and is intended to combat "sick building syndrome," a problem in many energy-efficient structures whose windows are sealed to save fuel.

The company found in tests that the error rate of keypunch operators dropped by almost 50 percent following exposure to a lemon scent and almost 80 percent after exposure to lavender. The system is in use in several buildings in Japan, including a retirement complex. Future projects that are under development include casinos, airport terminals, and the interiors of airplanes and trains.[15]

an odor remover to increase salt consumption. In addition to other helpful tips about the many uses of salt, the company is advising homemakers to make their own air fresheners by filling orange peels with Morton Salt.[16]

Sound

Music and sound are also important to marketers. Consumers buy millions of dollars worth of sound recordings each year, advertising jingles maintain brand awareness, and background music creates desired moods.[17]

Many aspects of sound may affect people's feelings and behaviors. Two areas of research that have widespread applications in consumer contexts are the effects of background music on mood and the influence of speaking rate on attitude change and message comprehension.

THE SOUND OF MUZAK The Muzak Corporation estimates that its recordings are heard by 80 million people every day. This so-called functional music is played in stores, shopping malls, and offices to either relax or stimulate consumers.

Research shows that workers tend to slow down during midmorning and midafternoon, so Muzak uses a system it calls "stimulus progression," in which the tempo increases during those slack times. Muzak has been linked to reductions in absenteeism among factory workers, and even the milk and egg output of cows and chickens is claimed to increase under its influence.[18]

TIME COMPRESSION *Time compression* is a technique used by broadcasters to manipulate perceptions of sound. It is a way to pack more information into a limited time by speeding up an announcer's voice in commercials. The speaking rate is typically accelerated to about 120 percent to 130 percent of normal. This effect is not detectable by most people; in fact, some tests indicate that consumers prefer a rate of transmission that is slightly faster than the normal speaking rate.[19]

The evidence for the effectiveness of time compression is mixed. It has been shown to increase persuasion in some situations and to reduce it in others. One explanation for a positive effect is that the listener uses a person's speaking rate to infer whether the speaker is confident; people seem to think that fast talkers must know what they are talking about.[20]

Another, more plausible, explanation is that the listener is given less time to elaborate in his or her mind on the assertions made in the commercial. The acceleration disrupts normal responses to the ad and changes the cues used to form judgments about its content. This change can either hinder or facilitate attitude change, depending on other conditions.[21]

Touch

Although relatively little research has been done on the effects of tactile stimulation on consumer behavior, common observation tells us that this sensory channel is important. Moods are stimulated or relaxed on the basis of sensations of the skin, whether from a luxurious massage or the bite of a winter wind. The Lubriderm skin lotion ad shown here dramatically illustrates the use of tactile qualities to reinforce product attributes.

Lubriderm Lotion restores lost moisture to heal and protect your skin.

Lubriderm Lotion
FOR DRY SKIN CARE
Created for Dermatologists.
Softens, smooths, moisturizes,
and protects.
Absorbs quickly.

This ad for Lubriderm lotion relies on the vivid imagery of a rough tactile sensation to communicate a primary product benefit. Courtesy of Warner Lambert, Inc.

Touch has even been shown to be a factor in sales interactions. In one study, for example, diners who were touched by waitpeople gave bigger tips, and food demonstrators in a supermarket who lightly touched customers had better luck in getting shoppers to try a new snack product and to redeem coupons for the brand.[22]

SYMBOLIC MEANING OF TACTILE CLUES: "SMOOTH AS SILK" People associate the textures of fabrics with underlying product qualities. The perceived richness or quality of the material in clothing, bedding, or upholstery is linked to its "feel," whether it is rough or smooth, flexible or inflexible. Silk is equated with luxury, while denim is considered practical and durable. Some of these tactile/quality associations are summarized in Table 2–1. Fabrics that are composed of scarce materials or that require a high degree of processing to achieve their smoothness or fineness tend to be more expensive and thus are seen as being higher-class. Similarly, lighter, more delicate textures are assumed to be feminine. Roughness is often positively valued for men,

TABLE 2–1 Tactile Oppositions in Fabrics

Perception	Male	Female	
High Class	Wool	Silk	Fine ↑
Low Class	Denim	Cotton	↓ Coarse

Heavy ◄──────► Light

while smoothness is sought by women. (When was the last time you saw a commercial in which a man was fretting about "dishpan hands?").

Taste

Our taste receptors obviously contribute to our experience of many products. Specialized companies called "flavor houses" keep busy trying to develop new tastes to please the changing palates of consumers. Their work has been especially important as consumers continue to demand good-tasting foods that are also low in calories and fat. When the Quaker Oats Company decided to capitalize on this trend by buying a small rice cake manufacturer, consumers complained that the cakes tasted like styrofoam, and sales were disappointing. A flavor house was hired to develop a rice cake that tasted like buttered popcorn. This new taste was perfected along with several others, and industry-wide sales of rice cakes now exceed $100 million a year.[23]

TASTE TESTING Food companies go to great lengths to ensure that their products taste as they should. Consider, for example, the procedure used by Nabisco as it monitors the quality of its cookies. The company uses a group of "sensory panelists" as cookie tasters. These consumers are recruited because they have superior sensory abilities, and they are then given six months of training. The panelists rate the products of Nabisco and its competitors (the specific types and brands being tested are kept secret) on a number of dimensions. These include "rate of melt," "fracturability and density," "molar packing" (the amount of cookie that sticks to the teeth), and the "notes" of the cookie, such as sweetness, saltiness, or bitterness. A typical evaluation session takes the group eight hours to rate just one sample of cookies.[24]

Blind Taste Tests. Are blind taste tests worth their salt? While taste tests often provide valuable information, their results can be misleading when it is forgotten that objective taste is only one component of product evaluation. The most famous example of this mistake concerns New Coke, Coca-Cola's answer to the Pepsi Challenge.[25] The new formulation was preferred to Pepsi in blind taste tests (in which the products were not identified) by an average of 55 percent to 45 percent in seventeen markets, yet New Coke ran into problems when it replaced the older version. People do not buy a cola for taste alone; they are buying intangibles like brand image as well.

Additional Example: Pepsi's "Slice" brand repeatedly failed taste tests when pitted against lemon-lime drinks, but the new product did quite well when its juice content was touted. See Tim Davis, "Taste Tests: Are the Blind Leading the Blind?" *Beverage World* (April 1987)6: 42.

Sometimes taste test failures can be overcome by repositioning the product. For example, Vernor's ginger ale did poorly in a taste test against leading ginger ales. When the research team instead introduced it as a new type of soft drink with a tangier taste, it won handily. As an executive noted, "People hated it because it didn't meet the preconceived expectations of what a ginger ale should be."[26]

Additional Example: A lot of recent business has been generated by the popularity of wine coolers and juice-added soft drinks. In an effort to differentiate products from competitors by introducing new, exotic tastes, the development of such tropical flavors as tamarind, passion fruit, and kiwi have gained momentum. See E.M. Curtin, "Pinpointing New Flavor Sensations," *Beverage World* (April 1988)2: 62.

Sensory Thresholds

If you have ever blown a dog whistle and watched pets respond to a sound you cannot hear, you know that there are some stimuli that people simply are not capable of perceiving. And, of course, some people are better able to pick up sensory information than are others.

The science that focuses on how the physical environment is integrated into our personal, subjective world is known as **psychophysics**. By understanding some of the physical laws that govern what we are capable of responding to, this knowledge can be translated into marketing strategies.

The Absolute Threshold

When we define the lowest intensity of a stimulus that can be registered on a sensory channel, we speak of a *threshold* for that receptor. The **absolute threshold** refers to the minimum amount of stimulation that can be detected on a sensory channel. The sound emitted by a dog whistle is too high to be detected by human ears, so this stimulus is beyond our auditory absolute threshold. The absolute threshold is an important consideration in designing marketing stimuli. A billboard might have the most entertaining copy ever written, but this genius is wasted if the print is too small for passing motorists to see it from the highway.

The Differential Threshold

The **differential threshold** refers to the ability of a sensory system to detect changes or differences between two stimuli. A commercial that is intentionally produced in black-and-white might be noticed on a color television because this decrease in the intensity of color differs from the program that preceded it. The same commercial being watched on a black-and-white television would not be seen as different and might be ignored altogether.

WANTING (OR NOT WANTING) CONSUMERS TO NOTICE A CHANGE The issue of when and if a change will be noticed by consumers is relevant to many marketing situations. Sometimes a marketer may want to ensure that a change is noticed, such as when merchandise is offered at a discount. In other situations, the fact that a change has been made is downplayed, as in the case of price increases or when a product is downsized.

A consumer's ability to detect a difference between two stimuli is *relative*. A whispered conversation that might be unintelligible on a noisy street can suddenly become public and embarrassing knowledge in a quiet library. It is the relative difference between the decibel level of the conversation and its surroundings, rather than the loudness of the conversation itself, that determines whether the stimulus will register.

The JND and Weber's Law. The minimum change in a stimulus that can be detected is also known as the **JND**, which stands for just noticeable difference. In the nineteenth century, a psychophysicist named Ernst Weber found that the amount of change that is necessary to be noticed is systematically related to the original intensity of the stimulus. The stronger the initial stimulus, the greater the change must be for it to be noticed. This relationship is known as **Weber's Law**. Many companies choose to update their packages periodically, making small changes that will not necessarily be noticed at the time. When a product icon is updated, the manufacturer does not want people to lose their identification with a familiar symbol.

A recent corporate *identity campaign*—in which a company tries to build a distinctive image for a line of products—illustrates the importance of phasing in an identity image by making incremental changes over time. When IBM sold its line of desktop printers, typewriters, and related supplies to an investment firm, the new company needed a new name and logo because the sales agreement stipulated that it would lose the rights to the IBM name in 1996. The new company wanted consumers to simultaneously perceive its product line as being new but also connected with the more familiar IBM image. A new name, Lexmark International, was selected from an initial list of 200 candidates, and a four-stage timetable was developed to phase in the Lexmark name over the five-year period in which the new company was entitled to use the IBM logo. A corporate advertising image cam-

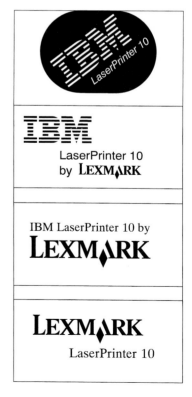

FIGURE 2–2 Evolution of the Lexmark Logo: The four stages illustrate the company's attempt to phase in the new identity by relying on the more familiar IBM image for as long as possible. Courtesy of Lexmark International, Inc.

paign, initiated to assist in the transition, included an ad asking consumers to "Imagine a brand-new company with more than 50 years of experience." The successive changes in the logo are shown in Figure 2–2.[27]

Subliminal Persuasion

Most marketers are concerned with creating advertising messages above consumers' thresholds. There is, however, another side to this story. A good number of consumers appear to believe that many advertising messages are, in fact, designed to be perceived unconsciously, or below the threshold of recognition. Another word for threshold is *limen*, and stimuli that fall below the limen are termed *subliminal*. **Subliminal perception** thus occurs when the stimulus is below the level of the consumer's awareness.

Subliminal Perception

Subliminal perception is a topic that has captivated the public for over thirty years, despite the fact that there is virtually *no proof* that this process has any effect on consumer behavior. A recent survey of American consumers found that almost two-thirds believe in the existence of subliminal advertising, and over one-half are convinced that this technique can get them to buy things they do not really want![28] In fact, most examples of subliminal perception that have been "discovered" are not subliminal at all; they are quite visible. Remember, if you can see it or hear it, it is *not* subliminal, because the stimulus is above the level of conscious awareness! Nonetheless, the continuing controversy about subliminal persuasion has been important in shaping the public's beliefs about advertising and marketers' ability to manipulate consumers against their will.

The public's fear of unconscious manipulation began with a widely popularized experiment that was performed in a New Jersey drive-in movie theater in September 1957. During a showing of the movie *Picnic*, a firm called the Subliminal Projection Company inserted messages that said "Drink Coca-Cola" and "Eat Popcorn" for 1/3000 second every five seconds. This rate was too fast for viewers to be aware that they had seen the images. Supposedly, sales of popcorn increased by almost 20 percent and consumption of Coke grew by almost 60 percent. These claims created an uproar across America as journalists and social critics expressed fears that social scientists would team up with advertisers to invade privacy and control consumers against their will. As one magazine put it at the time, consumers' minds had been "broken and entered."[29] This experiment was never replicated and has repeatedly been criticized. The design of the study was flawed in that other possible effects on consumption, such as the movie itself, the weather during the showing, and so on, could not be ruled out. Indeed, the executive responsible for the test later admitted that he had *made up* results to revive his failing research firm![30]

Subliminal Techniques

EMBEDS **Embeds** are tiny figures that are inserted into magazine advertising by use of high-speed photography or airbrushing. These hidden figures, usu-

Teaching Hint: An individual's perceptual threshold is usually defined as that stimulus value correctly detected 50 percent of the time, and many studies claiming to show subliminal effects present stimuli that may actually be noticed as much as 49 percent of the time. Responses may thus be due to weak—but not subliminal—stimulation. For example, when three of Pepsi's "Cool Cans" are stacked vertically, the designs form the word "sex" in one of the four designs produced. A company spokesman insisted that the letters were randomly generated combinations of the letters in the word "Pepsi," and the result was just a coincidence. In any case, the letters are clearly visible, and hence are not "subliminal" at all. See Timothy E. Moore, "Subliminal Advertising: What You See is What You Get," *Journal of Marketing* 46 (Spring 1982): 38–47; Patricia Winters, "S-E-X or Pepsi?" *Advertising Age* (August 20, 1990): 8.

ally of a sexual nature, supposedly exert strong but unconscious influences on innocent readers. Ice cubes are a prime culprit for accusations of this type of subliminal persuasion; critics often focus on ambiguous shapes in drinks as evidence for the use of this technique. For instance, one ad presented as evidence for the use of subliminal methods is a Gilbey's Gin ad in which the letters S E X are spelled out in the ice cubes. The belief that such messages are embedded in ice cubes has prompted other advertisers to poke fun of the technique in their own ads. Absolut Vodka, for example, proclaimed "Absolut Subliminal" in an ad in which the words "Absolut Vodka" were just discernible in the ice cubes in a glass of the featured drink, while the Seagram's gin ad shown here emphasizes the "hidden pleasure" in a glass of its beverage.

This Seagram's ad pokes fun at the belief that advertisers frequently embed pleasurable images in the ice cubes in pictures of drinks. Courtesy of The House of Seagram.

Research Report: Much of the furor surrounding embeds can be attributed to Wilson Bryan Key, who has written several books on "subliminal seduction." Systematic research studies, however, have found no evidence that embeds exert unconscious influence on unwitting consumers. See Wilson Bryan Key, *Subliminal Seduction* (New York: New American Library, Inc., 1973); Wilson Bryan Key, *Media Sexploitation* (Englewood Cliffs, N.J.: Prentice-Hall, 1976); Wilson Bryan Key, *The Clam-Plate Orgy* (Englewood Cliffs, N.J.: Prentice-Hall, 1980); W.E. Kilbourne, S. Painton, and D. Ridley, "The Effect of Sexual Embedding on Responses to Magazine Advertisements," *Journal of Advertising* 14 (1985)2: 48–56; Myron Gable, Henry T. Wilkens, Lynn Harris, and Richard Feinberg, "An Evaluation of Subliminally Embedded Sexual Stimuli in Graphics," *Journal of Advertising* 10 (1987)1: 26–30.

Q. CAN YOU FIND THE HIDDEN PLEASURE IN REFRESHING SEAGRAM'S GIN?

A. If you think this is just a bubble, look again.

AUDITORY MESSAGES In addition to subliminal visual messages, many consumers and marketers seem to be fascinated by the possible effects of messages hidden on sound recordings. An attempt to capitalize on subliminal auditory perception techniques is found in the growing market for self-help cassettes. These tapes, which typically feature the sound of waves crashing or some other natural setting, supposedly contain subliminal messages to help the listener stop smoking, lose weight, gain confidence, and so on. Despite the rapid growth of this market, there is little evidence that subliminal stimuli transmitted on the auditory channel can bring about desired changes in behavior.[31]

Along with the interest in hidden self-help messages on recordings, some consumers have become concerned about rumors of satanic messages recorded backward on rock records. The popular press has devoted much attention to such stories, and state legislatures have considered bills requiring warning labels about these messages. These backward messages do indeed appear on some albums, including Led Zeppelin's classic song "Stairway to Heaven," which contains the lyric ". . . there's still time to change." When played in reverse, this phrase sounds like "so here's to my sweet Satan." The novelty of such reversals might help to sell records, but the "evil" messages within have no effect.[32] Humans do not have a speech perception mechanism operating at an unconscious level that is capable of decoding a reversed signal.

LOW-LEVEL AUDITORY STIMULATION: "I WON'T STEAL." One technique, known as psycho-acoustic persuasion, does appear to work. Subtle acoustical messages such as "I am honest. I won't steal. Stealing is dishonest" are broadcast in more than 1000 stores in the United States to prevent shoplifting. Unlike subliminal perception, though, these messages are played at a (barely) audible level, using a technique known as threshold messaging.[33] After a nine-month test period, theft losses in one six-store chain declined almost 40 percent, saving the company $600,000.

Some evidence indicates, however, that these messages are effective only on individuals whose value systems make them predisposed to suggestion. For example, someone who might be thinking about taking something on a dare but who feels guilty about it might be susceptible to these messages, but they will not sway a professional thief or a kleptomaniac.[34]

Evaluating the Evidence

While some research by clinical psychologists suggests that people can be influenced by subliminal messages under very specific conditions, it is unlikely that these techniques would be of much use in marketing contexts. For one thing, effective messages must be very specifically tailored to individuals, rather than the mass messages required by advertising.[35] Other discouraging factors include the following issues.

1. There are wide individual differences in threshold levels. In order for a message to avoid conscious detection by consumers who have a low threshold, it would have to be so weak that it would not reach those who have a high threshold.

Additional Example: In a controversial and ultimately unsuccessful court case, the parents of two teenagers who had died in a suicide pact sued CBS Records and the heavy metal band Judas Priest for allegedly encouraging the teens' deaths by embedding the messages "Do it" and "Let's be dead" in the album "Stained Glass." See "Blaming Death's Hidden Messages," *Newsweek* (July 30, 1990): 58.

Teaching Hint: Relying on the Freudian theory that unconscious wishes can affect conscious feelings and behaviors, some research indicates that in very limited, controlled situations, influencing effects are obtained if an unconscious wish exists, the message is totally subliminal, and the stimulus precisely matches the unconscious wish. For example, stutterers who received the message *destroy mother* did not stutter more or less, since the stimulus had no relevance to their condition, but depressives did become more depressed when exposed to the same message. Thus, success in an advertising context is unlikely, since the messages are not carefully calibrated and presented on an individual level to specific individuals. See L.H. Silverman, "Psychoanalytic Theory: The Reports of My Death Are Greatly Exaggerated," *American Psychologist* 31 (September 1976): 621–37; Joel Saegert, "Why Marketing Should Quit Giving Subliminal Advertising the Benefit of the Doubt," *Psychology & Marketing* 4 (Summer 1987): 107–20.

2. Advertisers lack control over consumers' distance and position from a screen. In a movie theater, for example, only a small portion of the audience would be in exactly the right seats to be exposed to the subliminal message.
3. The consumer must be paying absolute attention to the stimulus. People watching a television program or a movie typically shift their attention periodically and might not even be looking when the stimulus is presented.
4. Even if the desired effect is induced, it operates only at a very general level. For example, a message might increase a person's thirst, but not necessarily for a specific drink. Because basic drives are affected, marketers could find that after all the bother and expense of creating a subliminal message, demand for competitors' products increases as well!

Perceptual Selection

Although we live in an "information society," we can have too much of a good thing. Consumers are often in a state of sensory overload, exposed to far more information than they are capable of or willing to process. People who have been in the middle of a noisy, crowded bar or party for several hours might feel the need to step outside periodically to take a break. A consumer can experience a similar overwhelmed feeling after being forced to sift through the claims made by hundreds of competing brands. Further, the competition for our attention is increasing steadily. In 1971 about 2600 television commercials ran each week; now stations carry more than 6000 during the same time period.[36]

Because the brain's capacity to process information is limited, consumers are very selective about what they pay attention to. The process of *perceptual selectivity* means that people attend to only a small portion of stimuli to which they are exposed. Consumers practice a form of psychic economy, picking and choosing among stimuli, to avoid being overwhelmed by **advertising clutter** of the type illustrated in the *Pensions & Investment Age* ad shown here. This overabundance of advertising stimuli highlights two important aspects of perceptual selectivity as they relate to consumer behavior: exposure and attention.

Exposure

Exposure is the degree to which people notice a stimulus that is within range of their sensory receptors. Consumers concentrate on some stimuli, are unaware of others, and even go out of their way to ignore some messages. An experiment by a Minneapolis bank illustrates consumers' tendencies to miss or ignore information in which they are not interested. After a state law was passed that required banks to explain details about money transfer in electric banking, the Northwestern National Bank distributed a pamphlet to 120,000 of its customers at considerable cost to provide the required information, which was hardly exciting bedtime reading. In one hundred of the mailings, a section in the middle of the pamphlet offered the reader $10.00 just for finding that paragraph. Not a single person claimed the reward.[37]

SELECTIVE EXPOSURE **Experience**, which is the result of acquiring stimulation, is one factor that determines how much exposure to a particular stimulus a

If this is happening to your print advertising, call (212)210-0227.

Getting noticed these days is tough enough.

And, if the media you use creates confusion with advertorials, inserts, bingo cards and enough other material designed to discourage all but the most persistent readers, you might as well call it quits even before you begin.

But, before you do, call *Pensions & Investments*.

Because, at *P&I*, we have a commitment to providing an uncluttered environment. Which gives advertisers who run with us a distinct competitive advantage.

And, because *P&I* offers you this environment, it explains why more decision makers from your target audience of financial and investment management executives make *P&I* priority reading over all other publications.

The *P&I* advantage incorporates another important idea, too.

It's simple -- each advertising unit generates an equal amount of additional editorial content. Your advertising dollars are reinvested into editorial, our readers get more news, and you get a more powerful newspaper.

Yet, none of this costs you any more. In fact, *P&I* advertising rates continue to be among the lowest in the business.

So, when you feel overwhelmed by the confusion, chaos and clutter in the publications you use to reach professionals in professional money, give us a call. We're here to help you stand out.

Pensions&Investments
The newspaper of corporate and institutional investing

| New York (212) 210-0227 | Chicago (312) 649-5280 | Boston (617) 248-6991 | Los Angeles (213) 651-3710 |

The photograph in this ad for *Pensions & Investment Age* illustrates how visual stimuli can cause advertising clutter, the sensory overload to which consumers are exposed in the marketplace. Courtesy of *Pensions and Investment Age;* Concept: W. Bisson; Copy: W. Bisson; Design: J. Hunt, Donna Klein.

person accepts. *Perceptual filters* based on consumers' past experiences influence what we decide to process.

Perceptual vigilance is a factor in selective exposure. Consumers are more likely to be aware of stimuli that relate to their current needs. These needs may be conscious or unconscious. A consumer who rarely notices car ads will become very much aware of them when he or she is in the market for a new car. A newspaper ad for a fast-food restaurant that would otherwise go unnoticed becomes significant when one glances at the paper in the middle of a five o'clock class.

Exposure to Television Messages: Consumers Take Control. The advent of the VCR has allowed consumers armed with remote control fast-forward buttons to be much more selective about which television messages they are exposed to. By "zipping," viewers fast-forward through commercials while playing recorded tapes of their favorite programs. A VCR marketed by

Mitsubishi in Japan even removes the need for zipping. It distinguishes between the different types of TV signals used to broadcast programs and commercials and automatically pauses during ads.[38]

How big an issue is "zipping," for marketers? The jury is still out on this question. In one survey, 69 percent of VCR owners said that they had increased their television viewing time, so overall exposure to commercials might actually be increased as people continue to purchase VCRs.[39]

Zipping has enhanced the need for advertising creativity. Interesting commercials do not get zipped as frequently. Evidence indicates that viewers are willing to stop fast-forwarding to watch an enticing or novel commercial. In addition, longer commercials and those that keep a static figure on the screen (such as a brand name or a logo) appear to counteract the effects of zipping; these executions are not as affected by a speed increase, since the figure remains in place.[40]

ADAPTATION Another factor affecting exposure is **adaptation**, the degree to which consumers continue to notice a stimulus over time. The process of adaptation occurs when consumers no longer pay attention to a stimulus because it is so familiar. Almost like drug addiction, a consumer can become "habituated" and require increasingly stronger "doses" of a stimulus for it to continue to be noticed. For example, a consumer en route to work might read a billboard message when it is first installed, but after a few days, it becomes part of the passing scenery.

Factors Leading to Adaptation. Generally, several factors can lead to adaptation.

- *Intensity:* Less intense stimuli (e.g., soft sounds or dim colors) habituate because they have less of a sensory impact.
- *Duration:* Stimuli that require relatively lengthy exposure in order to be processed tend to habituate because they require a long attention span.
- *Discrimination:* Simple stimuli tend to habituate because they do not require attention to detail.
- *Exposure:* Frequently encountered stimuli tend to habituate as the rate of exposure increases.
- *Relevance:* Stimuli that are irrelevant or unimportant will habituate because they fail to attract attention.

Attention

Attention is the degree to which consumers focus on stimuli within their range of exposure. Because consumers are being exposed to so many advertising stimuli, marketers are becoming increasingly creative in their attempts to gain attention for their products.

A dynamic package is one way to gain this attention. Recall that Gail was attracted by a distinctive candy bar that was placed at eye level, and the package essentially sold the product to her. Some consulting firms have established elaborate procedures to measure package effectiveness, using such instruments as an *angle meter*, which measures package visibility as a shopper moves down the aisle and views the package from different angles.

Data from *eye-tracking tests*, in which consumers' eye movements as they look at packages and ads are followed and measured, can result in subtle but powerful changes that influence their impact. For example, eye-tracking tests on an ad for Bombay gin showed that virtually no consumers were reading the message (in relatively small type) below the visual portion and that the Bombay bottle (also relatively small) positioned to the right of the visual portion was not seen by nine out of ten readers. The result was low recall scores for the ad. In a revised ad, the bottle's size was increased, and the message was emphasized. Recall scores for this version were almost 100 percent higher than for the original.[41]

COUNTERING ADVERTISING CLUTTER Many marketers are making specific attempts to counter the sensory overload caused by advertising clutter in order to call attention to their products. One expensive strategy involves buying large blocks of advertising space in a medium in order to dominate consumers' attention. Ralph Lauren filled 15 consecutive full pages in a single issue of *Vanity Fair* for this purpose.

Other companies are using "bookend ads," where a commercial for one product is split into parts that are separated by commercials for other products. The first part creates conflict, and the second resolves it. This technique motivates the viewer to keep watching in order to get the rest of the story. For example, an ad for Excedrin depicts a woman taking two tablets for her headache. She then reappears after a few other commercials have aired to announce that the headache is gone.[42]

Another solution has been to put ads in unconventional places, where there will be less competition for attention. These places include the backs of shopping carts, tunnels, sports stadiums, and even movies.[43] An executive at Campbell's Soup, commenting on the company's decision to place ads in church bulletins, noted, "We have to shake consumers up these days in order to make them take notice . . . . Television alone won't do that. Now we have to hit them with our ads where they shop and play and on their way to work."[44]

Cross-Cultural Example: Some advertisers, including Clorox, McDonald's, and Quaker Oats, have recently taken to printing part of their ads upside down to get the reader's attention. Perhaps reflecting a greater level of cultural involvement in advertising overseas, the editor of the Starch-Tested Copy newsletter noted, "I find people don't like to work at reading their ads . . . Americans don't like it. There's a disorienting aspect they find uncomfortable. The English, on the other hand, like it." Quoted in Stuart Elliott, "When Up Is Down, Does It Sell?," *New York Times* (February 21, 1992)2: D1.

MARKETING OPPORTUNITY

Even the music industry is trying new formats to reach potential buyers. MCA Records paid a major movie theater chain to play a music video by Tom Petty and the Heartbreakers prior to showing its scheduled movies, while Mercury Records launched a bus placard campaign in 18 cities to promote a new John Mellencamp album. As the senior vice president of marketing for MCA noted, "There is a real strong corollary between people who see films and buy music. And one thing you know for sure is that when they are in a movie house, you've got them. They are all looking at the screen."[45]

CREATING CONTRAST When many stimuli are competing to be noticed, one will receive attention to the extent that it differs from those around it. Stimuli that fall into *unpredictable patterns* often command a lot of attention. For example, the British Family Planning Association creatively drew consumers' attention to its message by featuring a pregnant male in its ads.

Size and color differences are also powerful ways to achieve contrast. A black-and-white object in a color ad is quite noticeable, as is a block of printed type surrounded by large amounts of white space. The size of the stimulus itself in contrast to the competition is also important. Readership of a magazine ad has been shown to increase in proportion to the size of the ad.[46]

This British Family Planning Association ad gets attention by relying on a stimulus that doesn't follow a familiar or predictable pattern. Source: Family Planning Association, United Kingdom.

Interpretation: Deciding What Things Mean

Interpretation is the meaning that people assign to sensory stimuli. Just as people differ in terms of the stimuli that they perceive, the eventual assignment of meanings to these stimuli varies as well. Two people can see or hear the same event, but their interpretation of it can be like night and day.

In a classic experiment, students at Princeton and Dartmouth viewed a movie of a particularly rough football game between the two schools. Although everyone was exposed to the same stimulus, the degree to which students saw infractions and the blame they assigned for those they did see, was quite different depending on which college they attended.[47] The assignment of meaning can be colored by what one expects or hopes to see.[48]

Consumers assign meaning to stimuli based on the schema, or set of beliefs, to which the stimulus is assigned. Certain properties of a stimulus will more likely evoke a schema than others. (This process is known as *priming*.) As evidenced by Gail's candy bar selection, a brand name can communicate expectations about product attributes and color consumers' perceptions of product performance by activating a schema. When Toro introduced a lightweight snow thrower, it was named the "Snow Pup." Sales were disappointing because the word pup called up a schema that grouped small, cuddly things together, which is not the desirable attributes for a snow thrower. When the product was renamed the "Snow Master," sales went up markedly.[49]

Stimulus ambiguity occurs when a stimulus is not clearly perceived or when it conveys a number of meanings. In such cases, consumers tend to project their own wishes and desires to assign meaning. Although ambiguity in product advertisements is usually undesirable to marketers, it can be used creatively to generate controversy or interest. For example, a popular ad for Benson & Hedges cigarettes featured a group of people sitting around a dinner table, while a man wearing only pajama bottoms stands in the background. This ambiguous character yielded valuable publicity for the company as people competed to explain the meaning of the mysterious "pajama man."

Stimulus Organization

People do not perceive a single stimulus in isolation. They tend to view it in terms of relationships with other events, sensations, or images. A number of perceptual principles describe how stimuli are perceived and organized.

THE GESTALT These principles are based on work in **Gestalt psychology**, a school of thought that maintains that people derive meaning from the *totality* of a set of stimuli, rather than from any individual stimulus. The German word *gestalt* roughly means whole, pattern, or configuration, and this perspective is best summarized by the saying "the whole is greater than the sum of its parts." The importance of a gestalt is underscored when consumers' interpretations of stimuli are affected by aesthetic, symbolic, or sensory qualities. Set in a context that is painfully familiar to most students, the

Additional Example: The Matex Corporation was experiencing sluggish results with a rust-proofing compound called "Thixo-Tex," because consumers could not perceive product qualities from this meaningless name. When the product's name was changed to "Rusty Jones," sales grew from $2 million to more than $100 million in four years. See Gail Tom, Teresa Barnett, William Lew, and Jodean Selmants, "Cueing the Consumer: The Role of Salient Cues in Consumer Perception," *Journal of Consumer Marketing* 4 (1987)2: 23–27; H. White, "Name Change to Rusty Jones Helps Polish Product's Identity," *Advertising Age* 2 (1980)18: 47–50

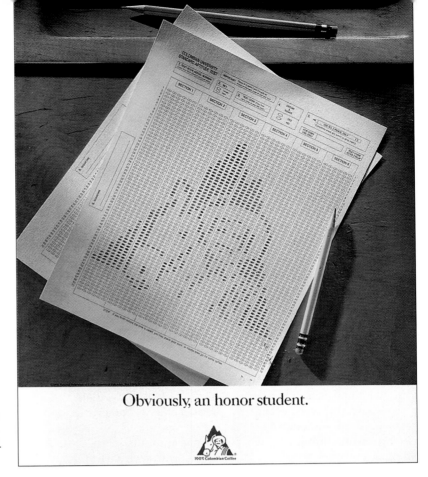

Obviously, an honor student.

This ad for Colombian coffee illustrates Gestalt principles of perception, in which the individual parts (the colored circles) are seen as a whole (the familiar symbol used to promote Colombian coffee). Courtesy of the National Federation of Coffee Growers of Colombia.

Colombian coffee ad shown here demonstrates the formation of a meaningful image from the individual colored circles on a Scantron sheet when viewed in totality. A piecemeal perspective that analyzes each component of the stimulus separately will be unable to capture the total effect. For instance, a "punk" black leather jacket and "preppie" khaki pants might

FIGURE 2–3 Principles of Stimulus Organization Derived from Gestalt Psychology

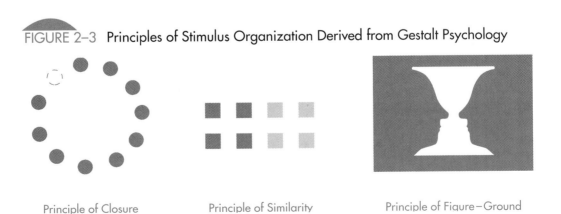

Principle of Closure   Principle of Similarity   Principle of Figure–Ground

look good separately, but the gestalt created when they are worn together would not be "right." The gestalt perspective provides several principles relating to the way stimuli are organized. Three of these principles, or perceptual tendencies, are illustrated in Figure 2–3.

Closure. The principle of **closure** implies that consumers tend to perceive an incomplete picture as complete. That is, we tend to fill in the blanks based on our prior experience. This principle explains why most of us have no trouble reading a neon sign even if one or two of its letters are burned out or filling in the blanks in an incomplete message, as illustrated by the J&B ad shown here. The principle of closure is also at work when we hear only part of a jingle or theme. Utilization of the principle of closure in marketing strategies encourages audience participation, which increases the chance that people will attend to the message.

Similarity. The **principle of similarity** tells us that consumers tend to group together objects that share similar physical characteristics. That is, they group like items into sets to form an integrated whole. Green Giant relied upon this principle when the company redesigned the packaging for its line of frozen vegetables. It created a "sea of green" look to unify all of its different offerings.

Figure–Ground. Another important principle is the **figure–ground relationship**, in which one part will dominate (the figure) while other parts recede into the background. This concept is easy to understand if one thinks literally of a photograph with a clear and sharply focused object (the figure) in the center. The figure is dominant, and the eye goes straight to it. The parts of the configuration that will be perceived as figure or ground can vary depending on the individual consumer as well as other factors. Similarly, in marketing messages that use the figure-ground principle, a stimulus can be made the focal point of the message or merely the context that surrounds the focus.

Symbolism in Marketing Messages

Every marketing message has three basic components: an object, a sign or symbol, and an interpretant. The *object* is the product that is the focus of the message (e.g., Marlboro cigarettes). The *sign* or *symbol* is the sensory imagery that represents the intended meanings of the object (e.g., the Marlboro cowboy). The *interpretant* is the meaning derived (e.g., rugged, individualistic, American). This relationship is diagrammed in Figure 2–4.

The use of symbols provides a powerful means for marketers to convey product attributes to consumers. For example, expensive cars, designer fashions, and diamond jewelry—all widely recognized symbols of success—frequently appear in ads to associate a product with affluence or sophistication.

FIGURE 2–4 Relationships of Components in Semiotic Analysis of Meaning

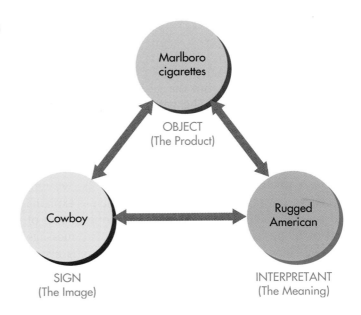

MARKETING PITFALL

Whether symbols are used to promote a product or to create identification for it, the interpretation or meaning may not always convey what the marketer intended. When the Coca-Cola Company was planning to expand into China in the 1920s, a translator developed a group of Chinese characters that phonetically resembled the company name. Since the product was new to the country, people would not recognize the Coca-Cola logo, so they had to rely upon the meaning as conveyed phonetically. Unfortunately, the Chinese characters that sounded like Coca-Cola translated to mean "bite the wax tadpole," and changes had to be made quickly.[50]

HYPERREALITY   One of the hallmarks of modern advertising is that it creates a condition that has been termed **hyperreality**. Hyperreality refers to the becoming real of what is initially simulation or "hype." Advertisers create new relationships between objects and interpretants by inventing new connections between products and benefits, such as equating Marlboro cigarettes with the American frontier spirit.[51] To a large extent, over time the true relationship between the symbol and reality is no longer possible to discern, and the "artificial" associations between product symbols and the real world may take on a life of their own. For example, Tasters' Choice coffee presents an ongoing series of "soap opera" commercials where a romantic relationship is slowly cultivated between two actors. The pink Energizer Bunny™ who began life in straight Eveready Battery commercials now goes gaily marching through fake commercials for such totally unrelated products as "Alarm" bath and shower soap—where the Bunny is appropriately dressed in rain gear. As illustrated by the film clips shown here, the Bunny's antics take the actors in these simulated commercials by surprise and usually the viewers as well.

The popular pink Energizer Bunny™, gaily marching through fake commercials, creates a condition of hyperreality in which product symbols take on a life of their own. Courtesy of the Eveready Battery Company, Inc.

Semiotics: The Study of Symbolism

For assistance in understanding how consumers interpret the meanings of symbols used in these communications, some marketers are turning to a field of study known as **semiotics**, which examines the correspondence between signs and symbols and their role in the assignment of meaning.[52] Semiotics is important to the understanding of consumer behavior, since consumers use products to express their social identities. Products have learned meanings, and we rely on advertising to figure out what those meanings are. As one set of researchers put it, ". . . advertising serves as a kind of culture/consumption dictionary; its entries are products, and their definitions are cultural meanings."[53]

According to semiotician Charles Sanders Peirce, signs are related to objects in one of three ways. Signs and symbols can resemble objects, be connected to them, or be conventionally tied to them.[54] An *icon* is a sign that resembles the product in some way (e.g., Bell Telephone uses an image of a bell to represent itself). An *index* is a sign that is connected to a product because they share some property (e.g., the pine tree on some of Spic and Span's cleanser products conveys the shared property of fresh scent). A *symbol* is a sign that is related to a product through either conventional or agreed-upon associations (e.g., the lion in Dreyfus Fund ads provides the

The complex symbolism in this Cognac Hennessy ad illustrates the different levels of meaning that can be conveyed in a picture. Reprinted with permission by Schieffelin & Somerset Co. All rights reserved.

conventional association with fearlessness that is carried over to the company's approach to investments).

The Cognac Hennessy ad illustrates some of the subtle semiotic processes that convey meaning in advertising. The product, cognac, is an upscale alcoholic beverage associated with a soft, smooth taste, luxurious surroundings, and a large price tag. The label is an *icon*—it literally represents the product. Silk is used as an *index* that shares properties with the cognac—it is smooth and also associated with luxury. The woman wrapped in a silk gown is a *symbol*—she stands for sex appeal, smoothness, and luxury. The creators of the ad hope that these properties will transfer to people's perceptions of the product.

Chapter Summary

• *Perception* is the process by which physical sensations such as sights, sounds, and smells are selected, organized, and interpreted. The eventual interpretation of a stimulus allows it to be assigned meaning.

• Marketing stimuli have important sensory qualities. We rely on colors, odors, sounds, tastes, and even the "feel" of products when forming evaluations of them.

• Not all sensations successfully make their way through the perceptual process. Many stimuli compete for our attention, and the majority are not noticed or accurately comprehended.

• People have different thresholds of perception. A stimulus must be presented at a certain level of intensity before it can be detected by sensory receptors. In addition, a consumer's ability to detect whether two stimuli are different (the *differential threshold*) is an important issue in many marketing contexts, such as changing a package design, altering the size of a product, or reducing its price.

• A lot of controversy has been sparked by so-called *subliminal persuasion* and related techniques, by which people are exposed to visual and audio messages below the threshold. Although evidence that subliminal persuasion is effective is virtually nonexistent, many consumers continue to believe that advertisers use this technique.

• Some of the factors that determine which stimuli (above the threshold level) do get perceived are the amount of exposure to the stimulus, how much attention it generates, and how it is interpreted. In an increasingly crowded stimulus environment, *advertising clutter* occurs when too many marketing-related messages compete for attention.

• A stimulus that is attended to is not perceived in isolation. It is classified and organized according to principles of perceptual organization. These principles are guided by a *gestalt*, or overall pattern. Specific grouping principles include closure, similarity, and figure–ground relationships.

• The final step in the process of perception is *interpretation*. Symbols help us to make sense of the world by providing us with an interpretation of a stimulus that is often shared by others. The degree to which the symbolism is consistent with our previous experience affects the meaning we assign to related objects. Every marketing message contains a relationship between the product, the sign or symbol, and the interpretation of meaning. A *semiotic* analysis involves the correspondence between stimuli and the meaning of signs.

- Signs function on several levels. The intended meaning may be literal (e.g., an icon like a street sign with a picture of children playing). The meaning may be indexical; it relies on shared characteristics (e.g., the red in a stop sign means danger). Finally, meaning can be conveyed by a symbol, where an image is given meaning by convention or by agreement by members of a society (e.g., stop signs are octagonal, while yield signs are triangular).

Key Terms

absolute threshold, p. 57
adaptation, p. 64
advertising clutter, p. 62
attention, p. 64
closure, p. 69
differential threshold, p. 57
embeds, p. 59
experience, p. 62

exposure, p. 62
figure–ground relationship, p. 70
Gestalt psychology, p. 67
hyperreality, p. 71
interpretation, p. 67
JND, p. 58
perception, p. 49
principle of similarity, p. 70

psychophysics, p. 57
schema, p. 50
semiotics, p. 72
sensation, p. 49
stimulus ambiguity, p. 67
subliminal perception, p. 59
Weber's Law, p. 58

Consumer Behavior Challenge

1. Many studies have shown that our sensory detection abilities decline as we grow older. Discuss the implications of the absolute threshold for marketers attempting to appeal to the elderly.
2. Assuming that some forms of subliminal persuasion may have the desired effect of influencing consumers, do you think the use of these techniques is ethical? Explain your answer.
3. Assume that you are a consultant for a marketer who wants to design a package for a new premium chocolate bar targeted to an affluent market. What recommendations would you provide in terms of such package elements as color, symbolism, and graphic design (remembering the grouping principles discussed in the chapter)? Give the reasons for your suggestions.
4. Do you believe that marketers have the right to use any or all public spaces to deliver product messages? Where would you draw the line in terms of places and products that should be restricted?
5. Find one ad that is rich in symbolism and perform a semiotic analysis of it. Identify each type of sign used in the ad and the product qualities being communicated by each. Comment on the effectiveness of the signs that are used to communicate the intended message.
6. Using magazines archived in the library, track the packaging of a spe-

cific brand over time. Find an example of gradual changes in package design that may have been below the JND.

7. Collect a set of current ads for one type of product (e.g., personal computers, perfumes, laundry detergents, or athletic shoes) from magazines, and analyze the colors employed. Describe the images conveyed by different colors, and try to identify any consistency across brands in terms of the colors used in product packaging or other aspects of the ads.

8. Find three ads for food products that present these products in a particular scene or setting. Report on the symbols used in the setting and how you believe the marketer intended them to be interpreted relative to the food product.

9. Look through a current magazine and select one ad that captures your attention over the others. Give the reasons why.

10. Find ads that utilize the techniques of contrast and novelty. Give your opinion of the effectiveness of each ad and whether the technique is likely to be appropriate for the consumers targeted by the ad.

CNN Connection

Sensory Marketing

CNN. A video segment is available to accompany this CNN Connection.

Singing magazine ads? In the battle to grab consumers' attention, marketers are finding other sources of ammunition. One approach has been called *sensory advertising*. It includes such techniques as singing ads (using micro chips embedded in magazine pages), 3-D glasses, elaborate pop-up ads in magazines, and scent strips to appeal to consumers on one or more sensory channels.

The practice of inserting perfumed strips in magazines is meeting resistance among some American consumers, especially those who are allergic to perfume and who find themselves bombarded with scents every time they open their mail. A small number of magazines, including *People, The New Yorker,* and *Mirabella,* are now providing scent-free issues to those who request them. For the rest of us, though, scent strips are here to stay: A survey of *Allure* readers found that 60% had purchased a fragrance.[1] However, help may be on the way: A German company is introducing a new technology that allows the scent to be released only by rubbing. The new method debuted in the October 1992 issue of *Allure.*[2]

[1]Deirdre Carmody, "When Readers Tell a Magazine That They Want to Smell It Like It Is," *New York Times* (May 11, 1992): D8.
[2]"Sense Those Scents?" *Adweek* (September 21, 1992): 24.

Notes

1. Kim Foltz, "Campaign on Harmony Backfires for Benetton," *New York Times* (November 20, 1989): D8.
2. Jerome S. Bruner, "On Perceptual Readiness," *Psychological Review* 64 (March 1957):123–52.
3. "The Lemon Juice That Wasn't," *Newsweek* (August 2, 1982): 53.
4. Gail Tom, Teresa Barnett, William Lew, and Jodean Selmants, "Cueing the Consumer: The Role of Salient Cues in Consumer Perception," *Journal of Consumer Marketing* 4 (1987)2: 23–27.
5. Elizabeth C. Hirschman and Morris B. Holbrook,"Hedonic Consumption: Emerging Concepts, Methods, and Propositions," *Journal of Marketing* 46 (Summer 1982): 92–101.
6. Woody Hochswender, "Battles So Real They Almost Hurt," *New York Times* (August 29, 1990): C1.
7. Ronald Alsop, "Color Grows More Important in Catch- ing Consumers' Eyes," *Wall Street Journal* (November 29, 1984): 37.
8. Alsop, "Color Grows More Important in Catching Consumers' Eyes."
9. "Court Refuses Trademark for Package Color," *Marketing News* (May 27, 1991): 25.
10. Anthony Ramirez, "Lessons in the Cracker Market: Nabisco Saved New Graham Snack," *New York Times* (July 5, 1990): D1.
11. "Ready for Purple Cars?" *Adweek* (January 20, 1992): 20.
12. Quoted in Cynthia Morris, "The Mystery of Fragrance," *Essence* 71 (May 1988)3: 71.
13. Deborah Toth, "To Relax or Stay Alert: New Mood-Altering Scents," *New York Times* (September 24, 1989): F15.
14. James LaRossa, Jr., "Home Fragrances Bloom in Wide-Open Field," *Home Textiles* 54 (May 8, 1989): 4.
15. "Environmental Fragrancing: The Muzak of the 90s," *Fragrance Forum* (Fall 1988); Toth, "To Relax or Stay Alert."
16 Eben Shapiro, "When It Rains, It Removes Odors," *New York Times* (October 6, 1992): D5.
17. Gail Tom, "Marketing with Music," *Journal of Consumer Marketing* 7 (Spring 1990): 49–53; J. Vail, "Music as a Marketing Tool," *Advertising Age* (November 4, 1985): 24.
18. Otto Friedrich, "Trapped in a Musical Elevator," *Time* 110 (December 10, 1984): 3.
19. James MacLachlan and Michael H. Siegel, "Reducing the Costs of Television Commercials by Use of Time Compression," *Journal of Marketing Research* 17 (February 1980): 52–57.
20. James MacLachlan, "Listener Perception of Time Compressed Spokespersons," *Journal of Advertising Research* 2 (April/May 1982): 47–51.
21. Danny L. Moore, Douglas Hausknecht, and Kanchana Thamodaran, "Time Compression, Response Opportunity, and Persuasion," *Journal of Consumer Research* 13 (June 1986): 85–99.
22. Jacob Hornik, "Tactile Stimulation and Consumer Response," *Journal of Consumer Research* 19 (December 1992).
23. Eben Shapiro, "The People Who Are Putting Taste Back on the Table," *New York Times* (July 22, 1990): F5.
24. Judann Dagnoli, "Cookie Tasters Chip in for Nabisco," *Advertising Age* (August 21, 1989): 58.
25. See Tim Davis, "Taste Tests: Are the Blind Leading the Blind?" *Beverage World* (April 1987)3: 43.
26. Quoted in Davis, "Taste Tests," 44.
27. Stuart Elliott, "Another Remarkable Story of the Brand-Name Lexicon," *New York Times* (August 13, 1992): D9. IBM is the world's ninth most popular brand.
28. Michael Lev, "No Hidden Meaning Here: Survey Sees Subliminal Ads," *New York Times* (May 3, 1991): D7.
29. *The New Yorker* (September 21, 1957): 33.
30. Erv Wolk, "Can Subliminal Ads Work for You?" *Modern Floor Coverings* (June 1986): 23.
31. Philip M. Merikle, "Subliminal Auditory Messages: An Evaluation," *Psychology & Marketing* 5 (1988)4: 355–72.
32. Timothy E. Moore, "The Case Against Subliminal Manipulation," *Psychology & Marketing* 5 (Winter 1988): 297–316.
33. Sid C. Dudley, "Subliminal Advertising: What Is the Controversy About?" *Akron Business and Economic Review* 18 (Summer 1987): 6–18; "Subliminal Messages: Subtle Crime Stoppers," *Chain Store Age Executive* (July 1987)2: 85; "Mind Benders," *Money* (September 1978): 24.
34. Moore, "The Case Against Subliminal Manipulation."
35. Joel Saegert, "Why Marketing Should Quit Giving Subliminal Advertising the Benefit of the Doubt," *Psychology & Marketing* 4 (Summer 1987): 107–20. See also Dennis L. Rosen and Surendra N. Singh, "An Investigation of Subliminal Embed Effect on Multiple Measures of Advertising Effectiveness," *Psychology & Marketing* 9 (March/April 1992): 157–73.
36. Foltz, *New York Times* (October 23, 1989).
37. "$10 Sure Thing," *Time* (August 4, 1980): 51.
38. David Kilburn, "Japanese VCR Edits Out the Ads," *Advertising Age* (August 20, 1990): 16.
39. Kate Lewin, "Getting Around Commercial Avoidance," *Marketing and Media Decisions* (December 1988)4: 116.
40. Craig Reiss, "Fast-Forward Ads Deliver," *Advertising Age* (October 27, 1986)2: 3; Steve Sternberg, "VCR's: Impact and Implications," *Marketing and Media*

Decisions 22 (December 1987)5: 100.

41. Elliot Young, "Overcoming the Zapping Problem in Magazines: New Learning from Eye Tracking Research," paper presented at Copy Research Workshop, Advertising Research Federation, New York, May 3, 1988.

42. Quoted in Kim Foltz, "Ads Popping Up All Over," *Newsweek* (August 12, 1985): 50.

43. "Traffic Now Tuned to Boston's Tunnel Radio," *New York Times* (August 1, 1982); Alison Fahey, "In the Lobby," *Advertising Age* (September 18, 1989); Kim Foltz, "Ads Popping Up All Over," *Newsweek* (August 12, 1985)2: 50.

44. Kim Foltz, *New York Times* (October 23, 1989): D11.

45. Michael Lev, "Music Industry Broadens Its Campaigns," *New York Times* (January 17, 1992): D15.

46. Roger Barton, *Advertising Media* (New York: McGraw-Hill, 1964).

47. Albert H. Hastorf and Hadley Cantril, "They Saw a Game: A Case Study," *Journal of Abnormal and Social Psychology* 49 (1954): 129–34.

48. Roberto Friedmann and Mary R. Zimmer, "The Role of Psychological Meaning in Advertising," *Journal of Advertising* 17 (1988)1: 31–40.

49. Tom et al., "Cueing the Consumer."

50. David A. Ricks, "Products That Crashed the Language Barrier," *Business and Society Review* (Spring 1983): 46–50.

51. Jean Baudrillard, *Simulations* (New York: Semiotext(e), 1983); A. Fuat Firat and Alladi Venkatesh, "The Making of Postmodern Consumption," in *Consumption and Marketing: Macro Dimensions*, eds. Russell Belk and Nikhilesh Dholakia (Boston: PWS-Kent, 1993); A. Furat Firat, "The Consumer in Postmodernity," in *Advances in Consumer Research* 18, eds, Rebecca H. Holman and Michael R. Solomon (Provo, Utah: Association for Consumer Research, 1991), 70–76.

52. See David Mick, "Consumer Research and Semiotics: Exploring the Morphology of Signs, Symbols, and Significance," *Journal of Consumer Research* 13 (September 1986): 196–213.

53. Teresa J. Domzal and Jerome B. Kernan, "Reading Advertising: The What and How of Product Meaning," *Journal of Consumer Marketing* 9 (Summer 1992): 48–64, p. 49.

54. Arthur Asa Berger, *Signs in Contemporary Culture: An Introduction to Semiotics* (New York: Longman, 1984); Mick, "Consumer Research and Semiotics"; Charles Sanders Peirce, in *Collected Papers*, eds. Charles Hartshorne, Paul Weiss, and Arthur W. Burks (Cambridge, Mass.: Harvard University Press, 1931–1958).

CHAPTER 3

Motivation

Buying, Having, and Being: Selections 10–11 from *Buying, Having, and Being: The Washington Post Consumer Behavior Companion*, Second Edition, accompany this chapter.

I t's been two years since Basil gave up smoking, drinking, and junk food. He now devotes the same enthusiasm to working out that he used to bring to partying. Basil has become a dedicated triathlete. Participating in this sport, which involves running, swimming, and biking, has become so important to Basil that he now structures his entire schedule around his training regimen. He even passed on an important class he needed for his major because the only open section was offered at the same time he did his daily five-mile run.

Basil has been so engrossed in the sport that his friends hardly see him anymore—he spends most of his free time (when not in training) reading magazines dedicated to the sport, shopping for special equipment like running shoes and Lycra tights for winter training, or traveling to triathalon events all over the country. His girlfriend, Judy, has even complained that lately he likes looking at himself in the mirror more than he likes looking at her.

Basil remains committed—he's nothing if not dedicated to the cause . . . .

Introduction

Some people are so involved in an activity that they can be termed *fanatic consumers*. Whether they are training for a triathalon, watching television, or playing music, these people tend to become totally engrossed in an activity to the point where such involvement has been called a "positive addiction." One survey of triathletes (like Basil), for example, found that intense commitment to the sport resulted in a highly modified daily schedule, unwillingness to stop training even if injured, major dietary changes, and—most relevant to marketers—a substantial financial commitment for travel to races, specialized clothing, and health club memberships.[1]

The forces that drive people to buy and use products are generally straightforward, as when a person purchases a pair of running shoes for everyday wear. As hard-core triathletes demonstrate, however, even the consumption of an everyday product like running shoes may also be related to deep-seated experiences. In some cases, these emotional responses create a deep commitment to the product, as the consumer in the Dingo boot ad at the beginning of this chapter illustrates. Sometimes, people are not even fully aware of the forces that drive them toward some products and away from others.

To understand motivation is to understand *why* consumers do what

Teaching Hint: Another example of high-involvement activity is voluntary high-risk consumption, such as skydiving and mountain climbing. For an interesting ethnographic account of such pursuits, see Richard L. Celsi, Randall L. Rose, and Thomas W. Leigh, "An Exploration of High-Risk Leisure Consumption Through Skydiving," *Journal of Consumer Research* 20 (June 1993): 1–23.

they do. We do everything for a reason, whether to quench a thirst, kill boredom, or attain some deep spiritual experience. Marketing students are taught from day one that the goal of marketing is to satisfy consumers' needs. However, this insight is useless unless we can discover *what* those needs are and *why* they exist.

The Motivation Process

Motivation refers to the processes that cause people to behave as they do. It occurs when a need is aroused that the consumer wishes to satisfy. Once a need has been activated, a state of tension exists that drives the consumer to attempt to reduce or eliminate the need. Marketers try to create products and services that will provide the desired benefits and permit the consumer to reduce this tension.

Figure 3–1 gives an overview of the motivation process. The sections to follow will elaborate on the components in this model, but in general the process works this way: A need is recognized by the consumer. This need may be *utilitarian* (i.e., a desire to achieve some functional or practical benefit, as when a person requires a pair of durable sneakers) or it may be *hedonic* (i.e., an experiential need, involving emotional responses or fantasies, as when Basil buys special running shoes for a triathalon event). The desired end state is the consumer's **goal**.

In either case, a discrepancy exists between the consumer's present state and some ideal state. This gulf creates a state of tension. The magnitude of this tension determines the urgency the consumer feels to reduce the tension. This degree of arousal is called a **drive.** A basic need can be satisfied any number of ways, and the specific path a person chooses is influenced by his or her unique set of experiences, cultural upbringing, and so on.

These factors combine to create a **want,** which is one manifestation of a need. For example, hunger is a basic need that must be satisfied by all; the lack of food creates a tension state that can be reduced by the intake of such

Figure 3–1 is available as Transparency 5.

FIGURE 3–1   An Overview of the Motivation Process

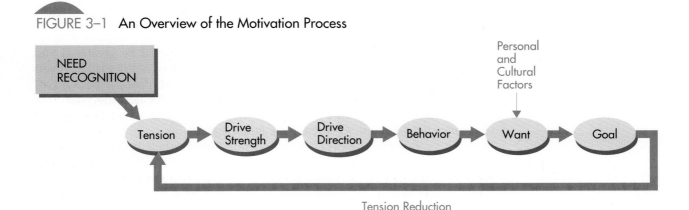

products as cheeseburgers, double fudge Oreo cookies, raw fish, or bean sprouts. The specific route to hunger reduction is culturally determined.

Once the goal is attained, tension is reduced and the motivation recedes (for the time being). Motivation can be described in terms of its *strength*, or the pull it exerts on the consumer, and its *direction*, or the particular way the consumer attempts to reduce motivational tension.

Motivational Strength

The degree to which a person is willing to expend energy to reach one goal as opposed to another reflects his or her underlying motivation to attain that goal. Many theories have been advanced to explain why people behave the way they do. Most share the basic idea that people have some finite amount of energy that must be directed toward certain goals.

Biological Versus Learned Needs

Early work on motivation ascribed behavior to *instinct*, the innate patterns of behavior that are universal in a species. This view is now largely discredited. For one thing, the existence of an instinct is difficult to prove or disprove. The instinct is inferred from the behavior it is supposed to explain (this type of circular explanation is called a *tautology*).[2] It is like saying that a consumer buys status symbols because he or she is motivated to attain status, which is hardly a satisfying explanation.

DRIVE THEORY *Drive theory* focuses on biological needs that produce unpleasant states of arousal (e.g., your stomach grumbles during a morning class). We are motivated to reduce the tension caused by this arousal. Tension reduction has been proposed as a basic mechanism governing human behavior.

In marketing, *tension* refers to the unpleasant state that exists if a person's consumption needs are not fulfilled. A person may be grumpy if he hasn't eaten, or he may be dejected or angry if he cannot afford that new car he wants. This state activates goal-oriented behavior, which attempts to reduce or eliminate this unpleasant state and return to a balanced one, is termed **homeostasis.**

Those behaviors that are successful in reducing the drive by eliminating the underlying need are strengthened and tend to be repeated. (This aspect of the *learning* process will be further discussed in Chapter 4.) Your motivation to leave class early in order to grab a snack would be greater if you hadn't eaten in 24 hours than if you had eaten only two hours earlier. If you did sneak out and got indigestion after, say, wolfing down a package of Twinkies, this behavior would be less likely to be repeated the next time you wanted a snack. One's degree of motivation, then, depends upon the distance between one's present state and the goal.

Drive theory, however, runs into difficulties when it tries to explain some facets of human behavior that run counter to its predictions. People often do things that *increase* a drive state rather than decrease it. For example, people may delay gratification. If you know you are going out for a lavish dinner, you might decide to forego a snack earlier in the day even though you are hungry at that time. In other cases, people deliberately watch erotic movies, even though these stimuli often increase sexual arousal rather than diminish it.

EXPECTANCY THEORY Most current explanations of motivation focus on cognitive factors rather than biological ones to understand what drives behavior. **Expectancy theory** suggests that behavior is largely pulled by expectations of achieving desirable outcomes—*positive incentives*—rather than pushed from within. We choose one product over another because we expect this choice to have more positive consequences for us. Thus the term *drive* is used here more loosely to refer to both physical and cognitive processes.

Consumer Involvement

Involvement refers to "the level of perceived personal importance and/or interest evoked by a stimulus (or stimuli) within a specific situation."[3] This definition implies that aspects of the person, the product, and the situation all combine to determine the consumer's motivation to process product-related information at a given point in time. When consumers are intent on doing what they can to satisfy a need, they will be motivated to pay attention and process any information felt to be relevant to achieving their goals.

On the other hand, a person may not bother to pay any attention to the same information if it is not seen as relevant to satisfying some need. One person who prides himself on his knowledge of exercise equipment may read anything he can find about the subject, spend his spare time in athletics stores, and so on, while another (lazier) person may skip over this information without giving it a second thought.

Involvement can be viewed as the motivation to process information.[4] To the degree that there is a perceived linkage between a consumer's needs, goals, or values, and product knowledge, the consumer will be motivated to pay attention to product information. When relevant knowledge is activated in memory, a motivational state is created that drives behavior (e.g., shopping). This subjective feeling of personal relevance is termed felt involvement. As felt involvement with a product increases, people devote more attention to ads related to the product, exert more cognitive effort to understand these ads, and focus their attention on the product-related information in them.[5]

FROM INERTIA TO PASSION The type of information processing that will occur thus depends upon the consumer's level of involvement. It can range from *simple processing,* where only the basic features of a message are considered, all the way to *elaboration,* where the incoming information is linked to one's preexisting knowledge systems.[6]

Degree of involvement can be conceived as a continuum, ranging from absolute lack of interest in a marketing stimulus at one end to obsession at the other. Consumption at the low end of involvement is characterized by **inertia,** where decisions are made out of habit because the consumer lacks the motivation to consider alternatives. At the high end of involvement, we can expect to

Research Report: Most marketing stimuli generate no active processing at all. For a recent study that equates the learning of marketing information with the processing of trivia, see Scott A. Hawkins and Stephen J. Hoch, "Low-Involvement Learning: Memory Without Evaluation," *Journal of Consumer Research* 19 (September 1992): 212–25.

This ad for lifestyle magazines targeted to men underscores the strategic value of reaching highly involved consumers. Courtesy of Times Mirror Magazines.

find the type of passionate intensity reserved for people and objects that carry great meaning to the individual. The ad for Times Mirror Magazines shown here emphasizes this type of high involvement. For the most part, however, a consumer's involvement level with products falls somewhere in the middle, and the marketing strategist must determine the relative level of importance to understand how much elaboration of product information will occur.

MARKETING OPPORTUNITY

The passion of some consumers for famous people demonstrates the high end of the involvement continuum. Celebrity worship is evident in activities ranging from autograph collections to the cement shrines at Graumann's Chinese

Theatre in Hollywood. Consumers can be described in terms of the intensity of their admiration for a celebrity. At the bottom of this intensity ladder are people who are uninvolved, oblivious, or even hostile to a celebrity.

As identification with a star increases, so does the consumer's degree of passion and desire to accumulate artifacts belonging to that star, or even to make actual contact with him or her. Groupies, for example, are people who follow celebrities, and often attempt to become a part of stars' lives by seducing them or even harassing them.

There are more than 1200 active fan clubs in the United States. These are composed of people who are devoted to an individual, whether a musician, race car driver, or soap opera star. While some clubs are spontaneously created by devoted fans, others are deliberately engineered by the stars themselves to perpetuate their worship. For example, singer Lionel Richie's clubs are run by his wife, and the merchandise purchased by members is subcontracted by the star.[7]

THE MANY FACES OF INVOLVEMENT As previously defined, involvement can take many forms. Basil could certainly be said to be involved with his running shoes, since they help to define and bolster his self-concept. This involvement seems to increase at certain times, as when he must prove himself in a triathalon. Alternatively, the act of buying the shoes may be very involving for people who are passionately devoted to shopping. To complicate matters further, advertisements, such as those produced for Nike or Adidas, may themselves be involving for some reason (e.g., because they make us laugh, cry, or inspire us to work harder).

It seems that involvement is a fuzzy concept, because it overlaps with other things and means different things to different people. Indeed, the consensus is that there are actually several broad types of involvement.[8]

Purchase Involvement. *Purchase involvement* is related to a consumer's level of interest in the buying process that is triggered by the need to consider a particular purchase. Many sales promotions are designed to increase purchase involvement.

In a contest sponsored by Dare perfume, for example, women submitted details of their most intimate trysts by letter or by phone to radio talk shows. The winning stories were edited into a romance novel published by Bantam Books. These books, in turn, were given away as a gift with the purchase of the perfume.[9]

Message-Response Involvement. *Message-response involvement* refers to the processing of marketing communications.[10] Television is considered a low-involvement medium, because it requires a passive viewer who exerts relatively little control (remote control "zipping" notwithstanding) over content. In contrast, print is a high-involvement medium. The reader is actively involved in processing the information and is able to pause and reflect on what he or she has read before moving on.[11] The role of message characteristics in changing attitudes is further discussed in Chapter 6.

Additional Example: To increase involvement, some recent campaigns have featured disguised products in blind taste-test challenges. Philip Morris updated its "Merit Taste Challenge" by introducing the "Mystery Taste Challenge" in 1991. Smokers send in a coupon for two free packs of an unnamed cigarette. This approach simultaneously stimulates sampling and enables the company to generate a data base to identify smokers of competitive brands. See Judann Dagnoli and Alison Fahey, "What's Behind the Mystery Ad?" *Advertising Age* (September 16, 1991): 17.

Research Report: Ads that are inconsistent with an evoked schema have been found to initiate more extensive processing, which is a mixed blessing: Evaluations tend to be most positive when a stimulus is moderately incongruent with a category, and extreme departures may decrease processing. See Ronald C. Goodstein, "Category-Based Applications and Extensions in Advertising: Motivating More Extensive Ad Processing," *Journal of Consumer Research* 20 (June 1993): 87–99. Joan Meyers-Levy and Alice M. Tybout, "Schema Congruity As a Basis for Product Evaluation," *Journal of Consumer Research* 16 (June 1989): 39–54; Douglas M. Stayman, Dana L. Alden, and Karen H. Smith, "Some Effects of Schematic Processing on Consumer Expectations and Disconfirmation Judgments," *Journal of Consumer Research* 19 (September 1992): 240–55.

Teaching Hint: Involvement level is an important consideration in political marketing. Not surprisingly, for example, people who are more interested in political campaigns and are more likely to vote are also more likely to watch candidates' debates and political conventions on television. See David R. Eppright, "Involvement and Party Affiliation Effects on Campaign Television Exposure, *Proceedings of the Annual Meeting of the Southern Marketing Association*, ed. Robert L. King, Richmond, Va., 1991, 94–97.

TABLE 3–1   A Scale to Measure Product Involvement

(Insert name of object to be judged)

important	_:_:_:_:_:_:_	unimportant*
of no concern	_:_:_:_:_:_:_	of concern to me
irrelevant	_:_:_:_:_:_:_	relevant
means a lot to me	_:_:_:_:_:_:_	means nothing to me*
useless	_:_:_:_:_:_:_	useful
valuable	_:_:_:_:_:_:_	worthless*
trivial	_:_:_:_:_:_:_	fundamental
beneficial	_:_:_:_:_:_:_	not beneficial*
matters to me	_:_:_:_:_:_:_	doesn't matter
uninterested	_:_:_:_:_:_:_	interested
significant	_:_:_:_:_:_:_	insignificant*
vital	_:_:_:_:_:_:_	superfluous
boring	_:_:_:_:_:_:_	interesting
unexciting	_:_:_:_:_:_:_	exciting
appealing	_:_:_:_:_:_:_	unappealing*
mundane	_:_:_:_:_:_:_	fascinating
essential	_:_:_:_:_:_:_	nonessential*
undesirable	_:_:_:_:_:_:_	desirable
wanted	_:_:_:_:_:_:_	unwanted*
not needed	_:_:_:_:_:_:_	needed

*Indicates item is reverse scored.

Items on the left are scored (1) low involvement to (7) high involvement on the right.

Totaling the 20 items gives a score from a low of 20 to a high of 140.

Source: Judith Lynne Zaichowsky, "Measuring the Involvement Construct," *Journal of Consumer Research* 12 (December 1985): 350. Reprinted with permission of The University of Chicago Press.

Ego Involvement. **Ego involvement** (sometimes termed *enduring involvement*) refers to the importance of a product to a consumer's self-concept. This concept implies a high level of social risk; the prospect of the product not performing its desired function may result in embarrassment or damage to the consumer's self-concept (Chapter 9 is devoted to the importance of the self-concept for consumer behavior issues). For example, Basil's running shoes are clearly an important part of his self-identity (i.e., they are said to have high *sign value*). This type of involvement is independent of particular purchase situations. It is an ongoing concern related to the self and hedonic experiences (e.g., the emotions felt as a result of using the product).[12]

MEASURING INVOLVEMENT   The measurement of involvement is important for many marketing applications. For example, research evidence indicates that a viewer who is more involved with a television show will also respond more positively to commercials contained in that show, and that these spots will have a greater chance of influencing his or her purchase intentions.[13] The many conceptualizations of involvement have led to some confusion about the best way to measure the concept. The scale shown in Table 3–1 is one widely used method.[14]

A pair of French researchers have argued that no single component of involvement is predominant. Recognizing that consumers can be involved with a product because it is a risky purchase and/or its use reflects upon or affects the self, they advocate the development of an *involvement profile* containing four components:[15]

- Importance and risk (the perceived importance of the product and the consequences of a bad purchase)
- Probability of making a bad purchase
- Pleasure value of the product category
- Sign value of the product category

These researchers asked a sample of housewives to rate a set of fourteen product categories on each of the above facets of involvement. The results are shown in Table 3–2. These data indicate that no single component captures consumer involvement, since this quality can occur for differ-

TABLE 3–2 Involvement Profiles for a Set of French Consumer Products

	Importance of Negative Consequences	Subjective Probability of Mispurchase	Pleasure Value	Sign Value
Dresses	121	112	147	181
Bras	117	115	106	130
Washing machines	118	109	106	111
TV sets	112	100	122	95
Vacuum cleaners	110	112	70	78
Irons	103	95	72	76
Champagne	109	120	125	125
Oil	89	97	65	92
Yogurt	86	83	106	78
Chocolate	80	89	123	75
Shampoo	96	103	90	81
Toothpaste	95	95	94	105
Facial soap	82	90	114	118
Detergents	79	82	56	63

Average product score = 100.

Source: Gilles Laurent and Jean-Noël Kapferer, "Measuring Consumer Involvement Profiles," *Journal of Marketing Research* 22 (February 1985): 45, Table 3. By permission of American Marketing Association.

ent reasons. For example, the purchase of a durable such as a vacuum cleaner is seen as risky, because one is stuck with a bad choice for many years. However, the vacuum cleaner does not provide pleasure (hedonic value), nor is it high in sign value (i.e., its use is not related to the person's self-concept). In contrast, chocolate is high in pleasure value but is not seen as risky or closely related to the self. Dresses and bras, on the other hand, appear to be involving for a combination of reasons.

Segmenting by Involvement Levels. A measurement approach of this nature allows consumer researchers to capture the diversity of the involvement construct, and it also provides the potential to use involvement as a basis for market segmentation. For example, a yogurt manufacturer might find that even though its product is low in sign value for one group of consumers, it might be highly related to the self-concept of another market segment, such as health-food enthusiasts or avid dieters. The company could adapt its strategy to account for the motivation of different segments to process information about the product. These variations are discussed in Chapter 6. Note also that involvement with a product class may vary across cultures. While this sample of French consumers rated champagne high in both sign value and personal value, the ability of champagne to provide pleasure or be central to self-definition might not transfer to other countries (e.g., Islamic cultures).

Strategies to Increase Involvement Although consumers differ in their level of involvement with respect to a product message, marketers do not have to just sit back and hope for the best. By being aware of some basic factors that increase or decrease attention, they can take steps to increase the likelihood that product information will get through. A consumer's motivation to process relevant information can be enhanced fairly easily by the marketer who uses one or more of the following techniques when designing persuasive communications.[17]

- Appeal to the consumers' hedonic needs. For example, ads using sensory appeals generate higher levels of attention.[18]

MULTICULTURAL DIMENSIONS

A recent study compared involvement levels of consumers from different countries for a number of products and services. When the researchers compared regular users of these items across countries, here are some differences in involvement that emerged (as measured by the scale in Table 3-1).[19]

- The Chinese are more involved with beer than are South Americans. Otherwise, the study found little differences for this category across countries.

- Involvement with soft drinks was relatively low in Canada and Sweden, but relatively high in (what was then) Yugoslavia and China.

- Blue jeans got the highest involvement score from Austrian consumers and the lowest from Swedes.

- Americans scored relatively high on involvement with air travel; Swedes, relatively low.

- French and Chinese subjects were most likely to be involved with going to the movies, while Mexicans were the least.

- Use novel stimuli, such as unusual cinematography, sudden silences, or unexpected movements in commercials.

- Use prominent stimuli, such as loud music and fast action, to capture attention in commercials. In print formats, larger ads increase attention. Also, viewers look longer at colored pictures as opposed to black-and-white.

- Include celebrity endorsers to generate higher interest in commercials. (This strategy will be discussed in Chapter 6).

Motivational Direction

Motives have direction as well as strength. They are goal oriented in that specific objectives are desired to satisfy a need. Most goals can be reached by a number of routes, and the objective of marketers is to convince consumers that the alternative they offer provides the best chance to attain the goal. For example, a consumer who decides that he needs a pair of jeans to help him reach his goal of being accepted by others or projecting an appropriate image can choose among Levi's, Wranglers, Guess, Calvin Klein, and many other alternatives, each of which promises to deliver certain benefits.

Needs Versus Wants

The specific way a need is satisfied depends upon the individual's unique history, learning experiences, and his or her cultural environment. The particular form of consumption used to satisfy a need is termed a *want*. For example, two classmates may feel their stomachs rumbling during a lunchtime lecture. If neither person has eaten since the night before, the strength of their respective needs (hunger) would be about the same. However, the way each person goes about satisfying this need might be quite different. The first person may be a health nut who fantasizes about gulping down a big handful of trail mix, while the second person may be equally aroused by the prospect of a greasy cheeseburger and fries.

This distinction between needs and wants is an important one, because it relates to the issue of whether marketers are actually capable of creating needs. That issue will be considered at the end of the chapter. For now, it is important to note that marketing strategies are more effective when they aim to influence the direction a consumer will take to satisfy a need rather than to create the need itself. Thus, a marketer will likely be more successful in convincing the "junk food junkie" to reach for the trail mix instead of the burger when hunger hits, rather than *creating* his or her hunger.

Types of Needs

People are born with a need for certain elements necessary to maintain life, such as food, water, air, and shelter. These are called *biogenic needs*. People have many other needs, however, that are not innate. *Psychogenic needs* are acquired in the process of becoming a member of a culture. These include the need for status, power, affiliation, and so on. Psychogenic needs reflect the priorities of a culture, and their effect on behavior will vary in different envi-

Teaching Hint: The Benetton apparel company has a reputation for creating controversial ads that generate a lot of publicity and public interest. Sometimes, however, fueling the fires of involvement can backfire. The company recently spent about $100,000 to sponsor a brochure, called "A Guide to Safer Sex," bound into *Spin* magazine, following an outcry about a campaign that used provocative news photographs. One such picture showed a man with AIDS at the moment of his death—with a Benetton logo superimposed over the photo. Several organizations decried the campaign, claiming that the company was exploiting concerns about AIDS for its own purposes. A spirited class discussion can be generated about the practice, sometimes called "point-of-purchase politics," of linking products to social causes. Stuart Elliott, "Brochure on AIDS Is the Latest Departure from Benetton," *New York Times* (April 29, 1992): D19.

ronments. For example, an American consumer may be driven to devote a good chunk of his income to products that permit him to display his wealth and status, while his Japanese counterpart may work equally hard to ensure that he does not stand out from his group. These differences in cultural values will be discussed in Chapter 15.

Consumers can also be motivated to satisfy either utilitarian or hedonic needs. The satisfaction of utilitarian needs implies that consumers will emphasize the objective, tangible attributes of products, such as miles per gallon in a car; the amount of fat, calories, and protein in a cheeseburger; and the durability of a pair of blue jeans. Hedonic needs are subjective and experiential; consumers may rely on a product to meet their needs for excitement, self-confidence, fantasy, and so on.[19] Of course, consumers may be motivated to purchase a product because it provides *both* types of benefits. For example, a mink coat may be bought because it feels soft and luxurious against the skin *and* because it keeps one warm on a snowy day.

Motivational Conflicts

A goal has *valence*; in addition to varying in its strength, it can be positive or negative. A positively valued goal is one toward which consumers direct their behavior; they are motivated to *approach* the goal and will seek out products that will be instrumental in attaining it. In the earlier example, Basil used his athletic equipment to help him improve his triathalon performance, his goal. However, not all behavior is motivated by the desire to approach a goal. In other cases, consumers are instead motivated to *avoid* a negative outcome. They will structure their purchases or consumption activities to reduce the chances of attaining this end result. For example, many consumers work hard to avoid rejection, a negative goal. They will stay away from products that they associate with social disapproval. Products such as deodorants and mouthwash frequently rely upon consumers' negative motivation by depicting the onerous social consequences of underarm odor or bad breath. Basil would most likely be especially vigilant about avoiding junk food as he prepared for an upcoming meet.

Because a purchase decision may involve more than one source of motivation, consumers often find themselves in situations where different motives, both positive and negative, conflict with one another. Since marketers are

FIGURE 3–2 **Three Types of Motivational Conflicts**

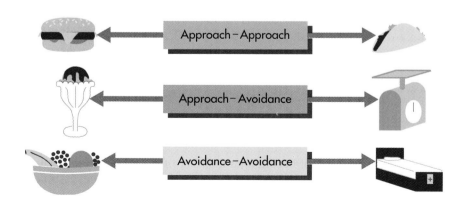

attempting to satisfy consumers' needs, they can also be helpful by providing possible solutions to these dilemmas. As shown in Figure 3–2, three general types of conflicts can occur: approach–approach, approach–avoidance, and avoidance–avoidance.

APPROACH–APPROACH CONFLICT   Here, a person must choose between two desirable alternatives. A student might be torn between going home for the holidays or going on a skiing trip with friends. Or, he or she might have to choose between two record albums.

Cognitive Dissonance.   The theory of **cognitive dissonance** is based on the premise that people have a need for order and consistency in their lives and that a state of tension is created when beliefs or behaviors conflict with one another. The conflict that arises when choosing between two alternatives may be resolved through a process of cognitive dissonance reduction, in which people are motivated to reduce this inconsistency (or dissonance) and thus eliminate unpleasant tension.[20]

A state of dissonance occurs when there is a logical inconsistency between two or more beliefs or behaviors. It often occurs when a consumer must make a choice between two products, where both alternatives usually possess both good and bad qualities. By choosing one product and not the other, the person gets the bad qualities of the chosen product and loses out on the good qualities of the unchosen one.

This loss creates an unpleasant, dissonant state that the person is motivated to reduce. People tend to convince themselves after the fact that the choice they made was the smart one by finding additional reasons to support the alternative they chose, or perhaps by "discovering" flaws with the option they did not choose. A marketer can resolve an approach–approach conflict by bundling several benefits together. For example, Miller Lite's claim that it is "less filling" *and* "tastes great" allows the drinker to "have his beer and drink it too."

APPROACH–AVOIDANCE CONFLICT   Many of the products and services we desire have negative consequences attached to them as well. We may feel guilty or ostentatious when buying a status-laden product or feel like a glutton when contemplating a box of Twinkies.

Some solutions to these conflicts include the proliferation of fake furs, which eliminate guilt about harming animals to make a fashion statement, and the success of diet foods, such as Weight Watchers, that promise good food without the calories. Many marketers try to overcome guilt by convincing consumers that they are deserving of luxuries (e.g., when the model for L'Oreal cosmetics claims "Because I'm worth it!").

AVOIDANCE–AVOIDANCE CONFLICT   Sometimes consumers find themselves caught "between a rock and a hard place." They may face a choice with two undesirable alternatives. A person may be faced with the option of either throwing more money into an old car or buying a new one. Marketers frequently address this conflict by messages that stress the unforeseen benefits of choosing one option (e.g., by emphasizing special credit plans to ease the pain of new-car payments).

Classifying Consumer Needs

Much research has been done on classifying human needs. On the one hand, some psychologists have tried to define a universal inventory of needs that could be traced systematically to explain virtually all behavior. One such effort, developed by Henry Murray, delineates a set of twenty needs that (sometimes in combination) result in specific behaviors. These needs include such dimensions as autonomy (being independent), defendance (defending the self against criticism), and even play (engaging in pleasurable activities).[21]

Others have focused on specific needs (which often are included in general models like Murray's) and their ramifications for behavior. For example, individuals with a high *need for achievement* strongly value personal accomplishment.[22] They place a premium on products and services that signify success because these consumption items provide feedback about the realization of their goals. These consumers are good prospects for products that provide evidence of their achievement. One study of working women found that those who were high in achievement motivation were more likely to choose clothing they considered businesslike, and less likely to be

Figure 3–3 is available as Transparency 6.

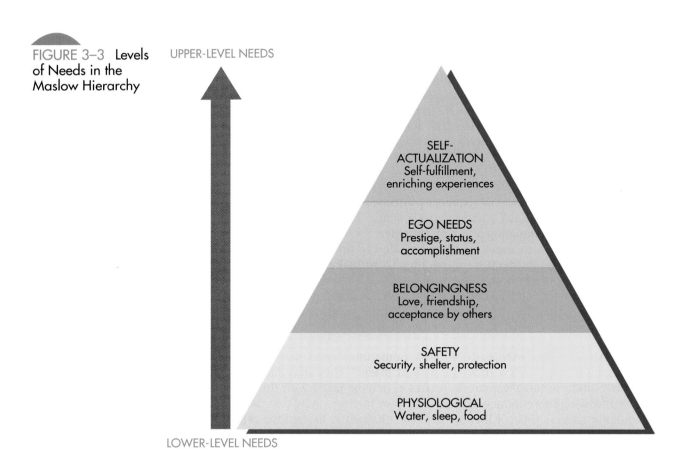

FIGURE 3–3 **Levels of Needs in the Maslow Hierarchy**

UPPER-LEVEL NEEDS

SELF-ACTUALIZATION
Self-fulfillment, enriching experiences

EGO NEEDS
Prestige, status, accomplishment

BELONGINGNESS
Love, friendship, acceptance by others

SAFETY
Security, shelter, protection

PHYSIOLOGICAL
Water, sleep, food

LOWER-LEVEL NEEDS

interested in apparel that accentuated their femininity.[23] Some other important needs that are relevant to consumer behavior include the following.

- *Need for affiliation* (to be in the company of other people):[24] This need is relevant to products and services that are consumed in groups and alleviate loneliness, such as team sports, bars, and shopping malls.
- *Need for power* (to control one's environment):[25] Many products and services allow consumers to feel that they have mastery over their surroundings, ranging from "hopped-up" muscle cars and loud boom boxes (large portable radios) to hotels, restaurants, and resorts that promise to respond to the customer's every whim.
- *Need for uniqueness* (to assert one's individual identity):[26] This need is satisfied by products that pledge to accentuate a consumer's distinctive qualities. For example, Cachet perfume claims to be "as individual as you are."

MASLOW'S HIERARCHY OF NEEDS One influential approach to motivation was proposed by the psychologist Abraham Maslow. Maslow's approach is a general one originally developed to understand personal growth and the attainment of "peak experiences."[27] Maslow formulated a hierarchy of needs, in which levels of motives are specified. A hierarchical approach implies that the order of development is fixed—that is, a certain level must be attained before the next, higher one is activated. This universal approach to motivation has been adapted by marketers because it (indirectly) specifies certain types of product benefits people might be looking for, depending upon the different stages in their development and/or their environmental conditions.

These levels are summarized in Figure 3–3. At each level, different priorities exist in terms of the product benefits a consumer is looking for. Ideally, an individual progresses up the hierarchy until his or her dominant motivation is a focus on "ultimate" goals, such as justice and beauty. Unfortunately, this state is difficult to achieve (at least on a regular basis); most of us have to be satisfied with occasional glimpses, or peak experiences. Examples of product appeals tailored to each level are provided in Table 3–3.

Transparency 7, a trade ad for a popcorn manufacturer, argues that bigger popcorn is a *need* for food establishments. Students will enjoy the explicit reference to the hierarchy of needs in the ad's copy.

TABLE 3–3 Maslow's Hierarchy and Marketing Strategies

Level of Hierarchy	Relevant Products	Example
Self-Actualization	Hobbies, travel, education	Club Med: "The antidote for civilization"
Ego Needs	Cars, furniture, credit cards, stores, country clubs, liquors	Royal Salute Scotch—"What the rich give the wealthy"
Belongingness	Clothing, grooming products, clubs, drinks	Pepsi—"You're in the Pepsi generation"
Safety	Insurance, alarm systems, retirement investments	Allstate Insurance—"You're in good hands with Allstate"
Physiological	Medicines, staple items, generics	Quaker Oat Bran—"It's the right thing to do"

Criticisms of the Maslow Hierarchy. The implication of Maslow's hierarchy is that one must first satisfy basic needs before progressing up the ladder (i.e., a starving man is not interested in status symbols, friendship, or self-fulfillment). This hierarchy is not set in stone. Its use in marketing has been somewhat simplistic, especially since the same product or activity can satisfy a number of different needs.

Sex, for example, is characterized as a basic biological drive. While this observation is true throughout most of the animal kingdom, it is obviously a more complicated phenomenon for humans. Indeed, this activity could conceivably fit into every level of Maslow's hierarchy. A sociobiologist, who approaches human behavior in terms of its biological origins, might argue that reproductive behavior provides security because it ensures continuation of a person's gene pool and the provision of children to care for the person in old age. Sex can also express love and affiliation at the belongingness level. In addition, sex is often used as a vehicle to attain status, domination over another, and to satisfy ego needs; it can be a significant determinant of self-respect. Finally, a sexual experience can be self-actualizing in that it may provide an ecstatic, transcendental experience.

Another problem with taking Maslow's hierarchy too literally is that it is culture-bound. The assumptions of the hierarchy may be restricted to Western culture. People in other cultures (or, for that matter, in Western culture) may question the order of the levels as specified. A religious person who has taken a vow of celibacy would not necessarily agree that physiological needs must be satisfied for self-fulfillment to occur.

Similarly, many Eastern cultures operate on the premise that the welfare of the group (belongingness needs) are more highly valued than needs of the individual (esteem needs). The point is that this hierarchy, while widely applied in marketing, should be valued because it reminds us that consumers may have different need priorities at different times (i.e., you have to walk before you can run) rather than because it *exactly* specifies a consumer's progression up the ladder of needs.

Hidden Motives: Probing Beneath the Surface

A motive is an underlying reason for behavior and not something researchers can see or easily measure. Furthermore, the same behavior can be caused by a number of different motives. To compound the problem of identifying motives, the consumer may be unaware of the actual need he or she is attempting to satisfy, or alternatively he or she may not be willing to admit that this need exists. Because of these difficulties, motives usually must be *inferred* by the analyst.

Although some consumer needs undoubtedly are utilitarian and fairly straightforward, some researchers feel that a great many purchase decisions are not the result of deliberate, logical decisions. To the contrary, people may do things to satisfy motives of which they are not even aware.

Consumer Behavior on the Couch: Freudian Theory

Sigmund Freud had a profound (if controversial) impact on many basic assumptions of human behavior. His work changed the way we view such topics as adult sexuality, dreams, and psychological adjustment. Freud developed the idea that much of human behavior stems from a fundamental conflict between a person's desire to gratify his or her physical needs and the necessity to function as a responsible member of society. This struggle is carried out in the mind among three systems. (Note: These systems do not refer to physical parts of the brain.)

The **id** is entirely oriented toward immediate gratification—it is the "party animal" of the mind. It operates according to the **pleasure principle;** behavior is guided by the primary desire to maximize pleasure and avoid pain. The id is selfish and illogical. It directs a person's psychic energy toward pleasurable acts without regard for any consequences.

The **superego** is the counterweight to the id. This system is essentially the person's conscience. It internalizes society's rules (especially as communicated by parents) and works to prevent the id from seeking selfish gratification.

Finally, the **ego** is the system that mediates between the id and the superego. It is in a way a referee in the fight between temptation and virtue. The ego tries to balance these two opposing forces according to the **reality principle.** It finds ways to gratify the id that will be acceptable to the outside world. These conflicts occur on an unconscious level, so the person is not necessarily aware of the underlying reasons for behavior. The Vivarin ad shown on page 96 uses these Freudian principles in a context designed to reach students.

According to Freudian theory, a person's development hinges on the way these systems interact in childhood. Aspects of Freudian theory are controversial, and his observations are not always accepted literally. For example, the bulk of Freud's insights were based on his own patients, a limited sample composed primarily of affluent Viennese housewives. Many feminists object to Freud's assumptions about the inferiority of women, ideas that were widely accepted in his time. Nonetheless, Freud had a profound impact on the fields of psychiatry and clinical psychology.

FREUD AND CONSUMERS Some of Freud's ideas have also been adapted by consumer researchers. In particular, his work highlights the potential importance of unconscious motives underlying purchases. The implication is that consumers cannot necessarily tell us their true motivation for choosing a product, even if we can devise a sensitive way to ask them directly.

The Freudian perspective also hints at the possibility that the ego relies on the symbolism in products to compromise between the demands of the id and the prohibitions of the superego. The person channels his or her unacceptable desire into acceptable outlets by using products that signify these underlying desires. This is the connection between product symbolism and motivation: The product stands for, or represents, a consumer's true goal, which is socially unacceptable or unattainable. By acquiring the product, the person is able to vicariously experience the forbidden fruit.

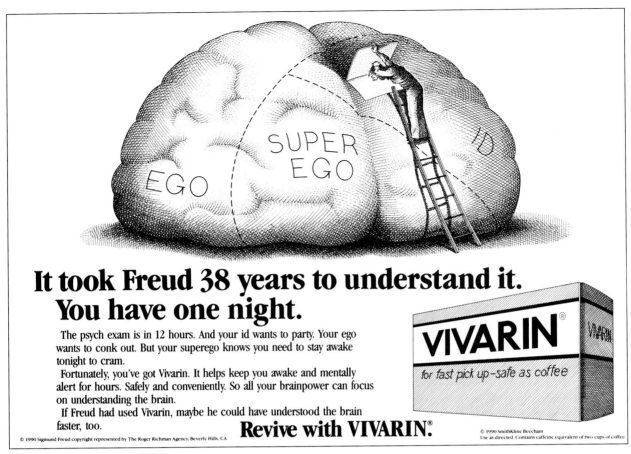
This ad for Vivarin stimulants depicts the three components of Freud's perspective on motivation and the unconscious. Licensed by The Roger Richman Agency, Inc., Beverly Hills, CA. Courtesy of Grey Advertising, Inc.

Sexual Symbolism. Most Freudian applications in marketing are related to the sexuality of products. For example, some analysts have speculated that a sports car is a substitute for sexual gratification for many men. Indeed, some men do seem inordinately attached to their cars and may spend many hours lovingly washing and polishing them. The Infiniti ad shown here reinforces the belief that cars symbolically satisfy consumers' sexual needs in addition to their functional ones by describing the J30 model as ". . . what happens when you cross sheet metal and desire."

Others focus on male-oriented symbolism—so-called phallic symbols—that appeals to women. Although Freud himself joked that "sometimes a cigar is just a cigar," many pop applications of Freud's ideas revolve around the use of objects that resemble sex organs (e.g., cigars, trees, or swords for men; tunnels for women). This focus stems from Freud's analysis of dreams, which were often interpreted as communicating repressed desires through symbols.

It's not a car.
It's an aphrodisiac.

You know that car you've always wanted? Really, really wanted? It's here. The new Infiniti J30 personal luxury sedan.

And its looks aren't all that will entice you.

For $33,400* the J30 is sure to impress you on a purely emotional level. With luxury details like the Bose audio system with a standard compact disc player. Soft gathered leather. Tasteful walnut trim. And a 24-hour Roadside Assistance Program that's standing by to do whatever it takes to keep you on the road.

Of course, the J30 is also equipped with a long list of impressive technological features. Like the variable valve timing system and the double isolated multi-link rear suspension. Three-sensor, three-channel ABS braking. And both driver's and passenger's side airbags.

But, in the end, what's really appealing about the new J30 is something far more than all its individual parts. Something indefinable. It's what happens when you cross sheet metal and desire.

INFINITI.

This Infiniti ad stresses the sensual dimension of car ownership. Courtesy of Infiniti Division, Nissan Motor Corporation U.S.A.

Motivational Research

The first attempts to apply Freudian ideas to understand the deeper meanings of products and advertisements were made in the 1950s as a perspective known as **motivational research** was developed. This approach was largely based on psychoanalytic (Freudian) interpretations, with a heavy emphasis on unconscious motives. A basic assumption is that socially unacceptable needs are channeled into acceptable outlets. Product use or avoidance is motivated by unconscious forces that often are determined in childhood.

This form of research relies on *depth interviews* with individual consumers. Instead of asking many consumers a few general questions about product usage and combining these responses with those of many other consumers in a representative statistical sample, this technique uses relatively few consumers but probes deeply into each person's purchase motivations. A depth interview might take several hours and is based on the assumption that the respondent cannot immediately articulate his or her latent, or underlying, motives. These can be derived only after careful questioning and interpretation on the part of a carefully trained interviewer.

This work was pioneered by Ernest Dichter, a psychoanalyst who was trained in Vienna in the early part of the century. Dichter conducted in-depth interview studies on over 230 different products, and many of his findings have been incorporated in actual marketing campaigns.[28] For example, Esso (now Exxon) for many years reminded consumers to "Put a Tiger in Your Tank" after Dichter found that people responded well to this powerful animal symbolism containing vaguely suggestive overtones. A summary of major consumption motivations identified using this approach appears in Table 3–4.

TABLE 3–4 Major Motives for Consumption as Identified by Ernest Dichter

Motive	Associated Products
Power–Masculinity–Virility	Power: Sugary products and large breakfasts (to charge oneself up), bowling, electric trains, hot rods, power tools
	Masculinity–virility: Coffee, red meat, heavy shoes, toy guns, buying fur coats for women, shaving with a razor
Security	Ice cream (feel like loved child again), full drawer of neatly ironed shirts, real plaster walls (feel sheltered), home baking, hospital care
Eroticism	Sweets (require licking), gloves (removed by women as a form of undressing), a man lighting a woman's cigarette (a tension-filled moment culminating in pressure, then relaxation)
Moral Purity–Cleanliness	White bread, cotton fabrics (connote chastity), harsh household cleaning chemicals (make housewives feel moral after using), bathing (Pontius Pilate washed blood from his hands), oatmeal (sacrifice, virtue)
Social Acceptance	Companionship: Ice cream (fun to share), coffee
	Love and affection: Toys (express love for children), sugar and honey (terms of affection)
	Acceptance: Soap, beauty products
Individuality	Gourmet foods, foreign cars, cigarette holders, vodka, perfume, fountain pens
Status	Scotch, ulcers, heart attacks, indigestion (because one has a high-stress, important job!), carpets (one does not live on bare earth like peasants)
Femininity	Cakes and cookies, dolls, silk, tea, household curios (all are light, decorative, and have a heavy tactile component)
Reward	Cigarettes, candy alcohol, ice cream, cookies
Mastery over Environment	Kitchen appliances, boats, sporting goods, cigarette lighters
Disalienation (a desire to feel connectedness to things)	Home decorating, skiing, morning radio broadcasts (to feel "in touch" with the world)
Magic–Mystery	Soups (have healing powers), paints (change the mood of a room), carbonated drinks (magical effervescent property), vodka (romantic history), unwrapping of gifts

Source: Adapted from Jeffrey F. Durgee, "Interpreting Dichter's Interpretations: An Analysis of Consumption Symbolism in *The Handbook of Consumer Motivations*," *Marketing and Semiotics: Selected Papers from the Copenhagen Symposium*, eds. Hanne Hartvig–Larsen, David Glen Mick, and Christian Alstead (Copenhagen, 1991).

CRITICISMS OF MOTIVATIONAL RESEARCH Motivational research has been attacked for two quite opposite reasons. Some feel it does not work, while others feel it works *too* well. On the one hand, social critics reacted much the same way they had to subliminal perception studies (see Chapter 2). They attacked this school of thought for giving advertisers the power to manipulate consumers.[29] On the other hand, many consumer researchers felt the research lacked sufficient rigor and validity, since interpretations were subjective and indirect.[30] Because conclusions are based on the analyst's own judgment and are derived from discussions with a small number of people, some researchers are dubious as to the degree to which these results can be generalized to a large market. In addition, because the original motivational researchers were heavily influenced by orthodox Freudian theory, their interpretations usually carried strong sexual overtones. This emphasis tends to overlook other plausible causes for behavior.

THE POSITIVE SIDE OF MOTIVATIONAL RESEARCH Motivational research had great appeal to at least some marketers for several reasons, some of which are detailed here.

Cost-Efficiency. Motivational research tends to be less expensive than large-scale, quantitative survey data because interviewing and data processing costs are relatively minimal.

Providing Insights. The knowledge derived from motivational research can possibly help to develop marketing communications that appeal to deep-seated needs and thus provide a more powerful hook to relate a product to consumers. Even if they are not necessarily valid for all consumers in a target market, these insights can be valuable when used in an exploratory way. For example, the rich imagery that may be associated with a product can be used creatively when developing advertising copy.

Intuitive Sense. Some of the findings seem intuitively plausible *after the fact*. For example, motivational studies concluded that coffee is associated with companionship, that people avoid prunes because they remind them of old age, and that men fondly equate the first car they owned as an adolescent with the onset of their sexual freedom.

Other interpretations were hard for some people to swallow, such as the observation that to a woman baking a cake symbolizes giving birth, or that men are reluctant to give blood because they feel that their vital fluids are being drained. On the other hand, some people do refer to a pregnant woman as "having a bun in the oven," and Pillsbury claims that "nothing says lovin' like something from the oven." Motivational research for the American Red Cross did find that men (but not women) tend to drastically overestimate the amount of blood that is taken during a donation. This group counteracted the fear of loss of virility by symbolically equating the act of giving blood with fertilization: "Give the gift of life." Despite its drawbacks, motivational research continues to be employed as a useful diagnostic tool. Its validity is enhanced, however, when used in conjunction with the other research techniques available to the consumer researcher.

Needs and Wants: Do Marketers Manipulate Consumers?

One of the most common and stinging criticisms of marketing is that marketing techniques (especially advertising) are responsible for convincing consumers that they "need" many material things and that they will be unhappy and somehow inferior people if they do not have these "necessities." The issue is a complex one, and is certainly worth considering: Do marketers give people what they want, or do they tell people what they *should* want? The American Association of Advertising Agencies' ad shown here emphasizes this theme.

Philosophers have approached this issue when considering the concept of free will. It has been argued that in order to claim that consumers are acting autonomously in response to ads, the capacity for free will and free action must be present. That is, the consumer must be capable of *indepen-*

This ad was created by the American Association of Advertising Agencies to counter charges that ads create artificial needs.   Courtesy of American Association of Advertising Agencies.

DESPITE WHAT SOME PEOPLE THINK, ADVERTISING CAN'T MAKE YOU BUY SOMETHING YOU DON'T NEED.

Some people would have you believe that you are putty in the hands of every advertiser in the country.

They think that when advertising is put under your nose, your mind turns to oatmeal.

It's mass hypnosis. Subliminal seduction. Brain washing. Mind control. It's advertising.

And you are a pushover for it.

It explains why your kitchen cupboard is full of food you never eat.

Why your garage is full of cars you never drive.

Why your house is full of books you don't read, TV's you don't watch, beds you don't use, and clothes you don't wear.

You don't have a choice. You are forced to buy.

That's why this message is a cleverly disguised advertisement to get you to buy land in the tropics.

Got you again, didn't we? Send in your money.

ADVERTISING
ANOTHER WORD FOR FREEDOM OF CHOICE.
American Association of Advertising Agencies

dently deciding what to do and not be prevented from carrying out that decision. This situation is probably true for purely informative advertising, where only the product or store information required to make a rational decision is provided. The case for persuasive advertising, where imagery or underlying motivations are tapped, is not as clear.[31] Three issues related to the complex relationship between marketing practices and consumers' needs are considered here.

Do Marketers Create Artificial Needs?

The marketing system has come under fire from both ends of the political spectrum. On the one hand, some members of the religious right believe that advertising contributes to the moral breakdown of society by presenting images of hedonistic pleasure, thus encouraging the pursuit of *secular humanism*. On the other hand, some leftists argue that the same deceitful promises of material pleasure function to buy off people who would otherwise be revolutionaries working to change the system.[32] Through advertising, then, the system creates demand that only its products can satisfy.

A Response: A need is a basic biological motive, while a want represents one way that society has taught us that the need can be satisfied. For example, while thirst is biologically based, we are taught to want Coca-Cola to satisfy that thirst rather than, say, goat milk. Thus, the need is already there; marketers simply recommend ways to satisfy it. A basic objective of advertising is to create awareness that these needs exist, rather than to create them. In some circumstances, however, the marketer can engineer an environment to make it more *probable* that a need will be activated. This occurs, for example, when movie theaters sell popcorn and bars supply free peanuts to patrons in order to stimulate thirst.

MARKETING OPPORTUNITY

The charge that businesses create artificial needs is relevant in the case of gasoline marketing. Oil companies have attempted to convince consumers of the need for premium gasolines, even though this need has been questioned by many people. As one automotive engineer noted, "'Oil company advertising has led people to the conclusion that more expensive fuels will make their car start easier, get more gas mileage, and last longer, ...' But in most cases this is untrue . . . . Your engine has to be designed to use that extra octane . . . . Otherwise, . . . the extra cost is just lining the pockets of the oil companies."

An oil industry executive wrote that "When prices go up a bit, people will come to their senses and premium volumes will diminish . . . . ." But for now, people buy higher-octane fuel for reasons that have nothing to do with car engines; one, he theorized, is "the use of premium as an expression of self-worth."[33] Is the need for higher octane a genuine one, or something manufactured by the oil companies by associating premium gasoline with power, status, manliness, and so on?

Is Advertising Necessary?

As social critic Vance Packard wrote over thirty years ago, "Large-scale efforts are being made, often with impressive success, to channel our unthinking habits, our purchasing decisions, and our thought processes by the use of insights gleaned from psychiatry and the social sciences."[34]

The economist John Kenneth Galbraith felt that radio and television are important tools to accomplish this manipulation of the masses. Since virtually no literacy is required to use these media, they allow repetitive and compelling communications to reach almost everyone.

Goods are arbitrarily linked to desirable social attributes. One influential critic even argued that the problem is that we are not materialistic *enough*—that is, we do not sufficiently value goods for the utilitarian functions they deliver, but instead focus on the irrational value of goods for what they symbolize. According to this view, for example, "Beer would be enough for us, without the additional promise that in drinking it we show ourselves to be manly, young at heart, or neighborly. A washing machine would be a useful machine to wash clothes, rather than an indication that we are forward-looking or an object of envy to our neighbors."[35]

A Response: Products are designed to meet existing needs, and advertising only helps to communicate their availability. Marketing overcomes some of the disadvantages of labor specialization, where most consumers are unfamiliar with the characteristics of mass-produced goods.[36] According to the *economics of information* perspective, advertising is an important source of consumer information.[37] This view emphasizes the economic cost of the time spent searching for products. Accordingly, advertising is a service for which consumers are willing to pay, since the information it provides reduces search time.

MULTICULTURAL DIMENSIONS

As Eastern Europe opens up to capitalism, some fear that consumers are being exploited as Western advertisements bombard them for products they didn't know they needed. In Poland, for example, previously taboo items like women's sanitary napkins are being advertised for the first time, and new markets are being created for products such as pet food. The actions of one Polish entrepreneur illustrate how a consumer's need for social approval can be channeled into a want for a product.

Beginning with an ad campaign featuring Miss Poland, he single-handedly created a market for electronic hair removers (Polish women usually do not shave their legs). He also persuaded a leading Polish fashion designer to announce that hairy legs were out of fashion in Europe, and he organized local beauty contests to find the best legs. At last report, he was selling 30,000 hair removers a month.[38]

Do Marketers Promise Miracles?

Consumers are led to believe through advertising that products have magical properties; they will do special and mysterious things for them that will transform their lives. They will be beautiful, have power over others' feelings, be successful, be relieved of all ills, and so on. In this respect, advertising functions like mythology does in primitive societies; it provides simple, anxiety-reducing answers to complex problems.

A Response: The effectiveness of advertising is overstated. There is little evidence that advertising creates patterns of consumption (though it may accelerate them). Instead, the marketing system creates a new way to satisfy an old need.

As an example, consider one analysis of the cigarette industry, which has been accused of using advertising to erode traditional taboos against smoking among women and the young. In the period between 1918 and 1940, the consumption of cigarettes increased steadily, but the overall level of *tobacco consumption* was unchanged. This finding suggests that the effect of advertising was to make people switch to cigarettes from cigars and pipes.[39] Advertising merely latched onto new consumption patterns, since cigarette smoking is more adaptable to a fast-paced urban lifestyle.

Advertisers simply do not know enough about people to manipulate them. Consider that the failure rate for new products ranges from 40 percent to 80 percent. In testimony before the Federal Trade Commission, one advertising executive observed that while people think that advertisers have an endless source of magical tricks and/or scientific techniques to manipulate people, in reality, the industry is successful when it tries to sell good products and unsuccessful when selling poor ones.[40]

Chapter Summary

- Marketers try to satisfy consumer needs, but the reasons any product is purchased can vary widely. The identification of consumer motives is an important step in ensuring that the appropriate needs will be met by a product.

- Traditional approaches to consumer behavior have focused on the abilities of products to satisfy rational needs (utilitarian motives), but hedonic motives (e.g., the need for exploration or for fun) also play a role in many purchase decisions.

- As demonstrated by Maslow's *hierarchy of needs,* the same product can satisfy different needs, depending upon the consumer's state at the time. In addition to his or her objective situation (e.g., have basic physiological needs already been satisfied?), the consumer's degree of involvement with the product must be considered.

- Since consumers are not necessarily able or willing to communicate their underlying needs to marketers, various techniques such as projective tests can be employed to indirectly assess these.

Key Terms

cognitive dissonance, p. 91

drive, p. 81

ego, p. 95

ego involvement, p. 86

expectancy theory, p. 83

goal, p. 81

homeostasis, p. 82

id, p. 95

inertia, p. 83

involvement, p. 83

motivation, p. 81

motivational research, p. 97

pleasure principle, p. 95

reality principle, p. 95

superego, p. 95

want, p. 81

Consumer Behavior Challenge

1. Describe three types of motivational conflicts, citing an example of each from current marketing campaigns.
2. Should consumer researchers have the ability (and the right) to probe into the consumer's unconscious? Is this a violation of privacy, or just another way to gather deep knowledge of purchase motivations?
3. Devise separate promotional strategies for an article of clothing, each of which stresses one of the levels of Maslow's hierarchy of needs.
4. What is the difference between a want and a need? Do marketers have the power to create needs?
5. Describe how a man's level of involvement with his car would affect how he is influenced by different marketing stimuli. How might you design a strategy for a line of car batteries for a segment of low-involvement consumers, and how would this strategy differ from your attempts to reach a segment of men who are very involved in working on their cars?
6. Interview members of a celebrity fan club. Describe their level of involvement with the "product," and devise some marketing opportunities to reach this group.
7. "High involvement is just a fancy term for expensive." Do you agree?

CNN *Connection*

 A video segment is available to accompany this CNN connection.

Sensation-Seeking Consumers

A thrill a minute! That's what many consumers seem to be searching for. Others are more content to watch someone else take the risks. Each person has an optimum stimulation level and is motivated to maintain that level. People who have a high level are called *sensation-seekers;* they are more likely to seek out activities that create high arousal.[1]

Sensation-seekers are good candidates for scary movies, bungee-jumping, and death-defying rollercoasters. The appetite for adventure has created a boom in demand for thrill rides in amusement parks, where sensation-seekers can elevate their pulses to their hearts' content. Theme parks have to cater to the needs of both low and high sensation-seekers, so they offer a range of attractions. Whether one wants to relax with one's favorite cartoon character or be spun up, around, and upside down, theme parks such as Disneyland, Six Flags, and Busch Gardens have become major sources of revenue for the travel and tourism industry.

[1]Marvin Zuckerman, *Sensation Seeking: Beyond the Optimum Level of Arousal* (Hillsdale, N.J.: Lawrence Erlbaum, 1979).

Notes

1. Ronald Paul Hill and Harold Robinson, "Fanatic Consumer Behavior: Athletics as a Consumption Experience," *Psychology & Marketing* 8 (Summer 1991): 79–100.
2. Robert A. Baron, *Psychology: The Essential Science* (Needham, Mass.: Allyn & Bacon, 1989).
3. John H. Antil, "Conceptualization and Operationalization of Involvement," in *Advances in Consumer Research* 11, ed. Thomas C. Kinnear (Provo, Utah: Association for Consumer Research, 1984), 203–09. The literature offers numerous approaches to the construct of involvement. See also Peter H. Bloch, "Involvement Beyond the Purchase Process: Conceptual Issues and Empirical Investigation," in *Advances in Consumer Research* 8, ed. Kent Monroe (Provo, Utah: Association for Consumer Research, 1981), 61–65; George S. Day, *Buyer Attitudes and Brand Choice Behavior* (Chicago: Free Press, 1970); Michael J. Houston and Michael L. Rothschild, "Conceptual and Methodological Perspectives on Involvement," in *Research Frontiers in Marketing: Dialogues and Directions*, ed. S.C. Jain (Chicago: American Marketing Association, 1978), 184–87; John L. Lastovicka and David Gardner, "Components of Involvement," in *Attitude Research Plays for High Stakes*, eds. John C. Maloney and Bernard Silverman (Chicago: American Marketing Association, 1979), 53–73; Andrew Mitchell, "Involvement: A Potentially Important Mediator of Consumer Behavior," in *Advances in Consumer Research* 6, ed. William L. Wilkie (Provo, Utah: Association for Consumer Research, 1979), 191–96.
4. Mitchell, "Involvement."
5. Richard L. Celsi and Jerry C. Olson, "The Role of

Involvement in Attention and Comprehension Processes," *Journal of Consumer Research* 15 (September 1988): 210–24.

6. Anthony G. Greenwald and Clark Leavitt, "Audience Involvement in Advertising: Four Levels," *Journal of Consumer Research* 11 (June 1984): 581–92.

7. Irving Rein, Philip Kotler, and Martin Stoller, *High Visibility* (New York: Dodd, Mead, 1987).

8. For a recent discussion of interrelationships between situational and enduring involvement, see Marsha L. Richins, Peter H. Bloch, and Edward F. McQuarrie, "How Enduring and Situational Involvement Combine to Create Involvement Responses," *Journal of Consumer Psychology* 1 (1992)2: 143–53.

9. Laurie Freeman, "Fragrance Sniffs Out Daring Adventures," *Advertising Age* (November 6, 1989): 47.

10. Rajeev Batra and Michael L. Ray, "Operationalizing Involvement as Depth and Quality of Cognitive Responses," in *Advances in Consumer Research* 10, eds. Alice Tybout and Richard Bagozzi (Ann Arbor, Mich.: Association for Consumer Research, 1983), 309–13.

11. Herbert E. Krugman, "The Impact of Television Advertising: Learning Without Involvement," *Public Opinion Quarterly* 29 (Fall 1965): 349–56.

12. Marsha L. Richins and Peter H. Bloch, "After the New Wears Off: The Temporal Context of Product Involvement," *Journal of Consumer Research* 13 (September 1986): 280–85.

13. Kevin J. Clancy, "CPMs Must Bow to 'Involvement' Measurement," *Advertising Age* (January 20, 1992): 26.

14. For a newer, modified version of this scale, see Edward F. McQuarrie and J. Michael Munson, "A Revised Product Involvement Inventory: Improved Usability and Validity," in *Advances in Consumer Research* 19, eds. John F. Sherry, Jr. and Brian Sternthal (Provo, Utah: Association for Consumer Research, 1992), 108–15.

15. Gilles Laurent and Jean-Noel Kapferer, "Measuring Consumer Involvement Profiles," *Journal of Marketing Research* 22 (February 1985): 41–53.

16. David W. Stewart and David H. Furse, "Analysis of the Impact of Executional Factors in Advertising Performance," *Journal of Advertising Research* 24 (1984)6: 23–26.

17. Morris B. Holbrook and Elizabeth C. Hirschman, "The Experiential Aspects of Consumption: Consumer Fantasies, Feelings, and Fun," *Journal of Consumer Research* 9 (September 1982): 132–40.

18. Deborah J. MacInnis, Christine Moorman, and Bernard J. Jaworski, "Enhancing and Measuring Consumers' Motivation, Opportunity, and Ability to Process Brand Information from Ads," *Journal of Marketing* 55 (October 1991): 332–53.

19. Data adapted from Judith Lynne Zaichkowsky and James H. Sood, "A Global Look at Consumers' Involvement and Use of Products," *International Marketing Review* 6 (1989)1: 20–34.

20. Leon Festinger, *A Theory of Cognitive Dissonance* (Stanford, Calif.: Stanford University Press, 1957).

21. See Paul T. Costa and Robert R. McCrae, "From Catalog to Classification: Murray's Needs and the Five-Factor Model," *Journal of Personality and Social Psychology* 55 (1988)2: 258–65; Calvin S. Hall and Gardner Lindzey, *Theories of Personality*, 2nd ed. (New York: John Wiley, 1970); James U. McNeal and Stephen W. McDaniel, "An Analysis of Need-Appeals in Television Advertising," *Journal of the Academy of Marketing Science* 12 (Spring 1984): 176–90.

22. See David C. McClelland, *Studies in Motivation* (New York: Appleton-Century-Crofts, 1955).

23. Mary Kay Ericksen and M. Joseph Sirgy, "Achievement Motivation and Clothing Preferences of White-Collar Working Women," in *The Psychology of Fashion*, ed. Michael R. Solomon (Lexington, Mass.: Lexington Books, 1985), 357–69.

24. See Stanley Schachter, *The Psychology of Affiliation* (Stanford, Calif.: Stanford University Press, 1959).

25. Eugene M. Fodor and Terry Smith, "The Power Motive as an Influence on Group Decision Making," *Journal of Personality and Social Psychology* 42 (1982): 178–85.

26. C.R. Snyder and Howard L. Fromkin, *Uniqueness: The Human Pursuit of Difference* (New York: Plenum Press, 1980).

27. Abraham H. Maslow, *Motivation and Personality*, 2nd ed. (New York: Harper & Row, 1970).

28. Ernest Dichter, *A Strategy of Desire* (Garden City, N.Y.: Doubleday, 1960); Ernest Dichter, *The Handbook of Consumer Motivations* (New York: McGraw-Hill, 1964); Jeffrey J. Durgee, "Interpreting Dichter's Interpretations: An Analysis of Consumption Symbolism in *The Handbook of Consumer Motivations*," unpublished manuscript, Rensselaer Polytechnic Institute, Troy, N.Y., 1989; Pierre Martineau, *Motivation in Advertising* (New York: McGraw-Hill, 1957).

29. Vance Packard, *The Hidden Persuaders* (New York: D. McKay, 1957).

30. Harold Kassarjian, "Personality and Consumer Behavior: A Review," *Journal of Marketing Research* 8 (November 1971): 409–18.

31. Roger Crisp, "Persuasive Advertising, Autonomy, and the Creation of Desire," *Journal of Business Ethics* 6 (1987): 413–18.

32. William Leiss, Stephen Kline, and Sut Jhally, *Social Communication in Advertising: Persons, Products, & Images of Well-Being* (Toronto: Methuen, 1986); Jerry Mander, *Four Arguments for the Elimination of Television* (New York: William Morrow, 1977).

33. Matthew L. Wald, "Looking for Savings as Gas Prices Rise," *New York Times* (May 27, 1989): 48.

34. Packard (1957), 11, quoted in Leiss et al., *Social Communication.*

35. Raymond Williams, "Advertising: The Magic System," in *Problems in Materialism and Culture* (London: New Left Books, 1962).

36. Leiss et al., *Social Communication.*

37. George Stigler, "The Economics of Information," *Journal of Political Economy* (1961): 69.

38. Steven Engelberg, "Advertising Pervades Poland, Turning Propoganda to Glitz," *New York Times* (May 26, 1992)2: Al.

39. Michael Schudson, *Advertising: The Uneasy Persuasion* (New York: Basic Books, 1984).

40. Quoted in Leiss et al., *Social Communications.*

SAFE DEPOSIT BOXES ARE FOR PRICELESS THINGS.

When you lose some things, they're lost forever.
That's why we think it's a good idea to keep your family heirlooms and sentimental treasures in a safer place than a shoebox. One of our safe deposit boxes, for instance. They're free for the first three months and safe forever.

CHAPTER 4

Learning and

Memory

Buying, Having, and Being: Selections 12–16 from *Buying, Having, and Being: The Washington Post Consumer Behavior Companion*, Second Edition, accompany this chapter.

As Joe and Ron are leaving the Flamingo Bar, Joe grabs a matchbook embossed with the bar's logo on his way out. Ron remarks, "What do you need that for? I didn't know you smoke." Joe just laughs and replies, "Ugh! No way I'd smoke. But I do happen to have the world's best matchbook collection." It turns out that for many years Joe has made it a habit to take a matchbook from every place he's been as a souvenir of that experience. He has hundreds of them, ranging from sleazy bars to elegant hotels. Some are linked to special memories, and occasionally Joe will go through his collection and allow his covers to conjure up these occasions in his mind.

There's the Tumble Inn, where he went after his fraternity initiation; Pier 4, the restaurant he went to on the night of his Senior Prom; and, of course, Wurlitzer's, where he first met Terri. Joe's never really gotten over Terri, and when he looks at that matchbook (with Terri's old phone number written inside), he can vividly remember her face and almost smell her perfume. It's gotten to the point where Joe just doesn't feel he's *really* been someplace unless he has a matchbook to commemorate his visit.

Sometimes Joe feels that the story of his life is written in the box where he keeps his precious matchbooks . . . .

Introduction

While Joe's attachment to his matchbook collection may be extreme, he is certainly not alone. The strong associations he has with these simple items illustrate one way that products are used by consumers: as memory markers. The ability of products (even cheap ones like matchbook covers) to evoke strong associations with past experiences also contributes to the current popularity of collecting everyday items that have little monetary value. "Collectibles" from the 1950s and 1960s are increasingly popular with middle-aged consumers, who are holding on to products that were initially designed to be throwaways. Dealers are doing a brisk business in such categories as cereal boxes, match covers, and (expired) credit cards.[1] The First Interstate Bank ad shown at the beginning of this chapter reflects the priceless value consumers place on the things they collect.

The Learning Process

Learning refers to a relatively permanent change in behavior that is caused by experience. This experience does not have to directly affect the learner; we can learn *vicariously* by observing events that affect others.[2] We also learn even when we are not trying. Consumers recognize many brand names and can hum many product jingles, for example, even for those product categories they themselves do not use. This casual, unintentional acquisition of knowledge is known as *incidental learning*. Like the concepts of perception and motivation discussed in the last two chapters, learning is a process. Our knowledge about the world is constantly being revised as we are exposed to new stimuli and receive ongoing feedback that allows us to modify behavior in other, similar situations.

The concept of learning covers a lot of ground, ranging from a consumer's simple association between a stimulus such as a product logo (e.g., Coca-Cola) and a response (e.g., "refreshing soft drink") to a complex series of cognitive activities (e.g., writing an essay on learning for a Consumer Behavior exam). Psychologists who study learning have advanced several theories to explain the learning process. These theories range from those focusing on simple stimulus-response connections to perspectives that regard consumers as complex problem solvers who learn abstract rules and concepts by observing others.

Behavioral Learning Theories

Behavioral learning theories assume that learning takes place as the result of responses to external events. Psychologists who subscribe to this viewpoint do not focus on internal thought processes. Instead, they approach the mind as a "black box" and emphasize the observable aspects of behavior, as depicted in Figure 4–1. The observable aspects consist of things that go into the box (the *stimuli,* or events perceived from the outside world) and things that come out of the box (the *responses,* or reactions to these stimuli).

This view is represented by two major approaches to learning: classical conditioning and instrumental conditioning. Just as Joe learned to associate his precious matchbook cover with unrequited love, people's experiences are shaped by the feedback they receive as they go through life.

Similarly, consumers respond to brand names, scents, jingles, and other marketing stimuli based upon the learned connections they have formed over time. People also learn that actions they take result in rewards and punishments, and this feedback influences the way they will respond in similar situations in the future. Consumers who receive compliments on a product choice will be more likely to buy that brand again, while those who get food poisoning at a new restaurant will not be likely to patronize it in the future.

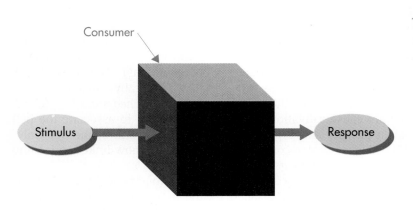

FIGURE 4–1 **The Consumer As a "Black Box": A Behaviorist Perspective on Learning**

How strong is the Chiquita name?
How many banana commercials can you sing?

Most people can't remember the TV commercials they saw last night as well as the Chiquita jingle they first heard in 1944.

In the 32 years since, Chiquita has come to be the first name that comes to mind for 9 out of every 10 consumers who buy bananas. Which is another reason why Chiquitas sell better than bananas.

Chiquita bananas today have a brand awareness of 92%. That's 30% higher than the awareness of the next leading brand..."what'sitsname?"

The Chiquita Banana jingle, largely due to its repetition over a number of years, has helped the product to create a high degree of awareness among consumers.   Used by permission of Chiquita Brands, Inc. All right reserved.

CLASSICAL CONDITIONING   Classical conditioning occurs when a stimulus that elicits a response is paired with another stimulus that initially does not elicit a response on its own. Over time, this second stimulus causes a similar response because it is associated with the first stimulus. This phenomenon was first demonstrated in dogs by Ivan Pavlov, a Russian physiologist doing research on digestion in animals.

Pavlov conducted a number of *conditioning trials* by pairing a neutral stimulus (a bell) with a stimulus known to cause a salivation response in dogs (he squirted dried meat powder into their mouths). The powder was an *unconditioned stimulus* (UCS) because it was naturally capable of causing the response. Over time, the bell became a *conditioned stimulus* (CS); it did not initially cause salivation, but the dogs learned to associate the bell with the meat powder and began to salivate at the sound of the bell only. The drooling of these canine consumers over a sound, now linked to feeding time, was a *conditioned response* (CR).

This basic form of classical conditioning demonstrated by Pavlov primarily applies to responses controlled by the autonomic (e.g., salivation) and nervous (e.g., eyeblink) systems. That is, it focuses on visual and olfactory cues that induce hunger, thirst, sexual arousal, and other basic drives discussed in Chapter 3. When these cues are consistently paired with conditioned stimuli such as brand names, consumers may learn to feel hungry, thirsty, or aroused when later exposed to the brand cues.

Classical conditioning can have similar effects for more complex reactions, too. Even a credit card becomes a conditioned cue that triggers greater spending, especially since it is a stimulus that is present only in situations where consumers are spending money. People learn they can make larger purchases when using credit cards, and they also have been found to leave larger tips than when using cash.[3] Small wonder that American Express reminds us, "Don't leave home without it."

Repetition. Conditioning effects are more likely to occur after the conditioned and unconditioned stimuli have been paired a number of times.[4] Repeated exposures increase the strength of stimulus-response associations and prevent the *decay* of these associations in memory.

Many classic advertising campaigns consist of product slogans that have been repeated so many times that they are etched in consumers' minds. The ad shown here brags about the high awareness of the Chiquita banana jingle ("I'm Chiquita banana, and I'm here to say . . .") and the effect this familiarity has had on sales. Conditioning will not occur or will take longer if the CS is only occasionally presented with the UCS. One result of this lack of association may be extinction, which occurs when the effects of prior conditioning are reduced and finally disappear.

Stimulus Generalization. **Stimulus generalization** refers to the tendency of stimuli similar to a CS to evoke similar, conditioned responses.[5] For example, Pavlov noticed in subsequent studies that his dogs would sometimes salivate when they heard noises that only *resembled* a bell (e.g., keys jangling). People react to other, similar stimuli in much the same way they responded to the original stimulus. A drug store's bottle of private brand mouthwash deliberately packaged to resemble Listerine mouthwash may evoke a similar response among consumers, who assume that this "me too" product shares other characteristics of the original.

M U L T I C U L T U R A L   D I M E N S I O N S

Many companies work hard to associate their products with high quality. Unfortunately, manufacturers of watches, recording tape, and even contraceptives have encountered a worldwide problem with stimulus discrimination: the proliferation of counterfeit goods bearing well-known brand names. Many of these goods are manufactured in Asia. It is estimated that South Korea alone is responsible for 60 percent to 70 percent of all counterfeited products. In parts of Asia, a fake Rolex watch can be had for $25 (a real one starts at about $1200); a fake Gucci handbag for $12 is a bargain compared to the real price of $120, and Ralph Lauren polo shirts go for $3 instead of $30 to $50.[6]

Stimulus Discrimination. **Stimulus discrimination** occurs when a stimulus similar to a CS is *not* followed by a UCS. When this happens, reactions are weakened and will soon disappear. Part of the learning process involves making a response to some stimuli but not to other, similar stimuli. Manufacturers of well-established brands commonly urge consumers not to buy "cheap imitations," because the results will not be what they expect.

OPERANT CONDITIONING **Operant conditioning**, also known as *instrumental conditioning,* occurs as the individual learns to perform behaviors that produce positive outcomes and to avoid those that yield negative outcomes. This learning process is most closely associated with the psychologist B.F. Skinner, who demonstrated the effects of instrumental conditioning by teaching animals to dance, play ping-pong, and so on by systematically rewarding them for desired behaviors.

While responses in classical conditioning are involuntary and fairly simple, those in instrumental conditioning are made deliberately to obtain a goal and may be more complex. The desired behavior may be learned over a period of time, as intermediate actions are rewarded in a process called *shaping.* For example, the owner of a new store may award prizes to shoppers just for coming in, hoping that over time they will continue to drop in and eventually buy something.

Also, classical conditioning involves the close pairing of two stimuli. Instrumental learning occurs as a result of a reward received *following* the desired behavior and takes place over a period where a variety of other behaviors are attempted and abandoned because they are not reinforced. A good way to remember the difference is to keep in mind that in instrumental learning, the response is performed because it is *instrumental* to gaining a reward or avoiding a punishment. Consumers over time come to associate with people that reward them and to choose products that make them feel good or satisfy some need.

Instrumental learning occurs in one of three ways. When the environment provides **positive reinforcement** in the form of a reward, the response is strengthened, and appropriate behavior is learned. For example, a woman who gets compliments after wearing Obsession perfume will learn that using this product has the desired effect, and she will be more likely to keep buying the product. **Negative reinforcement** also strengthens responses so that appropriate behavior is learned. A perfume company, for example, might run an ad showing a woman sitting home alone on a Saturday night because she did *not* use its fragrance. The message to be conveyed is that she could have *avoided* this negative outcome if only she had used the perfume. In contrast to situations where we learn to do certain things in order to *avoid* unpleasantness, **punishment** occurs when a response is followed by unpleasant events (such as being ridiculed by friends for wearing an offensive smelling perfume)—we learn not to repeat these behaviors.

To help in understanding the differences among these mechanisms, keep in mind that reactions from a person's environment to behavior can be either positive or negative and that these outcomes or anticipated outcomes can be applied or removed. That is, under conditions of both *positive reinforcement* and *punishment* the person receives a reaction after doing something. In contrast, negative reinforcement occurs when a negative outcome

Research Report: It is extremely difficult to study preconscious processing, since people have to be asked after exposure to a stimulus if they were aware of it. One recent study got around this problem by using the principle of *contralateral conduction*, which refers to the fact that stimuli are processed by different sides of the brain depending on where they appear relative to one's field of vision. When the verbal information in an ad was presented on the right and pictorial aspects appeared on the left, this format was preferred to others, even though the actual information in the ad did not change. This study showed support for the position that classical conditioning can occur *without* awareness. See Chris Janiszewski, "Preconscious Processing Effects: The Independence of Attitude Formation and Conscious Thought," *Journal of Consumer Research* 15 (September 1988): 199–209.

is *avoided*—the removal of something negative is pleasurable and hence is rewarding. Finally, when a positive outcome is no longer received, **extinction** is likely to occur (as when a woman no longer receives compliments on her perfume). Thus positive and negative reinforcement *strengthen* the future linkage between a response and an outcome because of the pleasant experience. This tie is *weakened* under conditions of both punishment and extinction because of the unpleasant experience. The relationships among these four conditions are easier to understand by referring to Figure 4–2.

An important factor in operant conditioning is the set of rules by which appropriate reinforcements are given for a behavior. The issue of what is the most effective *reinforcement schedule* to use is important to marketers, because it relates to the amount of effort and resources they must devote to rewarding consumers in order to condition desired behaviors.

Figure 4–2 is available as Transparency 8.

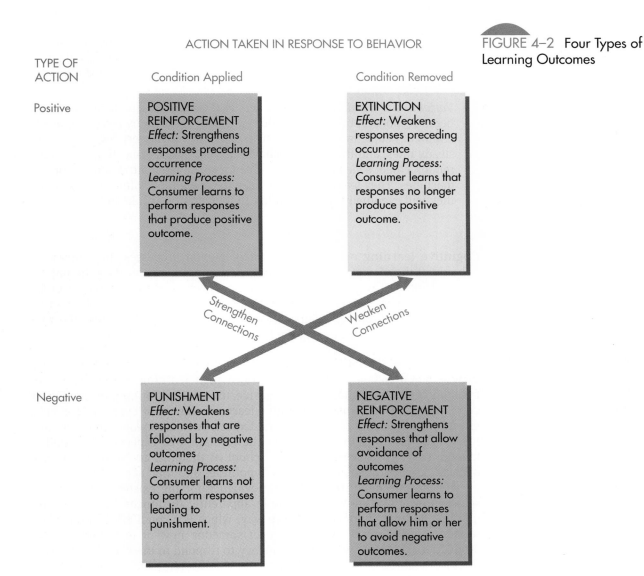

FIGURE 4–2 Four Types of Learning Outcomes

ACTION TAKEN IN RESPONSE TO BEHAVIOR

TYPE OF ACTION

Condition Applied

Condition Removed

Positive

POSITIVE REINFORCEMENT
Effect: Strengthens responses preceding occurrence
Learning Process: Consumer learns to perform responses that produce positive outcome.

EXTINCTION
Effect: Weakens responses preceding occurrence
Learning Process: Consumer learns that responses no longer produce positive outcome.

Strengthen Connections

Weaken Connections

Negative

PUNISHMENT
Effect: Weakens responses that are followed by negative outcomes
Learning Process: Consumer learns not to perform responses leading to punishment.

NEGATIVE REINFORCEMENT
Effect: Strengthens responses that allow avoidance of outcomes
Learning Process: Consumer learns to perform responses that allow him or her to avoid negative outcomes.

- *Fixed-interval reinforcement:* After a specified time period has passed, the first response that is made brings the reward. Under such conditions, people tend to respond slowly right after being reinforced, but their responses speed up as the time for the next reinforcement looms. For example, consumers may crowd into a store for the last day of its seasonal sale and not reappear again until the next one.

- *Variable-interval reinforcement:* The time that must pass before reinforcement is delivered varies around some average. Since the person does not know exactly when to expect the reinforcement, responses must be performed at a consistent rate. This logic is behind retailers' use of so-called *secret shoppers*; people who periodically test for service quality by posing as a customer at unannounced times. Since store employees never know exactly when to expect a visit, high quality must be constantly maintained.

- *Fixed-ratio reinforcement:* Reinforcement occurs only after a fixed number of responses. This schedule motivates people to continue performing the same behavior over and over. For example, a consumer might keep buying groceries at the same store in order to earn a prize after collecting fifty books of trading stamps.

- *Variable-ratio reinforcement:* The person is reinforced after a certain number of responses, but he or she does not know how many responses are required. People in such situations tend to respond at very high and steady rates, and this type of behavior is very difficult to extinguish. This reinforcement schedule is responsible for consumers' attraction to slot machines. They learn that if they keep throwing money into the machine, they will eventually win something (if they don't go broke first).

Cognitive Learning Theory

Cognitive learning occurs as a result of mental processes. In contrast to behavioral theories of learning, cognitive learning theory stresses the importance of internal mental processes. This perspective views people as problem solvers who actively use information from the world around them to master their environment. Supporters of this viewpoint also stress the role of creativity and insight during the learning process.

THE ISSUE OF CONSCIOUSNESS A lot of controversy surrounds the issue of whether or when people are aware of their learning processes. While behavioral learning theorists emphasize the routine, automatic nature of conditioning, proponents of cognitive learning argue that even these simple effects are based on cognitive factors: Expectations are created that a stimulus will be followed by a response (the formation of expectations requires mental activity). According to this school of thought, conditioning occurs because subjects develop conscious hypotheses and then act on them.

On the one hand, there is some evidence for the existence of nonconscious procedural knowledge. People apparently do process at least some information in an automatic, passive way, which is a condition that has been termed *mindlessness*.[7] When we meet someone new or encounter a new product, for example, we have a tendency to respond to the stimulus in terms of existing categories, rather than taking the trouble to formulate different ones. Our reactions are activated by a *trigger feature*, some stimulus that cues us toward a particular pattern. For example, men in one study rated a car in an ad as superior on a variety of characteristics if a seductive woman (the trigger feature) was present, despite the fact that the men did not believe the woman's presence actually had an influence.[8]

Nonetheless, many modern theorists are beginning to regard some instances of conditioning as cognitive processes, especially where expectations are formed about the linkages between stimuli and responses. Indeed, studies using *masking effects*, where it is difficult for subjects to learn CS/UCS associations, show substantial reductions in conditioning.[9] For example, an adolescent girl may observe that women on television and in real life seem to be rewarded with compliments and attention when they smell nice and wear alluring clothing. She figures out that the probability of these rewards occurring is greater when she wears perfume, and deliberately wears a popular scent to obtain the payoff of social acceptance.

OBSERVATIONAL LEARNING **Observational learning** occurs when people watch the actions of others and note the reinforcements *they* receive for their behaviors. This type of learning is a complex process; people store these observations in memory as they accumulate knowledge, perhaps using this information at a later point to guide their own behavior. This process of imitating the behavior of others is called *modeling*. For example, a woman shopping for a new kind of perfume may remember the reactions her friend received upon wearing a certain brand several months earlier, and she will base her behavior on her friend's actions.

In order for observational learning in the form of modeling to occur, four conditions must be met.[10] These factors are summarized in Figure 4–3.

1. The consumer's attention must be directed to the appropriate model, who for reasons of attractiveness, competence, status, or similarity is desirable to emulate.

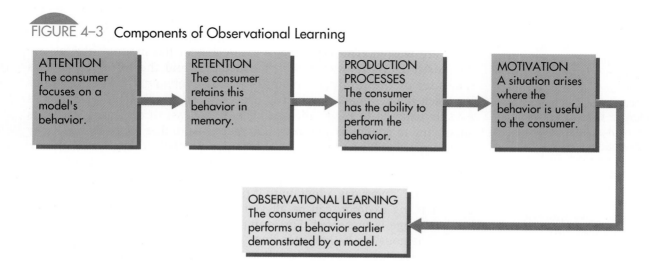

FIGURE 4–3 Components of Observational Learning

ATTENTION
The consumer focuses on a model's behavior.

RETENTION
The consumer retains this behavior in memory.

PRODUCTION PROCESSES
The consumer has the ability to perform the behavior.

MOTIVATION
A situation arises where the behavior is useful to the consumer.

OBSERVATIONAL LEARNING
The consumer acquires and performs a behavior earlier demonstrated by a model.

2. The consumer must remember what is said or done by the model.
3. The consumer must convert this information into actions.
4. The consumer must be motivated to perform these actions.

Marketing Applications of Learning Principles

Understanding how consumers learn is very important to marketers. After all, many strategic decisions are based on the assumption that consumers are continually accumulating information about products and that people can be "taught" to prefer some alternatives over others.

Behavioral Learning Applications

Many marketing strategies focus on the establishment of associations between stimuli and responses. Behavioral learning principles apply to many consumer phenomena, ranging from the creation of a distinctive brand image to the perceived linkage between a product and an underlying need.

USING CLASSICAL CONDITIONING The transfer of meaning from an unconditioned stimulus to a conditioned stimulus explains why "made-up" brand names like Marlboro, Coca-Cola, or IBM can exert such powerful effects on consumers. The association between the Marlboro Man and the cigarette is so strong that in some cases the company no longer even bothers to include the brand name in its ad. When nonsense syllables (meaningless sets of letters) are paired with such evaluative words as *beauty* or *success*, the meaning is transferred to the nonsense syllables. This change in the symbolic significance of initially meaningless words shows that complex meanings can be conditioned.[11]

These conditioned associations are crucial to many marketing strategies that rely on the creation and perpetuation of positive *brand equity*, a situation in which a brand has strong associations in a consumer's memory.[12] A product with brand equity holds a tremendous advantage in the marketplace.

Repetition. One advertising researcher argues that more than three exposures are wasted. The first creates awareness of the product, the second demonstrates its relevance to the consumer, and the third serves as a reminder of the product's benefits.[13] However, even this bare-bones approach implies that repetition is needed to ensure that the consumer is actually exposed to (and processes) the ad at least three times. Marketers attempting to condition an association must ensure that the consumers they have targeted will be exposed to the stimulus a sufficient number of times.

On the other hand, it is possible to have too much of a good thing: Consumers can become so used to hearing or seeing a marketing stimulus that they no longer pay attention to it (see Chapter 2). This problem, known as *advertising wearout,* can be alleviated by varying the way in which the basic message is presented. For example, the tax preparation firm of H&R Block is famous for its long-standing "Another of the seventeen reasons to use H&R Block . . ." campaign. Provigo's French supermarkets billboard

Research Report: After conducting extensive research, the Murjani clothing company found that people associated the Coca-Cola value and name with quality. They then approached Coca-Cola for permission to license the name and develop a line of Coca-Cola clothing. As one Murjani executive observed: "Because of the advertising Coke had done over the years, it turned out that people had a picture in their minds of what the clothes would look like." See Beth Sherman, "Coca-Cola Finds Murjani Clothes Are It," *Advertising Age* (June 9, 1986): S-4.

Les histoires de Mario.

Le poisson de Provigo.

One innovative way to employ repetition without causing wearout is illustrated by these related billboard images. Courtesy of Cossette Communications Marketing for Provigo Supermarkets, 1986.

campaign alleviates wearout by using a series of related billboards to tell its story, as illustrated by one set of the billboard images shown here.

Conditioning Product Associations. Advertisements often pair a product with a positive stimulus to create a desirable association. Various aspects of a marketing message, such as music, humor, or imagery, can affect conditioning. In one study, for example, subjects who viewed a slide of pens paired with either pleasant or unpleasant music were more likely to later select the pen that appeared with pleasant music.[14]

The order in which the conditioned stimulus and the unconditioned stimulus is presented can affect the likelihood that learning will occur. Generally speaking, the conditioned stimulus should be presented prior to the unconditioned stimulus. The technique of *backward conditioning*, such showing a soft drink (the UCS) and then playing a jingle (the CS) is generally not effective.[15] Because sequential presentation is desirable for conditioning to occur, classical conditioning is not very effective in static situations, such as in magazine ads, where (in contrast to TV or radio) the marketer cannot control the order in which the CS and the UCS are perceived.

Just as product associations can be formed, they can be *extinguished.* Because of the danger of extinction, a classical conditioning strategy may not be as effective for products that are frequently encountered, since there is no guarantee they will be accompanied by the CS. A bottle of Pepsi paired with the refreshing sound of a carbonated beverage being poured over ice may seem like a good example of conditioning. Unfortunately, the product would also be seen in many other contexts where this sound was absent, reducing the effectiveness of the conditioning.

By the same reasoning, a novel tune should be chosen over a popular one to pair with a product, since the popular song might also be heard in many situations where the product is not present.[16] Music videos in particular may serve as effective UCSs because they often have an emotional impact on viewers, and this effect may transfer to ads accompanying the video.[17]

Stimulus Generalization. The process of stimulus generalization is often central to branding and packaging decisions that attempt to capitalize on consumers' positive associations with an existing brand or company name, as illustrated by a haircutting establishment called United Hairlines.[18] In one twenty-month period, Procter & Gamble introduced almost ninety new prod-

This trade ad for King Features promotes the characters from the Blondie comic strip to potential licensers for use in their own advertising, with the expectation that positive attitudes toward these characters will be generalized to their products.
© King Features.

tling of the Berlin Wall). Recall of the past may have an effect on future behavior. For example, a college fund-raising campaign can get higher donations by evoking pleasant college memories. Some especially vivid associations are called *flashbulb memories*. These are usually related to some highly significant event. As one example, many people claim to remember exactly what they were doing when President Kennedy was assassinated in the early 1960s.

MEMORY SYSTEMS   According to the information-processing perspective, there are three distinct memory systems: sensory memory, short-term memory (STM), and long-term memory (LTM). Each plays a role in processing brand-related information. The interrelationships of these memory systems are summarized in Figure 4–5.

Sensory memory permits storage of the information we receive from our senses. This storage is very temporary; it lasts a couple of seconds at most. For example, a person might be walking past a donut shop and get a quick, enticing whiff of something baking inside. While this sensation would only last for a few seconds, it would be sufficient to allow the person to determine if he or she should investigate further. If the information is retained for further processing, it passes through an *attentional gate* and is transferred to short-term memory.

Short-term memory also stores information for a limited period of time, and its capacity is limited. Similar to a computer, this system can be regarded as *working memory;* it holds the information we are currently processing. Verbal input may be stored *acoustically* (in terms of how it sounds) or *semantically* (in terms of its meaning).[33]

The information is stored by combining small pieces into larger ones in a process known as "chunking." A *chunk* is a configuration that is familiar to the

Figure 4–5 is available as Transparency 9.

FIGURE 4–5   Relationships Among Memory Systems

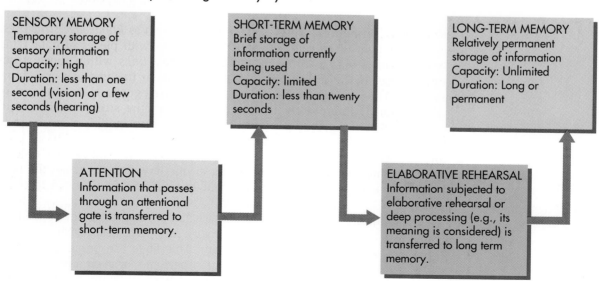

SENSORY MEMORY
Temporary storage of sensory information
Capacity: high
Duration: less than one second (vision) or a few seconds (hearing)

SHORT-TERM MEMORY
Brief storage of information currently being used
Capacity: limited
Duration: less than twenty seconds

LONG-TERM MEMORY
Relatively permanent storage of information
Capacity: Unlimited
Duration: Long or permanent

ATTENTION
Information that passes through an attentional gate is transferred to short-term memory.

ELABORATIVE REHEARSAL
Information subjected to elaborative rehearsal or deep processing (e.g., its meaning is considered) is transferred to long term memory.

person and can be manipulated as a unit. For example, a brand name can be a chunk that summarizes a great deal of detailed information about the brand.

Initially, it was believed that STM was capable of processing between five to nine chunks of information at a time, and for this reason phone numbers were designed to have seven digits.[34] It now appears that three to four chunks is the optimum size for efficient retrieval (seven-digit phone numbers can be remembered because the individual digits are chunked, so we may remember a three-digit exchange as one piece of information).[35]

Long-term memory is the system that allows us to retain information for a long period of time. In order for information to enter into long-term memory from short-term memory, *elaborative rehearsal* is required. This process involves thinking about the meaning of a stimulus and relating it to other information already in memory. Marketers sometimes assist in the process by devising catchy slogans or jingles that consumers repeat on their own.

Storing Information

Relationships among the types of memory are a source of some controversy. The traditional perspective, known as *multiple-store*, assumes that STM and LTM are separate systems. More recent research has moved away from the distinction between the two types of memory, instead emphasizing the interdependence of the systems. This work argues that depending upon the nature of the processing task, different levels of processing occur that *activate* some aspects of memory rather than others. These approaches are called **activation models of memory**.[36] The more effort it takes to process information (so-called "deep processing"), the more likely it is that information will be placed in long-term memory.

ASSOCIATIVE NETWORKS Activation models propose that an incoming piece of information is stored in an *associative network* containing many bits of related information organized according to some set of relationships. The consumer has organized systems of concepts relating to brands, stores, and so on.

Knowledge Structures. These storage units, known as *knowledge structures,* can be thought of as complex spider webs filled with pieces of data. This information is placed into *nodes* and *associative links* within these structures. Pieces of information that are seen as similar in some way are chunked together under some more abstract category. New, incoming information is interpreted to be consistent with the structure already in place.[37] According to the *hierarchical processing model,* a message is processed in a bottom-up fashion. Processing begins at a very basic level and is subject to increasingly complex processing operations that require greater cognitive capacity. If processing at one level fails to evoke the next level, processing of the ad is terminated and capacity is allocated to other tasks.[38]

Links form between nodes as an associative network is developed. For example, a consumer might have a network for "perfumes." Each node represents a concept related to the category. This node can be an attribute, a specific brand, a celebrity identified with a perfume, or even a related product. A network for perfumes might include concepts like the names Chanel,

Obsession, and Charlie, as well as attributes like sexy and elegant.

When asked to list perfumes, the consumer would recall only those brands contained in the appropriate category. This group is termed the **evoked set.** The task of a new entrant that wants to position itself as a category member (e.g., a new luxury perfume) is to provide cues that facilitate its placement in the appropriate category. A sample network for perfumes is shown in Figure 4–6.

Spreading Activation. A meaning can be activated indirectly; energy spreads across nodes of varying levels of abstraction. As one node is activated, other nodes associated with it also begin to be triggered. Meaning thus spreads across the network, bringing up concepts including competing brands and relevant attributes that are used to form attitudes toward the brand.

This process of *spreading activation* allows consumers to shift back and forth between levels of meaning. The way a piece of information is stored in memory depends upon the type of meaning assigned to it. This meaning type will in turn determine how and when the meaning is activated. For example, the *memory trace* for an ad could be stored in one or more of the following ways:

- Brand-specific—in terms of claims made for the brand
- Ad-specific—in terms of the medium or content of the ad itself
- Brand identification—in terms of the brand name
- Product category— in terms of how the product works or where it should be used, or in terms of experiences with the product
- Evaluative reactions—in terms of whether "that looks like fun"[39]

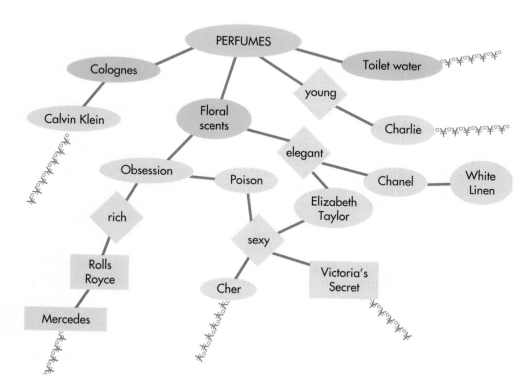

FIGURE 4–6 An Associative Network for Perfumes

Research Report: The identification of consumers' knowledge structures is integral to the research technique known as laddering, where a framework is developed to link perceived product attributes to terminal values. This application, also known as the means–end chain model, is discussed at length in the section on cultural values in Chapter 16. For an overview of the approach, see Thomas J. Reynolds and Jonathan Gutman, "Laddering Theory, Method, Analysis, and Interpretation," Journal of Advertising Research 28 (February/March 1988): 11–34.

Teaching Hint: Consumers process incoming information to be consistent with existing knowledge structures, and as a result incorrect inferences about a product may be made. In one national survey that examined the miscomprehension of advertisements and editorials, on average more than 20 percent of the material was incorrectly understood, while an additional 15 percent was not learned at all. See Jacob Jacoby and Wayne D. Hoyer, "The Comprehension–Miscomprehension of Print Communication: Selected Findings," Journal of Consumer Research 15 (March 1989): 434–44.

Levels of Knowledge. Knowledge is coded at different levels of abstraction and complexity. *Meaning concepts* are individual nodes (e.g., elegant). These may be combined into a larger unit, called a *proposition* (also known as a *belief*). A proposition links two nodes together to form a more complex meaning, which can serve as a single chunk of information. For example, a proposition might be that "Chanel is a perfume for elegant women." Propositions are in turn integrated to produce a complex unit known as a schema. A *schema* is a cognitive framework that is developed through experience. Information that is consistent with an existing schema is encoded more readily.[40] The ability to move up and down among levels of abstraction greatly increases processing flexibility and efficiency. For this reason, young children, who do not yet have well-developed schemas, are not able to make efficient use of purchase information compared to older children.[41]

One type of schema that is relevant to consumer behavior is a *script*, a sequence of procedures that is expected by an individual. For example, consumers learn *service scripts* that guide expectations and purchasing behavior in business settings. Consumers learn to expect a certain sequence of events, and they may become uncomfortable if the service departs from the script. A service script for a visit to the dentist might include such events as (1) drive to the dentist, (2) read old magazines in the waiting room, (3) hear name called and sit in dentist's chair, (4) dentist puts funny substance on my teeth, (5) dentist cleans my teeth, and so on. This desire to follow a script helps to explain why such service innovations as automatic bank machines and self-service gas stations have met with resistance by some consumers, who have trouble adapting to a new sequence of events.[42]

Retrieving Information

Retrieval is the process whereby information is accessed from long-term memory. As evidenced by the popularity of the game Trivial Pursuit, people have a vast quantity of information stored in their heads that is not necessarily available on demand. Although most of the information entered in long-term memory does not go away, it may be hard or impossible to retrieve unless the appropriate cues are present.

FACTORS INFLUENCING RETRIEVAL Some differences in retrieval ability are physiological. Older adults consistently display inferior recall ability for current items such as prescription information, though events that happened to them when they were younger may be recalled with great clarity.[43]

Other factors are situational, relating to the environment in which the message is delivered. Not surprisingly, recall is enhanced when the consumer pays more attention to the message in the first place. Some evidence indicates that information about a *pioneering brand* (the first brand to enter a market) is more easily retrieved from memory than follower brands because the product's introduction is likely to be distinctive and, for the time being, no competitors divert the consumer's attention.[44] In addition, descriptive brand names are more likely to be recalled than are those that do not provide adequate cues as to what the product is.[45]

The viewing environment of a marketing message also can affect recall.

Trivial Pursuit, a popular board game, tests consumers' memories of cultural happenings. TRIVIAL PURSUIT® is a registered trademark of Horn Abbot Ltd., under exclusive license to Parker Brothers and used with permission.

For example, commercials shown during baseball games yield the lowest recall scores among sports programs because the activity is stop-and-go rather than continuous. Unlike football or basketball, the pacing of baseball gives many opportunities for attention to wander even during play. Similarly, General Electric found that its commercials fared better in television shows with continuous activity, such as stories or dramas, compared to variety shows or talk shows that are punctuated by a series of acts.[46]

State-Dependent Retrieval. In a process termed *state-dependent retrieval,* people are better able to access information if their internal state is the same at the time of recall as when the information was learned.

This phenomenon, called the *mood congruence effect,* underscores the desirability of matching a consumer's mood at the time of purchase when

Research Report: Consumers make inferences if they are not provided with adequate information. Rather than simply ignoring omissions, they evaluate product descriptions with missing information more negatively. See Richard D. Johnson and Irwin P. Levin, "More Than Meets the Eye: The Effect of Missing Information on Purchase Evaluations," *Journal of Consumer Research* 12 (September 1985): 169–78

Research Report: According to the availability–valence model of communication effects, attitudes are influenced by the favorability of information that is available in memory at the time of judgment. One study found that subjects exposed to a pleasant odor recalled a greater percentage of happy memories than did those subjects who smelled an unpleasant odor. See Jolita Kiselius and Brian Sternthal, "Examining the Vividness Contro-versy: An Availability-Valence Interpre-tation," Journal of Consumer Re-search 12 (March 1986), 418–31; Howard Ehrlich-man and Jack N. Halpern, "Affect and Memory: Effects of Pleasant and Unpleas-ant Odors on Re-trieval of Happy and Unhappy Memories," Journal of Personality and Social Psychology 55 (1988)5: 769–79.

planning exposure to marketing communications. A consumer is more likely to recall an ad, for example, if his or her mood or level of arousal at the time of exposure is similar to that in the purchase environment. By recreating the cues that were present when the information was first presented, recall can be enhanced. For example, Life cereal uses a picture of "Mikey" from its commercial on the cereal box, which facilitates recall of brand claims and favorable brand evaluations.[47]

Familiarity. As a general rule, prior familiarity with an item enhances its recall. Indeed, this is one of the basic goals of marketers who are trying to create and maintain awareness of their products. The more experience a consumer has with a product, the better use he or she is able to make of product information.[48]

However, there is a possible fly in the ointment: As noted earlier in the chapter, some evidence indicates that extreme familiarity can result in *inferior* learning and/or recall. When consumers are highly familiar with a brand or an advertisement, they may attend to fewer attributes because they do not believe that any additional effort will yield a gain in knowledge.[49] For example, when consumers are exposed to the technique of *radio replay,* where the audio track from a television ad is replayed on the radio, they do very little critical, evaluative processing and instead mentally replay the video portion of the ad.[50]

Salience. The *salience* of a brand refers to its prominence or level of activation in memory. As noted in Chapter 2, stimuli that stand out in contrast to their environment are more likely to command attention, which, in turn, increases the likelihood they will be recalled. Almost any technique that increases the novelty of a stimulus also improves recall (a result known as the *von Restorff effect*).[51] This effect explains why unusual advertising or distinctive packaging tends to facilitate brand recall.[52]

Introducing a surprise element in an ad (e.g., the Energizer Bunny™ who unexpectedly marches through a commercial) can be particularly effec-

MARKETING OPPORTUNITY

One overlooked factor that contributes to advertising recall is the rhythm and beat of the verbal message. By stressing important words, cognitive overload is avoided because the commercial cues viewers to predict when they should be paying the most attention to the ad content. A technique called the TLK Picture Sort assesses the effect of rhythm on recall. Subjects are given a deck of still pictures from a commercial they have seen, and they sort them into "remember" and "don't remember" piles.

Commercials that score well on recall have an identifiable rhythmic stroke. Typically, the opening frames have an arousing sequence that hooks the viewer, and superior comprehension is found at the close of the commercial because curiosity and involvement build as the communication develops.[53]

tive in aiding recall even if it is not relevant to the factual information being presented.[54] In addition, so-called mystery ads, where the brand is not identified until the end of the ad, are more effective at building associations in memory between the product category and that brand—especially in the case of novel brands.[55]

Pictorial Versus Verbal Cues. There is some evidence for the superiority of visual memory over verbal memory, but this advantage is unclear because it is more difficult to measure recall of pictures.[56] However, the available data indicate that information presented in picture form is more likely to be recognized later[57] Certainly, visual aspects of an ad are more likely to grab a consumer's attention. In fact, eye-movement studies indicate that about 90 percent of viewers look at the dominant picture in an ad before they bother to view the copy.[58] While pictorial ads may enhance recall, however, they do not necessarily improve comprehension. One study found that television news items presented with illustrations (still pictures) as a backdrop result in improved recall for details of the news story, even though understanding of the story's content does not improve.[59] Visual imagery can be especially effective when it includes verbal cues that relate to the consumer's existing knowledge—as the Kraft cheese ad shown here does by linking the product's holes to the game of golf.

Research Report: Some research claims that consistency between verbal and visual aspects of an ad enhances recall, while other work argues that *different* information presented on the visual and verbal channels is more effective because it forces the consumer to concentrate more on the dual messages, which in turn enhances later recall. See Julie A. Edell and Richard Staelin, "The Information Processing of Pictures in Print Advertise-ments," *Journal of Consumer Research* 10 (June): 45–61; Michael Houston, Terry Childers, and Susan Heckler, "Picture-Word Consistency and the Elaborative Processing of Attributes," *Journal of Marketing Research* 24 (November 1987): 359–69.

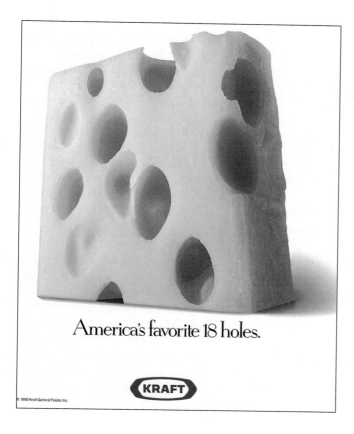

America's favorite 18 holes.

KRAFT

© 1990 Kraft General Foods, Inc.

This Kraft cheese ad uses a play on words to link the product to consumers' pre-existing knowledge to increase the chances that brand information will be stored in memory. Kraft is a registered trademark of Kraft General Foods, Inc. Reproduced with permission.

FACTORS INFLUENCING FORGETTING Marketers obviously hope that consumers will not forget about their products. However, in a poll of more than 13,000 adults, over half were unable to remember any specific ad they had seen, heard, or read in the last thirty days.[60] Forgetting is obviously a problem for marketers.

Decay and Interference. Early memory theorists assumed that memories fade due to the simple passage of time. In a process of **decay,** the structural changes in the brain produced by learning simply go away. Forgetting also occurs due to **interference;** as additional information is learned, it displaces the earlier information.

Stimulus-response associations will be forgotten if the consumers subsequently learn new responses to the same or similar stimuli in a process known as *retroactive interference.* Or, prior learning can interfere with new learning, a process termed *proactive interference.* Since pieces of information are stored as nodes in memory that are connected to one another by links, a meaning concept that is connected by a larger number of links is more likely to be retrieved. But, as new responses are learned, a stimulus loses its effectiveness in retrieving the old response.[61]

These interference effects help to explain problems in remembering brand information. Consumers tend to organize attribute information by brand.[62] Additional attribute information regarding a brand or similar brands may limit the person's ability to recall old brand information. Recall may also be inhibited if the brand name is composed of frequently used words. These words cue competing associations and result in less retention of brand information.[63]

In one study, brand evaluations deteriorated more rapidly when ads for the brand appeared with messages for twelve other brands in the *same* category than when the ad was shown with ads for twelve dissimilar products.[64] By increasing the salience of a brand, the recall of other brands can be impaired.[65] On the other hand, calling a competitor by name can result in poorer recall for one's own brand.[66]

Finally, a phenomenon known as the *part-list cueing effect* allows marketers to strategically utilize the interference process. When only a portion of the items in a category are presented to consumers, the omitted items are not as easily recalled. For example, comparative advertising that mentions only a subset of competitors (preferably those that the marketer is not very worried about) may inhibit recall of the *unmentioned* brands with which the product does not favorably compare.[67]

PRODUCTS AS MEMORY MARKERS As illustrated by Joe's matchbook collection, products and ads can themselves serve as powerful retrieval cues. Indeed, the three types of possessions most valued by consumers are furniture, visual art, and photos. The most common explanation for this attachment is the ability of these things to call forth memories of the past.[68] Products are particularly important as markers when our sense of past is threatened, as when a consumer's current identity is challenged due to some change in role caused by divorce, moving, graduation, and so on.[69] Products have *mnemonic* qualities that serve as a form of external memory, prompting consumers to retrieve episodic memories. For example, family photography allows consumers to create their own retrieval cues, with the 11 billion amateur photos taken annually forming a kind of external memory bank for our culture.

Researchers are just beginning to probe the effects of *autobiographical memories* on buying behavior. These memories appear to be one way that advertisements create emotional responses; ads that succeed in getting us to think about our own past also appear to get us to like these ads more—especially if the linkage between the nostalgia experience and the brand is strong.[70]

The Power of Nostalgia. **Nostalgia** has been described as a bittersweet emotion, where the past is viewed with both sadness and longing. This feeling was strongly experienced by Joe in the vignette at the beginning of the chapter.

One study of network television commercials found that about 10 percent of them contained some nostalgic reference, and this appeal was especially prevalent in the food and beverage categories.[71] In a recent survey of baby boomers, Bugs Bunny was the best-remembered cartoon character, Barbie was the favorite toy, and the boomers' favorite ad slogan was M&M's "Melts in your mouth, not in your hand."[72]

A stimulus is at times able to evoke a weakened response much later, an effect known as *spontaneous recovery*, and this reestablished connection may explain consumers' powerful nostalgic reactions to songs or pictures they have not been exposed to in many years. Some marketers are realizing the appeal nostalgia holds for many consumers. They are resurrecting *retro ads*, successful campaigns from the past that have been in retirement, as when Maypo cereal brought back its "I want my Maypo" slogan in the ad shown

Additional Example: The popularity of the movie "Rain Man" prompted Buick to reintroduce its old Roadmaster model, which was produced from 1936 to 1958. The characters in the movie drove a 1949 version across the country. After the division got letters from viewers suggesting the model be brought back, it redesigned the nameplate for a 1991 introduction. See Raymond Serafin, "Roadmaster Re-Enters Buick Fleet," Advertising Age (September 10, 1990): 28.

Maypo cereal brought back its original commercial ("I want my Maypo!") to appeal to consumers' nostalgic memories. Maypo photo courtesy of American Home Food Products.

here. The Coca-Cola Company went so far as to hire a detective agency to track down actors from a commercial made over twenty years earlier who gathered on a hilltop to sing "I'd Like to Buy the World a Coke." The original participants appeared with their children in a highly publicized ad called "Hilltop Reunion."[73]

Many companies are continuing to use their old, trademark characters, or are even bringing some out of retirement, including the Campbell Soup Kids, the Pillsbury Doughboy, Betty Crocker, and Planters' Mr. Peanut—who recently celebrated his seventy-fifth birthday with the company.[74]

MARKETING OPPORTUNITY

The souvenir industry depends upon consumers' desires to *tangibilize,* or give physical form to, their experiences as tourists. Indeed, the word souvenir is French for memory. Many opportunities exist to provide consumers with tangible markers of important events, although sometimes the end results are in questionable taste. A good case in point was the marketing of the visit of Pope John Paul II to the United States in 1987. The following are samples of some memorabilia that were offered to capitalize on this event:

- T-shirts picturing Budweiser beer mascot Spuds MacKenzie in papal hat and robe: The caption read "The Original Vatican Animal."
- A lawn sprinkler that shoots water from the out-turned palms of a plywood pope: The slogan read "Let Us Spray."
- A company called Popepourri Ltd. sold a papal ring made of gold plastic with red lips. According to the ring's creator, "When you kiss it, it'll kiss you back."[75]

Measuring Memory for Advertising

Because advertisers pay so much money to place their messages in front of consumers, they are naturally concerned that people will actually remember these messages at a later point. It seems that they have good reason to be concerned. In one study, less than 40 percent of television viewers made positive links between commercial messages and the corresponding products, only 65 percent noticed the brand name in a commercial, and only 38 percent recognized a connection to an important point.[76]

Even more sadly, only 7 percent of television viewers can recall the product or company featured in the most recent television commercial they watched. This figure represents less than half the recall rate recorded in 1965, and may be attributed to such factors as the increase of 30- and 15-second commercials and the practice of airing television commercials in clusters rather than in single-sponsor programs.[77]

A picture is worth a thousand words: Product icons—like the Jolly Green Giant who has appeared in ads and on packaging for more than thirty years—are a significant factor in product recognition. Courtesy of Pillsbury.

RECOGNITION VERSUS RECALL One indicator of good advertising is, of course, the impression it makes on consumers. But how can this impact be defined and measured? Two basic measures of impact are *recognition* and *recall*. In the typical recognition test, subjects are shown ads one at a time and asked if they have seen them before. In contrast, free recall tests ask consumers to independently produce previously acquired information and then perform a recognition check on it.

Under some conditions, these two memory measures tend to yield the same results, especially when the researchers try to keep the viewers' interest in the ads constant.[78] Generally, though, recognition scores tend to be more reliable and do not decay over time the way recall scores do.[79] Recognition scores are almost always better than recall scores because recognition is a simpler process and more retrieval cues are available to the consumer.

Both types of retrieval play important roles in purchase decisions. Recall tends to be more important in situations where consumers do not have product data at their disposal, and so they must rely upon memory to generate this information.[80] On the other hand, recognition is more likely to be an important factor in a store, where consumers are confronted with thousands of product options and information (i.e., external memory is abundantly available) and the task may simply be to recognize a familiar package.* For example, the Jolly Green Giant icon on packaging as shown here is quickly recognized by many consumers. The Giant first appeared in print ads in the 1930s, and his first appearance on television was in the 1960s.

THE STARCH TEST A widely used commercial measure of advertising recall for magazines is called the Starch test, a syndicated service founded in 1932. This service provides scores on a number of aspects of consumers' familiarity with an ad, including such categories as "noted," "associated," and "read most." It also scores the impact of the component parts of an overall ad, giving such information as "seen" for major illustrations and

Research Report: A mall-intercept study was conducted to examine the bogus recall of advertising slogans. The researchers found that bogus recall is more likely to occur among those cosumers who are younger and have lower education and income levels. It is also positively related to liking for the slogan and higher media usage. In addition, people who have more interest in a product category tend to claim higher recognition than do others. See Adam Finn, "Print Ad Recognition Readership Scores: An Information Process-ing Perspective," *Journal of Marketing Research* 25 (May 1988): 168–77; Myron Glassman and John B. Ford, "An Empirical Investigation of Bogus Recall, *Journal of the Academy of Marketing Science* 16 (Fall 1988): 38–42.

*Unfortunately, package recognition and familiarity can have a negative consequence in that warning labels may be ignored, since their existence is taken for granted and not really noticed.[81]

Research Report: The optimal location for a print ad is on a right-side page toward the front of the magazine. See Adam Finn, "Print Ad Recognition Readership Scores: An Information Processing Perspective," *Journal of Marketing Research* 25 (May 1988): 168–77.

"read some" for a major block of copy.[82] Such factors as the size of the ad, whether it appears toward the front or the back of the magazine, if it is on the right or left page, and the size of illustrations play an important role in affecting the amount of attention given to an ad as determined by Starch scores. The ad for Whittle Communications shown here highlights the problem of consumers noticing ads and processing them for recall and retrieval.

PROBLEMS WITH MEMORY MEASURES   While the measurement of an ad's memorability is important, the ability of existing measures to accurately assess these dimensions has been criticized for several reasons.

Response Biases.   Results obtained from a measuring instrument are not necessarily due to what is being measured, but rather to something else about the instrument or the respondent. This form of contamination is called a *response bias*. For example, people tend to give yes responses to

This ad for Whittle Communications emphasizes that consumers' memory for advertising is surprisingly limited and offers readers a solution to the problem of increasing an ad's memorability. Courtesy of Whittle Communications.

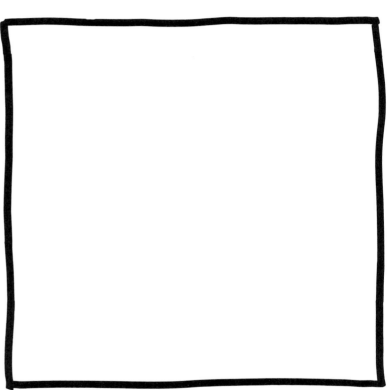

questions, regardless of what is asked. In addition, consumers often have an eagerness to be "good subjects" by pleasing the experimenter. They will try to give the responses they think he or she is looking for. In some studies, the claimed recognition of bogus ads (ads that have not been seen before) is almost as high as the recognition rate of real ads.[83]

Memory Lapses. Typical problems include *omitting* (leaving facts out), *averaging* (the tendency to "normalize" things and not report extreme cases), and *telescoping* (inaccurate recall of time).[84] These distortions call into question the accuracy of various product usage data bases that rely upon consumers to recall their purchase and consumption of food and household items. In one study, for example, people were asked to describe what portion of various foods—small, medium, or large—they ate in a normal meal. However, different definitions of medium were used (e.g., 3/4 cup versus 1 1/2 cups). Regardless of the measurement used, about the same number of people claimed they normally ate medium portions.[85]

MEMORY VERSUS FEELING Although techniques are being developed to increase the accuracy of memory scores, these improvements do not address the more fundamental issue of whether recall is necessary for advertising to have an effect. In particular, some critics argue that these measures do not adequately tap the impact of "feeling" ads where the objective is to arouse strong emotions rather than to convey concrete product benefits. Many ad campaigns, including those for Hallmark cards, Chevrolet, and Pepsi use this approach.[86] An effective strategy relies on a long-term buildup of feeling rather than on a one-shot attempt to convince consumers to buy the product.

Also, it is not clear that recall translates into preference. We may recall the benefits touted in an ad but not *believe* them. Or, the ad may be memorable because it is so obnoxious and the product becomes one we "love to hate." The bottom line: While recall is important, especially for creating brand awareness, it is not necessarily *sufficient* to alter consumer preferences. To accomplish this, more sophisticated attitude-change strategies are needed. These issues will be discussed in the next two chapters.

Research Report: Some researchers are adopting principles of signal detection theory to the measurement of advertising recognition. This perspective assumes that every piece of information has a certain strength in long-term memory. This strength increases with each exposure (including the first exposure). Both stimulus and distracter ads (those not seen before) have a strength value to begin with, but this value is changed with exposure during the experiment. Methodologies are being developed to account for the relative strength of old and new stimuli. See Surendra N. Singh, and Gilbert A. Churchill, Jr., "Response-Bias-Free Recognition Tests to Measure Adver-tising Effects," *Journal of Ad- vertising* Research (June/July 1987): 23-36; Armen Tashchian, J. Dennis White, and Sukgoo Pak, "Signal Detection Analysis and Advertising Recognition: An Introduction to Measurement and Interpretation Issues," *Journal of Marketing* 25 (November 1988): 397–405.

Chapter Summary

- *Learning* is a change in behavior that is caused by experience. Learning can occur through simple associations between a stimulus and a response, or via a complex series of cognitive activities.

- Behavioral learning theories assume that learning occurs as a result of responses to external events. *Classical conditioning* occurs when a stimulus that naturally elicits a response (an unconditioned stimulus) is paired with another stimulus that does not initially elicit this response. Over time, the second stimulus (the conditioned stimulus) comes to elicit the response as well.

- This response can also extend to other, similar stimuli in a process known as *stimulus generalization*. This process is the basis for such marketing strategies as licensing and family branding, where a consumer's positive associations with a product are transferred to other contexts.

- *Operant* or *instrumental conditioning* occurs as the person learns to perform behaviors that produce positive outcomes and avoid those that result in negative outcomes. While classical conditioning involves the pairing of two stimuli, instrumental learning occurs when reinforcement is delivered following a response to a stimulus. Reinforcement is positive if a reward is delivered following a response. It is negative if a negative outcome is avoided by *not* performing a response. Punishment occurs when a response is followed by unpleasant events. Extinction of the behavior will occur if reinforcement is no longer received.

- *Cognitive learning* occurs as the result of mental processes. For example, observational learning takes place when the consumer performs a behavior as a result of seeing someone else performing it and being rewarded for it.

- *Memory* refers to the storage of learned information. The way information is encoded when it is perceived determines how it will be stored in memory. The memory systems known as sensory memory, short-term memory, and long-term memory each play a role in retaining and processing information from the outside world.

- Information is not stored in isolation; it is incorporated into knowledge structures, where it is associated with other related data. The location of product information in *associative networks,* and the level of abstraction at which it is coded, help to determine when and how this information will be activated at a later time. Some factors that influence the likelihood of retrieval include the level of familiarity with an item, its salience (or prominence) in memory, and whether the information was presented in pictorial or written form.

- Products also play a role as memory markers; they are used by consumers to retrieve memories about past experiences (autobiographical memories) and are often valued for their ability to do this. This function also contributes to the use of *nostalgia* in marketing strategies.

- Memory for product information can be measured through either recognition or recall techniques. Consumers are more likely to recognize an advertisement if it is presented to them than to recall one without being given any cues.

Key Terms

activation models of memory, p. 126

behavioral learning theories, p. 111

classical conditioning, p. 112

cognitive learning, p. 116

decay, p. 132

encoding, p. 124

evoked set, p. 127

extinction, p. 115

interference, p. 132

learning, p. 110

long-term memory, p. 126

memory, p. 124

negative reinforcement, p. 114

nostalgia, p. 133

observational learning, p. 117

operant conditioning, p. 114

positive reinforcement, p. 114

and Familiarity Responses to Verbal Versus Visual Advertisements."

57. Terry Childers and Michael Houston, "Conditions for a Picture-Superiority Effect on Consumer Memory," *Journal of Consumer Research* 11 (September 1984): 643–54; Terry Childers, Susan Heckler, and Michael Houston, "Memory for the Visual and Verbal Components of Print Advertisements," *Psychology & Marketing* 3 (Fall 1986): 147–50.

58. Werner Krober-Riel, "Effects of Emotional Pictorial Elements in Ads Analyzed by Means of Eye Movement Monitoring," in *Advances in Consumer Research* 11, ed. Thomas C. Kinnear (Provo, Utah: Association for Consumer Research, 1984): 591–96.

59. Hans-Bernd Brosius, "Influence of Presentation Features and News Context on Learning from Television News," *Journal of Broadcasting & Electronic Media* 33 (Winter 1989): 1–14.

60. Raymond R. Burke and Thomas K. Srull, "Competitive Interference and Consumer Memory for Advertising," *Journal of Consumer Research* 15 (June 1988): 55–68.

61. Burke and Srull, "Competitive Interference and Consumer Memory for Advertising."

62. Johnson and Russo, "Product Familiarity and Learning New Information."

63. Joan Meyers-Levy, "The Influence of Brand Name's Association Set Size and Word Frequency on Brand Memory," *Journal of Consumer Research* 16 (September 1989): 197–208.

64. Michael H. Baumgardner, Michael R. Leippe, David L. Ronis, and Anthony G. Greenwald, "In Search of Reliable Persuasion Effects: II. Associative Interference and Persistence of Persuasion in a Message-Dense Environment," *Journal of Personality and Social Psychology* 45 (September 1983): 524–37.

65. Alba and Chattopadhyay, "Salience Effects in Brand Recall."

66. Margaret Henderson Blair, Allan R. Kuse, David H. Furse, and David W. Stewart, "Advertising in a New and Competitive Environment: Persuading Consumers to Buy," *Business Horizons* 30 (November/December 1987): 20.

67. Lynch and Srull, "Memory and Attentional Factors in Consumer Choice."

68. Russell W. Belk, "Possessions and the Extended Self," *Journal of Consumer Research* 15 (September 1988): 139–68.

69. Russell W. Belk, "The Role of Possessions in Constructing and Maintaining a Sense of Past," in *Advances in Consumer Research* 16, eds. Marvin E. Goldberg, Gerald Gorn, and Richard W. Pollay (Provo, Utah: Association for Consumer Research, 1989): 669–78.

70. Hans Baumgartner, Mita Sujan, and James R. Bettman, "Autobiographical Memories, Affect and Consumer Information Processing," *Journal of Consumer Psychology* 1 (January 1992): 53–82; Mita Sujan, James R. Bettman, and Hans Baumgartner (1992), "Autobiographical Memories and Consumer Judgments," Working Paper No. 183, Pennsylvania State University, University Park, 1992.

71. Lynette S. Unger, Diane M. McConocha, and John A. Faier, "The Use of Nostalgia in Television Advertising: A Content Analysis," *Journalism Quarterly* 63 (Fall 1991): 345–53.

72. "For Boomers, These Were a Few of Our Favorite Things," *Adweek* 10 (February 3, 1992): 16.

73. Marcus Mabry, "Rememberance of Ads Past," *Newsweek* (July 30, 1990): 42.

74. Stuart Elliott, "At 75, Mr. Peanut is Getting Expanded Role at Planters," *New York Times* (September 23, 1991): D15.

75. "The Selling of the Pope, American Style," *Newsweek* (June 29, 1987): 48.

76. "Only 38% of T.V. Audience Links Brands with Ads," *Marketing News* (January 6, 1984): 10.

77. "Terminal Television," *American Demographics* (January 1987): 15.

78. Richard P. Bagozzi and Alvin J. Silk, "Recall, Recognition, and the Measurement of Memory for Print Advertisements," *Marketing Science* (1983)2: 95–134.

79. Adam Finn, "Print Ad Recognition Readership Scores: An Information Processing Perspective," *Journal of Marketing Research* 25 (May 1988): 168–77.

80. Bettman, "Memory Factors in Consumer Choice."

81. Mark A. deTurck and Gerald M. Goldhaber, "Effectiveness of Product Warning Labels: Effects of Consumers' Information Processing Objectives," *Journal of Consumer Affairs* 23 (1989)1: 111–25.

82. Finn, "Print Ad Recognition Readership Scores."

83. Surendra N. Singh and Gilbert A. Churchill, Jr., "Response-Bias-Free Recognition Tests to Measure Advertising Effects," *Journal of Advertising Research* (June/July 1987): 23–36.

84. William A. Cook, "Telescoping and Memory's Other Tricks," *Journal of Advertising Research* 27 (February/March 1987): 5–8.

85. "On a Diet? Don't Trust Your Memory," *Psychology Today* (October 1989): 12.

86. Hubert A. Zielske and Walter A. Henry, "Remembering and Forgetting Television Ads," *Journal of Advertising Research* 20 (April 1980): 7–13.

1·9·8·9
ANO BRASILEIRO DE
**SEGURANÇA
NO TRÂNSITO**

CHAPTER 5

Attitudes

Buying, Having, and Being: Selections 17–18 from *Buying, Having, and Being: The Washington Post Consumer Behavior Companion*, Second Edition, accompany this chapter.

I t's Saturday night, and Nancy, Jan, and Lisa are out on the town. When the bartender at Eric's Pub comes over to take their drink orders, Nancy immediately orders her standard: a dry Stolichnaya martini, straight up, with a twist. Nancy takes her vodka seriously. Over the years, she's tried them all, and in her mind now, nothing will do but Stoly.

Jan, on the other hand, is more indecisive. She doesn't drink that often, and she can't really tell one concoction from another. Finally she says, "Oh, I don't really care. I guess your house white wine will be fine."

Lisa just shrugs and says, "Looks like it's going to be Pepsi for me. I'm the designated driver tonight." Robert, the bartender is impressed. "Now that's a nice change for you guys. I guess all the publicity on TV about drunk driving finally got to you." Lisa replies, "Hey, things are different these days! People know they can't party without accepting the consequences."

When the drinks are served, Nancy and Jan settle back and enjoy their beverages. Jan is especially pleased to find she really likes this particular white wine. I'll have to ask Eric which brand it is, she thinks.

Lisa eyes their frosty glasses as she munches some popcorn and drinks her Pepsi. These two owe me big time, she thinks, anticipating next Saturday night . . . .

The Power of Attitudes

As Lisa's willingness to serve as a designated driver (on a Saturday night!) shows, marketers can have a big impact on consumers' feelings, beliefs, and actions regarding many facets of their everyday lives. **Social marketing** involves the promotion of causes and ideas such as responsible drinking, energy conservation, and population control.[1] For example, a major campaign to combat drug use was undertaken by the Partnership for a Drug-Free America, a group organized by the American Association of Advertising Agencies. This campaign was the largest pro bono effort (meaning the ad agencies involved donated their services) in history. As one involved executive noted, "We are approaching the problem posed by the $110 billion illegal drug industry from a marketing point of view. What we're doing is competing with drug pushers for market share of nonusers."[2]

Manufacturers are also getting into social marketing as a way to encourage constructive behavior while promoting a positive public image. The Members Only apparel company, for example, has been especially active in this area. The company has funded $100 million worth of advertising to combat drug abuse and to encourage voter registration. One recent TV commercial includes images of past dictators such as Hitler and Mussolini as a way to remind people that the way to avoid future dictators is to vote. As another example, the General Motors ad shown here illustrates an attempt to persuade the company's Portuguese customers to wear their seat belts.

Cross-Cultural Example: The British government is an active proponent of social marketing. It is currently the country's third largest advertiser. Much of its expenditures are devoted to "selling" its social policies, including anti-drug and AIDS messages. See Steve Lohr, "Major British Advertiser: Government," New York Times (May 23, 1989): D1.

A storyboard for the Members Only television commercial described here is available as Transparency 10.

consumer's choice is reinforced by good or bad experiences with the product after purchase.

The possibility that consumers simply don't care enough about many decisions to carefully assemble a set of product beliefs and then evaluate them is important, because it implies that all of the concern about influencing beliefs and carefully communicating information about product attributes may largely be wasted. Consumers aren't necessarily going to pay attention anyway; they are more likely to respond to simple stimulus-response connections when making purchase decisions. For example, a consumer choosing among paper towels might remember that "Bounty is the quicker picker-upper" rather than bothering to systematically compare all of the brands on the shelf.

The notion of low involvement on the part of consumers is a bitter pill for some marketers to swallow. Who wants to admit that what they market is not very important or involving? A brand manager for, say, a brand of bubble gum or cat food may find it hard to believe that consumers don't put that much thought into purchasing her product since she spends many of her waking (and perhaps sleeping) hours thinking about it. This difference in perspective is illustrated in the restaurant ad shown here.

Steak is our life. All we ask is that you make it your lunch.

Smith & Wollensky.
The quintessential New York City steakhouse.
49th St. & 3rd Ave. (212)753-1530.

Winner of The *Wine Spectator's* 1987 Grand Award.

This ad for New York's famous Smith & Wollensky restaurant emphasizes that marketers and others associated with a product or service are often more involved with it than are their consumers. Courtesy of Smith & Wollensky Steakhouse, 797 3rd Avenue, NYC.

For marketers, the ironic silver lining to this low-involvement cloud is that under these conditions, consumers are not motivated to process a lot of complex brand-related information. Instead, they will be swayed by principles of behavioral learning, such as the simple responses caused by conditioned brand names, point-of-purchase displays, and so on. The *less* important the product to consumers, the *more* important are many of the marketing stimuli (e.g., packages, jingles) that must be devised to sell it. These factors will be explored at length in the next chapter.

Attitude as Affect

Researchers in recent years have begun to stress the significance of affect as a central aspect of an attitude. According to the *experiential hierarchy of effects*, consumers act on the basis of their emotional reactions (just as Lisa felt strongly about drunk drivers). Although the factors of beliefs and behavior still are recognized as playing a part, a consumer's overall evaluation of an attitude object is considered by many to be the core of an attitude.

The centrality of visceral feelings to an attitude is emphasized by the *Sports Illustrated* ad shown here. This perspective highlights the idea that

This *Sports Illustrated* ad, which emphasizes feelings, underscores the importance of affect in forming attitudes. John Iacono/Sports Illustrated.

attitudes can be strongly influenced by intangible product attributes, such as package design, and by consumers' reactions toward accompanying stimuli, such as advertising and even the brand name. As discussed in Chapter 3, resulting attitudes will be affected by consumers' hedonic motivations, such as how the product makes them feel or the fun its use will provide.

One important debate about the experiential hierarchy concerns the *independence* of cognition and affect. On the one hand, the *cognitive-affective model* argues that an affective judgment is but the last step in a series of cognitive processes. Earlier steps include the sensory registration of stimuli and the retrieval of meaningful information from memory to categorize these stimuli.[13]

THE INDEPENDENCE HYPOTHESIS The *independence hypothesis* takes the position that affect and cognition involve two separate, partially independent systems; affective responses do not always require prior cognitions.[14] A number one song on the *Billboard* Top 40 may possess the same attributes as many other songs (e.g., dominant bass guitar, raspy vocals, persistent downbeat), but beliefs about these attributes cannot explain why one song becomes a classic while another sharing the same characteristics winds up in the bargain bin at the local record store. The independence hypothesis does not *eliminate* the role of cognition in experience. It simply balances this traditional, rational emphasis on calculated decision making by paying more attention to the impact of aesthetic, subjective experience. This type of holistic processing is more likely to occur when the product is perceived as primarily expressive or delivers sensory pleasure rather than utilitarian benefits.[15]

ATTITUDE TOWARD THE ADVERTISEMENT Consumers' affective reactions to a product are influenced by their evaluations of its advertising, over and above their feelings about the product itself. The **attitude toward the advertisement (A_{ad})** is defined as a predisposition to respond in a favorable or unfavorable manner to a particular advertising stimulus during a particular exposure occasion. Determinants of A_{ad} include attitude toward the advertiser, evaluations of the ad execution itself, the mood evoked by the ad, and the degree to which the ad affects viewers' arousal levels.[16] A viewer's feelings about the context in which an ad appears can also influence brand attitudes. For example, attitudes about an ad and the brand depicted will be influenced if the consumer sees the ad while watching a favorite TV program.[17] The effects demonstrated by A_{ad} emphasize the importance of an ad's entertainment value on the purchase process.[18]

Feelings Elicited by Advertising. The feelings generated by an ad have the capacity to directly affect brand attitudes. Commercials can evoke a wide range of emotional responses, from disgust to happiness, as illustrated in the ad for an egg substitute on the next page. These reactions can in turn influence memory for advertising content.[19] At least three emotional dimensions have been identified in commercials: pleasure, arousal, and intimidation.[20] Specific types of feelings that can be generated by an ad include the following.[21]

- *Upbeat feelings:* amused, delighted, playful
- *Warm feelings:* affectionate, contemplative, hopeful
- *Negative feelings:* critical, defiant, offended

Teaching Hint: Recent evidence indicates that the effects of A_{ad} may be short-lived. In addition, a likable ad may even lower brand attitudes over time because it may focus attention away from brand claims. See Amitava Chattopadhyay and Prakash Nedungadi, "Does Attitude Toward the Ad Endure? The Moderating Effects of Attention and Delay," *Journal of Consumer Research* 19 (June1992): 26–33.

Research Report: While A_{ad} does appear to affect brand attitudes, its impact can be inflated when items measuring the two components are presented contiguously, rather than being separated by filler items. This effect is particularly pronounced for brands that are familiar to the respondent. See Karen A. Machleit and Arti Sahni, "The Impact of Measurement Context on the Relationship Between Attitude Toward the Ad and Brand Attitude for Familiar Brands," in *Advances in Consumer Research* 19, eds. John F. Sherry, Jr., and Brian Sternthal (Provo, Utah: Association for Consumer Research, 1992), 279–83.

Until now, your customers have had some definite opinions about healthier eggs.

Introducing EggStro'dnaire.™ EggStro'dnaire is an incredible alternative to shell eggs that will definitely increase your sales. And revolutionize your breakfast menu. All because they taste exactly like shell eggs. And not like egg substitutes.

EggStro'dnaire will sell. And not just to people with health concerns. But to anyone who likes eggs. And we can prove it.

In numerous scientific taste panels, blind taste tests with executive hotel chefs and restaurant menu tests, EggStro'dnaire's taste, texture and appearance proved to be indistinguishable from shell eggs.

Which isn't surprising since EggStro'dnaire is 98% real egg and 100% natural. With 78% less cholesterol, 67% less fat and 50% fewer calories than shell eggs. There are no artificial ingredients or preservatives. So they taste like the real McCoy.

And they're very convenient. EggStro'dnaire is available frozen in twelve, 16-oz. or six, 5-lb. cartons. Just thaw and use in any egg recipe.

For more information, talk to your distributor sales representative. Find out how EggStro'dnaire can definitely become your bread and butter.

EggStro'dnaire™
The healthy egg alternative.

Food Service
SANDOZNUTRITION

This ad for EggStro'dinaire, an egg substitute, illustrates that ads are capable of communicating negative feelings. Courtesy of Food Service Division, Sandoz Nutrition, Minneapolis, MN 55416.

MARKETING PITFALL

In a study of irritating advertising, researchers examined over 500 prime time network commercials that had registered negative reactions by consumers. The most irritating commercials were for feminine hygiene products, hemorrhoid medication or laxatives, and women's underwear. The researchers identified the following factors as contributors to irritation.[22]

- A sensitive product is shown (e.g., hemorrhoid medicine), and its use or package is emphasized.
- The situation is contrived or overdramatized.
- A person is put down in terms of appearance, knowledge, or sophistication.
- An important relationship is threatened (e.g., a marriage).
- There is a graphic demonstration of physical discomfort.
- Uncomfortable tension is created by an argument or by an antagonistic character.
- An unattractive or unsympathetic character is portrayed.

be receptive to communications urging her to play this role before heading out for an evening on the town. If she were opposed to this practice, these messages would probably not be considered.

Assimilation and Contrast. Messages that fall within the latitude of acceptance tend to be seen as *more* consistent with one's position than they actually are. This process is called an *assimilation effect*. On the other hand, messages falling in the latitude of rejection tend to be seen as even farther from one's position than they actually are, resulting in a *contrast effect*.

As a person becomes more involved with an attitude object, his or her latitude of acceptance gets smaller. In other words, the consumer accepts fewer ideas that are removed from his or her own position and tends to oppose even mildly divergent positions. This tendency is evident in ads that appeal to discriminating buyers, which claim that knowledgeable people will reject anything but the very best (e.g., "choosy mothers choose Jif"). On the other hand, relatively uninvolved consumers will consider a wider range of alternatives. They are less likely to be brand loyal and will be more likely to be brand switchers.[35]

BALANCE THEORY   **Balance theory** considers relations among elements a person might perceive as belonging together.[36] This perspective involves relations (always from the perceiver's subjective point of view) among three elements, so the resulting attitude structures are called *triads*. Each triad contains (1) a person and his or her perceptions of (2) an attitude object and (3) some other person or object. These perceptions can be either positive or negative. More important, people *alter* these perceptions in order to make relations among them consistent. The theory specifies that people desire relations among elements in a triad to be harmonious, or *balanced*. If they are not, a state of tension will result until somehow perceptions are changed and balance is restored.

Elements can be perceived as going together in one of two ways. They can have either a *unit relation*, where one element is seen as somehow belonging to or being a part of the other (something like a belief) or a *sentiment relation*, where the two elements are linked because one has expressed a preference (or dislike) for the other. A dating couple might be seen as having a positive sentiment relation. Upon getting married, they will have a positive unit relation. The process of divorce is an attempt to sever a unit relation.

To see how balance theory might work, consider the following scenario:

- Noreen would like to date Sal, who is in her Consumer Behavior class. In balance theory terms, Noreen has a positive sentiment relation with Sal.
- One day, Sal shows up in class wearing an earring. Sal has a positive unit relation with the earring. It belongs to him and is literally a part of him.
- Noreen does not like men who wear earrings. She has a negative sentiment relation with men's earrings.

According to balance theory, Noreen faces an unbalanced triad, and she will experience pressure to restore balance by altering some aspect of the triad as shown in Figure 5–2. She could, for example, decide that she does not like Sal after all. Or, her liking for Sal could prompt a change in her atti-

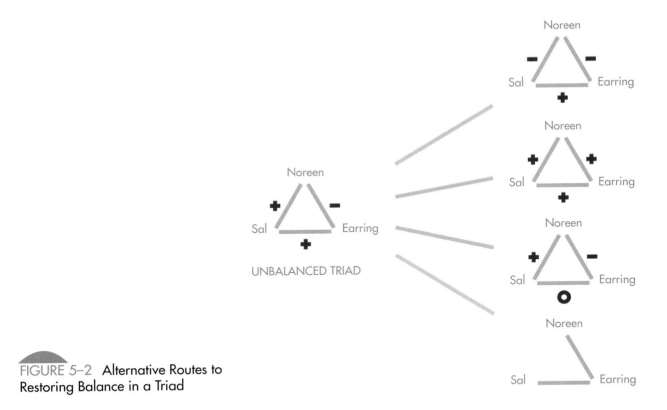

FIGURE 5–2 is available as Transparency 12.

FIGURE 5–2 Alternative Routes to Restoring Balance in a Triad

Teaching Hint: The easy way to determine if a triad is balanced is to use the multiplicative rule—a positive times a positive is positive, a positive times a negative is negative, and a negative times a negative is positive. Simply multiply all three signs in a triad to determine if it is stable.

tude toward earrings. She might even try to negate the unit relation between Sal and the earring by deciding that he must be only wearing it as part of a fraternity initiation (thus reducing the free-choice element). Finally, she could choose to "leave the field" by not thinking any more about Sal and his controversial earring.

Note that while the theory does not specify which of these routes will be taken, it does predict that one or more of Noreen's perceptions will probably change in order to achieve balance. While this distortion is most likely an oversimplified representation of most attitude processes, it helps to explain a number of consumer behavior phenomena.

Marketing Applications of Balance Theory. Balance theory reminds us that when perceptions are balanced, attitudes are likely to be stable. On the other hand, when inconsistencies are observed, we are more likely to observe changes in attitudes. Balance theory also helps to explain why consumers like to be associated with positively valued objects. Forming a unit relation with a popular product (e.g., buying and wearing fashionable clothing, driving a flashy car) may improve one's chances of being included as a positive sentiment relation in other people's triads.

Finally, balance theory is useful in accounting for the widespread use of celebrities to endorse products. In cases where a triad is not fully formed (e.g., perceptions about a new product or one about which the consumer does not yet have a well-defined attitude), the marketer can create a positive sentiment relation between the consumer and the product by depicting a positive unit relation between the product and a well-known personality. In other cases, behaviors are discouraged when admired people argue against them, as is the goal when athletes appear in anti-drug public service advertisements.

This balancing act is at the heart of celebrity endorsements, where it is hoped that the star's popularity will transfer to the product. This strategy will be considered at length in the next chapter. For now, it pays to remember that this creation of a unit relation between product and star can backfire if the public's opinion of the celebrity endorser shifts from positive to negative, as happened when Pepsi pulled an ad featuring Madonna after she was associated with a controversial music video involving religion and sex. The strategy can also cause trouble if the star-product unit relation is questioned, as happened when singer Michael Jackson, who also did promotions for Pepsi, subsequently confessed that he does not drink soda.

MARKETING OPPORTUNITY

Consumers often like to publicize their connections with successful people or organizations (no matter how tenuous the connection) to enhance their own standing. In balance theory terms, they are attempting to create a unit relation with a positively valued attitude object. This tactic has been called "basking in reflected glory."[37]

For example, a series of studies performed at Arizona State University showed how students' desire to identify with a winning image—in this case, ASU's football team—influenced their consumption behaviors. After the team played a game each weekend, observers went around campus and recorded the incidence of school-related items displayed by students (e.g., ASU T-shirts, caps, etc.). The frequency of these behaviors was related to the team's performance. If the team had won, students were more likely to show off their school affiliation (basking in reflected glory) than if the team had lost. This relationship was affected by the magnitude of the win—the bigger the point spread, the more likely were observers to note a sea of ASU insignias the following Monday.

The desire to bask in reflected glory by purchasing products associated with a valued attitude object has created numerous marketing opportunities. College bookstores reap over $400 million a year by selling items bearing their school's name and logo, and the total market for collegiate licensing amounts to about $750 million annually. The UCLA bookstore alone sells $5 million worth of Bruin items a year. Many schools now license their names (usually for a 6.5 percent royalty) to get a stake in this market. Because people tend to identify with successful teams, it is not surprising that the most successful licensing universities also happen to have renowned athletic programs, including Michigan, Ohio State, Florida, Penn State, Texas, Kentucky, Alabama, Florida State, Indiana, and Washington.[38]

Teaching Hint: The theory
specifically addresses the
linking of two attitude objects
by an **assertion** (usually a
person who is positively or
negatively regarded making
a statement about an object
that also is positively or negatively valued). One of the
advantages of the theory
compared to balance theory
is that it allows the analyst to
consider degrees of positivity
or negativity instead of global
good–bad judgments.

CONGRUITY THEORY   **Congruity theory** is yet another consistency theory that, like balance theory, specifically addresses how attitudes are affected when a person is linked to an object.[39] Congruity theory can help to answer two questions regarding the effectiveness of this strategy. Assuming that we can measure the appeal (positive or negative) of an endorser and the favorability of a product:

1. How big a boost would a product get by being paired with the endorser?
2. How will the *endorser's* reputation be affected by his or her connection with the product?

Congruity theory predicts that the value of the more negatively valued element will rise (as a company would hope) when linked to a positively valued one such as a popular personality. In addition, though, the positively valued element will be affected: Its ratings will be *diminished* by its association with the first element. The implication here is that a person or organization that is linked to some other entity does so at some risk. This process helps to explain why some media outlets are careful to select advertisers whose images are congruent with their own. For example, the high-fashion magazine *Mirabella* denies space to such mass market products as Maybelline and Avon cosmetics and Jaclyn Smith clothes for KMart. As its publisher explained, "We wanted to be perceived as a "department store"

FIGURE 5–3   A Hypothetical Example of Congruity Theory: A Model of Attitude Polarization

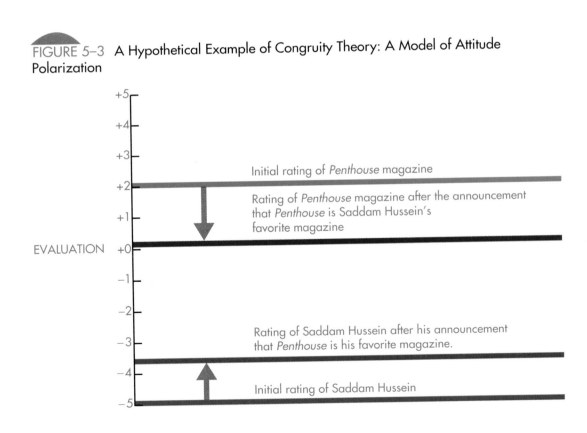

162   CHAPTER 5 • ATTITUDES

magazine. We're talking about Armani or Calvin Klein or Bulgari jewelry, not furnishing your home from Woolworth's."[40]

However, the two elements will not change equally: Change is inversely proportional to degree of *attitude polarization*. In plain English, this means that the more extremely related object will change its value less than will the more moderate one. To understand this effect, suppose that an extremely negative source (say, Saddam Hussein of Iraq) stated publicly that *Penthouse* (rated somewhat positively) was his favorite magazine. The image of *Penthouse* would drop to a greater degree than that of Hussein would rise. The attitude polarization process is depicted in Figure 5–3.

Congruity theory was used to investigate the impact of brand and retailer images on perceptions of quality. One catalyst for this study was the decision by the designer Halston (who had a very upscale image) to create a clothing line for J.C. Penney (a more downscale image). This study found that, consistent with congruity theory predictions, arrangements between stores and brands should be entered into carefully. While a store or brand can boost its image by associating itself with a more prestigious entity, the gain may happen at the expense of the other party.[41]

Additional Examples: *Conde Nast Travele*r magazine rejected ads for *Keebler Chips Deluxe Cookies*, and *Architectural Digest and Bon Appetit will not* accept pet food ads. See Karen Springen and Annetta Miller, "When Ads Don't Fit the 'Image'," *Newsweek* (January 22, 1990): 48.

Attitude Models

As noted earlier, a consumer's overall evaluation of a product appears to account for the bulk of his or her attitude. When market researchers want to assess attitudes, it is sometimes sufficient for them to simply ask consumers "How do you feel about Budweiser?" or "How satisfied are you with your grocery store?"

Attitude Measurement

Suppose a supermarket chain wanted to measure shoppers' attitudes toward its stores. The firm might administer one of the following types of attitude scales to consumers by mail, phone, or in person (see Chapter 1).[42]

Single-Item Scales. One simple way to assess consumer's attitudes toward a store or product is to ask them for their overall feelings about it. Such a global assessment does not provide much information about specific attributes, but it does give managers some sense of consumers' overall attitudes. This single-item approach often uses a *Likert scale*, which measures respondents' overall level of agreement or feelings about an attitude statement:

How satisfied are you with your grocery store?

Very satisfied	Satisfied	Somewhat satisfied	Not at all satisfied

Multiple-Item Batteries. Many attitude measures assess a set of beliefs about an issue and combine these reactions into an overall score. For example, the supermarket might ask customers to respond to a set of Likert scales and then combine consumers' responses into an overall measure of store satisfaction:

1. My grocery store has a good selection of produce.
2. My grocery store maintains sanitary conditions.
3. I never have trouble finding exotic foods at my grocery store.

| Agree strongly | Agree somewhat | Neither agree nor disagree | Disagree somewhat | Disagree strongly |

The *semantic-differential scale* is useful for a describing a person's set of beliefs about a company or brand, and it is also used to compare the images of competing brands. Respondents rate each attribute on a series of rating scales, where each end is anchored by adjectives or phrases:

My grocery store is

Dirty   1—2—3—4—5—6—7   Clean

Semantic-differential scales can be used to construct a *profile analysis* of the competition, where the images of several stores or products can be visually compared by plotting the mean ratings for each object on several attributes of interest. This simple technique can help to pinpoint areas where the product or store diverges sharply from the competitors (in either a positive or a negative way). The fictitious profiles of three different types of grocery stores are shown in Figure 5–4. Based on these findings, the management of

FIGURE 5–4 Hypothetical Profiles of Three Types of Food Stores

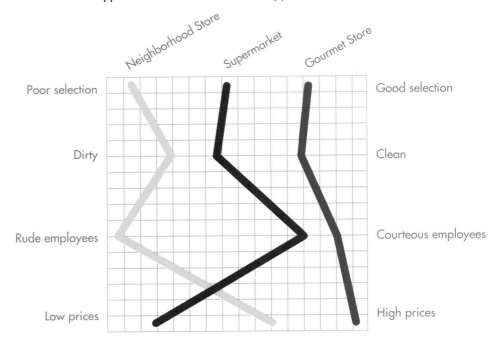

the supermarket chain might want to emphasize its low prices and/or try to improve its stores' selection and cleanliness.

Multi-Attribute Attitude Models

A simple response does not always tell us everything we need to know about either *why* the consumer feels a certain way toward a product or about what marketers can do to change the consumer's attitude. For this reason, **multi-attribute attitude models** have been extremely popular among marketing researchers. This type of model assumes that a consumer's attitude (evaluation) of an attitude object (A_0) will depend on the beliefs he or she has about several or many attributes of the object. The use of a multi-attribute model implies that an attitude toward a product or brand can be predicted by identifying these specific beliefs and combining them to derive a measure of the consumer's overall attitude.

Basic multi-attribute models specify three elements.[43]

- *Attributes* are characteristics of the A_0. Most models assume that the relevant characteristics can be identified. That is, the researcher can include those attributes that consumers take into consideration when evaluating the A_0. For example, scholarly reputation is an attribute of a university.
- *Beliefs* are cognitions about the specific A_0 (usually relative to others like it). A belief measure assesses the extent to which the consumer perceives that a brand possesses a particular attribute. For example, a student might have a belief that the University of Michigan has a strong academic standing.
- *Importance weights* reflect the relative priority of an attribute to the consumer. Although an A_0 can be considered on a number of attributes, some are likely to be more important than others (i.e., they will be given greater weight). And, these weights are likely to differ across consumers. In the case of universities, for example, one student might stress library resources, while another might weight athletic programs more heavily.

THE FISHBEIN MODEL The most influential multi-attribute model is called the Fishbein model, after its primary developer.[44] The model measures three components of attitude:

1. *Salient beliefs* people have about an A_0 (i.e., those beliefs about the object that are considered during evaluation)
2. *Object-attribute linkages*, or the probability that a particular object has an important attribute
3. *Evaluation* of each of the important attributes

Note, however, that the model makes some assumptions that may not always be warranted. It assumes that we have been able to adequately specify all of the relevant attributes that, for example, a student will use in evaluating his or her choices about which college to attend. The model also assumes that he or she will go through the process (formally or informally) of identifying a set of relevant attributes, weighing them, and summing them. Although this particular decision is likely to be highly involving, it is still possible that his or her attitude will instead be formed by an overall affective response (a process known as *affect-referral*).

Combining the Elements in a Multi-Attribute Model. By combining these three elements, a consumer's overall attitude toward an object can be computed (we'll see later how this basic equation has been modified to increase its accuracy). The basic formula is

$$A_{ijk} = \Sigma B_{ijk} I_{ik}$$

where i = attribute

j = brand

k = consumer

I = the importance weight given attribute i by consumer k

B = consumer k's belief regarding the extent to which brand j possesses attribute i

A = a particular consumer's (k's) attitude score for brand j

The overall attitude score (A) is obtained by multiplying a consumer's rating of each attribute for all of the brands considered, by the importance rating for that attribute.

To see how this basic multi-attribute model might work, let's suppose we want to predict which college a high school senior is likely to attend. After months of waiting, Saundra has been accepted to four schools. Since she must now decide among these, we would first like to know which attributes Saundra will consider in forming an attitude toward each school. We can then ask Saundra to assign a rating regarding how well each school performs on each attribute and also determine the relative importance of the attributes to her. An overall attitude score for each school can then be computed by summing scores on each attribute (after weighing each by its relative importance). These hypothetical ratings are shown in Table 5–1. Based on this analysis, it seems that Saundra has the most favorable attitude toward Smith. She is clearly someone who would like to attend an all-woman's school with a solid academic reputation rather than a school that offers a strong athletic program or a party atmosphere.

STRATEGIC APPLICATIONS OF THE MULTI-ATTRIBUTE MODEL Suppose you were the Director of Marketing for King County Community College, another school Saundra was considering. How might you use the data from this analysis to improve your image?

Capitalize on Relative Advantage. If one's brand is viewed as being superior on a particular attribute, consumers like Saundra need to be convinced that this particular attribute is an important one. For example, while Saundra rates King's social atmosphere highly, she does not believe this attribute is a valued aspect for a college. As King's Marketing Director, you

TABLE 5–1   The Basic Multi-Attribute Model: Saundra's College Decision

Attribute (i)	Importance (I)	Beliefs (B)			
		Smith	Princeton	Rutgers	King County Community College
Academic reputation	6	8	9	6	3
All women	7	9	3	3	3
Cost	4	2	2	6	9
Proximity to home	3	2	2	6	9
Athletics	1	1	2	5	1
Party atmosphere	2	1	3	7	9
Library facilities	5	7	9	7	2
Attitude score		163	142	153	131

Note: These hypothetical ratings are scored from 1 to 10, where higher numbers indicate "better" standing on an attribute. For a negative attribute (e.g., cost), higher scores indicate that the school is believed to have "less" of that attribute (i.e., to be cheaper).

might emphasize the importance of an active social life, varied experiences, or even the development of future business contacts forged through strong college friendships.

Strengthen Perceived Product/Attribute Linkages. A marketer may discover that consumers do not equate his or her brand with a certain attribute. This problem is commonly addressed by campaigns that stress the product's qualities to consumers (e.g., "new and improved"). Saundra apparently does not think much of King's academic quality, athletic programs, or library facilities. You might develop an informational campaign to improve these perceptions (e.g., "little known facts about King").

Add a New Attribute. Product marketers frequently try to create a distinctive position from their competitors by adding a product feature. King Community College might try to emphasize some unique aspect, such as a hands-on internship program for business majors that takes advantage of ties to the local community.

Influence Competitors' Ratings. Finally, you might try to decrease the positivity of competitors. This type of action is the rationale for a strategy of *comparative advertising*. One tactic might be to publish an ad that lists the tuition rates of a number of area schools, as well as their attributes

This Chrysler ad is an example of comparative advertising, where the attributes of competitors are specifically considered in the message. © 1989 Chrysler Corporation, used with permission.

with which King can be favorably compared, as the basis for emphasizing the value obtained for the money at King. Note that Chrysler has used this strategy in the comparative ad shown here.

Using Attitudes to Predict Behavior

Although multi-attribute models like the Fishbein model have been used by consumer researchers for many years, they have been plagued by a major problem: In many cases, knowledge of a person's attitude is *not* a very good predictor of behavior. In a classic demonstration of "do as I say, not as I do," many studies have obtained a very low correlation between a person's reported attitude toward something and his or her actual behavior toward it. Some researchers have been so discouraged that they have questioned whether attitudes are of any use at all in understanding behavior.[45]

The Extended Fishbein Model

The original Fishbein model, which focused on measuring a consumer's attitude toward a product, has been extended in several ways to improve its predictive ability. The newer version is called the **theory of reasoned action**.[46] This model contains several important additions to the original, and while the model is still not perfect, adoption of this version has improved on its ability to predict relevant behaviors in some cases.[47]

INTENTIONS VERSUS BEHAVIOR Many factors might interfere with performance of actual behavior, even if the consumer has sincere intentions. He or she might save up with the intention of buying a stereo system. In the interim, though, any number of things could happen: losing a job, getting mugged on the way to the store, or arriving at the store to find that the desired model is out of stock. It is not surprising, then, that in some instances past purchase behavior has been found to be a better predictor of future behavior than is a consumer's behavioral intention.[48] The theory of reasoned action aims to measure behavioral intentions, recognizing that certain uncontrollable factors inhibit prediction of actual behavior.

SOCIAL PRESSURE The theory acknowledges the power of other people in influencing behavior. Many of our behaviors are not determined in a vacuum. Much as we may hate to admit it, what we think others would *like* us to do may be more crucial than our own individual preferences.

In the case of Saundra's college choice, note that she was very positive about going to a predominantly female school. However, if she felt that this choice would be unpopular (perhaps her friends would think she was crazy), she might ignore or downgrade this preference when coming to a decision. A new element, the *subjective norm* (SN) was thus added to include the effects of what we believe other people think we should do. The value of SN is arrived at by including two other factors: (1) the intensity of a *normative belief* (NB) that others believe an action should be taken or not taken, and (2) the *motivation to comply* (MC) with that belief (i.e., the degree to which the consumer takes others' anticipated reactions into account when evaluating a course of action or a purchase).

ATTITUDE TOWARD BUYING The model now measures **attitude toward the act of buying** (A_{act}), rather than only the attitude toward the product itself. In other words, it focuses on the perceived consequences of a purchase. Knowing how someone feels about buying or using an object turns out to be more valid than merely knowing the consumer's evaluation of the object itself.[49] To understand this distinction, consider a problem that might arise when measuring attitudes toward condoms. Although a group of college students might have a positive attitude toward condoms, does this necessarily predict that they will buy and use them? Better prediction would be obtained by asking the students how likely they are to *buy* condoms. While a person might have a positive A_o toward condoms, A_{act} might be negative due to the embarrassment or the hassle involved.

Obstacles to Predicting Behavior

Despite improvements to the Fishbein model, problems arise when it is misapplied. In many cases, the model is used in ways for which it was not intended, or where certain assumptions about human behavior may not be warranted.[50] Other obstacles to predicting behavior follow.

- The model was developed to deal with actual behavior (e.g., taking a diet pill), not with the *outcomes* of behavior that are instead assessed in some studies (e.g., losing weight).

Research Report: One recent study assessed the effects of elements of the theory of reasoned action as well as past behavior in the context of coupon usage. See Richard P. Bagozzi, Hans Baumgartner, and Youjae Yi, "State Versus Action Orientation and the Theory of Reasoned Action: An Application to Coupon Usage," *Journal of Consumer Research* 18 (March 1992): 505–18.

Research Report: Other researchers have also advocated distinguishing between normative and personal motivations underlying behavior by adding another component, *personal normative beliefs* (NB_p) to the norm component of the theory of reasoned action. See Paul W. Miniard and Joel B. Cohen, "Modeling Personal and Normative Influences on Behavior," *Journal of Consumer Research* 10 (September 1983): 169–80.

- Some outcomes are beyond the consumer's control, such as when the purchase requires the cooperation of other people. For instance, a woman might *want* to get a mortgage, but this intention will be worthless if she cannot find a banker to give her one.

- The basic assumption that behavior is intentional may be invalid in a variety of cases, including impulsive acts, sudden changes in one's situation, novelty seeking, or even simple repeat buying. One study found that such unexpected events as having guests, changes in the weather, or reading articles about the healthfulness of certain foods exerted a significant effect on actual behaviors.[51]

Research Report: Emotional experiences have been studied as predictors of behavior. See Chris T. Allen, Karen A. Machleit, and Susan Schultz Kleine, "A Comparison of Attitudes and Emotions as Predictors of Behavior at Diverse Levels of Behavioral Experience," *Journal of Consumer Research* 18 (March 1992): 493–504.

- Measures of attitude often do not really correspond to the behavior they are supposed to predict, either in terms of the A_o or when the act will occur. One common problem is a difference in the level of *abstraction* employed. For example, knowing a person's attitude toward sports cars may not predict whether he or she will purchase a Nissan 300ZX. It is very important to match the level of specificity between the attitude and the behavioral intention.

- A similar problem relates to the *time-frame* of the attitude measure. In general, the longer the time between the attitude measurement and the behavior it is supposed to assess, the weaker the relationship will be. For example, predictability would improve markedly by asking consumers the likelihood that they would buy a house in the next week as opposed to within the next five years.

MULTICULTURAL DIMENSIONS

The theory of reasoned action has primarily been applied in Western settings. Certain assumptions inherent in the model may not necessarily apply to consumers from other cultures. Several cultural roadblocks diminish the universality of the theory of reasoned action.

- The model was developed to predict the performance of any voluntary act. Across cultures, however, many consumer activities, ranging from taking exams and entering military service to receiving an inoculation or even choosing a marriage partner, are not necessarily voluntary.

- The relative impact of subjective norms may vary across cultures. For example, Asian cultures tend to value conformity and "face-saving," so it is possible some subjective these consumers.

- The model measures behavioral intentions, and thus presupposes that consumers are actively thinking ahead and planning future behaviors. The intention concept assumes that consumers have a linear time sense; they think in terms of past, present, and future. As will be discussed in Chapter 10, this perspective on time is not held by all cultures.

- A consumer who forms an intention is (implicitly) claiming that he or she is in control of his or her actions. Some cultures (e.g., Muslim peoples) tend to be fatalistic and do not necessarily believe in the concept of free will. Indeed, one study comparing students from the United States, Jordan, and Thailand found evidence for cultural differences in assumptions about fatalism and control over the future.[52]

Lisa's attitudes about drinking and driving suggest that she is a socially responsible person. We might expect that her attitudes about the environment would be consistent with her general attitudes about social responsibility (as evidenced by her attitudes toward drinking and driving).

Your Simmons file for this chapter contains consumer attitudes on seventeen environmental issues. The disk also contains information on how willing consumers are to incur the cost of more "environmentally responsible" behavior. If "Green Marketing" is to succeed it is critical that marketers identify those consumer groups whose attitudes are most favorable to greater environmental responsibility.

Consider the demographic variables provided on your disk and generate a profile of those consumers whose attitudes are most consistent with the "Green Movement." Is this group also willing to pay for environmentally sound practices? Is education an important variable in distinguishing among different attitudes toward the environment? Is age? Why do you think these characteristics are (are not) good predictors of environmental attitudes? [*Hint:* It may be easier to work with the data if you average the index values across the "Agree" columns for the environmental issues.]

Notes

1. Seymour H. Fine, *Social Marketing: Promoting the Causes of Public and Nonprofit Agengies* (Boston: Allyn & Bacon, 1990); Katryna Malafarina and Barbara Loken, "Progress and Limitations of Social Marketing: A Review of Empirical Literature on the Consumption of Social Ideas," in *Advances in Consumer Research* 20, eds. Leigh McAllister and Michael Rothschild (Provo, Utah: Association for Consumer Research, in press).

2. Quoted in Cecelia Reed, "Partners for Life," *Advertising Age* (November 9, 1988): 122.

3. Dennis T. Lowry and David E. Towles, "Prime Time TV Portrayals of Sex, Contraception and Venereal Diseases," *Journalism Quarterly* 86 (Summer 1989): 347–52.

4. Quoted in Molly O'Neill, "Words to Survive Life With: None of This, None of That," *New York Times* (May 27, 1990): 1.

5. Bill Carter, "A Message on Drinking is Seen and Heard," *New York Times* (September 11, 1989): D11.

6. Robert A. Baron and Donn Byrne, *Social Psychology: Understanding Human Interaction*, 5th ed. (Boston: Allyn & Bacon, 1987).

7. Daniel Katz, "The Functional Approach to the Study of Attitudes," Public Opinion Quarterly 24 (Summer 1960): 163–204; Richard J. Lutz, "Changing Brand Attitudes through Modification of Cognitive Structure," *Journal of Consumer Research* 1 (March 1975): 49–59.

8. Russell H. Fazio, T.M. Lenn, and E.A. Effrein, "Spontaneous Attitude Formation," *Social Cognition* 2 (1984) :214–34.

9. Mason Haire, "Projective Techniques in Marketing Research," *Journal of Marketing* 14 (April 1950): 649–56.

10. Sharon Shavitt, "The Role of Attitude Objects in Attitude Functions," *Journal of Experimental Social Psychology* 26 (1990): 124–48; see also J.S. Johar and M. Joseph Sirgy, "Value-Expressive Versus Utilitarian Advertising Appeals: When and Why to Use Which Appeal," *Journal of Advertising* 20 (September 1991): 23–34.

11. Michael Ray, "Marketing Communications and the Hierarchy-of-Effects," in *New Models for Mass Communications*, ed. P. Clarke (Beverly Hills, Calif.: Sage, 1973), 147–76.

12. Herbert Krugman, "The Impact of Television Advertising: Learning Without Involvement," *Public Opinion Quarterly* 29 (Fall 1965): 349–56; Robert Lavidge and Gary Steiner, "A Model for Predictive Measurements of Advertising Effectiveness," *Journal of Marketing* 25 (October 1961): 59–62.

13. Punam Anand, Morris B. Holbrook, and Debra Stephens, "The Formation of Affective Judgments: The Cognitive-Affective Model Versus the Independence Hypothesis," *Journal of Consumer Research* 15 (December 1988): 386–91; Richard S. Lazarus, "Thoughts on the Relations Between Emotion and Cognition," *American Psychologist* 37 (1982)9: 1019–24.

14. Robert B. Zajonc, "Feeling and Thinking: Preferences Need No Inferences," *American Psychologist* 35 (1980)2: 151–75.

15. Banwari Mittal, "The Role of Affective Choice Mode in the Consumer Purchase of Expressive Products," *Journal of Economic Psychology* 4 (1988)9: 499–524.

16. Scot Burton and Donald R. Lichtenstein, "The Effect of Ad Claims and Ad Context on Attitude Toward the Advertisement," *Journal of Advertising*

17 (1988)1: 3–11; Karen A. Machleit and R. Dale Wilson, "Emotional Feelings and Attitude Toward the Advertisement: The Roles of Brand Familiarity and Repetition," *Journal of Advertising* 17 (1988)3: 27–35; Scott B. Mackenzie and Richard J. Lutz, "An Empirical Examination of the Structural Antecedents of Attitude Toward the Ad in an Advertising Pretesting Context," Journal of Marketing 53 (April 1989): 48–65; Scott B. Mackenzie, Richard J. Lutz, and George E. Belch, "The Role of Attitude Toward the Ad as a Mediator of Advertising Effectiveness: A Test of Competing Explanations,"*Journal of Marketing Research* 23 (May 1986): 130–43; Darrel D. Muehling and Russell N. Laczniak, "Advertising's Immediate and Delayed Influence on Brand Attitudes: Considerations Across Message-Involvement Levels," *Journal of Advertising* 17 (1988)4: 23–34; Mark A. Pavelchak, Meryl P. Gardner, and V. Carter Broach, "Effect of Ad Pacing and Optimal Level of Arousal on Attitude Toward the Ad," in Advances in Consumer Research 18, eds. Rebecca H. Holman and Michael R. Solomon (Provo, Utah: Association for Consumer Research, 1991), 94–99. Some research evidence indicates that a separate attitude is also formed regarding the brand name itself, see George M. Zinkhan and Claude R. Martin, Jr., "New Brand Names and Inferential Beliefs: Some Insights on Naming New Products," *Journal of Business Research* 15 (1987): 157–72.

17. John P. Murry, Jr., John L. Lastovicka, and Surendra N. Singh, "Feeling and Liking Responses to Television Programs: An Examination of Two Explanations for Media-Context Effects," *Journal of Consumer Research* 18 (March 1992): 441–51.

18. Barbara Stern and Judith Lynne Zaichkowsky, "The Impact of 'Entertaining' Advertising on Consumer Responses," *Australian Marketing Researcher* 14 (August 1991): 68–80.

19. Basil G. Englis, "Consumer Emotional Reactions to Television Advertising and Their Effects on Message Recall," in *Emotion in Advertising: Theoretical and Practical Explorations*, eds. S. Agres, J.A. Edell, and T.M. Dubitsky (Westport, Conn.: Quorum Books, 1990), 231–54.

20. Morris B. Holbrook and Rajeev Batra, "Assessing the Role of Emotions as Mediators of Consumer Responses to Advertising," *Journal of Consumer Research* 14 (December 1987): 404–20.

21. Marian Burke and Julie Edell, "Ad Reactions Over Time: Capturing Changes in the Real World," *Journal of Consumer Research* 13 (June 1986): 114–18.

22. David A. Aaker and Donald E. Bruzzone, "Causes of Irritation in Advertising," *Journal of Marketing* 49 (Spring 1985): 47–57.

23. Herbert Kelman, "Compliance, Identification, and Internalization: Three Processes of Attitude Change," *Journal of Conflict Resolution* 2 (1958): 51–60.

24. See Sharon E. Beatty and Lynn R. Kahle, "Alternative Hierarchies of the Attitude-Behavior Relationship: The Impact of Brand Commitment and Habit," *Journal of the Academy of Marketing Science* 16 (Summer 1988): 1–10.

25. Jack Brehm, A Theory of Psychological Reactance (New York: Academic Press, 1966).

26. Michael B. Mazis, Robert B. Settle, and D.C. Leslie, "Elimination of Phosphate Detergents and Psychological Reactance," *Journal of Marketing Research* 10 (1973): 390–95.

27. Greg J. Lessne and Elaine M. Notarantonio, "The Effect of Limits in Retail Advertisements: A Reactance Theory Perspective," *Psychology & Marketing* 5 (1988)1: 33–44.

28. Leon Festinger, *A Theory of Cognitive Dissonance* (Stanford, Calif.: Stanford University Press, 1957).

29. Chester A. Insko and John Schopler, Experimental *Social Psychology* (New York: Academic Press, 1972).

30. Robert E. Knox and James A. Inkster, "Postdecision Dissonance at Post Time," *Journal of Personality and Social Psychology* 8 (1968)4: 319–23.

31. Daryl J. Bem, "Self-Perception Theory," in Advan-ces in Experimental Social Psychology, ed. Leonard Berkowitz (New York: Academic Press, 1972), 1–62.

32. Jonathan L. Freedman and Scott C. Fraser, "Compliance Without Pressure: The Foot-in-the-Door Technique," *Journal of Personality and Social Psychology* 4 (August 1966): 195–202; for further consideration of possible explanations for this effect, see William DeJong, "An Examination of Self-Perception Mediation of the Foot-in-the-Door Effect," *Journal of Personality and Social Psychology* 37 (December 1979): 221–31; Alice M. Tybout, Brian Sternthal, and Bobby J. Calder, "Information Availability as a Determinant of Multiple-Request Effectiveness," *Journal of Marketing Research* 20 (August 1988): 280–90.

33. David H. Furse, David W. Stewart, and David L. Rados, "Effects of Foot-in-the-Door, Cash Incentives and Follow-ups on Survey Response," *Journal of Marketing Research* 18 (November 1981): 473–78; Carol A. Scott, "The Effects of Trial and Incentives on Repeat Purchase Behavior," *Journal of Marketing Research* 13 (August 1976): 263–69.

34. Muzafer Sherif and Carl I. Hovland, *Social Judgment: Assimilation and Contrast Effects in Communication and Attitude Change* (New Haven,

Conn.: Yale University Press, 1961).

35. Mark B. Traylor, "Product Involvement and Brand Commitment," *Journal of Advertising Research* (December 1981): 51–56.

36. Fritz Heider, *The Psychology of Interpersonal Relations* (New York: Wiley, 1958).

37. R.B. Cialdini, R.J. Borden, A. Thorne, M.R. Walker, S. Freeman, and L.R. Sloan, "Basking in Reflected Glory: Three (Football) Field Studies," *Journal of Personality and Social Psychology* 34 (1976): 366–75.

38. Howard G. Ruben, "College Stores Cash in on School Logos," *Daily News Record* (May 20, 1987): 1.

39. Charles E. Osgood and Percy H. Tannenbaum, "The Principle of Congruity in the Production of Attitude Change," *Psychological Review* 62 (1955): 42–55.

40. Quoted in Karen Springen and Annetta Miller, "When Ads Don't Fit the 'Image'," *Newsweek* (January 22, 1990): 48.

41. Jacob Jacoby and David Mazursky, "Linking Brand and Retailer Images: Do the Potential Risks Outweigh the Potential Benefits?" *Journal of Retailing* 60 (Summer 1984): 105–22.

42. A number of criteria beyond the scope of this book are important in evaluating methods of attitude measurement, including such issues as reliability, validity, and sensitivity. For an excellent treatment of attitude scaling techniques, see David S. Aaker and George S. Day, *Marketing Research*, 4th ed. (New York: Wiley, 1990).

43. William L. Wilkie, *Consumer Behavior* (New York: Wiley, 1986).

44. M. Fishbein, "An Investigation of the Relationships Between Beliefs About an Object and the Attitude Toward that Object," *Human Relations* 16 (1983): 233–40.

45. Allan Wicker, "Attitudes Versus Actions: The Relationship of Verbal and Overt Behavioral Responses to Attitude Objects," *Journal of Social Issues* 25 (Autumn 1969): 65.

46. Icek Ajzen and Martin Fishbein, "Attitude-Behavior Relations: A Theoretical Analysis and Review of Empirical Research," *Psychological Bulletin* 84 (September 1977): 888–918.

47. Morris B. Holbrook and William J. Havlena, "Assessing the Real-to-Artificial Generalizability of Multi-Attribute Attitude Models in Tests of New Product Designs," *Journal of Marketing Research* 25 (February 1988): 25–35; Terence A. Shimp and Alican Kavas, "The Theory of Reasoned Action Applied to Coupon Usage," *Journal of Consumer Research* 11 (December 1984): 795–809.

48. Richard P. Bagozzi, Hans Baumgartner, and Youjae Yi, "Coupon Usage and the Theory of Reasoned Action," in Advances in Consumer Research 18, eds. Rebecca H. Holman and Michael R. Solomon (Provo, Utah: Association for Consumer Research, 1991), 24–27; Edward F. McQuarrie, "An Alternative to Purchase Intentions: The Role of Prior Behavior in Consumer Expenditure on Computers," *Journal of the Market Research Society* 30 (October 1988): 407–37; Arch G. Woodside and William O. Bearden, "Longitudinal Analysis of Consumer Attitude, Intention, and Behavior Toward Beer Brand Choice," in Advances in Consumer Research 4, ed. William D. Perrault, Jr. (Ann Arbor, Mich.: *Association for Consumer Research*, 1977), 349–56.

49. Michael J. Ryan and Edward H. Bonfield, "The Fishbein Extended Model and Consumer Behavior," *Journal of Consumer Research* 2 (1975): 118–36.

50. Blair H. Sheppard, Jon Hartwick, and Paul R. Warshaw, "The Theory of Reasoned Action: A Meta-Analysis of Past Research with Recommendations for Modifications and Future Research," *Journal of Consumer Research* 15 (December 1988): 325–43.

51. Joseph A. Cote, James McCullough and Michael Reilly, "Effects of Unexpected Situations on Behavior-Intention Differences: A Garbology Analysis," *Journal of Consumer Research* 12 (September 1985): 188–94.

52. Joseph A. Cote and Patriya S. Tansuhaj, "Culture Bound Assumptions in Behavior Intention Models," in Advances in Consumer Research 16, ed. Thom Srull (Provo, Utah: *Association for Consumer Research*, 1989), 105–09.

53. Russell H. Fazio, Martha C. Powell, and Carol J. Williams, "The Role of Attitude Accessibility in the Attitude-to-Behavior Process," *Journal of Consumer Research* 16 (December 1989): 280–88.

54. Robert E. Smith and William R. Swinyard, "Attitude-Behavior Consistency: The Impact of Product Trial Versus Advertising," *Journal of Marketing Research* 20 (August 1983): 257–67.

55. Ida E. Berger and Andrew A. Mitchell, "The Effect of Advertising on Attitude Accessibility, Attitude Confidence, and the Attitude-Behavior Relationship," *Journal of Consumer Research* 16 (December 1989): 269–79.

56. Barbara Presley Noble, "After Years of Deregulation, a New Push to Inform the Public," *New York Times* (October 27, 1991): F5.

57. Mathew Greenwald and John P. Katosh, "How to Track Changes in Attitudes," American Demographics (August 1987): 46.

Some people are opposed to a very basic luxury:
Your freedom of choice.

SAGA
MINK
OF SCANDINAVIA

CHAPTER 6

Attitude Change and Persuasive Communications

Buying, Having, and Being: Selections 19–21 from *Buying, Having, and Being: The Washington Post Consumer Behavior Companion*, Second Edition, accompany this chapter.

When Beth got her big promotion, she decided this was the opportunity she'd been waiting for. She has always wanted a fur coat, even though she knows that recently this symbol of wealth and luxury has lost some of its appeal as people have become more concerned about animal rights. Just this morning, a newspaper columnist observed that the ". . . dried, dead, hairy animal skin—or if you insist, luxurious fur coat—has become as passé and vulgarly uncivilized as flogging one's servants."[1]

Beth's also heard about the animal rights activists who have made it increasingly difficult to buy, sell, and even wear fur. She remembers hearing about furriers who have had their store locks glued shut and who have received death threats. She also saw a news report about fur wearers being doused with red dye intended to resemble animal blood.

Nevertheless, now that Beth can afford to reward herself in a big way, she thinks about that coat she's always wanted. She longingly looks through Sunday's newspaper ads and finds a few for furs—most of them for sale at really good prices. Now she's eager to find a reason to justify her passion. Finally, she comes across some information distributed by the Fur Information Council of America, which asks "If fashion isn't about freedom of choice, what is?" Reading this information convinces her. She *will* buy her coat.

But she plans to be really careful about where she wears it . . . .

Changing Attitudes Through Communication

As consumers, we are constantly bombarded by messages inducing us to change our attitudes. The passionate debate about whether consumers should wear fur illustrates some of the tactics used to change attitudes (fur sales have declined by 25 percent since the 1980s).[2] For example, groups such as People for the Ethical Treatment of Animals have run hard-hitting ads to influence consumers' opinions about buying fur. In a parody of the long-running ads for Blackglama furs—which depict famous women wrapped in furs and bear the caption "What Becomes a Legend Most?"—the PETA ad shown here features Cassandra Petersen (a.k.a. horror-show hostess and cult heroine Elvira) asking, "What Disgraces a Legend Most?"

On the other hand, the fur industry claims that the animals, which often kill each other in the wild anyway, are treated humanely.[3] Research conducted by the fur industry showed that most consumers felt they were entitled to wear fur, but needed reassurance in the face of the social pressures confronting them. The ad for Saga furs shown at the beginning of this chapter attempts to address this need. As a result of such efforts, some fur wearers are beginning to flaunt their furs to show their resentment at being told what to wear. In London, women staged a "National Wear Your Fur Day," and they demonstrated in Berkeley Square with posters demanding freedom of dress.[4]

As the battle over wearing fur illustrates, persuasion attempts can range

What disgraces a legend most?

FUR IS DEAD

Model: Cassandra Petersen   Photo: David Goldner

PETA
PEOPLE FOR THE ETHICAL TREATMENT OF ANIMALS
Washington, DC 20015 · (301) 770-7444

A group called People for the Ethical Treatment of Animals (PETA) is attempting to change consumers' attitudes toward the wearing of fur coats. In this ad, which is intended to reduce the social desirability of wearing fur, actress Cassandra Petersen is used in a parody of a long-running fur campaign that featured famous women wearing furs. Courtesy of People for the Ethical Treatment of Animals (PETA)

The PETA ad shown here is available as Transparency 13.

from logical arguments to graphic pictures, and from intimidation by peers to celebrity spokespeople. This chapter will review some of the factors that help to determine the effectiveness of such communication devices. Of course, much activity by marketing practitioners involves the design and execution of messages that are supposed to affect buying behavior, so many of the topics covered in other chapters bear on this issue as well.

For now, however, the focus will be on some basic aspects of communication that specifically help to determine how and if attitudes will be created or modified. This objective relates to **persuasion,** which refers to an active attempt to change attitudes. Persuasion is the central goal of many marketing communications.

Suppose that a perfume company wants to create an advertising campaign for a new fragrance. As it plans this campaign, it must develop a message that will create desire for the perfume in potential consumers. A number of questions must be answered:

- Who will be depicted as using the scent in an ad? Should it be linked to a glamorous celebrity? A career woman? A rock star? The source of a message helps to determine consumers' acceptance of it as well as their desire to try the product.

- How should the message be constructed? Should it emphasize the negative consequences of smelling badly? Should it directly compare the fragrance with others already on the market or maybe present a fantasy where a princess is swept off her feet by a dashing knight after she applies the scent? Product benefits can be expressed in many ways.

- What media should be used to transmit the message? Should it be depicted in a print ad? On television? Sold door-to-door? If a print ad is produced, should it be run in the pages of *Vogue? Good Housekeeping? The National Enquirer?* Sometimes *where* something is said can be as important as *what* is said. Ideally, the attributes of the product should be matched to those of the medium. For example, magazines with high prestige are more effective at communicating messages about overall product image and quality, while specialized, expert magazines do a better job at conveying factual information.[5]

- What characteristics of the target market might influence the ad's acceptance? If targeted users are frustrated in their daily lives, these women might be more receptive to a fantasy appeal. If they don't tend to wear perfume, they may not pay any attention to a traditional perfume ad at all.

This chapter discusses the **communications model**, which specifies that a number of elements are necessary for communication to be achieved. The chapter focuses on two important components of this model—the source and the message—and, in the final section, compares their effectiveness in persuading consumers to change their attitudes.

In this model, a *source* must choose and encode a message (i.e., initiate the transfer of meaning by choosing appropriate symbolic images that represent that meaning). This meaning must be put in the form of a *message*. There are many ways to say something, and the structure of the message has a big effect on how it is perceived. The message must be transmitted via a *medium,* which could be television, radio, magazines, billboards, personal contact, and so on. The message is then decoded by one or more *receivers,* who interpret the symbols in light of their own experiences. Finally, *feedback* must be received by the source, who uses the reactions of receivers to modify aspects of the message. The communications process is depicted in Figure 6–1.

Figure 6–1 is available as Transparency 14.

FIGURE 6–1 The Communications Model

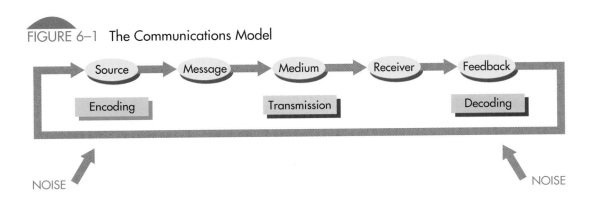

TABLE 6–1   The World's Ten Highest-Paid Athletes

Rank	Athlete	Sport	Millions of Dollars		
			Winnings	Other Income	Total
1	Evander Holyfield	Boxing	$60.0	$0.5	$60.5
2	Mike Tyson	Boxing	30.0	1.5	31.5
3	Michael Jordan	Basketball	2.8	13.2	16.0
4	George Foreman	Boxing	14.0	0.5	14.5
5	Ayrton Senna	Auto racing	12.0	1.0	13.0
6	Alain Prost	Auto racing	10.0	1.0	11.0
7	Razor Ruddock	Boxing	10.0	0.2	10.2
8	Arnold Palmer	Golf	0.3	9.0	9.3
9	Nigel Mansell	Auto racing	8.0	1.0	9.0
10	Jack Nicklaus	Golf	0.5	8.0	8.5

Note: Other income is an estimate of endorsement income, exhibition fees, and incentive bonuses.

Source: Adapted from Peter Newcomb, "Madonna Is the Model," *Forbes* 80 (August 19, 1991). Reprinted by permission of FORBES Magazine. © Forbes, Inc., 1991.

Sodas of the Stars. A good illustration of an extensive reliance on star power is the battle between Coke and Pepsi, two mature products that rely heavily upon celebrity endorsements. As observed by the consultant who designed Coke's logo: "Coke and Pepsi aren't in the product business anymore . . . . They're in the image business, in show business. There is almost no differentiation between Coke and Pepsi, so they have run out of things to say about their products. They have to do it via image."[28] Coca-Cola's stable of endorsers includes such figures as hockey player Wayne Gretzky, George Michael, model Elle MacPherson, Roger Rabbit, and the rap group Run-DMC. Pepsi has employed David Bowie, Michael J. Fox, Dwight Gooden, Madonna, and Tina Turner, among many others.

MULTICULTURAL DIMENSIONS

Some celebrities choose to maintain their credibility by endorsing products only in other countries, so these ads will not be seen by consumers in their own land. Many celebrities who do not do many American advertisements appear frequently in Japan. Mel Gibson endorses Asahi beer, Sly Stallone appears for Kirin beer, Sean Connery plugs Ito hams, and the singer Sheena Easton was featured in ads for Shochu liquor—dressed in a kimono and wig. Even the normally reclusive comedian and film director Woody Allen was featured in a campaign for a large Tokyo department store.[29]

Coke regularly polls consumers to see how closely they identify the product with a set of 18 attributes, such as young, modern, warm, and so on. When a dip in ratings on an attribute is detected, ads are created to bolster that image. Coke reacted to one ratings decline by using rock star George Michael in ads to reassure Coke drinkers that Coke is young and modern.

EFFECTIVENESS OF CELEBRITY ENDORSEMENTS Famous people can be effective because they are credible, attractive, or both, depending on the reasons for their fame. Ross Perot is unlikely to be a "sex symbol," but he may be quite effective at advocating use of a financial product. On the other hand, Vanna White may not be perceived as highly expert (except perhaps at turning letters on game shows), but she might be a persuasive source for a message about perfume or clothing.

Wanted: Believable Celebrities. The effectiveness of celebrities as communications sources often depends upon their perceived credibility. Consumers may not trust a celebrity's motives for endorsing a product, or they may question the star's competence to critically evaluate the product's claims. This "credibility gap" appears to be widening. In a recent one-year period, for example, the number of consumers who find celebrity advertising "less than credible" jumped to 52 percent. The greatest erosion of confidence comes from younger consumers, 64 percent of whom thought that celebrities appeared in ads just for the money.[30] The lack of credibility is aggravated by incidences where celebrities endorse products that they do not really believe in, or in some cases do not use. In 1978, the situation was so bad that the Federal Trade Commission announced that it would go after celebrities who made false claims in advertising. One casualty of that effort was the singer Pat Boone, who was forced to stop his endorsement of an acne cream.

Testing Celebrity Images. For celebrity campaigns to be effective, the endorser must have a clear and popular image. Many promotional strategies employing stars fail for this reason, such as unsuccessful attempts to market fragrances by Candice Bergen, Michael Jackson, and even the late artist Salvador Dali.

The images of celebrities are often pretested to increase the probability of consumer acceptance. One widely used technique is the so-called "Q" rating (Q stands for quality) developed by a market research company. This rating considers two factors in surveys: consumers' level of familiarity with a name and the number of respondents who indicate that a person, program, or character is a favorite. While not the most sophisticated research technique, the Q rating acknowledges that mere *familiarity* with a celebrity's name is not sufficient to gauge popularity since some widely known people are also widely disliked. Celebrities with low Q ratings include athlete Bruce Jenner, Michael Jackson, Gene Simmons, Wayne Newton, Madonna, and Cyndi Lauper. Some with high ratings are Stevie Wonder, Billy Joel, Phil Collins, George Michael, Whitney Houston, Cher, and Dolly Parton.[31]

THE SLEEPER EFFECT While in general more positive sources tend to increase attitude change, exceptions can occur. Sometimes a source can be obnoxious or disliked and still manage to be effective at getting the product's message across. A case in point is Mr. Whipple, the irritating but well-

Additional Examples: Former football quarterback Johnny Unitas was sued by a group of investors for endorsing a mortgage firm. The founder subsequently went to jail for fraud. Actress Jamie Lee Curtis jeopardized her relationship with Hertz by going topless in the movie *Trading Places*. Ringo Starr went into treatment for alcohol abuse after plugging Sun Country wine coolers, and Eric Clapton did spots for Michelob despite being a recovering drug addict. See "A Celebrity Malpractice? Hurt Investors Try to Sack a Quarterback," *Newsweek* (December 23, 1985): 65; James Cox, "Star-Struck Advertisers Lean on Celebs," *USA Today* (June 20, 1990): 80.

Research Report: One exception to the rule that highly credible sources are more persuasive is when speakers with low credibility advocate a position incongruous with their own interests. For example, a drug dealer, while not well-regarded by many, might be very effective in an anti-drug campaign. See Brian Sternthal, Ruby Dholakia, and Clark Leavitt, "The Persuasive Effects of Source Credibility: Tests of Cognitive Response," *Journal of Consumer Research* 4 (1978)4: 252–60.

known television character who for many years scolded customers: "Please don't squeeze the Charmin!"

In some instances the differences in attitude change between positive sources and less positive sources seem to get erased over time. After a while people appear to "forget" about the negative source and wind up changing their attitudes anyway. This process is known as the **sleeper effect**.[32]

The explanation for the sleeper effect is a subject of debate, as is the more basic question regarding whether and when it really exists. Initially, the *dissociative cue hypothesis* proposed that over time the message and the source become disassociated in the consumer's mind. The message remains on its own in memory, causing the delayed attitude change termed the sleeper effect.[33] A more recent explanation is the *availability-valence hypothesis*, which emphasizes the selectivity of memory owing to limited capacity.[34] If the associations linked to the negative source are less available than those linked to the message information, the residual impact of the message enhances persuasion. Consistent with this view, the sleeper effect has been obtained only when the message was encoded deeply; it had stronger associations in memory than did the source.[35]

Communications Model: The Message

A major study of over 1000 commercials identified factors that appear to determine whether or not a commercial message will be persuasive. The single most important feature was whether the communications contained a brand-differentiating message. In other words, did the communication stress a unique attribute or benefit of the product? Other good and bad elements are depicted in Table 6–2.[36]

TABLE 6–2 Positive and Negative Effects of Elements in Television Commercials

Positive Effects	Negative Effects
Showing convenience of use	Extensive information on components, ingredients, or nutrition
Showing new product or improved features	
Background cast (people incidental to message)	Outdoor setting (message gets lost)
Indirect comparison to other products	Large number of on-screen characters
Demonstration of the product in use	Graphic displays
Demonstration of tangible results(e.g., bouncy hair)	
An actor playing the role of an ordinary person	
No principal character (more time devoted to the product)	

Source: Adapted from David W. Stewart and David H. Furse, "The Effects of Television Advertising Execution on Recall, Comprehension, and Persuasion," *Psychology & Marketing* 2 (Fall 1985): 135–60. Copyright © 1985 by John Wiley & Sons, Inc. Reprinted by permission.

Characteristics of the message itself help to determine its impact on attitudes. These variables include how the message is said as well as what is said. Some of the issues facing marketers include the following.

- Should the message be conveyed in words or pictures?
- How often should the message be repeated?
- Should a conclusion be drawn, or should this be left up to the listener?
- Should both sides of an argument be presented?
- Is it effective to explicitly compare one's product to competitors?
- Should a blatant sexual appeal be used?
- Should negative emotions, such as fear, ever be aroused?
- How concrete or vivid should the arguments and imagery be?
- Should the ad be funny?

Sending the Message

WORDS VERSUS PICTURES The saying "one picture is worth a thousand words" captures the idea that visual stimuli can economically deliver big impact, especially when the communicator wants to influence receivers' emotional responses. For this reason, advertisers often place great emphasis on vivid and creative illustrations or photography.[37]

On the other hand, a picture is not always as effective at communicating factual information. Ads that contain the same information, presented in either visual or verbal form, have been found to elicit different reactions. The verbal version affects ratings on the utilitarian aspects of a product, while the visual version affects aesthetic evaluations.[38] Verbal elements are more effective when reinforced by an accompanying picture, especially if the illustration is *framed* (the message in the picture is strongly related to the copy).[39]

Because it requires more effort to process, a verbal message is most appropriate for high-involvement situations, such as in print contexts where the reader is motivated to really pay attention to the advertising. Because verbal material decays more rapidly in memory, more frequent exposures are needed to obtain the desired effect. Visual images, in contrast, allow the receiver to *chunk* information at the time of encoding (see Chapter 4 on memory processes). Chunking results in a stronger memory trace that aids retrieval over time.[40]

Visual elements may affect brand attitudes in one of two ways. First, the consumer may form inferences about the brand and change his or her beliefs because of an illustration's imagery. For example, people who saw an ad for a facial tissue accompanied by a photo of a sunset were more likely to believe that the brand came in attractive colors. Second, brand attitudes may be affected more directly; for example, a strong positive or negative reaction elicited by the visual elements will influence the consumer's attitude toward the ad (A_{ad}), which will then affect brand attitudes (A_b). This *dual component model* of brand attitudes is illustrated in Figure 6–2.[41]

VIVIDNESS Both pictures and words can differ in *vividness*. Powerful descriptions or graphics command attention and are more strongly embedded in memory. The reason may be because they tend to activate mental imagery, while abstract stimuli inhibit this process.[42] Of course, this effect can cut both ways: Negative information presented in a vivid manner may result in more negative evaluations at a later time.[43]

Research Report: Even the size and color of illustrations can have a strong impact on responses to an ad and in causing attitude change. The use of one-color newspaper ads in a field study resulted in 41 percent more sales volume than when the same ads were run in black-and-white. See Andrew A. Mitchell and Jerry C. Olson (1981), "Are Product Attribute Beliefs the Only Mediator of Advertising Effects on Brand Attitude?" *Journal of Marketing Research* 18 (1981)3: 318–32; R. Sparkman and L.M. Austin, "The Effect on Sales of Color in Newspaper Advertisements," *Journal of Advertising* 9 (1980): 39–42.

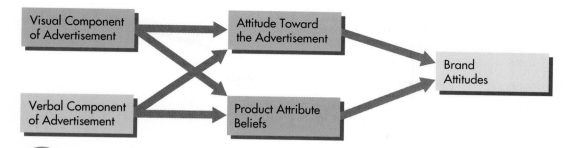

FIGURE 6–2 **Effects of Visual and Verbal Components of Advertisements on Brand Attitudes** Source: Andrew A. Mitchell, "The Effect of Verbal and Visual Components of Advertisements on Brand Attitudes and Attitude Toward the Advertisement," *Journal of Consumer Research* 13 (June 1986): 21. Reprinted by permission of The University of Chicago Press.

The concrete discussion of a product attribute in ad copy also influences the importance of that attribute, because more attention is drawn to it. For example, the copy for a watch that read "According to industry sources, three out of every four watch breakdowns are due to water getting into the case" was more effective than this version: "According to industry sources, many watch breakdowns are due to water getting into the case."[44]

REPETITION Repetition can be a two-edged sword for marketers. As noted in Chapter 4, multiple exposures to a stimulus are usually required for learning (especially conditioning) to occur. Contrary to the saying "familiarity breeds contempt," people tend to like things that are more familiar to them, even if they were not that keen on them initially.[45] This phenomenon is known as the *mere exposure effect*. On the other hand, too much repetition creates *habituation*, where the consumer no longer pays attention to the stimulus because of fatigue or boredom. Excessive exposure can cause *advertising wear-out*, which can result in negative reactions to an ad after seeing it too much.[46]

Two-Factor Theory. The fine line between familiarity and boredom has been explained by the **two-factor theory**, which proposes that two separate psychological processes are operating when a person is repeatedly exposed to an ad. The positive side of repetition is that it increases familiarity and thus reduces uncertainty about the product. The negative side is that over time boredom increases with each exposure. At some point the amount of boredom incurred begins to exceed the amount of uncertainty reduced, resulting in wear-out. This pattern is depicted in Figure 6–3. Its effect is especially pronounced in cases where each exposure is of a fairly long duration (such as a sixty-second commercial).[47]

The theory implies that advertisers can overcome this problem by limiting the amount of exposure per repetition (such as using fifteen-second spots). They can also maintain familiarity but alleviate boredom by slightly varying the content of ads over time through campaigns that revolve around a common theme, although each spot may be different. For example, H&R Block systematically presents different reasons to use their firm for tax preparation.

Teaching Hint: Attempts to influence attitudes by highlighting the behavior of other people in the same situation are more successful when put into concrete terms. For example, a commercial that features five people explaining their product choice is more vivid than the abstract claim "four out of five consumers chose Brand X." See Michael R. Solomon, Sarah Drenan, and Chester A. Insko, "Popular Induction: When is Consensus Information Informative?" *Journal of Personality* 49 (1981)2: 212–24.

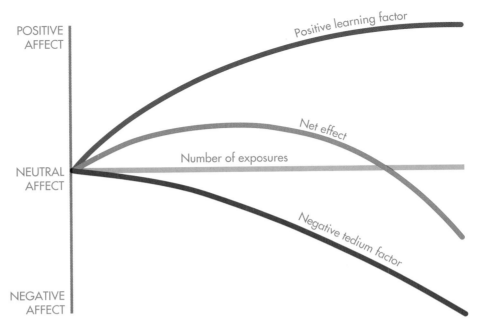

POSITIVE AFFECT

Positive learning factor

Net effect

Number of exposures

NEUTRAL AFFECT

Negative tedium factor

NEGATIVE AFFECT

FIGURE 6–3 Two-Factor Theory and Advertising Wear-Out Source: Adapted from Arno J. Rathans, John L. Swasy, and Lawrence Marks, "Effects of Television Commercial Repetition. Receiver Knowledge," *Journal of Marketing Research* 23 (February 1986): 50–61, Figure 1, p. 51. By permission of American Marketing Association.

Constructing the Argument

Many marketing messages are similar to debates or trials, where someone presents arguments and tries to convince the receiver to shift his or her opinion accordingly. The way the argument is presented can thus be very important.

ONE- VERSUS TWO-SIDED ARGUMENTS Most messages merely present one or more positive attributes about the product or reasons to buy it. These are known as *supportive arguments*. An alternative is to use a *two-sided message*, where both positive and negative information is presented. Research has indicated that two-sided ads can be quite effective, yet they are not widely used.[48]

Why would a marketer want to devote advertising space to publicizing a product's negative attributes? Under the right circumstances, the use of *refutational arguments* where a negative issue is raised and then dismissed can be quite effective. This approach can increase source credibility by reducing reporting bias. Also, people who are skeptical about the product may be more receptive to a balanced argument instead of a "whitewash."[49] In one novel application, a Chateau Potelle winery ad included both positive and negative reviews of a wine by two experts. The ad suggested that consumers develop their own taste rather than relying on reviews in wine magazines.[50]

This is not to say that the marketer should go overboard in presenting major problems with the product. In the typical refutational strategy, relatively minor attributes are discussed that may present a problem or fall short when compared with competitors. These drawbacks are then refuted by emphasizing positive, important attributes. For example, Avis got a lot of mileage out of claiming to be only "No. 2," while an ad for Volkswagen woefully described one of its cars as a "lemon" because there was a scratch on the glove compartment chrome strip.[51] A two-sided strategy appears to be the most effective when the audience is well educated (and is presumably more impressed by a balanced argument).[52] It is also best to use when receivers are not already loyal to the product; "preaching to the converted" about possible drawbacks may raise doubts unnecessarily.

DRAWING CONCLUSIONS   A related factor is the issue of whether the argument should draw conclusions, or whether the points should merely be presented, permitting the consumer to arrive at his or her own. Should the message only say "Our brand is superior," or should it add "You should buy our brand"? On the one hand, consumers who make their own inferences instead of having them spoon-fed will form stronger, more accessible attitudes. On the other, leaving the conclusion ambiguous increases the chance that the desired attitude will not be formed.

The response to this issue depends upon the consumers' motivation to process the ad and the complexity of the arguments. If the message is personally relevant, people will pay attention to it and spontaneously form inferences. However, if the arguments are hard to follow or consumers' motivation to follow them is lacking, it is safer for the ad to draw conclusions.[53]

COMPARATIVE ADVERTISING   In 1971, the FTC issued guidelines that encouraged advertisers to name competing brands in their ads. This action was taken to improve the information available to consumers in ads.[54] **Comparative advertising** refers to a strategy where a message compares two or more specifically named or recognizably presented brands and makes a comparison of them in terms of one or more specific attributes.[55] For example, Schering-Plough claimed that "New OcuClear relieves three times longer than Visine," and Bristol-Myers stated that "New Liquid Vanish really does clean tough rust stains below the water line better than Lysol."

This strategy has yielded mixed results. While some comparative ads result in desired attitude change or positive A_{ad}, they have also been found to be lower in believability and may result in more source derogation (i.e., the consumer may doubt the credibility of a biased presentation).[56]

Comparative ads do appear to be effective in the case of new products. Here, they are superior in anchoring a new brand closer to a dominant one and in building a clear brand image. However, if the aim is to compare the new brand with the market leader in terms of specific product attributes, merely saying it is as good or better than the leader is not sufficient. For example, the use of the claim "Spring has the same fluoride as Crest" in a study resulted in attitude change for the fictitious product, while the more global statement "Preferred by Europeans in comparison with Crest" did not.[57]

Research Report: Another factor that may influence the persuasive potential of a message is syntactic complexity. For example, the statement "Trident gum is sugarless" is less complex than the statement "Trident gum does not contain sugar." These alternatives can make a difference, especially when motivation to process the statement is relatively low.   See Tina M. Lowrey, "The Relation Between Syntactic Complexity and Advertising Persuasiveness," in *Advances in Consumer Research* 19, eds. John F. Sherry, Jr. and Brian Sternthal, (Provo, Utah: Association for Consumer Research, 1992), 270–74.

Teaching Hint: Direct comparative ads are most effective when they encourage differentiation between the two brands, especially when they lower consumers' perceptions of the comparison brand. This effect is particularly robust when the attribute in question is typical of the product category.   See Cornelia Pechmann and S. Ratneshwar, "The Use of Comparative Advertising for Brand Positioning: Association Versus Differentiation," *Journal of Consumer Research* 18 (September 1991): 145–60.

M A R K E T I N G   P I T F A L L

Many consumers are skeptical about claims made or implied in advertising, and some ads are challenged after being aired, either by the government, by concerned citizens, or by a competitor. About half of those challenged are either modified or taken off the air completely. In some cases, the company makes an attempt to correct the misinformation. An example is a recent Volvo ad that was challenged by the Texas attorney general's office. In an ad showing a row of cars being crushed by a pickup truck, only the Volvo was unharmed, but the investigation revealed that the Volvo used in the ad had been specially reinforced for the shoot. The company later ran ads acknowledging that the dramatization had been faked.

When a marketer makes a specific comparative claim relative to a competing product, he or she must be prepared for the possibility that the rival company will respond with a lawsuit. Many companies have gotten involved in complex lawsuits after using the comparative approach, and the costs of such litigation are high for both parties. As one judge who was involved in a ten-year court battle being fought between two makers of rival analgesics noted, "Small nations have fought for their very survival with less resources."

As a result of these and other incidents, marketers are learning to exercise extra care when making product claims, and some are beginning to supply disclaimers to protect themselves against lawsuits.[58]

Types of Message Appeals

EMOTIONAL VERSUS RATIONAL APPEALS A few years ago, both Toyota and Nissan introduced a large luxury car that sold for over $40,000. The two companies chose very different ways to communicate their product's attributes, as seen in the ads shown here. Toyota's advertising for its Lexus model used a rational appeal, with ads concentrating on the large number of technical advancements incorporated in the car's design. Print ads were dominated by copy describing these engineering features.

In sharp contrast, Nissan's controversial campaign for its Infiniti used an emotional appeal. The new model was introduced with a series of print and television ads that did not even discuss the car at all. The ads instead focused on the Zen-like experience of driving and featured long shots of serene landscapes. As one executive involved with the campaign explained, "We're not selling the skin of the car; we're selling the spirit."[59] While these ads were innovative, most American consumers had trouble grasping the Japanese conception of luxury. Later ads for the Infiniti emphasized functional features of the car to compensate for this initial confusion.

The goal of an emotional appeal is to establish a connection between the product and the consumer, a strategy known as *bonding* .[60] Emotional appeals have the potential to increase the chance the message will be perceived, they may be more likely to be retained in memory, and they can also increase the consumer's involvement with the product. Although Nissan's gamble on emphasizing the aesthetic aspects of its product did not pay off in this case, other emotional appeals are quite effective. Many companies turned to this strategy after realizing that consumers do not find many differences among brands, especially those in well-established, mature categories. Ads for products ranging from cars (Lincoln Mercury) to

Teaching Hint: Perceptual vigilance presents a paradox: How can the perceptual system screen out a stimulus when the stimulus must be noticed in order to be avoided? The process highlights the importance of not viewing perception as a single, discrete experience, but as a chain of events beginning with an input and ending with conscious recognition. Perception thus represents the conscious termination of a sequence of nonconscious processes. See Michael H. Erdelyi, "A New Look at the New Look: Perceptual Defense and Vigilance," *Psychological Review* 81 (1974)1: 1–25.

These ads demonstrate rational versus emotional message appeals. At the time of the initial ad campaign for the new Infiniti automobiles, the ads for rival Lexus (top) emphasized design and engineering, while the ads for Infiniti (bottom) did not even show the car. Courtesy of Lexus. Courtesy of INFINITI®. A division of Nissan Motor Corporation, USA.

cards (Hallmark) focus instead on emotional aspects. Mercury's capitalization on emotional attachments to old rock songs succeeded in lowering the median age of their consumers for some models by ten years.[61]

The precise effects of rational versus emotional appeals are hard to gauge. Though recall of ad contents tends to be better for "thinking" ads than for "feeling" ads, conventional measures of advertising effectiveness (e.g., day-after recall) may not be adequate to assess cumulative effects of emotional ads. These open-ended measures are oriented toward cognitive responses, and feeling ads may be penalized because the reactions are not as easy to articulate.[62]

While they can make a strong impression, emotional appeals also run the risk of not getting across an adequate amount of product-related infor-

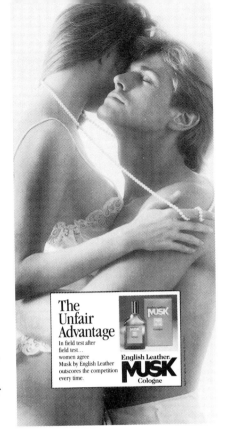

This ad for English Leather musk cologne relies on a sexual appeal, a strategy that appears to be effective when such appeals are related to the product and not used merely to grab attention. Courtesy of MEM Company, Inc.

mation. This potential problem is reminding some advertisers that the arousal of emotions is functional only to the extent that it sells the product. Procter & Gamble's original ads for Bounce fabric softener showed a happy young couple dancing to the song "Jump," with the message that Bounce is for clothes "you can't wait to jump into." In more recent spots, a woman discusses why the product makes her clothes feel and smell better. It is still somewhat emotional and experiential, but the main selling point of "softness without static cling" is driven home.[63]

SEX APPEALS   Under the assumption that "sex sells," many campaigns—for everything from perfumes to autos—feature heavy doses of erotic suggestions that range from subtle hints to blatant displays of skin. Perhaps not surprisingly, female nudity in print ads generates negative feelings and tension among female consumers, while men's reactions are more positive.[64]

Does Sex Work?   Although the use of sex does appear to draw attention to an ad, its use may actually be counterproductive to the marketer. Ironically, a provocative picture can be too effective; it attracts so much attention that it hinders processing and recall of the ad's contents. Sexual appeals appear to be ineffective when used merely as a "trick" to grab attention. They do, however, appear to work when the product is *itself* sexually related, such as in the ad shown here for English Leather Musk cologne, a product intended to enhance interpersonal attraction.

"BALDNESS. HANDSOME IN A MAN, BEAUTIFUL IN A CHICKEN."

Frank Perdue

To me, nothing is more attractive than a chicken with skin as smooth as silk.

Not only is it lovely to look at. But since it doesn't have all those feathers, pinfeathers and hairs you'll find on some other chickens, you don't have to clean it.

That's the beauty of Perdue. I remove that unwanted hair and stubble from my fresh, delicious chickens. Which is why they come with a money-back guarantee. Instead of unsightly extras.

So if a store sells you a chicken that needs a shave and a haircut, take it back. And demand a refund. Then demand Perdue. It's one good-looking chicken. And I can tell you firsthand, good looks go a long way in the chicken business.

IT TAKES A TOUGH MAN TO MAKE A TENDER CHICKEN.

Teaching Hint: One reason for the mixed findings regarding humor is that humorous appeals increase in persuasiveness over time—humor creates generalized arousal, resulting in a more active memory trace process and an enhancement of cognitive processing in the long term. (This effect would not show up on conventional measures of ad effectiveness that are taken immediately following exposure to the humorous ad.) See H. Bruce Lammers, Laura Leibowitz, George E. Seymour, and Judith E. Hennessey, "Humor and Cognitive Responses to Advertising Stimuli: A Trace Consolidation Approach," *Journal of Business Research* 11 (1983): 173–85.

Perdue has relied heavily on humor in its messages by focusing on the resemblance between Frank Perdue and the company's product to promote its chickens. Courtesy of Scali MacCabe Scaves, Inc.

HUMOROUS APPEALS The use of humor can be tricky, particularly since what is funny to one person may be offensive or incomprehensible to another. Specific cultures may have different senses of humor and also use funny material in diverse ways. For example, commercials in the United Kingdom are more likely to use puns and satire than in the United States.[65]

Does Humor Work? Overall, humorous advertisements, such as the one shown here featuring Frank Perdue, do get attention. One study found that recognition scores for humorous liquor ads were better than average. However, the verdict is mixed as to whether humor affects recall or product

Additional Example: A recent attempt by Subaru to satirize the typical commercial for sports cars backfired. In one TV commercial for the SVX, the announcer claims the car "can reach speeds of 140 miles an hour." This statement is followed by the question: "How important is that, with extended urban gridlock, gas at $1.38 a gallon, and highways full of patrolmen?" Unfortunately, auto safety groups didn't seem to get the joke; focusing on the mph claim, they called the ads "offensive and totally inappropriate." See Randall Rothenberg, "When Jokes Backfire, Campaigns Explode," *New York Times* (August 26, 1991): D6.

Research Report: Some evidence indicates that downscale, more traditional consumers are more susceptible to fear appeals. See J.L. Burnett and R.L. Oliver, "Fear Appeal Effects in the Field: A Segmentation Approach," *Journal of Marketing Research* 16 (1976): 181–90.

attitudes in a significant way.[66] One function it may play is to provide a source of *distraction*. A funny ad inhibits the consumer from counterarguing, thereby increasing the likelihood of message acceptance.[67]

Humor is more likely to be effective when the brand is clearly identified and the funny material does not "swamp" the message. This danger is similar to that of beautiful models diverting attention from copy points. Subtle humor is usually better, as is humor that does not make fun of the potential consumer. Finally, humor should be appropriate to the product's image. An undertaker or a bank might want to avoid humor, while other products adapt to it quite well. Sunsweet pitted prunes quadrupled sales based on their claim, "Today the pits, tomorrow the wrinkles."[68]

FEAR APPEALS **Fear appeals** highlight the negative consequences that can occur unless the consumer changes a behavior or an attitude. This strategy is widespread; fear appeals are used in over 15 percent of all television ads.[69] The arousal of fear is a common tactic for public policy issues, such as convincing consumers to stop smoking or to drive safely (i.e., to reduce physical risk). It can also be applied to social risk issues by threatening one's success with the opposite sex, career, and so on. This tactic has been half-jokingly called "slice of death."

Does Fear Work? Fear appeals are usually most effective when only a moderate amount of fear is induced. The relationship between fear and attitude change is *nonmonotonic*.[70] As shown in Figure 6–4, increasing levels of fear do not result in increased change; the relationship instead resembles an inverted U-shaped curve. If the threat is too great, the audience tends to deny that it exists as a way to rationalize the danger. A study that manipulated subjects' degree of anxiety about AIDS, for example, found that condom ads were evaluated most positively when a moderate amount of fear was induced. In this context, copy that promoted the use of the condom because "Sex is a risky business" (moderate fear) resulted in more attitude change than either a low fear appeal that instead emphasized the product's sensitivity or a high fear appeal that discussed the certainty of death from AIDS.[71] Similarly, scare tactics have not been as effective as hoped in getting teen-agers to decrease their use of alcohol or drugs. Teens simply tune out the message or deny its relevance to them.[72]

FIGURE 6–4 **The Relationship Between Fear and Attitude Change**

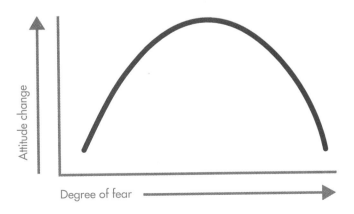

Attitude change

Degree of fear

I never shower alone.

And neither should you. Because simply by hanging this free card in your shower, you could save your own life.

You see, this shower card will show you how to do monthly breast self examination. And remind you to do it. This is vitally important. Because even though 1 in 10 women will develop breast cancer, 90% of those cancers are controllable if detected early.

So send for your free Coors/High Priority Shower Card today. Then put it in your shower and use it. And if you're over 35, ask your doctor about getting a mammogram. Because in the fight against cancer, we're not alone.

HIGH PRIORITY
Breast Cancer Research/Information Network
of the AMC Cancer Research Center

Coors

© 1987 Adolph Coors Company, Golden, Colorado 80401
Brewer of Fine Quality Beers Since 1873.

For your free Coors/High Priority Shower Card, send this coupon to the AMC Cancer Research Center at: Shower Card, Box 1987, Denver, CO 80201.

NAME
ADDRESS
CITY   STATE   ZIP   CO
One card per coupon. Offer good while supplies last.

Cher, High Priority
Charter Member

Fear appeals have a greater chance of being effective if they also provide consumers with a possible solution to the problem. Here, celebrity Cher gives concrete advice about breast self-examinations. Courtesy of Coors Brewing Company and AMC Cancer Research Center.

Some of the most effective fear appeals try to convey a moral lesson by creating a powerful character who demonstrates how to avoid negative outcomes. For example General Motors' Mr. Goodwrench personifies the concept of "good car-maintenance," appealing to the desire to avoid an accident or death by properly maintaining one's car. Mr. Goodwrench's enemy is consumer inertia (not getting one's car serviced regularly). By embodying struggles or other evil forces in made-up characters, some threatening aspects are softer than they would be if a real person were used.[73]

Fear appeals appear to be most effective when the consumer is already afraid of the problem discussed in the ad. The threats should not be excessive, and a solution to the problem should be presented (otherwise, consumers will tune out the ad since they can do nothing to solve the problem).[74] This technique is at work in the ad shown here, where the actress Cher advises readers about doing breast self-examinations. Appeals also work better when source credibility is high.[75]

Research Report: Research on the effectiveness of fear appeals has yielded mixed results. One reason may be due to the assumption that a specific type of message will uniformly generate a high level of fear among all consumers. For a review of this research, see Herbert J. Rotfeld, "Fear Appeals and Persuasion: Assumptions and Errors in Advertising Research," *Current Issues and Research in Advertising* 11 (1988)1: 21–40

MARKETING OPPORTUNITY

Gun manufacturers are capitalizing on women's fears regarding personal protection and home defense. According to the National Rifle Association, between 15–20 million women own guns. At least three manufacturers have introduced guns for women. One company makes a .32 magnum model called a "Bonnie," to go with a .38 "Clyde" for his-and-hers shooting. Smith & Wesson introduced the LadySmith, a revolver with a slimmed-down grip.[76] The company's ads have been criticized for preying on the fears of women. They include such copy as "The world is different today than when you grew up" and "Personal security is a very real issue." A magazine called *Women & Guns*, started in 1989 now goes to over 25,000 readers.[77] In addition to gun safety, it features articles on firearm fashions. The cover of a recent issue featured an attractive woman wearing a pistol holder strapped above her knee with the caption "Self-Defense Goes Thigh High."

The Message as Art Form: Metaphors Be with You

Marketers may be thought of as storytellers who supply visions of reality similar to those provided by authors, poets, and artists. These communications take the form of stories because the product benefits they describe are intangible and must be given tangible meaning by expressing them in a form that is concrete and visible. Advertising creatives rely (consciously or not) on various literary devices to communicate these meanings.

For example, a product or service might be personified by a character such as Mr. Goodwrench, the Jolly Green Giant, or the California Raisins. Many ads take the form of an allegory, where a story is told about an abstract trait or concept that has been personified as a person, animal, vegetable, and so on.

A **metaphor** involves the use of an explicit comparison, such as A is B (e.g., "United Airlines is your friend in faraway places"). The device was used literally by Reebok to equate its Metaphors line of shoes with comfort, as seen in the ad shown here. Metaphors allow the marketer to activate meaningful images and apply them to everyday events. In the stock market, "white knights" battle "hostile raiders" using "poison pills," while Tony the Tiger allows us to equate cereal with strength, and the Merrill Lynch bull sends the message that the company is "a breed apart."[78]

Resonance is another type of literary device that is frequently used in advertising. It is a form of presentation that combines a play on words with a relevant picture. Table 6–3 gives some examples of actual ads that rely on the principle of resonance. While metaphor substitutes one meaning for another by connecting two things that are in some way similar, resonance uses an element that has a double meaning, such as a pun where there is a similarity in the sound of a word but a difference in meaning. For example, an ad for a diet strawberry shortcake dessert might bear the copy "berried treasure" so that qualities associated with buried treasure—being rich, hidden and associated

Reebok uses the metaphor "Pretty as a picture" to promote its line of Metaphors shoes. Reprinted by permission of Reebok International Ltd.

TABLE 6–3 Some Examples of Advertising Resonance

Product/Headline	Visual
Embassy Suites: This Year, We're Unwrapping Suites by the Dozen	Chocolate kisses with hotel names underneath each
Toyota auto parts: Our Lifetime Guarantee May Come as a Shock	Man holding a shock absorber
Bucks filter cigarettes: Herd of These?	Cigarette pack with a picture of a stag
Bounce fabric softener: Is There Something Creeping Up Behind You?	Woman's dress bunched up on the back of her due to static
Pepsi: This Year, Hit the Beach Topless	Pepsi bottle cap lying on the sand
ASICS athletic shoes: We Believe Women Should be Running the Country	Woman jogging in a rural setting

Source: Adapted from Edward F. McQuarrie and David Glen Mick, "On Resonance: A Critical Pluralistic Inquiry into Advertising Rhetoric," *Journal of Consumer Research* 19 (September 1992): Table 1, 182. Reprinted with permission of The University of Chicago Press.

with adventurous pirates—are conveyed for the brand. Because the text departs from expectations, it creates a state of tension or uncertainty on the part of the viewer until he or she figures out the wordplay. Once the consumer "gets it," he or she may prefer the ad over a more straightforward message.[79]

FORMS OF STORY PRESENTATION Just as a story can be told in words or pictures, the way the audience is addressed can also make a difference. Commercials are structured like other art forms, borrowing conventions from literature and art as they communicate their messages.[80]

One important distinction is between a *drama* and a *lecture*.[81] A lecture is like a speech where the source speaks directly to the audience in an attempt to inform them about a product or persuade them to buy it. Because a lecture clearly implies an attempt at persuasion, the audience will regard it as such. Assuming listeners are motivated to do so, the merits of the message will be weighed, along with the credibility of the source. Cognitive responses, such as counterargumentation, will occur. The appeal will be accepted to the extent that it overcomes objections and is congruent with a person's beliefs.

In contrast, a drama is similar to a play or movie. While an argument holds the viewer at arm's length, a drama draws the viewer into the action. The characters only indirectly address the audience; they interact with each other about a product or service in an imaginary setting. Dramas attempt to be experiential—to involve the audience emotionally. In *transformational* advertising, the consumer associates the experience of product usage with some subjective sensation. Thus, ads for the Infiniti attempted to transform the "driving experience" into a mystical, spiritual event.

The Source Versus the Message: Sell the Steak or the Sizzle?

Two major components of the communications model, the source and the message, have been reviewed. Which aspect has the most impact on persuading consumers to change their attitudes? Should marketers worry more about *what* is said, or *how* it's said and *who* says it?

The answer is, it depends. Variations in a consumer's level of involvement, as discussed in Chapter 3, result in the activation of very different cognitive processes when a message is received. Research indicates that this level of involvement will determine which aspects of a communication are processed. The situation appears to resemble a traveler who comes to a fork in the road: One or the other path is chosen, and this path has a big impact on the factors that will make a difference in persuasion attempts.

The Elaboration Likelihood Model

The **elaboration likelihood model (ELM)** assumes that once a consumer receives a message he or she begins to process it.[82] Depending upon the personal relevance of this information, one of two routes to persuasion will be followed. Under conditions of high involvement, the consumer takes the *central route to persuasion*. Under conditions of low involvement, a *peripheral route* is taken instead. This model is diagrammed in Figure 6–5.

Research Report: In one study on transformational advertising, projective measures were used to determine if subjects' exposure to prior advertising would affect product usage experiences. A hiking scene was rated as more enjoyable when Coors was present relative to Lowenbrau, while the reverse was found when a barbecue scene was substituted. Coors' advertising has relied on an outdoor theme, while Lowenbrau concentrates on more social settings. See David A. Aaker and Douglas M. Stayman, "Implementing the Concept of Transformational Advertising," *Psychology & Marketing* 9 (May/June 1992): 237–53.

Research Report: When a consumer is more motivated to process an ad because it is relevant to his or her goals, the impact of central processing on brand attitudes is increased and that of peripheral cues is decreased. For a recent discussion, see Scott B. MacKenzie and Richard A. Spreng, "How Does Motivation Moderate the Impact of Central and Peripheral Processing on Brand Attitudes and Intentions?" *Journal of Consumer Research* 18 (March 1992): 519–29.

CNN Connection

The Sneaker War

CNN. A video segment is available to accompany this CNN connection.

In the $5 billion war to sell you a pair of athletic shoes, major manufacturers pull out all the stops to get consumers to sit up and take notice of their product communication. In the "old days," sneakers were a functional product, and ads would be more likely to emphasize a shoe's durability than its ability to somehow make the person who wears it popular in school or awesome on the basketball court.

Nowadays, however, the picture has changed: Athletic shoes are largely image-driven, and often rely on their association with admired people for their appeal (just as predicted by balance theory).

In today's ferocious battle for market share, a celebrity endorsement is a favorite weapon. Companies like Nike and Reebok, who compete fiercely against each other, pay millions to superstar athletes such as Michael Jordan and Bo Jackson to endorse their shoes. These compnaies are betting big money that fans who revere these athletes will try to acquire a "touch of greatness" by buying their shoes as well. Even sports figures like managers, coaches, and referees who don't actually play the game are credible and potent product endorsers. And in the sneaker war, since athletic shoes have become for many a fashion rather than a fitness statement, singing stars like Michael Jackson and Paula Abdul have also been deployed as highly-paid weapons.

SIMMONS Connection

SIMMONS Connection: Data for this exercise is on the Simmons Data Disk inside the back cover of your Instructor's Annotated Edition.

Data File: Politically Sensitive Products

In the end, Beth decides that she will treat herself to the fur coat she has always wanted. Although her own attitudes about wearing fur products are probably more positive than negative, she is well aware of the growing outcry against the use of fur. For example, she appears to have been influenced by recent press coverage of the treatment of animals. Beth also seems concerned with the "political correctness" of wearing animal fur. The fact that she is going to be careful about when she wears her new fur coat illustrates her awareness that for some people wearing fur is "politically incorrect."

One issue of concern to anyone interested in influencing consumers' attitudes and behaviors is the question of how well attitudes predict behavior. Just because someone says they are against the killing of animals for their fur or that they object to the way that veal is raised does not necessarily mean that they will not wear a fur coat or eat a veal cutlet.

The Simmons file for this chapter contains information about the consumption of a group of "sensitive" products. These products are considered sensitive because for many people it is just not "politically correct" to consume them. The data file contains a cross-tabulation of environmental attitudes with a variety of "politically sensitive" products. The question for you to consider is: How well do these attitudes relate to consumers' actual behavior? Are consumers who express concern about the environment less likely to use products such as weed killers? Are they also less likely to wear fur coats? Do they substitute synthetic for real fur?

Notes

1. Quoted in Cyndee Miller, "The Fur Flies as Fashion Foes Pelt It Out Over Animal Rights," *Marketing News* 2 (December 4, 1989): 2.

2. Nina Darnton, "Revolt of the Fur Bearers," *Newsweek* (January 6, 1992): 49.

3. Quoted in Miller, "The Fur Flies as Fashion Foes Pelt It Out Over Animal Rights": 8.

4. Darnton, "Revolt of the Fur Bearers."

5. Gert Assmus, "An Empirical Investigation into the Perception of Vehicle Source Effects," *Journal of Advertising* 7 (Winter 1978): 4–10; for a more thorough discussion of the pros and cons of different media, see Stephen Baker, *Systematic Approach to Advertising Creativity* (New York: McGraw-Hill, 1979).

6. Carl I. Hovland and W. Weiss, "The Influence of Source Credibility on Communication Effectiveness," *Public Opinion Quarterly* 15 (1952): 635–50.

7. Herbert Kelman, "Processes of Opinion Change," *Public Opinion Quarterly* 25 (Spring 1961): 57–78; Susan M. Petroshuis and Kenneth E. Crocker, "An Empirical Analysis of Spokesperson Characteristics on Advertisement and Product Evaluations," *Journal of the Academy of Marketing Science* 17 (Summer 1989): 217–26.

8. Kenneth G. DeBono and Richard J. Harnish, "Source Expertise, Source Attractiveness, and the Processing of Persuasive Information: A Functional Approach," *Journal of Personality and Social Psychology* 55 (1988)4: 541–46.

9. Hershey H. Friedman and Linda Friedman, "Endorser Effectiveness by Product Type," *Journal of Advertising Research* 19 (1979)5: 63–71.

10. S. Ratneshwar and Shelly Chaiken, "Comprehension's Role in Persuasion: The Case of Its Moderating Effect on the Persuasive Impact of Source Cues," *Journal of Consumer Research* 18 (June 1991): 52–62.

11. "Jim Palmer Pitches 'Style' for Jockey," *New York Times* (August 29, 1982).

12. "Robber Makes It Biggs in Ad," *Advertising Age* (May 29, 1989): 26.

13. Alice H. Eagly, Andy Wood, and Shelly Chaiken, "Causal Inferences About Communicators and Their Effect in Opinion Change," *Journal of Personality and Social Psychology* 36 (1978)4: 424–35.

14. Rick Marin, "The Stepford Channel," *New York Times* (October 4, 1992)2: 1v.

15. Barry Meier, "TV Commercials That Go On and On," *New York Times* (January 27, 1990): 54.

16. Karen K. Dion, "What is Beautiful is Good," *Journal of Personality and Social Psychology* 24 (December 1972): 285–90.

17. Michael J. Baker and Gilbert A. Churchill, Jr., "The Impact of Physically Attractive Models on Advertising Evaluations," *Journal of Marketing Research* 14 (November 1977): 538–55; Marjorie J. Caballero and William M. Pride, "Selected Effects of Salesperson Sex and Attractiveness in Direct Mail Advertisements," *Journal of Marketing* 48 (January 1984): 94–100; W. Benoy Joseph, "The Credibility of Physically Attractive Communicators: A Review," *Journal of Advertising* 11 (1982)3: 15–24; Lynn R. Kahle and Pamela M. Homer, "Physical Attractiveness of the Celebrity Endorser: A Social Adaptation Perspective," *Journal of Consumer Research* 11 (1985)4: 954–61; Judson Mills and Eliot Aronson, "Opinion Change as a Function of Communicator's Attractiveness and Desire to Influence," *Journal of Personality and Social Psychology* 1 (1965): 173–77.

18. Leonard N. Reid and Lawrence C. Soley, "Decorative Models and the Readership of Magazine Ads," *Journal of Advertising Research* 23 (1983)2: 27–32.

19. Marjorie J. Caballero, James R. Lumpkin, and Charles S. Madden, "Using Physical Attractiveness as an Advertising Tool: An Empirical Test of the Attraction Phenomenon," *Journal of Advertising Research* (August/September 1989): 16–22.

20. Baker and Churchill, Jr., "The Impact of Physically Attractive Models on Advertising Evaluations"; George E. Belch, Michael A. Belch, and Angelina Villareal, "Effects of Advertising Communications: Review of Research," in *Research in Marketing* (Greenwich, Conn.: JAI Press, 1987)9, 59–117; A.E. Courtney and T.W. Whipple, *Sex Stereotyping in Advertising* (Lexington, Mass.: Lexington Books, 1983).

21. Kahle and Homer, "Physical Attractiveness of the Celebrity Endorser."

22. Baker and Churchill, Jr., "The Impact of Physically Attractive Models on Advertising Evaluations."

23. Michael A. Kamins, "Celebrity and Noncelebrity Advertising in a Two-Sided Context," *Journal of Advertising Research* 29 (June-July 1989): 34; Joseph M. Kamen, A.C. Azhari, and J.R. Kragh, "What a Spokesman Does for a Sponsor," *Journal of Advertising Research* 15 (1975)2: 17–24; Lynn Langmeyer and Mary Walker, "A First Step to Identify the Meaning in Celebrity Endorsers," in *Advances in Consumer Research* 18, eds. Rebecca H. Holman and Michael R. Solomon (Provo, Utah: Association for Consumer Research, 1991), 364–71.

24. Jeffrey Burroughs and Richard A. Feinberg, "Using Response Latency to Assess Spokesperson Effectiveness," *Journal of Consumer Research* 14 (September 1987): 295–99.

25. Pamela G. Hollie, "A Rush for Singers to Promote Goods," *New York Times* (May 14, 1984): D1

26. Judith Graham, "Sponsors Line Up for Rockin' Role," *Advertising Age* (December 11, 1989): 50.

27. Hollie, "A Rush for Singers to Promote Goods."

28. Quoted in Douglas C. McGill, "Star Wars in Cola Advertising," *New York Times* (March 22, 1989): D1.

29. Marie Okabe, "Fading Yen for Foreign Stars in Ads," *Singapore Straits-Times* (1986).

30. Thomas R. King, "Credibility Gap: More Consumers Find Celebrity Ads Unpersuasive," *Wall Street Journal* (July 5, 1989): B5.31. Bruce Haring, "Company Totes Up Popularity Quotients," *Billboard Magazine* 101 (1989): 12.

32. Anthony R. Pratkanis, Anthony G. Greenwald, Michael R. Leippe, and Michael H. Baumgardner, "In Search of Reliable Persuasion Effects: III. The Sleeper Effect Is Dead, Long Live the Sleeper Effect," *Journal of Personality and Social Psychology* 54 (1988): 203–18.

33. Herbert C. Kelman and Carl I. Hovland, "Reinstatement of the Communication in Delayed Measurement of Opinion Change," *Journal of Abnormal Psychology* 4, 48 (1953)3: 327–35.

34. Darlene Hannah and Brian Sternthal, "Detecting and Explaining the Sleeper Effect," *Journal of Consumer Research* (September 1984)11: 632–42.

35. David Mazursky and Yaacov Schul, "The Effects of Advertisement Encoding on the Failure to Discount Information: Implications for the Sleeper Effect," *Journal of Consumer Research* 15 (June 1988): 24–36.

36. David W. Stewart and David H. Furse, "The Effects of Television Advertising Execution on Recall, Comprehension, and Persuasion," *Psychology & Marketing* 2 (Fall 1985): 135–60.

37. R.C. Grass and W.H. Wallace, "Advertising Communication: Print Vs. TV," *Journal of Advertising Research* 14 (1974): 19–23.

38. Elizabeth C. Hirschman and Michael R. Solomon, "Utilitarian, Aesthetic, and Familiarity Responses to Verbal Versus Visual Advertisements," in *Advances in Consumer Research* 11, ed. Thomas C. Kinnear (Provo, Utah: Association for Consumer Research, 1984), 426–31.

39. Andrew A. Mitchell and Jerry C. Olson, "Are Product Attribute Beliefs the Only Mediator of Advertising Effects on Brand Attitude?" *Journal of Marketing Research* 18 (1981)3: 318–32.

40. Terry L. Childers and Michael J. Houston, "Conditions for a Picture-Superiority Effect on Consumer Memory," *Journal of Consumer Research* 11 (September 1984): 643–54.

41. Andrew A. Mitchell, "The Effect of Verbal and Visual Components of Advertisements on Brand Attitudes and Attitude Toward the Advertisement," *Journal of Consumer Research* 13 (June 1986): 12–24.

42. John R. Rossiter and Larry Percy, "Attitude Change Through Visual Imagery in Advertising," *Journal of Advertising Research* 9 (1980)2: 10–16.

43. Jolita Kiselius and Brian Sternthal, "Examining the Vividness Controversy: An Availability-Valence Interpretation," *Journal of Consumer Research* 12 (March 1986): 418–31.

44. Scott B. Mackenzie, "The Role of Attention in Mediating the Effect of Advertising on Attribute Importance," *Journal of Consumer Research* 13 (September 1986): 174–95.

45. Robert B. Zajonc, "Attitudinal Effects of Mere Exposure," Monograph, *Journal of Personality and Social Psychology* 8 (1968): 1–29.

46. George E. Belch, "The Effects of Television Commercial Repetition on Cognitive Response and Message Acceptance," *Journal of Consumer Research* 9 (June 1982): 56–65; Marian Burke and Julie Edell, "Ad Reactions Over Time: Capturing Changes in the Real World," *Journal of Consumer Research* 13 (June 1986): 114–18; Herbert Krugman, "Why Three Exposures May Be Enough," *Journal of Advertising Research* 12 (December 1972): 11–14.

47. Robert F. Bornstein, "Exposure and Affect: Overview and Meta-Analysis of Research, 1968–1987," *Psychological Bulletin* 106 (1989)2: 265–89; Arno Rethans, John Swasy, and Lawrence Marks, "Effects of Television Commercial Repetition, Receiver Knowledge, and Commercial Length: A Test of the Two-Factor Model," *Journal of Marketing Research* 23 (February 1986): 50–61.

48. Linda L. Golden and Mark I. Alpert, "Comparative Analysis of the Relative Effectiveness of One- and Two-Sided Communication for Contrasting Products," *Journal of Advertising* 16 (1987); Kamins, "Celebrity and Noncelebrity Advertising in a Two-Sided Context"; Robert B. Settle and Linda L. Golden, "Attribution Theory and Advertiser Credibility," *Journal of Marketing Research* 11 (May 1974): 181–85.

49. See Alan G. Sawyer, "The Effects of Repetition of Refutational and Supportive Advertising Appeals," *Journal of Marketing Research* 10 (February 1973): 23–33; George J. Szybillo and Richard Heslin, "Resistance to Persuasion: Inoculation Theory in a Marketing Context," *Journal of Marketing Research* 10 (November 1973): 396–403.

50. Lawrence M. Fisher, "Winery's Answer to Critics: Print Good and Bad Reviews," *New York Times* (January 9, 1991): D5.

51. Golden and Alpert, "Comparative Analysis of the Relative Effectiveness of One- and Two-Sided Communication for Contrasting Products."

52. Belch et al., "Effects of Advertising Communications."

53. Frank R. Kardes, "Spontaneous Inference Processes in Advertising: The Effects of Conclusion Omission and Involvement on Persuasion," *Journal of Consumer Research* 15 (September 1988): 225–33.

54. Belch et al., "Effects of Advertising Commun-ications."

55. Cornelia Dröge and Rene Y. Darmon, "Associative Positioning Strategies Through Comparative Advertising: Attribute vs. Overall Similarity Approaches," *Journal of Marketing Research* 24 (1987): 377–89; D. Muehling and N. Kangun, "The Multidimensionality of Comparative Advertising: Implications for the FTC," *Journal of Public Policy and Marketing* (1985): 112–28; Beth A. Walker and Helen H. Anderson, "Reconceptualizing Comparative Advertising: A Framework and Theory of Effects," in *Advances in Consumer Research* 18, eds. Rebecca H. Holman and Michael R. Solomon (Provo, Utah: Association for Consumer Research, 1991), 342–47; William L. Wilkie and Paul W. Farris, "Comparison Advertising: Problems and Potential," *Journal of Marketing* 39 (October 1975): 7–15; R.G. Wyckham, "Implied Superiority Claims," *Journal of Advertising Research* (February/March 1987): 54–63.

56. Stephen A. Goodwin and Michael Etgar, "An Experimental Investigation of Comparative Advertising: Impact of Message Appeal, Information Load, and Utility of Product Class," *Journal of Marketing Research* 17 (May 1980): 187–202; Gerald J. Gorn and Charles B. Weinberg, "The Impact of Comparative Advertising on Perception and Attitude: Some Positive Findings," *Journal of Consumer Research* 11 (September 1984): 719–27; Terence A. Shimp and David C. Dyer, "The Effects of Comparative Advertising Mediated by Market Position of Sponsoring Brand," *Journal of Advertising* 3 (Summer 1978): 13–19; R. Dale Wilson, "An Empirical Evaluation of Comparative Advertising Messages: Subjects' Responses to Perceptual Dimensions," in *Advances in Consumer Research* 3, ed. B.B. Anderson (Ann Arbor, Mich.: Association for Consumer Research, 1976), 53–57.

57. Dröge and Darmon, "Associative Positioning Strategies Through Comparative Advertising: Attribute vs. Overall Similarity Approaches."

58. Dottie Enrico, "Guaranteed! Greatest Advertising Story Ever Told!" *Newsday* (October 16, 1991): 43; Bruce Buchanan and Doron Goldman, "Us Vs. Them: The Minefield of Comparative Ads," *Harvard Business Review* 38 (May–June 1989)7: 50.

59. Michael Lev, "For Car Buyers, Technology or Zen," *New York Times* (May 22, 1989): D1.

60. "Connecting Consumer and Product," *New York Times* (January 18, 1990): D19.

61. Edward F. Cone, "Image and Reality," *Forbes* (December 14, 1987): 226.

62. H. Zielske, "Does Day-After Recall Penalize 'Feeling' Ads?" *Journal of Advertising Research* 22 (1982): 19–22.

63. Cone, "Image and Reality."

64. Belch et al., "Effects of Advertising Commun-ications"; Courtney and Whipple, "Sex Stereotyping in Advertising"; Michael S. LaTour, "Female Nudity in Print Advertising: An Analysis of Gender Differences in Arousal and Ad Response," *Psychology & Marketing* 7 (1990)1: 65–81; B.G. Yovovich, "Sex in Advertising—The Power and the Perils," *Advertising Age* (May 2, 1983): M4–M5.

65. Marc G. Weinberger and Harlan E. Spotts, "Humor in U.S. Versus U.K. TV Commercials: A Comparison," *Journal of Advertising* 18 (1989)2: 39–44.

66. Thomas J. Madden, "Humor in Advertising: An Experimental Analysis," working paper No. 83–27, University of Massachusetts, 1984; Thomas J. Madden and Marc G. Weinberger, "The Effects of Humor on Attention in Magazine Advertising," *Journal of Advertising* 11 (1982)3: 8–14; Weinberger and Spotts, "Humor in U.S. Versus U.K. TV Commercials."

67. David Gardner, "The Distraction Hypothesis in Marketing," *Journal of Advertising Research* 10, (1970): 25–30.

68. "Funny Ads Provide Welcome Relief During These Gloom and Doom Days," *Marketing News* (April 17, 1981): 3.

69. Lynette S. Unger and James M. Stearns, "The Use of Fear and Guilt Messages in Television Advertising: Issues and Evidence," in 1983 AMA Educators' Proceedings, eds. Patrick E. Murphy et al. (Chicago: American Marketing Association, 1983), 16–20.

70. Michael L. Ray and William L. Wilkie, "Fear: The Potential of an Appeal Neglected by Marketing," *Journal of Marketing* 34 (1970)1: 54–62.

71. Ronald Paul Hill, "An Exploration of the Relationship Between AIDS-Related Anxiety and the Evaluation of Condom Advertisements," *Journal of Advertising* 17 (1988)4: 35–42.

72. Randall Rothenberg, "Talking Too Tough on Life's Risks?" *New York Times* (February 16, 1990): D1.

73. Barbara B. Stern, "Medieval Allegory: Roots of Advertising Strategy for the Mass Market," *Journal of Marketing* 52 (July 1988): 84–94.

74. Judith Waldrop, "They're Coming to Take You Away (Fear as a Form of Persuasion)," *American Demographics* (June 15, 1988): 2; John F. Tanner, Jr., James B. Hunt, and David R. Eppright, "The Protection Motivation Model: A Normative Model of Fear Appeals," *Journal of Marketing* 55 (July 1991): 36–45.

75. Brian Sternthal and C. Samuel Craig, "Fear Appeals: Revisited and Revised," *Journal of Consumer Research* 1 (December 1974): 22–34.

76. Anonymous, "A Drive to Woo Women—And Invigorate Sales," *New York Times* (April 2, 1989).

77. Carrie Goerne, "Gun Companies Target Women: Foes Call it 'Marketing to Fear'," *Marketing News* (August 31, 1992)2: 1.

78. Stern, "Medieval Allegory."

79. Edward F. McQuarrie and David Glen Mick, "On Resonance: A Critical Pluralistic Inquiry into Advertising Rhetoric," *Journal of Consumer Research* 19 (September 1992): 180–197.

80. See Linda M. Scott, "The Troupe: Celebrities as Dramatis Personae in Advertisements," in *Advances in Consumer Research* 18, eds. Rebecca H. Holman and Michael R. Solomon (Provo, Utah: Association for Consumer Research, 1991), 355–63; Barbara Stern, "Literary Criticism and Consumer Research: Overview and Illustrative Analysis," *Journal of Consumer Research* 16 (1989): 322–34; Judith Williamson, *Decoding Advertisements* (Boston: Marion Boyars, 1978).

81. John Deighton, Daniel Romer and Josh McQueen, "Using Drama to Persuade," *Journal of Consumer Research* 16 (December 1989): 335–43.

82. Richard E. Petty, John T. Cacioppo, and David Schumann, "Central and Peripheral Routes to Advertising Effectiveness: The Moderating Role of Involvement," *Journal of Consumer Research* 10 (1983)2: 135–46.

83. Jerry C. Olson, Daniel R. Toy, and Philip A. Dover, "Do Cognitive Responses Mediate the Effects of Advertising Content on Cognitive Structure?" *Journal of Consumer Research* 9 (1982)3: 245–62.

84. Julie A. Edell and Andrew A. Mitchell, "An Information Processing Approach to Cognitive Responses," in *Research Frontiers in Marketing: Dialogues and Directions*, ed. S.C. Jain (Chicago: American Marketing Association, 1978).

85. See Mary Jo Bitner and Carl Obermiller, "The Elaboration Likelihood Model: Limitations and Extensions in Marketing," in *Advances in Consumer Research* 12, eds. Elizabeth C. Hirschman and Morris B. Holbrook (Provo, Utah: Association for Consumer Research, 1985), 420–25; Meryl P. Gardner, "Does Attitude Toward the Ad Affect Brand Attitude Under a Brand Evaluation Set?" *Journal of Marketing Research* 22 (1985): 192–98; C.W. Park and S.M. Young, "Consumer Response to Television Commercials: The Impact of Involvement and Background Music on Brand Attitude Formation," *Journal of Marketing Research* 23 (1986): 11–24; Petty, Cacioppo, and Schumann, "Central and Peripheral Routes to Advertising Effectiveness"; for a discussion of how different kinds of involvement interact with the ELM, see Robin A. Higie, Lawrence F. Feick, and Linda L. Price, "The Importance of Peripheral Cues in Attitude Formation for Enduring and Task-Involved Individuals," in *Advances in Consumer Research* 18, eds. Rebecca H. Holman and Michael R. Solomon (Provo, Utah: Association for Consumer Research, 1991), 187–93.

86. J. Craig Andrews and Terence A. Shimp, "Effects of Involvement, Argument Strength, and Source Characteristics on Central and Peripheral Processing in Advertising," *Psychology & Marketing* 7 (Fall 1990): 195–214.

87. Richard E. Petty, John T. Cacioppo, Constantine Sedikides, and Alan J. Strathman, "Affect and Persuasion: A Contemporary Perspective," *American Behavioral Scientist* 31 (1988)3: 355–71.

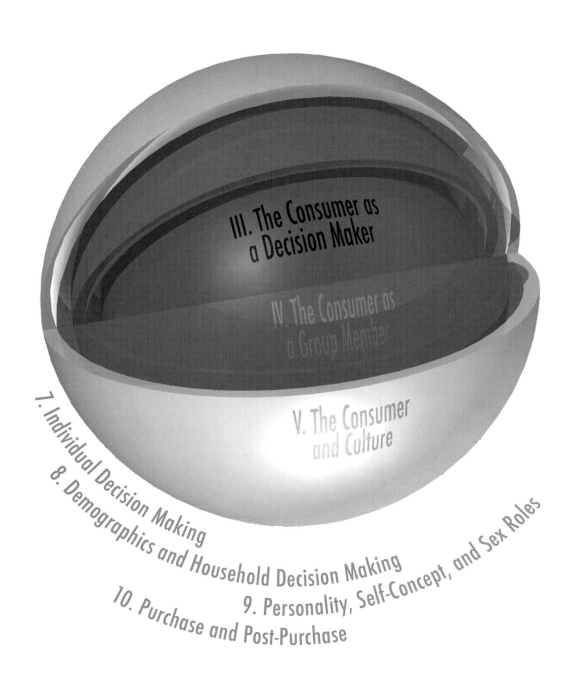

III. The Consumer as
a Decision Maker

IV. The Consumer as
a Group Member

V. The Consumer
and Culture

The Consumer

as a Decision

Maker

This section looks at how consumers use products in their daily lives, with emphasis on how we make decisions regarding the purchase and usage of goods and services. Chapter 7 begins with a focus on the steps that occur in individual decision making and then follows the consumer as he or she becomes aware of a need and tries to satisfy this need by evaluating and selecting products and services that (hopefully) will provide the best solution.

Since many consumer decisions are in fact made jointly by two or more individuals (and often at the household level), Chapter 8 considers elements of family decision making and also discusses how children in the household enter into these decisions. Chapter 9 examines how products are used to modify the images of ourselves that we try to transmit to others and how marketers affect our evaluations of a very important "product": ourselves.

The section concludes with Chapter 10, which focuses on how environmental factors—whether time pressure or the design of a shopping mall—affect consumer decisions. Recognizing that our concern with consumer behavior issues by no means stops at the point-of-purchase, this chapter also discusses postpurchase issues, such as determinants of consumer satisfaction with products and how people go about disposing of them after use.

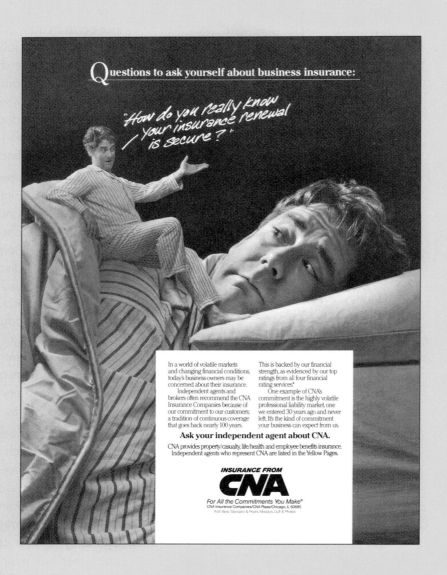

experiential perspective stresses the gestalt, or totality, of the product or service. Marketers in these areas focus on measuring consumers' affective responses to products or services and develop offerings that elicit appropriate subjective reactions and employ effective symbolism.

Types of Consumer Decisions

One helpful way to characterize the decision-making process is to consider the amount of effort that goes into the decision each time it must be made. Consumer researchers have found it convenient to think in terms of a continuum, which is anchored on one end by **habitual decision making** and at the other extreme by **extended problem solving**. Many decisions fall somewhere in the middle and are characterized by **limited problem solving**. This continuum is presented in Figure 7–2.

EXTENDED PROBLEM SOLVING   Decisions involving extended problem solving correspond most closely to the traditional decision-making perspective. As indicated in Table 7–1, the extended problem-solving process is usually initiated by a motive that is fairly central to the self-concept (see Chapter 9), and the eventual decision is perceived to carry a fair degree of risk. The consumer tries to collect as much information as possible, both from memory (internal search) and from outside sources (external search). Based on the importance of the decision, each product alternative is carefully evaluated. The evaluation is often done by considering the attributes of one brand at a time and seeing how each brand's attributes shape up to some set of desired characteristics.

TABLE 7–1   Characteristics of Limited Versus Extended Problem Solving

	Limited Problem Solving	Extended Problem Solving
Motivation	Low risk and involvement	High risk and involvement
Information Search	Little search	Extensive search
	Information processed passively	Information processed actively
	In-store decision making likely prior to store visits	Multiple sources consulted
Alternative Evaluation	Weakly held beliefs	Strongly held beliefs
	Only most prominent criteria used	Many criteria used
	Alternatives perceived as perceived basically similar	Significant differences among alternatives
	Noncompensatory strategy used	Compensatory strategy used
Purchase	Limited shopping time; may prefer self-service	Many outlets shopped if needed
	Choice often influenced by in desirable	Communication with store per sonnel store displays often

Additional Example: Consumers at times even treat advertisements as conjectures about product performance. People may not totally believe claims made in ads, but these ads may prompt them to engage in further information search and product trial to determine if the claims are true or not. When evidence regarding a product's quality is ambiguous, advertising can be persuasive when it is presented with some performance evidence. This is a good reason for advertisers to encourage product trial. See Stephen J. Hoch and Young-Won Ha, "Consumer Learning: Advertising and the Ambiguity of Product Experience," *Journal of Consumer Research* 13 (September 1986): 221–33.

LIMITED PROBLEM SOLVING Limited problem solving is usually more straightforward and simple. Buyers are not as motivated to search for information or to rigorously evaluate each alternative. People instead use simple *decision rules* to choose among alternatives. These cognitive shortcuts enable them to fall back on general guidelines instead of having to start from scratch every time a decision is to be made.

HABITUAL DECISION MAKING Both extended and limited problem-solving modes involve some degree of information search and deliberation, varying in the degree to which these activities are undertaken. At the other end of the choice continuum, however, are decisions that are made with little to no conscious effort. Many purchase decisions are so routinized that we may not realize we've made them until we look in our shopping carts. Choices characterized by *automaticity* are performed with minimal effort and without conscious control.[5] While this kind of thoughtless activity may seem dangerous or at best stupid, it is actually an efficient way to operate. The development of habitual, repetitive behavior allows consumers to minimize the time and energy spent on mundane purchase decisions. This strategy allows them to save their real effort for important decisions requiring careful scrutiny.

Problem Recognition

Problem recognition occurs whenever the consumer sees a significant difference between his or her current state of affairs and some desired or ideal state. The consumer perceives there is a problem to be solved, which may be small or large, simple or complex. A person who unexpectedly runs out of gas on the highway has a problem, as does the person who becomes dissatisfied with the image of his or her car, even though there is nothing mechanically wrong with it. Although the quality of Billy's TV had not

FIGURE 7–3 Problem Recognition: Shifts in Actual or Ideal States

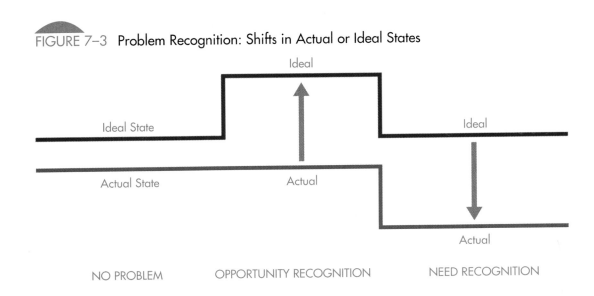

changed, for example, his standard of comparison was altered, and he was confronted with a need he did not have prior to watching his friend's TV.

Problem Creation

Figure 7–3 shows that a problem can arise in one of two ways. As in the case of the person running out of gas, the quality of the consumer's actual state can move downward (*need recognition*). On the other hand, as in the case of the person who craves a newer, flashier car, the consumer's ideal state can move upward (*opportunity recognition*). Either way, a gulf occurs between the actual state and the ideal state.[6] In Billy's case, a problem was perceived as a result of opportunity recognition; his ideal state in terms of television reception was altered.

Need recognition can occur in several ways. The quality of the person's actual state can be diminished simply by running out of a product, by buying a product that turns out not to adequately satisfy needs, or by creating new needs (e.g., deciding to buy a house). Opportunity recognition often occurs when a consumer is exposed to different or better-quality products. This shift often occurs because the person's circumstances have somehow changed, as when an individual goes to college or gets a new job. As the person's frame of reference shifts, a variety of purchases are made to adapt to the new environment.

Teaching Hint: Evidence suggests that for some consumers, problem recognition tends to be triggered mainly by a change in desired state while others only recognize a problem when their actual states change. The former type of consumer tends to enjoy shopping more and to consult more information sources. These consumers are likely to be opinion leaders or innovators. See Gordon C. Bruner, "Problem Recognition Styles and Search Patterns: An Empirical Investigation," *Journal of Retailing* 62 (Fall 1986): 281-97.

MARKETING PITFALL

A common structure for advertisements has been to present a person who has a physical or social problem and then "miraculously" show how the product will resolve it. Some marketers have gone so far as to *invent* a problem and then offer a remedy for it. In the 1940s, for example, the Talon zipper was touted as a cure for gaposis, the horrifying condition that develops when puckers appear around the buttons on a woman's skirt. Listerine, which was originally sold to fight dandruff, carried warnings about "bottle bacillus," which caused "infectious dandruff." Geritol gave us a remedy for "tired blood," and Wisk detergent drew our attention to the shame of "ring around the collar."[7]

Even when real problems are depicted in ads, the offered solutions are sometimes overly simplistic, implying that the problem will disappear if the product is used. One analysis of over 1000 television ads found that about eight in ten suggest that the problem will be resolved within seconds or minutes after using the product. In addition, 75 percent of the ads make definite claims that the product will solve the problem, and over 75 percent imply that this solution is a one-step process—all the consumer needs to do is buy the product, and the problem will go away.[8] Consumers, however, are becoming more cynical and less susceptible to such claims. As many marketers are discovering, consumers of the 1990s are more receptive to realistic ads that provide solid information about the product. In addition, both the government and consumer groups are now taking a more active interest in product claims, and marketers are being more cautious about the content of their ads.

MARKETERS' ROLE IN PROBLEM CREATION   While problem recognition can and does occur naturally, this process is often spurred by marketing efforts. For example, as the ad shown here demonstrates, Arm & Hammer has been particularly successful in identifying a succession of new problems its product can solve. Many marketing communications are designed to make consumers aware that they have a problem and then (conveniently) provide a solution.

Building Primary Versus Secondary Demand.   In some cases, marketers attempt to create *primary demand*, where consumers are encouraged to use a product or service regardless of the brand they choose. Such needs are often encouraged in the early stages of a product's life cycle, as, for example, when microwave ovens were first introduced. *Secondary demand,* where consumers are prompted to prefer a specific brand over others, can

This ad for Arm & Hammer demonstrates the strategy of identifying new problems an existing product can solve. By permission of Church & Dwight Co., Inc.

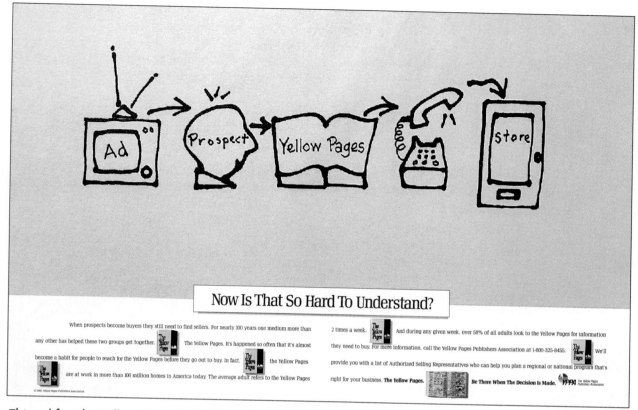

This ad for The Yellow Pages highlights the use of its product by consumers during the information search stage of making a purchase decision. Courtesy of Yellow Pages Publishers Association.

occur only if primary demand already exists. At this point, marketers must convince consumers that a problem can best be solved by choosing their brand over others in a category.

Information Search

Once a problem has been recognized, consumers need adequate information to resolve it. **Information search** is the process in which the consumer surveys his or her environment for appropriate data to make a reasonable decision. The Yellow Pages ad shown here illustrates one sequence of events that might occur during information search.

Types of Search

A consumer may explicitly search the marketplace for specific information after a need has been recognized (a process called *prepurchase search*.) On the other hand, many consumers, especially veteran shoppers, enjoy hunting for information and keeping track of developments just for the fun of it

An ad for *Bride's* magazine, which is available as Transparency 18, demonstrates that important events like weddings often generate many product needs requiring extensive information search. The magazine is a specialized information source designed to help meet those needs when they arise.

TABLE 7–2 A Framework for Consumer Information Search

Prepurchase Search	Ongoing Search
Determinants	
Involvement in the purchase	Involvement with the product
Market environment	Market environment
Situational factors	Situational factors
Motives	
To make better purchase decisions	Build a bank of information for future use
Experience fun and pleasure	
Outcomes	
Increased product and market knowledge	Increased product and market knowledge leading to:
	—future buying efficiencies
Better purchase decisions	—personal influence
Increased satisfaction with the purchase outcome	Increased impulse buying
	Increased satisfaction from search with other outcomes

Source: Peter H. Block, Daniel L. Sherrell, and Nancy M. Ridgway, "Consumer Search: An Extended Framework," *Journal of Consumer Research* 13 (June 1986): 120. Reprinted with permission by The University of Chicago Press.

Research Report: The nature of consumers' information search instigated by a new product is mediated by the extent to which it is similar or dissimilar to existing categories stored in memory. Exhibiting an inverted-U function, consumers appear to consider a set of relevant attributes in greater depth at moderate levels of discrepancy than at low or high levels. See Julie L. Ozanne, Merrie Brucks, and Dhruv Grewal, "A Study of Information Search Behavior During the Categorization of New Products," *Journal of Consumer Research* 18 (March 1992): 452.

(i.e., *browsing*) or because they like to maintain current information for future use. They engage in *ongoing search*.[9] Some differences between these two search modes are described in Table 7–2.

INTERNAL VERSUS EXTERNAL SEARCH Information sources can be roughly broken down into two kinds: internal and external. As a result of prior experience and simply living in a consumer culture, each of us often has some degree of knowledge about many products already in memory. When confronted with a purchase decision, we may engage in *internal search* by scanning our own memory banks to assemble information about different product alternatives (see Chapter 4).

DELIBERATE VERSUS "ACCIDENTAL" SEARCH Our existing knowledge of a product may be the result of *directed learning*, where on a previous occasion we had already searched for relevant information or experienced some of the alternatives. A parent who bought a birthday cake for one child last month, for example, probably has a good idea of the best kind to buy for another child this month.

Alternatively, we may have acquired information in a more passive manner. Even though a product may not be of interest, exposure to advertising, packaging, and sales promotion activities may result in *incidental learn-*

ing. Mere exposure over time to conditioned stimuli and observations of others results in the learning of much material that may not be needed for some time after the fact, if ever. For marketers, this result is a benefit of steady, "low-dose" advertising, since product associations are established and maintained until the time they are needed.[10]

In some cases, we may be so expert about a product category (or at least believe we are) that no additional search is undertaken. Frequently, however, our own existing state of knowledge is not satisfactory to make an adequate decision, and we must go outside of ourselves for more information. The sources we consult for advice vary: They may be impersonal and marketer-dominated sources, such as retailers and catalogs; they may be friends and family members; or they may be unbiased third parties such as *Consumer Reports*.[11] The ad for *Nation's Business* shown here highlights the important role of print media during information search.

This ad for *Nation's Business* magazine emphasizes the high level of consumer involvement often associated with print media that provide needed information. Reprinted by permission, *Nation's Business Magazine*.

Additional Example: While on average Americans take two weeks to shop for a car, buyers of luxury cars take twice as long. For this reason, manufacturers are increasingly emphasizing the shopping experience by investing in elaborate showrooms and furnishings. Some Nissan Infiniti showrooms even have "contemplation zones," quiet areas where a customer can sit and think about his or her choices. The shopping experience will be considered at length in Chapter 10. See "Zen and the Art of Buying a Car," *New York Times* (September 8, 1991): F10.

Teaching Hint: Relative to novices, experts tend to process alternatives by brand rather than by attribute. Because experts have a better sense of what criteria should be important, it is easier for them to collect this information. See James R. Bettman and C. Whan Park, "Effects of Prior Knowledge and Experience and Phase of the Choice Process on Consumer Decision Processes: A Protocol Analysis," *Journal of Consumer Research* 7 (December 1980): 234–48.

The Economics of Information

The traditional decision-making perspective incorporates the *economics-of-information approach* to the search process; it assumes that consumers will gather as much data as is needed to make an informed decision. Consumers form expectations of the value of additional information and continue to search to the extent that the rewards of doing so (i.e., the *utility*) exceed the costs. This utilitarian assumption also implies that the most valuable units of information will be collected first. Additional pieces will be absorbed only to the extent that they are seen as adding to what is already known.[12] In other words, people will put themselves out to collect as much information as possible, as long as the process of gathering it is not too onerous or time consuming.[13]

DO CONSUMERS ALWAYS SEARCH RATIONALLY? The assumption of rational search is not always supported. The amount of external search for most products is surprisingly small, even when additional information would most likely benefit the consumer. For example, lower-income shoppers, who have more to lose by making a bad purchase, actually search less prior to buying than do more affluent people.[14] Like our friend Billy, some consumers typically visit only one or two stores and rarely seek out unbiased information sources prior to making a purchase decision, especially when little time is available to do so.[15] This pattern is especially prevalent for decisions regarding durables, even when these products represent significant investments. One study of Australian car buyers found that more than a third had made only two or fewer trips to inspect cars prior to buying one.[16]

This tendency to avoid external search is less prevalent when consumers consider the purchase of symbolic items, such as clothing. In those cases, not surprisingly, people tend to do a fair amount of external search, although most of it involves seeking the opinions of peers.[17] While the stakes may be lower financially, these self-expressive decisions may be seen as having dire social consequences if the wrong choice is made. The level of perceived risk, a concept to be discussed shortly, is high.

Brand Switching. In addition, consumers are often observed to engage in brand switching, even if their current brand satisfies their needs. Sometimes, it seems that people just like to try new things—they are interested in *variety seeking.* The tendency of consumers to shift brand choices over time means that marketers can never rest assured that once they have won a customer, he or she is necessarily theirs forever.[18]

Determinants of Information Search

As a general rule, search activity is greater when the purchase is important, when there is a need to learn more about the purchase, and when the relevant information is easily obtained and utilized.[19] Consumers differ in the amount of search they tend to undertake, regardless of the product category in question. All things being equal, younger, better-educated people who enjoy the shopping/fact-finding process tend to conduct more information search. Women are more inclined to search than are men, as are those who place greater value on style and the image they present.[20]

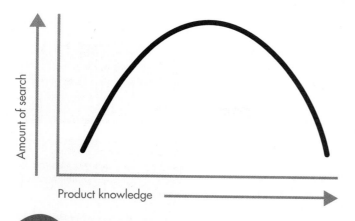

FIGURE 7–4 The Relationship Between Amount of Information Search and Product Knowledge

Research Report: One widely used device to study the search process in the laboratory is the Information Display Board (IDB). This board is a brand x attribute matrix that allows subjects to access product information in any order they would like prior to making a choice (almost like the game show Concentration). Researchers can trace the order of subjects' choices and assess the quality of their eventual decisions. This technique does have some drawbacks: The choice situations are somewhat artificial, and a structure is imposed on the subjects that they may not necessarily use in real life (e.g., brands and attributes to choose from are not neatly laid out). Nonetheless, the IDB has been an important tool for consumer researchers and policy makers who are concerned with maximizing the quality of product information available to consumers. See Jacob Jacoby, Robert W. Chestnut, Karl C. Weigl, and William Fisher, "Pre-Purchase Information Acquisition: Description of a Process Methodology, Research Paradigm and Pilot Investigation," in *Advances in Consumer Research* 3, ed. Beverlee B. Anderson (Ann Arbor, Mich.: Association for Consumer Research, 1976), 306–14; Charles M. Schaninger and Donald Sciglimpaglia, "The Influence of Cognitive Personality Traits and Demographics on Consumer Information Acquisition," *Journal of Consumer Research* 8 (September 1981): 208–16; Merrie Brucks, "The Effects of Product Class Knowledge on Information Search Behavior," *Journal of Consumer Research* 12 (June 1985): 1–16.

THE CONSUMER'S PRIOR EXPERTISE   Should prior product knowledge make it more or less likely that consumers will engage in search? Products experts and novices use very different procedures during decision making. Novices who know little about a product should be the most motivated to find out more about it. However, experts are more familiar with the product category, so they should be able to better understand the meaning of any new product information they might acquire.

Amount of Search.   So, who searches more? The answer is neither: Search tends to be greatest among those consumers who are *moderately* knowledgeable about the product. There is an inverted-U relationship between knowledge and external search effort, as shown in Figure 7–4. People with very limited expertise may not feel they are capable of searching extensively. In fact, they may not even know where to start. Billy, who did not spend a lot of time researching his purchase, is representative of this situation. He visited one store, and only looked at brands with which he was already familiar. In addition, he focused on only a small number of product features. On the other hand, people who are extremely knowledgeable in the area can rely heavily on their own memories for information (internal search), so they may not search very much either.[21]

Type of Search.   The type of search undertaken by people with varying levels of expertise differs as well. Because experts have a better sense of what information is relevant to the decision, they tend to engage in *selective search*, which means their efforts are more focused and efficient. In contrast, novices are more likely to rely upon the opinions of others and to rely upon "nonfunctional" attributes, such as brand name and price, to distinguish among alternatives. They may also process information in a "top-down" rather than a "bottom-up" manner, focusing less on details than on the big picture. For instance, they may be more impressed by the sheer amount of technical information presented in an ad than by the actual significance of the claims made.[22]

Research Report: Companies can take a variety of measures to reduce consumers' perceived risk by providing signals of quality. One such signal is a warranty. Experimental evidence indicates that in general a high-quality firm will choose a stronger warranty than will a low-quality firm, so consumers can infer quality from the warranty signal. Polling students as to other available quality signals will help to stimulate class discussion about types of perceived risk. See William Boulding and Amna Kirmani (1992), "An Experimental Examination of Signalling Theory: Do Consumers Perceive Warranties as Signals of Quality?" unpublished manuscript, Duke University, Durham, N.C., 1992.

TYPE OF RISK	BUYERS MOST SENSITIVE TO IT	PURCHASES MOST SUBJECT TO IT
Monetary	Risk capital consists of money and property. Those with relatively little income and wealth are most vulnerable.	High-ticket items that require a substantial expenditure are most subject to this form of risk.
Functional	Risk capital consists of alternate means of performing the function or meeting the need. Practical consumers are most sensitive.	Products or services whose purchase and use requires the buyer's exclusive commitment and precludes redundancy.
Physical	Risk capital consists of physical vigor, health, and vitality. Those who are elderly, frail, or in ill health are most vulnerable.	Mechanical or electrical goods (such as vehicles, flammables), drugs and medical treatment, food and beverages.
Social	Risk capital consists of self-esteem and self-confidence. Those who are insecure and uncertain are most sensitive.	Socially visible or symbolic goods such as clothes, jewelry, cars, homes, or sports equipment are most subject to it.
Psychological	Risk capital consists of affiliations and status. Those lacking respect or attractiveness to peers are most sensitive.	Expensive personal luxuries that may engender guilt, durables, and services whose use demands self-discipline or sacrifice.

FIGURE 7–5 Five Forms of Buyer Risk

PERCEIVED RISK As a rule, purchase decisions that involve extensive search also entail some kind of **perceived risk**, or the belief that the product has potentially negative consequences. Perceived risk may be present if the product is expensive or is complex and hard to understand. Alternatively, perceived risk can be a factor when a product choice is visible to others and we run the risk of embarrassment if the wrong choice is made.

Figure 7–5 lists five basic kinds of risk—including both objective (e.g., physical danger) and subjective factors (e.g., social embarrassment)—as well as the products subject to each type. As this figure notes, consumers with greater "risk capital" are less affected by perceived risks associated with the products. For example, a highly self-confident person would be less worried about the social risk inherent in a product, while a more vulnerable, insecure consumer might be reluctant to take a chance on a product that might not be

S'alternative.

This ad for Sunkist lemon juice attempts to establish a new category for the product by re-positioning it as a salt substitute. Courtesy of Sunkist Growers, Inc.

Consumers are often faced with choices between noncomparable categories, where a number of attributes exist that cannot be directly related to one another (the old problem of comparing apples and oranges). The comparison process is easier when consumers can derive an overlapping category that encompasses both items (e.g., entertainment, value, usefulness) and then rate each alternative in terms of that superordinate category.[29]

Prototypicality. If a product is a really good example of a category, it is more familiar to consumers, and, as a result, is more easily recognized and recalled.[30] Judgments about category attributes tend to be disproportionately influenced by the characteristics of category exemplars.[31] In a sense, brands that are strongly associated with a category get to "call the shots" by defining the evaluative criteria that should be used to evaluate all category members.

Stimulating Interest. Being a bit less than prototypical is not necessarily a bad thing. Products that are moderately unusual within their product category may stimulate more information processing and positive evaluations, since they are neither so familiar that they will be taken for granted nor so discrepant that they will be dismissed.[32] A brand that is strongly discrepant may occupy a unique niche position, while those that are moderately discrepant remain in a differentiated position within the general category.[33]

Locating Products. Product categorization can also affect consumers' expectations regarding the places they can locate a desired product. If products do not clearly fit into categories (e.g., is a rug furniture?), consumers' ability to find them or make sense of them may be affected. For instance, a frozen dog food that had to be thawed and cooked failed in the market, partly because people could not adapt to the idea of buying dog food in the frozen foods section.

Research Report: A consumer's selection of a category he or she will use during the evaluation process can be affected by the examples of the category presented. Category priming affects the likelihood that desired criteria will be used in evaluations. Marketers can have a hand in determining what criteria are used by consumers to evaluate alternatives by framing these criteria in certain ways. This means that the buyer's initial reference point can be altered, perhaps by raising or lowering a buyer's initial expectations of product performance. See James R. Bettman and Mita Sujan, "Effects of Framing on Evaluation of Comparable Alternatives by Expert and Novice Consumers," *Journal of Consumer Research* 14 (September 1987): 141–54; Paul M. Herr, "Priming Price: Prior Knowledge and Context Effects," *Journal of Consumer Research* 16 (June 1987): 67–75; Christopher P. Puto, "The Framing of Buying Decisions," *Journal of Consumer Research* 14 (December 1987): 301–15.

Choosing Among Alternatives

Once the relevant options from a category have been assembled, a choice must be made among them. Recall that the decision rules that guide choice can range from very simple and quick strategies to complicated processes requiring a lot of attention and cognitive processing.

EVALUATIVE CRITERIA When Billy was looking at different television sets, recall that he focused on one or two product features and that several others were completely ignored. He narrowed down his choices by only considering two specific brand names, and from the Prime Wave and Precision models, he chose one that featured stereo capability.

The **evaluative criteria** are the dimensions used to judge the merits of competing options. In comparing alternative products, Billy could have chosen from among any number of criteria, ranging from very functional attributes (does this TV come with remote control?) to experiential ones (does this TV's sound reproduction make me imagine I'm in a concert hall?). The specific evaluative criteria used vary among people and also across cultures. For example, the appeal to consumers in the ad for the Swedish chocolate drink shown here is based on the product's nutritional value, while American consumers would more likely be interested in the taste or calorie content of this type of product.

Another important point is that criteria on which products differ carry more weight in the decision process. If all brands being considered rate equally well on one attribute (e.g., if all TVs come with remote control), consumers will have to find other attributes to make a choice. Those attributes that are actually used to differentiate among choices are *determinant attributes.*

Marketers can play a role in educating consumers about which criteria should be used as determinant attributes. For example, consumer research by Church & Dwight indicated that many consumers view the use of natural ingredients as a determinant attribute. The result was promotion of a toothpaste made from baking soda, which the company already manufactured for its Arm & Hammer brand.[34]

The decision about which attributes to use is the result of *procedural learning,* where a person undergoes a series of cognitive steps before making a choice. These steps include identifying important attributes, remembering whether competing brands differ on those attributes, and so on. In order for a marketer to effectively recommend a new decision criterion, his or her communication should convey three pieces of information.[35]

1. It should point out that there are significant differences among brands on the attribute.
2. It should supply the consumer with a decision-making rule, such as *if* (deciding among competing brands), *then* (use the attribute as a criterion).
3. It should convey a rule that can be easily integrated with how the person has made this decision in the past. Otherwise, the recommendation is likely to be ignored since it requires too much mental work.

Consumers consider sets of product attributes by using different rules, depending upon the complexity of the decision, their involvement in it, and

FULL AV KRAFT.

TILL SKILLNAD FRÅN LÄSK.

Claiming the product is "full of strength," this ad for Pucko, a Swedish chocolate drink, emphasizes an evaluation criterion based on nutritional value, whereas American consumers might evaluate a similar product based on taste or calorie content.   Photographer: Kurt Wass. Courtesy of Forsman & BodenFors.

so on. One way to differentiate among decision rules is to divide them into those that are *compensatory* versus those that are *noncompensatory*. To aid the discussion of some of these rules, the attributes of TV sets considered by Billy are summarized in Table 7–3.

NONCOMPENSATORY DECISION RULES Simple decision rules are **noncompensatory**, and a product with a low standing on one attribute cannot make up for this position by being better on another attribute. In other words, people simply eliminate all options that do not meet some basic standards. A consumer like Billy who uses the decision rule "Only buy well-known brand names" would not consider a new brand, even if it was equal or superior to existing ones. When people are less familiar with a product category or not very motivated to process complex information, they tend to use simple, noncompensatory rules.[36]

TABLE 7–3 Hypothetical Alternatives for a TV Set

Attribute	Importance Ranking	Brand Ratings		
		Prime Wave	Precision	Kamashita
Size of screen	1	Excellent	Excellent	Excellent
Stereo broadcast capability	2	Poor	Excellent	Good
Brand reputation	3	Excellent	Excellent	Poor
On-screen programming	4	Excellent	Poor	Poor
Cable ready	5	Good	Good	Good
Sleep timer	6	Excellent	Poor	Good

The Lexicographic Rule. When the *lexicographic rule* is used, the brand that is the best on the most important attribute is selected. If two or more brands are seen as being equally good on that attribute, the consumer then compares them on the second most important attribute. This selection process goes on until the tie is broken. In Billy's case, since both the Prime Wave and Precision models were tied on his most important attribute (a 27" screen), the Precision was chosen because of its rating on this second most important attribute—its stereo capability.

The Elimination-by-Aspects Rule. Again, brands are evaluated on the most important attribute under the *elimination-by-aspects rule*. In this case, though, specific cutoffs are imposed. For example, if Billy had been more interested in having a sleep timer on his TV (i.e., if it had a higher importance ranking), he might have stipulated that his choice "must have a sleep timer." Since the Prime Wave model had one and the Precision did not, the Prime Wave would have been chosen.

The Conjunctive Rule. While the two former rules involve processing by attribute, the *conjunctive rule* entails processing by brand. As with the elimination-by-aspects procedure, cutoffs are established for each attribute. A brand is chosen if it meets all of the cutoffs, while failure to meet any one cutoff means it will be rejected. If none of the brands meet all of the cutoffs, the choice may be delayed, the decision rule may be changed, or the cutoffs themselves may be modified.

If Billy had stipulated that all attributes had to be rated "good" or better, he would not have been able to choose any of the options. He might then have modified his decision rule, conceding that it was not possible to attain these high standards in the price range he was considering. In this case, Billy could perhaps decide that it was not so important to have on-screen programming, so the Precision model could again be considered.

COMPENSATORY DECISION RULES Unlike noncompensatory decision rules, **compensatory rules** give a product a chance to make up for its shortcomings. Consumers who employ these rules tend to be more involved in the purchase and thus are willing to exert the effort to consider the entire picture in a more exacting way. The willingness to let good and bad product qualities balance out can result in quite different choices. For example, if Billy were not concerned about having stereo reception, he might have chosen the Prime Wave model. But because this brand did not feature this highly ranked attribute, it doesn't stand a chance when he uses a noncompensatory rule.

Simple and Complex Compensation. Two basic types of compensatory rules have been identified. When using the *simple additive rule,* the consumer merely chooses the alternative having the largest number of positive attributes. This choice is most likely to occur when his or her ability or motivation to process information is limited. One drawback to this approach for the consumer is that some of these attributes may not be very meaningful or important. An ad containing a long list of product benefits may be persuasive, despite the fact that many of the benefits included are actually standard within the product class.[37] The more complex version is known as the *weighted additive rule.* When using this rule, the consumer also takes into account the relative importance of positively rated attributes, essentially multiplying brand ratings by importance weights. If this process sounds familiar, it should. The calculation process strongly resembles the multi-attribute attitude model described in Chapter 5.

Heuristics: Mental Shortcuts

Instead of carefully calculating importance weights, consumers often employ decision rules that allow them to use some dimensions as substitutes for others. Especially where limited problem solving occurs prior to making a choice, consumers often fall back upon **heuristics**, or mental rules of thumb that lead to a speedy decision. These rules range from the very general, (e.g., "Higher-priced products are higher quality products" or "Buy the same brand I bought last time") to the very specific (e.g., "Buy Domino, the brand of sugar my mother always bought").[38]

For example, Billy relied on certain assumptions as substitutes for prolonged information search. In particular, he assumed the selection at Zany Zack's would be more than sufficient, so he did not bother to shop any of Zack's competitors. This assumption served as a shortcut to more extensive information processing.[39] Sometimes these shortcuts may not be in consumers' best interests. A consumer who personally knows one or two people who have had problems with a particular make of car, for example, might assume he or she would have similar trouble with it and thus overlook the model's overall excellent repair record.[40] The influence of such assumptions may be enhanced if the product has an unusual name, which makes it *and* the experiences with it more distinctive.[41]

RELYING ON A PRODUCT SIGNAL One frequently used shortcut is the tendency to infer hidden dimensions of products from observable attributes. The aspect of the product that is visible acts as a *signal* of some underlying

Additional Example: Another heuristic has been termed the false consensus effect. People tend to overestimate the amount that others agree with them. They often tend to assume, for example, that their own brand preferences are more typical than they actually are. One reason for this is that instances where others have agreed with them tend to be more available in memory.

TABLE 7–4 Common Market Beliefs

Brand	All brands are basically the same.
	Generic products are just name brands sold under a different label at a lower price.
	The best brands are the ones that are purchased the most.
	When in doubt, a national brand is always a safe bet.
Store	Specialty stores are a great place to familiarize yourself with the best brands, but once you figure out what you want, it's cheaper to buy it at a discount outlet.
	A store's character is reflected in its window displays.
	Sales people in specialty stores are more knowledgeable than other sales personnel.
	Larger stores offer better prices than small stores.
	Locally owned stores give the best service.
	A store that offers a good value on one of its products probably offers good values on all of its items.
	Credit and return policies are most lenient at large department stores.
	Stores that have just opened usually charge attractive prices.
Prices/Discounts/Sales	Sales are typically run to get rid of slow-moving merchandise.
	Stores that are constantly having sales don't really save you any money.
	Within a given store, higher prices generally indicate higher quality.

quality. Such inferences explain why someone trying to sell a used car takes great pains to be sure the car's exterior is clean and shiny: Potential buyers often judge the vehicle's mechanical condition by its appearance.[42]

When product information is incomplete, judgments are often derived from beliefs about *covariation*, or associations among events.[43] For example, a consumer may form an association between product quality and the length of time a manufacturer has been in business. Other signals or attributes believed to co-exist with good or bad products include well-known brand names, country of origin, price, and the retail outlets that carry the product.

Unfortunately, consumers tend to be poor estimators of covariation. Their beliefs persist despite evidence to the contrary. Similar to the consistency principle discussed in Chapter 5, people tend to see what they are looking for. They will look for product information that confirms their guesses. In one experiment, consumers sampled four sets of products to determine if price and quality were related. Those who believed in this relationship prior to the study elected to sample higher-priced products, thus creating a sort of self-fulfilling prophecy.[44]

MARKET BELIEFS AS HEURISTICS Consumers often form specific beliefs about relationships in the marketplace. These beliefs then become the shortcuts that guide their decisions—whether or not they are accurate.[42] Our friend Billy's decisions were influenced by his **market beliefs**. Recall, for instance, that he chose to shop at a large "electronics supermarket" because

Advertising and Sales Promotion	"Hard sell" advertising is associated with low-quality products.
	Items tied to "giveaways" are not a good value (even with the freebee).
	Coupons represent real savings for customers because they are not offered by the store.
	When you buy heavily advertised products, you are paying for the label, not higher quality.
Product/Packaging	Largest sized containers are almost always cheaper per unit than smaller sizes.
	New products are more expensive when they're first introduced; prices tend to settle down as time goes by.
	When you are not sure what you need in a product, it's a good idea to invest in the extra features, because you'll probably wish you had them later.
	In general, synthetic goods are lower in quality than goods made of natural materials.
	It's advisable to stay away from products when they are new to the market; it usually takes the manufacturer a little time to work the bugs out.

Source: Adapted from Calvin P. Duncan, "Consumer Market Beliefs: A Review of the Literature and an Agenda for Future Research," in *Advances in Consumer Research*, ed. Marvin E. Goldberg, Gerald Gorn, and Richard W. Pollay (Provo, Utah: Association for Consumer Research, 1990)17: 729–35.

he assumed the selection would be better (though the prices would be lower). A large number of market beliefs have been identified. Some of these are listed in Table 7–4. How many do you share?

PRICE AS A HEURISTIC Do higher prices mean higher quality? The assumption of a *price–quality relationship* is one of the most pervasive market beliefs.[46] Novice consumers may in fact consider price as the only relevant product attribute. Experts also consider this information, although in these cases price tends to be used for its informational value, especially for products (e.g., virgin wool) that are known to have wide quality variations in the marketplace. When this quality level is more standard or strictly regulated (e.g., Harris Tweed sportcoats), experts do not weigh price in their decisions. For the most part, this belief is justified; you do tend to get what you pay for. However, let the buyer beware: The price–quality relationship is not always justified.[47]

BRAND NAMES AS A HEURISTIC Branding is a marketing strategy that often functions as a heuristic. People form preferences for a favorite brand and then may literally never change their minds in the course of a lifetime. In a study of the market leaders in 30 product categories by the Boston Consulting Group, it was found that 27 of the brands that were number one in 1930 are still number one today. These brands include such perennial favorites as Ivory Soap, Campbell's Soup, and Gold Medal Flour.[48]

A brand that exhibits that kind of staying power is treasured by marketers, and for good reason. Brands that dominate their markets are as much as 50 percent more profitable than their nearest competitors.[49] A survey of 3000 consumers on brand power in Japan, Europe, and the United States combined awareness and esteem scores to produce the following list of the most positively regarded brand names around the world.[50]

1. Coca-Cola	6. Disney
2. IBM	7. Honda
3. Sony	8. Toyota
4. Porsche	9. Seiko
5. McDonald's	10. BMW

Consumers' attachments to certain brands, such as Marlboro, Coca-Cola, Gerber, and Levi's, are so powerful that this loyalty is often considered as a positive product attribute in and of itself. Brand equity can actually be quantified in terms of *goodwill*, defined as the difference between the market value and the book value of a brand. Recently, the British company Grand Metropolitan actually decided to record brand names it had acquired on its balance sheets, including these intangible assets in its financial reports to shareholders.[51] Marlboro is the most valuable brand name in the world. It was recently valued at $31.2 billion.[52]

Inertia. Many people tend to buy the same brand just about every time they go to the store. This consistent pattern is often due to **inertia**, where a brand is bought out of habit merely because less effort is required. If another product comes along that is for some reason easier to buy (e.g., it is cheaper or the original product is out of stock), the consumer will not hesitate to do so. A competitor who is trying to change a buying pattern based on inertia often can do so rather easily, because little resistance to brand switching will be encountered if some reason to do so is apparent. Since there is little to no underlying commitment to the product, such promotional tools as point-of-purchase displays, extensive couponing, or noticeable price reductions may be sufficient to "unfreeze" a consumer's habitual pattern.

Brand Loyalty. This kind of fickleness will not occur if true **brand loyalty** exists. In contrast to inertia, brand loyalty is a form of repeat purchasing behavior reflecting a conscious decision to continue buying the same brand. This concept thus refers to a pattern of purchases over time where actual decision making occurs.[53] For brand loyalty to exist, a pattern of repeat purchase must be accompanied by an underlying positive attitude toward the brand. Brand loyalty may be initiated by customer preference based on objective reasons, but after the brand has been around for a long time and is heavily advertised it can also create an emotional attachment, either by being incorporated into the consumer's self-image or because it is associated with prior experiences.[54] Purchase decisions based on brand loyalty are thus simplified and may even become habitual. The Honda ad shown here emphasizes this type of purchase decision.

Compared to an inertia situation where the consumer passively accepts a brand, a brand loyal consumer is actively (sometimes passionately)

Consumer Behavior Challenge

1. If people are not always rational decision makers, is it worth the effort to study how these decisions are made? What techniques might be employed to understand experiential consumption and to translate this knowledge into marketing strategy?

2. List three product attributes that can be used as quality signals and provide an example of each.

3. Why is it difficult to place a product in a consumer's evoked set after it has already been rejected? What strategies might a marketer use in an attempt to accomplish this goal?

4. Define the three levels of product categorization described in the chapter. Diagram these levels for a health club.

5. Discuss two different noncompensatory decision rules and highlight the difference(s) between them. How might the use of one rule versus another result in a different product choice?

6. Choose a friend or parent who grocery shops on a regular basis and keep a log of their purchases of common consumer products over the semester. Can you detect any evidence of brand loyalty in any categories based upon consistency of purchases? If so, talk to the person about these purchases. Try to determine if his or her choices are based upon true brand loyalty or based on inertia. What techniques might you use to differentiate between the two?

7. Form a group of three. Pick a product and develop a marketing plan based upon each of the three approaches to consumer decision making: rational, experiential, and behavioral influence. What are the major differences in emphasis among the three perspectives? Which is the most likely type of problem-solving activity for the product you have selected? What characteristics of the product make this so?

8. Locate a person who is about to make a major purchase. Ask that person to make a chronological list of all the information sources consulted prior to making a decision. How would you characterize the types of sources used (i.e., internal versus external, media versus personal, etc.)? Which sources appeared to have the most impact on the person's decision?

9. Perform a survey of country-of-origin stereotypes. Compile a list of five countries and ask people what products they associate with each. What are their evaluations of the products and likely attributes of these different products? The power of a country stereotype can also be demonstrated in another way. Prepare a brief description of a product, including a list of features, and ask people to rate it in terms of quality, likelihood of purchase, and so on. Make several versions of the description, varying only the country from which it comes. Do ratings change as a function of the country-of-origin?

10. Ask a friend to "talk through" the process he or she used to choose one brand over others during a recent purchase. Based on this description, can you identify the decision rule that was most likely employed?

CNN Connection

CNN A video segment is available to accompany this CNN Connection.

To Tell the Truth: Package Labeling

Do people look before they buy, and is it worth doing so? Manufacturers provide a great deal of information on package labels, and in theory a rational decision maker would weigh all of this information carefully, compare alternatives, and arrive at a responsible decision. While the chapter noted that in many cases consumers do not bother with these steps in the decision process, they are not entirely to blame: The data may not be accurate or useful anyway.

While many consumers actively search for products claiming to be "fat free" or good for the environment, they may not be getting what they think. Although efforts to regulate and improve the provision of product content information waned in the deregulation era of the 1980s, the U.S. Government is now taking a more active interest in specifying exactly what manufacturers are permitted to claim about their products. On the nutritional front, for example, some products claiming to be "fat free" have had to eliminate this claim, and efforts are underway to provide consumers with nutritional information that is easier to use (e.g., specifying what proportion of a product's calories are derived from fat).

Similarly, increased concern with the effects of products on the environment has meant that more consumers are regarding this dimension as a determinant attribute during the decision-making process: About three-fourths of consumers have expressed willingness to pay extra for products that are good for the environment. Unfortunately, the resulting boom in "green marketing" was accompanied by abuse, as some manufacturers, eager to climb on the eco-friendly bandwagon, made inaccurate claims about their products. Again, the government has begun to crack down on misleading claims by such companies as Borden, 3M, and Alberto-Culver, and efforts are underway to develop more uniform "green" standards. Still, after all is said and done, it is also up to consumers to incorporate this information in the decision-making process so that they can make wise choices. After all, you can lead a horse to water, but you can't make him drink . . . .

Notes

1. John C. Mowen, "Beyond Consumer Decision Making," *Journal of Consumer Marketing* 5 (1988)1: 15–25.
2. Richard W. Olshavsky and Donald H. Granbois, "Consumer Decision Making—Fact or Fiction," *Journal of Consumer Research* 6 (September 1979): 93–100.
3. James R. Bettman, "The Decision Maker Who Came In from the Cold," Presidential Address, in *Advances in Consumer Research* 20, eds. Leigh McAllister and Michael Rothschild (Provo, Utah: Association for Consumer Research, in press); John W. Payne, James R. Bettman, and Eric J. Johnson, "Behavioral Decision Research: A Constructive Processing Perspective," *Annual Review of Psychology* 4 (1992): 87–131; for an overview of recent developments in individual choice models, see Robert J. Meyer and Barbara E. Kahn, "Probabilistic Models of Consumer Choice Behavior," in *Handbook of Consumer Behavior*, eds. Thomas S. Robertson and Harold H. Kassarjian (Englewood Cliffs, NJ: Prentice-Hall, 1991), 85–123.
4. Mowen, "Beyond Consumer Decision Making."
5. Joseph W. Alba and J. Wesley Hutchinson, "Dimensions of Consumer Expertise," *Journal of Consumer Research* 13 (March 1987): 411–54.
6. Gordon C. Bruner III and Richard J. Pomazal, "Problem Recognition: The Crucial First Stage of

the Consumer Decision Process," *Journal of Consumer Marketing* 5 (1988)1: 53–63.

7. Ross K. Baker, "Textually Transmitted Diseases," *American Demographics* (December 1987): 64.

8. Julia Marlowe, Gary Selnow, and Lois Blosser, "A Content Analysis of Problem-Resolution Appeals in Television Commercials," *The Journal of Consumer Affairs* 23 (1989)1: 175–94.

9. Peter H. Bloch, Daniel L. Sherrell, and Nancy M. Ridgway, "Consumer Search: An Extended Framework," *Journal of Consumer Research* 13 (June 1986): 119–26.

10. Girish Punj, "Presearch Decision Making in Consumer Durable Purchases," *Journal of Consumer Marketing* 4 (Winter 1987): 71–82.

11. H. Beales, M.B. Jagis, S.C. Salop, and R. Staelin, "Consumer Search and Public Policy," *Journal of Consumer Research* 8 (June 1981): 11–22.

12. Itamar Simonson, Joel Huber, and John Payne, "The Relationship Between Prior Brand Knowledge and Information Acquisition Order," *Journal of Consumer Research* 14 (March 1988): 566–78.

13. George J. Stigler, "The Economics of Information," *Journal of Political Economy* 69 (June 1961): 213–25.

14. Cathy J. Cobb and Wayne D. Hoyer, "Direct Observation of Search Behavior," *Psychology & Marketing* 2 (Fall 1985): 161–79.

15. Sharon E. Beatty and Scott M. Smith, "External Search Effort: An Investigation Across Several Product Categories," *Journal of Consumer Research* 14 (June 1987): 83–95; William L. Moore and Donald R. Lehmann, "Individual Differences in Search Behavior for a Nondurable," *Journal of Consumer Research* 7 (December 1980): 296–307.

16. Geoffrey C. Kiel and Roger A. Layton, "Dimensions of Consumer Information Seeking Behavior," *Journal of Marketing Research* 28 (May 1981): 233–39; see also Narasimhan Srinivasan and Brian T. Ratchford, "An Empirical Test of a Model of External Search for Automobiles," *Journal of Consumer Research* 18 (September 1991): 233–42.

17. David F. Midgley, "Patterns of Intepersonal Information Seeking for the Purchase of a Symbolic Product," *Journal of Marketing Research* 20 (February 1983): 74–83.

18. Barbara E. Kahn, "Understanding Variety-Seeking Behavior From a Marketing Perspective," unpublished manuscript, University of Pennsylvania, University Park, 1991; Leigh McAlister and Edgar A. Pessemier, "Variety-Seeking Behavior: An Interdisciplinary Review," *Journal of Consumer Research* 9 (December 1982): 311–22.

19. Girish N. Punj and Richard Staelin, "A Model of

20. Cobb and Hoyer, "Direct Observation of Search Behavior"; Moore and Lehmann, "Individual Differences in Search Behavior for a Nondurable"; Punj and Staelin, "A Model of Consumer Search Behavior for New Automobiles."

21. James R. Bettman and C. Whan Park, "Effects of Prior Knowledge and Experience and Phase of the Choice Process on Consumer Decision Processes: A Protocol Analysis," *Journal of Consumer Research* 7 (December 1980): 234–48.

22. Alba and Hutchinson, "Dimensions of Consumer Expertise"; Bettman and Park, "Effects of Prior Knowledge and Experience and Phase of the Choice Process on Consumer Decision Processes"; Merrie Brucks, "The Effects of Product Class Knowledge on Information Search Behavior," *Journal of Consumer Research* 12 (June l985): 1–16; Joel E. Urbany, Peter R. Dickson, and William L. Wilkie, "Buyer Uncertainty and Information Search," *Journal of Consumer Research* 16 (September 1989): 208–15.

23. Robert J. Sutton, "Using Empirical Data to Investigate the Likelihood of Brands Being Admitted or Readmitted Into an Established Evoked Set," *Journal of the Academy of Marketing Science* 15 (Fall 1987): 82.

24. John R. Hauser and Birger Wernerfelt, "An Evaluation Cost Model of Consideration Sets," *Journal of Consumer Research* 16 (March 1990): 393–408.

25. Alba and Hutchison, "Dimensions of Consumer Expertise"; Joel B. Cohen and Kunal Basu "Alternative Models of Categorization: Toward a Contingent Processing Framework," *Journal of Consumer Research* 13 (March 1987): 455–72.

26. Eleanor Rosch, "Principles of Categorization," in *Recognition and Categorization*, eds. E. Rosch and B.B. Lloyd (Hillsdale, N.J.: Lawrence Erlbaum, 1978).

27. Michael R. Solomon, "Mapping Product Constellations: A Social Categorization Approach to Symbolic Consumption," *Psychology & Marketing* 5 (1988)3: 233–58.

28. Elizabeth C. Hirschman and Michael R. Solomon, "Competition and Cooperation Among Culture Production Systems," in *Marketing Theory: Philosophy of Science Perspectives*, eds. Ronald F. Bush and Shelby D. Hunt (Chicago: American Marketing Association, 1982), 269–72.

29. Michael D. Johnson, "The Differential Processing of Product Category and Noncomparable Choice Alternatives," *Journal of Consumer Research* 16 (December 1989): 300–09.

30. Mita Sujan, "Consumer Knowledge: Effects on Evaluation Strategies Mediating Consumer Judgments," *Journal of Consumer Research* 12 (June 1985): 31–46.
31. Rosch, "Principles of Categorization."
32. Joan Meyers-Levy and Alice M. Tybout, "Schema Congruity as a Basis for Product Evaluation," *Journal of Consumer Research* 16 (June 1989): 39–55.
33. Mita Sujan and James R. Bettman, "The Effects of Brand Positioning Strategies on Consumers' Brand and Category Perceptions: Some Insights from Schema Research," *Journal of Marketing Research* 26 (November 1989): 454–67.
34. Jack Trout, "Marketing in Tough Times," *Boardroom Reports* (October 1992)2: 8.
35. Amna Kirmani and Peter Wright, "Procedural Learning, Consumer Decision Making and Marketing Communication," *Marketing Letters* (1992).
36. C. Whan Park, "The Effect of Individual and Situation-Related Factors on Consumer Selection of Judgmental Models," *Journal of Marketing Research* 13 (May 1976): 144–51.
37. Joseph W. Alba and Howard Marmorstein, "The Effects of Frequency Knowledge on Consumer Decision Making," *Journal of Consumer Research* 14 (June 1987): 14–25.
38. Wayne D. Hoyer, "An Examination of Consumer Decision Making for a Common Repeat Purchase Product," *Journal of Consumer Research* 11 (December 1984): 822–29; Calvin P. Duncan, "Consumer Market Beliefs: A Review of the Literature and an Agenda for Future Research," in *Advances in Consumer Research* 17, eds. Marvin E. Goldberg, Gerald Gorn, and Richard W. Pollay (Provo, Utah: Association for Consumer Research, 1990), 729–35.
39. Robert A. Baron, *Psychology: The Essential Science* (Boston: Allyn & Bacon, 1989); Valerie S. Folkes, "The Availability Heuristic and Perceived Risk," *Journal of Consumer Research* 15 (June 1989): 13–23; Daniel Kahneman and Amos Tversky, "Prospect Theory: An Analysis of Decision Under Risk," *Econometrica* 47 (1979): 263–91.
40. Michael R. Solomon, Sarah Drenan, and Chester A. Insko, "Popular Induction: When is Consensus Information Informative?" *Journal of Personality* 49 (1981)2: 212–24.
41. Folkes, "The Availability Heuristic and Perceived Risk."
42. Beales et al., "Consumer Search and Public Policy."
43. Gary T. Ford and Ruth Ann Smith, "Inferential Beliefs in Consumer Evaluations: An Assessment of Alternative Processing Strategies," *Journal of Consumer Research* 14 (December 1987): 363–71; Deborah Roedder John, Carol A. Scott, and James R. Bettman, "Sampling Data for Covariation Assessment: The Effects of Prior Beliefs on Search Patterns," *Journal of Consumer Research* 13 (June 1986): 38–47; Gary L. Sullivan and Kenneth J. Berger, "An Investigation of the Determinants of Cue Utilization," *Psychology & Marketing* 4 (Spring 1987): 63–74.
44. John et al., "Sampling Data for Covariation Assessment."
45. Duncan, "Consumer Market Beliefs."
46. Chr. Hjorth-Andersen, "Price as a Risk Indicator," *Journal of Consumer Policy* 10 (1987): 267–81.
47. David M. Gardner, "Is There a Generalized Price-Quality Relationship?" *Journal of Marketing Research* 8 (May 1971): 241–43; Kent B. Monroe, "Buyers' Subjective Perceptions of Price," *Journal of Marketing Research* 10 (1973): 70–80.
48. Richard W. Stevenson, "The Brands With Billion-Dollar Names," New York Times (October 28, 1988): A1.
49. Ronald Alsop, "Enduring Brands Hold Their Allure by Sticking Close to Their Roots," *Wall Street Journal,* centennial ed. (1989): B4.
50. Laura Clark, "Porsche Top Auto Brand Name; Honda, Toyota, BMW Follow in U.S., Japan, Europe Survey," *Automotive News* (December 12, 1988): 62.
51. "What's in a Name?" *The Economist* (August 27, 1988): 62.
52. Stuart Elliott, "What's in a Name? Perhaps Billions," *New York Times* (August 12, 1992): D6.
53. Jacob Jacoby and Robert Chestnut, *Brand Loyalty: Measurement and Management* (New York: Wiley, 1978).
54. Anne B. Fisher, "Coke's Brand Loyalty Lesson," *Fortune* (August 5, 1985): 44.
55. Jacoby and Chestnut, Brand Loyalty.
56. Ronald Alsop, "Brand Loyalty is Rarely Blind Loyalty," *Wall Street Journal* (October 19, 1989): B1.
57. Alsop, "Brand Loyalty is Rarely Blind Loyalty."
58. Dennis Kneale, "Glitzy Brands Make Small Impressions: in Fragrances, Fashion, Many Favor Familiar," *Wall Street Journal* (December 15, 1989): B1.
59. Judith Waldrop, "Educating the Customer," *American Demographics* (September 1991)4: 44.
60. Barbara C. Garland and Marti J. Rhea, "American Consumers: Profile of an Import Preference Segment," *Akron Business and Economic Review* 19 (Summer 1988): 20–29.
61. Richard Ettenson, Janet Wagner, and Gary Gaeth,

"Evaluating the Effect of Country of Origin and the 'Made in the U.S.A.' Campaign: A Conjoint Approach," *Journal of Retailing* 64 (Spring 1988): 85–100; C. Min Han and Vern Terpstra, "Country-of-Origin Effects for Uni-National & Bi-National Products," *Journal of International Business* 19 (Summer 1988): 235–55; Michelle A. Morganosky and Michelle M. Lazarde, "Foreign-Made Apparel: Influences on Consumers' Perceptions of Brand and Store Quality," *International Journal of Advertising* 6 (Fall 1987): 339–48.

62. Gary M. Erickson, Johny K. Johansson, and Paul Chao, "Image Variables in Multi-Attribute Product Evaluations: Country-of-Origin Effects," Journal of *Consumer Research* 11 (September 1984): 694–99.

63. Sung-Tai Hong and Robert S. Wyer, Jr., "Effects of Country-of-Origin and Product–Attribute Information on Product Evaluation: An Information Processing Perspective," *Journal of Consumer Research* 16 (September 1989): 175–87; Majorie Wall, John Liefeld, and Louise A. Heslop, "Impact of Country-of-Origin Cues on Consumer Judgments in Multi-Cue Situations: A Covariance Analysis," *Journal of the Academy of Marketing Science* 19 (1991)2: 105–13.

CHAPTER 8

Demographics

and Household

Decision Making

Buying, Having, and Being: Selections 24–26 from *Buying, Having, and Being: The Washington Post Consumer Behavior Companion*, Second Edition, accompany this chapter.

Tuesday is grocery shopping day, and L.J. is accompanying his Mom to the store. He doesn't usually go along, and he kind of thinks Tina, his mom, would rather go without him. She spends less and gets home faster without him, she says. But he's going today anyway, partly to be sure that she picks out cool stuff for his eleventh birthday party. The Ninja Turtles tablecloth and cupcakes were OK last year, but he's close to being a teenager now and he plans to lobby heavily for the right food and decorations. Yeah, he wants stuff that's with it—maybe heavy metal, featuring bands like Metallica or Fingers of Death.

First, though, they have to get the family's regular shopping out of the way. Tina gets a little exasperated as L.J. and his little brother argue over the best type of dog food to get for Sherman, their new puppy. Finally, at Tina's urging, they move on to the next aisle, where she quickly throws two cans of tuna fish into the cart. She starts to move on, but from behind her she hears L.J. say: "Whoa, Ma! Just chill for a minute here! You're not really going to buy that brand, are you? Don't you know that they still use nets to catch their tuna—those nets kill hundreds of innocent dolphins every year!" This was news to Tina. After getting over her initial irritation at being told how to shop by a kid who can't even clean up his room, she realizes that L.J. is making a lot of sense.

As she puts the offending cans back on the shelf, she remarks, "Gee, L.J., I guess I should send you to do the shopping from now on. If you could only drive, I'd really have it easy . . . ."

Joint Decision Making

Kids are becoming a major force in persuading their parents to clean up their act when it comes to the environment. One study showed that one-third of parents have changed their shopping habits to be more environmentally conscious because of information they received from their children. Teen groups like YES (Youth for Environmental Sanity) travel around the country preaching environmental consciousness. So-called "green teens" have been instrumental in projects ranging from home and school recycling to persuading tuna companies to stop buying tuna caught in nets that also capture dolphins. Many companies are becoming aware of young peoples' influence in everyday family buying decisions, and some are trying extra hard to convince green teens that their products are environmentally friendly.[1]

L.J.'s influence on Tina's choice of an environmentally safe product illustrates that many consumer decisions are made jointly. The *individual* decision-making process described in detail in Chapter 7 is, in many cases, overly simplistic. In fact, more than one person may actually be involved in any stage of the problem-solving sequence, from initial problem recognition and information search to evaluation of alternatives and product choice. For example, as the photo at the beginning of this chapter reminds us, the decision to get a pet is often jointly made by family members. The kids may be instrumental in persuading their reluctant parents to get a dog or a cat, while the parents may be responsible for the information search to determine what kind to get or where to get it. Then, the entire family may be involved in actually selecting the puppy or kitten that will soon become another family member.

This chapter examines the importance of the household unit for many purchase decisions, and it also considers how such characteristics as family structure and the stage of life of household members influence both the demand for products and the way decisions regarding these products are made. The chapter concludes by focusing on how children learn to be consumers and how marketers cater to this important constituency in the household.

Defining the Modern Family

The **extended family** was once the most common family unit. It consisted of three generations living together and often included not only the grandparents, but aunts, uncles, and cousins. As evidenced by the Cleavers of "Leave It To Beaver" and other television families of the 1950s, the **nuclear family**— a mother and a father and one or more children (perhaps with a sheepdog thrown in for good measure)—became the model family unit over time. However, many changes have occurred since the days of Beaver Cleaver. Alhough people may continue to conjure up an image of the typical American family based on old shows like "Leave it to Beaver," "Father Knows Best," and "Ozzie and Harriet," demographic data show that this ideal image of the family is no longer a realistic picture.

Demographics are statistics that measure a population's characteristics, such as birth rate, age distribution, income, and so on. The U.S. Census Bureau is a major source of demographic data on families, but many private firms gather additional data on specific population groups. The changes and trends revealed in demographic studies are of great interest to marketers, because the data can be used to locate and predict the size of markets for many products, ranging from home mortgages to brooms and can openers. In addition, changes in consumers' family structures, such as the upheaval caused by divorce, often represent opportunities for marketers as normal purchasing patterns become unfrozen and people make new choices about products and brands.[2]

Describing the Family

In taking the national census every ten years, the U.S. Census Bureau regards *any* occupied housing unit as a *household*, regardless of the relationships among people living there. A **family household**, as defined by the Census Bureau, contains at least two people who are related by blood or marriage. While the Census Bureau and other survey firms compile a massive amount of data on family households, certain categories are of particular interest to marketers.

Additional Example: Whittle Communications has compiled a list of 850,000 newly-weds by monitoring wedding license files and tracking customer requests at Zales Jewelers. These customers are mailed a free magazine, called *New Marriage*, for which Prudential Insurance has exclusive advertising rights. See Brad Edmondson, "With This Magazine I Thee Wed," *American Demographics* (June 1987): 24.

GROWTH AND DISTRIBUTION OF FAMILY HOUSEHOLDS The last half of this century has seen a major shift in where Americans live. Historically, the population was concentrated in northeastern and midwestern urban areas. Largely through the widespread availability of automobiles, consumers migrated, and suburban areas grew dramatically.

Recently, people have been pushing out even farther beyond cities. *Exurbs*, smaller towns ringing suburbs, have grown the most rapidly. Consumers are still reporting a greater desire to live in towns and villages than in cities, and some experts predict that this trend will continue.[3] This growth has been concentrated in the southern and western United States and accounts for about 90 percent of the population growth that has occurred since 1980 as a result of migration from the North and Midwest.[4]

AGE OF THE FAMILY Since 1980, the under-25, married couple age group declined by one-third, while the 65 + couples group increased by about 15 percent.[5] Overall, consumers between 35 and 44 were responsible for the largest increase in the number of households, growing by almost 40 percent since 1980.[6] Half of all family householders will fall into this age group by the year 2000. People are waiting longer to get married: According to the U.S. Census Bureau, the average age of marriage is now 24 for women and 26 for men. This trend has implications for businesses ranging from catering to cutlery.

Children in the Family. Worldwide, surveys show that almost all women want smaller families than they did a decade ago. Family size is dependent on such factors as educational level, the availability of birth control, and religion.[7] Approximately 3.8 million babies are born annually in the United States. This number peaked in 1988, ending a rising trend that began in 1977. Marketers keep a close eye on the population's birth rate (also called *fertility rate*) to gauge how the pattern of births will affect demand for products in the future.

The *fertility rate* is determined by the number of births per year per 1000 women of child-bearing age. The U.S. fertility rate increased dramatically in the late 1950s and early 1960s, the period of the so-called baby boomers. It declined in the 1970s and began to climb again in the 1980s as baby boomers began to have their own children in a "baby boomlet."

The current figure is about 66 babies born annually for every 1000 women between the ages of 15 and 44, a rate almost half that during the baby boom period. Demographers predict that the fertility rate will continue to decline, even though the number of fertile women between 15 and 44 will grow.[8] Despite the fact that half of American women between the ages of 18 and 34 expect to have children, births will fall because most women are on the older edge of this age group.[9]

MARKETING OPPORTUNITY

Nine million preschoolers are involved in child-care programs, most of them in the 600,000 licensed facilities now in operation in the United States. However,

dogs (for $100, and the veil is extra), a $48 black dinner jacket, and a $30 trench coat.[29]

- A veterinarian in Maryland offers holistic medicine for pets. He features natural foods, acupuncture, and chiropractic massages. The doctor also sells the Rodeo Drive Fragrance Collection, a set of spray colognes for dogs.[30]

- A 25-minute video, titled "Doggie Adventure," was produced for dogs. Shot with a camera balanced two feet off the ground, it takes viewers on a romp from a dog's perspective.[31]

- Pet accessories for sale include a pet safety belt for the car and a heated water bed. The Pet Set, a store in Atlanta, offers mink coats, marble feeding bowls, brass beds, jogging suits, and toothpaste for consumers' furry friends.[32]

The Family in the Marketplace

Although the "Leave It to Beaver" ideal of the American family is no longer an accurate picture of consumers' real lives, marketers recognize that families and other household units still tend to function according to the traditional pattern of mom, dad, and kids. For example, the kitchen, where food and household products are often shown, is usually dominated by a mother figure (not necessarily a woman), who dispenses love and food and maintains the home. The den is reserved for a father figure who is the source of wise counsel and advice. Bedrooms are usually used as personal space (often of children), where comforting reassurances are given and confidential problems are resolved.[33]

Targeting the Family

Many marketers have focused on the renewed interest in family life brought about by the more flexible definitions of what constitutes a family.[34] While families were indeed out of fashion in the 1960s and 1970s, being seen by some as an infringement on personal freedom, 90 percent of the respondents in one recent survey confirmed that family life was one of the most important things to them.[35]

The Club Med organization is one marketer that has changed with the times. More than a half-million members are married, and members' median age is 37. Many Club Meds, which now have Mini Clubs for kids aged 2 to 11, switched in the 1980s from havens for "swinging singles" to family destinations. Some clubs even have a staff to warm bottles and take care of babies as young as four months old.[36] The company has changed its advertising slogan from "The antidote to civilization" to "Take home a Club Med vacation" and is even airing television commercials during Saturday morning children's programming.[37]

The renewed priority on the family and other changes such as increasing birth and marriage rates have been emphasized by direct mail strategists. For example, Kimberly-Clark purchases a list of new parents from a vendor that scans local birth announcements. Every three months these con-

Soft Sheen Products, the largest marketer of ethnic hair-care products, is entering the baby category. An ad introducing a product line called Baby Love, which is specifically designed to meet the needs of African-American and Hispanic babies, is available as Transparancy 19.

sumers are mailed a free magazine explaining changes in infant behavior, along with coupons for Huggies diapers.

Other advertisers are also climbing on the bandwagon. Companies ranging from Heinz and Polycell (in the United Kingdom) to Gitano jeans and Johnson outboard motors are revamping their campaigns.[38] As the ad shown here indicates, Gitano, for example, traditionally positioned as jeans for seductive women, is now spending $3 million on its "Spirit of Family" campaign that depicts an all-American family image. As a company executive explains, "Even though the Gitano ads of the past have been of a self-confident, sexy woman, they've updated with the times. Now, we see that the family is what is important."[39]

Effects of Family Structure on Consumption

Family structure can affect consumer behavior in a variety of ways. A family's needs and expenditures vary depending on such factors as the number of people (children and adults) in the family, their ages, and whether one, two, or more adults are employed outside of the home.

Two important factors that determine how a couple spends time and money are whether they have children and whether the woman works. Couples with children generally have higher expenses (ranging from food to utility bills).[40] In addition, a recently married couple makes very different expenditures than one with young children, who in turn are quite different from a couple with children in college, and so on. Families with working mothers also must often make allowances for such expenses as day care and a work wardrobe for the woman.

THE FAMILY LIFE CYCLE Recognizing that family needs and expenditures change over time, the concept of the **family life cycle** (FLC) has been widely used by marketers. This form of classification combines trends in income and family composition with the changes in demands placed upon this income. As we age, our preferences for products and activities tend to change. In many cases, our income levels tend to rise (at least until retirement), so that we can afford more as well. In addition, many purchases that must be made at an early age do not have to be repeated very often. For example, we tend to accumulate durable goods, such as large appliances, and only replace them as necessary.

This focus on longitudinal changes in priorities is particularly valuable in predicting demand for specific product categories over time. For example, the money spent by a couple with no children on dinners out and vacations will probably be diverted for quite different purchases after the birth of a child. While a number of models have been proposed to describe family life cycle stages, their usefulness has been limited because in many cases they have failed to take into account such important social trends as the changing role of women, the acceleration of alternative lifestyles, childless and delayed-child marriages, and single-parent households.

Three variables are necessary to encompass these changes: age, marital status, the presence or absence of children in the home and their ages. In addition, our definition of marital status (at least for analysis purposes)

Among the companies that have revamped their images to stress the family, Gitano has replaced its traditional focus on young, single adults (top) with a family theme (bottom). Courtesy of THE AD GROUP, New York, N.Y.; in-house agency: The Gitano Group, Inc.

must be relaxed to include any couple living together who are in a long-term relationship. Thus, while roommates might not be considered "married," a man and woman who have established a household would be, as would two homosexual men who have a similar understanding.

When these changes are considered, this approach allows us to identify a set of categories that include many more types of family situations.[41] These categories, which are listed in Table 8–1, are derived by dividing consumers into groups in terms of age, whether there is more than one adult present, and whether there are children. For example, a distinction is made between the consumption needs of people in the Full Nest I category (where the youngest child is less than six), the Full Nest II category (where the youngest child is older than six), the Full Nest III category (where the youngest child is older than six and the parents are middle-aged), and the

TABLE 8–1 The Family Life Cycle: An Updated View

	Age of Head of Household		
	Under 35	**35–64**	**Over 64**
One adult in household	Bachelor I	Bachelor II	Bachelor III
Two adults in household	Young couple	Childless couple	Older couple
Two adults plus children in household	Full nest I	Delayed full nest	
	Full nest II	Full nest III	

Source: Adapted from Mary C. Gilly and Ben M. Enis, "Recycling the Family Life Cycle: A Proposal for Redefinition," in *Advances in Consumer Research* 9, ed. Andrew A. Mitchell (Ann Arbor, Mich.: Association for Consumer Research, 1982), 271–76, Figure 1, p. 274.

Table 8–1 is available as Transparency 20.

Teaching Hint: The J. Walter Thompson advertising agency developed an alternative typology, called Lifestages, to better describe the growing numbers of single consumers who do not fit into traditional FLC categories. The five stages include such classifications as At-Home Singles (average age 22), and Mature Singles (divorced or separated, average age 45). See Gary Levin, "JWT Researches Stages, Not Ages," *Advertising Age* (June 26, 1989): 30.

Delayed Full Nest (where the parents are middle-aged but the youngest child is younger than six).

As might be expected, consumers classified into these categories show marked differences in consumption patterns. Young bachelors and newlyweds have the most "modern" sex-role attitudes, are the most likely to engage in exercise, to go out to bars, concerts, movies, and restaurants, and to go out dancing; and they consume more alcohol. Families with young children are more likely to consume health foods such as fruit, juice, and yogurt, while those made up of single parents and older children buy more junk foods. The dollar value of homes, cars, and other durables is lowest for bachelors and single parents, but increases as people go through the full nest and childless couple stages. Perhaps reflecting the bounty of wedding gifts, newlyweds are the most likely to own appliances such as toaster ovens and electric coffee grinders. Babysitter and day care usage is, of course, highest among single-parent and full-nest households, while home maintenance services (e.g., lawnmowing) are most likely to be employed by older couples and bachelors.

The growth of these additional categories creates many opportunities for enterprising marketers. For example, divorced people undergo a process of transition to a new social role. This change is often accompanied by the disposition of possessions linked to the former role and the need to acquire a set of possessions that help to express the person's new identity as he or she experiments with new lifestyles. While these changes, and others like them, tend to be overlooked by traditional perspectives on the FLC,[42] the Toyota ad shown here is designed to appeal to people who have moved from the young singles stage to a full-nest stage.

Decision Makers in the Family

Traditionally, some buying decisions, termed **autocratic decisions**, were usually made by one or the other spouse. Men, for instance, often had sole responsibility for selecting a car, while most decorating choices fell to

DISCOVER COROLLA. AGAIN.

"I love what you do for me."

TOYOTA

It's a safe bet you first discovered Corolla early in your driving career. After all, Corolla was introduced in 1968, back when hair was long, skirts were short, and cars stretched a city block. But now it's the nineties. And just as you've changed over the past twenty-five years, so has Corolla. Introducing the all-new 1993 Toyota Corolla. With an interior that's bigger, more comfortable, so you can stretch your legs, not your patience. A larger, more powerful engine.* And an abundance of safety features, including a standard driver-side air bag† side-door impact beams, and available Anti-lock Brakes. Yet with all these changes, it's still a Corolla. Which, after all, is what drove you to discover it in the first place. Take a look at the new 1993 Toyota Corolla. Call 1-800-GO-TOYOTA for a brochure and location of your nearest dealer. And discover again what you need in a car today.

INTRODUCING THE ALL-NEW
1993 TOYOTA COROLLA.

©1992 Toyota Motor Sales, U.S.A., Inc. Buckle Up! Do it for those who love you. *1.8-liter engine standard on LE and DX models. †Always use your seatbelts. Driver-side air bag is a supplemental restraint system.

This Toyota ad targets consumers who have moved from the young singles stage to a full-nest stage in the family life cycle. Courtesy of Toyota Motor Sales, USA Inc.

women. Other decisions, such as vacation destinations, were made jointly; these are known as **syncratic decisions**.

The nature of consumer decision making within a particular product category is an important issue for marketers, so that they know whom to target and whether or not they need to reach both spouses to influence a decision. For example, when market research in the 1950s indicated that women were playing a larger role in household purchasing decisions, lawn-mower manufacturers began to emphasize the rotary mower over other power mowers. Rotary mowers, which conceal the cutting blades and engine, were often depicted being used by young women and smiling grandmothers to downplay fears of injuries.[43]

Four factors appear to determine the degree to which decisions will be made jointly or by one or the other spouse.[44]

1. *Sex-role stereotypes:* Couples who believe in traditional sex-role stereotypes tend to make individual decisions for sex-typed products (i.e., those considered to be "masculine" or "feminine").
2. *Spousal resources:* The spouse who contributes more resources to the family has the greater influence.
3. *Experience:* Individual decisions are made more frequently when the couple has gained experience as a decision-making unit.
4. *Socio-economic status:* Joint decisions are made more by middle-class families than in either higher- or lower-class families.

Sex Roles and Decision-Making Responsibilities

With many women now working outside of the home, men are participating more in nurturing, family-related activities. Overall, the degree to which a couple adheres to traditional sex-role norms determines how much their allocation of responsibilities will fall along familiar lines and how their consumer decision-making responsibilities will be allocated.

In traditional families (and especially those with low educational levels), women are primarily responsible for family financial management—the man makes it, and the woman spends it.[45] Each spouse "specializes" in certain activities.[46] The pattern is different among families where spouses adhere to more modern sex-role norms. These couples believe that there should be more shared participation in family maintenance activities. In these cases, husbands assume more responsibility for laundering, house-

MULTICULTURAL DIMENSIONS

Japan's increasing modernization is causing some radical changes in its family structure—not all of them good. Although traditional sex roles are quite robust in Japan, recently women are starting to rebel against the inevitability of getting married young and staying home with babies. The number of unmarried people older than 30 has doubled in the last 20 years.

Women report that they are getting fed up with playing housekeeper to men who lounge around the house when they are not at work. Many have instead chosen to live with their families, save their money, and travel. Some married women are also starting to complain about their husbands, who have been described as "absentee fathers." Japanese fathers spend so

much time working that more than a quarter of children surveyed said their Dads never take them for a walk or play games with them. Due to long work hours, a typical Japanese father has only 36 minutes a day available to spend with his kids. About 60 percent of Japanese men typically do not eat breakfast at home, and about 30 percent regularly miss dinner.

To counteract these trends, the Japanese Government is offering a "reward" of 5000 yen per month (about $38) for couples who have a second child and twice that amount for a third child. Many Japanese women are angered and insulted by this policy, claiming that the government is treating them like machines.[47]

cleaning, grocery shopping, and so on, in addition to such traditionally "male" tasks as home maintenance and garbage removal.[48]

MAINTAINING THE KIN NETWORK Despite recent changes in decision-making responsibilities, women still are primarily responsible for the continuation of the family's *kin-network system*. They perform the rituals intended to maintain ties among family members, both immediate and extended. This function includes such activities as coordinating visits among relatives, calling and writing family members, sending greeting cards, making social engagements, and so on.[49] This organizing role means that women often make important decisions about the family's leisure activities, choices regarding whom to see and where to see them, and so on.

Spousal Influence

In terms of family decision making, the **synoptic ideal** calls for the husband and wife to take a common view and act as joint decision makers. According to this ideal, they would very thoughtfully weigh alternatives, assign one another well-defined roles, and calmly make mutually beneficial consumer decisions. The couple would act rationally, analytically, and use as much information as possible to maximize joint utility. In reality, however, spousal decision making is often characterized by the use of influence or methods that are likely to reduce conflict. A couple "reaches" rather than "makes" a decision. This process has been described as "muddling through."[50]

One common technique for simplifying the decision-making process is the use of *heuristics* (see Chapter 7). Some decision-making patterns frequently observed when a couple makes decisions in buying a new house illustrate the use of heuristics.

1. The couple's areas of common preference are based upon salient, objective dimensions rather than more subtle, hard-to-define cues. For example, a couple may easily agree on the number of bedrooms they need in the new home, but will have more difficulty achieving a common view of how the home should look.
2. The couple agrees on a system of task specialization, where each is responsible for certain duties or decision areas and does not interfere on the other's "turf." For many couples, these assignments are likely to be influenced by their perceived sex roles. For example, the wife may scout out houses in advance that meet their requirements, while the husband determines whether the couple can obtain a mortgage.
3. Concessions are based on the intensity of each spouse's preferences. One spouse will yield to the influence of the other in many cases simply because his or her level of preference for a certain attribute is not particularly intense, where in other situations he or she will be willing to exert effort to obtain a favorable decision.[51] In cases where intense preferences for different attributes exist, rather than attempt to influence each other, spouses will "trade off" a less-intense preference for a more strongly felt one. For example, a husband who is somewhat indifferent about kitchen design may give in to his wife, but expect that in turn he will be allowed to design his own garage workshop.

Research Report: Spouses are generally unable to accurately identify how much influence they and their partners have in the decision-making process, much less predict their partners' preferences. Indeed, because spouses tend to be fairly similar, research suggests that they are better off relying upon their *own* preferences rather than inferring their mates' when predicting what their spouses will like. See Harry L. Davis, Stephen J. Hoch, and E.K. Easton Ragsdale, "An Anchoring and Adjustment Model of Spousal Predictions," *Journal of Consumer Research* 13 (June 1986): 25–37; Rosann L. Spiro, "Persuasion in Family Decision-Making," *Journal of Consumer Research* 9 (March 1983): 393–402; J.S. Hopper, C. Burns, and N.L. Sherrell, "An Assessment of the Reliability and Validity of Husband and Wife Self-Report Purchase Decision Making Measures," *Journal of the Academy of Marketing Science* 17 (Summer 1989): 227–34.

Research Report: One recent study on the adoption of product innovations found that a wife tends to exert more control over the new product adoption decisions of her husband rather than vice-versa. See David J. Burns, "Husband-Wife Innovative Decision Making: Exploring the Effect of Family Power," *Psychology & Marketing* 9 (May/June 1992): 175–89.

TABLE 8–2 Kids' Influence on Household Purchases

Top 10 Selected Products	Industry Sales ($ billions)	Influence Factor (%)	Sales Influence ($ billions)
Fruit snacks	0.30	80	0.24
Frozen novelties	1.40	75	1.05
Kids' beauty aids	1.20	70	0.84
Kids' fragrances	0.30	70	0.21
Toys	13.40	70	9.38
Canned pasta	0.57	60	0.34
Kids' clothing	18.40	60	11.04
Video games	3.50	60	2.10
Hot cereals	0.74	50	0.37
Kids' shoes	2.00	50	1.00

Source: "Charting the Children's Market," *Adweek* (February 10, 1992): 42. Reprinted with permission of James J. McNeal, Texas A&M University, College Station, Texas.

Cross-Cultural Example: In one study of Singaporean families, almost half of the families surveyed felt that their children had significantly influenced major purchase decisions, including the family's dwelling. See William R. Swinyard and Cheng Peng Sim, "Perception of Children's Influence on Family Decision Processes," *Journal of Consumer Marketing* 4 (Winter 1987): 25–38.

Research Report: Shopping goods (e.g., clothing) tend to be purchased jointly by parent and child, but specialty goods such as records and movie tickets are likely to be purchased by the child alone. See George P. Moschis, "The Role of Family Communication in Consumer Socialization of Children and Adolescents," *Journal of Consumer Research* 11 (March 1985): 898–913.

The Influence of Children

Anyone who has had the "delightful" experience of grocery shopping with one or more children in tow knows that kids often have a say in what their parents buy, especially for products like cereal.[52] It has been estimated that children between the age of 4 and 12 spend or influence their parents to spend about $140 billion a year.[53] Table 8–2 documents kids' influence in ten different product categories.

Parental yielding occurs when a parental decision maker is influenced by a child's request and "surrenders." The strategies kids use to request purchases were documented in a recent study. While most children simply asked for things, some other common tactics included saying they had seen it on television, saying that a sibling or friend has it, bargaining by offering to do chores, and so on. Other actions were less innocuous; they included directly placing the object in the cart and continuous pleading.[54]

The Intimate Corporation: Family Decision Making

The decision process within a household unit in some ways resembles a business conference. Certain matters are put on the table for discussion, different members may have different priorities and agendas, and there may be some jockeying for position or power struggles to rival any tale of corporate intrigue. In just about every living situation, whether a conventional family, students sharing a sorority house or apartment, or some other nontraditional arrangement, group members seem to take on different roles just as purchasing agents, engineers, account executives, and others do within a company.

Household Decision Roles

A number of specific roles are played when a decision must be made by either a private household or some other decision-making unit, such as the buying center in a large company.[55] Depending on the decision, some or all of the group members may be involved, and one person may play any number (or even all) of these roles. Indeed, a person living alone may be thought of as a "corporation of one." He or she makes the "executive" decision to initiate a project and is also responsible for information collection and making a purchase. The roles that may be played are as follows.

- *Initiator:* the person who brings up the idea or need.
- *Gatekeeper(s):* the person(s) who conducts the information search and controls the flow of information available to the group.
- *Influencer(s):* the person(s) who tries to sway the outcome of the decision. Some people may be more motivated to get involved, and participants also differ in terms of the amount of power they have to convince others of their choice.
- *Buyer(s):* the person(s) who actually makes the purchase. The buyer may or may not actually use the product. This person may pay for the item, actually procure it, or both.
- *User(s):* the person(s) who winds up using the product or service.

TYPES OF DECISIONS   Two basic types of decisions are made by families.[56] In a *consensual purchase decision*, the group agrees on the desired purchase, differing only in terms of how it will be achieved. In these circumstances, the family will most likely engage in problem solving and consider alternatives until the means for satisfying the group's goal is found. For example, a household considering adding a dog to the family but concerned about who will take care of it might draw up a chart assigning individuals to specific duties.

In other cases, life is not so easy. In an *accommodative purchase decision*, group members have different preferences or priorities and cannot agree on a purchase that will satisfy the minimum expectations of all involved. It is here that bargaining, coercion, compromise, and the wielding of power are all likely be used to achieve the primary goal of agreement on the purchase itself. Family decisions often are characterized by an accommodative rather than a consensual decision.

SOURCES OF CONFLICT   Conflict occurs when there is not complete correspondence in family members' needs and preferences. Some specific factors determining the degree of family decision conflict include the following.[57]

- *Interpersonal need* (a person's level of investment in the group): A child in a family situation may care more about what his or her family buys for the house than will a college student who is temporarily living in a dorm.

Research Report: Children's input tends to be greatest in the early stages of the decision-making process, where they play an important role in problem recognition and information search. See George Belch, Michael A. Belch, and Gayle Ceresino, "Parental and Teenage Child Influences in Family Decision Making," *Journal of Business Research* 13 (April 1985): 163–76; D.R. Howard and R. Madrigal, "Who Makes the Decision: The Parent or the Child? The Perceived Influence of Parents and Children on the Purchase of Recreation Services," *Journal of Leisure Research* 22 (1990)3: 244–58.

Additional Examples: Prompted by research showing that children exert a major influence on family vacation decisions, travel-and-leisure firms are getting into the act. Hyatt Hotels recently initiated a Camp Hyatt Kids Council to evaluate its Camp Hyatt program, Delta Air Lines formed a Fantastic Flier Club (complete with a mascot, Dusty, the Delta Air Lion), and Embassy Suites has licensed Garfield the cartoon cat as its spokescharacter. See Claudia H. Deutsch, "Younger Set Leads the Way on the Road," *New York Times* (December 1, 1991): F10; Betsy Spethmann, "Young Travelers Exposed to Hyatt Touch," *Advertising Age* (February 10, 1992) S-6: 294.

- *Product involvement and utility* (the degree to which the product in question will be used or will satisfy a need): A family member who is an avid coffee drinker will obviously be more interested in the purchase of a new coffeemaker to replace a malfunctioning one than a similar expenditure for some other item.

- *Responsibility* (for procurement, maintenance, payment, and so on): People are more likely to have disagreements about a decision if it entails long-term consequences and commitments. For example, a family decision about getting a dog may involve conflict regarding who will be responsible for walking it and feeding it.

- *Power* (or the degree to which one family member exerts influence over the others in making decisions): In traditional families, the husband tends to have more power than the wife, who in turn has more than the oldest child, and so on. In family decisions, conflict can arise when one person continually uses the power he or she has within the group to satisfy his or her priorities. For example, if L.J. believed that his life would end if he did not have a heavy metal birthday party, he might be more willing to resort to extreme tactics to influence his parents, perhaps by throwing a tantrum or refusing to participate in family chores.

In general, decisions will involve conflict among family members to the extent that they are somehow important or novel and/or if individuals have strong opinions about good and bad alternatives. The degree to which these factors generate conflict determines the type of decision the family will make.

Development of Children: Consumers-in-Training

International Example: The craze to acquire Nintendo games, Barbie dolls, and other juvenile delights is certainly not confined to the United States: Toys 'R' Us expects to have over 400 international units in operation by 1997. The store is adapting its operations to suit local tastes. It sells porcelain dolls in Japan and wooden toys in Germany. Its version of Monopoly in Hong Kong stores replaces Boardwalk and Park Place with swank suburbs like Sheko and Repulse Bay. See Annetta Miller, "The World 'S' Ours," *Newsweek* (March 23, 1992)2: 46.

Children often play important roles in family consumer decision making, and they are gaining responsibility as consumers in their own right. They continue to support the toy and candy industries, of course, but now they also buy and/or influence the purchase of many other products as well.

For better or for worse, the new generation is, as the bumper sticker proclaims, "Born to Shop." Shopping now ranks among the top seven interests and activities of America's children.[58] Over 80 percent of young respondents in one survey said their primary wish was to have more money to buy things.[59]

Consumer Socialization Sources

Children do not spring from the womb with consumer skills already in memory. Learning the dos and don'ts of being a consumer involves a long and complex process with many influences lending a hand. **Consumer socialization** has been defined as the process ". . . by which young people acquire skills, knowledge, and attitudes relevant to their functioning in the marketplace."[60] Where does this knowledge come from? Friends and teachers certainly participate in this process. For instance, children talk to one another about consumer products, and this tendency increases with age.[61]

Especially for young children, though, the two primary socialization sources are the family and the media.

FAMILY INFLUENCE Parents' influences in consumer socialization are both direct and indirect. They deliberately try to instill their own values about consumption in their children ("you're going to learn the value of a dollar"). Parents also determine the degree to which their children will be exposed to other information sources, such as television, salespeople, and peers.[62] Parents serve as significant models for observational learning (see Chapter 4). Children learn about consumption by watching their parents' behavior and imitating it. This modeling is facilitated by marketers who package adult products in child versions.

Parental Style. Three dimensions combine to produce different "segments" of parental styles. Parents characterized by certain styles have been found to socialize their children differently.[63] For example, "authoritarian parents," who are hostile, restrictive, and emotionally uninvolved, do not have warm relationships with their children, are active in filtering the types of media to which their children are exposed, and tend to have negative views about advertising. "Neglecting parents" also do not have warm relationships, but they are more detached from their children and do not exercise much control over what their children do. In contrast, "indulgent parents" communicate more with their children about consumption-related matters and are less restrictive. They believe that children should be allowed to learn about the marketplace without much interference.

LEARNING FROM TELEVISION It's no secret that kids watch a lot of television. As a result, they are constantly bombarded with messages about consumption, both contained in commercials and in the shows themselves. According to **cultivation theory**, the media teaches people about a culture's values and myths. The more a child is exposed to television, whether the show is "LA Law" or "Teenage Mutant Ninja Turtles," the more he or she will accept the images depicted there as real.[64]

In addition to the large volume of programming targeted directly to children, kids also are exposed to idealized images of what it is like to be an adult. Since children over the age of six do about a quarter of their television viewing during prime time, they are affected by programs and commercials targeted to adults. For example, young girls exposed to adult lipstick commercials learn to associate lipstick with beauty.[65]

Sex-Role Socialization

Children pick up on the concept of gender identity (see Chapter 9) at an earlier age than was previously believed—perhaps as young as age one or two. By the age of three, most children categorize driving a truck as masculine and cooking and cleaning as feminine.[66] Even cartoon characters who are portrayed as helpless are more likely to wear frilly or ruffled dresses.[67]

CHILD'S PLAY One function of child's play is to rehearse for adulthood. Children "act out" different roles they might assume later in life and learn

Many companies, such as Guess, design clothing for children that differs little from adult versions. Courtesy of GUESS: Art Director: Paul Marciano. Photographer: Dominick Guiwmot.

Teaching Hint: Expectations regarding sex-typed toys also are reinforced at the time of purchase. Salespeople in toy stores have been found to recommend stereotypical choices when asked for advice by shoppers. See Glenn Collins, "New Studies on 'Girl Toys' and 'Boy Toys," *New York Times* (February 13, 1984): D1.

about the expectations others have of them. The toy industry provides the props children use to perform these roles.[68] As the Guess ad shown here demonstrates, many apparel items are being designed to resemble those that will continue to be used in adulthood.

Often "traditional" sex roles are stressed in children's products; the same item may be designed and positioned differently for boys and girls. Huffy, for example, manufactures bicycles for both boys and girls. The boys' versions have names like "Sigma" and "Vortex," and they are described as having ". . . maxed-out features that'll pump your pulse." The girls' version is more sedate. It is called "Sweet Style," and it comes in pink or purple. As a company executive described it in contrast to the boys' bikes, the girls' model ". . . is a fashion bike. It's not built for racing or jumping—just the look."[69]

Cognitive Development

The ability of children to make mature, "adult" consumer decisions obviously increases with age (not that grownups always make mature decisions).

Kids can be segmented by age in terms of their stage of **cognitive development**, or ability to comprehend concepts of increasing complexity. Some recent evidence indicates that young children are able to learn consumption-related information surprisingly well, depending on the format in which the information is presented (e.g., learning is enhanced if a videotaped vignette is presented to small children repeatedly).[70]

PIAGETIAN STAGES OF DEVELOPMENT The foremost proponent of the idea that children pass through distinct stages of cognitive development was the Swiss psychologist Jean Piaget, who believed that each stage is characterized by a certain cognitive structure the child uses to handle information.[71]

AN ALTERNATIVE TO PIAGET Many developmental specialists no longer believe that children necessarily pass through these fixed stages at the same time. An alternative approach regards children as differing in *information-processing capability*, or ability to store and retrieve information from memory (see Chapter 4). The following three segments have been identified by this approach.[72]

1. *Limited:* Below the age of 6, children do not employ storage and retrieval strategies.
2. *Cued:* Children between the ages of 6 and 12 employ these strategies, but only when prompted.
3. *Strategic:* Children 12 and older spontaneously employ storage and retrieval strategies.

This sequence of development underscores the notion that children do not think like adults, and they cannot be expected to use information the same way. It also reminds us that they do not necessarily form the same conclusions as adults do when presented with product information. For example, kids are not as likely to realize that something they see on television is not "real," and as a result they are more vulnerable to persuasive messages.

Children in the Marketplace

Kids are a "dream target" to some marketers because they are brand conscious and they are not price sensitive.[73] Most children also possess a surprisingly high degree of knowledge about products and brands, and they attribute positive and negative characteristics to others depending upon their product usage. Stereotypes about adults who own different styles of cars and houses are almost fully developed by the sixth grade.[74] Elementary school children also make judgments about other kids depending on the brand of jeans they wear (e.g., Calvin Klein vs. Sears) or even the types of video games they own.[75]

To kids, even the lunch box means more than a container for a bologna sandwich. As one collector put it, "When you're a kid, it's not what you drive, it's what you carry that gives you status in the blackboard jungle."[76] A lunch box is a fashion item. The characters depicted on it express a child's grasp of what is "in." Carrying a box with outdated figures or babyish ones may contribute to social suicide, and the choice of the right lunch box to buy is frequently the source of conflict between parents and children.

Research Report: In one classic demonstration of cognitive development, Piaget poured the contents of a glass of lemonade into a taller, thinner glass. Five-year-olds thought that this glass had more liquid than the other glass, while six-year-olds were unsure, and the seven-year-olds knew there was no difference. The younger children's judgment was determined by the shape of the glass itself, while the older children knew that the same amount of liquid had merely been transferred. One example of the relevance to consumerism is that unlike their older counterparts, children in the preoperational stage expect a package to determine the size of the contents. See Jean Piaget, "The Child and Modern Physics," *Scientific American* 196 (1957)3: 46–51; Kenneth D. Bahn, "How and When Do Brand Perceptions and Preferences First Form? A Cognitive Developmental Investigation," *Journal of Consumer Research* 13 (December 1986): 382–93; Gary Soldow, "Ability of Children to Understand the Product Package," *Journal of Public Policy and Marketing* (1985): 55–68.

Teaching Hint: Lunch boxes have become so embedded in American popular culture that the American Museum of National History maintains a display of classic boxes. Mickey Mouse, the first licensed lunch box character, appeared in 1935, but the boom began in 1950 with Hopalong Cassidy. The best-selling box of all time is the Disney School Bus (driven by Goofy). See N.R. Kleinfeld, "Another August Under the 'Whine Sign'," *New York Times* (August 6, 1989): D1.

Additional Examples: The Young American's Bank in Denver was the first bank established specifically for children. It specifies an age range for its clientele (12–22) and offers loans in addition to other services. F.A.O. Schwarz, a famous toy store in New York City, offers youth credit cards and checking accounts and opened the First Children's Bank in its Fifth Avenue store. Kids can make deposits alone, but withdrawals require an adult's signature. See Leonard Sloane, "Banks Children Can Call Their Own," *New York Times* (October 15, 1988): 38.

Targeting Children: More Than Child's Play

Although three product categories—toys, cereals, and candy or snacks—account for more than three-quarters of all ads on Saturday morning television, marketers are promoting children's versions of products ranging from personal stereos (Sony) to tissues (Scott Paper).[77] While numerous groups have objected to both the products and strategies used in targeting children, four out of five adults have no objections to ads for clothing or toys directed to kids, and a majority also accept the concept of directly advertising such products as cereals, shampoo, pet foods, movies (G-rated), and records.[78]

More than a third of girls aged 9 to 11 are regular users of deodorant, perfume, and nail polish. What's more, almost a third of boys and girls in the same age bracket use hair mousse! Mattel sells stick-on painted fingernails, and Maybelline features bubblegum flavored lip gloss. As one Maybelline market researcher explains the company's strategy, "They start out playing with lip gloss and nail color. Then they move into blusher and eye shadow."[79] This rationale is also behind the L'eggs hosiery ad shown here.

GETTING A HEAD START ON BRAND LOYALTY While marketers' interest in kids has a lot to do with what they are able to buy now, in many cases

This L'eggs ad shows how some companies begin to cultivate future customers at an early age. Courtesy of SARA LEE HOSIERY.

they are as or more interested in what they will spend *later*. Some forward-looking companies are realizing that brand loyalties form at an early age and are devising strategies to cement bonds with their future markets.

The McDonald's Corporation was a pioneer of this concept. The company regards children as three markets in one. First, they appeal directly to kids by offering meal kits, parties, playgrounds, and so on. Second, they realize the child's role as an influencer in family decision making, so advertising often encourages family trips to their restaurants. Finally, they regard children as their future market, realizing that today's kids will someday be bringing *their* children to the Golden Arches.[80]

Other marketers also are trying to cultivate this future market. This is why the Army, Marines, and Air Force advertise in *Boys' Life* magazine and why Levi Strauss & Company entered the children's market with My First Levi's (a line of corduroy and denim diaper covers, pants, and shirts) when sales of adult jeans began to slump.[81]

Market Research and Children

Despite their buying power, relatively little real data on children's preferences or influences on spending patterns is available. Compared to adults, kids are difficult subjects for market researchers. They tend to be undependable reporters of their own behavior, they have poor recall, and they often do not understand abstract questions.[82] This problem is compounded in Europe, where some countries restrict marketers' ability to interview children.

Still, market research can pay off, and many companies, as well as a number of specialized firms, have been successful researching some aspects of this segment.[83] After interviewing elementary school kids, Campbell's Soup discovered that kids like soup, but are afraid to admit it, because they associate it with "nerds." The company decided to reintroduce the Campbell kids in its advertising after a prolonged absence, but they are now slimmed-down and more athletic to reflect an updated, "un-nerdy" image.[84] Similarly, Oscar Mayer is attempting to impart a "cool" look to lunch meat, as shown in the company's cafeteria poster depicted on page 274.

Product Testing. A particularly helpful type of research with children is product testing. Young subjects can provide a valuable perspective on what products will succeed with other kids. One candy company has a Candy Tasters Club, composed of 1200 kids aged 6 to 16, that evaluates its product ideas. For example, the group nixed the idea of a Batman lollipop, claiming that the superhero was too macho to be a sucker.[85] The Fisher-Price Company maintains a nursery known as the Playlab. Children are chosen from a waiting list of 4000 to play with new toys, while staff members watch from behind a one-way mirror.[86] Other techniques include ethnographic research, where researchers hang out with kids or videotape them as they shop. The most successful interviewers are those who try not to be "adultcentric" (i.e., as an adult authority figure who assumes that children's beliefs are just unreal fantasies); they act as a friend to the children and are willing to use a variety of projective techniques and props to get children to express themselves in their own terms.[87]

Teaching Hint: Marketers wishing to target children may need to redesign their facilities and services to accommodate this segment. Some suggested changes include the addition of children's activities at vacation resorts (as Club Med is already doing), more innovative children's menus at restaurants, and supervised play areas at stores and supermarkets. See William R. Swinyard and Cheng Peng Sim, "Perception of Children's Influence on Family Decision Processes," *Journal of Consumer Marketing* 4 (Winter 1987): 25–38; Monte Williams, "Parental Guidance Lost on This Crop: From Peanut Butter to the Family's Wheels, Kids a Big Influence," *Advertising Age* (July 30, 1990): 26; George J. Szybillo, Arlene Sosanie, and Aaron Tenenbein, "Should Children Be Seen But Not Heard," *Journal of Advertising Research* 17 (December 1977): 7–13; David Zuckerman, "How To's of Menu Design and Marketing; Children's Menus: Not Just Kid Stuff," *Restaurant Management* (February 1988): 50–54.

Additional Example: Even IBM has begun to hire teachers to consult on software needs as it competes with Apple to win young (and hopefully long-term) customers. As an IBM executive explained, "Let's face it, we want to help these teachers and kids, but we also don't want kids growing up on Apple Computer, Inc. machines." Quoted in Stan Kolodziej, "Substitute Teacher: PC's + Students = Early Brand Loyalty," *Computerworld* 22 (June 1988): 10–13.

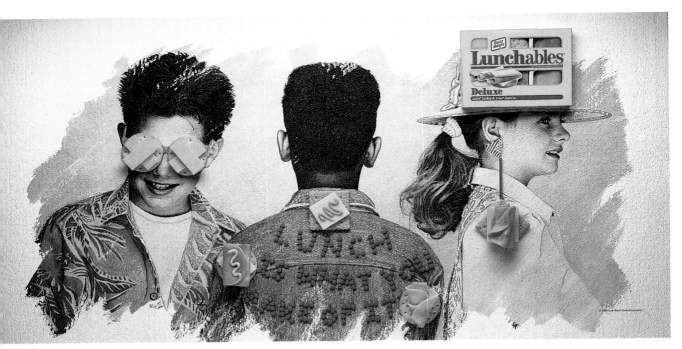

Recognizing that kids influence food purchases, Oscar Mayer attempts to create a positive image for its lunch meats in this poster for use in school cafeterias. Courtesy of Oscar Mayer Foods Corporation. The Oscar Mayer rhomboid, Lunch Is What Your Make Of It, and Lunchables are trademarks of Oscar Mayer Foods Corporation, Madison, Wisconsin.

Teaching Hint: A recent content analysis of cartoon programs found that while all shows studied contained some violence, those that were linked to toy merchandisers exhibited a higher level. Discussion of this pattern can be used to generate class discussion about the desirability of "program-length toy commercials" and the degree to which these should be regulated. See B. Carol Eaton and Joseph R. Dominick, "Product-Related Programming and Children's TV: A Content Analysis," *Journalism Quarterly* 68 (Spring/Summer 1991): 67–75.

Advertising to Children: An Ethical Minefield

Since children differ in their abilities to process product-related information, many serious ethical issues are raised when advertisers try to appeal directly to them.[88] Kids tend to accept what they see on television as real, and they do not necessarily understand the persuasive intent of commercials—that they are paid advertisements. Preschool children may not have the ability to make any distinctions between programming and commercials.

Kids' cognitive defenses are not yet sufficiently developed to filter out commercial appeals, so in a sense altering their brand preferences may be likened to "shooting fish in a barrel," as one critic put it.[89] Although some ads include a *disclaimer*, which is a disclosure intended to clarify a potentially misleading or deceptive statement, the evidence suggests that young children do not adequately understand these either.[90]

Is It a Program or a Commercial? The problem with children's processing of commercials has been exacerbated by television programming that essentially showcases toys (e.g., Jem, G.I. Joe, Transformers). This format has been the target of a lot of criticism because it blurs the line between programming and commercials (much like "infomercials" for adults, as described in Chapter 6).[91] Parents' groups object to such shows because, as one mother put it, the ". . . whole show is one big commercial."[92]

MEASURING COMPREHENSION Children's level of understanding is especially hard to assess, since preschoolers are not very good at verbal responses. One way around this problem is to show children pictures of kids in different scenarios, and ask them to point to which sketch corresponds to what a commercial is trying to get them to do. In the example shown in Figure 8–1, a child who points to sketch 1 after seeing a cereal commercial (depicting the act of buying the product) as opposed to, say, sketches 2 or 3 (where children are eating the cereal or sharing it with friends) would be said to understand the underlying intent of the commercial. Sketch 1 was in fact selected by only 7.5 percent of four-year-olds, but 20 percent of five-year-olds.[93]

Protective Measures. It has been suggested that children should be better educated as to how advertising works and encouraged to question what they see on television, perhaps through public-service advertising.[94] Of some help is *Penny Power,* a kids' version of *Consumer Reports* aimed at 9- to 14-year-olds. It has been estimated that 20 percent of the advertising complaints received come from children, most of whom read *Penny Power.*[95]

In addition, the Children's Advertising Review Unit (CARU) of the Council of Better Business Bureaus, Inc., maintains industry guidelines in such areas as product claims (e.g., is it clear how the toy actually looks and works?), the use of fantasy elements (e.g., are they clearly "just pretend"?), sales pressure techniques (e.g., suggesting that the child will be better than others if he or she owns the product), endorsements by program characters, and disclosures and disclaimers (e.g., "you or your parents have to put it together" versus "assembly required").[96]

The FCC recently ruled that advertising in shows produced for children under the age of 12 cannot exceed 12 minutes an hour on weekdays and 10.5 minutes an hour on weekends. In Europe, regulations are confusing, because each country still has different rules. For example, the Netherlands

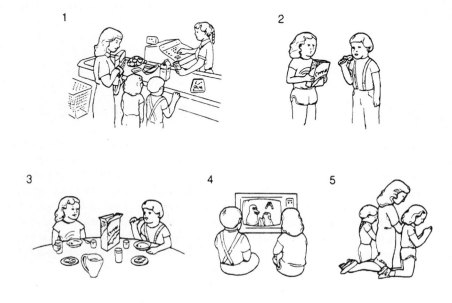

FIGURE 8–1 Sketches to Measure Children's Perceptions of the Intent of Commercials. Source: M. Carole Macklin, "Preschoolers' Understanding of the Informational Function of Television Advertising," *Journal of Consumer Research* 14 (September 1987): 234. Reprinted with permission by The University of Chicago Press.

bars ads for sweets before 8 p.m., the ads cannot feature children under age 14, and a toothbrush must appear on the screen for at least part of the commercial, while Spain and Germany ban ads for war toys.[97]

ETHICAL ISSUES IN ADVERTISING TO CHILDREN   *Are Advertising Tactics Unfair?* Consumers Union has accused major marketers of launching an "unfair advertising assault" on children. Among other issues, the consumer advocate group cited tactics used in schools. These include hidden advertising messages, samples, sponsorship of teaching materials, and donation of equipment in exchange for product labels.

The Response: Marketers claim that their participation in school programs is responsible and appropriate, noting that their contributions are welcomed by parents, teachers, and students.[98]

Is Television Advertising Unfair? The Federal Trade Commission provided one view on this issue in a recent report by noting the unfair state that occurs when the brand loyalty of a gullible eight-year-old child is being courted by the considerable professional and monetary resources devoted to television commercials, including sound effects and lighting specialists, psychological analysts, scriptwriters, and so on.[99]

The Response: Some observers argue that most children (at least those over the age of seven) do recognize the selling intent of commercials and have the right to receive (tasteful) advertising information.

Does Advertising Encourage Poor Product Choices? According to the Federal Trade Commission, many people are concerned, for example, that food advertising distorts nutritional habits, negating any nutrition education imparted by the schools or parents through its heavy emphasis on sugared cereals, snacks, and drinks that account for over half of all products advertised.[100]

The Response: Supporters of children's advertising argue that it helps children to make informed decisions. Also, they feel that it is up to parents to decide which products are inappropriate for their children. Paralleling recent debates about cigarette advertising, they feel it is the products that should be banned, not the advertising.

M A R K E T I N G   P I T F A L L

An organization of health groups called Coalition on Smoking or Health petitioned the Federal Trade Commission in 1991 to prohibit R.J. Reynolds Tobacco Company from using Old Joe, the camel character used by the company to promote its Camel cigarettes. The group called the Camel ads "the most egregious example in recent history of tobacco advertising targeted at children." It cited three studies in the *Journal of the American Medical Association* to document its assertions. One study found that the "smooth character" in Camel advertising increased the company's share of the children's cigarette market from 0.5% before the campaign to 32.8% by the end of 1991. A second study estimated that sales of Camels to kids rose from $6 million to $476 million and that children aged 12 to 13 exhibited the highest recognition of the Camel campaign. A third study found that six-year-olds were almost as likely to recognize that Joe Camel represents Camel cigarettes as they were that Mickey Mouse represents the Disney Channel. In 1993, the FTC recommended an outright ban on the Old Joe campaign.

The company has also come under fire for merchandising Joe Camel accessories that seem to appeal to young people, such as beach shoes with the word Camel on the soles that leave the word behind you when you walk on the sand. The company calls these "Camel tracks." The company refutes these claims, and recently began a campaign in both English and Spanish that urges kids not to smoke. One of the ads says "Don't create a smokescreen between you and your friends."[101]

Does Advertising Create Parent–Child Conflict? According to critics, "The child is unwittingly turned into an 'assistant salesman.' He sells, he nags, until he breaks down the sales resistance of his parent."[102]

The Response: Supporters point to the low level of complaints received from parents about advertising. They feel that children's product requests are a natural part of the parent–child relationship, and according to one industry source, often provide an opportunity for parent–child discussions.[103]

Does Advertising Contribute to Undesirable Socialization? Critics argue that advertising teaches the virtues of materialism, impulsive choice, and immediate gratification.

The Response: Supporters counter that advertising actually *helps* children prepare for the real world. Indeed, the CARU Guidelines recommend the following: "Advertisers are urged to capitalize on the potential of advertising to influence social behavior by developing advertising that addresses itself to social standards generally regarded as positive and beneficial."[104]

Chapter Summary

- *Demographics* are statistics that measure a population's characteristics. Some of the most important of these relate to family structure, e.g., the birth rate, the marriage rate, and the divorce rate.

- A *household* is an occupied housing unit. The number and type of U.S. households is changing in many ways, including increasing movement by consumers to southern and western states, delays in getting married and having children, and in the composition of family households, which increasingly are headed by a single parent.

- New perspectives on the *family life cycle*—and the changes in consumption needs as people move through different stages—are forcing marketers to adapt their traditional perspectives to include such groups as homosexuals, divorcees, and childless couples.

- Families must be understood in terms of their decision-making dynamics. Many purchase decisions are made with the input of two or more people, each of whom may play different roles (e.g., gathering information versus actually making the purchase). Spouses in particular have different priorities and exert varying amounts of influence in terms of effort and power. Children are also increasingly influential during a widening range of purchase decisions.

- Children undergo a process of *socialization,* whereby they learn how to be consumers. Some of this knowledge is instilled by parents and friends, but a lot of it comes from exposure to mass media and advertising. Since children are in some cases so easily persuaded, the ethical aspects of marketing to them are hotly debated among consumers, academics, and marketing practitioners.

Key Terms

autocratic decisions, p. 262

cognitive development, p. 271

consumer socialization, p. 268

cultivation theory, p. 269

demographics, p. 253

extended family, p. 253

family household, p. 253

family life cycle, p. 260

nuclear family, p. 253

parental yielding, p. 266

syncratic decisions, p. 263

synoptic ideal, p. 265

Consumer Behavior Challenge

1. Do you think market research should be performed on children? Give the reasons for your answer.
2. What do you think of the practice of companies and survey firms collecting public data (e.g., from marriage licenses, birth records, or even death announcements) to compile targeted mailing lists? State your opinion from both a consumer's and marketer's perspective.
3. Marketers have been criticized for donating products and services to educational institutions in exchange for free promotion. Is this a fair exchange, in your opinion, or should corporations be prohibited from attempting to influence youngsters in school?
4. For each of the following five product categories—groceries, automobiles, vacations, furniture, and appliances—describe the ways in which you believe a married couple's choices would be affected if they had children.
5. In identifying and targeting newly divorced couples, do you think marketers are exploiting these couples' situations? Are there instances where you think marketers may actually be helpful to them? Support your answers with examples.

6. Arrange to interview two married couples, one younger and one older. Prepare a response form listing five product categories—groceries, furniture, appliances, vacations, and automobiles—and ask each spouse to indicate, without consulting the other, whether purchases in each category are made by joint or unilateral decisions and to indicate whether the unilateral decisions are made by the husband or the wife. Compare each couples' responses for agreement between husbands and wives relative to who makes the decisions and compare both couples' overall responses for differences relative to the number of joint versus unilateral decisions. Report your findings and conclusions.

7. Collect ads for three different product categories in which the family is targeted. Find another set of ads for different brands of the same items in which the family is not featured. Prepare a report on the effectiveness of the approaches.

8. Observe the interactions between parents and children in the cereal section of a local grocery store. Prepare a report on the number of children who expressed preferences, how they expressed their preferences, and how parents responded, including the number who purchased the child's choice.

9. Watch three hours of children's programming on commercial television stations and evaluate the marketing techniques used in the commercials in terms of the ethical issues raised in the final section of this chapter. Report your findings and conclusions.

10. Select a product category, and using the life-cycle stages given in the chapter, list the variables that will affect a purchase decision for the product by consumers in each stage of the cycle.

11. Consider three important changes in modern family structure. For each, find an example of a marketer who has attempted to be conscious of this change as reflected in product communications, retailing innovations, or other aspects of the marketing mix. If possible, also try to find examples of marketers who have failed to keep up with these developments.

CNN Connection

CNN A video segment is available to accompany this CNN connection.

Teens Go Shopping

"Who's running this house, anyway?" As the number of single-parent or dual-income families rises, more teens are being enlisted to take on family responsibilities. As the chapter notes, teens have always been an important market for products like records and cosmetics. Now, though, their influence is being felt by makers of other products as well.

It has been estimated that 30 percent of teen-aged boys and 50 percent of teen-aged girls do grocery shopping for their families on a regular basis. While a few companies like Oscar Mayer have taken the lead in developing food products designed to appeal to teens, many are as yet reluctant to view teens as primary shoppers. As the number of teenagers in the population increases, however, watch out for a change in focus over the coming years. As kids are forced to grow up faster in our evolving society, it is inevitable that they will be entrusted with a wider range of consumer decisions.

The Young American's Bank in Denver even offers a credit card to teens and pre-teens. Although the card only offers a $100 credit limit and requires the applicant to have a source of income (an allowance is acceptable), this concept—if successful—may for better or for worse turn on a younger generation to the appeal of "plastic." And, the growth in teens' disposable income is not just an American phenomenon. Young people in Japan are spending money like it is going out of style. Despite the extremely high cost of living, Japan's emphasis on status and fashion has created a boom market for flashy clothes, exotic foods, and teen idols that have whipped Japanese teenagers into a spending frenzy.

SIMMONS Connection

SIMMONS Connection: Data for this exercise is on the Simmons Data Disk inside the back cover of your Instructor's Annotated Edition.

Data File: Gender-Based Purchasing Decisions

Just as L.J. influenced his mother's choice of what to buy in the supermarket, many other purchase decisions are not made in isolation. Many purchase decisions are made after consultation with other members of our households. Nonetheless, many marketers have been criticized for making stereotypic assumptions about the purchase decisions that are made by male as compared with female members of a household.

So, most ads for power tools are targeted at men, while most ads for floor-cleaning products are targeted at women. But for many products, this separation of decision makers may not hold up. For example, who decides what brand of beer to purchase or whether to purchase an umbrella for the outdoor dining set? The extent to which Tina and her husband (and children) engage in joint purchase decisions may be related to the specific products they are buying. But, it may also be related to their own characteristics as consumers.

It is very important that marketers understand how different groups of consumers go about making purchase decisions. In your Simmons file for this chapter, measures of the influence exerted by male members of a household are cross-tabulated against several demographic and psychographic measures. In general, which decisions are dominated by men? Which are dominated by women? Pick a product category where women dominate the pur-

chase decision. Is there a target market where the role that men play in this decision is more equal to that of women? How can you explain this? [*Hint:* Low index values for these measures of male influence indicate a high degree of influence exerted by female members of the household].

Notes

1. Nancy Marx Better, "Green Teens," *New York Times Magazine* (March 8, 1992)3: 44; Howard Schlossberg, "Kids Teach Parents How to Change Their Buying Habits," *Marketing News* (1992): 8.
2. Alan R. Andreasen, "Life Status Changes and Changes in Consumer Preferences and Satisfaction," *Journal of Consumer Research* 11 (December 1984): 784–94.
3. Cheryl Russell, "Bright Lights, Big City," *American Demographics* (August 1988): 13.
4. Judith Waldrop and Thomas Exter, "What the 1990 Census Will Show," *American Demographics* (January 1990): 20; Judith Waldrop and Thomas Exter, "Fast-Track States," *American Demographics* (January 1990): 24.
5. Judith Waldrop, "The Fashionable Family," *American Demographics* (March 1988): 22.
6. "The Big Picture," *American Demographics* (March 1989): 22–27; Thomas G. Exter, "Middle-Aging Households," *American Demographics* (July 1992): 63.
7. Karen Hardee-Cleaveland, "Is Eight Enough?" *American Demographics* (June 1989): 60.
8. Thomas Exter, "Peak-a-boo (Recent Baby Boomlet)," *American Demographics* (December 1988): 63.
9. Cheryl Russell, "Is Big Back?" *American Demographics* (May 1988): 15.
10. Blayne Cutler, "McChild Care," *American Demographics* (September 1989): 20.
11. Judith Waldrop, "A Lesson in Home Economics," *American Demographics* (August 1989): 26.
12. Mary Lou Padilla and Garry L. Landreth, "Latchkey Children: A Review of the Literature," *Child Welfare* 68 (July/August 1989): 445.
13. Judith Waldrop and Thomas Exter, "Lone Lifestyle," *American Demographics* (January 1990): 27.
14. Joe Schwartz, "After School," *American Demographics* (June 1987): 60.
15. "Men on Their Own," *American Demographics* (July 1987): 62.
16. Christy Fisher, "Census Data May Make Ads More Single-Minded," *Advertising Age* (July 20, 1992): 2.
17. Stephanie Shipp, "How Singles Spend," *American Demographics* (April 1988): 22–27.
18. Joe Schwartz, "Family Traditions: Although Radically Changed, the American Family Is as Strong as Ever," *American Demographics* (March 1987): 9.
19. Diane Crispell, "Three's a Crowd," *American Demographics* (January 1989): 34.
20. "Mothers Bearing a Second Burden," *New York Times* (May 14, 1989): 26.
21. Thomas Exter, "Disappearing Act," *American Demographics* (January 1989): 78.
22. "The Big Picture," *American Demographics*.
23. Cheryl Russell, "Throw Out the Script," *American Demographics* (September 1990): 2.
24. Constance Sorrentino, "The Changing Family in International Perspective," *Monthly Labor Review* (March 1990): 41.
25. Martha Farnsworth Riche, "Somebody's Baby," *American Demographics* (February 1988): 10.
26. Clinton R. Sanders, "The Animal 'Other': Self Definition, Social Identity, and Companion Animals," in *Advances in Consumer Research* 16, ed. Marvin E. Goldberg, Gerald Gorn, and Richard W. Pollay, (Provo, Utah: Association for Consumer Research, 1989).
27. Jeffrey P. Rosenfeld, "Barking Up the Right Tree," *American Demographics* (May 1987): 40.
28. Quoted in Youssef M. Ibrahim, "French Love for Animals: Too Fervent?" *New York Times* (February 2, 1990): A5.
29. Woody Hochswender, "The Cat's Meow," *New York Times* (May 16, 1989): B7.
30. Judann Dagnoli, "Toothcare for Terriers," *Advertising Age* (November 20, 1989): 8.
31. "For Fido, Broccoli and Yogurt," *New York Times* (April 16, 1989).
32. N.R. Kleinfeld, "Limos and Fine Food: Ah, It's a Dog's Life," *New York Times* (May 3, 1990): C1.
33. Robert Passikoff and Rebecca H. Holman, "The

Semiotics of Possession and Commercial Communication," in *Marketing and Semiotics: New Directions in the Study of Signs for Sale*, ed. Jean Umiker-Sebeok (Berlin: Mouton de Guyter, 1987): 375–90.

34. David Cheal, "The Ritualization of Family Ties," *American Behavioral Scientist* 31 (July/August 1988): 632.

35. "Families Come First," *Psychology Today* (September 1988): 11.

36. "Club Med in a Family Way," *American Demographics* (January 1987): 25.

37. Stuart Elliott, "Club Med Says It's for Families," *New York Times* (October 8, 1991): D22.

38. Alison Fahey, "Lamaze Testing 'Seal': Program Delivers America's Newest Parents," *Advertising Age* (March 26, 1990): 4.

39. "Connecting Consumer and Product," *New York Times* (January 18, 1990): D19; Maryellen Gordon, "Gitano's New Ad Campaign to Emphasize Family Spirit," *Woman's Wear Daily* (August 16, 1989): 11; David Reed, "Heinz and Polycell Get in the Family Way," *Marketing* (October 27, 1988): 9.

40. Waldrop, "A Lesson in Home Economics."

41. These categories are an adapted version of an FLC model proposed by Gilly and Enis (1982). Based upon a recent empirical comparison of several competing models, Schaninger and Danko found that this framework outperformed others, especially in terms of its treatment of nonconventional households, though they recommend several improvements to this model as well. See Mary C. Gilly and Ben M. Enis, "Recycling the Family Life Cycle: A Proposal for Redefinition," in *Advances in Consumer Research* 9, ed. Andrew A. Mitchell (Ann Arbor, Mich.: Association for Consumer Research, 1982), 271–76; Charles M. Schaninger and William P. Drake, "A Conceptual and Empirical Comparison of Alternate Household Life Cycle Markets," *Journal of Consumer Research* 19 (March 1993): 580–94.

42. James H. McAlexander, John W. Schouten, and Scott D. Roberts, "Consumer Behavior and Divorce," in *Research in Consumer Behavior* (Greenwich, Conn.: JAI Press, 1992); Michael R. Solomon, "The Role of Products as Social Stimuli: A Symbolic Interactionism Perspective," *Journal of Consumer Research* 10 (December 1983): 319–29; Melissa Martin Young, "Disposition of Possession During Role Transitions," in *Advances in Consumer Research* 18, eds. Rebecca H. Holman and Michael R. Solomon (Provo, Utah: Association for Consumer Research, 1991), 33–39.

43. Thomas Hine, *Populuxe* (New York: Alfred A. Knopf, 1986).

44. Gary L. Sullivan and P.J. O'Connor, "The Family Purchase Decision Process: A Cross-Cultural Review and Framework for Research," *Southwest Journal of Business & Economics* (Fall 1988): 43.

45. Dennis L. Rosen and Donald H. Granbois, "Determinants of Role Structure in Family Financial Management," *Journal of Consumer Research* 10 (September 1983): 253–58.

46. Robert F. Bales, *Interaction Process Analysis: A Method for the Study of Small Groups* (Reading, Mass.: Addison-Wesley, 1950).

47. Peter Hartcher, "Absentee Fathers," *World Press Review* 34 (October 1987): 59; Kurimoto Kazuo, "Under New Management," *Unesco Courier* (July 1989): 28–33; Kay Itoi and Bill Powell, "Take a Hike, Hiroshi," *Newsweek* (August 10, 1992)2: 38; Steven R. Weisman, "In Crowded Japan, A Bonus for Babies Angers Women," *New York Times* (January 30, 1991)2: A1.

48. Alma S. Baron, "Working Parents: Shifting Traditional Roles," *Business* 37 (January/March 1987): 36; William J. Qualls, "Household Decision Behavior: The Impact of Husbands' and Wives' Sex Role Orientation," *Journal of Consumer Research* 14 (September 1987): 264–79; Charles M. Schaninger and W. Christian Buss, "The Relationship of Sex-Role Norms to Household Task Allocation," *Psychology & Marketing* 2 (Summer 1985): 93–104.

49. Micaela DiLeonardo, "The Female World of Cards and Holidays: Women, Families, and the Work of Kinship," *Signs* 12 (Spring 1942): 440–53.

50. C. Whan Park, "Joint Decisions in Home Purchasing: A Muddling-Through Process," *Journal of Consumer Research* 9 (September 1982): 151–62; see also William J. Qualls and Francoise Jaffe, "Measuring Conflict in Household Decision Behavior: Read My Lips and Read My Mind," in *Advances in Consumer Research* 19, eds. John F. Sherry, Jr. and Brian Sternthal (Provo, Utah: Association for Consumer Research, 1992), 522–31.

51. Kim P. Corfman and Donald R. Lehmann, "Models of Cooperative Group Decision-Making and Relative Influence: An Experimental Investigation of Family Purchase Decisions," *Journal of Consumer Research* 14 (June 1987): 1–13.

52. Charles Atkin, "Observation of Parent-Child Interaction in Supermarket Decision-Making," *Journal of Marketing* 42 (October 1978): 41–45.

53. Sharen Kindel, "They May be Small, But They Spend Big," *Adweek* (February 10, 1992)2: 38.

54. Leslie Isler, Edward T. Popper and Scott Ward, "Children's Purchase Requests and Parental Responses: Results From a Diary Study," *Journal of Advertising Research* 27 (October/November 1987): 28–39.

55. Fred E. Webster and Yoram Wind, *Organizational Buying Behavior* (New York: Prentice-Hall, 1972).

56. Harry L. Davis, "Decision Making Within the Household," *Journal of Consumer Research* 2 (March 1972): 241–60; Michael B. Menasco and David J. Curry, "Utility and Choice: An Empirical Study of Wife/Husband Decision Making," *Journal of Consumer Research* 16 (June 1989): 87–97.

57. Daniel Seymour and Greg Lessne, "Spousal Conflict Arousal: Scale Development," *Journal of Consumer Research* 11 (December 1984): 810–21.

58. Horst H. Stipp, "Children as Consumers," *American Demographics* (February 1988): 27.

59. Melissa Turner, "Kids' Marketing Clout Man-Sized," *Atlanta Journal* (February 18, 1988): E10.

60. Scott Ward, "Consumer Socialization," in *Perspectives in Consumer Behavior*, ed. Harold H. Kassarjian and Thomas S. Robertson (Glenville, Ill.: Scott, Foresman, 1980): 380.

61. Thomas Lipscomb, "Indicators of Materialism in Children's Free Speech: Age and Gender Comparisons," *Journal of Consumer Marketing* (Fall 1988): 41–46.

62. George P. Moschis, "The Role of Family Communication in Consumer Socialization of Children and Adolescents," *Journal of Consumer Research* 11 (March 1985): 898–913.

63. For a recent study, see Les Carlson, Sanford Grossbart, and J. Kathleen Stuenkel, "The Role of Parental Socialization Types on Differential Family Communication Patterns Regarding Consumption," *Journal of Consumer Psychology* 1 (1992)1: 31–52.

64. See Patricia M. Greenfield, Emily Yut, Mabel Chung, Deborah Land, Holly Kreider, Maurice Pantoja, and Kris Horsley, "The Program-Length Commercial: A Study of the Effects of Television/Toy Tie-Ins on Imaginative Play," *Psychology & Marketing* 7 (Winter 1990): 237–56 for a study on the effects of commercial programming on creative play.

65. Gerald J. Gorn and Renee Florsheim, "The Effects of Commercials for Adult Products on Children," *Journal of Consumer Research* 11 (March 1985): 962–67.

66. Glenn Collins, "New Studies on 'Girl Toys' and 'Boy Toys'," *New York Times* (February 13, 1984): D1.

67. Susan B. Kaiser, "Clothing and the Social Organization of Gender Perception: A Developmental Approach," *Clothing and Textiles Research Journal* 7 (Winter 1989): 46–56.

68. Lori Schwartz and William Markham, "Sex Stereotyping in Children's Toy Advertisements," *Sex Roles* 12 (January 1985): 157–70.

69. Brad Edmondson, "Snakes, Snails, and Puppy Dogs' Tails," *American Demographics* (October 1987): 18.

70. Laura A. Peracchio, "How Do Young Children Learn to be Consumers? A Script-Processing Approach," *Journal of Consumer Research* 18 (March 1992): 425–40.

71. Jean Piaget, "The Child and Modern Physics," *Scientific American* 196 (1957)3: 46–51.

72. Deborah L. Roedder, "Age Differences in Children's Responses to Television Advertising: An Information-Processing Approach," *Journal of Consumer Research* 8 (September 1981): 144–53.

73. Turner, "Kids' Marketing Clout Man-Sized."

74. Russell W. Belk, Kenneth D. Bahn, and Robert N. Mayer, "Developmental Recognition of Consumption Symbolism," *Journal of Consumer Research* 9 (June 1982): 4–17.

75. Robert N. Mayer and Russell W. Belk, "Fashion and Impression Formation Among Children," in *The Psychology of Fashion*, ed. Michael R. Solomon (Lexington, Mass.: Lexington Books, 1985): 293–308.

76. Quoted in N.R. Kleinfeld, "Another August Under the 'Whine Sign'," *New York Times* (August 6, 1989): D1.

77. Patricia Sellers, "The ABC's of Marketing to Kids," *Fortune* (May 8, 1989): 114; Turner, "Kids' Marketing Clout Man-Sized."

78. Edmondson, "Snakes, Snails and Puppy Dogs' Tails."

79. Quoted in Linda Wells, "Babes in Makeup Land," *New York Times Magazine* (August 13, 1989): 46.

80. Graham, "Children's Hour."

81. Joe Agnew, "Children Come of Age as Consumers," *Marketing News* (December 4, 1987): 8.

82. Janet Simons, "Youth Marketing: Children's Clothes Follow the Latest Fashion," *Advertising Age* (February 14, 1985): 16.

83. Stipp, "Children as Consumers"; See Laura A. Peracchio, "Designing Research to Reveal the Young Child's Emerging Competence," *Psychology & Marketing* 7 (Winter 1990): 257–76, for details regarding the design of research on children.

84. "Kid Power," *Forbes* (March 30, 1987): 9–10.

85. Dena Kleiman, "Candy to Frighten Your Parents

With," *New York Times* (August 23, 1989): C1.

86. Laura Shapiro, "Where Little Boys Can Play with Nail Polish," *Newsweek* (May 28, 1990): 62.

87. Cindy Clark,(1991), "Putting Aside Adultcentrism: Child-Centered Ethnographic Research, unpublished manuscript, C.D. Clark Limited, 1991; Cindy Clark, "Some Practical In's and Out's of Studying Children as Consumers," paper presented at the AMA Research Roundtable, March 1986.

88. Gary Armstrong and Merrie Brucks, "Dealing with Children's Advertising: Public Policy Issues and Alternatives," *Journal of Public Policy and Marketing* 7 (1988): 98–113.

89. Bonnie Reece, "Children and Shopping: Some Public Policy Questions," *Journal of Public Policy and Marketing* (1986): 185–94.

90. Mary Ann Stutts and Garland G. Hunnicutt, "Can Young Children Understand Disclaimers in Television Commercials," *Journal of Advertising* 16 (Winter 1987): 41–46.

91. Steve Weinstein, "Fight Heats Up Against Kids' TV 'Commershows'," *Marketing News* (October 9, 1989): 2.

92. Alan Bunce, "Are TV Ads Turning Kids Into Consumers?" *Christian Science Monitor* (August 11, 1988): 1.

93. M. Carole Macklin, "Preschoolers' Understanding of the Informational Function of Television Advertising," *Journal of Consumer Research* 14 (September 1987): 229–39.

94. Merrie Brucks, Gary M. Armstrong, and Marvin E. Goldberg, "Children's Use of Cognitive Defenses Against Television Advertising: A Cognitive Response Approach," *Journal of Consumer Research* 14 (March 1988): 471–82.

95. Michael deCourcy Hines, "Young Consumers: Perils and Power," *New York Times* (February 11, 1989):

52; Oscar Suris, "Selling to Savvy Young Buyers," *Orlando Sentinel* (September 10, 1989): F8.

96. Rita Weisskoff, "Current Trends in Children's Advertising," *Journal of Advertising Research* (February/March 1985): 12–14.

97. Edmund L. Andrews, "F.C.C. Limits Ads on TV Shows Aimed at Children," *New York Times* (April 10, 1991): D6; Laurel Wentz, "Playing by the Same Rules: Harmonization of Children's Ads Sought Via Self-Regulation," *Advertising Age* (December 2, 1991): S-2.

98. Judann Dagnoli, "Consumers Union Hits Kids Advertising," *Advertising Age* (July 23, 1990): 4.

99. Federal Trade Commission, "FTC Staff Report on Television Advertising to Children" (Washington, D.C.: Government Printing Office, 1979).

100. Federal Trade Commission, "FTC Staff Report on Television Advertising to Children," cited in Armstrong and Brucks, "Dealing with Children's Advertising."

101. Judann Dagnoli, "'JAMA' Lights New Fire Under Camel's Ads," *Advertising Age* (December 16, 1991)2: 3; Stuart Elliott, "Adoring or Abhoring the Camel," *New York Times* (July 29, 1992): D17; Eben Shapiro, "The FTC Staff Recommends the Ban on Joe Camel Campaign," *Wall Street Journal* (August 11, 1993): B1.

102. Federal Trade Commission, "FTC Staff Report on Television Advertising to Children, quoted in Armstrong and Brucks, "Dealing with Children's Advertising."

103. Television Information Office (1986), 8, quoted in Armstrong and Brucks, "Dealing with Children's Advertising."

104. Children's Advertising Review Unit (1983), 5, quoted in Armstrong and Brucks, "Dealing with Children's Advertising."

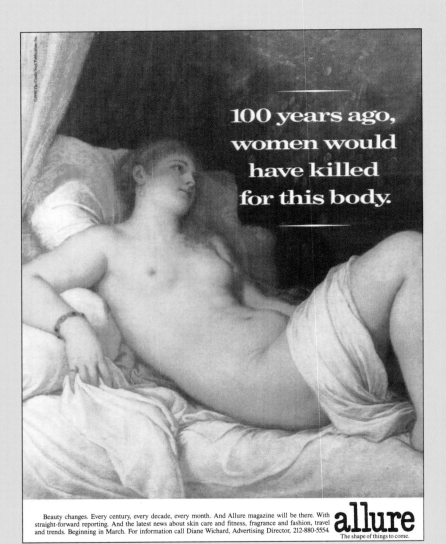

100 years ago, women would have killed for this body.

Beauty changes. Every century, every decade, every month. And Allure magazine will be there. With straight-forward reporting. And the latest news about skin care and fitness, fragrance and fashion, travel and trends. Beginning in March. For information call Diane Wichard, Advertising Director, 212-880-5554.

allure
The shape of things to come.

CHAPTER 9

Personality,

Self-Concept,

and Sex Roles

Buying, Having, and Being: Selections 27–32 from *Buying, Having, and Being: The Washington Post Consumer Behavior Companion*, Second Edition, accompany this chapter.

S uzy is trying to concentrate on the report her client is expecting by five o'clock. Suzy has always worked hard to maintain this important account for the firm, but today she keeps getting distracted thinking about her date last night with Rob. Although things seemed to go okay, why couldn't she shake the feeling that Rob regarded her more as a friend than as a potential romantic partner?

During her lunch hour, Suzy decides to take a break and catch up on some of the magazines she hasn't had time to read lately. Leafing through *Glamour* and *Cosmopolitan* at her desk, Suzy is struck by all of the articles about ways to be more attractive by dieting, exercise, and wearing sexy clothes. Suzy begins to feel depressed as she looks at the models in the many advertisements for perfumes, apparel, and makeup. Each woman is more glamorous and beautiful than the next. She could swear that some of them must have had breast implants and other assorted "adjustments"—women just don't look that way in real life.

In her down mood, Suzy even entertains the thought that maybe she should look into cosmetic surgery. Even though she's never considered herself unattractive, who knows—maybe a new nose or larger breasts are what it will take to turn Rob around. On second thought, though, is he even worth thinking about it? . . .

Perspectives on the Self

Suzy is not alone in feeling that her physical appearance and possessions affect her "value" as a person. Consumers' insecurities about their appearance are rampant: It has been estimated that 72 percent of men and 85 percent of women are unhappy with at least one aspect of their appearance.[1] Many products, from cars to cologne, are bought because the person is trying to highlight or hide some aspect of the self. This chapter focuses on the self and will discuss how consumers' feelings about themselves shape their consumption practices, particularly as they strive to fulfill their society's expectations about how a male or female should look and act.

Exposure to ads can trigger a process of *social comparison*, where the person tries to evaluate his or her self by comparing it to other people and media images. This form of comparison appears to be a basic human motive, and many marketers have tapped into this need by supplying idealized images of happy, attractive people who just happen to be using their products. A recent study illustrates this process of social comparison. It showed that female college students do tend to compare their physical appearance with models who appear in advertising. Furthermore, study participants who were exposed to beautiful women in advertisements afterwards expressed lowered satisfaction with their *own* appearance, as compared to other participants who did not view ads with models.[2] Another study demonstrated that young women's perceptions of their body shapes and sizes can be altered after being exposed to as little as thirty minutes of television programming.[3]

The 1980s were called the "Me Decade" because for many this time was

Teaching Hint: The value placed on individuality and a distinction between an inner and an outer self developed with the self-consciousness wrought by Puritanism between 1500 and 1800. The notion of secular fulfillment (and the conflict between an individual's needs and those of society) that drives much of modern-day hedonistic marketing was a dominant issue in the Romantic period (the late eighteenth and early nineteenth century). See Roy F. Baumeister, Dianne M. Tice, and Debra G. Hutton, "Self-Presentational Motivations and Personality Differences in Self-Esteem," *Journal of Personality* 57 (September 1989): 547–75.

marked by an absorption with the self. While it seems natural to think about each consumer having a self, this concept is actually a relatively new way of regarding people and their relationship to society. The idea that each single human life is unique, rather than a part of a group, only developed in late medieval times (between the eleventh and fifteenth centuries). The notion that the self is an object to be pampered is even more recent. In addition, the emphasis on the unique nature of the self is much greater in Western societies.[4] Many Eastern cultures instead stress the importance of a collective self, where the person's identity is derived in large measure from his or her social group.

The self can be understood from many different theoretical vantage points. From a psychoanalytic, or Freudian, perspective, the self is a system of competing forces riddled with conflict (see Chapter 3). Behaviorists tend to regard the self as a collection of conditioned responses. From a cognitive orientation, the self is an information processing system, an organizing force that serves as a nucleus around which new information is processed.[5]

Self-Concept

Self-concept refers to the attitude a person holds toward him- or herself. Just as a consumer has an attitude toward Pepsi or democracy, the self is also a subject of evaluation. An overall self-attitude is frequently positive, but not always; there are certainly parts of the self that are evaluated more positively than others. For example, Suzy felt better about her professional identity than she did about her feminine identity.

COMPONENTS OF THE SELF-CONCEPT Compared to other attitudes, the self-concept is a very complex structure. It is composed of many attributes, some of which are given greater emphasis in determining overall self-attitude. Attributes of self-concept can be described along such dimensions as their content (e.g., facial attractiveness versus mental aptitude), positivity or negativity (i.e., self-esteem), intensity, stability over time, and accuracy (i.e., the degree to which one's self-assessment corresponds to reality).[6] As will be seen later in the chapter, consumers' self-assessments can be quite distorted, especially with regard to their physical appearance.

Personality

To understand the nature of the self, some theorists focus on the concept of **personality,** which refers to a person's unique psychological makeup and how it consistently influences the way a person responds to his or her environment. In recent years, the nature of the personality construct has been hotly debated. Many studies have found that people tend to not behave consistently across different situations and that they do not seem to exhibit stable personalities. In fact, some researchers feel that personality does not really exist at all, but rather is merely a convenient way to describe the behavior of other people.

This argument is a bit hard to accept intuitively, possibly because we tend to see others in a limited range of situations, and so to us, people do act consistently. On the other hand, we each know that we are not all that consistent; we may be wild and crazy at times and the model of respectability at others.

Teaching Hint: According to objective self-awareness (OSA) theory, our conscious attention flips back and forth between the self and the external world. When a person is in an OSA state, he or she sees the self as others do, which usually arouses negative feelings, because we are often critical of the image we see. A somewhat similar perspective regards self-awareness as a feedback loop, much like the regulatory mechanism in a thermostat. We check our current self against our goals, altering our behavior if necessary to get back on track. See S. Duval and R.A. Wicklund, *A Theory of Objective Self-Awareness* (New York: Academic Press, 1972); Charles S. Carver and Michael F. Scheier, *Attention and Self-Regulation: A Control-Theory Approach to Human Behavior* (New York: Springer-Verlag, 1981); see also M. Joseph Sirgy, "Self-Cybernetics: Toward an Integrated Model of Self-Concept Processes," *Systems Research* 7 (1990)1: 19–32.

Teaching Hint: Materialism has been conceptualized as a personality trait, while later work has regarded the construct as a value, which will be discussed in that context later in the book. For discussions of the trait perspective, see Russell W. Belk, "Materialism: Trait Aspects of Living in the Material World," *Journal of Consumer Research* 12 (December 1985): 265–80; Dennis Cole, Newell D. Wright, M. Joseph Sirgy, Rustan Kosenko, Don Rahtz, and H. Lee Meadow, "Testing the Reliability and Validity of Belk's and Richins' Materialism Scales," in *Proceedings of the Academy of Marketing Science* (1992); Seth R. Ellis, "A Factor Analytic Investigation of Belk's Structure of the Materialism Construct," in *Advances in Consumer Research* 19, eds. John F. Sherry, Jr. and Brian Sternthal (Provo, Utah: Association of Consumer Research, 1992), 688.

Research Report: The trait of innovativeness is particularly relevant to many marketing applications, insofar as its measurement can aid researchers in assigning consumers to adopter categories. Differences in the adoption of product innovations will be discussed in Chapter 17. For recent advances in measurement of this trait, see Ronald E. Goldsmith and Charles F. Hofacker, "Measuring Consumer Innovativeness," *Journal of the Academy of Marketing Science* 19 (1991)3: 209–21; Gordon R. Foxall and Ronald E. Goldsmith, "Personality and Consumer Research: Another Look," *Journal of the Market Research Society* 30 (1988)2: 111–25.

While certainly not all psychologists have abandoned the idea of personality, many now recognize that a person's underlying characteristics are but one part of the puzzle and that situational factors often play a very large role in determining behavior.[7] (This realization underscores the potential importance of segmenting according to situations, a concept discussed in Chapter 10.)

TRAIT THEORY One approach to personality is to focus on the quantitative measurement of **traits**, or identifiable characteristics that define a person. For example, people can be distinguished by the degree to which they are socially outgoing (the trait of extroversion). Some specific traits that are relevant to consumer behavior include: innovativeness (the degree to which a person likes to try new things); materialism (amount of emphasis placed on acquiring and owning products); self-consciousness (the degree to which a person deliberately monitors and controls the image of the self that is projected to others),[8] and need for cognition (the degree to which a person likes to think about things and by extension expend the necessary effort to process brand information).

Problems with Trait Theory in Consumer Research. Since large numbers of consumers can be categorized in terms of their standing on various traits, these approaches can in theory be used for segmentation purposes. If a car manufacturer, for example, could determine that drivers who fit a trait profile are more likely to prefer a car with certain features, this match could be used to great advantage. The notion that consumers buy products that are extensions of their personalities makes intuitive sense. This idea is endorsed by many marketing managers, who try to create brand personalities that will appeal to different types of consumers.

However, the use of standard personality trait measurements to predict product choices has met with mixed success at best. In general, marketing researchers simply have not been able to predict consumers' behaviors on the basis of measured personality traits. A number of explanations have been offered for these equivocal results.[9]

- Many of the scales are not sufficiently valid or reliable; they do not adequately measure what they are supposed to measure, and their results may not be stable over time.

- Personality tests are often developed for specific populations (e.g., mentally ill people); these tests are then "borrowed" and applied to the general population where their relevance is questionable.

- The tests often are not administered under the appropriate conditions; they may be given in a classroom or over a kitchen table by people who are not properly trained.

- The researchers often make changes in the instruments to adapt them to their own situations, in the process deleting or adding items and renaming variables. These *ad hoc* changes dilute the validity of the measures and also reduce researchers' ability to compare results across consumer samples.

- Many trait scales are intended to measure gross, overall tendencies (e.g., emotional stability or introversion); these results are then used to make predictions about purchases of specific brands.

This Sony Walkman ad uses a variety of props to emphasize its appeal to all sides of a consumer's personality. Courtesy of Sony Corporation of America.

SYMBOLIC INTERACTIONISM If each person potentially has many social selves, how does each develop and how do we decide which self to "activate" at any point in time? The sociological tradition of **symbolic interactionism** stresses that relationships with other people play a large part in forming the self.[27] This perspective maintains that people exist in a symbolic environment and the meaning attached to any situation or object is determined by the interpretation of these symbols. As members of society, we learn to agree on shared meanings. Thus, we "know" that a red light means stop, the "golden arches" means fast food, and "blondes have more fun."

Like other social objects, the meanings of consumers themselves are defined by social consensus. The consumer interprets his or her own identity, and this assessment is continually evolving as he or she encounters new situations and people. In symbolic interactionist terms, we negotiate these meanings over time. Essentially the consumer poses the question:

"Who am I in this situation?" The answer to this question is greatly influenced by those around us: "Who do other people think I am?" We tend to pattern our behavior on the perceived expectations of others in a form of *self-fulfilling prophecy*. By acting the way we *assume* others expect us to act, we wind up confirming these perceptions.

The Looking-Glass Self. This process of imagining the reactions of others toward us is known as "taking the role of the other," or the "looking-glass self."[28] According to this view, a process of *reflexive evaluation* occurs when the individual attempts to define the self, and it operates as a sort of psychological sonar: We take readings of our own identity by "bouncing" signals off of others. The looking-glass image we receive will differ depending upon whose views we are considering. Like the distorted mirrors in a funhouse, our appraisal of who we are can vary, depending upon whose perspective we are taking. A confident career woman like Suzy may sit morosely at a bar or discotheque, imagining that others see her as an unattractive, woman with little sex appeal (whether these perceptions are true or not).

Consumption and Self-Concept

By extending the dramaturgical perspective a bit further, it is easy to see how the consumption of products and services contributes to the definition of the self. For an actor to play a role convincingly, he or she needs the correct props, stage setting, and so on. Consumers learn that different roles are accompanied by *constellations* of products and activities that help to define these roles.[29] Some "props" are so important to the roles we play that they can be viewed as a part of the *extended self*, a concept to be discussed shortly.

Products That Shape the Self: You Are What You Consume

The reflected self helps to shape self-concept, which implies that people see themselves as they imagine others see them. Since what others see includes a person's clothing, jewelry, furniture, car, and so on, it stands to reason that these products also help to determine the perceived self. A consumer's products place him or her into a social role, which helps to answer the question "Who am I now?"

People use an individual's consumption behaviors to help them make judgments about who that person is. In addition to considering a person's clothes, grooming habits, and so on, we make inferences about personality based on a person's choice of leisure activities (e.g., squash versus bowling), food preferences (e.g., vegetarians versus "steak-and-potatoes" people), cars, home decorating choices, and so on. People who are shown pictures of someone's living room, for example, are able to make surprisingly accurate guesses about that consumer's personality.[30] In the same way that a consumer's use of products influences others' perceptions, the same products can help to determine his or her *own* self-concept.[31]

A consumer exhibits *attachment* to an object to the extent that it is used by that person to maintain self-concept.[32] Objects can act as a sort of security blanket by reinforcing our identities, especially in unfamiliar situations. For example, students who decorate their dorm rooms with personal items are less likely to drop out of college. This coping process may protect the self from being diluted in a strange environment.[33]

The use of consumption information to define the self is especially important when an identity is yet to be adequately formed, as occurs when a consumer plays a new or unfamiliar role. **Symbolic self-completion theory** predicts that people who have an incomplete self-definition tend to complete this identity by displaying symbols associated with it.[34] The Yes Clothing ad shown here relies on this perspective by emphasizing the confidence one gains by wearing the right fashions. Adolescent boys may use "macho" products like cars and cigarettes to bolster their developing masculinity; here, products are a sort of "social crutch" to be leaned upon during a period of uncertainty.

In emphasizing the notion that looking the right way gives one confidence, this Yes Clothing ad relies on symbolic self-completion theory to appeal to consumers. © Philippe Berthome for No Comment!

Loss of Self. The contribution of possessions to self-identity is perhaps most apparent when these treasured objects are lost or stolen. One of the first acts performed by institutions that want to repress individuality and encourage group identity, such as prisons or convents, is to confiscate personal possessions.[35] Victims of burglaries and natural disasters commonly report feelings of alienation, depression, or of being "violated." One consumer's comment after being robbed is typical: "It's the next worse thing to being bereaved; it's like being raped."[36] Burglary victims exhibit a diminished sense of community, less feelings of privacy, and take less pride in their houses' appearance than do their neighbors.[37]

Self/Product Congruence

Because many consumption activities are related to self-definition, it is not surprising to learn that consumers demonstrate consistency between their values and attitudes and the things they buy.[38] **Self-image congruence models** predict that products will be chosen when their attributes match some aspect of the self.[39] These models assume a process of cognitive matching between these attributes and the consumer's self-image.[40] While results are somewhat mixed, the ideal self appears to be more relevant as a comparison standard for highly expressive social products such as perfume. In contrast, actual self is more relevant for everyday, functional products. These standards are also likely to vary by usage situation. For example, a consumer might want a functional, reliable car to commute to work everyday, but a flashier model with more "zing" when going out on a date in the evening.

Research tends to support the idea of congruence between product usage and self-image. One of the earliest studies to examine this process found that car owners' ratings of themselves tended to match their perceptions of their cars. Pontiac drivers, for example, saw themselves as more active and flashier than did Volkswagen drivers.[41] Congruity also has been found between consumers and their most-preferred brands of beer, soap, toothpaste, and cigarettes relative to their least-preferred brands, as well as between consumers' self-images and their favorite stores.[42] Some specific attributes that have been found to be useful in describing some of the matches between consumers and products include rugged/delicate, excitable/calm, rational/emotional, and formal/informal.[43]

PROBLEMS WITH THE CONGRUENCE CONCEPT While these findings make some intuitive sense, we cannot blithely assume that consumers will always buy products whose "personality" characteristics match their own. It is not clear that consumers really see aspects of themselves in down-to-earth, functional products that don't have very complex or human-like images. It is one thing to consider a brand personality for an expressive, image-oriented product like perfume and quite another to impute human characteristics to a toaster.

Another problem is the old "chicken-and-egg" question: Do people buy

Teaching Hint: A common way to assess these matches is to use a technique known as a Q-sort. Consumers sort various products into categories according to the extent each is associated or not associated with the self. See M. Joseph Sirgy, "Self-Concept in Consumer Behavior: A Critical Review," *Journal of Consumer Research* 9 (December 1982): 287–300.

Research Report: People are more likely to rate more socially desirable products as similar to themselves; person/product congruence also increases with ownership. See George E. Belch and E. Laird Landon, Jr., "Discriminant Validity of a Product-Anchored Self-Concept Measure," *Journal of Marketing Research* 24 (May 1977): 252–56.

products because they are seen as similar to the self, or do they *assume* that these products must be similar because they have bought them? The similarity between a person's self-image and the images of products purchased does tend to increase with ownership, so this explanation cannot be ruled out.

The Extended Self

As noted earlier, many of the props and settings consumers use to define their social roles in a sense become a part of their selves. Those external objects that we consider a part of us comprise the **extended self**. In some cultures, people literally incorporate objects into the self—they lick new possessions, take the names of conquered enemies (or in some cases eat them), or bury the dead with their possessions.[44]

Many material objects, ranging from personal possessions and pets to national monuments or landmarks, help to form a consumer's identity. Just about everyone can name a valued possession that has a lot of the self "wrapped up" in it, whether it is a treasured photograph, a trophy, an old shirt, a car, or a cat. Indeed, it is often possible to construct a pretty accurate "biography" of someone just by cataloguing the items on display in his or her bedroom or office.

In one study on the extended self, people were given a list of items that ranged from electronic equipment, facial tissues, and television programs to parents, body parts, and favorite clothes. They were asked to rate each in terms of its closeness to the self. Objects were more likely to be considered a part of extended self if "psychic energy" was invested in them by expending effort to obtain them or because they were personalized and kept for a long time.[45]

LEVELS OF THE EXTENDED SELF Four levels of the extended self are used by consumers to define themselves. These range from very personal objects to places and things that allow people to feel like they are rooted in their environments.[46]

- *Individual level:* Consumers include many of their personal possessions in self-definition. These products can include jewelry, cars, clothing, and so on. The saying "You are what you wear" reflects the belief that one's things are a part of what one is.

- *Family level:* This part of the extended self includes a consumer's residence and the furnishings in it. The house can be thought of as a symbolic body for the family and is often a central aspect of identity.

- *Community level:* It is common for consumers to describe themselves in terms of the neighborhood or town from which they come. For farm families or residents with close ties to a community, this sense of belonging is particularly important.

- *Group level:* Our attachments to certain social groups also can be considered a part of self. A consumer may feel that landmarks, monuments, or sports teams are a part of the extended self.

Additional Example: Pets are often an integral part of the extended self. Many consumers are devoted to their pets and regard them as family members. This link is so strong that people often infer the features of owners from their pets. See Marcel Heiman, "Man and His Pet," in *Motivations in Play, Games, and Sports*, eds. Ralph Slovenko and James A. Knight (Springfield, Ill.: Charles C. Thomas, 1967), 329–48.

Research Report: The degree to which people incorporate their communities into their selves helps to predict how cohesive and safe a neighborhood will be. One study that examined suburban areas found a relationship between the use of "territorial markers," such as shrubs, to indicate one's property and a willingness to defend one's neighborhood. Another group of researchers also found that residents who personalize their homes by displaying property markers and holiday decorations were more attached to their communities and that these actions also deterred property crimes. See Julian J. Edney, "Property, Possession and Performance: A Field Study of Human Territoriality," *Journal of Applied Social Psychology* 2 (1972)3: 275–82; Barbara B. Brown and Carol M. Werner, "Social Cohesiveness, Territoriality, and Holiday Decorations: The Influence of Cul-de-Sacs," *Environment and Behavior* 17 (September 1985): 539–65.

Hello?

You snore.

And you steal all the covers. What time did you leave?

Six-thirty. You looked like a toppled Greek statue lying there. Only some tourist had swiped your fig leaf. I was tempted to wake you up.

I miss you already.

You're going to miss something else. Have you looked in the bathroom yet?

Why?

I took your bottle of Paco Rabanne cologne.

What on earth are you going to do with it…give it to a secret lover you've got stashed away in San Francisco?

I'm going to take some and rub it on my body when I go to bed tonight. And then I'm going to remember every little thing about you… and last night.

Do you know what your voice is doing to me?

You aren't the only one with imagination. I've got to go; they're calling my flight. I'll be back Tuesday. Can I bring you anything?

My Paco Rabanne. And a fig leaf.

Paco Rabanne.
A cologne for men.
What is remembered is up to you.

This Paco Rabanne ad illustrates that norms are changing with regard to male (and female) sex roles. Courtesy of Ogilvy & Mather New York.

Sex Roles

Sexual identity is a very important component of a consumer's self-concept. People often conform to their culture's expectations about what those of their sex should do. Of course, these guidelines change over time, and they can differ radically across societies. The ad for Paco Rabanne shown here illustrates one marketer's contribution to these changing norms; it blurs the boundaries between the sexes and promotes male sensuality. Because sexual identity of both men and women is considered by many to be a crucial aspect of self-concept, the rest of this chapter focuses on this dimension of the self.

Gender Differences in Socialization

A society's assumptions about the proper roles of men and women is communicated in terms of the ideal behaviors that are stressed for each sex. For example, an activity such as Christmas shopping is widely regarded as "women's work."[47] In many societies, males are controlled by *agentic goals*, which stress self-assertion and mastery. Females, on the other hand, are taught to value *communal goals*, such as affiliation and the fostering of harmonious relations.[48] Assumptions about sex roles are deeply engrained in marketing communications. Consider, for example, the Curad ad shown

(MUSIC Throughout)

ANNCR (VO): A Curad Bandage brings out the mother in all of us.

Especially a

Curad Flexible Bandage.

It's soft...Comforting...

and it stays in place...Even on a bending place.

And Curad is the Ouchless Bandage.

It sticks to the skin not the sore.

So the next time...

you have to mother someone...

mother 'em with a Curad.

This storyboard for Curad emphasizes women's maternal instincts in promoting a traditional sex role. Courtesy of CURAD Bandages.

here, which appeals to women's maternal instinct: One would not expect to see the parallel phrase "*Father* 'em with a Curad."

MACHO MARKETERS The field of marketing has been largely defined by men, so it tends to be dominated by male values. Competition rather than cooperation is stressed, and the language of warfare and domination is often used. Strategists often use distinctly masculine concepts: "market penetration" or "competitive thrusts," for example. Academic marketing articles also emphasize agentic rather than communal goals. The most pervasive theme is power and control over others. Other themes include instrumentality (manipulating people for the good of an organization) and competition. This bias may diminish in coming years, as more marketing researchers begin to stress such factors as emotions and aesthetics in purchase decisions.[49]

Gender Versus Sexual Identity

Sex role identity is a state of mind as well as body. A person's biological gender (i.e., male or female) does not totally determine whether he or she will exhibit **sex-typed traits,** or characteristics that are stereotypically associated with one sex or the other. A consumer's subjective feelings about his or her sexuality are crucial as well. Unlike maleness and femaleness, masculinity and femininity are *not* biological characteristics. A behavior considered masculine in one culture may not be viewed as such in another. For example, the norm in the United States is that males should be "strong" and repress tender feelings ("real men don't eat quiche"), and male friends avoid touching each other (except in "safe" situations such as on the football field). In some Latin and European cultures, however, it is common for men to hug one another. Each society determines what "real" men and women should and should not do. The Bijan ad shown here interprets the contrasting ways in which women are viewed in different cultures.

SEX-TYPED PRODUCTS   Many products (other than quiche) also are *sex-typed;* they take on masculine or feminine attributes, and consumers often associate them with one sex or another.[50] The car, for example, has long been thought of as a masculine product. The sextyping of products is often

This ad for Bijan illustrates how sex roles identities are culturally bound by contrasting the expectations of how women should be in two different countries. Coutesy of Bijan. Photographer Jim Koch.

TABLE 9-2 Sex-Typed Products

Masculine	Feminine
Pocket knife	Scarf
Tool kit	Baby oil
Shaving cream	Bedroom slippers
Briefcase	Hand lotion
35 mm camera	Clothes dryer
Stereo system	Food processor
Scotch	Wine
IRA account	Long-distance phone service
Wall paint	Facial tissue

Source: Adapted from Kathleen Debevec and Easwar Iyer, "Sex Roles and Consumer Perceptions of Promotions, Products, and Self: What Do We Know and Where Should We Be Headed," in *Advances in Consumer Research*, ed. Richard J. Lutz (Provo, Utah: Association for Consumer Research, 1986)13: 210–14.

created or perpetuated by marketers (e.g., Princess telephones, boys' and girls' toys, and Luvs color-coded diapers). Some sex-typed products are listed in Table 9–2.

ANDROGYNY Masculinity and femininity are not opposite ends of the same dimension. **Androgyny** refers to the possession of both masculine and feminine traits.[51] Researchers make a distinction between sex-typed people, who are stereotypically masculine or feminine, and androgynous people, whose mixture of characteristics allows them to function well in a variety of social situations.

Differences in sex-role orientation can influence responses to marketing stimuli, although evidence for the strength of this factor is unclear.[52] For example, research evidence indicates that females are more likely to undergo more elaborate processing of message content, so they tend to be more sensitive to specific pieces of information when forming a judgment, while males are more influenced by overall themes.[53] In addition, women with a relatively strong masculine component in their sex-role identity prefer ad portrayals that include nontraditional women.[54] Some research indicates that sex-typed people are more sensitive to the sex-role depictions of characters in advertising, although women appear to be more sensitive to gender role relationships than are men.[55]

In one study, subjects read two versions of a beer advertisement, couched in either masculine or feminine terms. The masculine version contained phrases like "X Beer has the strong aggressive flavor that really asserts itself with good food and good company . . . ," while the feminine version made claims like "Brewed with tender care, X Beer is a full-bodied beer that goes down smooth and gentle . . . ." People who rated themselves as highly masculine or highly feminine preferred the version that was

Teaching Hint: The decision about how to portray a man or a woman (for example, whether a woman's family, sexuality, or professional life be emphasized) should take into consideration the intended function of the product. Consumers are most comfortable with role portrayals that are consistent with the product in question—a family role should be emphasized for family products, and so on. See Lawrence H. Wortzel and John M. Frisbie, "Women's Role Portrayal Preferences in Advertisements: An Empirical Study," *Journal of Marketing* 38 (October 1974): 41–46.

described in (respectively) very masculine or feminine terms.[56] Sex-typed people in general are more concerned with ensuring that their behavior is consistent with their culture's definition of gender appropriateness.

Female Sex Roles

Sex roles for women are changing rapidly. Social changes, such as the dramatic increase in the proportion of women working outside of the home, have created an upheaval in the way women are regarded by men, the way they regard themselves, and in the products they choose to buy. Modern women now play a greater role in decisions regarding traditionally male purchases. For example, women now buy approximately 40 percent of all condoms sold.[57]

The character of Rosie the Riveter was created during World War II to symbolize the efforts of American women to take the place of men on factory production lines.

SEGMENTING WORKING WOMEN In the 1949 movie *Adam's Rib,* Katharine Hepburn played a stylish and competent lawyer. This film was one of the first to show that a woman can have a successful career and still be happily married. Historically, married women have worked outside of the home, especially during wartime, as the Word War II poster of Rosie the Riveter shows. However, the presence of women in positions of authority is a fairly recent phenomenon. The evolution of a new managerial class of women has forced marketers to change their traditional assumptions about women as they target this growing market.

Subsegments of Working Women. Ironically, it seems that in some cases marketers have overcompensated for their former emphasis on women as housewives. Many attempts to target the vast female working market tend to depict all working women in glamorous, executive positions. This portrayal ignores the facts that the majority of working women do not hold such jobs and that many work because they have to, rather than for self-fulfillment. This diversity means that all women should not be expected to respond to marketing campaigns that stress professional achievement or the glamour of the working life. Adult women can be segmented into four groups:

1. Housewives who do not plan to work outside of the home.
2. Housewives who plan to work at some point. (The women in this group may be staying at home only temporarily—until small children grow old

Cross-Cultural Example: The traditional demarcation between men and women is perpetuated in Japanese comic books, which are widely read by children and adults (they comprise over 25 percent of Japan's publishing industry). Female characters in these books tend to have lives centered around their husbands and children. Negative consequences occur when they try to pursue professional careers. See Sean Ledden and Fred Fejes, "Female Gender Role Patterns in Japanese Comic Magazines," *Journal of Popular Culture* 21 (Summer 1987): 155–70.

M U L T I C U L T U R A L D I M E N S I O N S

Some countries are redefining the role of women at a faster pace than others. This process tends to reflect the rate at which women are working outside of the home. For example, the percentage of active women (defined as those not in school, retired, or disabled), who are in the workforce is approximately 65 percent in the United States, while 50 percent of Italian women are employed, and only 37 percent work in Venezuela.[58]

Many cultures appear to be undecided about accepting an updated version of the female sex role. For example, while it is not unusual for Russian women to work as physicians, pilots, or scientists, the ideal of women as anchor of the family is still dominant in that culture. When a female cosmonaut landed at the Salyut-7 space station, the flight engineer greeted her by saying "We've got an apron ready for you, Sveta.

It's as if you've come home. Of course, we have a kitchen for you; that'll be where you work."[59]

One of the most marked changes in sex roles is occurring in Japan. Traditional Japanese wives stay home and care for children while their husbands work late and entertain clients. The good Japanese wife is expected to walk two paces behind her husband. However, these patterns are changing as women are less willing to live vicariously through their husbands.[60] More than half of Japanese women aged 25 to 29 are either working or looking for a job.[61] Japanese marketers and advertisers are beginning to depict women in professional situations (though still usually in subservient roles) and even to develop female market segments for such traditionally male products as automobiles.

Teaching Hint: A growing number of women are deciding to isolate themselves from men when they vacation; one guidebook lists over 400 women-only tours. While some are targeted to lesbians, others are designed to teach traditionally male skills or to bond with other women.

Teaching Hint: Initially, manufacturers tried to sell slower electric cars to women. When women said they preferred internal-combustion engines, the manufacturers replaced hand cranks with electric starters and enclosed the vehicles to appease them. See Sandra Salmans, "When an It Is Labeled a He or a She," *New York Times* (November 16, 1989): C1.

Teaching Hint: Prompted by concerns about how advertising portrayed women, The National Advertising Review Board in 1975 issued a checklist for advertisers to consider when creating or approving an ad. These guidelines caution against perpetuating sexual stereotypes, such as portraying women as weak, over-emotional, or subservient to men. Marketers, by and large, have responded to this challenge, though with mixed success. Note that even Virginia Slims, which bases its campaign on women's progress, still says "You've come a long way, baby!" See *Advertising and Women: A Report on Advertising Portraying or Directed to Women* (New York: The National Advertising Review Board, 1975).

enough to enter school, for example—and are thus not to be grouped with those housewives who have voluntarily chosen a domestic lifestyle.)

3. Career-oriented working women who value professional success and the trappings of achievement.
4. "Just-a-job" women who work primarily because they need the money.[62]

Appealing to Independence and Mobility. Whether or not they work outside of the home, many women have come to value greater independence and respond positively to marketing campaigns that stress the freedom to make their own lifestyle decisions. The American Express Company has been targeting women for a long time, but the company found that its "Do you know me?" campaign did not appeal to women as much as to men. A campaign aimed specifically at women instead features confident women using their American Express cards. By depicting women in active situations, the company greatly increased its share of the woman's credit card market.[63]

The desire for independence by women has also affected the car market. While men traditionally were primarily responsible for choosing and purchasing cars, this situation is changing radically and car makers are scrambling to keep up with it. While most car advertising is still male-oriented, women are increasingly depicted as serious buyers. More than six in ten of new car buyers under the age of 50 are female.[64]

Some of the most successful advertising targeted to women has been genderless. As one advertising executive who does automotive work commented, "You don't have to show a chiffon dress and high heels to get women to read the ad." Genderless ads have worked particularly well for Chevrolet's Geo line: Over 70 percent of the buyers of its Storm and Prizm models are women.[65] Women also are more sensitive to the aesthetics of the car showroom. They are more likely to notice and be turned off if the selling floor is dirty, and they are more likely to shop more dealers before buying. Hyundai has responded to this difference by designing car dealerships to resemble shopping malls, emphasizing a light and airy atmosphere.[66]

THE DEPICTION OF WOMEN IN ADVERTISING As implied by the ads for Virginia Slims cigarettes—"You've come a long way, baby!"—attitudes about the female sex role have changed remarkably in this century. Still, women continue to be depicted by advertisers and the media in stereotypical ways. Analyses of ads in such magazines as *Time, Newsweek, Playboy*, and even *Ms.* have shown that the large majority of women included were presented as sex objects or in traditional roles.[67] Similar findings have been obtained in the United Kingdom.[68] One of the biggest culprits may be rock videos, which tend to reinforce traditional women's roles. The women portrayed in these videos are usually submissive, and their primary attribute is high physical attractiveness. Recent evidence also indicates an increase in the amount of lingerie and nudity contained in rock videos.[69]

Ads may also reinforce negative stereotypes. Women often are portrayed as stupid, submissive, temperamental, or as sexual objects who exist solely for the pleasure of men. A recent ad for Newport cigarettes illustrates how the theme of female submission may be perpetuated. The copy "Alive with pleasure!" is accompanied by a photo of a woman in the woods, playfully hanging from a pole being carried by two men. The underlying message may be interpreted as two men bringing home their captured prey.[70]

Updated Images. Although women continue to be depicted in traditional roles, this situation is changing as advertisers scramble to catch up with reality. Women are now as likely as men to be central characters in television commercials. Still, while males increasingly are depicted as spouses and parents, women are still more likely than men to be seen in domestic settings. Also, about 90 percent of all narrators in commercials are male. The deeper male voice apparently is perceived as more authoritative and credible.[71]

Some modern ads now feature role-reversal, where women occupy traditional men's roles. In other cases, women are portrayed in romantic situations, but they tend to be more sexually dominant. Ironically, current advertising is more free to emphasize traditional female traits now that sexual equality is becoming more of an accepted fact. This freedom is demonstrated in a German poster for a women's magazine. The caption reads "Today's women can sometimes show weakness, because they are strong."

Cross-Cultural Example: The degree to which men and women are presented in traditional roles varies across cultures, as might be expected. For example, compared to advertising in the United States, Australian commercials do not emphasize sex-role differences as much, while Mexican commercials emphasize them a bit more. See Mary C. Gilly, "Sex Roles in Advertising: A Comparison of Television Advertisements in Australia, Mexico, and the United States," *Journal of Marketing* 52 (April 1988): 75–85.

MARKETING PITFALL

The R.J. Reynolds Tobacco Company created controversy with its "Smooth Character" campaign for Camel cigarettes. Designed to update the brand's image for a younger audience, ads feature "Old Joe," the company's traditional spokescamel, who presents tips on how to become a "smooth character." One tip suggested a way to impress a person at the beach: ". . . run into the water, grab someone and drag her back to shore . . . . The more she kicks and screams, the better." Several women's rights groups complained, and the ad was pulled.[72]

Male Sex Roles

While the traditional conception of the ideal male as a tough, aggressive, muscular man who enjoys "manly" sports and activities is not dead, society's definition of the male role is evolving. Men are allowed to be more compassionate and to have close friendships with other men. In contrast to the depiction of macho men who do not show feelings, some marketers are promoting men's "sensitive" side. An emphasis on male bonding has been the centerpiece of many ad campaigns, especially for beer companies.[73]

The prototype of the "new man" was expressed in the positioning statement for Paco Rabanne Pour Homme, a cologne that attempted to focus on this new lifestyle: "Paco Rabanne Pour Homme is a prestige men's fragrance for the male who is not a cliched stereotype, the man who understands and accepts the fluidity of male/female relationships." The ideal personality of the target consumer for the cologne was described by the company with adjectives like confident, independent, romantic, tender, and playful.[74]

Additional Example: In a commercial for Cascade dishwasher powder, two men have anxiety attacks because their dates are due for a dinner party and their glasses are spotted. See Kim Foltz, "In Ads, Men's Image Becomes Softer," *New York Times* (March 26, 1990): D12.

MARKETING OPPORTUNITY

As sex roles for males evolve, formerly "feminine products" like fragrances and hair coloring have been successfully marketed to men in recent years. Cosmetics companies are now attempting to expand the male market even further. So far, the most profitable products are treatments for baldness, but some companies are trying togo even further.

Estee Lauder, for example, sells four different male skin-care lines. Older men are somewhat resistant to the concept of skin care, and cosmetics marketers cannot use the same appeals they might employ when communicating to female consumers. As one industry consultant noted, "If you tell a man that a product makes his razor burn feel better or it makes him look healthier, he's more likely to respond. The cosmeticky language doesn't work." As explained by an executive with the Bic Corporation, which has a new line of disposable razors for men with different skin types, "Perhaps men's changing role make it easier for some to acknowledge they had sensitive skin."[75] Lancome sells an Anti-Wrinkle Creme and an Anti-Aging Eye Balm for men. These and other companies are optimistic about the prospects of appealing to a generation of younger men who will be more open than their older counterparts to cosmetics and skin-care products traditionally designed for women.[76]

The Joys of Fatherhood. Males' lifestyles are changing to allow greater freedom of expression in clothing choices, hobbies such as cooking, and so on. Men also are getting more involved in parenting, and advertising campaigns for such companies as Kodak, Omega watches, and Pioneer electronics stress the theme of fatherhood.[77] Still, this change is coming slowly. A commercial for 7-Eleven stores showed two men out for a walk, each pushing a stroller. As they near a 7-Eleven, they begin to push their strollers faster until they are racing. As the campaign's creative director explained, "We showed them engaged in a competition to make it easier for men to accept the concept of taking care of children."[78]

WHAT'S GOOD FOR THE GOOSE . . . Men as well as women often are depicted in a negative fashion in advertising. They frequently come across as helpless or bumbling. As one advertising executive put it, "The woman's movement raised consciousness in the ad business as to how women can be depicted. The thought now is, if we can't have women in these old-fashioned traditional roles, at least we can have men being dummies."[79] An organization called Men's Rights, Inc., identifies ads that demean men by depicting them as incompetent, panicked, smelling bad, and so on.[80]

From Cheesecake to Beefcake. In a twist on traditional portrayals, advertising is increasingly depicting men as sex objects or, as known in the industry, as "beefcake."[81] A recent campaign for Sansabelt trousers has the theme

"What women look for in men's pants." Ads feature a woman who confides, "I always lower my eyes when a man passes [pause] to see if he's worth following." One female executive commented, ". . . turnabout is fair play . . . . If we can't put a stop to sexism in advertising . . . at least we can have some fun with it and do a little leering of our own."[82]

Gay and Lesbian Consumers

The gay and lesbian community is in many ways a highly desirable market segment. It numbers at least 25 million people and consists of many consumers who are affluent, highly educated, and brand loyal. One survey of readers of urban gay newspapers found their average income to be almost $37,000, which is three times the national average. Nearly 60 percent had a college education (compared to 18 percent of the national population).

It has been estimated that between 6 and 16 percent of the U.S. adult population is homosexual. While, to say the least, this market segment is a sizable one, gay and lesbian consumers are still largely ignored by marketers.[83] This situation is starting to change, however, as some marketers are acknowledging the upscale demographic profile of these consumers. Remy Martin, for example, advertises its cognac in local gay media with great success. Both Stolichnaya and Absolut vodkas also recently began to advertise in these media, as have Bugle Boy Industries and the Adolph Coors Company.[84]

Experts believe more mainstream companies will jump on board once they realize the market potential of this group,[85] as has already happened in Australia, where Toyota dealers are targeting gay consumers with ads in an Australian gay magazine that feature male couples. Although the dealers were fearful of the general public's reaction, the response appears to have been positive. An employee at one Toyota dealer in Sydney remarked that the only criticism is "why aren't we showing two women?"[86]

Additional Example: Men's vulnerability was also the centerpiece of an ad campaign for Champion Athletic Apparel. In one execution, four soccer players hold their crotches with pained expressions and the ad reads "There's no such thing as a free kick. It's just a question of who pays." See Lena Williams, "Bodies Go Public: It's Men's Turn Now," *New York Times* (October 31, 1990): C1.

Body Image

A person's physical appearance is a large part of his or her self-concept. **Body image** refers to a consumer's subjective evaluation of his or her physical self. This image is not necessarily accurate. A man may think of himself as being more muscular than he really is, or a woman may feel she appears fatter than is the case. In fact, it is not uncommon to find marketing strategies that exploit consumers' tendencies to distort their body images by preying upon insecurities about appearance, thereby creating a gap between the real and ideal physical self and, consequently, the desire to purchase products and services to narrow that gap.

Body Cathexis

A person's feelings about his or her body can be described in terms of **body cathexis**. *Cathexis* refers to the emotional significance of some object or idea to a person, and some parts of the body are more central to self-concept than are others. One study of young adults' feelings about their bodies found that these respondents were the most satisfied with their hair and eyes and had the least positive feelings about their waists. These feelings also were related to usage of grooming products. Consumers who were more satisfied with their bodies were more frequent users of such "preening" products as hair conditioner, blower dryers, cologne, facial bronzer, tooth polish, and pumice soap.[87]

MARKETING OPPORTUNITY

An estimated 43 million Americans have a physical disability. This number is bound to increase as the population ages. While this group has long been ignored in the marketplace, recently such major marketers as Budweiser, Levi Strauss, McDonald's, and Reebok have employed disabled actors in their advertising and major retailers such as Nordstrom, Target, Eddie Bauer, and KMart are increasingly featuring the disabled in their catalogs. A recent ad campaign for Safeway Foods called "Nobody Does it Better," which depicts ordinary people doing their jobs, illustrates this new attitude. One segment features a letter carrier reading a letter to a blind woman, and another portrays a professor in a wheelchair teaching a class. The Americans with Disabilities Act, which prohibits employers from discriminating against the disabled, has created opportunities as many companies are investing in facilities that feature greater accessibility for the handicapped. To recoup this investment, these companies are working hard to attract more disabled customers and employees. In the process, they are waking up to the existence of a large niche that has been overlooked by many marketers.[88]

Ideals of Beauty

A person's satisfaction with the physical image he or she presents to others is affected by how closely that image corresponds to the image valued by his or her culture. An **ideal of beauty** is a particular model, or exemplar, of appearance. Female ideals of beauty include physical features (e.g., large lips or small lips, big breasts or small breasts) as well as such aspects as clothing styles, cosmetics, hairstyles, skin tone (pale versus tan), and musculature (petite, athletic, voluptuous). These ideals often are summed up in a sort of cultural shorthand. We may talk about a "vamp," a "girl-next-door," or an "ice queen," or we may refer to specific women who have come to embody an ideal, such as Cher, Marilyn Monroe, or Princess Grace.

An ideal of beauty functions as a sort of cultural yardstick. Consumers compare themselves to some standard and are dissatisfied with their appearance to the extent that they don't match up to it. Ideals of beauty, however, vary radically across cultures and even over time within the same society.

cedure is more likely to be selected.[113] Although some of these procedures have generated controversy due to possible negative side effects, it is unclear whether potential medical problems will deter large numbers of women from choosing surgical options to enhance their (perceived) femininity.

The importance of breast size to self-concept resulted in an interesting and successful marketing strategy undertaken by an underwear company. While conducting focus groups on bras, an analyst noted that small-chested women typically reacted with hostility when discussing the subject. They would unconsciously cover their chests with their arms as they spoke and felt that their needs were ignored by the fashion industry. To meet this overlooked need, the company introduced a line of A-cup bras called "A-OK" and depicted wearers in a positive light. A new market segment was born. A California company, in contrast, recently took the opposite tack: Taking a page from the craze for pump sneakers, they introduced Top Secret, a bikini with built-in, inflatable "falsies" as a "remedy" for flat-chested women.[114]

BODY DECORATION AND MUTILATION   The body is adorned or altered in some way in every culture. Decorating the self serves a number of purposes.[115]

- *To separate group members from nonmembers:* Chinook Indians of North America pressed the head of a newborn between two boards for a year, permanently altering its shape. In our society, teens go out of their way to adopt distinctive hair and clothing styles that will separate them from adults.

- *To place the individual in the social organization:* Many cultures engage in puberty rites, where a boy symbolically becomes a man. Young men in Ghana paint their bodies with white stripes to resemble skeletons to symbolize the death of their child status. In Western culture, this rite may involve some form of mild self-mutilation or engaging in dangerous activities.

- *To place the person in a gender category:* The Tchikrin Indians of South America insert a string of beads in a boy's lip to enlarge it. Western women wear lipstick to enhance femininity. At the turn of the century, small lips were fashionable because they represented women's submissive role at that time.[116] Today, big, red lips are provocative and indicate an aggressive sexuality. Some women, including a number of famous actresses and models, receive collagen injections or lip inserts to create large, pouting lips (known in the modeling industry as "liver lips").[117]

- *To enhance sex-role identification:* The modern use of high heels, which podiatrists agree are a prime cause of knee and hip problems, backaches, and fatigue, can be compared with the traditional Oriental practice of foot-binding to enhance femininity. As one doctor observed, "When they [women] get home, they can't get their high-heeled shoes off fast enough. But every doctor in the world could yell from now until Doomsday, and women would still wear them."[118]

- *To indicate desired social conduct:* The Suya of South America wear ear ornaments to emphasize the importance placed in their culture on listening and obedience. In Western society gay men may wear an earring to signal how they expect to be treated.

- *To indicate high status or rank:* The Hidates Indians of North America

International Example: Cosmetic surgery is booming in China, and many of the operations appear to be intended to give patients more of a Western look. The most common operations are to make rounder eyes and bigger noses. See Nicholas D. Kristof, "Changing the Face of China, One Face at a Time," *New York Times* (June 19, 1991): A4.

wear feather ornaments that indicate how many people they have killed. In our society, some people wear glasses with clear lenses, even though they do not have eye problems, to increase their perceived status.

- *To provide a sense of security:* Consumers often wear lucky charms, amulets, rabbits' feet, and so on to protect them from the "evil eye." Some modern women wear a "mugger whistle" around their necks for a similar reason.

Tattoos. Tattoos are one popular form of body adornment. This body art can be used to communicate aspects of the self to onlookers and may serve some of the same functions that other kinds of body painting do in primitive cultures. Tattoos (from the Tahitian ta-tu) have deep roots in folk art. Until recently, the images were crude and were primarily either death symbols (e.g., a skull), animals (especially panthers, eagles, and snakes), pinup women, or military designs. More current influences include science-fiction themes, Japanese symbolism, and tribal designs.

A tattoo may be viewed as a fairly risk-free way of expressing an adventurous side of the self. Tattoos have a long history of association with people who are socially disvalued. For example, the faces and arms of criminals in sixth-century Japan were tattooed as a means to identify them, as were Massachusetts prison inmates in the nineteenth century. These emblems are often used by marginal groups, such as bikers or Japanese yakuze (gang members), to express group identity and solidarity.

Chapter Summary

- Consumers' *self-concepts* are reflections of their attitudes toward themselves. Whether these attitudes are positive or negative, they will help to guide many purchase decisions; products can be used to bolster self-esteem or to "reward" the self.

- Many product choices are dictated by the consumer's perceived similarity between his or her personality and attributes of the product. The *symbolic interactionist perspective* on the self implies that each of us actually has many selves, and a different set of products is required as props to play each. Many things other than the body can also be viewed as part of the self. Valued objects, car, homes, and even attachments to sports teams or national monuments are used to define the self, when these are incorporated into the extended self.

- A person's *sex-role identity* is a major component of self-definition. Conceptions about masculinity and femininity, largely shaped by society, guide the acquisition of "sex-typed" products and services.

- Advertising and other media play an important role in socializing consumers to be male and female. While traditional women's roles have often been perpetuated in advertising depictions, this situation is changing somewhat. The media do not always portray men accurately either.

- A person's conception of his or her body also provides feedback to self-image. A culture communicates certain ideals of beauty, and consumers go to great lengths to attain these. Many consumer activities involve manipulating the body, whether through dieting, cosmetic surgery, tattooing, or so forth.

- Sometimes these activities are carried to an extreme, as people try too hard to live up to cultural ideals. One example is found in eating disorders, where women in particular become obsessed with thinness.

Key Terms

androgyny, p. 303
body cathexis, p. 309
body image, p. 309
extended self, p. 299
fantasy, p. 292

ideal of beauty, p. 310
personality, p. 289
self-concept, p. 289
self-image congruence models, p. 298
sex-typed traits, p. 302

symbolic interactionism, p. 295
symbolic self-completion theory, p. 297
trait, p. 290

Consumer Behavior Challenge

1. How might the creation of a self-conscious state be related to consumers who are trying on clothing in dressing rooms? Does the act of preening in front of a mirror change the dynamics by which people evaluate their product choices? Why?
2. Is it ethical for marketers to encourage infatuation with the self?
3. List three dimensions by which the self-concept can be described.
4. Compare and contrast the real versus the ideal self. List three products for which each type of self is likely to be used as a reference point when a purchase is considered.
5. Watch a set of ads featuring men and women on television. Try to imagine the characters with reversed roles (i.e., the male parts played by women and vice versa). Can you see any differences in assumptions about sex-typed behavior?
6. To date, the bulk of advertising targeted to gay consumers has been placed in exclusively gay media. If it was your decision to make, would you consider using mainstream media as well to reach gays, who constitute a significant proportion of the general population? Or, remembering that members of some targeted segments have serious objection about this practice, especially when the product (e.g., liquor, cigarettes) may be viewed as harmful in some way, do think gays should be singled out at all by marketers?
7. Do you agree that marketing strategies tend to have a male-oriented bias? If so, what are some possible consequences for specific marketing activities?
8. In the past, some marketers have been reluctant to use disabled people in advertising out of fear they would be seen as patronizing or that their ads would be depressing. Should the disabled be viewed as a distinct market segment, or should marketers continue to assume that their wants and needs are the same as the rest of the mainstream market?

CNN Connection

CNN. A video segment is available to accompany this CNN connection.

The Beauty Ideal

"Are women prisoners of their femininity? Some feminists argue that our culture maintains an unrealistic standard of beauty, and women spend their lives in a futile effort to match up to it. They diet, spend hours doing their makeup, and even have fat suctioned out of their thighs to conform to male expectations. In the professional world, a lot of conflict still exists about the degree to which appearance should play a role in evaluations of competence. Women are not alone in their pursuit of perfection. Although many deny it, men are also obsessed with how they look. As the chapter notes, men's usage of cosmetics, hair coloring, and even cosmetic surgery is growing as marketers are turning their attention to this underdeveloped market for appearance-related products. Men spend over a billion dollars a year on fragrances, and well over $150 million a year on hair and skin products. They, too, are to some degree "slaves" to their culture's definition of sex-role perfection.

This obsession is certainly not unique to the United States. Western beauty standards are being exported overseas and have made a particularly strong impact in status-conscious Japan. In a country where fashion reigns supreme, designer clothes, leisure activities, and even food choices can be an expression of the extended self. While the Japanese are avid importers of the latest in Western food and drink, they are also beginning to exhibit the eating disorders that have plagued Western cultures for some time. Incidences of anorexia nervosa and bulimia are on the rise as the Japanese strive to emulate the thin and chic Western beauty standard they have admired from afar.

SIMMONS Connection

SIMMONS Connection: Data for this exercise is on the Simmons Data Disk inside the back cover of your Instructor's Annotated Edition.

Data File: Consumers' Self-Concepts

Suzy is concerned with her appearance—her physical self. She is thinking about some of the options available for her in her quest to change her appearance. Suzy seems willing to consider cosmetic surgery to "correct" some of her perceived imperfections or to "improve" upon her natural physical endowments. The social comparison process described in this chapter may lead some consumers to feel that they should "adjust" themselves so that they come closer to an idealized image. Some have argued that the motivation underlying this willingness to adjust oneself to fit a culturally defined ideal is rooted in one's self-concept.

The Simmons file for this chapter contains information about consumers' self-concepts. The cross-tabulations relate the use of several health-care products, such as contact lenses and diet-control products, to consumers' self-concepts. What self-concept factors are most related to the use of such products as contact lenses, diet-control products, health spas, and so on? How are these self-concept dimensions related to consumer demographics? [Hint: You may want to refer to the Self file on your Simmons disk to answer the question about demographics.]

Notes

1. Daniel Goleman, "When Ugliness is Only in Patient's Eye, Body Image Can Reflect Mental Disorder," *New York Times* (October 2, 1991): C13.

2. Marsha L. Richins, "Social Comparison and the Idealized Images of Advertising," *Journal of Consumer Research* 18 (June 1991): 71–83; M. Wayne DeLozier and C. William Roe, "Marketing to the Homosexual (Gay) Market: A Profile and Strategy Implicatons," in *Proceedings of the Southern Marketing Association*, ed. Robert L. King (Richmond, Va.: Southern Marketing Association, 1991), 107–09; Richard V. Weekes, "Gay Dollars," *American Demographics* (October 1989)2: 45.

3. Philip N. Myers, Jr., and Frank A. Biocca, "The Elastic Body Image: The Effect of Television Advertising and Programming on Body Image Distortions in Young Women," *Journal of Communication* 42 (Summer 1992): 108–33; Dennis Rodkin, "Untapped Niche Offers Marketers Brand Loyalty," *Advertising Age* (July 9, 1990): S-2.

4. Harry C. Triandis, "The Self and Social Behavior in Differing Cultural Contexts," *Psychological Review* 96 (1989)3: 506–20; H. Markus and S. Kitayamak, "Culture and the Self: Implications for Cognition, Emotion, and Motivation," *Psychological Review* 98 (1991): 224–53.

5. Anthony G. Greenwald and Mahzarin R. Banaji, "The Self as a Memory System: Powerful, But Ordinary," *Journal of Personality and Social Psychology* 57 (1989)1: 41–54; Hazel Markus, "Self-Schemata and Processing Information About the Self," *Journal of Personality and Social Psychology* 35 (1977): 63–78.

6. Morris Rosenberg, *Conceiving the Self* (New York: Basic Books, 1979); M. Joseph Sirgy, "Self-Concept in Consumer Behavior: A Critical Review," *Journal of Consumer Research* 9 (December 1982): 287–300.

7. See J. Aronoff and J.P. Wilson, *Personality in the Social Process* (Hillsdale, N.J.: Erlbaum, 1985); Walter Mischel, *Personality and Assessment* (New York: Wiley, 1968).

8. Linda L. Price and Nancy Ridgway, "Development of a Scale to Measure Innovativeness," in *Advances in Consumer Research* 10, eds. Richard P. Bagozzi and Alice M. Tybout (Ann Arbor, Mich.: Association for Consumer Research, 1983), 679–84; Russell W. Belk, "Three Scales to Measure Constructs Related to Materialism: Reliability, Validity, and Relationships to Measures of Happiness," in *Advances in Consumer Research* 11, ed. Thomas C. Kinnear (Ann Arbor, Mich.: Association for Consumer Research, 1984), 291; Mark Snyder, "Self-Monitoring Processes," in *Advances in Experimental Social Psychology*, ed. Leonard Berkowitz (New York: Academic Press, 1979), 85–128; Gordon R. Foxall and Ronald E. Goldsmith, "Personality and Consumer Research: Another Look," *Journal of the Market Research Society* 30 (1988)2: 111–25; Ronald E. Goldsmith and Charles F. Hofacker, "Measuring Consumer Innovativeness," *Journal of the Academy of Marketing Science* 19 (1991)3: 209–21; Curtis P. Haugtvedt, Richard E. Petty, and John T. Cacioppo, "Need for Cognition and Advertising: Understanding the Role of Personality Variables in Consumer Behavior," *Journal of Consumer Psychology* 1 (1992)3: 239–60.

9. Jacob Jacoby, "Personality and Consumer Behavior: How Not to Find Relationships," in *Purdue Papers in Consumer Psychology, No. 102* (Lafayette, Ind.: Purdue University, 1969); Harold H. Kassarjian and Mary Jane Sheffet, "Personality and Consumer Behavior: An Update," in *Perspectives in Consumer Behavior*, 4th ed., eds. Harold H. Kassarjian and Thomas S. Robertson (Glenview, Ill.: Scott, Foresman and Company, 1991), 291–353; John Lastovicka and Erich Joachimsthaler, "Improving the Detection of Personality Behavior Relationships in Consumer Research," *Journal of Consumer Research* 14 (March 1988): 583–87.

10. J.G. Hull and A.S. Levy, "The Organizational Functions of the Self: An Alternative to the Duval and Wicklund Model of Self-Awareness," *Journal of Personality and Social Psychology* 37 (1979): 756–68; Jay G. Hull, Ronald R. Van Treuren, Susan J. Ashford, Pamela Propsom, and Bruce W. Andrus, "Self-Consciousness and the Processing of Self-Relevant Information," *Journal of Personality and Social Psychology* 54 (1988)3: 452–65.

11. Arnold W. Buss, *Self-Consciousness and Social Anxiety* (San Francisco: W.H. Freeman, 1980); Lynn Carol Miller and Cathryn Leigh Cox, "Public Self-Consciousness and Makeup Use," *Personality and Social Psychology Bulletin* 8 (1982)4: 748–51; Michael R. Solomon and John Schopler, "Self-Consciousness and Clothing," *Personality and Social Psychology Bulletin* 8 (1982)3: 508–14.

12. Morris B. Holbrook, Michael R. Solomon, and Stephen Bell, "A Re-Examination of Self-Monitoring and Judgments of Furniture Designs," *Home Economics Research Journal* 19 (September 1990): 6–16; Snyder, "Self-Monitoring Processes."

13. Mark Snyder and Steve Gangestad, "On the Nature of Self-Monitoring: Matters of Assessment, Matters of Validity," *Journal of Personality and Social Psychology* 51 (1986): 125–39.

14. Emily Yoffe, "You Are What You Buy," *Newsweek* (June 4, 1990): 59.

15. Roy F. Baumeister, Dianne M. Tice, and Debra G. Hutton, "Self-Presentational Motivations and Personality Differences in Self-Esteem," *Journal of Personality* 57 (September 1989): 547–75; Ronald J.

Faber, "Are Self-Esteem Appeals Appealing?" in *Proceedings of the 1992 Conference of The American Academy of Advertising*, ed. Leonard N. Reid (1992), 230–35.

16. B. Bradford Brown and Mary Jane Lohr, "Peer-Group Affiliation and Adolescent Self-Esteem: An Integration of Ego-Identity and Symbolic-Interaction Theories," *Journal of Personality and Social Psychology* 52 (1987)1: 47–55.

17. Jeffrey F. Durgee, "Self-Esteem Advertising," *Journal of Advertising* 14 (1986)4: 21.

18. Ernest Dichter, *Handbook of Consumer Motivations* (New York: McGraw-Hill, 1964).

19. Sigmund Freud, *New Introductory Lectures in Psychoanalysis* (New York: Norton, 1965).

20. Harrison G. Gough, Mario Fioravanti, and Renato Lazzari, "Some Implications of Self Versus Ideal-Self Congruence on the Revised Adjective Check List," *Journal of Personality and Social Psychology* 44 (1983)6: 1214–20.

21. Steven Jay Lynn and Judith W. Rhue, "Daydream Believers," *Psychology Today* (September 1985): 14.

22. Blayne Cutler, "Anything For A Thrill," *American Demographics* (August, 1988): 38.

23. Frank G. Wells, "Travel and Tourism 1983 to the Year 2003," *Vital Speeches of the Day*, delivered at Reno, Nev., October 29, 1987.

24. Peter S. Greenberg, "Hotels Play Up Fantasies," *Asbury Park Press* (May 27, 1990): El.

25. Erving Goffman, *The Presentation of Self in Everyday LIfe* (Garden City, N.Y.: Doubleday, 1959).

26. Julie Skur Hill, "Purchasing Habits Shift for Execs," *Advertising Age* (April 27, 1992): I–16.

27. George H. Mead, *Mind, Self and Society* (Chicago: University of Chicago Press, 1934).

28. Charles H. Cooley, *Human Nature and the Social Order* (New York: Scribner's, 1902).

29. Michael R. Solomon and Henry Assael, "The Forest or the Trees?: A Gestalt Approach to Symbolic Consumption," in *Marketing and Semiotics: New Directions in the Study of Signs for Sale*, ed. Jean Umiker-Sebeok (Berlin: Mouton de Gruyter, 1987), 189–218.

30. Jack L. Nasar, "Symbolic Meanings of House Styles," *Environment and Behavior* 21 (May 1989): 235–57; E.K. Sadalla, B. Verschure, and J. Burroughs, "Identity Symbolism in Housing," *Environment and Behavior* 19 (1987): 599–87.

31. Michael R. Solomon, "The Role of Products as Social Stimuli: A Symbolic Interactionism Perspective," *Journal of Consumer Research* 10 (December 1983): 319–28; Robert E. Kleine, III, Susan Schultz-Kleine, and Jerome B. Kernan, "Mundane Everyday Consumption and the Self: A Conceptual Orientation and Prospects for Consumer Research," in *Advances in Consumer Research* 19, eds. John F. Sherry, Jr. and Brian Sternthal (Provo, Utah: Association for Consumer Research, 1992), 411–15; Newell D. Wright, C.B. Claiborne, and M. Joseph Sirgy, "The Effects of Product Symbolism on Consumer Self-Concept," in *Advances in Consumer Research* 19, eds. John F. Sherry, Jr., and Brian Sternthal (Provo, Utah: Association for Consumer Research, 1992), 311–18.

32. A. Dwayne Ball and Lori H. Tasaki, "The Role and Measurement of Attachment in Consumer Behavior," *Journal of Consumer Psychology* 1 (1992)2: 155–72.

33. William B. Hansen and Irwin Altman, "Decorating Personal Places: A Descriptive Analysis," *Environment and Behavior* 8 (December 1976): 491–504.

34. R.A. Wicklund and P.M. Gollwitzer, *Symbolic Self-Completion* (Hillsdale, N.J.: Lawrence Erlbaum, 1982).

35. Erving Goffman, *Asylums* (New York: Doubleday, 1961).

36. Quoted in Floyd Rudmin, "Property Crime Victimization Impact on Self, on Attachment, and on Territorial Dominance," *CPA Highlights*, Victims of Crime Supplement 9 (1987)2: 4–7.

37. Barbara B. Brown, "House and Block as Territory," paper presented at the Conference of the Association for Consumer Research, San Francisco, 1982.

38. Deborah A. Prentice, "Psychological Correspondence of Possessions, Attitudes, and Values," *Journal of Personality and Social Psychology* 53 (1987)6: 993–1002.

39. Sak Onkvisit and John Shaw, "Self-Concept and Image Congruence: Some Research and Managerial Implications," *The Journal of Consumer Marketing* 4 (Winter 1987): 13–24. For a related treatment of congruence between advertising appeals and self-concept, see George M. Zinkhan and Jae W. Hong, "Self-Concept and Advertising Effectiveness: A Conceptual Model of Congruency, Conspicuousness, and Response Mode," in *Advances in Consumer Research* 18, eds. Rebecca H. Holman and Michael R. Solomon (Provo, Utah: Association for Consumer Research, 1991), 348–54.

40. C.B. Claiborne and M. Joseph Sirgy, "Self-Image Congruence as a Model of Consumer Attitude Formation and Behavior: A Conceptual Review and Guide for Further Research," paper presented at the Academy of Marketing Science Conference, New Orleans, 1990.

41. Al E. Birdwell, "A Study of Influence of Image Congruence on Consumer Choice," *Journal of Business* 41 (January 1964): 76–88; Edward L. Grubb and

Gregg Hupp, "Perception of Self, Generalized Stereotypes, and Brand Selection," *Journal of Marketing Research* 5 (February 1986): 58–63.

42. Ira J. Dolich, "Congruence Relationship Between Self-Image and Product Brands," *Journal of Marketing Research* 6 (February 1969): 80–84; Danny N. Bellenger, Earle Steinberg, and Wilbur W. Stanton, "The Congruence of Store Image and Self Image as It Relates to Store Loyalty," *Journal of Retailing* 52 (1976)1: 17–32; Ronald J. Dornoff and Ronald L. Tatham, "Congruence Between Personal Image and Store Image," *Journal of the Market Research Society* 14 (1972)1: 45–52.

43. Naresh K. Malhotra, "A Scale to Measure Self-Concepts, Person Concepts, and Product Concepts," *Journal of Marketing Research* 18 (November 1981): 456–64.

44. Ernest Beaglehole, *Property: A Study in Social Psychology* (New York: MacMillan, 1932).

45. M. Csikszentmihalyi and Eugene Rochberg-Halton, *The Meaning of Things: Domestic Symbols and the Self* (Cambridge, Mass.: Cambridge University Press, 1981).

46. Russell W. Belk, "Possessions and the Extended Self," *Journal of Consumer Research* 15 (September 1988): 139–68.

47. Eileen Fischer and Stephen J. Arnold, "More than a Labor of Love: Gender Roles and Christmas Gift Shopping," *Journal of Consumer Research* 17 (December 1990): 333–45.

48. Joan Meyers-Levy, "The Influence of Sex Roles on Judgment," *Journal of Consumer Research* 14 (March 1988): 522–30.

49. ElizaBeth C. Hirschman, "A Feminist Critique of Marketing Theory: Toward Agentic-Communal Balance," working paper, School of Business, Rutgers University, New Brunswick, N.J., l990.

50. Kathleen Debevec and Easwar Iyer, "Sex Roles and Consumer Perceptions of Promotions, Products, and Self: What Do We Know and Where Should We Be Headed," in *Advances in Consumer Research* 13, ed. Richard J. Lutz (Provo, Utah: Association for Consumer Research, 1986), 210–14.

51. Sandra L. Bem, "The Measurement of Psychological Androgyny," *Journal of Consulting and Clinical Psychology* 42 (1974): 155–62; Deborah E.S. Frable, "Sex Typing and Gender Ideology: Two Facets of the Individual's Gender Psychology That Go Together," *Journal of Personality and Social Psychology* 56 (1989)1: 95–108.

52. See D. Bruce Carter and Gary D. Levy, "Cognitive Aspects of Early Sex-Role Development: The Influence of Gender Schemas on Preschoolers' Memories and Preferences for Sex-Typed Toys and

Activities," *Child Development* 59 (1988): 782–92; Bernd H. Schmitt, France Le Clerc, and Laurette Dube-Rioux, "Sex Typing and Consumer Behavior: A Test of Gender Schema Theory," *Journal of Consumer Research* 15 (June 1988): 122–27.

53. Carol Gilligan, *In a Different Voice: Psychological Theory and Women's Development* (Cambridge, Mass.: Harvard University Press, 1982); Joan Meyers-Levy and Durairaj Maheswaran, "Exploring Differences in Males' and Females' Processing Strategies," *Journal of Consumer Research* 18 (June 1991): 63–70.

54. Lynn J. Jaffe and Paul D. Berger, "Impact on Purchase Intent of Sex-Role Identity and Product Positioning," *Psychology & Marketing* (Fall 1988): 259–71.

55. Sandra L. Bem, "Gender Schema Theory: A Cognitive Account of Sex Typing," *Psychological Review* 88 (July 1981): 354–64; Keren A. Johnson, Mary R. Zimmer, and Linda L. Golden, "Object Relations Theory: Male and Female Differences in Visual Information Precessing," in *Advances in Consumer Research* 14, eds. Melanie Wallendorf and Paul Anderson, (Provo, Utah: Association for Consumer Research, 1986), 83–87.

56. Leila T. Worth, Jeanne Smith, and Diane M. Mackie, "Gender Schematicity and Preference for Gender-Typed Products," *Psychology & Marketing* 9 (January 1992): 17-30.

57. Blayne Cutler, "Condom Mania," *American Demographics* (June 1989): 17.

58. Denise Rusoff, "British Women Get the Jobs," *American Demographics* (December 1987): 54; Rena Bartos, "Marketing to Women: The Quiet Revolution," *Marketing Insights* (June 1989): 61.

59. John F. Burns, "An Apron For Soviet Woman in Space," *New York Times* (August 28, 1982): D1.

60. Laurel Anderson and Marsha Wadkins, "The New Breed in Japan: Consumer Culture," unpublished manuscript, Arizona State University, Tempe, 1990.

61. Doris L. Walsh, "A Familiar Story," *American Demographics* (June 1987): 64.

62. Rena Bartos, "Marketing to Women."

63. B. Abrams, "American Express is Gearing New Ad Campaign to Women," *Wall Street Journal* (August 4, 1983): 23.

64. Julie Candler, "Woman Car Buyer—Don't Call Her a Niche Anymore," *Advertising Age* (January 21, 1991): S-8.

65. Candler, "Woman Car Buyer—Don't Call Her a Niche Anymore."

66. Frieda Curtindale, "Marketing Cars to Women," *American Demographics* (November 1988): 28.

67. "Ads' Portrayal of Women Today is Hardly Innovative," *Marketing News* (November 6, 1989): 12; Jill Hicks Ferguson, Peggy J. Kreshel, and Spencer F. Tinkham, "In the Pages of *Ms.*: Sex Role Portrayals of Women in Advertising," *Journal of Advertising* 19 (1990)1: 40–51.

68. Sonia Livingstone and Gloria Greene, "Television Advertisements and the Portrayal of Gender," *British Journal of Social Psychology* 25 (1986): 149–54; L.Z. McArthur and B.G. Resko, "The Portrayal of Men and Women in American Television Commercials," *Journal of Social Psychology* 97 (1975): 209–20.

69. Richard C. Vincent, "Clio's Consciousness Raised? Portrayal of Women in Rock Videos, Re-examined," *Journalism Quarterly* 66 (1989): 155.

70. Richard Edel, "American Dream Vendors," *Advertising Age* (November 9, 1988): 153.

71. Daniel J. Brett and Joanne Cantor, "The Portrayal of Men and Women in U.S. Television Commercials: A Recent Content Analysis and Trends Over 15 Years," *Sex Roles* 18 (1988): 595–609.

72. Judann Dagnoli, "Groups Smoking Over Camel Ad," *Advertising Age* (July 17, 1989): 49.

73. Gordon Sumner, "Tribal Rites of the American Male," *Marketing Insights* (Summer 1989): 13.

74. Margaret G. Maples, "Beefcake Marketing: The Sexy Sell," *Marketing Communications* (April 1983): 21–25.

75. Quoted in Diana Minardi, "The '90s Man: Cowboy or Wimp?" *Adweek* (June 29, 1992)2: 34.

76. Linda Wells, "Flirting With Men," *New York Times Magazine* (April 9, 1989): 64.

77. "Changing Conceptions of Fatherhood," *USA Today* (May 1988): 10.

78. Quoted in Kim Foltz, "In Ads, Men's Image Becomes Softer," *New York Times* (March 26, 1990): D12.

79. Quoted in Jennifer Foote, "The Ad World's New Bimbos," *Newsweek* (January 25, 1988): 44.

80. Mary Jung, "Watchdog Group Lashes Out At Ads That Demean Men," *Marketing News* (March 27, 1989): 2.

81. Maples, "Beefcake Marketing."

82. Quoted in Lynn G. Coleman, "What Do People Really Lust After in Ads?" *Marketing News* (November 6, 1989): 12.

83. DeLozier and Roe "Marketing to the Homosexual (Gay) Market: A Profile and Strategy Implications,"; Weekes, "Gay Dollars."

84. Rodkin, "Untapped Niche Offers Marketers Brand Loyalty."

85. Anne O'Malley, "The Gay Nineties," *The Marketer* (1990)2: 12.

86. Geraldine Fabrikant, "Australian Car Ads Aim at Gay Buyers," *New York Times* (December 24, 1991): D7.

87. Dennis W. Rook, "Body Cathexis and Market Segmentation," in *The Psychology of Fashion*, ed. Michael R. Solomon (Lexington, Mass.: Lexington Books, 1985), 233–41.

88. Carrie Goerne, "Marketing to the Disabled: New Workplace Law Stirs Interest in Largely Untapped Market," *Marketing News* (September 14, 1992)3: 1; "Retailers Find a Market, and Models, in Disabled," *New York Times* (August 6, 1992): D4.

89. Michael R. Solomon and Richard Ashmore, "The Language of Beauty," paper presented at the International Institute on Marketing Meaning, Indianapolis, Ind., 1989.

90. Lois W. Banner, *American Beauty* (Chicago: The University of Chicago Press, 1980).

91. David M. Garner, Paul E. Garfinkel, Donald Schwartz, and Michael Thompson, "Cultural Expectations of Thinness in Women," *Psychological Reports* 47 (1980): 483–91.

92. Kathleen Boyes, "The New Grip of Girdles is Lightened by Lycra," *USA Today* (April 25, 1991): 6D.

93. "Girls at 7 Think Thin, Study Finds," *New York Times* (February 11, 1988): B9.

94. Jennifer Stoffel, "What's New in Weight Control," *New York Times* (November 26, 1989): F17.

95. Stoffel, "What's New in Weight Control."

96. "How Much is *Too Fat*?" *USA Today* (February 1989): 8.

97. *American Demographics* (May 1987): 56.

98. Deborah Marquardt, "A Thinly Disguised Message," *Ms.* 15 (May 1987): 33.

99. Vincent Bozzi, "The Body in Question," *Psychology Today* 22 (February 1988): 10.

100. Elaine L. Pedersen and Nancy L. Markee, "Fashion Dolls: Communicators of Ideals of Beauty and Fashion," paper presented at the International Conference on Marketing Meaning, Indianapolis, Ind., 1989; Dalma Heyn, "Body Hate," *Ms.* (August 1989): 34.

101. "Big Women, Big Profits," *Newsweek* (February 25, 1991): 48; Monica Gonzales, "Fashionably Large," *American Demographics* (August 1988): 18.

102. Debra A. Zellner, Debra F. Harner, and Robbie I. Adler, "Effects of Eating Abnormalities and Gender on Perceptions of Desirable Body Shape," *Journal of Abnormal Psychology* 98 (February 1989): 93–96.

103. Robin T. Peterson, "Bulimia and Anorexia in an Advertising Context," *Journal of Business Ethics* 6 (1987): 495–504.

104. Jane E. Brody, "Personal Health," *New York Times* (February 22, 1990): B9.

105. Christian S. Crandall, "Social Contagion of Binge

Eating," *Journal of Personality and Social Psychology* 55 (1988): 588–98.

106. Judy Folkenberg, "Bulimia: Not For Women Only," *Psychology Today* (March 1984): 10.

107. Eleanor Grant, "The Exercise Fix: What Happens When Fitness Fanatics Just Can't Say No?" *Psychology Today* 22 (February 1988): 24.

108. John W. Schouten, "Selves in Transition: Symbolic Consumption in Personal Rites of Passage and Identity Reconstruction," *Journal of Consumer Research* 17 (March 1991): 412–25.

109. Monica Gonzalez, "Want a Lift?" *American Demographics* (February 1988): 20.

110. Annette C. Hamburger and Holly Hall, "Beauty Quest," *Psychology Today* (May 1988): 28.

111. Emily Yoffe, "Valley of the Silicone Dolls," *Newsweek* (November 26, 1990): 72.

112. Keith Greenberg, "What's Hot: Cosmetic Surgery," *Public Relations Journal* (June 1988): 23.

113. Jerry Adler, "New Bodies For Sale," *Newsweek* (May 27, 1985): 64.

114. Melinda Beck, "Glad You Aren't Here," *Newsweek* (August 10, 1992): 46.

115. Ruth P. Rubinstein, "Color, Circumcision, Tatoos, and Scars," in *The Psychology of Fashion*, ed. Michael R. Solomon (Lexington, Mass.: Lexington Books, 1985), 243–54; Peter H. Bloch and Marsha L. Richins, "You Look 'Mahvelous': The Pursuit of Beauty and Marketing Concept," *Psychology & Marketing* 9 (January 1992): 3–16.

116. Sondra Farganis, "Lip Service: The Evolution of Pouting, Pursing, and Painting Lips Red," *Health* (November 1988): 48–51.

117. Michael Gross, "Those Lips, Those Eyebrows; New Face of 1989 (New Look of Fashion Models)," *New York Times Magazine* (February 13, 1989): 24.

118. Quoted in "High Heels: Ecstasy's Worth the Agony," *New York Post* (December 31, 1981).

CHAPTER 10

Purchase and
Postpurchase

Buying, Having, and Being: Selections 33–37 from *Buying, Having, and Being: The Washington Post Consumer Behavior Companion,* Second Edition, accompany this chapter.

Mark is really psyched. The big day has actually arrived: He's going to buy a car! He hasn't had time to shop around, but he's had his eye on that silver 1987 Camaro parked in the lot of Ron's Auto-Rama. Although the sticker says $2999, Mark figures he can probably get this baby for a cool $2000—Ron's looks like just the kind of place where they're hungry to move some cars. Mark dreads the prospect of haggling over the price, but he hopes to convince the salesman to take his offer, especially since he can write a check for the full amount today. He's been working two jobs to save up for that car, and a little more suffering in the showroom will be worth it.

At the Auto-Rama lot, big signs on all the cars proclaim that today is Ron's Auto-Rama Rip Us Off Day! Things look better than Mark expected—maybe he can get the Camaro for even less than he had planned. He heads for the Camaro and is a bit surprised when a salesperson who introduces herself as Rhoda comes over to him. He had expected to be dealing with a middle-aged man in a loud sport coat (a stereotype he has about used-car salespeople), but this is more good luck: He figures he won't have to be so tough when dealing with a woman who looks to be about his age.

Rhoda laughs when he offers her $1800 for the Camaro, pointing out that she can't take such a low bid for such a sweet car to her boss or she'll lose her job. Rhoda's enthusiasm for the car convinces him all the more that he has to have it. When he finally writes a check for $2700, he's exhausted from all the haggling. What an ordeal! In any case, Mark figures he'll get his money back when he sells the car in a few years, and he did manage to convince Rhoda to sell him the car for less than the sticker price.

Actually, he's not only pleased with the car, but with himself—he's a tougher negotiator than he thought . . . .

Introduction

Many consumers dread the act of buying a car. Although the ritual of haggling over price is a time-honored one in the automobile industry, change is in the wind. A growing number of dealerships (about 2 percent of the total) are responding to consumer's reluctance to enter into battle by introducing a "no-dicker" policy—the sticker price is the only price. The Saturn division of General Motors encourages this policy, as does Ford for sales of its Escort model. While the profit per car tends to be smaller, dealers who have gone

FIGURE 10–1   Issues Related to Purchase and Postpurchase Activities

this route report they more than make up for this loss due to increased sales volume. Industry research indicates that these dealers are both better liked and busier than are traditional dealers. The new approach seems especially likely to benefit women and minority buyers, who (research indicates) are less likely to negotiate than are white males.[1]

Figure 10–1 is available as Transparency 24.

Mark's experience in buying a car illustrates some of the concepts to be discussed in this chapter. Making a purchase is often not a simple, routine matter of going to a store and quickly picking out something. As illustrated in Figure 10–1, a consumer's choices are affected by many personal factors, such as his or her mood, whether there is time pressure to make the purchase, and the particular situation or context for which the product is needed. In some situations, like the purchase of a car or a home, the salesperson or realtor plays a pivotal role in the final selection.

The store environment also exerts a big influence: Shopping is like a performance of a play, where the customer is involved as either an audience member or an active participant. The quality of this performance is affected by the other cast members (e.g., salespeople or other shoppers), as well as by the setting of the play (e.g., the image of a particular store and particular store and the "feeling" it imparts to the shopper) and props (e.g., store decorations and promotional materials that try to influence the shopper's decisions). The Tandy Corporation's new Incredible Universe consumer electronics stores exemplify this approach to shopping. As one executive observed, ". . . we put on a show everyday. We have 300 cast members [not salespeople], in scenes, with props and costumes to educate our 'guests' about the latest in electronic wizardry."[2]

In addition, a lot of important consumer activity occurs *after* a product has been purchased and brought home. After using a product, the consumer must decide whether he or she is satisfied with it. The satisfaction process is especially important to savvy marketers who realize that the key to success is not selling a product one time, but rather forging a relationship with the consumer so that he or she will continue to buy one's products in the future. Finally, just as Mark thought about the resale value of his car, we must also consider how consumers go about disposing of products and how secondary markets (e.g., used car dealers) often play a pivotal role in product acquisition. This chapter considers many issues related to purchase and postpurchase phenomena.

Situational Effects on Consumer Behavior

A situation is defined by factors over and above characteristics of the person and of the product. Situational effects can be behavioral (e.g., entertaining friends) or perceptual (e.g., being depressed, or feeling pressed for time).[3] Common sense tells us that people tailor their purchases to specific occasions or that the way we feel at a specific point in time affects what we feel like buying or doing.

One reason for this variability is that the role a person plays at any time is partly determined by his or her *situational self-image*: "Who am I right now?" (see Chapter 9).[4] Someone trying to impress his date by playing the role of "man-about-town" may spend more lavishly, ordering champagne instead of beer and buying flowers—purchases he would never consider when he is hanging out with his friends, slurping beer, and playing the role of "one of the boys." As this example demonstrates, knowledge of what

This South African ad for Volkswagen emphasizes that brand criteria can differ depending upon the situation in which the product will be used. Courtesy of Volkswagen of South Africa.

consumers are doing at the time a product is consumed can improve predictions of product and brand choice.[5]

Situational Segmentation

By systematically identifying important usage situations, market segmentation strategies can be developed to position products that will meet the specific needs arising from these situations. Many product categories are amenable to this form of segmentation. For example, consumers' furniture choices are often tailored to specific settings. We prefer different styles for a city apartment, beach house, or an executive suite. Similarly, motorcycles can be distinguished in terms of what riders use them for, including commuting, riding them as dirt bikes, using them on a farm versus highway travel, and so on.[6] The South African ad for Volkswagen shown here emphasizes the versatility of the Volkswagen bus for different situations.

CONSTRUCTING A SITUATIONAL SEGMENTATION MATRIX Table 10–1 gives one example of how situations can be used to fine-tune a segmentation strategy. By listing the major contexts where a product is used (e.g., snow skiing and sunbathing for a suntan lotion) and the different users of the product, a matrix can be constructed that identifies specific product features that should be emphasized for each situation. For example, a lotion manufacturer might promote the fact that the bottle floats and is hard to lose during the summer, but tout its antifreeze formula during the winter season.

Physical and Social Surroundings

A consumer's physical and social environment can make a big difference in motives for product usage and also affect how the product is evaluated. Important cues include the person's physical surroundings, as well as the amount and type of other consumers also present in that situation.

CO-CONSUMERS As will be seen in the next chapter, many of a consumer's purchase decisions are significantly affected by the groups or social settings in which these occur. In some cases, the sheer presence or absence of other patrons ("co-consumers") in a setting can be a determinant attribute (see Chapter 7), such as when an exclusive resort or boutique promises to provide privacy to privileged customers. At other times, the presence of others can have positive value. A sparsely attended ball game or an empty bar can be depressing sights.

The presence of large numbers of people in a consumer environment increases arousal levels, so a consumer's subjective experience of a setting tends to be more intense. This polarization, however, can be both positive and negative. While the presence of other people creates a state of arousal, the consumer's actual experience depends upon his or her *interpretation* of this arousal. It is important to distinguish between *density* and *crowding* for this reason. The former term refers to the actual number of people occupying a space, while the psychological state of crowding exists only if a negative affective state occurs as a result of this density.[7] For example, 100

Additional Example: Hallmark Cards owes much of its success to identifying situations that merit the purchase of a greeting card. As a way to smooth out demand between holidays, the company is now trying a new niche: "non-occasion" cards for both kids and adults. For example: "You're getting a card and it's not even your birthday, That's because you don't have to have a birthday to be special to me—I love you ALL the time!" See Isadore Barmash, "Sending the Very Best, for No Particular Reason," *New York Times* (June 9, 1991): F12.

Research Report: Businesses segment their markets in terms of local weather conditions. See Joe Schwartz, "Climate-Controlled Customers," *American Demographics* (March 1992): 24–33.

TABLE 10-1 A Person–Situation–Segmentation Matrix for Suntan Lotion

Situations	Young Children		Teenagers		Adult Women		Adult Men		Situation Benefits/Features
	Fair Skin	Dark Skin	Fair Skin	Dark Skin	Fair Skin	Dark Skin	Fair Skin	Dark Skin	
Beach/boat sunbathing	Combined insect repellent				Summer perfume				a. Windburn protection b. Formula and container can stand heat c. Container floats and is distinctive (not easily lost)
Home-poolside sunbathing					Combined moisturizer				a. Large pump dispenser b. Won't stain wood, concrete, furnishings
Sunlamp bathing					Combined moisturizer and massage oil				a. Designed specifically for type lamp b. Artificial tanning ingredient
Snow skiing					Winter perfume				a. Special protection from special light rays and weather b. Antifreeze formula
Person benefit/ features	Special protec-tion		Special protec-tion		Special protec-tion		Special protec-tion		
	a. Protection critical b. Non-poisonous		a. Fit in jean pocket b. Used by opinion leaders		Female perfume		Male perfume		

Source: Peter R. Dickson, "Person-Situation: Segmentation's Missing Link," *Journal of Marketing* 46 (Fall 1982): 62. By permission of American Marketing Association.

students packed into a classroom designed for 75 may be unpleasant for all concerned, but the same number of people jammed together at a party occupying a room of the same size might just make for a great party.

In addition, the type of consumers who patronize a store or service can serve as a store attribute. We may infer something about a store by examining its customers. For this reason, some restaurants require men to wear a jacket for dinner (and supply one if they don't), and bouncers of some "hot" nightspots hand-pick patrons they will admit based on whether they have the right "look" for the club. To paraphrase the comedian Groucho Marx, "I would never join a club that would have me for a member."

MARKETING OPPORTUNITY

Developments in the coin-operated laundry business illustrate how a traditionally depressing experience can be repositioned as a fun, social event. Many laundries have taken to installing bars, tanning salons, and exercise machines to encourage customers to look forward to doing their laundry. The Videotown Laundrette in Manhattan features a 6000 title videocassette library, and Suds & Duds in Greensboro, North Carolina, has a snack bar, pool hall, and big-screen television.[8]

Temporal Factors

Time is one of consumers' most limiting resources. We talk about "making time" or "spending time," and we are frequently reminded that "time is money." Our perspectives on time can affect many stages of decision making and consumption, such as needs that are stimulated, the amount of information search we undertake, and so on. Common sense tells us that more careful information search and deliberation occurs when we have the luxury of taking our time. A meticulous shopper who would normally price an item at three different stores before buying it might be found running through the mall at 9 p.m. on Christmas Eve, furiously scooping up anything left on the shelves that might serve as a last-minute gift.

ECONOMIC TIME   Time is an economic variable; it is a resource that must be divided among activities.[9] Consumers try to maximize satisfaction by allocating time to the appropriate combination of tasks. Of course, people's allocation decisions differ; we all know people who seem to play all of the time, and others who are workaholics. An individual's priorities determine his or her *timestyle*.[10]

Time Poverty.   Many consumers believe they are more pressed for time than ever before. This feeling may, however, be due more to perception than to fact. People may just have more options for spending their time and feel pressured by the weight of all of these choices. The average working day at the turn of the century was ten hours (six days per week), and women did 27 hours of housework per week, compared to under five hours weekly now. Of course, one reason for this difference is that men are sharing these burdens more.[11] Still, about a third of Americans report always feeling rushed—up from 25 percent of the population in 1964.[12]

This sense of time poverty has made consumers very responsive to marketing innovations that allow them to save time. As an executive at Campbell's Soup observed, "Time will be the currency of the 1990s."[13] This priority has created new opportunities for services as diverse as photograph processing, optometrists, and car repair, where speed of delivery has become an important attribute.[14] To cater to this need, a Chicago funeral home even offers drive-through service, where viewers can see a loved one

Consumers can be characterized in terms of their pattern of time allocation, or "timestyle." A time model allocation model is available as Transparency 25.

International Example: Japanese consumers are even more pressed for time. When Tokyo residents were asked what they would do if given one extra hour per day, almost half said they would sleep (compared to about 20 percent of Los Angeles residents who were asked this question). See *A New Partnership: New Values and Attitudes of the New Middle Generation in Japan and the U.S.A.* (Tokyo: Dentsu Institute for Human Studies, 1989).

on a screen without taking the time to leave their cars. The owner notes, "The working person doesn't have time to come in. They want to see the body but they don't want to wait."[15]

Polychronicity. With the increase in time poverty, researchers also are noting a rise in *polychronic activity*, where consumers do more than one thing at a time.[16] One area where this type of activity is especially prevalent is eating. Consumers often do not allocate a specific time to dining, but instead eat on the run. In a recent poll, 64 percent of respondents said they usually do something else while eating. As one food industry executive commented, "We've moved beyond grazing and into gulping."[17]

PSYCHOLOGICAL TIME The psychological dimension of time, or how it is experienced, is an important factor in *queuing theory*, the mathematical study of waiting lines. A consumer's experience of waiting can radically influence his or her perceptions of service quality. Although we assume that something must be pretty good if we have to wait for it, the negative feelings aroused by long waits can quickly turn off customers.

Marketers have adopted a variety of "tricks" to minimize psychological

MULTICULTURAL DIMENSIONS

To most Western consumers, time is a neatly compartmentalized thing: We wake up in the morning, go to school or work, come home, eat dinner, go out, go to sleep . . . wake up and do it all over again. This perspective is called *linear separable time* (or Christian time); events proceed in an orderly sequence and different times are well-defined: "There's a time and a place for everything." There is a clear sense of past, present, and future. Many activities are performed as the means to some end that will occur later, as when people "save for a rainy day."

This conception of time is not universal. Large cultural differences exist in terms of people's time perspectives.[18] Some cultures run on *procedural time* and ignore the clock completely. People decide to do something "when the time is right." Alternatively, in *circular* or *cyclic time,* people are governed by natural cycles, such as the regular occurrence of the seasons (a perspective found in many Latino

cultures). To these consumers, the notion of the future does not make sense, because that time will be much like the present. Since the concept of future value does not exist, these consumers often prefer to buy an inferior product that is available now to waiting for a better one that may be available later. Also, it is hard to convince people who function on circular time to buy insurance or save for the future when they do not endorse this concept.

When groups of college students were asked to draw a picture of time, the resulting sketches in Figure 10–2 illustrate some of these different temporal perspectives.[19] The drawing at the top represents procedural time; there is lack of direction from left to right and little sense of past, present, and future. The two drawings in the middle denote cyclical time, with regular cycles designated by markers. The bottom drawing represents linear time, with a segmented time line moving from left to right in a well-defined sequence.

waiting time. These techniques range from altering customers' perceptions of a line's length to providing distractions that divert attention away from waiting.[20]

- One hotel chain, after receiving excessive complaints about the wait for elevators, installed mirrors near the elevator banks. People's natural tendency to check their appearance reduced complaints, even though the actual waiting time was unchanged.

- Airline passengers often complain of the time they must wait to claim their baggage. In one airport, they would walk one minute from the plane to the baggage carousel and then wait seven minutes for their luggage. By changing the layout so that the walk to the carousel took six minutes and bags arrived two minutes after that, complaints were almost entirely eliminated.

- McDonald's uses a multiple-line system, where each server deals with a separate line of people. Wendy's uses a multistage system, where the first server takes orders, the second prepares burgers, the third pours drinks, and so on. While Wendy's lines are longer, customers move continuously through stages, so signs of progress can be seen and psychological time is reduced. Similarly, Disneyland often disguises the length of its lines by bending them around corners so that customers are prevented from judging the actual size of the line and anticipated waiting time.

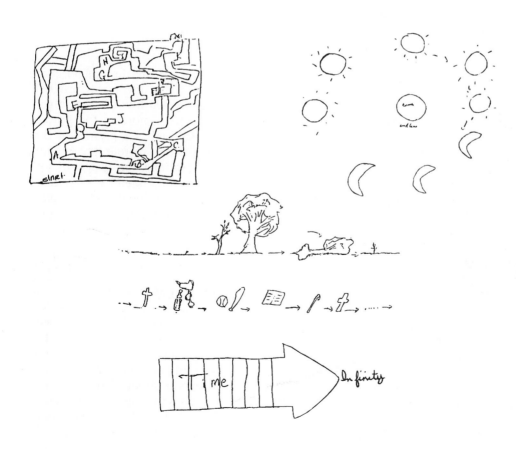

FIGURE 10–2 Drawings of Time Source: Esther S. Page-Wood, Carol J. Kaufman, and Paul M. Lane, "The Art of Time," *Proceedings of the Academy of Marketing Science* (1990).

MARKETING PITFALL

An emphasis on speed resulted in some serious public relations problems for Domino's Pizza, which guarantees delivery within thirty minutes. Critics claimed that this policy encouraged reckless driving and backed up this charge with some damaging statistics. In 1989, more than a dozen lawsuits, stemming from death or serious injuries caused by delivery people rushing to make the half-hour deadline, were filed against the company. The employee death rate was 50 per 100,000 equal to that suffered in the mining industry.[21] The company now qualifies its claim by stipulating that safety factors must be considered during delivery.

Time-of-Day. Some products and services are believed to be appropriate for certain times and not for others. One study of fast food preferences found that consumers were more likely to choose Wendy's over other fast food outlets for an evening meal when not rushed than when they were pressed for time.[22] Also, we may be more receptive to advertising messages at certain times (who wants to hear a beer commercial at 7:00 in the morning?). There is some evidence that consumers' arousal levels are lower in the morning than in the evening, which affects their style and quality of information processing.[23]

Antecedent States

A person's mood or physiological condition active at the time of purchase can have a big impact on what is bought and can also affect how products are evaluated.[24] One reason is that behavior is directed toward certain goal states, as was discussed in Chapter 3. People spend more in the grocery store if they have not eaten for a while because food is a priority at that time. In addition, the person'sparticular social identity, or role that is being played at a given time, will be influential.[25] For example, one aspect of situational role is the degree to which a consumer's ethnic identity, or *felt ethnicity*, is activated during a purchase situation. When people are reminded of this connection, they are more likely to tailor their product choices along ethnic lines.[26]

MOOD A consumer's mood can have a big impact on purchase decisions. For example, stress can impair information-processing and problem-solving abilities.[27] Two dimensions determine if a shopper will react positively or negatively to a store environment. These are *pleasure* and *arousal*. A person can enjoy or not enjoy a situation, and he or she can feel stimulated or not. As Figure 10–3 indicates, different combinations of pleasure and arousal levels result in a variety of emotional states. For example, an arousing situation can be either distressing or exciting, depending on whether the context is positive or negative (e.g., a street riot versus a street festival such as Mardi Gras). Maintaining an "up" feeling in a pleasant context is one factor behind the success of theme parks like Disney World, which try to provide consistent doses of carefully calculated stimulation to patrons.[28]

FIGURE 10–3 Dimensions of Emotional States Source: James Russell and Geraldine Pratt, "A Description of the Affective Quality Attributed to Environment," *Journal of Personality and Social Psychology* 38 (August 1980): 311–322. Copyright © 1980 by the American Psychological Association. Adapted by permission.

A specific mood is some combination of these two factors. For example, the state of happiness is high in pleasantness and moderate in arousal, while elation would be high on both dimensions.[29] In general, a mood state (either positive or negative) biases judgments of products and service in that direction.[30] Put simply, consumers like things better when they are in a good mood. When in positive moods, consumers process ads with less elaboration. They pay less attention to specifics of the message and rely more on heuristic processing (see Chapter 7).[31]

Moods can be affected by store design, the weather, or other factors specific to the consumer. In addition, music and television programming can affect mood, which has important consequences for commercials.[32] When consumers hear happy music or watch happy programs, they have more positive reactions to commercials, especially to emotional messages.[33]

Figure 10–3 is available as Transparency 26.

Shopping Motives

People often shop even though they do not necessarily intend to buy anything at all, while others have to be dragged to a mall. Shopping is a way to acquire needed products and services, but social motives for shopping also are important. Shopping motives can include the following.[34]

- *Social experiences:* The shopping center or department store has replaced the traditional town square or county fair as a community gathering place. Many people (especially in suburban or rural areas) may have no place else to go to spend their leisure time.

- *Sharing of common interests:* Stores frequently offer specialized goods that allow people with shared interests to communicate.

- *Interpersonal attraction:* Shopping centers are a natural place to congregate. The shopping mall has become a central "hangout" for teenagers. It also represents a controlled, secure environment for other groups, such as the elderly.

- *Instant status:* As every salesperson knows, some people savor the experience of being waited on, even though they may not necessarily buy anything. One men's clothing salesman offered this advice: ". . . remember their size, remember what you sold them last time. Make them feel important! If you can make people feel important, they are going to come back. Everybody likes to feel important!"[35]
- *"The thrill of the chase":* Some people pride themselves on their knowledge of the marketplace. Unlike Mark, they may relish the process of haggling and bargaining, viewing it almost as a sport.

SHOPPING ORIENTATIONS Many people seem to be falling out of love with shopping. In 1987, a survey done for Neiman-Marcus and American Express found that 50 percent of the respondents liked shopping as much as they liked watching television, and 17 percent found shopping as pleasurable as romance! Just two years later, though, more than half of the respondents in another survey said that they hated browsing in stores as much as they loathed housework.[36]

Which way is it? Do people hate to shop or love it? It depends. Consumers can be segmented in terms of their **shopping orientation**, or general attitudes about shopping. These orientations may vary depending on the particular product categories and store types considered. Mark hates to shop for a car, but he may love to browse in record stores. Several shopping types have been identified.[37]

- *The economic consumer:* a rational, goal-oriented shopper who is primarily interested in maximizing the value of his or her money.
- *The personalized consumer:* a shopper who tends to form strong attachments to store personnel ("I shop where they know my name").
- *The ethical consumer:* a shopper who likes to help out the underdog and will support locally owned stores against big chains.
- *The apathetic consumer:* one who does not like to shop and sees it as a necessary but unpleasant chore.
- *The recreational shopper:* a person who views shopping as a fun, social activity—a preferred way to spend leisure time.

The Purchase Environment

Additional Example: The Mall of America in Bloomington, Minnesota, is the size of 78 football fields (9.5 million square feet). The center features an amusement park, 18 movie theaters, and 100 nightclubs and restaurants. See "Attention Shoppers," *U.S. News & World Report* (July 31, 1989): 66.

We see bumper stickers and T-shirts everywhere: "Shop 'til you drop." "When the going gets tough, the tough go shopping." "Born to shop." Like it or not, shopping is a dominant activity for many consumers. On the average, American consumers spend about 6 percent of their waking hours shopping. Only about half of this time is devoted to shopping for groceries and other basics.[38]

The competition for shoppers is getting rougher amongst retailers. Between 1974 and 1984, total retail square footage in the United States grew by 80 percent, but the population grew by only 12 percent. About 200 million square feet of shopping mall space is added every year.[39] Retailers must now offer something extra to lure shoppers, whether that something is excitement or just plain bargains.[40]

Non-Store Shopping

The competition for customers is becoming even more intense as non-store alternatives that bring retail services to the home continue to multiply. Popular non-store alternatives include mail-order catalogs, television shopping networks, salespersons who make house calls (e.g., the Avon lady), and home shopping parties (e.g., Tupperware). The growth of computerized home shopping systems (e.g., Prodigy) has been somewhat slow in the United States, compared to France, where the Minitel System offers about 8000 information services and is connected to more than 3.7 million home terminals.[41] Another emerging trend is to bring retailing to the office, as demonstrated by the Spiegel ad shown here. This approach makes sense, because people are working longer hours and earning more money but are leaving themselves less free time in which to spend it.

Additional Example: In the United States, information services such as the Prodigy system offered by Sears and IBM allow consumers with modem-equipped computers to order airline tickets, do their banking, and get updates on local events. See Marianne Meyer, "Attention Shoppers!" *Marketing and Media Decisions* 23 (May 1988).

Recognizing that modern women have many time pressures, Spiegel brings retailing to the office.
© Copyright 1991, Spiegel, Inc.

Finding that many of its female customers are no longer home during the day, even Avon has expanded its distribution network to the office, where representatives make presentations during lunch and coffee breaks. Similarly, Tupperware features "rush-hour parties" at the end of the work-day and now finds that about 20 percent of its sales are made outside of homes. An employee of Mary Kay cosmetics, another company adapting this strategy, offered another explanation for its success: "Working women buy more in the office because they are not looking at the wallpaper that needs replacing. They feel richer away from home."[42]

M A R K E T I N G   P I T F A L L

In 1988, 12.4 billion mail-order catalogs were mailed, twice the number sent in 1980. This figure amounts to fifty catalogs for every man, woman, and child in the United States. While $30 billion worth of merchandise was ordered as a result, there are signs that this market is reaching the saturation point as more retailers jump on the direct marketing bandwagon. In addition to increasing competition, rising postal costs have elevated mailing expenses by as much as 30 percent. To economize, many mailers are abandoning their scattershot approach by developing more targeted mailing lists or producing different editions, each catering to a specialized group. L.L. Bean, for example, distributes twenty-two separate catalogs, including one just for fly fishermen.[43]

The Shopping Experience

Store-loyal consumers are prized by retailers. They will routinely visit a small set of stores without considering others or doing much in the way of comparative pre-purchase search. However, consumers now have an abundance of choices regarding where to shop, including the non-store alternatives. For this reason, people do not tend to be as store loyal as they once were.[44]

RETAILING AS THEATER Shopping malls have tried to gain the loyalty of shoppers by appealing to their social motives as well as providing access to desired goods. The mall is often a focal point in a community. In the United States, 94 percent of adults visit a mall at least once a month. More than half of all retail purchases (excluding autos and gasoline) are made in a mall.

Malls are becoming giant entertainment centers, almost to the point where their traditional retail occupants seem like an afterthought. It is now typical to find such features as carousels, miniature golf, or batting cages in a suburban mall. As one retailing executive put it, "Malls are becoming the new mini-amusement parks."[45] The importance of creating a positive, vibrant, and interesting image has led innovative marketers to blur the line between shopping and theater. Both shopping malls and individual stores must create environments that stimulate people and allow them to shop and be simultaneously entertained.[46] The following are among the best "performers."[47]

- Bloomingdale's department store is noted for its elaborate store-wide promotions, often based upon the culture of a selected country. During these events the entire store is transformed, with each department featuring unusual merchandise from the country. These promotions are accompanied by lavish parties, food, and entertainment associated with that country.

- Babyland (the home of Cabbage Patch dolls) does not have a sales staff. Instead, the company offers "doctors," "nurses," and "adoption officers." Dolls are never "sold," they are adopted. Every fifteen minutes, Bunny Bees hover over the cabbage patch and inseminate the cabbages. These cabbages quiver, and the leaves open, displaying a newborn Cabbage Patch baby.

- Ralph Lauren's Madison Avenue store is in a refurbished mansion, and the decor is consistent with the company's image of aristocratic gentility and the good life. The store is furnished with expensive antiques and tapestries, and cocktails and canapés are served in the evening. Even cleaning supplies are carried by maintenance staff in Lauren shopping bags.

- At Nike's showcase Nike Town stores, as indicated in the photo shown here, sports memorabilia is showcased along with Nike products in a futuristic atmosphere where see-through tubes carry stock to the selling floor. Video screens display Michael Jordan slam-dunking, and one can hear the sound of dribbling basketballs in the background. Merchandise in the store's water sports section is displayed on surf boards and there is a salt-water fish tank on the wall, while TV monitors embedded in the floor play underwater scenes.

Teaching Hint: Some retailers, especially those in the grocery business, are taking a lesson from the airlines and are encouraging store loyalty with programs that reward "frequent shoppers." Participants can earn points toward merchandise by buying particular brands in the store. In some cases, this process is part of a "discount-for-data" system, where consumers agree to have their purchases tracked by a computer in exchange for product discounts. Such companies as Kraft, Campbell's, Del Monte, Procter & Gamble, and General Foods now participate in these programs. See Cynthia Crossen, "If You Are What You Eat, They've Got Your Number," *Wall Street Journal* (August 31, 1989): B1; Stan Rapp, "Frequent Flyers Move Over, Here Comes the Frequent Shopper," *Direct Marketing* 51 (January 1989): 70.

The Nike Town Store in Portland, Oregon, provides an innovative, futuristic atmosphere designed to enhance the shopping experience. © Christopher Kean.

STORE IMAGE   With so many stores competing for customers, how do consumers pick one over another? Like products, stores may be thought of as having "personalities." Some stores have very clearly defined images (either good or bad). Others tend to blend into the crowd. They may not have anything distinctive about them and may be overlooked for this reason. This personality, or **store image**, is composed of many different factors. Store features, coupled with such consumer characteristics as shopping orientation, help to predict which shopping outlets people will prefer.[48] Some of the important dimensions of a store's profile are location, merchandise suitability, and the knowledge and congeniality of the sales staff.[49]

Store Gestalt.   When shoppers think about stores, they may not say, "Well, that place is fairly good in terms of convenience, the salespeople are acceptable, and services are good." They are more likely to say, "That place gives me the creeps," or "I always enjoy shopping there." Consumers evaluate stores both in terms of both their specific attributes *and* a global evaluation, or *gestalt* (see Chapter 2).[50] This overall feeling may have more to do with such intangibles as interior design and the types of people one finds in the store than with such aspects as return policies or credit availability. As a result, some stores are likely to consistently be in consumers' evoked sets, while others will never be considered.[51]

Atmospherics.   Because a store's gestalt is now recognized to be a very important aspect of the retailing mix, attention is increasingly paid to **atmospherics,** or the "conscious designing of space and its various dimensions to evoke certain effects in buyers."[52] These dimensions include colors, scents, and sounds.

Many elements of store design can be cleverly controlled to attract customers and produce desired effects on consumers. Light colors impart a feeling of spaciousness and serenity, and signs in bright colors create excitement. In one subtle but effective application, fashion designer Norma Kamali replaced fluorescent lights with pink ones in department store dressing rooms. The light had the effect of flattering the face and banishing wrinkles, making female customers more willing to try on (and buy) the company's bathing suits.[53]

In addition to visual stimuli, all sorts of cues can influence behaviors.[54] For example, patrons of country-and-western bars drink more when the jukebox music is slower. According to a researcher, "Hard drinkers prefer listening to slower paced, wailing, lonesome, self-pitying music . . . ."[55] Similarly, music can affect eating habits. Another study found that diners who listened to loud, fast music ate more food. In contrast, those who listened to Mozart or Brahms ate less and more slowly. The researchers concluded that diners who choose soothing music at mealtimes can increase weight loss by at least five pounds a month![56]

In-Store Decision Making

Despite all their efforts to "pre-sell" consumers through advertising, marketers increasingly are recognizing the significant degree to which many purchases are influenced by the store environment. It has been estimated that about two out of every three supermarket purchases are decided in the aisles. The proportion of unplanned purchases is even higher for some product categories. It is estimated that 85 percent of candy and gum, almost 70 percent of cosmetics, and 75 percent of oral hygiene purchases are unplanned.[57] Despite all the talk about rational, planning consumers, most enter the store relatively unprepared. Approximately 90 percent of shoppers do *not* use store circulars, 80 percent do without coupons, and 70 percent do not even bother with a shopping list.[58]

SPONTANEOUS SHOPPING When a shopper is prompted to buy something while in the store, one of two different processes may be at work.

Unplanned Buying. Unplanned buying may occur when a person is unfamiliar with a store's layout or perhaps when under some time pressure. Or, a person may be reminded to buy something by seeing it on a store shelf. About one-third of unplanned buying has been attributed to the recognition of new needs while within the store.[59]

Impulse Buying. **Impulse buying** occurs when the person experiences a sudden urge that he or she cannot resist.[60] For this reason, so-called impulse items such as candy and gum are conveniently placed near the checkout. Similarly, many supermarkets have installed wider aisles to encourage browsing, and the widest tend to contain products with the highest margin. Low mark-up items that are purchased regularly tend to be stacked high in narrower aisles, to allow shopping carts to speed through.[61]

Planning Versus Impulse Shopping. Shoppers can be categorized in terms of how much advance planning they do. *Planners* tend to know what products and specific brands they will buy beforehand, *partial planners* know they need certain products, but do not decide on specific brands until they are in the store, and *impulse purchasers* do no advance planning whatsoever.[62] Figure 10–4 was drawn by a consumer, participating in a study on consumers' shopping experiences, who was asked to sketch a typical impulse purchaser.

Research Report: One recent survey found that on average a coupon user needs to see an increase of 42 percent in the value of a coupon to try a new brand. For example, if a person redeems a 50 cent coupon for a product he/she already uses, that person would require one for 70 cents to try a new brand. See "Coupons—at the Right Price—Can Torpedo Brand Loyalty," *Advertising Age* (May 18, 1992): 52.

M A R K E T I N G   P I T F A L L

Cents-off coupons and rebates are widely used by manufacturers and retailers to induce consumers to switch brands.[63] While coupons are an important aspect of many promotions, evidence regarding their effectiveness at luring *new* customers is mixed. Households that already use the couponed brand are more likely to redeem the coupon, and most customers revert to their original brand after a coupon promotion.[64] As a result, a company that adopts a couponing strategy intended to attract brand switchers may find itself "preaching to the converted."

Similarly, rebate offers are not always used by consumers for several reasons, including a short expiration date, a requirement to purchase a greater quantity than is needed, and difficulty in finding or removing the proof-of-purchase seal.[65]

DRAW-A-PICTURE

1. Think about your image of what kind of person an impulse buyer is. In the space provided below draw a picture of your image of a typical impulse buyer who is about to make an impulse purchase. Be creative and don t worry about your artistic skills! If you feel that some features of your drawing are unclear, don t hesitate to identify them with a written level.

2. After you have completed your drawing imagine what is going through your character s mind as he or she is about to make their impulse purchase. Then write down your shopper s thoughts in a speech balloon (like you might see in a cartoon strip) that connects to your character s head.

FIGURE 10–4   One Consumer's Image of an Impulse Buyer   Source: Dennis Rook, "Is Impulse Buying (Yet) a Useful Marketing Concept?" unpublished manuscript, University of Southern California, Los Angeles, 1990, fig. 7-A.

POINT-OF-PURCHASE STIMULI Because so much decision making apparently occurs while the shopper is in the purchasing environment, retailers are beginning to pay more attention to the amount of information in their stores, as well as to the way it is presented. It has been estimated that impulse purchases increase by 10 percent when appropriate displays are used. Each year, U.S. companies spend more than $13 billion on **point-of-purchase stimuli (POP)**. A point-of-purchase stimulus can be an elaborate product display or demonstration, a coupon-dispensing machine, or even someone giving out free samples of a new cookie in the grocery aisle.

Displays. The first elaborate (and highly successful) point-of-purchase display was developed for L'eggs pantyhose. The company believes that this strategy builds impulse traffic[66] and now has even more sophisticated displays, as shown in the photo here.
Some other dramatic POP displays include the following.[67]

- *Timex:* A still-ticking watch sits in the bottom of a filled aquarium.
- *Elizabeth Arden:* The company introduced "Elizabeth," a computer and video makeover system that allows customers to test out their images with different shades of makeup, without having to actually apply the products

The L'eggs display (inset) is one of the best known and earliest point-of-purchase displays. The newer version is also shown here.   Courtesy of SARA LEE HOSIERY.

first. Similarly, the Novell Corporation's line of Clarion cosmetics features a computer to help women select the right shades for them.[68]

- *Tower Records:* A music sampler allows customers to hear records before buying them and to custom-design their own recordings by mixing and matching singles from assorted artists.

- *Nabisco:* A display for the company's Fruit Wheats cereal emits the scent of fresh raspberries.

MARKETING PITFALL

Although POP techniques can potentially aid consumers by providing them with more helpful information about nutrition and product safety, so far this promise has not been fulfilled. Research conducted in over 300 supermarkets indicates that POP nutritional signage had no effect on the purchase behavior of customers. One positive aspect for participating outlets: The sheer presence of the signs did improve their store image among customers.[69]

- *Trifari:* This company offers paper punch-out versions of its jewelry so that customers can "try on" the pieces at home.
- *Charmin:* Building on the familiar "Please don't squeeze the Charmin" theme, the company deploys the Charmin Squeeze Squad. Employees hide behind stacks of the toilet tissue and jump out and blow horns at any "squeezers" they catch in the aisles.
- *The Farnam Company:* As somber music plays in the background, a huge plastic rat draped in a black shroud lies next to a tombstone to promote the company's Just One Bite rat poison.

Place-Based Media. Advertisers are also being more aggressive about hitting consumers with their messages, wherever they may be. *Place-based media* is a growing specialized medium that targets consumers based on locations in which the message is delivered. These places can be anything from airports, doctors' offices, college campuses, or health clubs. Turner Broadcasting System has begun such ventures as Checkout Channel for grocery stores and Airport Channel, and it has even tested McDTV for McDonald's restaurants.[70] Even MTV is getting into the act: Its new Music Report, to be shown in record stores, is a two-hour "video capsule" featuring video spots and ads for music retailers and corporate sponsors. An MTV executive observed, "They're already out there at the retail environment. They're ready to spend money."[71]

A company called Privy Promotions is even beginning to sell ad space on restroom walls in stadiums. For $2,000, the company will mount a framed ad for a year in a restroom stall, above a sink, or ". . . wherever it looks nice and appropriate," according to Privy's president. He claims ". . . it's a decided opportunity for an advertiser to reach a captive audience . . . ."[72]

Much of the growth in point-of-purchase activity has been in new electronic technologies.[73] Some stores feature talking posters that contain a human body sensor that speaks up when a shopper approaches. The Point-of-Purchase Radio Corporation offers in-store radio networks that are now used by about sixty grocery chains.[74] As illustrated in the trade ad for VideOcart shown here, new shopping carts have a small screen that displays advertising, which is keyed to the specific areas of the store through which the cart is wheeled.[75] In-store video displays allow advertisers to reinforce major media campaigns at the point of purchase.[76]

Some of the most interesting innovations can be found in state-of-the-art vending machines, which now dispense everything from Hormel's microwaveable chili and beef stew and Ore-Ida french fries to software. French consumers

MULTICULTURAL DIMENSIONS

Due to their frenetic lifestyles, the Japanese are avid users of vending machines. These machines dispense virtually all of life's necessities, plus many luxuries people in other countries would not consider obtaining from a machine. The list includes jewelry, fresh flowers, frozen beef, pornography, business card, underwear and even the names of possible dates.[77]

The VideOcart represents a new generation of point-of-purchase advertising. Courtesy of VideOcart, Inc.

can even purchase Levi's jeans from a machine called "Libre Service," which offers the pants in ten different sizes. The customer uses a seatbelt to find his or her size, and the jeans sell for about $10 less than the same versions sold in more conventional stores.

The Salesperson

One of the most important in-store factors is the salesperson, who attempts to influence the buying behavior of the customer.[78] This influence can be understood in terms of **exchange theory**, which stresses that every interaction involves an exchange of value. Each participant gives something to the other and hopes to receive something in return.[79]

RESOURCE EXCHANGE What "value" does the customer look for in a sales interaction? There are a variety of resources a salesperson might offer. He or she, for example, might offer expertise about the product to make the shopper's choice easier. Alternatively, the customer may be reassured because the salesperson is an admired or likable person whose tastes are similar and is seen as someone who can be trusted.[80] Mark's car purchase, for example, was strongly influenced by the age and sex of Rhoda, the salesperson with whom he negotiated

THE SALES INTERACTION A buyer/seller situation is like many other dyadic encounters (two-person groups); it is a relationship where some agreement must be reached about the roles of each participant: A process of *identity negotiation* occurs.[81] For example, if Rhoda immediately establishes herself as an all-knowing expert (and Mark accepts this position), she is likely to have more influence over him through the course of the relationship. Some of the factors that help to determine a salesperson's role (and relative effectiveness) are his or her age, appearance, educational level, and motivation to sell.[82]

In addition, more effective salespersons usually know their customers'

International Example: People from different cultures may stress certain attributes at the bargaining table. Research suggests that French negotiators are influenced by the personal characteristics of their counterparts across the table (especially that person's similarity to themselves), and the British tend to emphasize status or role. In contrast, these factors do not sway Americans as much. They are more affected by the actual conditions during negotiations and stress the importance of problem solving and information exchange. Chinese negotiators tend to be extremely competitive, while in Japan sellers defer to buyers and tend to reciprocate when offers of cooperation are made. See Nigel C.G. Campbell, John L. Graham, Alain Jolibert, and Hans Gunther, "Marketing Negotiations in France, Germany, the United Kingdom, and the United States," *Journal of Marketing* 52 (April 1988): 49–62.

Teaching Hint: The relationship marketing perspective may help to explain why female salespeople tend to be more productive, even though women are underrepresented in sales. One speculation for this difference is that women are less threatening, more empathetic, and better listeners than their male counterparts. See Lee Boyan, "Who's More Productive?" *American Salesman* (November 1989): 16.

traits and preferences better than do ineffective salespersons, since this knowledge allows them to adapt their approach to meet the needs of the specific customer.[83] The ability to be adaptable is especially vital when customers and salespeople differ in terms of their *interaction styles*.[84] Consumers, for example, vary in the degree of assertiveness they bring to interactions. At one extreme, nonassertive people believe that complaining is not socially acceptable and may be intimidated in sales situations. Assertive people are more likely to stand up for themselves in a firm but nonthreatening way, while aggressives may resort to rudeness and threats if they do not get their way.[85]

RELATIONSHIP MARKETING The strategic perspective that stresses the long-term, human side of buyer/seller interactions is called **relationship marketing**. This view recognizes that ". . . the sale merely consummates the courtship. Then the marriage begins. How good the marriage is depends on how well the relationship is managed by the seller."[86] Like a romantic involvement, long-term sales relationships typically go through five phases.[87]

1. *Awareness:* The buyer enters the market, perhaps becoming aware of local brands.
2. *Exploration:* The buyer undergoes search and trial. A minimal investment is made in the relationship. Norms and expectations begin to develop.
3. *Expansion:* The buyer and seller start to become more interdependent as the relationship becomes solidified.
4. *Commitment:* A pledge is made (it may be done implicitly) to continue the relationship (e.g., a customer may come to refer to someone as "my hairdresser").
5. *Dissolution:* The relationship will dissolve, unless steps are taken to keep it together. One way for the seller to prevent dissolution is to construct *exit barriers*, making it difficult for the buyer to separate. Examples of exit barriers include delayed rebates (customers must accumulate proof-of-purchase seals over time), frequent flier programs (which make it less tempting to switch airlines), or rental deposits.

Postpurchase Satisfaction

Consumer satisfaction or **dissatisfaction (CS/D)** is determined by the overall feelings, or attitude, a person has about a product after it has been purchased. Consumers are engaged in a constant process of evaluating the things they buy as these products are integrated into their daily consumption activities.[88]

Perceptions of Product Quality

Just what do consumers look for in products? That's easy: They want quality and value. Especially because of foreign competition, claims of product quality have become strategically crucial to maintaining a competitive advantage.[89] Consumers use a number of cues to infer quality, including brand name, price, and even their own estimates of how much money has been put into a new product's advertising campaign.[90] These cues, as well

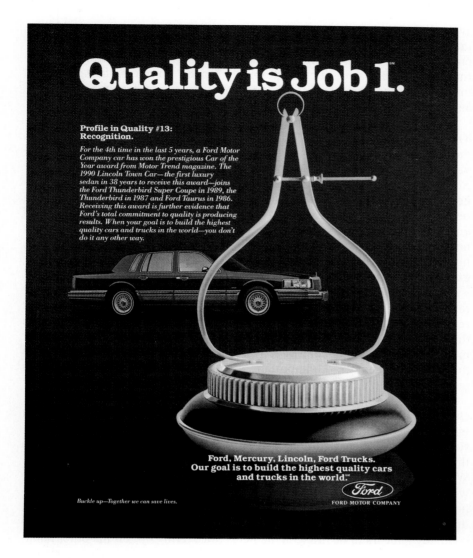

Quality is Job 1.℠

**Profile in Quality #13:
Recognition.**

For the 4th time in the last 5 years, a Ford Motor Company car has won the prestigious Car of the Year award from Motor Trend magazine. The 1990 Lincoln Town Car—the first luxury sedan in 38 years to receive this award—joins the Ford Thunderbird Super Coupe in 1989, the Thunderbird in 1987 and Ford Taurus in 1986. Receiving this award is further evidence that Ford's total commitment to quality is producing results. When your goal is to build the highest quality cars and trucks in the world—you don't do it any other way.

**Ford, Mercury, Lincoln, Ford Trucks.
Our goal is to build the highest quality cars
and trucks in the world."**

Ford

FORD MOTOR COMPANY

Buckle up—Together we can save lives.

This ad for Ford relies on a common claim about "quality." Courtesy of Ford Motor Company.

as others such as product warranties and follow-up letters from the company, are often used by consumers to relieve perceived risk and assure themselves that they have made smart purchase decisions.[91]

While everyone wants quality, it is not clear exactly what it means. Certainly, many manufacturers claim to provide it. The Ford Motor Company ad shown here emphasizes "*Quality* is job 1." Similar claims that have been made at one time or another by car manufacturers include the following.[92]

Lincoln-Mercury: ". . . the highest *quality* cars of any major American car company"

Chrysler: ". . . *quality* engineered to be the best"

GMC trucks: ". . . *quality* built yet economical"

Oldsmobile: ". . . fulfilling the *quality* needs of American drivers"

Audi: ". . . *quality* backed by our outstanding new warranty"

Research Report: A study of major appliance purchases found that 33 percent of those consumers who were satisfied with the brand they bought repurchased that brand at a later time. In contrast, only 7 percent of dissatisfied customers stuck with the same brand. Further, between 17 percent and 25 percent of major appliance purchases resulted in dissatisfaction. A manufacturer with a market share of 5 percent would thus lose $31 million if dissatisfaction with its products was equal to the industry average. See Joseph W. Newman and Richard A. Werbel, "Multivariate Analysis of Brand Loyalty for Major Household Appliances," *Journal of Marketing Research* 10 (November 1973): 404–09.

WHAT IS QUALITY? In the book *Zen and the Art of Motorcycle Maintenance*, a cult hero of college students in an earlier generation literally went crazy trying to figure out the meaning of quality.[93] Marketers appear to use the word quality as a catch-all term for "good." Because of its wide and imprecise usage, the attribute of "quality" threatens to become a meaningless claim. If everyone has it, what good is it?

THE IMPORTANCE OF EXPECTATIONS Satisfaction or dissatisfaction is more than a reaction to the actual performance quality of a product or service. It is influenced by prior expectations regarding the level of quality. According to the **expectancy disconfirmation model**, consumers form beliefs about product performance based upon prior experience with the product and/or communications about the product that imply a certain level of quality.[94] When something performs the way we thought it would, we may not think much about it. If, on the other hand, it fails to live to expectations, negative affect may result. And, if performance happens to exceed our expectations, we are satisfied and pleased.

To understand this perspective, think about different types of restaurants. People expect to be provided with sparkling clear glassware at fancy restaurants, and they might become upset if they discover a grimy glass. On the other hand, we may not be surprised to find fingerprints on our beer mug at a local greasy spoon; we may even shrug it off because it contributes to the place's "charm." An important lesson emerges for marketers from this perspective: Don't overpromise.[95]

Quality and Product Failures. The power of quality claims is most evident when they are not fulfilled, as when a company's product fails in some way. Here, consumers' expectations are dashed, and dissatisfaction results. In these situations, marketers immediately take steps to reassure customers. When the company confronts the problem truthfully, consumers often are willing to forgive and forget, as was the case for Tylenol (product tampering), Chrysler (disconnecting odometers on executives' cars and reselling them as new), or Perrier (traces of benzene found in the water). When the company appears to be dragging its heels or covering up, on the other hand, consumer resentment will grow, as occurred during Union Carbide's chemical disaster in India and with Exxon following the massive Alaskan oil spill caused by its tanker, the *Exxon Valdez*.

ACTING ON DISSATISFACTION If a person is not happy with a product or service, what can be done? Essentially, a consumer has three different courses of action that can be taken (more than one can be taken).[96]

1. *Voice response:* The consumer can appeal directly to the retailer for redress (e.g., a refund).
2. *Private response:* Express dissatisfaction about the store or product to friends and/or boycott the store. As will be discussed in Chapter 11, negative word of mouth (WOM) can be very damaging to a store's reputation.
3. *Third-party response:* The consumer can take legal action against the merchant, register a complaint with the Better Business Bureau, or perhaps write a letter to the newspaper.

A number of factors influence which route is eventually taken. The consumer may in general be an assertive or a meek person. Action is more likely to be taken for expensive products such as household durables, cars, and clothing than for inexpensive products.[97] Also, if the consumer does not believe that the store will respond well to a complaint, the person will be more likely to simply switch brands than fight.[98] Ironically, marketers should actually *encourage* consumers to complain to them: People are more likely to spread the word about unresolved negative experiences to their friends than they are to boast about positive occurrences.

Product Disposal

Because people often do form strong attachments to products, the decision to dispose of something may be a painful one. One function performed by possessions is to serve as anchors for our identities: Our past lives on in our things.[99] This attachment is exemplified by the Japanese, who ritually "retire" worn-out sewing needles, chopsticks, and even computer chips by burning them as thanks for good service.[100]

Although some people have more trouble than others in discarding things, even a "pack rat" does not keep everything. Consumers must often dispose of things, either because they have fulfilled their designated functions, or possibly because they no longer fit with consumers' view of themselves. Concern about the environment coupled with a need for convenience has made ease of product disposal a key attribute in categories from razors to diapers.

Disposal Options

When a consumer decides that a product is no longer of use, several choices are available. The person can either (1) keep the item, (2) temporarily dispose of it, or (3) permanently dispose of it. In many cases, a new product is acquired even though the old one still functions. Some reasons for this replacement include a desire for new features, a change in the person's environment (e.g., a refrigerator is the wrong color for a freshly painted kitchen), or a change in the person's role or self-image.[101] Figure 10–5 provides an overview of consumers' disposal options.

RECYCLING The issue of product disposition is doubly vital because of its enormous public policy implications. We live in a throw-away society, which creates problems for the environment and also results in a great deal of unfortunate waste. For instance, it has been estimated that U.S. consumers discard $4.5 billion worth of food every year.[102] Training consumers to recycle has become a priority in many countries. The United States alone puts about three-quarters of the 100 million tons of solid waste it generates into landfills, more than half of which will be full by the mid-1990s.[103] This problem is not unique to the United States. Tokyo is expected to run out of landfill space by 1995, and the Japanese stress the social value of recycling. Most citizens comply and are encouraged by garbage trucks that periodically rumble through the streets playing classical music or children's songs.[104]

Research Report: In one survey, 57 percent of respondents said they regularly avoided buying certain products for environmental reasons, and 80 percent are willing to pay a little more for an environmentally friendly product. See Carl Frankel, "Blueprint for Green Marketing," *American Demographics* (April 1992)4: 34.

Teaching Hint: One recent telephone survey found that women were more likely to participate in recycling activities than were male respondents. This finding can be used to stimulate discussion about decision-making dynamics in families regarding recycling. See David Bejou and Debbie M. Thorne, "Exploring the Differences Between Recyclers and Non-Recyclers: The Roles of Demographics and Personal Factors," in *Marketing: Toward the Twenty-First Century*, ed. Robert L. King (Richmond, Va.: The Southern Marketing Association, 1991), 110–15; see also Jacob Hornik, Michelle Madansky, Joseph Cherian, and Chem Narayna, "Consumer's Recycling Behavior: A Meta-Analysis," in *Marketing Technical Report and Reprint Series* (Chicago, Ill.: The University of Chicago, 1992).

Teaching Hint: The "inability to discard worn-out or worthless objects even when they have no sentimental value" is described by psychiatrists as a symptom of an obsessive-compulsive personality disorder. See Lynda W. Warren, Sennae C. Ostrom, and Anne H. Rosenfeld, "Pack Rats: World-Class Savers," *Psychology Today* (February 1988): 58.

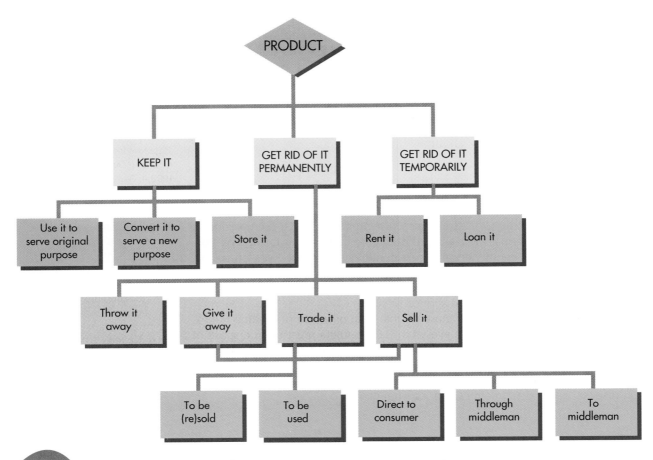

FIGURE 10–5 Consumers' Disposal Options Source: Jacob Jacoby, Carol K. Bern-
ing, and Thomas F. Dietvorst, "What About Disposition?" *Journal of Marketing* 41 (April
1977): 23. By permission of American Marketing Association.

Lateral Cycling: Junk Versus "Junque"

Interesting consumer processes occur during **lateral cycling**, where already-
purchased objects are sold to others or exchanged for still other things. Many
purchases are made second-hand, rather than new. The reuse of other people's things is especially important in our throw-away society because, as one
researcher put it, ". . . there is no longer an 'away' to throw things to."[105]

Flea markets, garage sales, classified advertisements, bartering for services, hand-me-downs, and the black market all represent important alternative marketing systems that operate in addition to the formal
marketplace. For example, the number of used-merchandise retail establishments has grown at about ten times the rate of other stores.[106] While traditional marketers have not paid much attention to used-product sellers,
factors such as concern about the environment, demands for quality, and
cost and fashion consciousness are conspiring to make these "secondary"

Teaching Hint: Most treatments of marketing ignore
the underground economy.
Students are likely to have
had some contact with these
operations, whether the gray
market for computers or the
black market to obtain drugs,
etc. One avenue of product
disposal is the channel for
stolen goods. For a recent
account of the dynamics of the
criminal "fence," see Ronald Paul
Hill, "Criminal Receiving: The
'Fence' as Marketer," *Journal of
Public Policy & Marketing* (1992).

markets more important.[107] Interest in antiques, period accessories, and specialty magazines catering to this niche is increasing. Other growth areas include student markets for used computers and textbooks, as well as ski swaps, where millions of dollars of used ski equipment is exchanged.

Chapter Summary

- The *act of purchase* can be affected by many factors. These include the consumer's antecedent state (e.g., his/her mood, time pressure, or disposition toward shopping). Time is an important resource that often determines how much effort and search will go into a decision. Mood can be affected by the degree of pleasure and arousal present in a store environment.

- The *usage context* of a product can be a basis for segmentation; consumers look for different product attributes depending upon the use to which they intend to put their purchase. The presence or absence of other people—and the types of people they are—can also affect a consumer's decisions.

- The *shopping experience* is a pivotal part of the purchase decision. In many cases, retailing is like theater—the consumer's evaluation of stores and products may depend upon the type of "performance" he or she witnesses. This evaluation can be influenced by the actors (e.g., salespeople), the setting (the store environment), and props (e.g., store displays). A *store image*, like a brand personality, is determined by a number of factors, such as perceived convenience, sophistication, knowledgeability of salespeople, and so on. With increasing competition from non-store alternatives, the creation of a positive shopping experience has never been more important.

- Since many purchase decisions are not made until the time the consumer is actually in the store, *point-of-purchase* (POP) stimuli are very important sales tools. These include product samples, elaborate package displays, place-based media, and in-store promotional materials such as "shelf talkers." POP stimuli are particularly useful in stimulating impulse buying, where a consumer yields to a sudden urge for a product.

- The consumer's encounter with a salesperson is a complex and important process. The outcome can be affected by such factors as the salesperson's similarity to the customer and his or her perceived credibility.

- The perspective called *relationship marketing* stresses the desirability of building a long-term relationship with the consumer. Like a romantic relationship, it develops in stages of increasing familiarity and identification.

- *Consumer satisfaction* is determined by the person's overall feeling toward the product after purchase. Many factors influence perceptions of product quality, including price, brand name, and product performance. Satisfaction is often determined by the degree to which a product's performance is consistent with the consumer's prior expectations of how well it will function.

- *Product disposal* is an increasingly important problem. Recycling is one option that will continue to be stressed as consumers' environmental awareness grows. Products may also be introduced by consumers into secondary markets during a process of *lateral cycling*, which occurs when objects are bought and sold second-hand, fenced, or bartered.

Key Terms

atmospherics, p. 340

consumer satisfaction or dissatisfaction (CS/D), p. 346

exchange theory, p. 345

expectancy disconfirmation model, p. 348

impulse buying, p. 341

lateral cycling, p. 350

point-of-purchase stimuli (POP), p. 342

relationship marketing, p. 346

shopping orientation, p. 336

store image, p. 340

The Consumer Behavior Challenge

1. Discuss some of the motivations for shopping as described in the chapter. How might a retailer adjust his or her strategy to accommodate these motivations?
2. A number of court cases in recent years have attempted to prohibit special interest groups from distributing literature in shopping malls. Mall management claims that these centers are private property. On the other hand, these groups argue that the mall is the modern-day version of the town square and as such is a public forum. Find some recent court cases involving this free-speech issue, and examine the arguments pro and con. What is the current status of the mall as a public forum? Do you agree with this concept?
3. What are some positive and negative aspects of requiring employees who interact with customers to wear some kind of uniform or to mandate a dress code in the office?
4. Think about exceptionally good and bad salespeople you have encountered in the past. What qualities seem to differentiate them?
5. List the five stages of a long-term service relationship. How can a practitioner of relationship marketing incorporate each stage into his or her strategy?
6. Discuss the concept of "timestyle." Based on your own experiences, how might consumers be segmented in terms of their timestyles?
7. Compare and contrast different cultures' conceptions of time. What are some implications for marketing strategy within each of these frameworks?
8. The movement away from a "disposable consumer society" toward one that emphasizes creative recycling creates many opportunities for marketers. Can you identify some?
9. Conduct naturalistic observation at a local mall. Sit in a central location and observe the activities of mall employees and patrons. Keep a log of the nonretailing activity you observe (e.g., special performances, exhibits, socializing, etc.). Does this activity enhance or detract from business conducted at the mall?

10. Select three competing clothing stores in your area and conduct a store image study for them. Ask a group of consumers to rate each store on a set of attributes and plot these ratings on the same graph. Based on your findings, are there any areas of competitive advantage or disadvantage you could bring to the attention of store management? (Note: This technique was described in Chapter 5.)

11. Using Table 10–1 as a model, construct a person/situation segmentation matrix for a brand of perfume.

12. What applications of queuing theory can you find employed among local services? Interview consumers who are waiting on lines to determine how (if at all) this experience affects their satisfaction with the service.

13. The store environment is heating up as more and more companies put their promotional dollars into point-of-purchase efforts. Shoppers are now confronted by videos at the checkout counter, computer monitors attached to their shopping carts, and so on. Place-based media even expose us to ads in nonshopping environments. Recently, a health club in New York was forced to remove TV monitors that showed advertising on the Health Club Media Networks, claiming that they interfered with workouts. Do you feel that these innovations are overly intrusive? At what point might shoppers "rebel" and demand some peace and quiet while shopping? Do you see any market potential in the future for stores that "countermarket" by promising a "hands-off" shopping environment?

CNN Connection

CNN A video segment is available to accompany this CNN Connection.

The "New" Car Salesperson

Many consumers dread the very thought of entering an automobile showroom. One reason is the unsavory reputation of car salespeople, who are known (accurately or not) for being aggressive and fast-talking. In today's fiercely competitive marketplace, auto dealers can no longer afford to foster that kind of reputation.

As noted at the beginning of the chapter, many are changing with the times, and some have even eliminated bargaining by introducing "no-dicker" sticker prices. Others are dismantling the car salesman stereotype by employing female salespeople. This new breed appears to be effective for at least two reasons: Women may be less threatening and thus make better listeners than men,[1] and greater numbers of women are either buying cars for their own use or are more involved in the decision making process with their husbands, so they may respond better when another woman is sitting across the table.

Car dealers are also taking other steps to increase the attractiveness of the sales environment. Showroom interiors are being redesigned to resemble posh retail environments, and some dealers are providing such amenities as play areas for children, comfortable waiting lounges with office facilities, and even diaper-changing areas.

[1] Lee Boyan, "Who's More Productive?" *American Salesman* (November 16, 1989).

Notes

1. Michelle Krebs, "Moving Out the Cars with a 'No-Dicker Sticker,'" *New York Times* (October 11, 1992): F12; "No-dicker Car Dealers Gaining Popularity," *Marketing News* (September 28, 1992): 19.

2. Quoted in Lawrence M. Fisher, "A Store Just for 'Guests,'" *New York Times* (September 20, 1992): F7.

3. Pradeep Kakkar and Richard J. Lutz, "Situational Influence on Consumer Behavior: A Review," in *Perspectives in Consumer Behavior*, 3rd ed., eds. Harold H. Kassarjian and Thomas S. Robertson (Glenview, Ill.: Scott, Foresman and Company, 1981), 204–14.

4. Carolyn Turner Schenk and Rebecca H. Holman, "A Sociological Approach to Brand Choice: The Concept of Situational Self-Image," in *Advances in Consumer Research* 7, ed. Jerry C. Olson (Ann Arbor, Mich.: Association for Consumer Research, 1980), 610–14.

5. Russell W. Belk, "An Exploratory Assessment of Situational Effects in Buyer Behavior," *Journal of Marketing Research* 11 (May 1974): 156–63; U.N. Umesh and Joseph A. Cote, "Influence of Situational Variables on Brand-Choice Models," *Journal of Business Research* 16 (1988)2: 91–99; see also J. Wesley Hutchinson and Joseph W. Alba, "Ignoring Irrelevant Information: Situational Determinants of Consumer Learning," *Journal of Consumer Research* 18 (December 1991): 325–45.

6. Peter R. Dickson, "Person-Situation: Segmentation's Missing Link," *Journal of Marketing* 46 (Fall 1982): 56–64.

7. Daniel Stokols, "On the Distinction Between Density and Crowding: Some Implications for Future Research," *Psychological Review* 79 (1972): 275–77.

8. Keith Bradsher, "There's More to Coin Laundries Than Just Getting the Wash Done," *New York Times* (January 7, 1990): 38.

9. Carol Felker Kaufman, Paul M. Lane, and Jay D. Linquist, "Exploring More Than 24 Hours a Day: A Preliminary Investigation of Polychronic Time Use," *Journal of Consumer Research* 18 (December 1991): 392–401.

10. Laurence P. Feldman and Jacob Hornik, "The Use of Time: An Integrated Conceptual Model," *Journal of Consumer Research* 7 (March 1981): 407–19; see also Michelle M. Bergadaa, "The Role of Time in the Action of the Consumer," *Journal of Consumer Research* 17 (December 1990): 289–302.

11. Robert J. Samuelson, "Rediscovering the Rat Race," *Newsweek* (May 15, 1989): 57.

12. John P. Robinson, "Time Squeeze," *Advertising Age* (February 1990): 30–33.

13. Quoted in Judann Dagnoli, "Time—The Currency of the 90's," *Advertising Age* (November 13, 1989): S-2.

14. Leonard L. Berry, "Market to the Perception," *American Demographics* (February 1990): 32.

15. Quoted in Isabel Wilkerson, "New Funeral Options for Those in a Rush," *New York Times* (February 25, 1989): A16.

16. Lane, Kaufman, and Lindquist, "Exploring More Than 24 Hours a Day."

17. Quoted in Kleiman, "Fast Food?": C12.

18. Robert J. Graham, "The Role of Perception of Time in Consumer Research," *Journal of Consumer Research* 7 (March 1981): 335–42.

19. Esther S. Page-Wood, Carol J. Kaufman, and Paul M. Lane, "The Art of Time," in *Proceedings of the Academy of Marketing Science* (1990).

20. David H. Maister, "The Psychology of Waiting Lines," in *The Service Encounter: Managing Employee/Customer Interaction in Service Businesses*, eds. John A. Czepiel, Michael R. Solomon, and Carol F. Surprenant (Lexington, Mass.: Lexington Books, 1985), 113–24.

21. Eric N. Berg, "Fight on Quick Pizza Delivery Grows," *New York Times* (August 29, 1989): D6.

22. Kenneth E. Miller and James L. Ginter, "An Investigation of Situational Variation in Brand Choice Behavior and Attitude," *Journal of Marketing Research* 16 (February 1979): 111–23.

23. Jacob Hornik, "Diurnal Variation in Consumer Response," *Journal of Consumer Research* 14 (March 1988): 588–91.

24. Laurette Dube and Bernd H. Schmitt, "The Processing of Emotional and Cognitive Aspects of Product Usage in Satisfaction Judgments," in *Advances in Consumer Research* 18, eds. Rebecca H. Holman and Michael R. Solomon (Provo, Utah: Association for Consumer Research, 1991), 52–56; Lalita A. Manrai and Meryl P. Gardner, "The Influence of Affect on Attributions for Product Failure," in *Advances in Consumer Research* 18, eds. Rebecca H. Holman and Michael R. Solomon (Provo, Utah: Association for Consumer Research, 1991), 249–54.

25. Peter J. Burke and Stephen L. Franzoi, "Studying Situations and Identities Using Experimental Sampling Methodology," *American Sociological Review* 53 (August 1988): 559–68.

26. Douglas M. Stayman and Rohit Deshpande, "Situational Ethnicity and Consumer Behavior," *Journal of Consumer Research* 16 (December 1989): 361–71.

27. Kevin G. Celuch and Linda S. Showers, "It's Time To Stress *Stress* : The Stress-Purchase/Consumption Relationship," in *Advances in Consumer Research* 18, eds. Rebecca H. Holman and Michael R. Solomon (Provo, Utah: Association for Consumer Research, 1991), 284–89; Lawrence R. Lep-

IV. The Consumer as a Group Member

V. The Consumer and Culture

SECTION

IV

The Consumer

as a Group

Member

This section explores the types of groups that define our social identities. Chapter 11 provides an overview of group processes and discusses the reasons we are motivated to conform to the expectations of our fellow group members. It also considers how some individuals in particular (called "opinion leaders") are likely to influence the consumption behavior of others in a group. Chapter 12 focuses on factors that dictate a person's social class and how membership in a social class exerts a strong pull on what we buy with the money we make. This chapter also considers more broadly how the economic conditions of a society at any point in time will affect the purchase decisions of group members.

Money and education alone do not explain what we buy or do; we must also know more about consumer lifestyles to understand the consumption patterns that reflect what people do with their disposable time and income. This important segmentation variable is covered in Chapter 13. Finally, Chapters 14 and 15 discuss the ways that our unique religious and ethnic backgrounds help to stamp our social identities and also how similarities such as common ages or places of residence unite us. While each chapter in this section "slices up" consumers in a different way, all of them taken together underscore the complex ways we forge common identities with those around us.

CHAPTER 11

Group Influence
and Opinion
Leadership

Buying, Having, and Being: Selections 38–41 from *Buying, Having, and Being: The Washington Post Consumer Behavior Companion*, Second Edition, accompany this chapter.

Z achary leads a secret life. During the week, he is a button-down stock analyst for a major investment firm. The weekend is another story. Come Friday evening, it's off with the Brooks Brothers suit and on with the black leather, as he trades in his BMW for his treasured Harley-Davidson motorcycle. A dedicated member of HOG (Harley Owners Group), Zachary belongs to the faction of Harley riders known as "RUBs" (rich urban bikers). Everyone in his group wears expensive leather vests with Harley insignias and owns customized "Low Riders." Just this week, Zack finally got his new Harley belt buckle that his fellow riders had pointed out to him in *Hog Tails* magazine—now he won't have to take any more ribbing from them about his old "wimpy" belt.

Zack has spent a lot of money on his bike and on outfitting himself to be like the rest of the group. But it's worth it. Zachary feels a real sense of brotherhood with his fellow RUBs. The group rides together in two-column formation to bike rallies that sometimes attract up to 300,000 cycle enthusiasts. What a sense of power he feels when they're all cruising together—it's them against the world!

Of course, an added benefit is the business networking he's been able to accomplish during his weekend jaunts with his fellow professionals who also wait for the weekend to "ride on the wild side."[1] Sometimes sharing a secret can pay off in more ways than one . . . .

Reference Groups

Humans are social animals. We all belong to groups, try to please others, and take cues about how to behave by observing the actions of those around us. In fact, our desire to "fit in" or to identify with desirable individuals or groups is the primary motivation for many of our purchases and activities. We will often go to great lengths to please the members of a group whose acceptance we covet.[2]

Zachary's biker group is an important part of his identity, and this membership influences many of his buying decisions. He has spent many thousands of dollars on parts and accessories since acquiring his identity as a RUB. As the Harley-Davidson ad shown here makes clear, fellow riders are united by their consumption choices so that total strangers feel an immediate bond with each other when they meet.

Zachary doesn't model himself after just *any* biker—only the people with whom he really identifies can exert that kind of influence on him. For example, Zachary's group doesn't have much to do with outlaw clubs, which are primarily composed of blue-collar riders sporting Harley tattoos. The members of his group also have only polite contact with "Ma and Pa" bikers, whose bikes are the epitome of comfort, featuring such niceties as

When was the last time you met a stranger and knew he was a brother?

A chance meeting on the highway turns into an immediate connection.

The glimmer of recognition between two people who are not just passing strangers. Two Harley® riders.

If you're one of these riders, you know: The two of you have been through quite a few of the same things. Like going out for a quick morning ride and not coming back until dark. Following a squiggly line on a map just for the pure fun of it. Forgetting to stop and eat. Common experiences that become a shared obsession.

It's this kind of obsession that inspired the Harley-Davidson® FXR series—The Super Glide,® the Low Riders® and the Sport Glide.®

its look and sound as much as for its ground-gobbling torque, the Big Twin will move you in ways you'd never imagined.

When you ride a Harley for the first time, something clicks. You won't look at another Harley rider as a stranger again. Because chances are, that is where your first on-the-road thumbs up is coming from.

You'll understand. It means "way to go." It means you've got more in common than bug-splattered leathers.

It means welcome to the family.

Six different Harleys that share a common mission. Putting a rider at one with the road. They have a go-anywhere versatility that takes them from short cruise to long haul without ever missing a beat. A lot of that versatility comes from a sport chassis and a 39mm fork that allows both stability and sure handling. Which means that any FXR is as much at home on the interstate as it is on a winding back road. At the heart of it all is the 80 cubic inch Evolution® engine, isolation-mounted for a smooth and comfortable ride. Famous for

Through and Through.

We care about you. Sign up for a MSF rider course today. Ride with your headlight on and watch out for the other person. Always wear a helmet, proper eyewear and protective clothing. Protect your privilege to ride by joining the AMA.   © 1990 Harley-Davidson Inc.

This Harley-Davidson ad underscores the concept of referent power that emanates from common experiences by emphasizing that Harley riders share a bond of "brotherhood." Courtesy of Harley-Davidson Motor Company.

radios, heated handgrips, and floorboards. Essentially, only the RUBs comprise Zachary's *reference group.*

A **reference group** is ". . . an actual or imaginary individual or group conceived of having significant relevance upon an individual's evaluations, aspirations, or behavior."[3] Reference groups influence consumers in three ways. These influences, *informational*, *utilitarian*, and *value-expressive*, are described in Table 11–1 and discussed in this chapter. The chapter focuses on how other people, whether fellow bikers, co-workers, friends, and family, or just casual acquaintances influence our purchase decisions. It considers how our preferences are shaped by our group memberships, by our desire to please or be accepted by others, or even by the actions of famous people whom we've never even met. Finally, it explores why some people are more influential than others in affecting consumer's product preferences, and how marketers go about finding those people and enlisting their support in the persuasion process.

TABLE 11–1 Three Forms of Reference Group Influence

1. Informational Influence	• The individual seeks information about various brands of the product from an association of professionals or independent group of experts. • The individual seeks information from those who work with the product as a profession. • The individual seeks brand-related knowledge and experience (such as how Brand A's performance compares to Brand B's) from those friends, neighbors, relatives, or work associates who have reliable information about the brands. • The brand the individual selects is influenced by observing a seal of approval of an independent testing agency (such as *Good Housekeeping*). • The individual's observation of what experts do influences his or her choice of a brand (such as observing the type of car that police drive or the brand of television that repairmen buy).
2. Utilitarian Influence	• To satisfy the expectations of fellow work associates, the individual's decision to purchase a particular brand is influenced by their preferences. • The individual's decision to purchase a particular brand is influenced by the preferences of people with whom he or she has social interaction. • The individual's decision to purchase a particular brand is influenced by the preferences of family members. • The desire to satisfy the expectations that others have of him or her has an impact on the individual's brand choice.
3. Value-Expressive Influence	• The individual feels that the purchase or use of a particular brand will enhance the image others have of him or her. • The individual feels that those who purchase or use a particular brand possess the characteristics that he or she would like to have. • The individual sometimes feels that it would be nice to be like the type of person that advertisements show using a particular brand. • The individual feels that the people who purchase a particular brand are admired or respected by others. • The individual feels that the purchase of a particular brand would help show others what he or she is or would like to be (such as an athlete, successful business person, good parent, etc.).

Source: Adapted from C. Whan Park and V. Parker Lessig, "Students and Housewives: Differences in Susceptibility to Reference Group Influence," *Journal of Consumer Research* 4 (September 1977): 102. Reprinted with permission by The University of Chicago Press.

Types of Reference Groups

Although two or more people are normally required to form a group, the term *reference group* often is used a bit more loosely to describe *any* external influence that provides social cues.[4] The referent may be a cultural figure and have an impact on many people (e.g., Malcolm X) or a person or group whose influence is confined to the consumer's immediate environment (e.g., Zachary's biker club). Reference groups that affect consumption can include parents, fellow motorcycle enthusiasts, the Democratic party, or even the Chicago Bears and bands like the Red Hot Chili Peppers.

Dewar's has successfully used noncelebrities as endorsers in its "Profiles" campaign, which is now being adapted to other countries, as this Spanish ad illustrates. Courtesy of Schenley Industries Inc.

Obviously, some groups and individuals exert a greater influence than others and for a broader range of consumption decisions. For example, our parents may play a pivotal role in forming our values toward many important issues, such as attitudes about marriage or where to go to college. This type of influence is **normative influence**—that is, the reference group helps to set and enforce fundamental standards of conduct. In contrast, a Harley-Davidson club might exert **comparative influence**, where decisions about specific brands or activities are affected.[5]

FORMAL VERSUS INFORMAL GROUPS A reference group can take the form of a large, formal organization that has a recognized structure, complete with a charter, regular meeting times, and officers. Or it can be small and informal, such as a group of friends or students living in a dormitory.

Marketers tend to be more successful at influencing formal groups because they are more easily identifiable and accessible.

In general, small, informal groups exert a more powerful influence on individual consumers. These groups tend to be more involved in our day-to-day lives and to be more important to us, because they are high in normative influence. Larger, formal groups tend to be more product- or activity-specific and thus are high in comparative influence.

MEMBERSHIP VERSUS ASPIRATIONAL REFERENCE GROUPS While some reference groups consist of people the consumer actually knows, others are composed either of people the consumer can *identify* with or admire. Not surprisingly, many marketing efforts that specifically adopt a reference group appeal concentrate on highly visible, widely admired figures (such as well-known athletes or performers).

Identificational Reference Groups. Since people tend to compare themselves to others who are similar, they often are swayed by knowing how people like them conduct their lives. For this reason, many promotional strategies include "ordinary" people whose consumption activities provide informational social influence. For example, MasterCard shifted the focus of its advertising away from glamorous, affluent lifestyles of professionals to relatively ordinary activities like those of a young man furnishing his first apartment (and, of course, using his MasterCard to pay for it). The campaign's slogan: "For the Way We Really Live."[7]

The likelihood that people will become part of a consumer's identificational reference group is affected by several factors, including the following.

- *Propinquity:* As physical distance between people decreases and opportunities for interaction increase, relationships are more likely to form. Physical nearness is called *propinquity*. An early study on friendship patterns in a housing complex showed this factor's strong effects: Residents were much more likely to be friends with the people next door than with those who lived only two doors away. And, people who lived next to a staircase had more friends than those at the ends of a hall (presumably, they were more likely to "bump into" people using the stairs).[8] Physical structure has a lot to do with who we get to know and how popular we are.

- *Mere exposure:* We come to like persons or things simply as a result of seeing them more often, which is known as the *mere exposure phenomenon*.[9] Greater frequency of contact, even if unintentional, may help to determine one's set of local referents. The same effect holds when evaluating works of art, or even political candidates.[10] One study predicted 83 percent of the winners of political primaries solely by the amount of media exposure given to candidates.[11]

- *Group cohesiveness: Cohesiveness* refers to the degree that members of a group are attracted to each other and value their group membership. As the value of the group to the individual increases, so too does the likelihood that the group will guide consumption decisions. Smaller groups tend to be more cohesive, because it is more difficult to relate to larger groups of people. By the same token, groups often try to restrict mem-

Research Report: Human consumers are not alone: Even cockroaches and rats have been found to prefer familiar stimuli over novel ones! See H.A. Cross, C.G. Halcomb, and W. Matter, "Imprinting or Exposure Learning in Rats Given Early Auditory Stimulation," Psychonomic Science 10 (1967): 223–34; R.B. Zajonc, H.M. Markus, and W. Wilson, "Exposure Effects and Associative Learning," Journal of Experimental Social Psychology 10 (1974): 248–63

bership to a select few, which increases the value of membership to those who are admitted. Exclusivity of membership is a benefit often touted by credit card companies, book clubs, and so on, even though the actual membership base might be fairly large.

Aspirational Reference Groups. The MasterCard campaign noted previously is taking a bit of a risk, since most credit card advertising is "aspirational." As one executive noted, "In this industry, you market to who you want to be, rather than who you are."[12] *Aspirational reference groups* are composed of idealized figures such as successful business people, athletes, or performers. The Hart, Schaffner & Marx ad shown here, which features real executives rather than models, relies on the aspirational reference group perspective to appeal to business people who aspire to be successful executives.

Demonstrating the aspirational reference group perspective, this Hart, Schaffner & Marx ad uses real executives rather than models wearing the company's clothing to appeal to consumers aspiring to be successful executives. Courtesy of Hart, Schaffner & Marx.

While the consumer may have no direct contact with reference groups, they can have powerful influences on his or her tastes and preferences, because they provide guidance as to the types of products used by admired people.[13] For example, one study that included business students who aspired to the "executive" role found a strong relationship between products they associated with their *ideal selves* (see Chapter 9) and those they assumed would be owned or used by executives.[14]

POSITIVE VERSUS NEGATIVE REFERENCE GROUPS   Reference groups may exert *either* a positive or a negative influence on consumption behaviors. In most cases, consumers model their behavior to be consistent with what they think the group expects of them. In some cases, though, a consumer may try to distance him- or herself from other people or groups that function as *avoidance groups*. He or she may carefully study the dress or mannerisms of a disliked group (e.g., "nerds," "druggies," or "preppies") and scrupulously avoid buying anything that might identify him or her with that group. For example, rebellious adolescents often resent parental influence and may deliberately do the opposite of what their parents would like as a way of making a statement about their independence. As Romeo and Juliet discovered, nothing makes a dating partner more attractive than a little parental opposition.

Figure 11–1 is available as Transparency 27.

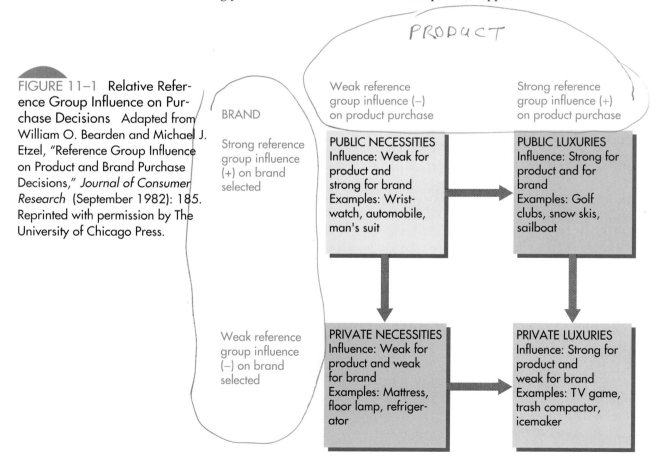

FIGURE 11–1   Relative Reference Group Influence on Purchase Decisions   Adapted from William O. Bearden and Michael J. Etzel, "Reference Group Influence on Product and Brand Purchase Decisions," *Journal of Consumer Research* (September 1982): 185. Reprinted with permission by The University of Chicago Press.

PRODUCT

BRAND

Weak reference group influence (–) on product purchase

Strong reference group influence (+) on product purchase

Strong reference group influence (+) on brand selected

PUBLIC NECESSITIES
Influence: Weak for product and strong for brand
Examples: Wristwatch, automobile, man's suit

PUBLIC LUXURIES
Influence: Strong for product and for brand
Examples: Golf clubs, snow skis, sailboat

Weak reference group influence (–) on brand selected

PRIVATE NECESSITIES
Influence: Weak for product and weak for brand
Examples: Mattress, floor lamp, refrigerator

PRIVATE LUXURIES
Influence: Strong for product and weak for brand
Examples: TV game, trash compactor, icemaker

When Reference Groups Are Important

Reference group influences are not equally powerful for all types of products and consumption activities. For example, products that are not very complex, that are low in perceived risk, and that can be tried prior to purchase are less susceptible to personal influence.[15] In addition, the specific impact of reference groups may vary. At times they may determine the use of certain products rather than others (e.g., owning or not owning a computer, eating junk food versus health food), while at other times they may have specific effects on brand decisions within a product category (e.g., wearing Levi's jeans versus Calvin Klein jeans, or smoking Marlboro cigarettes rather than Virginia Slims).

Two dimensions that influence the degree to which reference groups are important are whether the purchase is to be consumed publicly or privately and whether it is a luxury or a necessity. As a rule, reference group effects are more robust for purchases that are (1) luxuries rather than necessities (e.g., sailboats), since products that are purchased with discretionary income are subject to individual tastes and preferences, while necessities do not offer this range of choices; and (2) socially conspicuous or visible to others (e.g., living room furniture or clothing) since consumers do not tend to be swayed as much by the opinions of others if their purchases will never be observed by anyone but themselves.[16] The relative effects of reference group influences on some specific product classes are shown in Figure 11–1.

The Power of Reference Groups

Social power refers to ". . . the capacity to alter the actions of others."[17] To the degree that you are able to make someone else do something, whether they do it willingly or not, you have power over that person. The following classification of *power bases* can help us to distinguish among the reasons a person can exert power over another, the degree to which the influence is allowed voluntarily, and whether this influence will continue to have an effect in the absence of the power source.[18]

Referent Power. If a person admires the qualities of a person or a group, he or she will try to imitate those qualities by copying the referent's behaviors (e.g., choice of clothing, cars, leisure activities) as a guide to forming consumption preferences, just as Zack's preferences were affected by his fellow bikers. Prominent people in all walks of life can affect people's consumption behaviors by virtue of product endorsements (e.g., Michael Jordan for Air Nike), distinctive fashion statements (e.g., Madonna's use of lingerie as outerwear), or championing causes (e.g., Jerry Lewis' work for muscular dystrophy). Referent power is important to many marketing strategies because consumers voluntarily change behaviors to please or identify with a referent.

Information Power. A person can have power simply because he or she knows something others would like to know. Editors of trade publications such as *Women's Wear Daily* often possess power due to their ability to compile and disseminate information that can make or break individual designers or companies. People with information power are able to influence consumer opinion by virtue of their (assumed) access to the "truth."

International Example: A recent study examined reference group effects in both the United States and Thailand and also distinguishes between family and peer groups. See Terry L. Childers and Akshay R. Rao, "The Influence of Familial and Peer-based Reference Groups on Consumer Decisions," *Journal of Consumer Research* 19 (September 1992): 198–221.

This GM card is one of the many affinity cards, or special credit cards, designed to encourage consumer identification with group membership. Photograph © David E. Dempster.

▲ MARKETING OPPORTUNITY

One of the most recent and widespread applications of reference group influences to consumer behavior is **affinity marketing**. This strategy allows consumers to underscore their identification with some organization by attaching the group's identification to aspects of their personal life.

In the most common form of affinity marketing, banks promote special credit cards known as *affinity cards*, which can be tied to a membership group, such as a church or college alumni organization, or to a symbolic group, like an NFL team or a rock group.[19] Priests and nuns have been targeted to adopt the Caritas card, issued by Catholic charities,[20] and even Elvis has appeared on an affinity card. Use of these cards has surged since 1985, when rules regarding what could be pictured on a credit card were relaxed.

Numerous companies have also jumped on the bandwagon and are now offering these special credit cards, as illustrated by the GM affinity card shown here. Current estimates indicate that over 2700 different affinity cards are available and that they are carried by over 26 million people.[21]

Legitimate Power. Sometimes people are granted power by virtue of social agreements, such as the power given to policemen and professors. The legitimate power conferred by a uniform is recognized in many consumer contexts, including teaching hospitals, where medical students don white coats

EVERY WEEKNIGHT McLAUGHLIN BRINGS THE AUTHORITIES IN FOR QUESTIONING.

When Emmy-award winning host John McLaughlin grills the experts, you can bet the experts talk. On subjects ranging from business to politics to medicine to media. So if you're looking for upscale audience awareness, tap the audience that's already aware.

McLaughlin is just part of a potent prime time line-up on CNBC—The Consumer News and Business Channel—new from NBC. Stay tuned.

Consumer News & Business Channel

For information contact: Marie Skelly, New York (212) 664-7012; Annette Leiderman, Eastern Territories (212) 664-7838; Bill Holt, Detroit (313) 643-9033; Dale Hopkins, West Coast & Chicago (818) 840-4979. © 1989 CNBC Inc. A Service of NBC

This ad for the McLaughlin show emphasizes viewers' appreciation of expert power, which frequently sways consumer decisions. Courtesy of CNBC.

to enhance their aura of authority with patients, and banks, where tellers' uniforms communicate trustworthiness.[22] This form of power may be "borrowed" by marketers to influence consumers. For example, an ad featuring a model wearing a white doctor's coat can add an aura of legitimacy or authority to the presentation of the product.

Expert Power. Expert power is derived from possessing a specific knowledge or skill. Consumers are often influenced by experts who are assumed to be able to evaluate products in an objective, informed way. As the CNBC ad shown here indicates, this power base also underlies the appeal of so-called "talking heads" television shows, where panels of authorities dissect issues of interest to consumers.

The power of celebrity experts can be measured by their visibility on talk shows, lecture circuits, and so on. Prominent economists, for example, can receive between $5000 and $20,000 for a speech, depending on their level of perceived expertise. One analysis of economist superstars noted these requirements for success:[23]

- Affiliation with an elite university, think tank, or investment house
- Author of a slim, easy-reading book that yields a vision of the future
- An advisory relationship with at least one presidential candidate

The need to provide evidence of expert power creates other marketing opportunities, ranging from the provision of certificates and diplomas to coaching for licensing exams. A number of industries where the criteria for expertise are poorly defined are grappling with the need for *credentialing*, or defining what knowledge and experience is necessary to make a person an expert and providing a mechanism to weed out people who do not meet these criteria. Hitting close to home, the American Marketing Association periodically debates the need for licensing of its members as a way to boost the perceived professionalism of marketing research as a discipline.

Reward Power. When a person or group has the means to provide positive reinforcement (see Chapter 4), that entity will have power over a consumer to the extent that this reinforcement is valued or desired. The reward may be tangible, as occurs when an employee is given a raise. Or, the reward may be intangible: Social approval or acceptance is often what is exchanged in return for molding one's behavior to a group or buying the products expected of group members. The Everlast ad shown here humorously acknowledges others' power to reward us for "correct" product choices.

Coercive Power. While coercive power often is effective in the short-term, it does not tend to produce permanent attitudinal or behavioral change. Surveillance of some sort is usually required to make people do something they do not wish to do. Fortunately, coercive power is rarely employed in marketing situations. However, elements of this power base are evident in fear appeals, intimidation in personal selling, and some campaigns that emphasize the negative consequences that might occur if people do not use a product.

Conformity

Conformity refers to a change in beliefs or actions as a reaction to real or imagined group pressure. In order for a society to function, its members develop **norms,** or informal rules that govern behavior. If such a system of agreements did not evolve, chaos would result. Imagine the confusion if a

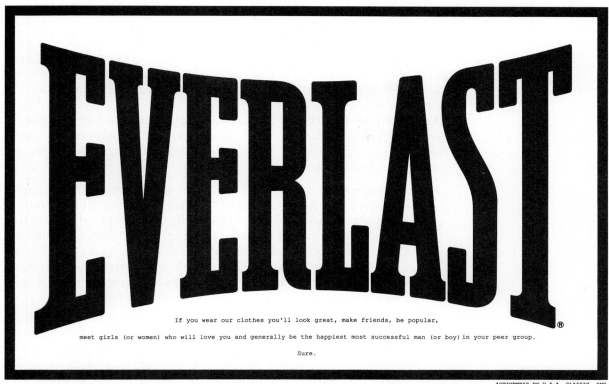

This ad for Everlast pokes fun at the power of peer groups to reward people for wearing the right clothes. Courtesy of Goldsmith/Jeffrey, Inc., N.Y.

simple norm such as stopping for a red traffic light did not exist. While norms change slowly over time, there is general agreement within a society about which ones should be obeyed, and we adjust our way of thinking to conform to these norms.

Unspoken rules govern many aspects of consumption. In addition to norms regarding appropriate use of clothing and other personal items, we conform to rules that include gift giving (we expect birthday presents from loved ones and get upset if they do not materialize), sex roles (men often are expected to pick up the check on a first date), and personal hygiene (we are expected to shower regularly to avoid offending others).

Types of Social Influence

Just as the bases for social power can vary, the process of social influence operates in several ways.[24] Sometimes a person is motivated to model the behavior of others because this mimicry is believed to yield rewards such as social approval or money. At other times, the social influence process occurs simply because the person honestly does not *know* the correct way to respond and is using the behavior of the other person or group as a cue to ensure that

Research Report: The research technique known as ethnomethodology is applied by violating minor social norms to observe the consequences. For example, students might stand in an elevator backward or serve a dessert before a main course to observe people's reactions. See Harold Garfinkel, *Studies in Ethnomethodology* (Englewood Cliffs, N.J.: Prentice-Hall, 1967).

he or she is responding correctly.[25] **Normative social influence** occurs when a person conforms to meet the expectations of a person or group.

In contrast, **informational social influence** refers to conformity that occurs because the group's behavior is taken as evidence about reality: If other people respond in a certain way in an ambiguous situation, we may mimic their behavior because this appears to be the correct thing to do.[26]

REASONS FOR CONFORMITY   Conformity is not an automatic process, and many factors contribute to the likelihood that consumers will pattern their behavior after others.[27] Among the factors that affect the likelihood of conformity are the following.

- *Cultural pressures:* Different cultures encourage conformity to a greater or lesser degree. The American slogan "Do your own thing" in the 1960s reflected a movement away from conformity and toward individualism. In contrast, Japanese society is characterized by the dominance of collective well-being and group loyalty over individuals' needs. As illustrated in the film clips shown here, the French-Canadian commercial, which emphasizes the "power of cooperation," encourages readers to conform by joining the credit union because so many others already have.

- *Fear of deviance:* The individual may have reason to believe that the group will apply *sanctions* to punish behavior that differs from the group's. It is not unusual to observe adolescents shunning a peer who is "different" or a corporation passing over a person for promotion because he or she is not a "team player."

- *Commitment:* The more a person is dedicated to a group and values membership in it, the more motivated he or she will be to follow the dictates of the group. Rock groupies and followers of television evangelists may do anything that is asked of them, and terrorists may be willing to die for the good of their cause. According to the *principle of least interest*, the person or group that is least committed to staying in a relationship has the most power, because that party won't be susceptible to threatened rejection.[28]

- *Group unanimity, size, and expertise:* As groups gain in power, compliance increases. It is often harder to resist the demands of a large num-

These clips from a commercial for Desjardins Credit Union in Quebec illustrate an appeal to people's need to conform when it says, "Two out of three people from Quebec do business with us. They must have a good reason." (The tagline reads, "Desjardins. The incredible power of cooperation.") Courtesy of Mouvement des caisses Desjardins (Quebec).

ber of people than just a few, and this difficulty is compounded when the group members are perceived to know what they are talking about.

- *Sex differences:* It has often been assumed that women are more susceptible than men to interpersonal influence, since they are more sensitive to social cues and tend to be more group-oriented and cooperative in nature. However, recent indications show this reasoning as flawed: Both men and women who possess feminine personality traits tend to conform more (see Chapter 9).[29]

Social Comparison: "How'm I Doing?"

Informational social influence implies that sometimes we look to the behavior of others to provide a yardstick about reality. **Social comparison theory** asserts that this process occurs as a way to increase the stability of one's self-evaluation, especially when physical evidence is unavailable.[30] Social comparison even applies to choices for which there is no objectively correct answer. Such stylistic decisions as tastes in music and art are assumed to be a matter of individual choice, yet people often assume that some types are "better" or more "correct" than others.[31] If you have ever been responsible for choosing the music to play at a party, you can probably appreciate the social pressure involved in choosing the right "mix."

CHOOSING COMPARISON GROUPS Although people often like to compare their judgments and actions to those of others, they tend to be selective about precisely whom they will use as benchmarks. Similarity between the consumer and others used for social comparison boosts confidence that the information is accurate and relevant (though we may find it more threatening to be outperformed by someone similar to ourselves).[32] We tend to value the views of obviously dissimilar others only when we are reasonably certain of our own.[33]

Birds of a Feather. In general people tend to choose a *co-oriented peer*, or a person of equivalent standing, when undergoing social comparison. For example, a study of adult cosmetics users found that women were more likely to seek information about product choices from similar friends to reduce uncertainty and to trust the judgments of similar others.[34] The same effects have been found for evaluations of products as diverse as men's suits and coffee.[35]

Compliance and Obedience

The discussion of persuasive communications in Chapter 6 indicated that source and message characteristics have a big impact on the likelihood of influence. Influencers have been found to be more successful at gaining compliance if they are perceived to be confident or expert.[36] In addition, the way a request is phrased can influence the likelihood of compliance.

TACTICAL REQUESTS The way a request for compliance is phrased or structured can make a difference. One well-known sales tactic, which was also described in Chapter 5, is known as the *foot-in-the-door technique*, where the consumer is first asked a small request and then is hit up for something

Research Report: A recent study examined the effects of peer pressure on drug and alcohol use. See Randall L. Rose, William O. Bearden, and Jesse E. Teel, "An Attributional Analysis of Resistance to Group Pressure Regarding Illicit Drug and Alcohol Consumption," *Journal of Consumer Research* 19 (June 1992): 1–13

bigger.[37] This term is adapted from door-to-door selling. Experienced sales-people know that they are much more likely to make a sale if they first convince a customer to let them in the house to deliver a sales pitch. Once the person has agreed to this small request, it is more difficult to refuse a larger one, since the consumer has legitimized the salesperson's presence by entering into a dialogue. He or she is no longer a threatening stranger at the door.

Other variations on this strategy include the *low-ball technique*, where a person is asked for a small favor and is informed after agreeing to it that it will be very costly, or the *door-in-the-face technique*, where a person is first asked to do something extreme (a request that is usually refused) and then is asked to do something smaller. In each of these cases, people tend to go along with the smaller request, possibly because they feel guilty about denying the larger one.[38]

GROUP EFFECTS ON INDIVIDUAL BEHAVIOR With more people in a group, it becomes less likely any one member will be singled out for attention. People in larger groups or those in situations where they are likely to be unidentified tend to focus less attention on themselves, so normal restraints on behavior are reduced. You may have observed that people sometimes behave more wildly at costume parties or on Halloween night than they do normally. This phenomenon is known as **deindividuation**, where individual identities get submerged within a group.

Shopping Patterns. Shopping behavior changes when people do it in groups. For example, people who shop with at least one other person tend to make more unplanned purchases, buy more, and cover more areas of a store than those who go alone.[39] These effects are due to both normative and informational social influence. Group members may be convinced to buy something to gain the approval of the others, or they may simply be exposed to more products and stores by pooling information with the group. For these reasons, retailers would be well advised to encourage group shopping activities.

Social Loafing. *Social loafing* refers to the fact that people do not devote as much to a task when their contribution is part of a larger group effort.[40] Waitresses are painfully aware of social loafing: People who eat in groups tend to tip less per person than when they are eating alone.[41] For this reason, many restaurants automatically tack on a fixed gratuity for groups of six or more.

The Risky Shift. There is some evidence that decisions made by groups differ from those that would be made by each individual. In many cases, group members show a greater willingness to consider riskier alternatives following group discussion than they would if each member made his or her own decision with no discussion. This change is known as the *risky shift*.[42]

Several explanations have been advanced to explain this increased riskiness. One possibility is that something similar to social loafing occurs. As more people are involved in a decision, each individual is less accountable for the outcome, so *diffusion of responsibility* occurs.[43] Another explanation is termed the *value hypothesis*. In this case, riskiness is a culturally valued characteristic, and social pressures operate on individuals to conform to attributes valued by society.[44]

Evidence for the risky shift is mixed. A more general effect appears to be that group discussion tends to increase **decision polarization**. Whichever direction the group members were leaning before discussion began, toward a risky choice or toward a conservative choice, becomes even more extreme in that direction after discussion. Group discussions regarding product purchases tend to create a risky shift for low-risk items, but they yield even more conservative group decisions for high-risk products.[45]

Resistance to Influence

Many people pride themselves on their independence, unique style, or ability to resist the best efforts of salespeople and advertisers to buy products.[48] Indeed, individuality should be encouraged by the marketing system: Innovation creates change and demand for new products and styles.

ANTICONFORMITY VERSUS INDEPENDENCE It is important to distinguish between *independence* and *anticonformity*, where defiance of the group is the actual object of behavior.[49] Some people will go out of their way *not* to buy whatever happens to be in at the moment. Indeed, they may spend a lot of time and effort to ensure that they will not be caught in style. This behavior is a bit of a paradox, since in order to be vigilant about not doing what is expected, one must always be aware of what is expected. In contrast, truly independent people are oblivious to what is expected; like the "loner" in the Ford audio systems ad shown here, they "march to their own drummers."

The Need for Freedom. People have a deep-seated need to preserve freedom of choice. When they are threatened with a loss of this freedom, they try to overcome this loss. This negative emotional state is termed **reactance**.[50] For example, efforts to censor books, television shows, or rock music because some people find the content objectionable may result in an *increased* desire for these products by the public.[51] Similarly, extremely overbearing promo-

This ad for Ford audio systems targets nonconformists by depicting a "loner" who prefers the wide open spaces to groups of people. Courtesy of Ford Motor Company.

tions that tell consumers they must or should use a product may wind up losing more customers in the long run, even those who were already loyal to the advertised brand! Reactance is more likely to occur when the perceived threat to one's freedom increases and as the threatened behavior's importance to the consumer also increases.

The Need for Uniqueness. If you have ever shown up at a party wearing the same outfit as someone else, you know how upsetting the discovery can be. Some psychologists believe this reaction is a result of a need for uniqueness.[52] Consumers who have been led to believe they are not unique are more likely to try to compensate by increasing their creativity, or even to engage in unusual experiences. In fact, this need could be one explanation for the purchase of relatively obscure brands. People may try to establish a unique identity by deliberately *not* buying market leaders.

Word-of-Mouth Communication

Despite the abundance of formal means of communication (such as newspapers, magazines, and television), much information about the world actually is conveyed by individuals on an informal basis. If you think carefully about the content of your own conversations in the course of a normal day, you will probably agree that much of what you discuss with friends, family members, or co-workers is product-related: Whether you compliment someone on her dress and ask her where she bought it, recommend a new restaurant to a friend, or complain to your neighbor about the shoddy treatment you got at the bank, you are engaging in **word-of-mouth communication** (WOM). Recall, for example, that many of Zachary's biker purchases were directly initiated by comments and suggestions from his fellow RUBs.

Information obtained from those we know or talk with directly tends to be more reliable and trustworthy than that received through more formal channels, and unlike advertising, it is often backed up by social pressure to conform with these recommendations.[53] The importance of personal, informal product communication to marketers is underscored by one advertising executive, who stated "Today, 80 percent of all buying decisions are influenced by someone's direct recommendations."[54]

The Dominance of WOM

Communications theorists began in the 1950s to challenge the assumption that advertising is the primary determinant of purchases: It is now generally accepted that advertising is more effective at reinforcing existing product preferences than at creating new ones.[55] Studies in both industrial and consumer purchase settings underscore the idea that while information from impersonal sources is important for creating brand awareness, word-of-mouth is relied upon in the later stages of evaluation and adoption.[56] The more positive information a consumer gets about a product from peers, the more likely he or she will adopt the product.[57] The influence of others' opinions is at times even more powerful than one's own perceptions. In one study of furniture choices, consumers' estimates of how much their friends

Research Report: Word-of-mouth communication has also been shown to be a stronger determinant of bank patronage than is advertising. See W. Thomas Anderson, Jr., and Linda L. Golden, "Bank Promotion Strategy," *Journal of Advertising Research* 24 (April/May 1984): 53–65.

Additional Example: Over 60 percent of the patrons at Club Med's Western Hemisphere resorts came because of personal recommendations (not counting referrals from travel agents). See Barnaby Feder, "Those With Things to Sell Love Word-of-Mouth Ads," *New York Times* (June 23, 1992): D18.

Additional Example: A company can initiate the discussion, as exemplified in an strategy implemented in 1905 by Sears that the company called "Iowaization." As a plan to distribute its catalogs, Sears wrote to all of its current customers in Iowa asking them to first pass on catalogs to friends and then send the company the names of those who had received them. The company tracked incoming orders and awarded premiums to each original "distributor" based on the number of orders it received. Sales boomed in Iowa, and the company took this "Iowaization" to the rest of America. See Stuart Ewen and Elizabeth Ewen, *Channels of Desire: Mass Images and the Shaping of American Consciousness* (New York: McGraw-Hill, 1982), 66.

Additional Example: Ninety percent of the U.S. adult population knew that President Kennedy had been assassinated within forty-five minutes of the first news account, and half heard the news from another person rather than directly from the mass media. See B.S. Greenberg, "Diffusion of News of the Kennedy Assassination," *Public Opinion Quarterly* 28 (1964): 225–32.

would like the furniture was a better predictor of purchase than their *own* evaluations.[58]

FACTORS INITIATING WOM Most WOM campaigns happen spontaneously, as a product begins to develop a regional following, as was the case with Ben & Jerry's ice cream. Occasionally, a "buzz" is intentionally created. For example, Henry Weinhards' Private Reserve, a super-premium beer in the Pacific Northwest, was first introduced at selected bars where bartenders had been briefed on the brand's unusual brewing process. The beer was introduced to stores only after demand from bar patrons mounted.[59]

Product-related conversations can be motivated by a number of factors.[60]

- A person might be highly involved with a type of product or activity and get pleasure in talking about it. Computer hackers, avid birdwatchers, and "fashion plates" seem to share the ability to steer a conversation toward their particular interest.

- A person might be knowledgeable about a product and use conversations as a way to let others know it. Thus, word-of-mouth communication sometimes enhances the ego of the individual who wants to impress others with his or her expertise.

- A person might initiate such a discussion out of a genuine concern for someone else. We often are motivated to ensure that people we care about buy what is good for them, do not waste their money, and so on.

- One way to reduce uncertainty about the wisdom of a purchase is to talk about it. Talking gives the consumer an opportunity to generate more supporting arguments for the purchase and to garner support for this decision from others.

EFFICIENCY OF WOM Interpersonal transmissions can be quite rapid. The producers of the movie *Batman* showed a trailer to 300 Batman fans months prior to its release to counteract widespread anger about the casting of Michael Keaton as the star. The filmmakers attribute the film's eventual huge success to the positive word-of-mouth that quickly spread following the screening.[61]

WOM is especially powerful in cases where the consumer is relatively unfamiliar with the product category. Such a situation would be expected in cases where the product is new (e.g., medications to prevent hair loss) or is technologically complex (e.g., CD players). As one example, the strongest predictor of a person's intention to buy a residential solar water heating system was found to be the number of solar heating users the person knows.[62]

Negative WOM

Word-of-mouth is a two-edged sword that can cut both ways for marketers. Informal discussions among consumers can make or break a product or store. And, negative word-of-mouth is weighted *more* heavily by consumers than are positive comments. Especially when making a decision about trying a product innovation, the consumer is more likely to pay attention to negative information than positive information and to relate news of this experience to others.[63]

RUMORS: DISTORTION IN THE WORD-OF-MOUTH PROCESS In the 1930s, "professional rumor mongers" were hired to organize word-of-mouth campaigns to promote clients' products and criticize those of competitors.[64] A rumor, even if it has no basis in fact, can be a very dangerous thing. As information is transmitted among consumers, it tends to change. The resulting message usually does not at all resemble the original.

Social scientists who study rumors have examined the process by which information gets distorted. The British psychologist Frederic Bartlett used the method of *serial reproduction* to examine this phenomenon. As in the game of "Telephone," a subject is asked to reproduce a stimulus, such as a drawing or a story. Another subject is given this reproduction and asked to copy that, and so on. This technique is shown in Figure 11–2. Bartlett found that distortions almost inevitably follow a pattern: They tend to change from ambiguous forms to more conventional ones as subjects try to make them consistent with pre-existing schemas. This process, known as *assimilation*, is characterized by *leveling*, where details are omitted to simplify the structure, or *sharpening*, where prominent details are accentuated.

In general, people have been shown to prefer transmitting good news rather than bad, perhaps because they like to avoid unpleasantness or dis-

Figure 11–2 is available as Transparency 28.

Original Drawing

FIGURE 11–2 The Transmission of Misinformation: These drawings provide a classic example of the distortions that can occur as information is transmitted from person to person. As each participant reproduces the figure, it gradually changes from an owl to a cat. Source: Kenneth J. Gergen and Mary Gergen, *Social Psychology* (New York: Harcourt Brace Jovanovich, 1981), 365, fig. 10–3; adapted from F. C. Bartlett, *Remembering* (Cambridge, England: Cambridge University Press, 1932).

like arousing hostility. The result is known as the MUM effect.[65] However, this reluctance does not appear to occur when companies are the topic of conversation. Corporations such as Procter & Gamble and McDonald's have been the subjects of rumors about their products, sometimes with noticeable effects on sales.

Rumors are thought to reveal the underlying fears of a society. For example, one rumor regarding snakes coming out of teddy bears imported from the Orient was interpreted to signify Western consumers' apprehensions about Asian influences. While rumors sometimes die out by themselves, in other instances a company may take direct action to counteract them. A French margarine was rumored to contain contaminants, and the company addressed this in its advertising by referring to the story as "The rumor that costs you dearly."[66]

Several marketers in Indonesia, including Nestlé, recently have been hurt by rumors that their foods contain pork, which is prohibited to the 160 million Muslim consumers in that country. Islamic preachers, or mullahs, responded to these rumors by warning consumers not to buy products that might be tainted with pork fat. Nestlé spent more than $250,000 on an ad campaign to counteract the rumors, and a noodle manufacturer plans to spend up to $500,000 to salvage its brand.[67]

CONSUMER BOYCOTTS Sometimes a negative experience can trigger an organized and devastating response, as when a consumer group organizes a *boycott* of a company's products. About 100 boycott campaigns (including threats to boycott if a company does not change some policy) are currently in effect. These efforts can include protests against everything from the use of products from a politically undesirable country (as when Proctor & Gamble used Salvadoran beans for its Folgers coffee) to the inclusion of obscene or inflammatory song lyrics (as when law enforcement organizations threatened to boycott Time Warner after it distributed a rap song by Ice-T entitled "Cop Killer").

Boycotts are not always effective—studies show that only 18 percent of Americans participate in them. However, those who do are disproportionately upscale and well-educated, so they are a group companies especially don't want to alienate. One increasingly popular solution used by marketers is setting up a joint task force with the boycotting organization to try to iron out the problem. McDonald's recently used this approach with the Environmental Defense Fund, which was concerned about its use of polystyrene containers and bleached paper. The company agreed to test a composting program and to switch to plain brown bags.[68]

Opinion Leadership

Although consumers get information from personal sources, they do not tend to ask just *anyone* for advice about purchases. If you decide to buy a new stereo, you will most likely seek advice from a friend who knows a lot about sound systems. This friend may own a sophisticated system, or he or she may subscribe to specialized magazines like *Stereo Review* and spend free time browsing through electronics stores. On the other hand, you may have another friend who has a reputation for being stylish and who spends

Additional Example:
McDonald's action did not, however, mollify animal-rights groups. They continue to call for a boycott because the chain does not offer a vegetarian sandwich! See Marcus Mabry, Marcus, "Do Boycotts Work?" *Newsweek* (July 6, 1992)3: 56.

his free time reading *Gentlemen's Quarterly* and shopping at trendy boutiques. While you might not bring up your stereo problem with him, you may take him with you to shop for a new fall wardrobe.

The Nature of Opinion Leadership

Everyone knows people who are knowledgeable about products and whose advice is taken seriously by others. These individuals are **opinion leaders**. An opinion leader is a person who is frequently able to influence others' attitudes or behaviors.[69] Opinion leaders are extremely valuable information sources for a number of reasons.

1. They are technically competent and thus are convincing because they possess expert power.[70]
2. They have prescreened, evaluated, and synthesized product information in an unbiased way, so they possess knowledge power.[71] Unlike commercial endorsers, opinion leaders do not actually represent the interests of one company. They are more credible because they have no "axe to grind."
3. They tend to be socially active and highly interconnected in their community.[72] They are likely to hold office in community groups and clubs and to be active outside of the home. As a result, opinion leaders often have legitimate power by virtue of their social standing.
4. They tend to be similar to the consumer in terms of their values and beliefs, so they possess referent power. Note that while opinion leaders are set apart by their interest or expertise in a product category, they are more convincing to the extent that they are *homophilous* rather than *heterophilous*. *Homophily* refers to the degree that a pair of individuals is similar in terms of education, social status, and beliefs.[73] Effective opinion leaders tend to be slightly higher than those they influence in terms of status and educational attainment, but not so high as to be in a different social class.
5. Opinion leaders often are among the first to buy new products, so they absorb much of the risk. This experience reduces uncertainty for others who are not as courageous. And, while company-sponsored communications tend to focus exclusively on the positive aspects of a product, this hands-on experience makes opinion leaders more likely to impart *both* positive and negative information about product performance.

THE EXTENT OF AN OPINION LEADER'S INFLUENCE When marketers and social scientists initially developed the concept of the opinion leader, it was assumed that certain influential people in a community would exert an overall impact on group members' attitudes. Later work, however, began to question the assumption that there is such a thing as a *generalized opinion leader*, somebody whose recommendations are sought for all types of purchases. Very few people are capable of being expert in a number of fields. Sociologists distinguish between those who are *monomorphic*, or experts in a limited field, and those who are *polymorphic*, or experts in several fields.[74] Even the opinion leaders who are polymorphic tend to concentrate on one broad domain, such as electronics or fashion.

Teaching Hint: While opinion leaders often encourage the adoption of new products, at times they can exert a negative influence on novelty and risk taking, especially if they find the product to be deficient or if it violates the community's expectations or standards. Opinion leaders uphold the dominant norms in a community. If these norms favor conservatism, non-innovativeness may be stressed. For example, religious leaders may be influential in discouraging the use of various product categories such as alcohol and contraceptives. See G. Appa Rao and Everett Rogers, "Caste and Formal Education in Interpersonal Diffusion of an Innovation in Two Indian Villages," *Indian Journal of Extension Education* 16 (1980): 1–9.

Research on opinion leadership generally indicates that while opinion leaders do exist for multiple product categories, expertise tends to overlap across similar categories. It is rare to find a generalized opinion leader. An opinion leader for home appliances is likely to serve a similar function for home cleaners, but not for cosmetics. In contrast, a *fashion opinion leader* whose primary influence is on clothing choices may also be consulted for recommendations on cosmetics purchases, but not necessarily on microwave ovens.[75]

OPINION LEADERS VERSUS OTHER CONSUMER TYPES Early conceptions of the opinion leader role also assumed a static process: The opinion leader absorbs information from the mass media and in turn transmits these data to opinion receivers. This view has turned out to be overly simplified; it confuses the functions of several different types of consumers.

Innovative Communicators. Opinion leaders may or may not be purchasers of the products they recommend. Early purchasers are known as *innovators.* Opinion leaders who are *also* early purchasers have been termed *innovative communicators.* One study identified a number of characteristics of college men who were innovative communicators for fashion products. These men were among the first to buy new fashions, and their fashion opinions were incorporated by other students in their own clothing decisions. Other characteristics of the men included the following.[76]

- They were socially active.
- They were appearance-conscious and narcissistic (i.e., they were quite fond of themselves and self-centered).
- They were involved in rock culture.
- They were heavy magazine readers, including *Playboy* and *Sports Illustrated.*
- They were likely to own more clothing, and a broader range of styles, than other students.
- Their intellectual interests were relatively limited.

Opinion Seekers. Opinion leaders also are likely to be *opinion seekers.* They are generally more involved in a product category and actively search for information. As a result, they are more likely to talk about products with others and to solicit others' opinions as well. Contrary to the static view of opinion leadership, most product-related conversation does not take place in a "lecture" format, where one person does all of the talking. A lot of product-related conversation is prompted by the situation and occurs in the context of a casual interaction rather than as formal instruction.[77] One study, which found that opinion seeking is especially high for food products, revealed that two-thirds of opinion seekers also view themselves as opinion leaders.[78] This updated view of interpersonal product communication is contrasted with the traditional view in Figure 11–3.

Market Mavens. Consumers who are expert in a product category may not actively communicate with others, while other consumers may have a more general interest in being involved in product discussions. A consumer category called the **market maven** has been proposed to describe people who

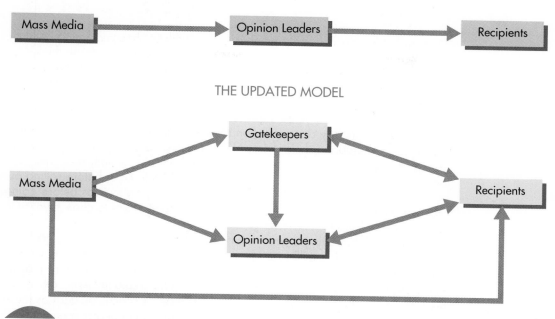

FIGURE 11–3 Perspectives on the Communications Process

Figure 11–3 is available as Transparency 29.

are actively involved in transmitting marketplace information of all types. Market mavens are not necessarily interested in certain products and may not necessarily be early purchasers of products. They come closer to the function of a generalized opinion leader because they tend to have a solid overall knowledge of how and where to procure products. The following scale items, where respondents indicate how much they agree or disagree, have been used to identify market mavens.[79]

1. I like introducing new brands and products to my friends.
2. I like helping people by providing them with information about many kinds of products.
3. People ask me for information about products, places to shop, or sales.
4. If someone asked me where to get the best buy on several types of products, I could tell him or her where to shop.
5. My friends think of me as a good source of information when it comes to new products or sales.
6. Think about a person who has information about a variety of products and likes to share this information with others. This person knows about new products, sales, stores, and so on, but does not necessarily feel he or she is an expert on one particular product. How well would you say this description fits you?*

*Although it is possible to identify market mavens within a study population using this type of scale, to date no clear demographic profile that characterizes this type has been identified.

Opinion leadership is heavily emphasized in athletic shoe marketing. Athletic shoes are very much a fashion statement and a phenomenon largely fueled by inner city kids, despite price tags of $100 and more. Many of the sneaker styles originate in the inner city and then spread outward by word-of-mouth. As one marketer noted, "The urban kid stands for hard-core experience . . . . That, to a youth in the suburbs, represents authenticity."

Manufacturers pay close attention to these inner-city trendsetters and try to woo them to "endorse" their styles. Nike flew over twenty owners of sporting goods stores in urban areas to Chicago to find out how to influence inner-city kids. Converse spent a year talking to groups of kids in cities before rolling out its Bold line, and Avia tests its models on inner-city focus groups before going national. Reebok does its part by repaving basketball courts to curry favor with young opinion leaders.

In addition to paying a few major athletes to endorse shoes (Michael Jordan earns about $1.6 million a year to endorse Nike's Air Jordans), sneaker companies pay many high school and college coaches to outfit team players with their footwear, since this provides exposure and credibility when other kids see their role models wearing a certain type of shoe. A coach can earn as much as $200,000 a year to participate in this kind of promotional arrangement.[80]

Teaching Hint: Although Nike and Reebok dominate the athletic shoe market, the power of influential publications to stir up consumer interest was seen first-hand by Hyde Athletic Industries. After the company's Saucony Jazz 3000 shoes got the *Consumer Reports* top rating for good value, sales soared. Since the magazine's core readership prides itself on being product experts, the subscriber is likely to contain a high proportion of influential opinion leaders. This example can propel the class into a discussion of the power of reviewers to make or break a product or service (e.g., restaurants or movies). Should a few individuals possess such power? See Eben Shapiro, "Getting a Running Shoe in the Door," *New York Times* (August 13, 1992)2: D1.

Surrogate Consumers. In addition to everyday consumers who are influential in influencing others' purchase decisions, a class of marketing intermediary called the **surrogate consumer** is an active player in many categories. A surrogate consumer is a person who is hired to provide input into purchase decisions. Unlike the opinion leader or market maven, the surrogate is usually compensated for this involvement.

Interior decorators, stockbrokers, professional shoppers, or college consultants can all be thought of as surrogate consumers. Whether or not they actually make the purchase on behalf of the consumer, surrogates' recommendations can be enormously influential. The consumer in essence relinquishes control over several or all decision-making functions, such as information search, evaluation of alternatives, or the actual purchase. For example, a client may commission an interior decorator to redo her house, while a broker may be entrusted to make crucial buy/sell decisions on behalf of investors. The involvement of surrogates in a wide range of purchase decisions tends to be overlooked by many marketers, who may be mistargeting their communications to end consumers instead of to the surrogates who are actually sifting through product information.[81]

Identifying Opinion Leaders

Because opinion leaders are so central to consumer decision making, marketers are quite interested in identifying influential people for a product category. In fact, many ads are intended to reach these influentials rather than the average consumer, especially if the ads contain a lot of technical information. The average television purchaser probably would not be excited by an ad for a Pioneer projection television that claims to have a lens with a "maximum bore of 160 mm" and a "new high-voltage stabilizing circuit." On the other hand, an electronics buff might be quite impressed by this information and in turn take it into consideration when recommending a projection television to a more naive friend.

Unfortunately, since most opinion leaders are everyday consumers and are not formally included in marketing efforts, they are harder to find. A celebrity or an influential industry executive is by definition easy to locate. He or she has national or at least regional visibility or may be listed in published directories. In contrast, opinion leaders tend to operate at the local level and may influence five to ten consumers rather than an entire market segment. In some cases, companies have been known to identify influentials and involve them directly in their marketing efforts, hoping to create a "ripple effect" as these consumers sing the company's praises to their friends. Many department stores, for example, have fashion "panels," usually composed of adolescent girls, who provide input into fashion trends, participate in fashion shows, and so on.

Because of the difficulties involved in identifying specific opinion leaders in a large market, most attempts to do so instead focus on exploratory studies where the characteristics of representative opinion leaders can be identified and then generalized to the larger market. This knowledge helps marketers to target their product-related information to appropriate settings and media. For example, one attempt to identify financial opinion leaders found that these consumers were more likely to be involved in managing their own finances and tended to use a computer to do so. They also were more likely to follow their investments on a daily basis and to read books and watch television shows devoted to financial issues.[82]

THE SELF-DESIGNATING METHOD The most commonly used technique to identify opinion leaders is simply to ask individual consumers whether they consider themselves to be opinion leaders.

Problems with Self-Designation. While respondents who report a greater degree of interest in a product category are more likely to be opinion leaders, the results of surveys intended to identify self-designated opinion leaders must be viewed with some skepticism. Some people have a tendency to inflate their own importance and influence, while others who really are influential might not admit to this quality.[83] Just because we transmit advice about products does not mean other people *take* that advice. For someone to be considered a *bona fide* opinion leader, his or her advice must actually be heard and heeded by opinion seekers. An alternative is to select certain group members (*key informants*) who in turn are asked to identify opinion leaders. The success of this approach hinges on locating those who have accurate knowledge of the group and on minimizing their response biases (e.g., the tendency to inflate one's own influence on the choices of others).

While the self-designating method is not as reliable as a more systematic analysis (where individual claims of influence can be verified by asking others

Additional Example: The Roper Organization has been tracking a group it calls "Influentials" since 1945. To qualify as an Influential, a person must have done at least three community activities in one year (e.g., attending a public meeting, holding office in a local organization, etc.). Comprising about 10 percent of the population, Influentials entertain, travel, and spend money on hobbies at a higher rate than the general population. See Rebecca Piirto, "The Influentials," *American Demograpics* (October 1992)6: 30.

Research Report: Professional opinion leaders are doctors or scientists who obtain specialized information from technical journals and other practitioners. One study that examined some choices of materials used by prosthodontists (crown and bridge restoration specialists) traced the colleagues who tended to be contacted for advice and found a small set of peers who were influential in determining choices around the country. See Dorothy Leonard-Barton, "Experts as Negative Opinion Leaders in the Diffusion of a Technological Innovation," *Journal of Consumer Research* 11 (March 1985): 914–26.

whether the person is really influential), it does have the advantage of being easy to administer to a large group of potential opinion leaders. In some cases not all members of a community are surveyed. One of the original measurement scales developed for self-designation of opinion leaders is shown in Figure 11–4.

SOCIOMETRY Sociometric methods, which trace communication patterns among group members, allow researchers to systematically map out the interactions that take place among group members. By interviewing participants and asking them who they go to for product information, those who tend to be sources of product-related information can be identified. While this method is the most precise, it is very hard and expensive to implement, since it involves very close study of interaction patterns in small groups. For this reason, sociometric techniques are best applied in a closed, self-contained social setting, such as in hospitals, prisons, and army bases, where members are largely isolated from other social networks.

Tracing Referrals. Many professionals and services marketers depend primarily upon word-of-mouth to generate business. In many cases consumers recommend a service provider to a friend or coworker, and in other cases other

FIGURE 11–4 Opinion Leadership Scale Source: Charles W. King and John O. Summers, "Overlap of Opinion Leadership Across Consumer Product Categories," *Journal of Marketing Research* 7 (February 1970): 43–50. By permission of American Marketing Association.

Research Report: Several studies have provided updates on the content and validity of the original King and Summers scale. See, for example, Terry L. Childers, "Assessment of the Psychometric Properties of an Opinion Leadership Scale," *Journal of Marketing Research* 23 (May 1986): 184–88; Ronald E. Goldsmith and Rene Desborde, "A Validity Study of a Measure of Opinion Leadership," *Journal of Business Research* 22 (1991): 11–19.

1. In general, do you like to talk about _____ with your friends?
   Yes ___ –1   No ___ –2
2. Would you say *you give very little information, an average amount of information, or a great deal of information* about _____ to your friends?
   You give very little information   ___ –1
   You give an average amount of information   ___ –2
   You give a great deal of information   ___ –3
3. During the *past six months,* have *you told anyone* about _____?
   Yes ___ –1   No ___ –2
4. Compared with your circle of friends, are you *less likely, about as likely,* or *more likely* to be asked for advice about _____?
   Less likely to be asked   ___ –1
   About as likely to be asked   ___ –2
   More likely to be asked   ___ –3
5. If you and your friends were to discuss _____, what part would you be most likely to play? Would you *mainly listen* to your friends' ideas or would *you try to convince them* of your ideas?
   You mainly listen to your friends' ideas   ___ –1
   You try to convince them of your ideas   ___ –2
6. Which of these happens more often? Do *you tell your* friends about _____, or do *they tell* you about _____?
   You tell them about_____ ___ –1
   They tell you about_____ ___ –2
7. Do you have the feeling that you are generally regarded by your friends and neighbors as a good source of advice about _____?
   Yes ___ –1   No ___ –2

CNN Connection

Bad-Mouthing a Product

 A video segment is available to accompany this CNN Connection.

A soda that sterilizes black men? This rumor almost destroyed a soft drink called Tropical Fantasy. As discussed in this chapter, negative word-of-mouth can be a nuisance to a big company like Proctor & Gamble, but it can be a death blow to a small business—especially when the bad rap is unfounded. Sales were growing for the small New York company, especially when it began selling a 20-ounce bottle of the drink for 49 cents. All that changed, however, when the fliers began appearing on city streets. The crude, misspelled messages claimed that the soda was manufactured by the Ku Klux Klan and contained stimulants that caused sterilization in black men. Concerned consumers got the city to test the product, but no trace of any drug was found. No one could pinpoint who was behind the fliers, although some employees believed that workers for rival firms were to blame. Ironically, the company employs mostly minority workers whose jobs would be lost if everyone swallowed the story.

SIMMONS Connection

SIMMONS Connection: Data for this exercise is on the Simmons Data Disk inside the back cover of your Instructor's Annotated Edition.

Data File: Motorcycle Ownership

As the opening vignette suggests, Zachary's "secret life" may not be all that unusual. The biker groups known as RUBs represent a growing biker subculture. And, RUBs are clearly a far cry from the Hell's Angels groups that until recently were associated with Harley-Davidson motorcycles. Sharp distinctions seem to exist between the outlaw clubs, the RUBs, and the "Ma and Pa" bikers.

Your Simmons file for this chapter contains information about the type and size of motorcycle owned by various consumer groups. Assume that the largest markets for motorcycles in the United States are the RUBs and the outlaw bikers. What sorts of motorcycles do these two groups of consumers prefer? Although RUBs and outlaw bikers are probably similar in age (18 to 34 years old), they most likely differ in several other ways. RUBs are probably more highly educated and they may also earn more. Can you identify any differences in the motorcycles preferred by these two groups of riders? How does marital status influence the likelihood of ownership of a "major hog" (a bike whose engine is larger than 1,000 cc)?

Notes

1. Details adapted from John W. Schouten and James H. McAlexander, "Market Impact of a Consumption Subculture: The Harley-Davidson Mystique," in *Proceedings of the 1992 European Conference of the Association for Consumer Research*, eds. Fred van Raaij and Gary Bamossy (Amsterdam, 1992).

2. Joel B. Cohen and Ellen Golden, "Informational Social Influence and Product Evaluation," *Journal of Applied Psychology* 56 (February 1972): 54–59; Robert E. Burnkrant and Alain Cousineau, "Informational and Normative Social Influence in Buyer Behavior," *Journal of Consumer Research* 2 (December 1975): 206–15; Peter H. Reingen, "Test of a List Procedure for Inducing Compliance with a Request to Donate Money," *Journal of Applied Psychology* 67 (1982): 110–18.

3. C. Whan Park and V. Parker Lessig, "Students and Housewives: Differences in Susceptibility to Reference Group Influence," *Journal of Consumer Research* 4 (September 1977): 102–10.

4. Kenneth J. Gergen and Mary Gergen, *Social Psychology* (New York: Harcourt Brace Jovanovich, 1981).

5. Harold H. Kelley, "Two Functions of Reference Groups," in *Basic Studies in Social Psychology*, eds. Harold Proshansky and Bernard Siedenberg (New York: Holt, Rinehart and Winston, 1965), 210–14.

6. David Murrow, "Dewar's Profiles Travel Well," *Advertising Age* (August 14, 1989): 28.

7. Anthony Ramirez, "Mastercard's Shift from Glamour," *New York Times* (April 9, 1990): D1.

8. L. Festinger, S. Schachter, and K. Back, *Social Pressures in Informal Groups: A Study of Human Factors in Housing* (New York: Harper, 1950).

9. R.B. Zajonc, H.M. Markus, and W. Wilson, "Exposure Effects and Associative Learning," *Journal of Experimental Social Psychology* 10 (1974): 248–63.

10. D.J. Stang, "Methodological Factors in Mere Exposure Research," *Psychological Bulletin* 81 (1974): 1014–25; R.B. Zajonc, P. Shaver, C. Tavris, and D. Van Kreveid, "Exposure, Satiation and Stimulus Discriminability," *Journal of Personality and Social Psychology* 21 (1972): 270–80.

11. J.E. Grush, K.L. McKeogh, and R.F. Ahlering, "Extrapolating Laboratory Exposure Research to Actual Political Elections," *Journal of Personality and Social Psychology* 36 (1978): 257–70.

12. Ramirez, "Mastercard's Shift from Glamour."

13. A. Benton Cocanougher and Grady D. Bruce, "Socially Distant Reference Groups and Consumer Aspirations," *Journal of Marketing Research* 8 (August 1971): 79–81; James E. Stafford, "Effects of Group Influences on Consumer Brand Preferences," *Journal of Marketing Research* 3 (February 1966): 68–75.

14. Cocanaugher and Bruce, "Socially Distant Reference Groups and Consumer Aspirations."

15. Jeffrey D. Ford and Elwood A. Ellis, "A Re-examination of Group Influence on Member Brand Preference," *Journal of Marketing Research* 17 (February 1980): 125–32; Thomas S. Robertson, *Innovative Behavior and Communication* (New York: Holt, Rinehart and Winston, Inc., 1980), Chapter 8.

16. William O. Bearden and Michael J. Etzel, "Reference Group Influence on Product and Brand Purchase Decisions," *Journal of Consumer Research* 9 (1982)2: 183–94.

17. Gergen and Gergen, *Social Psychology*, 312.

18. J.R.P. French, Jr., and B. Raven, "The Bases of Social Power," in *Studies in Social Power*, ed. D. Cartwright (Ann Arbor, Mich.: Institute for Social Research, 1959), 150–67.

19. Judith Waldrop, "Plastic Wars," *American Demographics* (November 1988): 6.

20. Elaine Santoro, "Catholic Charities Credit Card Unveiled," *Fund Raising Management* 20 (April 1989): 10.

21. Judith Graham, "Affinity Card Clutter: Number of Tie-Ins Raises Doubts About Continued Use," Special Report: Financial Services Marketing, *Advertising Age* (November 14, 1988): S1; Waldrop, "Plastic Wars."

22. Michael R. Solomon, "Packaging the Service Provider," *The Service Industries Journal* 5 (March 1985): 64–72.

23. Augustin Hedberg, "Lights! Camera! Economists!" (celebrity economists), *Money* (October 1987): 118.

24. See Robert B. Cialdini, *Influence: Science and Practice*, 2nd ed. (New York: Scott, Foresman, 1988), for an excellent and entertaining treatment of this process.

25. For the seminal work on conformity and social influence, see Solomon E. Asch, "Effects of Group Pressure Upon the Modification and Distortion of Judgments," in *Group Dynamics* , eds. D. Cartwright and A. Zander (New York: Harper and Row, 1953); Richard S. Crutchfield, "Conformity and Character," *American Psychologist* 10 (1955): 191–98; Muzafer Sherif, "A Study of Some Social Factors in Perception," *Archives of Psychology* 27 (1935): 187.

26. Burnkrant and Cousineau, "Informational and Normative Social Influence in Buyer Behavior."

27. For a recent attempt to measure individual differences in proclivity to conformity, see William O. Bearden, Richard G. Netemeyer, and Jesse E. Teel, "Measurement of Consumer Susceptibility to Interpersonal Influence," *Journal of Consumer Research* 15 (March 1989): 473–81.

28. John W. Thibaut and Harold H. Kelley, *The Social Psychology of Groups* (New York: John Wiley, 1959); W.W. Waller and R. Hill, *The Family, a Dynamic Interpretation* (New York: Dryden, 1951).

29. Sandra L. Bem, "Sex Role Adaptability: One Consequence of Psychological Androgyny," *Journal of Personality and Social Psychology* 31 (1975): 634–43.

30. Leon Festinger, "A Theory of Social Comparison Processes," *Human Relations* 7 (May 1954): 117–40.

31. Chester A. Insko, Sarah Drenan, Michael R. Solomon, Richard Smith, and Terry J. Wade, "Conformity as a Function of the Consistency of Positive Self-Evaluation with Being Liked and Being Right," *Journal of Experimental Social Psychology* 19 (1983): 341–58.

32. Abraham Tesser, Murray Millar, and Janet Moore, "Some Affective Consequences of Social Comparison and Reflection Processes: The Pain and Pleasure of Being Close," *Journal of Personality and Social Psychology* 54 (1988)1: 49–61.

33. L. Wheeler, K.G. Shaver, R.A. Jones, G.R. Goethals, J. Cooper, J.E. Robinson, C.L. Gruder, and K.W. Butzine, "Factors Determining the Choice of a Comparison Other," *Journal of Experimental Social Psychology* 5 (1969): 219–32.

34. George P. Moschis, "Social Comparison and Informal Group Influence," *Journal of Marketing Research* 13 (August 1976): 237–44.

35. Burnkrant and Cousineau, "Informational and Normative Social Influence in Buyer Behavior"; M. Venkatesan, "Experimental Study of Consumer Behavior Conformity and Independence," *Journal of Marketing Research* 3 (November 1966): 384–87.

36. Harvey London, *Psychology of the Persuader* (Morristown, N.J.: Silver Burdett/General Learning Press, 1973); William J. McGuire, "The Nature of Attitudes and Attitude Change," in *The Handbook of Social Psychology*, eds. G. Lindzey and E. Aronson (Reading, Mass.: Addison-Wesley, 1968), 3; N. Miller, G. Naruyama, R.J. Baebert, and K. Valone, "Speed of Speech and Persuasion," *Journal of Personality and Social Psychology* 34 (1976): 615–24.

37. J.L. Freedman and S. Fraser, "Compliance Without Pressure: the Foot-in-the-Door Technique," *Journal of Personality and Social Psychology* 4 (1966): 195–202.

38. R.B. Cialdini, J.E. Vincent, S.K. Lewis, J. Catalan, D. Wheeler, and B.L. Darby, "Reciprocal Concessions Procedure for Inducing Compliance: The Door-in-the-Face Effect," *Journal of Personality and Social Psychology* 31 (1975): 200–15.

39. Donald H. Granbois, "Improving the Study of Customer In-Store Behavior," *Journal of Marketing* 32 (October 1968): 28–32.

40. B. Latane, K. Williams, and S. Harkins, "Many Hands Make Light the Work: The Causes and Consequences of Social Loafing," *Journal of Personality and Social Psychology* 37 (1979): 822–32.

41. S. Freeman, M. Walker, R. Borden, and B. Latane, "Diffusion of Responsibility and Restaurant Tipping: Cheaper by the Bunch," *Personality and Social Psychology Bulletin* 1 (1978): 584–87.

42. Nathan Kogan and Michael A. Wallach, "Risky Shift Phenomenon in Small Decision-Making Groups: A Test of the Information Exchange Hypothesis," *Journal of Experimental Social Psychology* 3 (January 1967): 75–84; Nathan Kogan and Michael A. Wallach, *Risk Taking* (New York: Holt, Rinehart and Winston, 1964); Arch G. Woodside and M. Wayne DeLozier, "Effects of Word-of-Mouth Advertising on Consumer Risk Taking," *Journal of Advertising* (Fall 1976): 12–19.

43. Kogan and Wallach, *Risk Taking.*

44. Roger Brown, *Social Psychology* (New York: The Free Press, 1965).

45. David L. Johnson and I.R. Andrews, "Risky Shift Phenomenon Tested with Consumer Product Stimuli," *Journal of Personality and Social Psychology* 20 (1971): 382–85; see also Vithala R. Rao and Joel H. Steckel, "A Polarization Model for Describing Group Preferences," *Journal of Consumer Research* 18 (June 1991): 108–118.

46. Len Strazewski, "Tupperware Locks in New Strategy," *Advertising Age* (February 8, 1988): 30.

47. Peter Wilkinson, "For Your Eyes Only," *Savvy Woman* (January 1989): 68.

48. Gergen and Gergen, *Social Psychology.*

49. L.J. Strickland, S. Messick, and D.N. Jackson, "Conformity, Anticonformity and Independence: Their Dimensionality and Generality," *Journal of Personality and Social Psychology* 16 (1970): 494–507.

50. Jack W. Brehm, *A Theory of Psychological Reactance* (New York: Academic Press, 1966).

51. R.D. Ashmore, V. Ramchandra, and R. Jones, "Censorship as an Attitude Change Induction," paper presented at meetings of Eastern Psychological Association, New York, 1971; R.A. Wicklund and J. Brehm, *Perspectives on Cognitive Dissonance* (Hillsdale, N.J.: Lawrence Erlbaum, 1976).

52. C.R. Snyder and H.L. Fromkin, *Uniqueness: The Human Pursuit of Difference* (New York: Plenum Press, 1980).

53. Johan Arndt, "Role of Product-Related Conversations in the Diffusion of a New Product," *Journal of Marketing Research* 4 (August 1967): 291–95.

54. Quoted in Barbara B. Stern and Stephen J. Gould, "The Consumer as Financial Opinion Leader," *Jour-*

nal of Retail Banking 10 (Summer 1988): 43–52.

55. Elihu Katz and Paul F. Lazarsfeld, *Personal Influence* (Glencoe, Ill.: Free Press, 1955).

56. John A. Martilla, "Word-of-Mouth Communication in the Industrial Adoption Process," *Journal of Marketing Research* 8 (March 1971): 173–78; see also Marsha L. Richins, "Negative Word-of-Mouth by Dissatisfied Consumers: A Pilot Study," *Journal of Marketing* 47 (Winter 1983): 68–78.

57. Arndt, "Role of Product-Related Conversations in the Diffusion of a New Product."

58. James H. Myers and Thomas S. Robertson, "Dimensions of Opinion Leadership," *Journal of Marketing Research* 9 (February 1972): 41–46.

59. Barnaby J. Feder, "Those With Things to Sell Love Word-of-Mouth Ads," *New York Times* (June 23, 1992): D18.

60. James F. Engel, Robert J. Kegerreis, and Roger D. Blackwell, "Word of Mouth Communication by the Innovator," *Journal of Marketing* 33 (July 1969): 15–19.

61. Bill Barol, "Batmania," *Newsweek* (June 26, 1989): 70.

62. Dorothy Leonard-Barton, "Experts as Negative Opinion Leaders in the Diffusion of a Technological Innovation," *Journal of Consumer Research* 11 (March 1985): 914–26.

63. Richard J. Lutz, "Changing Brand Attitudes through Modification of Cognitive Structure," *Journal of Consumer Research* 1 (March 1975): 49–59; for some suggested remedies to bad publicity, see Mitch Griffin, Barry J. Babin, and Jill S. Attaway, "An Empirical Investigation of the Impact of Negative Public Publicity on Consumer Attitudes and Intentions," in *Advances in Consumer Research* 18, eds. Rebecca H. Holman and Michael R. Solomon (Provo, Utah: Association for Consumer Research, 1991), 334–41; Alice M. Tybout, Bobby J. Calder, and Brian Sternthal, "Using Information Processing Theory to Design Marketing Strategies," *Journal of Marketing Research* 18 (1981): 73–79.

64. Charles W. King and John O. Summers, "Overlap of Opinion Leadership Across Consumer Product Categories," *Journal of Marketing Research* 7 (February 1970): 43–50.

65. A. Tesser and S. Rosen, "The Reluctance to Transmit Bad News," in *Advances in Experimental Social Psychology*, ed. L. Berkowitz (New York: Academic Press, 1975), 8.

66. John Leo, "Psst! Wait 'Till You Hear This: A Scholar Says Rumors Reveal Our Fears and Desires," *Time* (March 16, 1987): 76.

67. Sid Astbury, "Pork Rumors Vex Indonesia," *Advertising Age* (February 16, 1989): 36.

68. Marcus Mabry, "Do Boycotts Work?" *Newsweek*

(July 6, 1992)3: 35.

69. Everett M. Rogers, *Diffusion of Innovations*, 3rd ed. (New York: Free Press, 1983).

70. Leonard-Barton, "Experts as Negative Opinion Leaders in the Diffusion of a Technological Innovation"; Rogers, *Diffusion of Innovations.*

71. Herbert Menzel, "Interpersonal and Unplanned Communications: Indispensable or Obsolete?" in *Biomedical Innovation* (Cambridge, Mass.: MIT Press, 1981), 155–63.

72. Meera P. Venkatraman, "Opinion Leaders, Adopters, and Communicative Adopters: A Role Analysis," *Psychology & Marketing* 6 (Spring 1989): 51–68.

73. Rogers, *Diffusion of Innovations.*

74. Robert Merton, *Social Theory and Social Structure*, (Glencoe, Ill.: Free Press, 1957).

75. King and Summers, "Overlap of Opinion Leadership Across Consumer Product Categories"; see also Ronald E. Goldsmith, Jeanne R. Heitmeyer, and Jon B. Freiden, "Social Values and Fashion Leadership," *Clothing and Textiles Research Journal* 10 (Fall 1991): 37–45; J.O. Summers, "Identity of Women's Clothing Fashion Opinion Leaders," *Journal of Marketing Research* 7 (1970): 178–85.

76. Steven A. Baumgarten, "The Innovative Communicator in the Diffusion Process," *Journal of Marketing Research* 12 (February 1975): 12–18.

77. Russell W. Belk, "Occurrence of Word-of-Mouth Buyer Behavior as a Function of Situation and Advertising Stimuli," in *Combined Proceedings of the American Marketing Association, Series No. 33*, ed. Fred C. Allvine (Chicago: American Marketing Association, 1971), 419–22.

78. Lawrence F. Feick, Linda L. Price, and Robin A. Higie, "People Who Use People: The Other Side of Opinion Leadership," in *Advances in Consumer Research* 13, ed. Richard J. Lutz (Provo, Utah: Association for Consumer Research, 1986), 301–05.

79. For discussion of the marke maven construct, see Lawrence F. Feick and Linda L. Price, "The Market Maven," *Managing* (July 1985): 10; scale items adapted from Lawrence Feick and Linda Price, "The Market Maven: A Diffuser of Marketplace Information," *Journal of Marketing* 51 (January 1987), 83-87.

80. Gerald Eskenazi, "Once a Canvas Shoe, Now a Big-Time Player," *New York Times* (March 11, 1990): 1.

81. Michael R. Solomon, "The Missing Link: Surrogate Consumers in the Marketing Chain," *Journal of Marketing* 50 (October 1986): 208–18.

82. Stern and Gould, "The Consumer as Financial Opinion Leader."

83. William R. Darden and Fred D. Reynolds, "Predict-

ing Opinion Leadership for Men's Apparel Fashions," *Journal of Marketing Research* 1 (August 1972): 324–28. A modified version of the opinion leadership scale with improved reliability and validity can be found in Terry L. Childers, "Assessment of the Psychometric Properties of an Opinion Leadership Scale," *Journal of Marketing Research* 23 (May l986), 184-88.

84. "Referrals Top Ads as Influence on Patients' Doctor Selections," *Marketing News* (January 30, 1987): 22.

85. Peter H. Reingen, Brian L. Foster, Jacqueline Johnson Brown, and Stephen B. Seidman, "Brand Congruence in Interpersonal Relations: A Social Network Analysis," *Journal of Consumer Research* 11 (December 1984): 771–83; see also James C. Ward and Peter H. Reingen, "Sociocognitive Analysis of Group Decision Making Among Consumers," *Journal of Consumer Research* 17 (December 1990): 245–62.

86. Peter H. Reingen and Jerome B. Kernan, "Analysis of Referral Networks in Marketing: Methods and Illustration," *Journal of Marketing Research* 23 (November 1986): 370–78.

Whether it's a swift horse, a smart hound or an agile car, the English have long known the importance of good breeding.

JAGUAR

CHAPTER 12

Social Class

and Economic

Influences

Buying, Having, and Being: Selections 42–44 from *Buying, Having, and Being: The Washington Post Consumer Behavior Companion*, Second Edition, accompany this chapter.

F inally, the big day has come! Phil is going home with Marilyn to meet her parents. Phil had been doing some contracting work at the publishing company where Marilyn works, and it was love at first sight. Even though Phil had attended "The School of Hard Knocks" on the streets of Brooklyn and Marilyn was fresh out of Vassar, somehow they knew they could work things out despite their vastly different backgrounds. Marilyn's been hinting that the Caldwells have money, but Phil doesn't feel intimidated. After all, he knows plenty of guys from his old neighborhood who have wheeled and dealed their way into six figures; he guesses he can handle one more big shot in a silk suit, flashing a roll of bills and showing off his expensive modern furniture with mirrors and gadgets everywhere you look.

When they arrive at the family estate in Connecticut, Phil looks for a Rolls-Royce or a Jaguar parked in the circular driveway just like on "Dynasty," but sees only a Jeep Cherokee—which, he decides, must belong to one of the servants. Once inside, Phil is surprised by how simply the house is decorated and by how shabby everything seems. The hall entryway is covered with a faded Oriental rug, and all of the furniture looks really old—in fact, there doesn't seem to be a new stick of furniture anywhere, just a lot of antiques.

Phil is even more surprised when he meets Mr. Caldwell. He had half expected Marilyn's father to be wearing a tuxedo and holding a large glass of cognac like the people on "Lifestyles of the Rich and Famous." In fact, Phil had put on his best black Italian suit in anticipation and wore his large cubic zirconium pinky ring so this guy would know that he had some money too.

When Marilyn's father emerges from his study wearing an old rumpled cardigan sweater and tennis sneakers, Phil clearly realizes he's definitely not in the old neighborhood . . . .

Introduction

As Phil's eye-opening experience at the Caldwells suggests, there are many ways to spend money, and a wide gulf exists between those who have it and those who don't. Perhaps an equally wide one exists between those who have had it for a long time and those who "made it the hard way—by earning it!" This chapter begins by briefly considering how general economic conditions affect the way consumers allocate their money. Then, reflecting the adage that says "The rich are different," it will explore how people who occupy different positions in society consume in very different ways. Whether a skilled worker like Phil or a child of privilege like Marilyn, a person's social class has a profound impact on what he or she does with money and on how consumption choices reflect the person's "place" in society.

As this chapter illustrates, these choices play another purpose as well. The specific products and services we buy are often intended to make sure *other* people know what our social standing is—or what we would like it to be. Products are frequently bought and displayed as markers of social class; they are valued as *status symbols*. Indeed, it is quite common for a product to be positioned on the basis of its (presumed) placement in the social hierarchy.

Within this hierarchy, each hen has a position in which she is submissive to all of the hens above her and dominates all of the ones below her (hence, the origin of the term *pecking order*).[7]

People are no different. They also develop a pecking order where they are ranked in terms of their relative standing in society. This standing determines their access to such resources as education, housing, and consumer goods. And people try to improve their ranking by moving up in the social order whenever possible. This desire to improve one's lot in life and often to let others know that one has done so is at the core of many marketing strategies.

While every culture has its social hierarchies, variations in terms of how explicit these distinctions are can be observed. Stratification of one sort or another is universal, even in societies that officially disdain such a process. For example, in China, a supposedly classless society, many Chinese are irritated by the children of top party officials, who are called *gaoganzidi*. These offspring have a reputation for laziness, enjoying material pleasures, and getting the best jobs by virtue of their family connections. They are thus a privileged class in a classless society.[8]

SOCIAL CLASS AFFECTS ACCESS TO RESOURCES Just as marketers try to carve society into groups for segmentation purposes, sociologists have developed ways to describe meaningful divisions of society in terms of people's relative social and economic resources. Some of these divisions involve political power, while others revolve around purely economic distinctions. Karl Marx felt that position in a society was determined by one's relationship to the *means of production*. Some people (the haves) control resources, and they use the labor of others to preserve their privileged positions. The have-nots lack control and depend on their own labor for survival, so these people have the most to gain by changing the system. Distinctions among people that entitle some to more than others are perpetuated by those who will benefit by doing so.[9]

The sociologist Max Weber showed that the rankings people develop are not one-dimensional. Some involve prestige or "social honor" (he called these *status groups*), some rankings focus on power (or *party*) and some revolve around wealth and property (*class*).[10]

SOCIAL CLASS AFFECTS TASTE AND LIFESTYLES The term **social class** is now used more generally to describe the overall rank of people in a society. People who are grouped within the same social class are approximately equal in terms of their social standing in the community. They work in roughly similar occupations, and they tend to have similar lifestyles by virtue of their income levels and common tastes. These people tend to socialize with one another and share many ideas and values regarding the way life should be lived.[11]

Social class is as much a state of being as it is of having: As Phil saw, class is also a question of what one *does* with one's money and how one defines his or her role in society. Although people may not like the idea that some members of society are better off or "different" than others, most consumers do acknowledge the existence of different classes and the effect of class membership on consumption. As one wealthy woman observed when asked to define social class:

> I would suppose social class means where you went to school and how far. Your intelligence. Where you live . . . . Where you send your children to school. The hobbies you have. Skiing, for example, is higher than the snowmobile . . . . It can't be [just] money, because nobody ever knows that about you for sure.[12]

MARKETING PITFALL

J.C. Penney found out the hard way about class identification. This retailer traditionally had a very strong identification with the lower-middle class, and these consumers felt great loyalty to the store. In recent years, the company tried to change its image and go upscale by featuring higher-priced designer clothes and boutique accessory items. It was not successful, however, in convincing wealthier consumers of this change. Penney's is now returning to its roots, with promotions featuring "priced-right" apparel instead of designer goods.[13]

Social Stratification

In school, it always seems that some kids are more popular. They have access to many resources, such as special privileges, fancy cars, large

MULTICULTURAL DIMENSIONS

England is an extremely class-conscious country, and at least until recently, consumption patterns were preordained in terms of one's inherited position and family background. Members of the upper class were educated at schools like Eton and Oxford and spoke like Henry Higgins in *My Fair Lady*. Remnants of this rigid class structure can still be found. "Hooray Henrys" (wealthy young men) play polo at Windsor and hereditary peers still dominate the House of Lords.

The dominance of inherited wealth appears to be fading in Britain's traditionally aristocratic society. According to a recent survey, 86 of the 200 wealthiest people in England made their money the old-fashioned way: They earned it. Even the sanctity of the Royal Family, which epitomizes the aristocracy, has been diluted because of tabloid exposure and the antics of younger family members who have been transformed into celebrities more like rock stars than royalty. As one observer put it, ". . . the royal family has gone down-market . . . to the point that it sometimes resembles soap opera as much as grand opera."[14]

allowances, or dates with other popular classmates. At work, some people are put on the fast track and are promoted to high-prestige jobs, given higher salaries, and perhaps such perks as a parking space, a large office, or the keys to the executive washroom.

In virtually every context, some people seem to be ranked higher than others. Patterns of social arrangements evolve whereby some members get more resources than others by virtue of their relative standing, power, and/or control in the group.[15] The phenomenon of **social stratification** refers to this creation of artificial divisions in a society: ". . . those processes in a social system by which scarce and valuable resources are distributed unequally to status positions that become more or less permanently ranked in terms of the share of valuable resources each receives."[16]

ACHIEVED VERSUS ASCRIBED STATUS If you think back to groups you've belonged to, both large and small, you'll probably agree that in many instances some members seem to get more than their fair share of goodies, while other individuals are not so lucky. Some of these resources may have gone to people who earned them through hard work or diligent study. This allocation is due to *achieved status*. Other rewards may have been obtained because the person was lucky enough to be born rich or beautiful. Such good fortune reflects *ascribed status*. Whether rewards go to *the best and the brightest* or to someone who happens to be related to the boss, allocations are rarely equal within a social group. Most groups exhibit a structure, or **status hierarchy,** in which some members are somehow better off than others. They may have more authority or power, or they are simply better liked or respected.

CLASS STRUCTURE IN THE UNITED STATES The United States supposedly does not have a rigid, objectively defined class system. Nevertheless, America has tended to maintain a stable class structure in terms of income distribution. Unlike other countries, however, what *does* change are the groups (ethnic, racial, and religious) that have occupied different positions within this structure at different times.[17]

The most influential and earliest attempt to describe American class structure was proposed by W. Lloyd Warner in 1941. Warner identified six social classes:[18]

1. Upper Upper
2. Lower Upper
3. Upper Middle
4. Lower Middle
5. Upper Lower
6. Lower Lower

Note that these classifications imply (in ascending order) some judgment of desirability in terms of access to such resources as money, education, and luxury goods. Variations on this system have been proposed over the years, but these six levels summarize fairly well the way social scientists think about class. A more current view of the American status structure is provided in Figure 12–1.

International Example: Reflecting the British redistribution of wealth away from the aristocracy and toward self-made businesspeople, the richest man in the United Kingdom is now Paul Raymond, who deposed the Duke of Westminster for the title. Raymond's business ventures include ownership of several nightclubs, and he publishes the sex magazines "Men Only," "Club International," and "Mayfair." The *London Times* noted that "there is more money these days in porn than inherited property." See "Duke is No Longer Britain's Richest Man," *New York Times* (December 1, 1992): D5.

Teaching Hint: The popular British television series "Upstairs, Downstairs" is an example of the explicit portrayal of class differences. An impenetrable gulf separates the "upstairs" characters from those who reside "downstairs." See Arthur A. Berger, *Signs in Contemporary Culture: An Introduction to Semiotics* (New York: Longman, 1984).

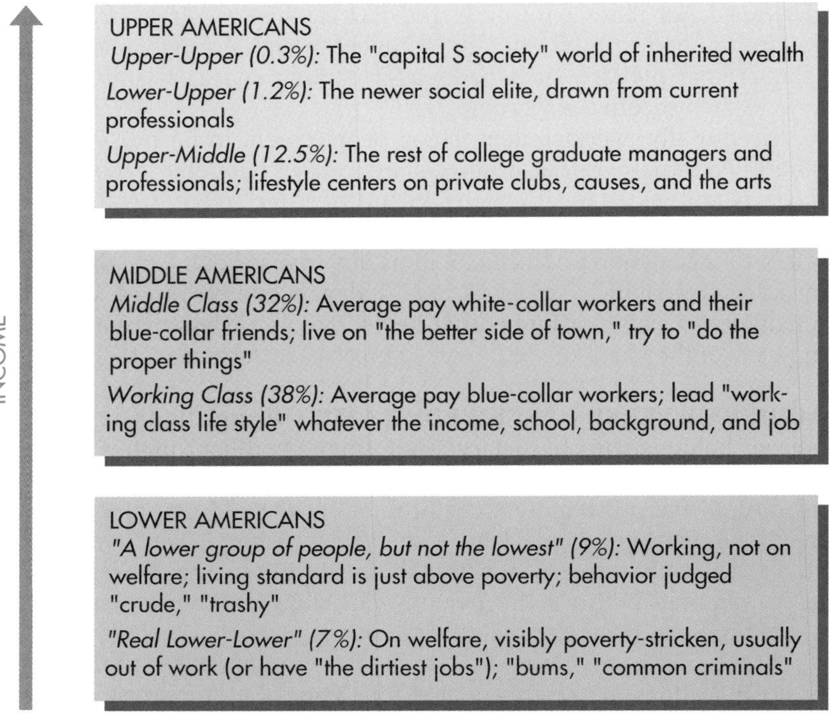

FIGURE 12–1   A Contemporary View of the American Class Structure   Source: Richard P. Coleman, "The Continuing Significance of Social Class to Marketing," *Journal of Consumer Research* 10 (December 1983): 265–80. Reprinted with permission of The University of Chicago Press

Figure 12–1 is available as Transparency 30.

Research Report: A recent ethnographic study gives a poignant account of how homeless women adapt to life in a shelter.   See Ronald Paul Hill, "Homeless Women, Special Possessions, and the Meaning of 'Home,' An Ethnographic Case Study," *Journal of Consumer Research* 18 (December 1991): 298.

SOCIAL MOBILITY   To what degree do people tend to change their social classes? In some societies, such as India, one's social class is very difficult to change, but America is known as a country where "any man (or woman?) can grow up to be President." **Social mobility** refers to the ". . . passage of individuals from one social class to another . . . ."[19]

Direction of Movement.   This passage can be upward, downward, or even horizontal. *Horizontal mobility* refers to movement from one position to another roughly equivalent in social status, like becoming a nurse instead of an elementary school teacher. *Downward mobility* is, of course, not very desirable, but this pattern is unfortunately quite evident in recent years as farmers and other displaced workers have been forced to go on welfare rolls or have joined the ranks of the homeless. A conservative estimate is that 600,000 Americans are homeless on a given day.[20]

Despite that discouraging trend, demographics in fact decree that there must be *upward mobility* in our society. The middle and upper classes reproduce less than the lower classes (an effect known as *differential fertility*), and they tend to restrict family size below replacement level. Therefore, so the reasoning goes, positions of higher status over time must be filled by those of lower status.[21] Overall, though, the offspring of blue-collar consumers tend also to be blue-collar while the offspring of white-collar consumers also tend to wind up as white-collars.[22] People tend to improve their positions over time, but these increases are not usually dramatic enough to catapult them from one social class to another.

Components of Social Class

When we think about a person's social class, there are a number of pieces of information we may consider. Two major ones are occupation and income (a third important factor is educational attainment, which is strongly related to income and occupation).

OCCUPATIONAL PRESTIGE   In a system where (like it or not) a consumer is defined to a great extent by what he or she does for a living, *occupational prestige* is one way to evaluate the "worth" of people. Hierarchies of occupational prestige tend to be quite stable over time, and they also tend to be similar in different societies. Similarities in occupational prestige have been found in countries as diverse as Brazil, Ghana, Guam, Japan, and Turkey.[23] A typical ranking includes a variety of professional and business occupations at the top (e.g., CEO of a large corporation, physician, and even college professor), while those jobs hovering near the bottom include shoe shiner, ditchdigger, and garbage collector. Because a person's occupation tends to be strongly linked to his or her use of leisure time, allocation of family resources, political orientation, and so on, this variable is often considerable to be the single best proxy for social class.

INCOME   The distribution of wealth is of great interest to social scientists and to marketers, since it determines what groups have the greatest buying power and market potential. Wealth is by no means distributed evenly across the classes. The top fifth of the population controls about 75 percent of all assets.[24]

THE RELATIONSHIP BETWEEN INCOME AND SOCIAL CLASS   Although consumers tend to equate money with class, the precise relationship between other aspects of social class and income is not clear and has been the subject of debate among social scientists.[25] The two are by no means synonymous, which is why many people with a lot of money try to use it to upgrade their social class (i.e., the "nouveaux riches"). One problem is that even if a family increases household income by adding wage-earners, each additional job is likely to be of lower status. For example, a housewife who gets a part-time job is not as likely to get one that is of equal or greater status than the primary wage-earner's. In addition, the extra money earned often is not pooled toward the common good of the family. It is instead used by the individual for his or her own personal spending. More money does not then result in increased status or changes in consumption patterns, since it tends to be devoted to buying *more* of the usual rather than upgrading to higher-status products.[26]

The following general conclusions can be made regarding the relative value of social class (i.e., place of residence, occupation, cultural interests, etc.) versus income in predicting consumer behavior:

- Social class appears to be a better predictor of purchases that have symbolic aspects, but low to moderate prices (e.g., cosmetics, liquor).
- Income is a better predictor of major expenditures that do not have status or symbolic aspects (e.g., major appliances).
- Both social class and income data are needed to predict purchases of expensive, symbolic products (e.g., cars, homes).

Measurement of Social Class

Because social class is a complex concept that depends on a number of factors, not surprisingly it has proven difficult to measure. Early measures included the Index of Status Characteristics developed in the 1940s and the Index of Social Position developed in the 1950s.[27] These indices used various combinations of individual characteristics (e.g., income, type of housing) to arrive at a label of class standing. A more current measurement instrument is shown in Figure 12–2.

Figure 12–2 is available as Transparency 31.

American consumers generally have little difficulty placing themselves in either the working class (lower middle class) or middle class. Also, the number who reject the idea that such categories exist is rather small.[28] The proportion of consumers identifying themselves as working-class tended to rise until about 1960, but it has been declining since. The ad for Street Cars shoes shown here is an unabashed attempt to appeal to working-class males. The

This ad for Street Car shoes is targeted to the "working-class American," who is not keen on paying $100 for a pair of shoes nor $60 for a haircut. Courtesy of Jim Arndt Photography.

Interviewer circles code numbers (for the computer) which in his/her judgment best fit the respondent and family. Interviewer asks for detail on occupation, then makes rating. Interviewer often asks the respondent to describe neighborhood in own words. Interviewer asks respondent to specify income—a card is presented the respondent showing the eight brackets—and records R's response. If interviewer feels this is over-statement or under, a "better-judgment" estimate should be given, along with explanation.

EDUCATION:

	Respondent	Respondent's Spouse
Grammar school (8 yrs or less)	–1	–1
Some high school (9 to 11 yrs)	–2	–2
Graduated high school (12 yrs)	–3	–3
Some post high school (business, nursing, technical, 1 yr college)	–4	–4
Two, three years of college—possibly Associate of Arts degree	–5	–5
Graduated four-year college (B.A./B.S.)	–7	–7
Master's or five-year professional degree	–8	–8
Ph.D. or six/seven-year professional degree	–9	–9

R's Age ___   Spouse's Age ___

OCCUPATION PRESTIGE LEVEL OF HOUSEHOLD HEAD: Interviewer's judgment of how head of household rates in occupational status.

(Respondent's description—asks for previous occupation if retired, or if R. is widow, ask husband's:_____)

Chronically unemployed—"day" laborers, unskilled; on welfare	–0
Steadily employed but in marginal semi-skilled jobs; custodians, minimum pay factory help, service workers (gas attendants, etc.)	–1
Average-skill assembly-line workers, bus and truck drivers, police and firefighters, route deliverymen, carpenters, brickmasons	–2
Skilled craftsmen (electricians), small contractors, factory foremen, low-pay salesclerks, office workers, postal employees	–3
Owners of very small firms (2–4 employees), technicians, salespeople, office workers, civil servants with average level salaries	–4
Middle management, teachers, social workers, lesser professionals	–5
Lesser corporate officials, owners of middle-sized businesses (10–20 employees), moderate-success professionals (dentists, engineers, etc.)	–7
Top corporate executives, "big successes" in the professional world (leading doctors and lawyers), "rich" business owners	–9

AREA OF RESIDENCE: Interviewer's impressions of the immediate neighborhood in terms of its reputation in the eyes of the community.

Slum area: people on relief, common laborers	–1
Strictly working class: not slummy but some very poor housing	–2
Predominantly blue-collar with some office workers	–3
Predominantly white-collar with some well-paid blue-collar	–4
Better white-collar area: not many executives, but hardly any blue-collar either	–5
Excellent area: professionals and well-paid managers	–7
"Wealthy" or "society"-type neighborhood	–9

TOTAL SCORE _____

TOTAL FAMILY INCOME PER YEAR:

Under $5,000	–1	$20,000 to 24,999	–5
$5,000 to $9,999	–2	$25,000 to $34,999	–6
$10,000 to 14,999	–3	$35,000 to 49,999	–7
$15,000 to $19,999	–4	$50,000 and over	–8

Estimated Status _____

(Interviewer's estimate:_____ and explanation _____)

R's MARITAL STATUS: Married ___ Divorced/Separated ___ Widowed ___ Single ___ (CODE:___)

FIGURE 12–2 Example of a Computerized Status Index. Source: Richard P. Coleman, "The Continuing Significance of Social Class to Marketing," *Journal of Consumer Research* 10 (December 1983): 265–80. Reprinted with permission of The University of Chicago Press.

targeted consumers are intended to identify with the man depicted in the picture, who thinks it's ridiculous to spend $100 for a pair of shoes or $60 for a haircut.

Blue-collar workers with relatively high prestige jobs still tend to view themselves as working-class, even though their income levels may be equivalent to many white-collar workers.[29] This fact reinforces the idea that the labels of "working-class" or "middle-class" are very subjective. Their meanings say at least as much about self-identity as they do about economic well-being.

PROBLEMS WITH MEASURES OF SOCIAL CLASS Market researchers were among the first to propose that people from different social classes can be distinguished from each other in important ways. While some of these dimensions still exist, others have changed.[30] Unfortunately, many of these measures are badly dated and are not as valid today for a variety of reasons, four of which are discussed here.[31]

Changes in Family Structure. Most measures of social class were designed to accommodate the traditional nuclear family, with a male wage-earner in the middle of his career and a female full-time homemaker. Such measures have trouble accounting for two-income families, young singles living alone, or households headed by women that are so prevalent in today's society (see Chapter 8).

Anonymity. Another problem with measuring social class is attributable to the increasing anonymity of our society. Earlier studies relied on the *reputational method,* where extensive interviewing was done within a community to determine the reputations and backgrounds of individuals (see the discussion of sociometry in Chapter 11). This information, coupled with the tracing of interaction patterns among people, provided a very comprehensive view of social standing within a community.

This approach is virtually impossible to implement in most communities today. One compromise is to interview individuals to obtain demographic data and to combine these data with the subjective impressions of the interviewer regarding the person's possessions and standard of living. An example of this approach appeared in Figure 12–2. Note that the accuracy of this questionnaire relies largely on the interviewer's judgment, especially regarding the quality of the respondent's neighborhood. These impressions are in danger of being biased by the interviewer's own circumstances, which may affect his or her standard of comparison. This potential problem highlights the need for adequate training of interviewers, as well as for some attempt to cross-validate such data, possibly by employing multiple judges to rate the same area.

Status Inconsistency. One problem with assigning people to a social class is that they may not be equal in their standing on all of the relevant dimensions. A person might come from a low-status ethnic group but have a high-status job, while another may live in a fancy part of town but did not finish high school. The concept of **status crystallization** was developed to assess the impact of inconsistency on the self and social behavior.[32] It was thought that since the rewards from each part of such an "unbalanced" person's life would be variable and unpredictable, stress would result. People who exhibit such inconsistencies tend to be more receptive to social change than are those whose identities are more firmly rooted.

A related problem occurs when a person's social class standing creates expectations that are not met. Some people find themselves in the not-unhappy position of making more money than is expected of those in their social class. This situation is known as an *overprivileged* condition and is usually defined as an income that is at least 25 percent to 30 percent over the median for one's class.[33] In contrast, *underprivileged* consumers, who earn at least 15 percent less than the median, must often devote their consumption priorities to sacrificing in order to maintain the appearance of living up to class expectations.

Lottery winners are examples of consumers who become overprivileged virtually overnight. As attractive as winning is to many people, it has its problems. Consumers with a certain standard of living and level of expectations may have trouble adapting to sudden affluence and engage in flamboyant and irresponsible displays of wealth. Ironically, it is not unusual for lottery winners to report feelings of depression in the months after cashing in. They may have trouble adjusting to an unfamiliar world, and they frequently experience pressure from friends, relatives, and business people to "share the wealth."

One New York winner who was featured prominently in the media is a case in point. He was employed as a mail porter until winning $5 million. After winning the lottery, he divorced his wife and married his girlfriend. She wore a $13,000 gown to the ceremony and the couple arrived in a horse-drawn carriage. Other purchases included a Cadillac with a Rolls Royce grill and a $5,000 car phone. This individual later denied rumors that he was heavily in debt due to his extravagant spending.[34]

WOMEN AND SOCIAL CLASS   The traditional assumption is that husbands define a family's social class, while wives must live it. Women borrow their social status from their husbands.[35] Indeed, the evidence indicates that physically attractive women tend to "marry up" in social class to a greater extent than attractive men. Women trade the resource of sexual appeal, which historically has been one of the few assets they were allowed to possess, for the economic resources of men.[36] (This tradeoff is another application of exchange theory discussed in Chapter 10.)

The accuracy of this assumption in today's world must be questioned. Many women now contribute equally to the family's well-being and work in positions of comparable or even greater status than their spouses. *Cosmopolitan* magazine offered this revelation:

> Women who've become liberated enough to marry any man they please, regardless of his social position, report how much more fun and spontaneous their relationships with men have become now that they no longer view men only in terms of their power symbols.[37]

Employed women tend to average both their own and their husband's respective positions when estimating their own subjective status.[38] Nevertheless, a prospective spouse's social class is often an important "product attribute" when evaluating alternatives in the interpersonal marketplace (as

Phil and Marilyn were to find out). *Cosmopolitan* also discussed this dilemma, implying that social class differences are still an issue in the dating game:

> You've met the (almost) perfect man. You both adore Dashiell Hammett thrillers, Mozart, and Doonesbury. He taught you to jet ski; you taught him the virtues of tofu . . . . The glitch? You're an executive earning ninety-thousand dollars a year. He's a taxi driver . . . .[39]

How Social Class Affects Purchase Decisions

Different products and stores are perceived by consumers to be appropriate for certain social classes.[40] Working-class consumers tend to evaluate products in more utilitarian terms such as sturdiness or comfort rather than style or fashionability. They are less likely to experiment with new products or styles, such as modern furniture or colored appliances.[41] More affluent people living in the suburbs tend to be concerned about appearance and body image, so they are more avid consumers of diet foods and drinks compared to people in more downscale small towns. These differences mean that the cola market, for example, can be segmented by social class.[42] Consumption differences often reflect underlying differences in lifestyle priorities, as the ad shown here for Libbey glass products vividly illustrates.

Class Differences in Worldview

A major social class difference involves the *worldview* of consumers. The world of the working-class (i.e., the lower-middle class) is more intimate and constricted. For example, working-class men are likely to name local sports figures as heroes and are less likely to take long vacation trips to out-of-the way places.[43] Immediate needs, such as a new refrigerator or TV, tend to dictate buying behavior for these consumers, while the higher classes tend to focus on more long-term goals, such as saving for college tuition or retirement.[44]

Working-class consumers depend heavily on relatives for emotional support and tend to orient themselves in terms of the community rather than the world at large. They are more likely to be conservative and family-oriented. Maintaining the appearance of one's home and property is a priority, regardless of the size of the house. While they would like to have more in the way of material goods, working-class people do not necessarily envy those who rank above them in social standing.[45] The maintenance of a high-status lifestyle is sometimes not seen as worth the effort. As one blue-collar consumer commented: "Life is very hectic for those people. There are more breakdowns and alcoholism. It must be very hard to sustain the status, the clothes, the parties that are expected. I don't think I'd want to take their place."[46]

The blue-collar consumer quoted here may be right. While good things appear to go hand in hand with higher status and wealth, the picture is not

Teaching Hint: Because the higher classes have broader social networks and control of informational resources, it has been proposed that consumers from these strata will more readily adopt technological innovations that permit information flow and communication. For a discussion, see James E. Fisher and Paul D. Boughton (1991), "Information, Technology and Social Class," in *Marketing: Toward the Twenty-First Century*, ed. Robert L. King, (Richmond, Va.: Southern Marketing Association, 1991), 11.

Whatever your customers love to do for fun, Libbey refreshes them along the way. Libbey offers glasses to fit any lifestyle and specific taste. □ You can satisfy your customers' preferences and reflect your store's distinctiveness, too. □ Contact your Libbey representative today for a personal viewing. We will come out to see you with so many choices, we know it will be very refreshing indeed.

Libbey
America's Glassmaker™

"Peach cooler, please."

"Gimme a brew."

This ad for Libbey Glass implies that there are social class differences in leisure activities and preferred beverages. Courtesy of Libbey Glass Inc.

that clear. The social scientist Emile Durkheim observed that suicide rates are much higher among the wealthy, and wrote in 1897, ". . . the possessors of most comfort suffer most."[48] The quest for riches has the potential to result in depression, deviant behavior, and ruin. In fact, a recent survey of affluent consumers (they made an average of $176,000 a year) supports this notion. Although these people are in the top 2.5 percent income bracket in America, only 14 percent said they are very well off.[48]

TASTE CULTURES   The concept of **taste cultures,** which differentiates people in terms of their aesthetic and intellectual preferences, is helpful in understanding the important yet subtle distinctions in consumption choices among the social classes. Taste cultures largely reflect education (and are also income-related).[49] A distinction is often made between low culture and high culture groups (and is discussed in more detail in Chapter 17). The ad for *US* magazine shown on page 418 attempts to appeal to consumers on the basis of value judgments about the cultural tastes of other classes.

While such perspectives have met with criticism due to the implicit value judgments involved, they are valuable because they recognize the existence of groupings based on shared tastes in literature, art, home decoration, and

The Libbey Glass ad is available as Transparency 32.

This ad for *US* magazine uses a strategy that relies on cultural tastes of consumers in different social classes. By *US Magazine* from *Ad Age* (7/24/89), By Straight Arrow Publishers, Inc. © 1989.

so on. In one of the classic studies of social differences in taste, researchers cataloged homeowners' possessions while asking more typical questions about income, occupation, and so on. Clusters of furnishings and decorative items that seemed to appear together with some regularity were identified, and different clusters were found depending upon the consumer's social status (see Figure 12–3). For example, religious objects, artificial flowers, and still-life portraits tended to be found together in relatively lower-status living rooms, while a cluster containing abstract paintings, sculptures, and modern furniture was more likely to appear in a higher-status home.[50]

Codes and Social Class. A semiotic approach to social class (see Chapter 2) focuses on differences in the types of *codes* (the ways meanings are expressed and interpreted by consumers) used within different social strata. Discovery of these codes is valuable to marketers, since this knowledge allows us to communicate to markets using concepts and terms most likely to be understood and appreciated by specific consumers.

The nature of these codes varies among social classes. *Restricted codes* are dominant among the working class, while *elaborated* codes tend to be used by the middle and upper classes. Restricted codes focus on the content of objects, not on relationships among objects. Elaborated codes, in contrast, are more complex and depend upon a more sophisticated worldview. Some differences between these two general types of codes are provided in Table 12–2. As this table indicates, these code differences extend to the way consumers approach such basic concepts as time, social relationships, and objects.

Marketing appeals that are constructed with these differences in mind will result in quite different messages. For example, a life insurance ad targeted to a lower-class person might depict in simple, straightforward terms a hard-working family man who feels good immediately after purchasing a policy. A more upscale appeal might depict a more affluent older couple surrounded by photos of their children and grandchildren and contain exten-

FIGURE 12–3   Living Room Clusters and Social Class   Source: Edward O. Laumann and James S. House, "Living Room Styles and Social Attributes: The Patterning of Material Artifacts in a Modern Urban Community," *Sociology and Social Research* 54 (April 1970): 321–42.

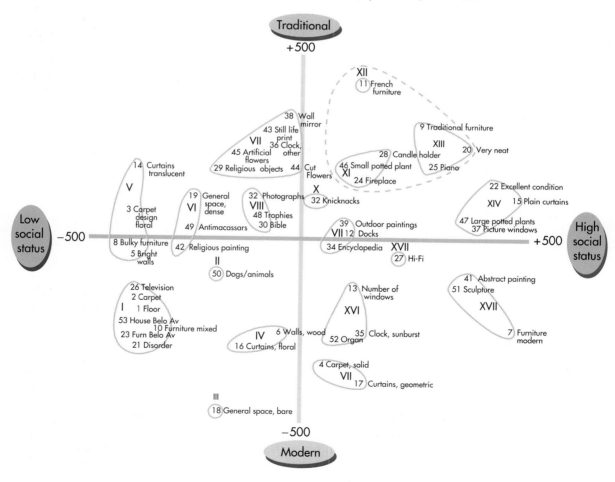

TABLE 12–2 Effects of Restricted Versus Elaborated Codes

	Restricted Codes	**Elaborated Codes**
General Characteristics	Emphasize description and contents of objects	Emphasize analysis and interrelationships between objects: hierarchical organization and instrumental connections
	Implicit meanings (context dependent)	Explicit meanings
Language	Few qualifiers, few adjectives or adverbs	Language rich in personal, individual qualifiers
	Concrete, descriptive, tangible symbolism	Large vocabulary, complex conceptual hierarchy
Social Relationships	Stress attributes of individuals over formal roles	Stress formal role structure, instrumental relationships
Time	Focus on present; have only general notion of future	Focus on instrumental relationship between present activities and future rewards
Physical Space	Rooms, spaces located in context of other rooms and places: e.g., "front room," "corner store"	Rooms, spaces identified in terms of usage; formal ordering of spaces: e.g., "dining room," "financial district"
Implications for Marketers	Stress inherent product quality, contents (or trustworthiness, goodness of "real-type") spokesperson	Stress difference, advantages vis-a-vis other products in terms of some autonomous evaluation criteria
	Stress implicit fit of product with total lifestyle	Stress product's instrumental ties to distant benefits
	Use simple adjectives, descriptors	Use complex adjectives, descriptors

Adapted from Jeffrey F. Durgee, "How Consumer Sub-Cultures Code Reality: A Look at Some Code Types," in *Advances in Consumer Research*, ed. Richard J. Lutz (Provo, Utah: Association for Consumer Research, 1986)13: 332.

sive copy emphasizing the satisfaction that comes from planning for the future and highlighting the benefits of a whole-life insurance policy. As another example, the ad for the Paisano Group Magazines shown here uses imagery and simple descriptors to appeal to the tastes and interests of lower-class young men.

Segmenting by Social Class: Targeting the Rich

Many marketers try to target affluent, upscale markets. This practice often makes sense, since these consumers obviously have the resources to expend on costly products (often with higher profit margins). However, it is a mistake to assume that everyone with a high income should be placed into the same market segment. As noted earlier, social class involves more than

This group of magazines distributed by the Paisano Group targets young lower-class males by appealing to their interests in cars, tattoos, and so on. Courtesy of Paisano Publications.

absolute income; it is also a way of life, and affluent consumers' interests and spending priorities are significantly affected by such factors as where they got their money, how they got it, and how long they have had it.[51]

For example, drivers in the luxury car market can be segmented. Some characteristics have been observed by industry experts.

- Cadillac owners want to be chauffeured. They are not very attentive to styling details or the car's color. Their primary interests are in comfort and the impression they make on others.
- Porsche owners prefer to drive themselves. They are more interested in performance than luxury. The color red is a favorite.
- Jaguar owners are more austere. They are interested in elegance and prefer darker colors.
- Mercedes owners like to feel they are in control. They tend to prefer muted shades of tan, gray, and silver.

OLD MONEY When people have enough money for all intents and purposes to buy just about anything they want, ironically social distinctions no longer revolve around the amount of money one has. Instead, it appears to be important to consider *where* the money came from and *how* it is spent. The "top-out-of-sight class" (e.g., the Rockefellers, DuPonts, Fords, etc.) live primarily on inherited money.

People who have made vast amounts of money from their own labor do not tend to be included in this select group, though their flamboyant consumption patterns may represent an attempt to prove their wealth.[52] The mere presence of wealth thus is not sufficient to achieve social prominence. It must be accompanied by a family history of public service and philanthropy, which is often manifested in tangible markers that enable these donors to achieve a kind of immortality (e.g., Rockefeller University, or the Whitney Museum).[53] "Old money" consumers tend to make distinctions among themselves in terms of ancestry and lineage rather than wealth.[55] The Jaguar ad shown here links the product to symbolic images of "old money" in the form of the English aristocracy and emphasis on "good breeding."

This Jaguar ad is intended to appeal to people who aspire to the "old money" class with its emphasis on good breeding and symbolic link to the English aristocracy.
Courtesy of Jaguar Cars Inc.

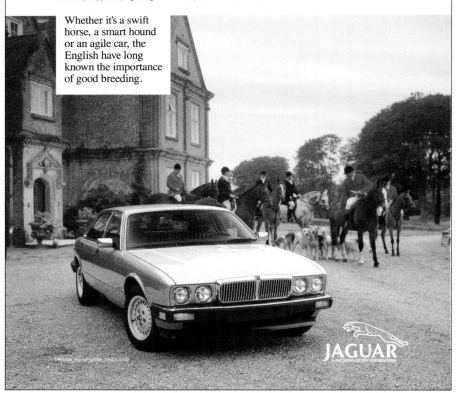

"Old money" consumers are often hard to identify. One commentator has called this group ". . . the class in hiding."[55] Following the Great Depression of the 1930s, monied families became more discreet about exhibiting their wealth, fleeing from mansions such as those found in Manhattan to hideaways in Virginia, Connecticut, and so on.

Old money people (like the Caldwells) are secure in their status. In a sense, they have been trained their whole lives to be rich. This group does not tend to be very interested in prominent displays of wealth: They can afford not to be. Surveys of "upper-affluent" Americans show that the wealthy downplay the importance of material goals and status. Less than 10 percent think owning a luxury car, antiques, or art is important, and only 7 percent believe that belonging to a prestigious club is worthwhile.[56] In addition, almost three-quarters describe themselves as thrifty and claim to shop at stores where a particular brand is cheapest.[57]

THE NOUVEAUX RICHES The Horatio Alger myth, where a person goes from "rags to riches" through hard work and a bit of luck, is still a powerful one in American society. Although many people do in fact become "self-made millionaires," they often encounter a problem after they have become wealthy and have changed their social status: They do not know how to be rich. Consumers who have achieved extreme wealth and relatively recently become members of upper social classes are known as the *nouveaux riches*, a term that is sometimes used in a derogatory manner to describe newcomers to the world of wealth.

MARKETING OPPORTUNITY

A California builder has a clear understanding of the needs of the *nouveaux riches*. He helps them to look like "old money." His company offers luxury homes that are completely furnished and outfitted to represent an idealized version of "the rich look."

The Tudor homes come complete with furniture, linens, and even stocked refrigerators. According to a description of these "packages," ". . . it is not just convenience [the builder] has to offer, it is security, the security that comes from knowing that the myriad inanimate objects that surround [the buyers] . . . from the Lenox china to the . . . Braun coffee makers are unmistakably appropriate to their place and station in the world." "People don't trust their own taste," says the builder.[58]

Status Anxiety. Many *nouveaux riches* are plagued by *status anxiety.* They monitor the cultural environment to ensure that they are doing the "right" thing, wearing the "right clothes," being seen at the "right" places (such as

The Trump Tower in Manhattan is a mecca for those who wish to engage in flamboyant consumption—and have the money to do so. © Ted - Thai/Sygma.

the Trump Tower in Manhattan shown in the photo here), using the "right" caterer, and so on.[59] Flamboyant consumption can thus be viewed as a form of symbolic self-completion, where the excessive display of symbols thought to denote "class" is used to make up for an internal lack of assurance about the "correct" way to behave (see Chapter 9). Advertising directed to this group often plays on these insecurities by emphasizing the importance of "looking the part." Clever merchandising supplies these consumers with the props necessary to masquerade by playing the role of old money people. For example, ads for *Colonial Homes* magazine feature consumers who ". . . have worked very hard to make it look like they never had to."

THE "GET SET" While the possession of wealth is clearly an important dimension of affluence, this quality may be as much determined by attitudes toward consumption as it is by level of income. Some marketers have identified a consumer segment composed of well-off, but not rich, people who desire the best products and services, even though they may have to be more selective about those items they are able to buy. These consumers are realistic about what they can afford and prefer to sacrifice in some areas so that they can have the best in others. Various advertising and marketing research agencies have labeled this segment with such terms as *Influentials*, the *New Grown-Ups*, and the *Get Set*. This group has been estimated to represent up to almost 70 percent of U.S. buying power.

While many upper-class brands tried in the past to downscale themselves to attract the mass market, there are some indications that this strategy is reversing. Because of the Get Set's emphasis on quality, one scenario is that marketers will encourage the masses to "buy up" into products associated with the upper classes, even if they are forced to buy less. A print campaign for Waterford Crystal exemplifies this approach. The theme line, "Steadfast in a world of wavering standards," is calculated to appeal to consumers who desire authenticity and lasting value.[60]

PROBLEMS WITH SOCIAL CLASS SEGMENTATION: A SUMMARY Social class remains an important way to categorize consumers. Many marketing strategies do target different social classes. However, marketers have failed to use social class information as effectively as they could for the following reasons:

- They have ignored status inconsistency.
- They have ignored intergenerational mobility.
- They have ignored subjective social class (i.e., the class a consumer identifies with rather than the one he or she objectively belongs to).
- They have ignored consumers' aspirations to change their class standing.
- They have ignored the social status of working wives.

The Quest for Status Symbols

People have a deep-seated tendency to evaluate themselves, their professional accomplishments, their material well-being, and so on, relative to others. The popular phrase "keeping up with the Joneses" (in Japan it's "keeping up with the Satos") refers to the comparison between one's standard of living and one's neighbors.

Satisfaction is a relative concept, however. We hold ourselves to a standard defined by others that is constantly changing. Unfortunately, a major motivation for the purchase and display of products is not to enjoy them, but rather to let others know that we can afford them. In other words, these products function as **status symbols**. The desire to accumulate these "badges of achievement" is summarized by the popular bumper sticker slogan: "He who dies with the most toys, wins."

International Example: The Japanese status craze is largely driven by the spending power of single women in their twenties. A typical clerical job pays about 170,000 yen per month (about $20,000 per year with bonus), but these consumers have a large amount of disposable income. They often live at home for free, and commuting costs are typically paid by their companies. As a result, they may be left with about 135,000 yen per year to spend on consumer goods. See "Japan's Consumer Boom: the Pricey Society," *The Economist* (September 9, 1989): 21.

MULTICULTURAL DIMENSIONS

Japan is a highly status-conscious society, where upscale, designer labels are quite popular, and new forms of status are always being sought. The quest for new symbols has reached the point where owning a traditional rock garden, formerly a vehicle for leisure and tranquillity, has become a sought-after item. Possession of a rock garden implies the presence of old money, since aristocrats traditionally were patrons of the arts. In addition, considerable assets are required to afford the required land in a country where real estate is extraordinarily costly. The scarcity of

land also helps to explain why the Japanese are fanatic golfers: Since a golf course takes up so much space, membership in a golf club is extremely valuable.[61]

Japanese consumers also place a high priority on the "snob appeal" of American and European products. For example, the status attached to acquiring the first taste of beaujolais nouveau wine from France each year has become a national obsession.[62] The frenzy to acquire expensive merchandise and Western culture has been dubbed the "prawns and Pavarotti phenomenon."[63]

CONSPICUOUS CONSUMPTION   The motivation to consume for the sake of consuming was first discussed by the social analyst Thorstein Veblen at the turn of the century. Veblen felt that a major role of products was for *invidious distinction*—they are used to inspire envy in others through display of wealth or power. Veblen coined the term **conspicuous consumption** to refer to people's desire to provide prominent visible evidence of their ability to afford luxury goods.

Veblen's work was motivated by the excesses of his time. He wrote in the era of the robber barons, where the likes of J.P. Morgan, Henry Clay Frick, William Vanderbilt, and others were building massive financial empires and flaunting their wealth by throwing lavish parties. Some of these events of excess became legendary, as described in this account:

> . . . there were tales, repeated in the newspapers, of dinners on horseback; of banquets for pet dogs; of hundred-dollar bills folded into guests' dinner napkins; of a hostess who attracted attention by seating a chimpanzee at her table; of centerpieces in which lightly clad living maidens swam in glass tanks, or emerged from huge pies; of parties at which cigars were ceremoniously lighted with flaming banknotes of large denominations.[64]

This flaunting of one's possessions even extended to wives: Veblen criticized the "decorative" role women were often forced to play as they were bestowed with expensive clothes, pretentious homes, and a life of leisure as a way to advertise the wealth of their husbands—a sort of "walking billboard." Such fashions as high-heeled shoes, tight corsets, billowing trains on dresses, and elaborate hairstyles all conspired to ensure that wealthy women could barely move without assistance, much less perform manual labor. Similarly, the Chinese practice of foot binding turned women into cripples, who had to be carried from place to place.

The Modern Potlach.   Veblen was inspired by anthropological studies of the Kwakiutl Indians, who lived in the Pacific Northwest. These Indians had a ceremony called a *potlach,* a feast where the host showed off his wealth and gave extravagant presents to the guests. The more one gave away, the better one looked to the others. Sometimes, the host would use an even more radical strategy to flaunt his wealth. He would publicly destroy some of his property to demonstrate how much he had.

This ritual was also used as a social weapon: Since guests were expected to reciprocate, a poorer rival could be humiliated by inviting him to a lavish potlach. The need to give away as much as the host, even though he could not afford it, would essentially force the hapless guest into bankruptcy. If this practice sounds "primitive," think for a moment about many modern weddings. Parents commonly invest huge sums of money to throw a lavish party and compete with others for the distinction of giving their daughter the "best" or most extravagant wedding, even if they have to save for twenty years to do it.

The Leisure Class.   This process of conspicuous consumption was, for Veblen, most evident among the *leisure class,* people for whom productive work is taboo. In Marxist terms, this reflects a desire to link oneself to ownership or control of the means of production, rather than to the production itself. Any evidence that one actually has to labor for a living is to be shunned, as suggested by the term the "idle rich."

Like the potlach ritual, the desire to convince others that one has a surplus of resources creates the need for evidence of this abundance. Accordingly, priority is given to consumption activities that use up as many resources as possible in non-constructive pursuits. This *conspicuous waste* in turn shows others that one has the assets to spare. Veblen noted that ". . . we are told of certain Polynesian chiefs, who, under the stress of good form, preferred to starve rather than carry their food to their mouths with their own hands."[65]

Many modern consumption practices can be understood in terms of conspicuous consumption. For example, this concept helps to explain how cultural ideals regarding desirable skin color for Caucasians have evolved over time. Despite medical warnings about skin cancer that are starting to force some "sun worshipers" to cut back on their exposure to the rays, the popularity of tanning products—and the willingness of many people to subject themselves to hours under ultraviolet lamps, as shown in the photo here—attests to the value Western culture places on a deep, dark tan. In fact, though, it is only recently that a tan has been valued, especially among women. Historically, women in Europe and America tried very hard to *avoid* any semblance of a tan: In the mid-1800s, they went so far as to paint their faces white![66]

Why the change? One explanation is that a tan results from excessive time spent outside. Traditionally the people who had to spend a lot of time out-of-doors were peasants toiling in the fields. A tan, therefore, was the sign of someone who worked for a living, and was thus avoided by those who did not. In the modern era, this trend is reversed. Since most people work inside, a tanned person is saying "I have the leisure time to sit outside and sun myself." Thus, a tan may be considered a form of conspicuous waste, since it is linked to sun-drenched beaches and trendy resorts. In our culture, then, a tan is in a sense a memento or souvenir of resources spent on leisure or nonconstructive activity. Indeed, the tanning salon industry may be said to owe its success to consumers' desires to pay for the illusion that they have idle time to soak up the sun.

Additional Example: Another contemporary example of conspicuous waste is the well-chronicled abuses of Imelda Marcos, the wife of the former Philippine ruler. Mrs. Marcos kept no less than 2700 pairs of shoes in her closets in Lalacanang Palace. See Lance Morrow, "The Shoes of Imelda Marcos," *Time* (March 31, 1986): 80.

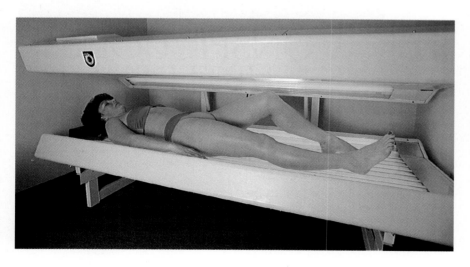

The tanning salon, or "electric beach," provides a quick way to obtain a tan, which is seen by many consumers as a status symbol conveying a life of leisure and wealth. © Tim Barnwell/Stock Boston

ARE STATUS SYMBOLS DEAD?   The use of material objects to display status is necessary in a large, anonymous society where reputation alone is insufficient to let people know who one is.[68] However, the ability of products to communicate status depends on their exclusivity. If too many people display the symbols, they lose their meaning. Indeed, a *need for uniqueness* is one important motivation for product choice.[69]

Fraudulent Symbolism.   Symbols that become too diffused are said to be **fraudulent symbols,** and their value becomes depleted, which creates a vacuum as new symbols are needed to differentiate the "in crowd" from the "masses.[9] This problem helps to explain the demise of "designer" products in

In a twist on conspicuous consumption, this ad for Halston jackets appeals to people who want to avoid the blatant display of status symbols. *Courtesy of Halston For Men Tailored Clothing.*

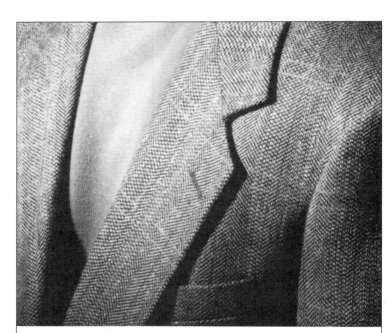

CONSPICUOUS SUBTLETY

One of the special fabrics that distinguishes Halston as being fashion conscious yet impeccably sensible clothing is Country Silk.™
Loomed in Scotland along the river Tweed this exclusive fabric is a unique blending of high quality wool and the best of silk.
Great weight, great feel, great looks and the perfect update of a classic sport coat by none other than Halston.

THE ONE LABEL YOU DON'T HAVE TO SEE TO KNOW IT'S THERE.

HALSTON
FOR MEN
1290 AVENUE OF THE AMERICAS, NEW YORK, N.Y. 10104 (212) 581 · 6510

the early to mid-1980s. While *signature goods* (e.g., designer jeans with someone's name written prominently on the rear end) were quite the rage for several years, their popularity eventually diminished because everyone wore them. They became exclusive clothing for the masses, a contradiction that could not last. For example, the designer Pierre Cardin alone has had more than 800 products licensed with his name.[70] As one consumer put it, "No more designer initials. Initials are in poor taste. Initials are tacky. The new thing is the uncluttered look. Dull, dull, dull, but chic, chic, chic."[71]

A survey by Grey Advertising categorized about 15 percent of the population as "UltraConsumers," people with a strong desire for ". . . luxury goods, go-go, and glitz."[72] A few years later, almost 60 percent of consumers fit into this category. More recent trends, however, indicate that people are, at least for now, satiated with status symbols. Another survey by a different agency found the three most popular status symbols to be running one's own business, international pleasure travel, and being the trustee of a cultural institution. This trend is illustrated by the tagline in the Halston ad shown here, which boasts of being "The one label you don't have to see to know it's there."

Parody Display. As the competition to accumulate status symbols escalates, sometimes the best tactic is to switch gears and go in reverse. One way to do this is to deliberately *avoid* status symbols—that is, to seek status by mocking it. This sophisticated form of conspicuous consumption has been termed **parody display**.[73] A good example of parody display is the home-furnishing style known as High Tech, which was in vogue a few years ago. This motif incorporated the use of industrial equipment (e.g., floors were covered with plates used on the decks of destroyers), and pipes and support beams were deliberately exposed.[74] This decorating strategy is intended to show that one is so witty and "in the know" that status symbols aren't necessary. Hence, the popularity of old, ripped blue jeans, and "utility" vehicles such as Jeeps among the upper classes. Thus, "true" status is shown by the adoption of product symbolism that is deliberately not fashionable.

Teaching Hint: There has been a sea-change in values regarding materialism from the 1980s to the 1990s. The construct of materialism as a social value will be further discussed in Chapter 16. While many marketers are moving toward simplicity, advertising for the upscale Charivari clothing stores bemoans this new trend and says: "Ripped jeans. Pocket Tees. Back to basics. Wake us up when it's over." Students can discuss whether it really is over: Is there still a market for status symbols? Is the yuppie (or some new incarnation) really dead?

MARKETING OPPORTUNITY

Since the products and activities that connote high status are always changing, a significant amount of marketing effort goes into educating consumers as to what specific symbols they should be displaying and to ensuring that a product is accepted in the pantheon of status symbols.

The need to display the "right" symbols has been a boon to the publishing industry, where a variety of "how-to books," magazines, and videos are available to school willing students of status. The concept of "dressing for success," where detailed instructions are provided to allow people to dress as if they are members of the upper middle class (at least the authors' versions of this) was one popular example.[75] This guidance has now spread to other areas of consumption, including "power lunching," (e.g., order "steak tartare" to intimidate your partner, since raw meat is a power food), office furnishings, and home decoration.

Chapter Summary

- The field of behavioral economics considers how consumers decide what to do with their money. In particular, *discretionary expenditures* are made only when people are able and willing to spend money on items above and beyond their basic needs. *Consumer confidence*—the state of mind consumers have about their own personal situation, as well as their feelings about their overall economic prospects—helps to determine whether they will purchase goods and services, take on debt, or save their money.

- In this decade, consumers overall have been relatively pessimistic about their future prospects. A lower level of resources has caused a shift toward an emphasis on quality products that are reasonably priced. Consumers are less tolerant of exaggerated or vague product claims, and they are more skeptical about marketing activities. Consumers in their twenties are particularly skeptical about the economy and marketing targeted to their age group.

- Virtually all groups make distinctions among members in terms of relative superiority, power, and access to valued resources. This *social stratification* creates a status hierarchy, where some goods are preferred over others and are used to categorize their owners' social class.

- A consumer's *social class* is determined by a number of factors, including education, occupation, and income.

- While income is an important indicator of social class, the relationship is far from perfect since social class is also determined by such factors as place of residence, cultural interests, and worldview.

- Purchase decisions are sometimes influenced by the desire to "buy up" to a higher social class or to engage in the process of *conspicuous consumption*, where one's status is flaunted by the deliberate and nonconstructive use of valuable resources. This spending pattern is a characteristic of the nouveaux riches, whose relatively recent acquisition of income, rather than ancestry or breeding, is responsible for their increased *social mobility*.

- Products often are used as status symbols to communicate real or desired social class. *Parody display* occurs when consumers seek status by deliberately avoiding fashionable products.

Key Terms

behavioral economics,
  p. 404

conspicuous consump-
  tion, p. 426

consumer confidence,
  p. 404

fraudulent symbols,
  p. 428

parody display, p. 429

social class, p. 407

social mobility, p. 410

social stratification,
  p. 409

status crystallization,
  p. 414

status hierarchy,
  p. 409

status symbols, p. 425

taste cultures, p. 417

Consumer Behavior Challenge

1. Sears, J.C. Penney, and, to a lesser degree, KMart, have made concerted efforts in recent years to upgrade their images and appeal to higher-class consumers. How successful have these efforts been? Do you believe this strategy is wise?

2. What are some of the obstacles to measuring social class in today's society? Discuss some ways to get around these obstacles.

3. What consumption differences might you expect to observe between a family characterized as underprivileged versus one whose income is average for its social class?

4. When is social class likely to be a better predictor of consumer behavior than mere knowledge of a person's income?

5. How do you assign people to social classes or do you? What consumption cues would you use (e.g., clothing, speech, cars, etc.) to determine social standing?

6. Thorstein Veblen argued that women were often used as a vehicle to display their husbands' wealth. Is this argument still valid today?

7. Given present environmental conditions and dwindling resources, what is the future of "conspicuous waste?" Can the desire to impress others with affluence ever be eliminated? If not, can it take on a less dangerous form?

8. Some people argue that status symbols are dead. Do you agree?

9. Using the Status Index presented in Figure 12–2, compute a social class score for people you know, including their parents if possible. Ask several friends (preferably from different places) to compile similar information for people they know. How closely do your answers compare? If you find differences, how can you explain them?

10. Compile a list of occupations, and ask a sample of students in a variety of majors (both business and nonbusiness) to rank the prestige of these jobs. Can you detect any differences in these rankings as a function of students' majors?

11. Compile a collection of ads that depict consumers of different social classes. What generalizations can you make about the reality of these ads and about the media in which they appear?

12. Identify a current set of fraudulent status symbols, and construct profiles of consumers who are wearing or using these products. Are these profiles consistent with the images portrayed in each product's promotional messages?

CNN Connection

CNN. A video segment is available to accompany this CNN Connection.

The Economy and Consumer Spending

For many consumers, decisions about what to buy now are based on what they think they can buy later. As discussed in the chapter, consumer confidence in the future of the economy is a vital determinant of current spending. If a consumer is optimistic about future prospects, money will flow freely for discretionary items. If that person is pessimistic, however, he or she may allocate the same income in very different ways.

Many American families have had to make big adjustments in their expectations during the recessionary period of the late 1980s and early 1990s. Even those who were not directly affected by the recession often displayed caution in the marketplace. More families took care to follow a budget and altered their leisure activities. A typical family might put more emphasis on eating at home, renting videos instead of going to the cinema, and perhaps be more receptive to bartering or pooling chores like babysitting with neighbors.

These alterations in the fabric of daily life are also felt by small business people, whose livelihoods are directly affected by consumer confidence. Retailers of many stripes have developed ways to tell if the economy is picking up or going into a downturn. Booksellers claim that people buy more fiction during a recession (to escape into fantasy?), restauranteurs see less weekday dinner traffic, and home appliance stores sell fewer big-ticket items. Although Government statistics give us the big picture, one need go no further than his or her own Main Street to really take the pulse of the economy.

SIMMONS Connection

SIMMONS Connection: Data for this exercise is on the Simmons Data Disk inside the back cover of your Instructor's Annotated Edition.

Data File: Index of Social Position

Phil seems a bit taken aback by the scene at his fiancee's parent's house. The understated style is a surprise to Phil, but it is often characteristic of "old money" families. As noted in this chapter, social class and income (or wealth) are not interchangeable. In many instances, consumers who possess equivalent levels of wealth exhibit striking differences in their buying behavior. As Phil discovered, different social class groups may be equally well-to-do, but may choose very different products and lifestyles.

The Simmons file for this chapter contains information about consumers' social class membership, which is the Simmons composite measure of Social Position. This index takes into account a person's occupation and their level of education. You will be able to compare the consumption patterns of different social class groups and compare these data to those of a high-income group (household income of more than $40,000.00).

If income alone was the most important determinant of what people consume, then we should not expect to find many differences between the top two or three social class categories (high-income groups) and consumers simply classified by their income (HHI of more than $40,000). What evidence do you find to support the idea that social class matters more than income alone? Which products are most "sensitive" to social class differences? Which are least sensitive? For each of these, explain why you think social class influences purchase decisions?

Hint: Simmon's uses a composite measure to capture social class information—the Index of Social Position. This index takes into account a person's occupation and their level of education. For example, someone with a graduate degree (MBA, Ph.D.) and employed as a high-level executive would fall into group I—highest social position. Someone who is a high-school graduate and who works in a semi-skilled occupation would fall into group IV. Figure 12–4 illustrates these five groups.

FIGURE 12–4 Groups I–V in the Simmons Index of Social Position

EDUCATION OF HOUSEHOLD HEAD

OCCUPATION OF HH HEAD	Graduate or Prof'l Training	College Graduate	Some College	High School Graduate	Some H.S. (10–11 Yrs)	Junior High School	8 Years or Less
Higher Executives / Major Professionals / Higher Proprietors	I (Upper Class)	II	II	II	II	III	III
Managers / Lesser Professionals / Large Proprietors	II	II	II	III	III	III	III
Administrators / Minor Professionals / Medium Proprietors / Large Farmers	II	III	III	III	III	IV	IV
Clerical/Sales Workers / Technicians / Small Proprietors / Medium Farmers	III	III	III	IV	IV	IV	IV
Skilled Workers / Small Farmers	III	III	IV	IV	IV	IV	V
Semi-Skilled Workers / Operators / Unskilled Workers	IV	IV	IV	IV	V	V	V
Homemakers / Students / Never Worked	IV	IV	V	V	V	V	V

Upper Middle Class • Lower Middle Class • Upper Lower Class • Lower Class

Notes

1. Fred van Raaij, "Economic Psychology," *Journal of Economic Psychology* 1 (1981): 1–24.
2. George Katona, "Consumer Saving Patterns," *Journal of Consumer Research* 1 (June 1974): 1–12.
3. Richard T. Curtin, "Indicators of Consumer Behavior: The University of Michigan Surveys of Consumers," *Public Opinion Quarterly* (1982): 340–352.
4. Joe Schwartz, "Hard Times Harden Consumers," *American Demographics* (May 1992): 10; "Today's Americans, in Tough Times and Beyond," in *Grey Matter Alert* (New York: Grey Advertising, Inc., 1991).
5. Cyndee Miller, "Sharper Image Revamps Product Line, Sells Items Consumers Can Actually Buy," *Marketing News* (May 11, 1992): 2.
6. Cyndee Miller, "Marketing to the Disillusioned," *Marketing News* (July 6, 1992)2: 6.
7. Floyd L. Ruch and Philip G. Zimbardo, *Psychology and Life,* 8th ed. (Glenview, Ill.: Scott Foresman, 1971).
8. Louise Do Rosario, "Privilege in China's Classless Society," *World Press Review* 33 (December 1986): 58.
9. Jonathan H. Turner, *Sociology: Studying the Human System*, 2nd ed. (Santa Monica, Calif.: Goodyear, 1981).
10. Turner, *Sociology*.
11. Richard P. Coleman, "The Continuing Significance of Social Class to Marketing," *Journal of Consumer Research* 10 (December 1983): 265–80; Turner, *Sociology*.
12. Quoted by Richard P. Coleman and Lee Rainwater, *Standing in America: New Dimensions of Class* (New York: Basic Books, 1978), 89.
13. Jil Curry, "One Year Later at J.C. Penney," *Chain Store Age—General Merchandise Trends* 63 (February 1987): 35.
14. Robin Knight, "Just You Move Over, 'Enry 'Iggins; A New Regard for Profits and Talent Cracks Britain's Old Class System," *U.S. News & World Report* 106 (April 24, 1989): 40.
15. Coleman and Rainwater, *Standing in America*.
16. Turner, *Sociology*.
17. James Fallows, "A Talent for Disorder (Class Structure)," *U.S. News & World Report* (February 1, 1988): 83.
18. Coleman, "The Continuing Significance of Social Class to Marketing"; W. Lloyd Warner with Paul S. Lunt, *The Social Life of a Modern Community* (New Haven, Conn.: Yale University Press, 1941).
19. Turner, *Sociology*, 260.
20. See Ronald Paul Hill and Mark Stamey, "The Homeless in America: An Examination of Possessions and Consumption Behaviors," *Journal of Consumer Research* 17 (December 1990): 303–21.
21. Joseph Kahl, *The American Class Structure* (New York: Holt, Rinehart and Winston, 1961).
22. Beeghley, *Social Stratification in America.*
23. Coleman and Rainwater, *Standing in America,* 220.
24. Turner, *Sociology*.
25. See Coleman "The Continuing Significance of Social Class to Marketing"; Charles M. Schaninger, "Social Class Versus Income Revisited: An Empirical Investigation," *Journal of Marketing Research* 18 (May 1981): 192–208.
26. Coleman, "The Continuing Significance of Social Class to Marketing."
27. August B. Hollingshead and Fredrick C. Redlich, *Social Class and Mental Illness: A Community Study* (New York: John Wiley, 1958).
28. Leonard Beeghley, *Social Stratification in America: A Critical Analysis of Theory and Research* (Santa Monica, Calif.: Goodyear, 1978).
29. R. Vanneman and F.C. Pampel, "The American Perception of Class and Status," *American Sociological Review* 42 (June 1977): 422–37.
30. Donald W. Hendon, Emelda L. Williams, and Douglas E. Huffman, "Social Class System Revisited," *Journal of Business Research* 17 (November 1988): 259.
31. Coleman, "The Continuing Significance of Social Class to Marketing."
32. Gerhard E. Lenski, "Status Crystallization: A Non-Vertical Dimension of Social Status," *American Sociological Review* 19 (August 1954): 405–12.
33. Richard P. Coleman, "The Significance of Social Stratification in Selling," in *Marketing: A Maturing Discipline, Proceedings of the American Marketing Association 43rd National Conference,* ed. Martin L. Bell (Chicago: American Marketing Association, 1960), 171–84.
34. Melinda Beck and Richard Sandza, "The Lottery Craze: Multimillion-Dollar Prizes Raise New Concerns That the Games Prey on the Poor," *Newsweek* (September 2, 1985): 16; Rhoda E. McKinney, "Has Money Spoiled the Lottery Millionaires," *Ebony* (December 1988): 150.
35. E. Barth and W. Watson, "Questionable Assumptions in the Theory of Social Stratification," *Pacific Sociological Review* 7 (Spring 1964): 10–16.
36. Zick Rubin, "Do American Women Marry Up?" *American Sociological Review* 33 (1968): 750–60.
37. Sue Browder, "Don't be Afraid to Marry Down," *Cosmopolitan* (June 1987): 236.
38. K.U. Ritter and L.L. Hargens, "Occupational Positions and Class Identifications of Married Working Women: A Test of the Asymmetry Hypothesis," *American Journal of Sociology* 80 (January 1975): 934–48.
39. Browder, "Don't Be Afraid to Marry Down": 236.
40. J. Michael Munson and W. Austin Spivey, "Product and Brand-User Stereotypes Among Social Classes: Implications for Advertising Strategy," *Journal of Advertising Research* 21 (August 1981): 37–45.

41. Stuart U. Rich and Subhash C. Jain, "Social Class and Life Cycle as Predictors of Shopping Behavior," *Journal of Marketing Research* 5 (February 1968): 41–49.

42. Thomas W. Osborn, "Analytic Techniques for Opportunity Marketing," *Marketing Communications* (September 1987): 49–63.

43. Coleman, "The Continuing Significance of Social Class to Marketing."

44. Jeffrey F. Durgee, "How Consumer Sub-Cultures Code Reality: A Look at Some Code Types," in *Advances in Consumer Research* 13, ed. Richard J. Lutz (Provo, Utah: Association for Consumer Research, 1986), 332–37.

45. David Halle, *America's Working Man: Work, Home, and Politics Among Blue-Collar Owners* (Chicago: The University of Chicago Press, 1984); David Montgomery, "America's Working Man," *Monthly Review* (1985): 1.

46. Quoted in Coleman and Rainwater, *Standing in America*, 139.

47. Durkheim (1958) quoted in Roger Brown, *Social Psychology* (New York: The Free Press, 1965).

48. Lenore Skenazy, "Affluent, Like Masses, Are Flush with Worries," *Advertising Age* (July 10, 1989): 55.

49. Herbert J. Gans, "Popular Culture in America: Social Problem in a Mass Society or Social Asset in a Pluralist Society?" in *Social Problems: A Modern Approach*, ed. Howard S. Becker (New York: Wiley, 1966).

50. Edward O. Laumann and James S. House, "Living Room Styles and Social Attributes: The Patterning of Material Artifacts in a Modern Urban Community," *Sociology and Social Research* 54 (April 1970): 321–42; see also Stephen S. Bell, Morris B. Holbrook, and Michael R. Solomon, "Combining Esthetic and Social Value to Explain Preferences for Product Styles With the Incorporation of Personality and Ensemble Effects," *Journal of Social Behavior and Personality* (1991)6: 243–74.

51. "Reading the Buyer's Mind," *U.S. News & World Report* (March 16, 1987): 59.

52. Paul Fussell, *Class: A Guide Through the American Status System* (New York: Summit Books, 1983), 29.

53. Elizabeth C. Hirschman, "Secular Immortality and the American Ideology of Affluence," *Journal of Consumer Research* 17 (June 1990): 31–42.

54. Coleman and Rainwater, *Standing in America*, 150.

55. Fussell, *Class*, 30.

56. Bickley Townsend, "What the Rich are Like," *American Demographics* (December 1987): 16.

57. Monica Gonzales, "Bargain Hunters," *American Demographics* (June 1989): 21.

58. Jerry Adler, "For Sale: The Rich Look," *Newsweek* (June 22, 1987): 80.

59. Jason DeParle, "Spy Anxiety; The Smart Magazine That Makes Smart People Nervous About Their Standing," *Washingtonian Monthly* (February 1989): 10.

60. Dennis Rodkin, "Wealthy Attitude Wins Over Healthy Wallet: Consumers Prove Affluence is a State of Mind," *Advertising Age* (July 9, 1990): S-4.

61. James Sterngold, "How Do You Define Status? A New BMW in the Drive. An Old Rock in the Garden," *New York Times* (December 28, 1989): C1.

62. David E. Sanger, "Japan Drinks Up France, with a Beaujolais Chaser," *New York Times* (November 17, 1989): A4.

63. "Japan's Consumer Boom: The Pricey Society," *The Economist* (September 9, 1989): 21.

64. John Brooks, *Showing Off in America* (Boston: Little, Brown, 1981), 13.

65. Thorstein Veblen, *The Theory of the Leisure Class* (1899; reprint, New York: New American Library, 1953), 45.

66. Lois W. Banner, *American Beauty* (Chicago, Ill.: University of Chicago Press, 1983).

67. Scott Dawson and Jill Cavell, "Status Recognition in the 1980's: Invidious Distinction Revisited," in *Advances in Consumer Research* 14, eds. Melanie Wallendorf and Paul Anderson (Provo, Utah: Association for Consumer Research, 1986), 487–91; William H. Form and Gregory P. Stone, "Urbanism, Anonymity, and Status Symbolism," *American Journal of Sociology* 62 (1957): 504–14; Erving Goffman, "Symbols of Class Status," *British Journal of Sociology* 2 (December 1951): 294–304; Georg Simmel, "Fashion," *Journal of Sociology* 62 (1904): 120–55.

68. C.R. Snyder and H.L. Fromkin, *Uniqueness: The Human Pursuit of Difference* (New York: Plenum Press, 1980).

69. Dawson and Cavell, "Status Recognition in the 1980's"; Goffman, "Symbols of Class Status."

70. Caroline Rennolds Milbank, "When Your Own Initials Are Not Enough: A Brief History of Status Symbols," *Avenue* (October 1990): 63.

71. Ron Alexander, "In the Mutable World of Chic, Designers' Initials Are Out, Simplicity Is In," *New York Times* (May 21, 1989): 54.

72. Alexander, "In the Mutable World of Chic, Designers' Initials Are Out, Simplicity Is In."

73. Brooks, *Showing Off in America*.

74. Brooks, *Showing Off in America*, 31–32.

75. For examples, see John T. Molloy, *Dress For Success* (New York: Warner Books, 1975); Vicki Keltner and Mike Holsey, *The Success Image* (Houston, Tex.: Gulf Publishing, 1982); and William Thourlby, *You Are What You Wear* (New York: New American Library, 1978).

CHAPTER 13

Lifestyles

Buying, Having, and Being: Selections 45–49 from *Buying, Having, and Being: The Washington Post Consumer Behavior Companion*, Second Edition, accompany this chapter.

J ackie and Hank are second-year associates in a high-powered Washington law firm. After a particularly grueling week, they are both looking forward to a well-deserved Sunday off (a rare occurrence).

Jackie is enthusiastically telling Hank about his plans. Since he no longer gets up early to work out every morning, he's going to sleep late in his new downtown condo. Then he's planned a luxurious, high-cholesterol champagne brunch with that lobbyist he's been dating. From there, it's on to the Kennedy Center for a matinee of *La Traviata* and a relaxed dinner at that new sushi bar he's heard so much about.

Hank just chuckles to himself: While Jackie's wasting his time at some opera, *he's* going to pop his new Randy Travis tape in the cassette player of his Trans Am and drive out to the Virginia countryside. He'll be spending the first half of the day in a duck blind. By four o'clock, he plans to be comfortably planted in front of the TV in his new Barcalounger to watch the Redskins beat the stuffing out of the Cowboys—an ideal "couch potato" afternoon!

Hank is sometimes amazed at how different he is from Jackie, who fancies himself a real urban sophisticate. They make the same salary and do almost identical things on the job all week long. How can their tastes be so different when it comes to the weekend? Oh well, Hank sighs to himself, that's why they make chocolate and vanilla . . . .

Lifestyles and Consumption Choices

Jackie and Hank strongly resemble one another demographically. They were both raised in middle-class households, have similar educational backgrounds, are about the same age, and they share the same occupation and income. However, as their leisure choices show, it would be a big mistake to assume that their consumption choices are similar as well. Jackie and Hank each choose products, services, and activities that help them define a unique *lifestyle*. This chapter first explores how marketers approach the issue of lifestyle and then how they use information about these consumption choices to tailor products and communications to individual lifestyle segments.

In traditional or collective societies, one's consumption options are largely dictated by class, caste, village, or family. In a modern consumer society, however, people are more free to select the set of products, services, and activities that define themselves and, in turn, create a social identity that is communicated to others. One's choice of goods and services indeed makes a statement about who one is and about the types of people with which one desires to identify.

Lifestyle can be described in terms of shared values or tastes, especially as these are reflected in consumption patterns. Lifestyle marketing recognizes that people sort themselves into groups on the basis of the things they like to do, how they like to spend their leisure time, and how they choose to spend their disposable income.[1] These choices in turn create opportunities for market segmentation strategies that recognize the potency of a consumer's chosen lifestyle in determining both the types of products purchased and the specific brands more likely to appeal to a designated lifestyle segment.

The Value of Lifestyle Marketing

Consumers often choose products, services, and activities over others because they are associated with a certain lifestyle. For this reason, lifestyle marketing strategies attempt to position a product by fitting it into this pattern of consumption. As an example of the power of this approach, take the case of Subaru. When this car manufacturer entered the U.S. market in the early 1970s, it had virtually no name recognition and struggled to compete with other, better-known imports. Subaru became the official car of the U.S. ski team and linked itself to the lifestyles of people who enjoy skiing. The company now has the highest market share for imports in several Snow Belt states.[2]

Because a goal of lifestyle marketing is to allow consumers to pursue their chosen ways to enjoy their lives and express their social identities, a key aspect of this strategy is to focus on product usage in social situations (see Chapter 10). The goal of associating a product with a social situation is a long-standing one for advertisers, whether the product is included in a round of golf, a family barbecue, or a night at a glamorous disco surrounded by "jetsetters."[3] Thus people, products, and settings are combined to express a certain consumption style, as diagrammed in Figure 13–1.

Lifestyle and Self-Definition

In an economic sense, one's lifestyle represents the way one has elected to allocate income, both in terms of relative allocations to different products and services and to specific alternatives within these categories.[4] Other somewhat similar distinctions have been made to describe consumers in terms of their broad patterns of consumption, such as those differentiating consumers by social class in terms of those who devote a high proportion of total expenditures to food, advanced technology, or to such information-intensive goods as entertainment and education.[5]

Additional Example: Recognizing that horse owners tend to have money, Chase Manhattan attempted its own version of lifestyle marketing by tapping directly into the "horsey set" with its Equine Card. In addition to a special credit card, this lifestyle marketing program included horse insurance, a newsletter, and equipment discounts. See Chester A. Swenson, "How to Sell to a Segmented Market," *Journal of Business Strategy* 9 (January–February 1988): 18.

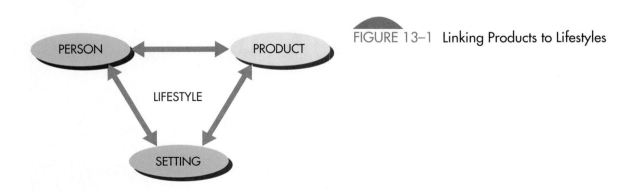

FIGURE 13–1 Linking Products to Lifestyles

These economic approaches are useful in tracking changes in broad societal priorities, but they do not begin to embrace the symbolic nuances that separate lifestyle groups. Lifestyle is more than the allocation of discretionary income. It is a statement about who one is in society and who one is not. Group identities, whether of hobbyists, athletes, or drug users, gel around forms of expressive symbolism. The self-definitions of group members are derived from the common symbol system to which the group is dedicated.

Such self-definitions have been described by a number of terms, including *lifestyle, taste public, consumer group, symbolic community*, and *status culture*.[6] The recreational vehicle ad shown here demonstrates how a market segment is defined by a particular allocation of time and money to a leisure activity. The ad's claim that the RV dealer has the product that ". . . says you're you!" implies that dedicated RVers derive a significant portion of their self-identities from the activities associated with this lifestyle.

This ad for Jayco motor homes targets a specific lifestyle segment and emphasizes self-identity, which is often derived from activities associated with a particular lifestyle. Courtesy of Jayco, Inc.

This GE ad features the principles of consumption constellations, in which complementary products from many different categories are integrated into a unified whole. Reproduced with permission of the copyright owner, General Electric Company.

Product Complementarity

Use of the term *lifestyle* implies that we must look at *patterns* of behavior to understand consumers. In many cases, products do not seem to "make sense" if unaccompanied by companion products (e.g., fast food and paper plates or a suit and tie) or are incongruous in the presence of others (e.g., a Chippendale chair in a high-tech office or Lucky Strike cigarettes with a solid gold lighter). As one study noted, ". . . all goods carry meaning, but none by itself . . . . The meaning is in the relations between all the goods, just as music is in the relations marked out by the sounds and not in any one note."[7] Interior designers rely on this principle when choosing items to furnish a room. A specific decorating *style* involves integrating products from many different categories—such as appliances, furnishings, knick-knacks, and even artwork—into a unified whole, as does the GE ad shown here.

Product complementarity occurs when the symbolic meanings of different products are related to each other.[8] These sets of products, termed **consumption constellations**, are used by consumers to define, communicate, and perform social roles.[9] For example, the American "Yuppie" of the 1980s was defined by such products as a Rolex watch, BMW automobile, Gucci briefcase, a squash racket, fresh pesto, white wine, and brie. Somewhat similar constellations could be found for "Sloane Rangers" in the United Kingdom and "Bon Chic bon Genres" in France. While people today take pains to avoid being classified as yuppies, this social role had a major influence on defining cultural values and consumption priorities in the 1980s.[10]

Consumption as a Goal

Members of "cargo cults" in the South Pacific literally worshipped cargo that was salvaged from crashed aircraft or washed ashore from ships. These people believed that these ships and planes were piloted by their ancestors, and they tried to attract them to their villages. During World War II, they went so far as to construct fake planes from straw in hopes of luring real ones.[11] While not everyone literally worships material goods in this way, things do play a central role in many people's lives. **Materialism** refers to the importance people attach to worldly possessions. Americans inhabit a highly materialistic society where people often gauge the worth of themselves and others in terms of how much they own.

We sometimes take the existence of an abundance of products and services for granted, until we remember how recent many of these developments are. For example, in 1950 two of five American homes did not have a telephone, and in 1940 half of all households still did not possess complete indoor plumbing. In contrast, many Americans now energetically seek "the good life," which abounds in material comforts. About 40 percent of households have two or more cars, and over $200 billion is spent on vacations in a year.[12] Advertising encourages this emphasis on consumption and increasingly portrays consumption as an end in itself, rather than as a means to attain well-being.[13]

The living standard of Europeans has also considerably increased in recent years. A Gallup study of 22,500 adults in 17 European countries found that ownership of such items as microwave ovens, VCRs, and cellular phones has "exploded" in recent years. And, 70 percent of European women are now using deodorant, which is a relatively new practice in many countries.[14]

INDIVIDUAL DIFFERENCES   Of course, not everyone stresses the value of materialism to the same degree. Individual differences have been found among consumers in terms of this emphasis. One approach partitions the value of materialism into three categories: success, centrality, and happiness.[15] The scale items used to measure these categories are shown in Table 13–1.

The Coca-Cola Invasion: Exporting Western Lifestyles

It is not unusual for cultures to borrow products, ideas, and symbols from each other, as the following examples illustrate.[16]

- In Peru, Indian boys can be found carrying rocks painted to look like transistor radios.
- In highland Papua New Guinea, tribesmen put Chivas Regal wrappers on their drums and wear Pentel pens instead of nosebones.
- Bana tribesmen in the remote highlands of Kako, Ethiopia, pay to watch "Pluto the Circus Dog" on a Viewmaster.
- When a Swazi princess marries a Zulu king, she wears red touraco wing feathers around her forehead and a cape of windowbird feathers and

TABLE 13-1   A Scale to Measure Categories of Materialism

Category	Scale Items
Success	• I admire people who own expensive homes, cars, and clothes. • Some of the most important achievements in life include acquiring material possessions. • I don't put much emphasis on the amount of material objects people own as a sign of success.* • The things I own say a lot about how well I'm doing in life. • I like to own things that impress people. • I don't pay much attention to the material objects other people own.*
Centrality	• I usually buy only the things I need.* • I try to keep my life simple, as far as possessions are concerned.* • The things I own aren't all that important to me.* • I enjoy spending money on things that aren't practical. • Buying things gives me a lot of pleasure. • I like a lot of luxury in my life. • I put less emphasis on material things than most people I know.*
Happiness	• I have all the things I really need to enjoy life.* • My life would be better if I owned certain things I don't have. • I wouldn't be any happier if I owned nicer things.* • I'd be happier if I could afford to buy more things. • It sometimes bothers me quite a bit that I can't afford to buy all the things I'd like.

Note: Respondents indicate whether they agree or disagree with each item on a 5-point scale. Items with an asterisk are reverse scored.

Source: Adapted from Marsha L. Richins and Scott Dawson, "A Consumer Values Orientation for Materialism and Its Measurement: Scale Development and Validation," *Journal of Consumer Research* 20 (December 1992), Table 3. Reprinted with permission of The University of Chicago Press.

---

oxtails. He is wrapped in a leopard skin. All is recorded on a Kodak movie camera while the band plays "The Sound of Music."

• In addition to traditional gifts of cloth, food, and cosmetics, Nigerian Hausa brides receive cheap quartz watches although they cannot tell time.

As indicated by these examples, many formerly remote cultures now incorporate Western objects into their traditional practices. In the process, the meanings of these objects are transformed and adapted to local tastes (at times in seemingly bizarre ways). Sometimes the process enriches local cultures, sometimes it produces painful stresses and strains the local fabric.

The West (and especially the United States) is a *net exporter* of popular culture. Western symbols in the form of images, words, and products have diffused throughout the world. This influence is eagerly sought by many consumers, who have learned to equate Western lifestyles in general and the English language in particular with modernization and sophistication.

Cross-Cultural Example:
Many Mexicans are upset by the creeping Americanization of their native culture. As evidence that the country is caught up in a wave of Americana, consider that the best-selling pinata figure is not of the traditional burro, but rather of Bart Simpson. See Tim Padgett, "The Gringos are Coming!" *Newsweek* (November 30, 1992): 55.

Foreign sales account for 70 percent of the revenues for the $20 billion a year American music business, and European networks buy about $600 million a year of American television (although it is important to realize that at this point, much of the American record and movie industries are in fact owned by foreign interests).[17]

Consumers in smaller, developing countries generally prefer products from established foreign producers and will often pay a premium for these items.[18] Chinese women, for example, are starting to demand Western cosmetics costing up to a quarter of their salaries, ignoring domestically produced competitors. As one Chinese executive noted, "Some women even buy a cosmetic just because it has foreign words on the package."[19]

Although a third of the world's countries have a per capita gross national product of less than $500, even poor Third World countries are influenced by images in Western media touting the virtue of elaborate consumption. For example, consider how the material expectations of consumers in the People's Republic of China have escalated. Twenty years ago, the Chinese strove to attain what they called the "three bigs": bikes, sewing machines, and wristwatches. This wish list was later modified to become the "new big six," adding refrigerators, washing machines, and televisions. At last count, the ideal is now the "eight new things." The list now includes *color* televisions, cameras, and video recorders.[20]

Mainland China is one of the newest markets to be opened up to American business and culture. Chinese television now carries commercials for the likes of Coca-Cola, Tang, and Contac cold capsules. Procter & Gamble manufactures goods like Pantene shampoo and Oil of Ulan locally (known as Oil of Olay in the United States). McDonald's recently opened a restaurant in Beijing that is the largest of its outlets in the world (and the only one with a Communist Party secretary). It has more than 700 seats and nearly 1000 employees, a few of whom are shown in the photo here. Many competed for these highly valued positions that are perceived to offer prestige and upward mobility.[21]

The casual American lifestyle being exported all over the world is exemplified by the McDonald's in Beijing, which seats over 700 people and has nearly 1000 employees who vied for positions in the chain's largest outlet. © Kees/Sygma.

This movie poster promotes the Tom Cruise film *Far and Away* to Japanese, who are huge fans of American popular culture. © Jeffrey Aaronson/Aspen Network.

The Japanese are particularly enthusiastic borrowers of Western culture. American music and movies are especially popular, perhaps because they strongly represent U.S. lifestyles and popular culture. In the photo shown here, a young couple is attracted to a poster advertising the American movie *Far and Away* in Japanese.

The Japanese often use Western words as a shorthand for anything new and exciting, even if they do not understand their meaning. The resulting phenomenon is known as "Japlish," where new Western sounding words are merged with Japanese. Cars are given names like Fairlady, Gloria, and Bongo Wagon. Consumers buy deodoranto (deodorant) and appuru pai (apple pie). Ads urge shoppers to stoppu rukku (stop and look), and products are claimed to be yuniku (unique).[22] English phrases often are used in puzzling ways. Coca-Cola cans say "I feel Coke & sound special," and a company called Cream Soda sells products with the slogan "Too old to die, too young to happy."[23]

CREEPING AMERICANISM: A NEGATIVE BACKLASH Some critics deplore the creeping Americanization of their cultures. Debates continue in Europe on the imposition of quotas that limit American television programming.[24] In Brazil, the most popular performing artist is a blond woman named Xuxa, who is backed by the Paquitas—seven girls with golden hair—and some Brazilians have expressed concern that their national idol is blond, even though the majority of her admirers clearly are not.[25]

The French have been the most outspoken opponents of creeping Americanization. They have banned the use of such English terms as *le drugstore, le fast food,* and even *le marketing.*[26] The French debate over Americanization was brought to a head by the 1992 opening of Euro Disney in a Paris suburb. In addition to the usual attractions, hotels with names like The Hotel New York, The Newport Bay Club, and The Hotel Cheyenne attempt to recreate portions of America. One critic described the theme park as "a horror made of cardboard, plastic, and appalling colors—a construction of hardened chewing gum and idiotic folklore taken straight out of comic book written for obese Americans."[27] The Disney organization appears to be unfazed by such criticism; the park expects to attract about 11 million visitors a year.

M A R K E T I N G   P I T F A L L

Cigarettes are among the most successful of Western exports. Asian consumers alone spend $90 billion a year on cigarettes, and U.S. tobacco manufacturers continue to push relentlessly into these markets. Cigarette advertising, often depicting glamorous Western models and settings, is found just about everywhere, on billboards, buses, storefronts, and clothing, and many major sports and cultural events are sponsored by tobacco companies. Some companies even hand out cigarettes and gifts in amusement areas, often to pre-teens.

A few countries have taken steps to counteract this form of Westernization. Singapore bans all promotions that mention a product's name. Hong Kong has prohibited cigarette ads from appearing on radio and TV. Japan and South Korea do not allow ads to appear in women's magazines. Industry executives argue that they are simply competing in markets that do little to discourage smoking (e.g., Japan issues health warnings like "Please don't smoke too much"), often against heavily-subsidized local brands with names like Long Life (Taiwan). The warnings and restrictions are likely to increase, however; smoking-related deaths have now overtaken communicable diseases for the "honor" of being Asia's #1 killer.[28]

Psychographics

Consider a marketer who wishes to target a student population. She identifies her ideal consumer as "a twenty-one-year-old senior marketing major living on a large university campus whose parents make between $30,000 and $60,000 per year." You may know a lot of people who fit this description. Do you think they are all the same? Would they all be likely to share common interests and buy the same products? Probably not, since their lifestyles are likely to differ considerably.

Knowledge of a market's demographics is essential to devising efficient marketing strategies (see Chapter 8). In many cases, however, these objec-

This ad for cable television underscores the vast differences in tastes and preferences among market segments and promotes the value of lifestyle segmentation. Courtesy of National Cable Television Association (NCTA).

tive characteristics are not sufficient to fine-tune strategies. As Jackie and Hank's lifestyle choices demonstrated, consumers can share the same demographic characteristics and still be very different people.

To "breathe life" into demographics, marketers turn to **psychographics**, which involves the ". . . use of psychological, sociological, and anthropological factors . . . to determine how the market is segmented by the propensity of groups within the market—and their reasons—to make a particular decision about a product, person, ideology, or otherwise hold an attitude or use a medium."[29] The cable television ad shown here promotes the value of tailoring messages to the tastes of specific market segments.

Psychographic research was developed in the 1960s and 1970s to address the shortcomings of two other types of consumer research: motivational research and quantitative survey research. *Motivational research*, which involves intensive one-to-one interviews and projective tests, yields a lot of information about a few people. The information, however, is often idiosyncratic and not very useful or reliable. At the other extreme, *quantitative survey research*, or large-scale demographic surveys, yields only a little information about a lot of people. As some researchers observed, ". . . The marketing manager who wanted to know why people ate the competitor's cornflakes was told '32 percent of the respondents said taste, 21 percent said flavor, 15 percent said texture, 10 percent said price, and 22 percent said don't know or no answer'."[29]

In many applications, the term psychographics is used interchangeably with lifestyle to denote the separation of consumers into categories based on differences in choices of consumption activities and product usage. To better understand psychographic factors, BBDO Worldwide uses a technique called Photosort, where consumers express their feelings about a brand by associating it with pictures of different types of people who they expect would use it. When the agency used the technique for General Electric, it found that respondents felt the brand was likely to be used by conservative, older people. To counteract that perception, GE developed its "Bring Good Things to Life" campaign. The Leo Burnett Agency has developed a technique called the Emotional Lexicon, which segments consumers in terms of the emotions elicited by different products.

While there are many psychographic variables that can be used to segment consumers, they all share the underlying principle of going beyond surface characteristics to understand consumers' motivations for purchasing and using products. Demographics allow us to describe *who* buys, but psychographics allow us to understand *why* they do.

Conducting a Psychographic Analysis

Some early attempts at lifestyle segmentation "borrowed" standard psychological scales (often used to measure pathology or personality disturbances) and tried to relate scores on these tests to product usage. As might be expected, such efforts were largely disappointing (see Chapter 9). These tests were never intended to be related to everyday consumption activities and yielded little in the way of explanation for purchase behaviors. The technique is more effective when the variables included are more closely related to actual consumer behaviors. If you want to understand purchases of household cleaning products, you are better off asking people about their attitudes toward household cleanliness than testing for personality disorders.

Most contemporary psychographic research attempts to group consumers according to some combination of three categories of variables—Activities, Interests, and Opinions—which are known as **AIOs.** Using data from large samples, marketers create profiles of customers who resemble each other in terms of their activities and patterns of product usage.[30] Some typical dimensions used to assess lifestyle are listed in Table 13–2. Typically, people are given a long list of statements and are asked to indicate how much they agree with each one. Lifestyle is thus "boiled down" by discovering how people spend their time, what they find interesting and important, and how they view themselves and the world around them, as well as demographic information.

Typically, the first step in conducting a psychographic analysis is to determine which lifestyle segments are producing the bulk of customers for a particular product. According to a very general rule of thumb frequently used in marketing research, the **20/80 rule,** only 20 percent of a product's users account for 80 percent of the volume of product sold. Researchers attempt to determine who uses the brand and try to isolate heavy, moder-

TABLE 13–2 Lifestyle Dimensions

Activities	Interests	Opinions	Demographics
Work	Family	Themselves	Age
Hobbies	Home	Social issues	Education
Social events	Job	Politics	Income
Vacation	Community	Business	Occupation
Entertainment	Recreation	Economics	Family size
Club membership	Fashion	Education	Dwelling
Community	Food	Products	Geography
Shopping	Media	Future	City size
Sports	Achievements	Culture	Stage in life cycle

Source: William D. Wells and Douglas J. Tigert, "Activities, Interests, and Opinions," *Journal of Advertising Research* 11 (August 1971): 27–35. ©1971 by The Advertising Research Foundation.

ate, and light users. They also look for patterns of usage and attitudes toward the product. In many cases, just a few lifestyle segments account for the majority of brand users.[31] Marketers primarily target these heavy users, even though they may constitute a relatively small number of total users.

After the heavy users are identified and understood, the brand's relationship to them is considered. Not all heavy users are the same. They may have quite different reasons for using the product. For instance, marketers at the beginning of the walking shoe craze assumed that purchasers were basically burned-out joggers. Subsequent psychographic research showed that there were actually several different groups of "walkers," ranging from those who walk to get to work to those who walk for fun. This realization resulted in shoes aimed at different segments, from Footjoy Joy-Walkers to Nike Healthwalkers.

USES OF PSYCHOGRAPHIC SEGMENTATION Psychographic segmentation can be used in a variety of ways.

- *To define the target market:* This information allows the marketer to go beyond simple demographic or product usage descriptions (e.g., middle-aged men or frequent users).

- *To create a new view of the market:* Sometimes marketers create their strategies with a "typical" customer in mind. This stereotype may not be correct because the actual customer may not match these assumptions. For example, marketers of a facial cream for women were surprised to find their key market was composed of older, widowed women rather than the younger, more sociable women to whom they were pitching their appeals.

- *To position the product:* Psychographic information can allow the marketer to emphasize features of the product that fit in with a person's lifestyle. Products targeted to people whose lifestyle profiles show a high need to be around other people might focus on the product's ability to help meet this social need.

- *To better communicate product attributes:* Psychographic information can offer very useful input to advertising creatives who must communicate something about the product. The artist or writer obtains a much richer mental image of the target consumer than that obtained through dry statistics, and this insight improves his or her ability to "talk" to that consumer. For example, research conducted for Schlitz beer found that heavy beer drinkers tended to feel that life's pleasures were few and far between. Commercials were developed using the theme that told these drinkers: "You only go around once, so reach for all the gusto you can."[32]

- *To develop overall strategy:* Understanding how a product fits, or does not fit, into consumers' lifestyles allows the marketer to identify new product opportunities, chart media strategies, and create environments most consistent and harmonious with these consumption patterns.

- *To market social and political issues:* Psychographic segmentation can be an important tool in political campaigns and can also be employed to find commonalities among types of consumers who engage in destructive behaviors, such as drug use or excessive gambling.

Psychographics and Social Marketing. A psychographic study of men aged 18 to 24 who drink and drive highlights the potential for this perspective to help in the eradication of harmful behaviors. This demographic segment accounts for a disproportionately high share of alcohol-related fatalities. Researchers divided this segment into four groups: "good timers," "well adjusted," "nerds," and "problem kids." They found that one group in particular—"good timers"—is more likely to believe that it is fun to be drunk, that the chances of having an accident while driving drunk are low, and that drinking increases one's appeal to the opposite sex. Since the study showed that this group is also the most likely to drink at rock concerts and parties, is most likely to watch MTV, and tends to listen to album-oriented rock radio stations, reaching "good timers" with a prevention campaign is easier and more efficient.[34]

MULTICULTURAL ⟨⟩ DIMENSIONS

A cross-country psychographic segmentation project conducted jointly by the Ogilvy and Mather advertising agency and an Australian research firm resulted in ten segments, including such categories as "basic needs" (traditional and passive), "look-at-me" (seek exciting and prosperous life), "visible achievement" (traditional values, seek "the good life"), "socially aware" (involved in environmental movements), and "fairer deal" (dissatisfied with their lives). Relatively few Australians were in the "visible achievement" segment, while high numbers of consumers in the United States, Canada, and Japan were. A disproportionate number of British consumers fell into the "fairer deal" group, while Germans were overrepresented in the "look-at-me" segment.[33]

The R.J. Reynolds Company introduced a new brand of cigarettes called Dakota in several test markets. The marketing plan, submitted to the company by an outside consulting firm, specifically targets the cigarette to 18- to 24-year-old women with a high school education or less who work in entry-level factory or service jobs. This segment is one of the few remaining demographic groups in the United States that exhibits an increase in smoking rates, so from a purely fiscal point of view it clearly has market potential.

The brand was developed to appeal to a lifestyle segment the company calls the "Virile Female." This woman has the following psychographic characteristics: Her favorite pastimes are cruising, partying, and going to hot rod shows and tractor pulls with her boyfriend, and her favorite TV shows are "Roseanne" and evening soap operas. Her chief aspirations are to get married in her early twenties and to spend time with her boyfriend, doing whatever he does. Over 100 public health officials signed a resolution asking that Dakota be withdrawn from the market, but R.J. Reynolds claims that the test brand was simply aimed at current Marlboro smokers and will not say whether or not it has plans to eventually introduce the brand.[35]

VALS

The most well-known and widely used segmentation system is **VALS (Values and Lifestyles)**, developed at what is now SRI International in California. Based on responses to a lengthy survey administered to about 1600 U.S. households in 1980, a researcher named Arnold Mitchell devised a system to place consumers into one of nine lifestyle clusters, or "VALS Types." The VALS system has been used by well over 200 corporations and advertising agencies in their marketing efforts. It has recently been updated to a new system called VALS 2.

THE ORIGINAL VALS SYSTEM   Originally, VALS combined two perspectives to create lifestyle clusters. One was based on the Maslow hierarchy of needs discussed in Chapter 3. Maslow's hierarchy stipulates that people's needs must be satisfied sequentially—that is, companionship is not a priority until physical needs are met, and so on. The second perspective was based on the distinction made by sociologist David Reisman between *inner-directed* people, who value personal expression and individual taste, and *outer-directed* people, who tend to be swayed by the behavior and reactions of others.

The VALS typology placed people in such categories as "achievers," "socially conscious," and "belongers," depending on their position in the Maslow hierarchy and whether their goals are inner or outer directed. For example, both "achievers" and "socially conscious" consumers are affluent, but outer-directed "achievers" are more oriented toward acquiring "power

The original VALS typology is available as Transparency 3.

symbols" (e.g., an impressive home) while the inner-directed "socially conscious" person would be more likely to buy a home equipped with energy-efficient systems (e.g., solar heating).

Throwing the Bull. A classic example of how VALS was used to modify a successful advertising campaign was in the strategy employed by Merrill Lynch. When the brokerage house shifted agencies in 1978, it had been using the theme "Bullish on America" for 12 years. The ad campaign featured a series of commercials showing a herd of bulls thundering across a plain. A VALS analysis, however, revealed that this approach appealed primarily to "belongers," mass-market consumers who want to fit in rather than stand out. In contrast, the Merrill Lynch target customers were "achievers": affluent business and government leaders who exhibit leadership and self-confidence and tend to be heavy investors. The ad agency thus shifted instead to a lone bull (symbolizing a strong individualist) and the theme became "A Breed Apart."

VALS 2 The original VALS system was widely used, but it was criticized on several grounds, such as the assumption that people tend to belong to only one VALS category and the possibility that many consumers who have the motivation to buy certain products do not necessarily have the incomes required to do so. Some of these concerns about the original VALS have been addressed in a revised version. Responding to some economic and demographic changes, the developers decided that this new psychographic system would *not* be as closely related to values and lifestyles. These changes include the evolution of a global economy and the increasing diversity of products and media that result in greater fragmentation of lifestyles.

VALS 2 divides people into eight groups that are determined both by psychological characteristics and "resources," which include such factors as income, education, energy levels, and eagerness to buy. VALS 2 appears to be easier to use, but it has abandoned some of the conceptual foundation on which the original VALS was based. In the VALS 2 structure, groups are arrayed vertically by resources and horizontally by self-orientation, as shown in Figure 13–2. The new top group is termed *actualizers*, who are successful consumers with many resources. This group is concerned with social issues and is open to change. The next three groups also have sufficient resources but differ in their outlooks on life:[36]

- *Fulfilleds* are satisfied, reflective, and comfortable. They tend to be practical and value functionality.
- *Achievers* are career-oriented and prefer predictability over risk or self-discovery.
- *Experiencers* are impulsive, young, and enjoy offbeat or risky experiences.

The next three groups have fewer resources:

- *Believers* have strong principles, and favor proven brands.
- *Strivers* are like achievers, but with fewer resources. They are very concerned about the approval of others.
- *Makers* are action-oriented and tend to focus their energies on self-sufficiency. They will often be found working on their cars, canning their own vegetables, or building their own houses.

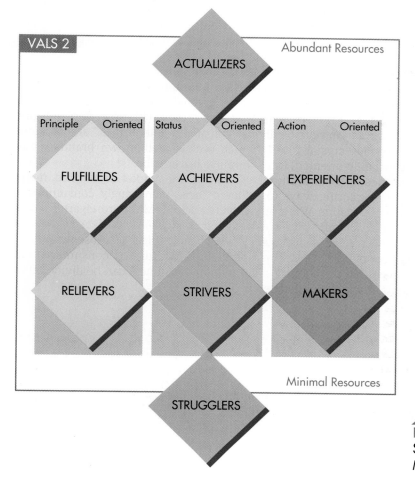

FIGURE 13–2 **VALS 2 Segmentation System** Source: SRI International, Menlo Park, CA.

- *Strugglers* are at the bottom of the ladder. They are most concerned with meeting the needs of the moment, and thus strongly resemble the survivor and sustainer groups they replaced.

Figure 13–2 is available as Transparency 35.

International Lifestyle Segmentation

VALS is by no means the only lifestyle segmentation scheme available. Researchers in a number of countries have developed psychographic strategies to apply to their own populations. One classification scheme, developed by McCann-Erickson London, segments British male and female consumers separately. Lifestyle categories in this system include such segments as "avant guardians" (interested in change), "pontificators" (traditionalists, very British), "chameleons" (follow the crowd), and "sleepwalkers" (contented underachievers).

A very popular Canadian campaign for Molson Export beer based its commercials on psychographic research showing target customers to be like boys who never grew up, who were uncertain about the future, and who were intimidated by women's new-found freedoms. Accordingly, the ads feature a group of men, "Fred and the boys," whose get-togethers emphasize male companionship, protection against change, and that the beer "keeps on tasting great."[37]

Consumers in Japan are sometimes called "life designers" to reflect the growing number who express themselves autonomously (much like inner-directed people). The equivalent of outer-directed has been termed *hitonami consciousness*, which translates as "aligning oneself with other people." One Japanese segmentation scheme divides consumers into "tribes" and includes among others the "crystal tribe" (which prefers well-known brands), "my home tribe" (family-oriented), and "impulse buyer tribe."[38]

As countries in Eastern Europe convert to free-market economies, many marketers are exploring ways to segment these increasingly consumption-oriented societies. Some Western products such as Marlboro cigarettes and McDonald's are already firmly entrenched in Russia. The D'Arcy Masius Benton & Bowles Advertising Agency, which has offices in Moscow and St. Petersburg, conducted a psychographic study of Russian consumers, and has proclaimed that the country's 150 million consumers can be divided into five segments,[39] which are detailed in Table 13–3.

TABLE 13–3 A Psychographic Segmentation of the Russian Market

Kuptsi (merchants)	Cossacks	Students	Business Exectutives	"Russian Souls"
% of all men				
30%	10%	10%	25%	25%
% of all women				
45%	10%	5%	10%	30%
Dominant Traits				
Reliant, nationalistic, practical, seeks value	Ambitious, independent, nationalistic, seeks status	Passive, scraping by, idealistic, practical	Ambitious, Western oriented, busy, concerned with status	Passive, follows others, fears choices, hopeful
Likely Preferences				
Car:				
Volkswagen	BMW	2CV	Mercedes	Lada
Cigarettes:				
Chesterfield	Dunhill	Marlboro	Winston	Marlboro
Liquor:				
Stolichnaya	Rémy Martin	Local vodka in Smirnoff bottles	Johnnie Walker	Smirnoff

Source: Stuart Elliott, "Sampling Tastes of a Changing Russia," *New York Times* (April 1, 1992): D1; adapted from *The Russian Consumer: A New Perspective and a Marketing Approach* (New York: D'Arcy Masius Benton & Bowles). Copyright ©1992 by The New York Times Company. Reprinted by permission.

Lifestyle Trends

One application of lifestyle analysis is to forecast **social trends,** or broad directions in which society is moving. Careful demographic analyses can, of course, provide valuable information regarding probable changes in social behavior, potential for different markets and product categories, and so on. For example, changes in birthrates can exert a huge impact on demand for products as diverse as baby food and life insurance. Still, this statistical portrait does not allow us to tap more subtle changes in priorities and values. For this reason, examinations of changes in orientations toward life, preferences for how one's leisure time is spent, and attitudes toward important social issues such as democracy, materialism, and religion can yield important insights on possible changes in consumption patterns.

Many observers have noted a shift toward *"neo-traditionalism,"* or marked conservative values, a renewed commitment to the family, and a tempering of the rampant materialism of the 1970s and 1980s. In the words of one observer, the 1990s have ushered in an emphasis on "romance, religion, and rattles."[40] This sentiment is clearly evident in the Liz Claiborne ad shown here, which depicts baby boomers who have apparently discovered that "Reality is the best fantasy of all," as the ad says.

A number of marketing research firms conduct ongoing lifestyle research to track changes in social trends. For example, the Lifestyle Monitor, now run

This ad for Realities by Liz Claiborne illustrates the shift in values from an emphasis in the 1980s on glitz to home-centered, down-to-earth activities in the 1990s. Courtesy of Altschiller Reitzfeld Tracy-Locke.

by the firm Yankelovich Clancy Shulman, interviews 2500 American adults annually. Advertising agency Backer Spielvogel Bates' Global Scan program divides markets in 18 countries into psychographic segments, and agency Ogilvy & Mather scans consumer trends with its New Wave program.[41] Since 1975, the DDB Needham Worldwide advertising agency has been conducting its Lifestyle Study, an ongoing study of changes in consumer behavior. The study uses a sample of 4000 adults, and the most recent report included the following findings, some of which are *not* consistent with the widely held belief that Americans are returning to "traditional values" in the 1990s.[42]

- Church attendance is slightly down, as is the percentage of people who agree that "Religion is an important part of my life."
- A third of adults agree that couples should live together before marriage, though there has been a sharp increase in the feeling that "Children are the most important thing in a marriage." Far fewer people (both men and women) agree that the "father should be the boss in the house."
- An increasing majority of Americans favor legalized abortion, but support for legalized marijuana remains at between 15–20 percent.
- Less people believe their family income is high enough to pay for important things, and fears about personal debt continue to rise.
- There is a steep drop in people who agree that "I am usually the first to try new products."
- There is a steep drop in those who agree that "Television is my primary form of entertainment."

Predicting Trends

Of course, trend forecasting is a bit like reading one's horoscope in the paper. Sometimes forecasts are so general they can't help but come true, and only some proportion of more specific ones actually do. The problem is, we don't know until after the fact which ones will. The following sections contain some recent predictions of trends we can expect in the rest of the 1990s (note that they sometimes contradict each other). Which will be accurate? Take your pick.

VOLUNTARY SIMPLICITY AND ENVIRONMENTALISM Consumers will forsake their pursuit of status symbols for a life that is ". . . outwardly simple and inwardly rich."[43] Look for a surge in camping and wilderness products. With the introduction of its Origins line of cosmetics, the Estee Lauder Company was the first major U.S. beauty company to bring natural, non-animal tested products in recyclable containers into department stores.[44] Concern for the environment, or the *green movement*, is also affecting marketing strategies for products ranging from diapers to fast food. Ecover, a Belgian detergent marketer, for example, appealed to consumers' environmental concerns in a tongue-in-cheek way by recycling its competitors' old TV commercials. The company used five black-and-white commercials from the l950s and superimposed a color picture of its brand over the competing brand while a voice-over explained that the old commercial had been recycled.[45]

DECREASED MATERIALISM AND EMPHASIS ON SELF-FULFILLMENT For many, the theme of the l980s was exemplified by the popular bumper sticker of the time that proclaimed, "He who dies with the most toys, wins." Status products like Godiva chocolate, filofax binders, and BMW cars watched their sales soar as consumers strove to acquire tokens of success. Today, though, things are somewhat different. Filofax was recently bought for a quarter of its 1987 value, while BMW now sells a model for $20,000—for an "affordable good time."[46] Even an indulgence like Godiva chocolate is being repositioned as an "accessible luxury" in the cost-conscious nineties.[47]

In the rest of this decade, consumers will instead value individualistic, unique experiences. Look for a boom in unusual vacation packages and highly segmented cable television stations. With the new emphasis on "value," more understated, inexpensive products, such as the Sensor razor from Gillette and clothing from the Gap, are benefiting from this trend. This shift in values is personified by the IMP (inner-motivated person) depicted in the ad shown here for *Harper's* magazine.

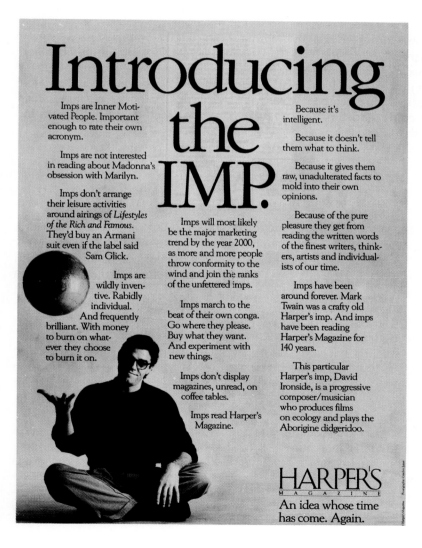

Reflecting the consumer trend toward self-fulfillment and away from materialism, this ad for *Harper's* magazine describes a lifestyle segment it dubs the IMP (inner-motivated person). Copyright © by *Harper's Magazine*. Reprinted with special permission.

TIME POVERTY The increase in working couples leads to greater value placed on convenience products and services that minimize time and effort spent in purchasing. Although couples where both partners work and couples where only one works both average two weekly trips to the market and spend about the same ($57.00 per trip), working couples spend 15 percent less time in the market. To facilitate this "race" through the market, some chains now display floor plans at the entrance.[49] Home delivery of food is growing twice as fast as take-out or drive-through. In addition, look for increased reliance on catalogs, professional shoppers, and home automation to occur.[48] The Japanese are leading the way in developing new convenience products. Recent time and money-saving hits in Japan include instant pasta, size-adjustable baby shoes, and tropical fish rentals.[50]

M A R K E T I N G   P I T F A L L

The convenience trend can be overdone. One company wanted to sell sheets in supermarkets, reasoning that working women would welcome this addition. They quickly found that consumers hated the idea. An important benefit of shopping for sheets is looking at a wide range of designs and colors, and fantasizing how one's bedroom would look with them. Consumers felt that a supermarket could not offer this diversity and that their mood would be too pragmatic while in the supermarket to fantasize. The idea was shelved.[51]

DISILLUSIONMENT OF WORKING WOMEN Women will discover that working outside of the home is not as "liberating" as they thought. Look for a return to traditional husband/wife roles to occur, as women abandon careers and stay home with the children.[52] Women are now more likely than men to say they "work very hard most of the time," and their use of pain relievers is growing dramatically.[53] In 1976, the values most likely to be endorsed by women were security and self-respect. By 1986, this emphasis had shifted to a paramount desire for warm relationships.[54]

DECREASED EMPHASIS ON NUTRITION AND EXERCISE People will stop being health fanatics. While Americans still appear to be concerned about their health, the obsession of many with diet and exercise appears to be subsiding. Americans appear to be adopting more of an "okay-in-moderation" outlook. Fewer consumers are avoiding salty products or foods with additives or report a willingness to pay more for "all natural" foods.[55] Opposition to the consumption of red meat also appears to have peaked.[56] In addition, fewer Americans are taking exercise classes, jogging, or playing tennis.[57]

Vitamin consumption is declining, and consumers appear to be balancing healthy behaviors with indulgences. Finding that 70 million people say they walk for exercise, Reebok is planning a major new emphasis on walking shoes—a far cry from the "run 'til you drop" attitude of a few years ago. The fastest-growing sports are now low-impact and home-centered, such as in-line skating and stair-climbing machines. And, while many consumers profess to look for low-fat, healthy foods, sales of premium ice creams, rich soups, fat-laden frozen food entrees, and fast food entrees like Wendy's Bacon Mushroom Melt are soaring.[58]

"COCOONING" Consumers will insulate themselves from such world problems as pollution and crime by staying home as much as possible: "They're going to go home and pull the covers over their heads, eat comfort food, watch VCRs, have babies, and stay married."[59] This emphasis on spending leisure time at home creates opportunities for such businesses as movie rentals, board games, and home spas. "Couch potatoes," like the one shown at the beginning of this chapter, will also be prime targets for the new wave of home shopping channels that will be appearing in the near future.

NONCONSUMPTION People will look for products and services that will help them to shed bad habits. In recent years, abstention from certain products and practices has become a way of life for many consumers who have adopted "non" as the code word for a lifestyle. Membership in support groups that help people to stop various forms of consumption, including alcohol, narcotics, gambling, overeating, and even sex, has doubled in the last decade. Some products have succeeded at positioning themselves in terms of attributes they do *not* possess. These include 7-UP ("The Un-Cola"), Club Med ("The antidote to civilization"), clear beer, and even Max Factor's "No color mascara."[60] In addition, the concept of "lite" versions of products has permeated everything from wine to ice cream.

Chapter Summary

- A consumer's *lifestyle* refers to the ways he or she chooses to spend time and money and how his or her values and tastes are reflected by consumption choices. Lifestyle research is useful to track societal consumption preferences and also to position specific products and services to different segments.

- Marketers segment by lifestyle differences, often by grouping consumers in terms of their *AIOs* (activities, interests, and opinions).

- *Psychographic techniques* attempt to classify consumers in terms of psychological, subjective variables in addition to observable characteristics (demographics). A variety of systems, such as VALS, have been developed to identify consumer "types" and to differentiate them in terms of their brand or product preferences, media usage, leisure time activities, and attitudes toward such broad issues as politics and religion.

- Interrelated sets of products and activities are associated with social roles to form *consumption constellations*. People often purchase a product or service because it is associated with a constellation that, in turn, is linked to a lifestyle they find desirable.

- Lifestyles change over time, and one application of lifestyle research is to track changes in priorities. Some major lifestyle trends in the 1990s include neo-traditionalism, self-fulfillment, and environmentalism.

Key Terms

AIOs, p. 448

consumption constella-
tions, p. 441

lifestyle, p. 438

materialism, p. 442

product complemen-
tarity, p. 441

psychographics, p. 447

social trends, p. 455

20/80 rule, p. 448

Values and Lifestyles
(VALS), p. 451

Consumer Behavior Challenge

1. Compare and contrast the concepts of lifestyle and social class.
2. In what situations is demographic information likely to be more useful than psychographic data, and vice-versa?
3. Alcohol drinkers vary sharply in terms of the number of drinks they may consume, from those who occasionally have one at a cocktail party to regular imbibers. Explain how the 20/80 rule applies to this product category.
4. Describe the underlying principles used to construct the VALS system. What are some positive and negative aspects of this approach to lifestyle segmentation?
5. What impact has the return to "neo-traditionalism" had on contemporary marketing strategies?
6. The chapter describes several apparent trends in lifestyles and values, including an emphasis on self-fulfillment, women's disaffection with careers, and a growth in environmentalism. Do you agree with these assessments? What do you believe to be the most important changes in values in the 1990s? Are these changes positive or negative?
7. Compile a set of recent ads that attempt to link consumption of a product with a specific lifestyle. How is this goal usually accomplished?
8. The chapter mentions that psychographic analyses can be used to market politicians. Conduct research on the marketing strategies used in a recent, major election. How were voters segmented in terms of values? Can you find evidence that communications strategies were guided by this information?
9. Construct separate ad campaigns for a cosmetics product targeted to the belonger, achiever, experiential, and societally conscious VALS types. How would the basic appeal differ for each group?
10. Using media targeted to the group, construct a consumption constellation for the social role of college students. What set of products, activities, and interests tend to appear in advertisements depicting "typical" college students? How realistic is this constellation? What factors might be operating to distort the correspondence of this constellation to reality?
11. The principle of market segmentation implies that a group of people sharing some set of characteristics will be singled out as the focus of a marketing strategy. Critics of targeted marketing argue that this is dis-

criminatory and unfair, especially if such a strategy encourages a group of people to buy a product that may be injurious to them or that they cannot afford. On the other hand, The Association of National Advertisers argues that banning targeted marketing constitutes censorship and is a violation of the First Amendment. Is segmentation an ethical marketing practice? Give the reasons for your answer.

12. Administer the Materialism Scale in Table 13–1 to a sample of business majors and another group of liberal arts majors. What predictions might you make regarding group differences on this value? For each statement, ask respondents to circle a number on a scale:

Strongly disagree   1   2   3   4   5   Strongly agree

Note: When scoring, be sure to remember that items marked with an asterisk are reverse scored. That is, a response of "5" should be scored as a "1," a "4" as a "2," and so on. Sum each person's score for each scale item, and calculate the average response for each sample. Do the two groups differ in terms of their mean responses?

13. If you were segmenting a consumer group in terms of their relative level of materialism, how might your advertising and promotional strategy take this difference into account? Construct two versions of an ad for a suntan lotion, one to appeal to a high materialism segment and one to appeal to a low materialism segment.

14. Due to increased competition and market saturation, marketers in industrialized countries increasingly are trying to develop Third World markets by encouraging people in underdeveloped countries to desire Western products. Should this practice be encouraged, even if the products being marketed may be harmful to consumers' health (e.g., cigarettes) or divert needed money away from the purchase of essentials? If you were a trade or health official in a Third World country, what guidelines, if any, might you suggest to regulate the import of luxury goods from advanced economies?

CNN Connection

 A video segment is available to accompany this CNN connection.

American Culture Around the World

Do Americans really have more fun? The Japanese seem to think so. They are enthusiastic consumers of American popular culture, and many companies are lining up to provide the Japanese with the means to emulate the U.S. lifestyle. One of the biggest successes has been scored by the Disney organization. The Tokyo Disneyland draws millions of Mickey and Minnie fans. The theme park is an American invention, and more than thirty are being planned throughout Asia. Although Japanese businesses are renowned for their organizational skills and high-tech abilities, American companies have a lock on the theme park market. The Japanese feel that Americans know how to have fun, and virtually all of the new parks are being developed by U.S. firms.

Although, as the chapter notes, the French have been less enthusiastic than the Japanese about importing some aspects of American culture, this resistance shows signs of breaking down (the new Euro Disney park is located in a suburb of Paris). While French cuisine is admired around the world, American food manufacturers are now trying to break into this market as well. Inspired by the success of McDonald's and other fast-food operations, French supermarket chains have been the target of recent promotions extolling the virtues of American cereal, juice, and, yes, even wine.

SIMMONS Connection

SIMMONS Connection: Data for this exercise is on the Simmons Data Disk inside the back cover of your Instructor's Annotated Edition.

Data File: Patterns of Consumption

Jackie and Hank are new to their careers as lawyers. Just as they are learning a great deal about what it means to perform their professional roles as lawyers in a high-powered Washington firm, they are also learning how to live the lifestyle associated with their profession. During such periods of transition, however, consumers often carry over patterns of consumption activities that characterized a previous period of their lives. For example, many recent college graduates continue the tradition of Thursday night partying for the first few years of their postgraduate singles life. This pattern gradually gives way to new activities that might be dictated by a new spouse, child, or career demands.

Although Jackie and Hank are both lawyers, they spend their leisure time in very different activities. And of course there are a range of products that are consumed as part of those activities—hunting gear for Hank and perhaps formal wear for Jackie's evenings at the opera. Although eventually their leisure activities may become more similar, marketers may miss several current opportunities. Clearly, Jackie and Hank share many current demographic similarities, such as income level, education level, and occupation, which provide little insight into their differences in leisure activities. However, by examining their product preferences, marketers might discover some important differences in the background of each.

Your Simmons file contains data for alcoholic beverages and automobiles and the associated demographic characteristics of users. You should generate a demographic profile for each product category (cars and alcoholic beverages) that highlights the differences between users of the following products.

Jackie's preferences:	Hank's preferences:
Champagne	Jack Daniels
BMW	Trans Am/Camaro

Now, consider each profile. Which of these best fits their current occupational role?

Notes

1. Benjamin D. Zablocki and Rosabeth Moss Kanter, "The Differentiation of Life-Styles," *Annual Review of Sociology* (1976): 269–97.
2. Chester A. Swenson, "How to Sell to a Segmented Market," *Journal of Business Strategy* 9 (January–February 1988): 18.
3. William Leiss, Stephen Kline, and Sut Jhally, *Social Communication in Advertising* (Toronto: Methuen, 1986).
4. Zablocki and Kanter, "The Differentiation of Life-Styles."
5. Mary Twe Douglas and Baron C. Isherwood, *The World of Goods* (New York: Basic Books, 1979).
6. Richard A. Peterson, "Revitalizing the Culture Concept," *Annual Review of Sociology* 5 (1979): 137–66.
7. Douglas and Isherwood, *The World of Goods*, 72–73.
8. Michael R. Solomon, "The Role of Products as Social Stimuli: A Symbolic Interactionism Perspective," *Journal of Consumer Research* 10 (December 1983): 319–29.
9. Michael R. Solomon and Henry Assael, "The Forest or the Trees?: A Gestalt Approach to Symbolic Consumption," in *Marketing and Semiotics: New Directions in the Study of Signs for Sale*, ed. Jean Umiker-Sebeok (Berlin: Mouton de Gruyter, 1988), 189–218; Michael R. Solomon, "Mapping Product Constellations: A Social Categorization Approach to Symbolic Consumption," *Psychology & Marketing* 5 (1988)3: 233–58.
10. Russell W. Belk, "Yuppies as Arbiters of the Emerging Consumption Style," in *Advances in Consumer Research* 13, ed. Richard J. Lutz (Provo, Utah: Association for Consumer Research, 1986), 514–19.
11. Russell W. Belk, "Possessions and the Extended Self," *Journal of Consumer Research* 15 (September 1988): 139–68; Melanie Wallendorf and Eric J. Arnould, "'My Favorite Things': A Cross-Cultural Inquiry into Object Attachment, Possessiveness, and Social Linkage," *Journal of Consumer Research* 14 (March 1988): 531–47.
12. Fabian Linden, "Who Has Buying Power?" *American Demographics* (August 1987): 4, 6.
13. Russell W. Belk and Richard W. Pollay, "Images of Ourselves: The Good Life in Twentieth Century Advertising," *Journal of Consumer Research* 11 (March 1985): 887–97.
14. "Europeans More Active as Consumers," *Marketing News* (June 10): 17.
15. Marsha L. Richins and Scott Dawson, "A Consumer Values Orientation for Materialism and Its Measurement: Scale Development and Validation," *Journal of Consumer Research* 20 (December 1992).
16. Eric J. Arnould and Richard R. Wilk, "Why Do the Natives Wear Adidas: Anthropological Approaches to Consumer Research," in *Advances in Consumer Research* 12 (Provo, Utah: Association for Consumer Research, 1985), 748–52.
17. John Huey, "America's Hottest Export: Pop Culture," *Fortune* (December 31, 1990)7: 50.
18. Chin Tiong Tan and John U. Farley: "The Impact of Cultural Patterns on Cognition and Intention in Singapore," *Journal of Consumer Research* 13 (March 1987): 540–44.
19. Quoted in Sheryl WuDunn, "Cosmetics from the West Help to Change the Face of China," *New York Times* (May 6, 1990): 16.

20. David K. Tse, Russell W. Belk, and Nan Zhou, "Becoming a Consumer Society: A Longitudinal and Cross-Cultural Content Analysis of Print Ads from Hong Kong, the People's Republic of China, and Taiwan," *Journal of Consumer Research* 15 (March 1989): 457–72; see also Annamma Joy, "Marketing in Modern China: an Evolutionary Perspective," *CJAS* (June 1990): 55–67, for a review of changes in Chinese marketing practices since the economic reforms of 1978.

21. Nicholas D. Kristof, "'Billions Served' (and That Was Without China)," *New York Times* (April 24, 1992): A4; James Sterngold, "The Awakening Chinese Consumer," *New York Times* (October 11, 1992): F1.

22. John F. Sherry, Jr., and Eduardo G. Camargo, "'May Your Life be Marvelous': English Language Labeling and the Semiotics of Japanese Promotion," *Journal of Consumer Research* 14 (September 1987): 174–88.

23. Bill Bryson, "A Taste for Scrambled English," *New York Times* (July 22, 1990): 10; Rose A. Horowitz, "California Beach Culture Rides Wave of Popularity in Japan," *Journal of Commerce* (August 3, 1989): 17; Elaine Lafferty, "American Casual Seizes Japan: Teenagers Go for N.F.L. Hats, Batman and the California Look," *Time* (November 13, 1989): 106.

24. Steven Greenhouse, "The Television Europeans Love, and Love to Hate," *New York Times* (August 13, 1989): 24.

25. James Brooke, "Brazil's Idol Is a Blonde, and Some Ask 'Why?'" *New York Times* (July 31, 1990): A4.

26. Sherry and Camargo, "May Your Life Be Marvelous."

27. Quoted in Alan Riding, "Only the French Elite Scorn Mickey's Debut," *New York Times* (1992)2: A1.

28. Mike Levin, "U.S. Tobacco Firms Push Eagerly into Asian Market," *Marketing News* (January 21, 1991)2: 2.

29. See Lewis Alpert and Ronald Gatty, "Product Positioning by Behavioral Life Styles," *Journal of Marketing* 33 (April 1969): 65–69; Emanuel H. Demby, "Psychographics Revisited: The Birth of a Technique," *Marketing News* (January 2, 1989): 21; William D. Wells, "Backward Segmentation," in *Insights into Consumer Behavior*, ed. Johan Arndt (Boston: Allyn & Bacon, 1968), 85–100.

29. William D. Wells and Douglas J. Tigert, "Activities, Interests, and Opinions," *Journal of Advertising Research* 11 (August 1971): 27.

30. Alfred S. Boote, "Psychographics: Mind Over Matter," *American Demographics* (April 1980): 26–29; William D. Wells, "Psychographics: A Critical Review," *Journal of Marketing Research* 12 (May 1975): 196–213.

31. Joseph T. Plummer, "The Concept and Application of Life Style Segmentation," *Journal of Marketing* 38 (January 1974): 33–37.

32. Berkeley Rice, "The Selling of Lifestyles," *Psychology Today* (March 1988): 46.

33. "Value Segments Help Define International Market," *Marketing News* (November 21, 1988): 17.

34. John L. Lastovicka, John P. Murry, Erich A. Joachimsthaler, Gurav Bhalla, and Jim Scheurich, "A Lifestyle Typology to Model Young Male Drinking and Driving," *Journal of Consumer Research* 14 (September 1987): 257–63.

35. Anthony Ramirez, "New Cigarettes Raising Issue of Target Market," *New York Times* (February 18, 1990): 28.

36. Martha Farnsworth Riche, "VALS 2," *American Demographics* (July 1989): 25.

37. Ian Pearson, "Social Studies: Psychographics in Advertising," *Canadian Business* (December 1985): 67.

38. Leiss et al., *"Social Communication in Advertising".*

39. Stuart Elliott, "Sampling Tastes of a Changing Russia," *New York Times* (April 1, 1992)2: D1.

40. Lenore Skenazy, "Welcome Home: Trend Experts Point to 'Neo-traditional'," *Advertising Age* (May 16, 1988): 38.

41. Rebecca Piirto, "Measuring Minds in the 1990s," *American Demographics* (December 1990)5: 31.

42. Data reported in Joseph M. Winski, "Who We Are, How We Live, What We Think," *Advertising Age* (January 20, 1992)2: 16.

43. Ronald D. Michman, "New Directions for Life-Style Behavior Patterns," *Business Horizons* (July–August 1984): 60.

44. Pat Sloan, "Cosmetics: Color it Green," *Advertising Age* (July 23, 1990): 1.

45. *Advertising Age* (May 2, 1992).

46. Kim Foltz, "As Baby Boomers Turn 40, Ammirati and BMW Adjust," *New York Times* (January 26, 1990): D17.

47. Judann Dagnoli, "Godiva Tones Down Luxury Image," *Advertising Age* (January 20, 1992): 54.

48. Michman, "New Directions for Life-Style Behavior Patterns."

49. Timothy Harris, "Fast and Easy: US Supermarkets Market Convenience Foods as Lifestyles," *Marketing* (October 29, 1987): 17.

50. *1989 Hit Products in Japan* (Tokyo: Dentsu Inc., 1989).

51. Judith Langer, "Where does the Consumer's Personal Style Fit In?" *American Demographics* (October 1987): 48.

52. Skenazy, "Welcome Home."

53. DDB Needham Worldwide's Life Style Study, reported in *Advertising Age* (September 24, 1990): 25.

54. Kahle et al., "Changes in Social Values in the United States During the Past Decade."

55. DDB Needham Worldwide's Life Style Study, 25.

56. Burdette Breidenstein, "Changes in Consumers' Attitudes Toward Red Meat and Their Effect on Marketing Strategy," *Food Technology* (January 1988): 112–16.

57. DDB Needham Worldwide's Life Style Study, 25.

58. Cathy Taylor, "Everything in Moderation," *Adweek* (August 17, 1992)2: 34; Yankelovich Clancy Shulman, "Physical Fitness: It's All in the Balance," *Adweek* (August 17, 1992)3: 36.

59. David Streitfeld, "What's Up, Trendwise?" *Washington Post* (November 28, 1988): D5.

60. Molly O'Neill, "Words to Survive Life With: None of This, None of That," *New York Times* (May 27, 1990): 1.

CHAPTER 14

Ethnic and
—
Religious
—
Groups
—

Buying, Having, and Being: Selections 50–54 from *Buying, Having, and Being: The Washington Post Consumer Behavior Companion*, Second Edition, accompany this chapter.

Maria, waking up early on Saturday morning, braces herself for a long day of errands and chores. As usual, her mother expects her to do the shopping and then help prepare the food for the big family gathering tonight. Of course, her older brother Roberto would never be asked to do the grocery shopping or help out in the kitchen—these are woman's jobs.

It seems like the Cruz family is constantly growing; Maria alone has five siblings, and sometimes she loses count of how many cousins live in her *barrio* (neighborhood). Family gatherings, like tonight's, make a lot of work, and Maria wishes that her mother would use prepared foods once in a while, especially on a Saturday when Maria has an errand or two of her own to do. But no, her mother insists on preparing most of her food from scratch and rarely uses any convenience products. And, of course, Maria has to pitch in and help.

Resigned, Maria watches a *telenovella* (soap opera) on Univision while she's getting dressed, and then she heads down to the *carniceria* (local mom-and-pop store) to buy a newspaper—there are almost forty different Spanish newspapers published in her area, and she likes to buy new ones occasionally. Then Maria buys the grocery items her mother wants; the list is full of well-known brand names like Casera and Goya that she gets all the time, so she's able to finish quickly. With any luck, she'll have a few minutes to go to the *mercado* (shopping center) to pick up that new tape by *Los Lobos* she's been saving to buy. She'll listen to it in the kitchen while she chops, peels, and stirs.

Maria smiles to herself: Despite all the negative publicity after the riots, LA is a great place to live and what could be better than spending an evening with *la familia* . . . .

Subcultures

Yes, Maria lives in Los Angeles, not Mexico City. One in four Californians is Latino. Within fifteen years, demographers predict that Southern California will essentially be a Latino subcontinent, culturally distinct from the rest of the United States.[1] Hispanic-Americans have much in common with members of other racial and ethnic groups who live in the United States. They observe the same national holidays, their expenditures are affected by the country's economic health, and they may join together in rooting for Team USA in the Olympics. Nonetheless, while American citizenship provides the raw material for some consumption decisions, others are profoundly affected by the enormous variations in the social fabric of the United States.

Consumers lifestyles are affected by group memberships *within* the society-at-large. These groups are known as **subcultures,** whose members share beliefs and common experiences that set them apart from others. While subcultural group memberships often have a significant impact on consumer behavior, some subcultural identifications are more powerful than others and so are the effects on consumption decisions. For marketing segmentation strategies that take subcultural membership into account to be successful, they must also consider the relative intensity of consumers' various affiliations.

Every consumer belongs to many subcultures. These include religious groups, age groups, ethnic groups, and even regional groups (e.g., Texans versus New Yorkers). Sometimes even leisure activities can evolve into a subculture, if this activity draws the consumer into a unique social situation with enough intensity. Consumers in these subcultures—whether "Dead Heads," retired people touring the country in Winnebagos, or members of youth gangs—create their own worlds, complete with their own norms, language, and product insignias (e.g., the skulls and roses used to signify the "Grateful Dead" subculture).

Major subcultural groups will be discussed in detail in this chapter and the next. This chapter focuses on ethnic and religious identification, and Chapter 15 considers consumer subcultures that are defined by people of a common age or area of residence. In some cases, the subcultures to be considered in this chapter are already widely used by marketers as a segmentation variable (e.g., race), while the potential of others is just beginning to be recognized (e.g., religion). It is important to keep in mind that these are by no means the *only* important ethnic and religious groups that marketers should know about. The United States is a melting pot of hundreds of diverse and interesting groups, from Italian- and Irish-Americans to Mormons and Seventh-Day Adventists. While this chapter only addresses several of the largest groups to represent this diversity, the omission of other groups should not be taken to mean that they are not of interest as well.

Research Report: One study has compared the validity of ethnicity scales. See Michel Laroche, Annamma Joy, Michael Hui, and Chankon Kim, "An Examination of Ethnicity Measures: Convergent Validity and Cross-Cultural Equivalence," in *Advances in Consumer Research* 18, eds. Rebecca H. Holman and Michael R. Solomon (Provo, Utah: Association for Consumer Research, 1991): 150–57.

Ethnic Subcultures

Ethnic and religious identity is often a significant component of a consumer's self-concept. An **ethnic subculture** consists of a self-perpetuating group of consumers who are held together by common cultural ties that is identified both by its members and by others as being a distinguishable category.[2]

In some countries, like Japan, ethnicity is almost synonymous with the dominant culture, since virtually everyone claims the same homogeneous cultural ties. In a heterogeneous society like the United States, however, many different cultures are represented, and consumers may expend great effort to keep their ethnic identification from being submerged into the mainstream of the dominant society. Membership in these groups often is predictive of such consumer variables as level and type of media exposure, food preferences, the wearing of distinctive apparel, political behavior, leisure activities, and even willingness to try new products.

Ethnic Stereotypes

Many subcultures have powerful stereotypes associated with them. Members of a subgroup are assumed to possess certain traits, even though these assumptions often are erroneous. The same trait can be cast either positively or negatively, depending upon the communicator's intentions and biases. For example, the Scottish stereotype in the United States is largely positive, so the supposed frugality of this ethnic group is viewed favorably. Scottish imagery has been used by the 3M company to denote value (e.g., Scotch tape) and also by a motel chain that offers inexpensive lodging. However, invoking the

Scottish "personality" might carry quite different connotations to consumers in Britain or Ireland. Thus, one person's "thrifty" is another's "stingy."

MARKETING USES OF ETHNIC STEREOTYPES Ethnic symbolism has been used in the past by marketers as a shorthand to connote certain product attributes. The subcultures involved often were minorities and the images employed were crude and unflattering. Blacks were depicted as subservient, Mexicans as bandits.[3] As the civil rights movement gave more power to minority groups and their rising economic status commanded respect from marketers, these negative stereotypes began to disappear. Frito-Lay responded to protests by the Hispanic community and stopped using the Frito Bandito character in 1971. Quaker Foods gave Aunt Jemima a makeover in 1989 to mark her hundredth birthday. In the words of a company spokesman, her new image reflects a youthful grandmother who "knows how to cook and enjoy it."

DE-ETHNICITIZATION Products that are marketed with an ethnic appeal are not necessarily intended for consumption only by the ethnic subculture from which they originate. **De-ethnicitization** refers to the process where a product formerly associated with a specific ethnic group is detached from its roots and marketed to other subcultures. This process is illustrated by the case of bagels, a bread product formerly associated with Jewish culture and now mass marketed. Recent variations include jalapeno bagels, blueberry bagels, and even a green bagel for St. Patrick's Day. A California company even markets tiny bagels as "bagel seeds."[4] A similar attempt to assimilate ethnic products into mainstream culture is underway by Goya Foods, a major marketer of Hispanic food products. As one company executive noted, "Several food items such as tacos . . . and burritos were once considered the domain of an ethnic group, and now they're mainstream."[5] To underscore this evolution, consider the fact that salsa is now the most popular condiment in the United States, outselling ketchup by $40 million.

MULTICULTURAL DIMENSIONS

Ethnic restaurants are a fast-growing segment of the food industry, whether in the United States, Canada, Europe, or Japan. For example, while restaurant patronage in the United States increased by 10 percent overall in a four-year period, the rate of increase was 43 percent for Mexican restaurants and 54 percent for Asian restaurants. Ethnic restaurants are a part of the internationalization of lifestyles, where consumers reach out for new experiences. A greater concentration of ethnic restaurants is found in the northeastern and western parts of the United States and in urban areas of Canada, with relatively fewer establishments in the South or the Midwest. Chinese is the most frequently served ethnic cuisine, followed closely by Mexican and Italian (these three types account for over 70 percent of all ethnic restaurants). Many other cuisines are underrepresented, or not represented at all, hinting at opportunities for entrepreneurs who wish to carve out a distinctive niche.[6]

New Ethnic Groups

The dominant American culture always exerted pressure on immigrants to divest themselves of their origins and become rapidly absorbed into the host culture. As President Theodore Roosevelt put it in the early part of the century, "We welcome the German or the Irishman who becomes an American. We have no use for the German or the Irishman who remains such."[8]

While the bulk of American immigrants historically came from Europe, immigration patterns have shifted dramatically in the latter part of this century. New immigrants are much more likely to be Asian or Hispanic. As these new waves of immigrants settle in the United States, marketers are attempting to track their consumption patterns and adjust their strategies accordingly. Figure 14–1 shows how new waves of immigrants are changing the ethnic composition of major American cities.

The U.S. Census Bureau estimates that the population of the United States, now numbering 255 million, will grow to 275 million by the year 2000. Much of this growth will be accounted for by members of non-white ethnic groups, and a substantial portion will be due to the immigration of people from other countries as opposed to citizens who are born in the United States. Three groups that will account for much of this growth are African-Americans, Hispanic-Americans, and Asian-Americans. The Hispanic

Cross-Cultural Example: Long-distance telephone carriers are cashing in on immigrant groups, who tend to call home frequently. Revenue from overseas calling is expected to reach $8.6 billion by 1996. In 1991, international telephone traffic accounted for 20 percent of the calls placed in the United States. See Jonathan Burton, "The Millions of New Immigrants Yearning to Call Home," *New York Times* (September 6, 1992): F4.

Figure 14–1 is available as Transparency 36.

FIGURE 14–1 **America's Newest Markets** Source: "Newest Markets," *American Demographics* (September 1988): 27. Reprinted with permission, © *American Demographics*.

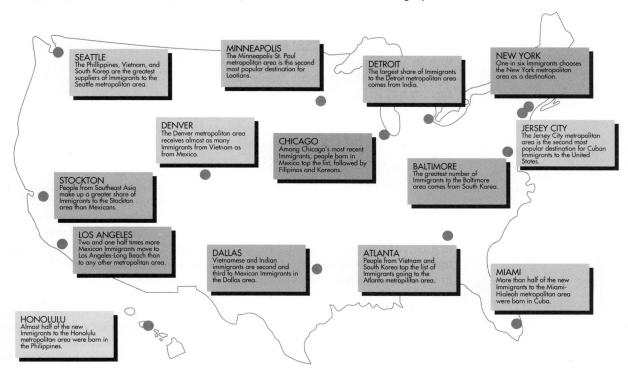

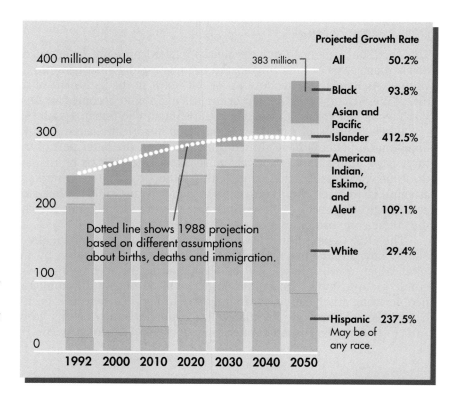

FIGURE 14–2 The Growth of the Nation: The Changing Racial Mix in the United States Source: Robert Pear, "New Look at the U.S. in 2050: Bigger, Older, and Less White," *New York Times* (December 4, 1992): A1. Copyright ©1992 by The New York Times Company. Reprinted by permission.

Figure 14–2 is available as Transparency 37.

population is projected to surpass the black population in the year 2013, at which time there will be 42.1 million Hispanic-Americans and 42 million African-Americans. The Asian-American population, while smaller in absolute numbers, is the fastest-growing racial group. This growth is largely due to immigration; the number of Asian immigrants who arrive in the United States each year is actually greater than the number who are born in the country.[9] The projected growth of major ethnic and racial groups until the year 2050 is shown in Figure 14–2.

African-Americans

African-Americans comprise a significant racial subculture and account for 12 percent of the U.S. population. While black consumers do differ in important ways from whites, the black market is hardly as homogeneous as many marketers seem to believe. Historically, blacks were separated from mainstream society (unfortunately, not by choice). More recently, though, increasing economic success and the many cultural contributions of this group that have been absorbed by mainstream white culture, have in some instances blurred the lines between American blacks and whites.

Indeed, some commentators have argued that black/white differences are largely illusory. Different consumption behaviors are more likely due to differences in income, the relatively high concentration of African-Americans in urban areas, and other dimensions of social class than by racial differences.

With some exceptions, the overall spending patterns of blacks and whites are roughly similar. Although the average black household income in 1984 was only 63 percent of whites', the proportions of monies allocated to different categories do not vary all that much. Both blacks and white spent about two-thirds of their incomes on housing, transportation, and food.[10]

Black/White Consumption Differences

Nonetheless, there clearly are some differences in consumption priorities and marketplace behaviors that demand marketers' attention.[11] One reason is the vast market potential of this group: If American blacks were a separate nation, their buying power would rank twelfth of any Western country.[12] Because of the growing economic power of this segment, black consumers often represent a fresh opportunity for otherwise saturated markets. The following are some important usage differences in some product categories.[13]

- Blacks account for only 2 percent of all spending on trucks and vans, while they account for almost a quarter of all spending on mass transit. This difference reflects the concentration of blacks in urban areas.
- Blacks purchase 10 percent of televisions, radios, and sound equipment.
- Blacks buy 17 percent of all encyclopedias and reference books sold.
- Blacks spend 28 percent more than other American consumers on baby products.
- Blacks buy 27 percent more cooking ingredients than average.
- Blacks buy more than one-half of all the cognac sold in the United States.
- Blacks comprise 19 percent of the market for toiletries and cosmetics, and 34 percent for hair-care products. Black women spend over $500 a year on health and beauty products, three times the rate of white women.

Cross-Cultural Example: Several major mass-market retailers, including KMart, Toys 'R' Us, and J.C. Penney, are making a concerted effort to woo minority shoppers. J.C. Penney, for example, opened "Authentic African" boutiques in 20 of its stores in 1991, and the company has plans to expand this operation to 350 of its outlets. See Carrie Goerne, "Retailers Boost Efforts to Target African-American Consumers," *Marketing News* (June 22, 1992): 2.

Additional Example: Glory Foods, Inc., announced plans to offer the first national line of packaged soul food (e.g., okra, collard greens). See "Packaged Soul," *Newsweek* (September 14, 1992): 6.

MARKETING OPPORTUNITY

Cosmetics lines developed specifically for black consumers have done well. Black skin can have 35 distinct undertones (as compared to seven for whites), so possibilities for different product formulations are much larger.[14] In a first for a major cosmetics company, Maybelline introduced a line of makeup products for black consumers called "Shades of You." Until now, major companies have opted to include shade ranges for darker skin as a part of their regular lines. Maybelline already sells the leading eye makeup brand for black women.[15]

Blacks and the Media

Blacks are heavy media users. Black households watch an average of ten hours of television a day, a rate 39 percent higher than the average Ameri-

99 99%/100%/100% PURE

Why is EBONY ranked by ADWEEK as one of the nation's hottest[1] magazines?

Why are EBONY's paid subscriptions up 22%?[2]

The answer is EBONY is pure black. Intentionally so. EBONY was created by blacks for blacks. Now, forty years later, our circulation is growing faster than ever before. Why? Because we give Black Americans a pure, positive view of their life and times. General media? They give a watered-down, diluted and sometimes biased view of the black experience. So, while some blacks read general market magazines and many watch television... they feel like outsiders looking in. Our readers live with EBONY. And EBONY's 100% credibility can be yours.

But you want more than the quality of EBONY's environment. You want reach, penetration and big numbers. Fine. You get all that in EBONY. We're the only mass medium truly welcomed into our increasingly affluent black households.

What's the value of all this reach and credibility? Sales.

EBONY boosts the selling power of your advertising. Proof? Many of our advertisers celebrate average sales increases of 48%.[3]

It's your choice. Try selling the $163 billion dollar[4] black consumer market with only general market media. Or use the only mass medium that sells 46% of that market with 100% credibility.

Go for the black. It's pure gold.

EBONY®

Nothing sells black consumers better.

For more information please call EBONY: New York (212) 586-2911, Chicago (312) 322-9200, Los Angeles (213) 386-5200.

1. ADWEEK, March, 1984.   2. Magazine Publishers Association, 1983 vs. 1982.   3. Wellington/Access Study, 1982.   4. U.S. Bureau of Labor Statistics.

Ebony is targeted to a solely black readership. Reprinted by permission of *EBONY* Magazine and Johnson Publishing Company, Inc.

can household. This segment tends to prefer established programming and is less likely to experiment with new offerings. As a result, they are more likely to be loyal to major networks, cable networks, and superstations such as WTBS, which attracts about 10 percent of the black viewing audience. In addition, readership of local morning daily newspapers (as opposed to major regional papers) is 30 percent higher than with adults overall, and blacks also are more likely to read classified ads and circulars.

BLACK REPRESENTATION IN MAINSTREAM MEDIA   Historically, blacks have not been well represented in mainstream advertising, but this situation is changing. Blacks now account for about one-quarter of the people depicted in ads (a rate even greater than their actual proportion of the overall population), and commercials are increasingly likely to be racially integrated.[16] The more striking and important change, though, is the way black people are portrayed on television. Unlike earlier shows that presented blacks in stereotyped roles, such as "Sanford and Son" and "The Jeffersons," most television roles created for blacks now tend to depict them as middle-to-upper-class individuals who also happen to be black (e.g., "The Cosby Show" or "The Fresh Prince of Bel Air").[17]

BLACK-ORIENTED MEDIA   Several major magazines, such as *Jet, Ebony, Essence,* and *Black Enterprise,* target this segment exclusively, and with great success. *Jet,* for example, claims to reach over 90 percent of the black male audience.[18] As the ad for *Ebony* shown here indicates, black media tend to depict consumers in their natural social environment and more positively than in the general media, so it is not surprising that many blacks gravitate to these magazines and newspapers.[19]

Targeted Advertising.   Advertising to blacks often is better executed when it is sensitive to important cues and avoids symbols irrelevant to the black subculture. For this reason, it is not uncommon for companies to commission a specialized agency to develop a separate ad campaign specifically targeted to the black market. Canadian Mist's general advertising campaign featured the motif Canada at its best and emphasized picturesque scenery and a rural lifestyle. A separate advertising program for blacks was developed by a black agency, which instead focused on style and an urban environment.[20]

Teaching Hint: Ethnic segmentation of the cigarette market is hardly a new phenomenon. A content analysis of cigarette ads appearing in *Life* and *Ebony* between 1950–1965 showed that the *Ebony* ads almost exclusively featured black models (primarily athletes), while none of these endorsements appears in *Life.* This advertising also was on average two to three years tardy in offering filtered cigarettes to black consumers. See Richard W. Pollay, Jung S. Lee, and David Carter-Whitney, "Separate, But Not Equal: Racial Segmentation in Cigarette Advertising," *Journal of Advertising* 21 (March 1992).

M A R K E T I N G   P I T F A L L

The R.J. Reynolds Tobacco Company ignited a lot of controversy when it announced plans to test-market a menthol cigarette, called Uptown, specifically to black consumers. Although the marketing of cigarettes to minorities is not a novel tactic, it was the first time a company explicitly acknowledged the strategy. Many critics immediately attacked the proposal, arguing that the campaign would exploit poor blacks. The publishers of black-oriented newspapers and magazines were caught in the middle, since they stood to receive substantial advertising revenues from the campaign. For example, approximately 10 percent of *Jet*'s advertising revenues come from cigarette advertising. For its part, the company claimed that its actions were a natural result of shrinking markets and the need to more finely target increasingly small segments.

Unlike other ethnic groups, which do not seem to display marked cigarette preferences, the tastes of black consumers are easy to pinpoint. According to the company, 69 percent of black consumers prefer menthol, more than twice the rate of smokers overall. After market research indicated that blacks tend to open cigarette packs from the bottom, the company decided to pack Uptowns with the filters facing down. Reynolds claimed that the product was not designed specifically for blacks, although it acknowledged that it was likely to attract a disproportionate share of black smokers. Following a storm of criticism by both private health groups and government officials (including the Secretary of Health and Human Services), the company announced that it was canceling its test-marketing plans. It would not comment on the likelihood that the cigarette would ever be introduced.[21]

Maximum Care For Beautiful Hair. MoistureMax.

MoistureMax protects all types of hair—relaxed, natural or pressed—from moisture loss caused by comb-ing, brushing, blow drying or hot styling.

MoistureMax's soothing, saturating formula of panthenol, lanolin, and jojoba oil penetrates hair to replenish natural moisture and restore sheen. Dryness, breakage and split ends simply melt away. So hair becomes easier to comb. Unlike other oil moisturizers, our feather-light formula contains no beeswax to weigh your hair down.

Try new MoistureMax Oil Sheen Spray when styling your hair. It gives you MoistureMax protection, while giving lasting sheen.

Keep beautiful hair in the family. With maximum care from MoistureMax.

Lustrasilk

Give Your Hair What It Needs Most. MoistureMax.

This ad for MoistureMax hair products promotes the stability of the black family. Courtesy of Lus-trasilk Corporation of America, Inc.

Family Emphasis. A Crest toothpaste ad done by a black agency had a powerful impact on target consumers. It depicted a simple act: A father lov-ingly showing his son how to knot a tie. The copy reads: "I'm going to be involved with my son as much as I can."[22] This idealized father/son rela-tionship often is taken for granted by whites, but it hits home to many black consumers, 40 percent of whom grow up in fatherless households.[23] Adver-tising has in general tried to promote a positive image of black men by stressing family involvement. This focus is reflected in the ad for Moisture-Max shown here.

The BUPPIE. This change also has been dictated by the growing black middle class and the emergence of the so-called BUPPIE, or Black YUPPIE.[24] Although some marketers assume that black consumers who have moved up the social ladder forsake their ethnic identities, this assumption does not appear to be the case. Middle-class blacks instead appear to span subcultures, exhibiting the attitudes of the white middle-class while still holding on to their black heritage. Black shoppers respond well to products that appeal to their racial pride.[25] This tact was taken in an ad targeted to blacks by Miller beer featuring a middle-class black man. The copy read, "He moved up, but not out." The McDonald's ad shown here was part of a campaign targeted to black consumers that was developed by an agency specializing in this market segment.

Black Celebrities. The use of black celebrities and sports figures is also on the rise. The proliferation of black role models appears to be reducing the racial

First date.

Her Mama insisted,
"OK, as long as you stay in the neighborhood."
His Dad suggested,
"Go someplace where you'll feel welcome and comfortable."
His wallet pleaded, "Take it easy man, easy."
He smoothly stated,
"And after the movie, we'll go to Mickey D's.®"

IT'S A GOOD TIME FOR THE GREAT TASTE®

© 1985 McDonald's Corporation

This ad for McDonald's was developed by a black agency for black markets. Courtesy of McDonald's Corporation.

Cross-Cultural Examples: Coca-Cola found that black consumers had trouble relating to its Max Headroom campaign for Sprite so it developed a separate campaign for this market. In two years, Sprite became the number one lemon-lime drink among blacks. Occasionally, specialized advertising actually turns out to be so universal it is adapted for the general market. The Kentucky Fried Chicken theme of "We Do Chicken Right," for example, was originally developed by a black agency exclusively for black consumers in the New York area. See Trudy Gallant-Stokes, "Black Marketing Marksmanship," Marketing Insights (Spring 1990): 101–4; Jeffrey L. Kovach, "Minority Sell: Ads Target Blacks, Hispanics, but . . . ," *Industry Week* (November 11,1985): 29.

distinctions formerly made by many. However, this strategy does not guarantee success with black consumers. For example, while Pepsi has used singer Michael Jackson in its ad campaigns, its research showed that he did not appeal to 25- to 40-year-old blacks, who interpreted his plastic surgery and eccentric behavior as a desire to distance himself from his black roots.[26] On the other hand, a black version of the popular cartoon character Bart Simpson became extremely popular in the black community in the early 1990s. Bart has been recast in the image of several black celebrities, including Malcolm X, Bob Marley (Rasta Bart), and Michael Jordan (Air Bart). Bart's popularity in the black subculture has been attributed to his status as an outsider with an attitude who battles established society.[27]

MARKETING OPPORTUNITY

The recent proliferation of ethnic dolls in America's toy stores reflects society's growing cultural diversity. While non-Caucasian dolls used to appear only in collections of dolls from around the world, all major manufacturers have now introduced ethnic dolls to the mass market. These new entrants include Kira, the Asian fashion doll, and Emmy, the African-American baby doll. As illustrated in the photo at the beginning of this chapter, Mattel recently introduced a trio of dolls named Shani (which means "marvelous" in Swahili), Asha, and Nichelle that represent the range of African-American facial features and skin tones. And, while Mattel has sold a black version of Barbie for over twenty years, it only recently began to promote the doll in television and print campaigns.[28]

Hispanic-Americans

The Hispanic subculture is a sleeping giant, a segment that was until recently largely ignored by many marketers. The growth and increasing affluence of this group has now made it impossible to overlook, and the Hispanic consumer is now diligently courted by many major corporations. For example, Pepsi sponsors local ethnic festivals in major cities, and the company also signed the music group Miami Sound Machine for its Latin promotions.[29]

The Hispanic Market

Demographically, two important characteristics of the Hispanic market are worth noting: First, it is a young market. The median age of Hispanic-Americans is 23.6, compared with the U.S. average of 32. Second, the Hispanic family is much larger than the rest of the population's. The average Hispanic household contains 3.5 people, compared to only 2.7 people for other U.S. households. These differences obviously affect the overall allocation of income to various product categories. For example, Hispanic households spend 15 percent to 20 percent more of their disposable income than the national average on groceries.[30] There are now over 19 million Hispanic consumers in the United States, and a number of factors make this market segment extremely attractive.

- Hispanics tend to be brand loyal, especially to brands from their country of origin. In one study, about 45 percent reported that they always buy their usual brand, while only one in five said they frequently switch brands.[31]

- Hispanics are highly concentrated by national origin, which makes them relatively easy to reach. Over 50 percent of all Hispanics live in the Los Angeles, New York, Miami, San Antonio, San Francisco, and Chicago metropolitan areas. For this reason, 70 percent of Avon's sales representatives in the Los Angeles area are Latino.[32]

- Education levels are increasing dramatically. In the period between 1984 and 1988, the number of Hispanics with four years of college increased by 51 percent. The number of men in managerial and professional jobs increased by 42 percent, and the corresponding increase of 61 percent for women was even more encouraging.[33]

THE ROLE OF THE CHURCH   While Hispanics traditionally have been predominantly Catholic, millions of Hispanics are leaving the Roman Catholic Church. It is estimated that about one in five Hispanics now practices some form of evangelical Protestantism. This change is ascribed to two factors: The evangelical Protestants have adopted sophisticated marketing techniques, such as providing local clergy with profiles of Hispanic communities in a campaign to convert large numbers of Hispanic Catholics, and the style of U.S. Catholicism is alien to many Hispanics. It tends to be more rational and bureaucratic and is not viewed by many as being responsive to the more emotional and mystical Hispanic religious experience. For example, the belief in miraculous healing that is prevalent in Latin American Catholicism does not tend to be emphasized in American churches.[34]

THE ROLE OF THE FAMILY   The importance of the family to Hispanics cannot be overstated. Preferences to spend time with family influence the structure of many consumption activities. As one illustration, the act of going to the movies has a different meaning for many Hispanics, who tend to regard this activity as a family outing. One study found that 42 percent of Hispanic moviegoers attend in groups of three or more, as compared with only 28 percent of Anglo consumers.[35]

Behaviors that underscore one's ability to provide well for the family are reinforced in this subculture. Clothing one's children well is regarded in particular as a matter of pride. In contrast, convenience and a product's ability to save time is not terribly important to the Hispanic homemaker, who is willing to purchase labor-intensive products if it means that her family will benefit. For this reason, a time-saving appeal short-circuited for Quaker Foods, which found that Hispanic women tend to cook Instant Quaker Oats on the stove, refrigerate it, and serve it later as a pudding.[36] This orientation also explains why generic products do not tend to do well in the Hispanic market; these consumers value the quality promised by well-known brand names.

The pervasiveness of the family theme can be seen in many marketing contexts. When Johnson Wax decided to enter the Hispanic market with Future floor polish, market research revealed that Hispanic consumers

Cross-Cultural Example:
Soft Sheen Products recently introduced Baby Love, the first line of products for black and Hispanic babies. This move represents the first entrant in a new segment of the ethnic hair-care industry, which generates about $200 million annually. See Kate Fitzgerald, "Hair-Care Eyes Ethnic Babies," *Advertising Age* (February 11, 1991): 8.

Cross-Cultural Example:
The first major American film to be simultaneously released in Spanish and English was "An American Tail." This was a very appropriate choice, since the movie told the story of a family of mice that immigrated to America. In the first week of its release, the Spanish-language theater in which the movie was shown recorded the second highest box office gross of any screen in the country. See "Bilingual Mice Go Hollywood," *American Demographics* (July 1987): 25.

Cross-Cultural Example:
After discovering that Hispanics tend to eat at home more than Anglos, Campbell's Soup developed a line of more than fifty food products under the Casera name, targeted to consumers of Caribbean origin. See Howard LaFranchi, "Media and Marketers Discover Hispanic Boom," *Christian Science Monitor* (April 20, 1988): 1.

cleaned their floors regularly, but did not wax them. As a result of this finding, the company's television commercial depicted a housewife standing on her dull floor and being asked: "We know your floors are clean, but do they shine?" Traditional gender roles are then reinforced as the husband leaps into the air, shouting *resalta* (outstanding).[37]

Appealing to Hispanic Subcultures

The behavior profile of the Hispanic consumer includes a need for status and a strong sense of pride. A high value is placed on self-expression and familial devotion. Some campaigns have played to Hispanics' fear of rejection and apprehension about loss of control and embarrassment in social situations. Conventional wisdom is to create action-oriented advertising and to emphasize a problem-solving atmosphere. Assertive role models who are cast in nonthreatening situations appear to be effective.[38]

Procter & Gamble is the biggest advertiser in Hispanic media. The company spends nearly $21 million a year catering to this segment. P&G also was one of the first to establish a Hispanic corporate marketing structure that has Hispanic group brand managers. It has focused on introducing products such as diapers, cleansers, and grooming products that capitalize on the youth and large family size prevalent among Hispanics.[39]

MARKETING BLUNDERS Many initial efforts by Americans to market to this subculture were, to say the least, counterproductive. Companies bumbled in their efforts to translate advertising adequately or to compose copy that could capture desired nuances. These mistakes do not occur so much anymore as marketers become more sophisticated in dealing with this market and as Hispanics themselves become involved in advertising production. The following are some translation mishaps that have occurred.[40]

- The Perdue slogan, "It takes a tough man to make a tender chicken," was translated as "It takes a sexually excited man to make a chick affectionate."
- Budweiser was promoted as the "queen of beers."
- A burrito was mistakenly called a *burrada*, which means big mistake.
- Braniff, promoting its comfortable leather seats, used the headline, *Sentado en cuero,* which was interpreted as "Sit naked."
- Coors beer's slogan to "get loose with Coors" appeared in Spanish as "get the runs with Coors."

HISPANIC IDENTITY Native language and culture are important components of Hispanic identity and self-esteem (about three-quarters of Latinos still speak Spanish when at home), and these consumers are very sympathetic to marketing efforts that acknowledge and emphasize the Hispanic cultural heritage.[41] More than 40 percent of Hispanic consumers say they deliberately attempt to buy products that show an interest in the Hispanic consumer, and this number jumps to over two-thirds for Cuban-Americans.[42]

Most Hispanic-Americans are avid consumers of soap operas, called *telenovellas.* Ethnic soap operas, shown on American television, are becoming big business. Univision, the biggest Spanish-language network, airs ten different ones each day. These shows are produced by Latin American net-

TABLE 14-1 Segmenting the Hispanic-American Subculture by Degree of Acculturation

Segment	Size	Status	Description	Characteristics
Established Adapters	17%	Upwardly mobile	Older, U.S. born; assimilated into U.S. culture	Relatively low identification with Hispanic culture
Young Strivers	16%	Increasingly important	Younger, born in U.S.; high motvation to succeed; expect to adapt to U.S. culture	Movement to reconnect with Hispanic roots
Hopeful Loyalists	40%	Largest segment, but shrinking	Working-class; traditional values	Slow to adapt to U.S. culture; Spanish is dominant language
Recent Seekers	27%	Growing segment	Newest immigrants; very conservative with high aspirations	Strongest identification with Hispanic background; little use of non-Hispanic media

Source: Adapted from a report by Yankelovich Clancy Shulman, described in "A Subculture With Very Different Needs," *Adweek* (May 11, 1992): 44. By permission of Yankelovich Partners, Inc.

works, but some viewers have complained that they do not address such problems of Hispanic-Americans as illegal immigration, getting a job, or speaking the language. The second-largest Spanish-language network, Telemundo, finally aired a *telenovella* about a U.S. Hispanic family in 1989.[43]

Level of Acculturation. A consumer's level of *acculturation* refers to the degree to which he or she has learned the ways of a different culture from the one in which he or she was originally raised. This factor is especially important when considering the Hispanic market, since the degree to which these consumers are integrated into the American way of life varies widely. For instance, about 38 percent of all Hispanics live in barrios, or predominantly Hispanic neighborhoods, which tend to be insulated from mainstream society.[44] Table 14–1 describes a recent attempt to segment Hispanic consumers in terms of degree of acculturation.

Differences in Cultural Integration. On one hand, many Cuban-American families with high educational levels fled Castro's regime in the late 1950s and early 1960s, worked hard for many years to establish themselves and are now firmly entrenched in the Miami political and economic establishment. Because of this affluence, businesses in South Florida now make an effort to target YUCAs (young, upwardly mobile Cuban-Americans),[45] as is the case in the ad shown on page 482 for a local radio station.

On the other hand, it is estimated that anywhere from 1.8 million to 5.4 million immigrants enter the country illegally each year. The majority of these people have less than a fifth-grade education and are concerned with fitting into their new country. Since they are eager to adapt to their new environment, these consumers tend to look for products they perceive to be more American, which may mean learning entirely new product categories.

Cross-Cultural Example: Recent evidence indicates that most minorities and a substantial portion of Anglo consumers believe Hispanics are underrepresented in the media. However, despite indications that Hispanic characters tend to be portrayed in a negative light, most consumers do not perceive that they are portrayed unfairly. See Ronald J. Faber, Thomas C. O'Guinn, and Timothy P. Meyer, "Televised Portrayals of Hispanics: A Comparison of Ethnic Perceptions," *International Journal of Intercultural Relations* 11 (1987): 155–69.

Who keeps Laura de Oña entertained?

Name: Laura de Oña.
Occupation: Attorney.
Age: 43.
Family: Mother of two.
Car: Mercedes Benz.
Hobbies: Playing tennis.
Last vacation spot: Hawaii
Latest book: *Atlas Shrugged*.
Radio Station: WQBA-FM, for the latest in Latin and American music.

The Super Q/FM listener profile is best represented by people like Laura de Oña. These career oriented, bilingual, educated Latins from 25 to 49 make up the majority of our listening audience. This Latin market in South Florida represents over $8.7 billion in spending power which most companies cannot ignore. You can reach this market by advertising on WQBA-FM.

For information contact Veronica Serra, National Sales Manager: WQBA AM/FM (305) 441-2073.

This trade ad for WQBA-FM, a South Florida radio station, describes its Hispanic listeners, who fit the profile of the YUCA (Young, Upwardly Mobile Cuban-American). *Courtesy of WQBA-FM Miami.*

The implication for marketers is that these consumers must be taught about a product (e.g., air freshener, which is not common in Central America) before they can be convinced to buy one brand over another.[46]

Leaving one's culture and family to go to a new place creates many needs that can only be partially addressed by products and services. Recent immigrants (both legal and illegal) encounter a strange culture and have often left family members behind. This frightening odyssey was incorporated by AT&T in its campaign to boost international calling volume. In a Spanish-language commercial called "Countryside," a young man says good-bye to his mother and promises to keep in touch. The announcer says, "The decision of leaving the family is based on a promise: Keeping it united."

Progressive Learning. The acculturation of Hispanic consumers may be understood in terms of the **progressive learning model**. This perspective assumes that people gradually learn a new culture as they increasingly come in contact with it. Thus, we would expect the consumer behavior of Hispanic-Americans to be a mixture of practices taken from their original culture and those of the new or *host culture*.[47]

Research has generally obtained results that support this pattern when factors such as shopping orientation, the importance placed on various product attributes, media preference, and brand loyalty are examined.[48] When the intensity of ethnic identification is taken into account, consumers who retained a strong ethnic identification differed from their more assimilated counterparts in the following ways.[49]

- They had a more negative attitude toward business in general (probably caused by frustration due to relatively low income levels).
- They were higher users of Spanish language media.
- They were more brand loyal.
- They were more likely to prefer brands with prestige labels.
- They were more likely to buy brands specifically advertised to their ethnic group.

SEGMENTING HISPANIC SUBCULTURES As with other large subcultural group, marketers are now beginning to discover that the Hispanic market is not homogeneous. Subcultural identity is not as much with being Hispanic as it is with the particular country of origin. Mexican-Americans, who make up about 62 percent of all Hispanic-Americans, also are the fastest-growing subsegment; their population has grown by 40 percent since 1980. In contrast, Cuban-Americans are by far the wealthiest subsegment, but they are also the smallest Hispanic ethnic group and are older on average than other Hispanics.[50] Because of large cultural differences among segments, it is important to address specific wants and needs of Hispanic subgroups. The Winn-Dixie supermarket chain, for example, promotes holidays and dishes native to individual countries and employs the theme: "Winn-Dixie *tiene el sabor de mi pais*" (Winn-Dixie has the flavor of my country).[51]

Research Report: The insulation of some Hispanics creates obstacles for conventional marketing research, due to such factors as low incidence of telephone ownership and the tendency to have unlisted numbers when a phone is available. The phone is primarily used to call only family and friends, and these consumers see no reason to publicize their number. A personal interview technique, using bilingual Hispanics as interviewers, is much more effective. See Sigredo A. Hernandez and Carol J. Kaufman, "Marketing Research in Hispanic Barrios: A Guide to Survey Research," *Marketing Research* (March 1990): 11–27.

M A R K E T I N G   P I T F A L L

While many corporations are just now waking up to the potential of the Hispanic market, others that sell harmful products such as junk food, cigarettes, and alcohol discovered this market long ago. Critics point to a high concentration of liquor stores and related advertising in Hispanic neighborhoods. Available evidence indicates that Mexican-born men stand a greater chance of dying of cirrhosis of the liver and that Hispanic men also are more likely to die of lung cancer than are Anglos. The smoking rate of fourth- and fifth-grade Hispanic boys is roughly five times that of Anglo boys.[52] In many cities, community action groups and others have begun programs to reverse these trends.

Asian-Americans

Although their numbers are still relatively small, Asian-Americans are the fastest-growing minority group in the United States. Marketers are just beginning to recognize their potential as a unique market segment. This subculture is attractive to marketers because Asian-Americans typically are hard working and many have above-average incomes. The average household incomes of Asian-Americans are more than $2000 greater than those of whites and $7000–$9000 higher than those of blacks and Hispanics.

This subculture places a very high priority on education and sends a large percentage of children to college. Of Asian-Americans over the age of 25, about a third have completed four or more years of college, twice the graduation rate of whites and more than quadruple that of blacks and Hispanics.[53]

Segmenting Asian-Americans

Despite its potential, this group is hard to market to, because it is actually composed of subgroups that are culturally diverse and speak many different languages and dialects. The term *Asian* refers to 20 ethnic groups, with Chinese being the largest and Filipino and Japanese second and third, respectively.[54] Also, although their birth rate is increasing at almost four times the rate of most other groups, Asian-Americans still comprise only about 2 percent of the population, so mass marketing techniques often are not viable to reach them.[55] Finally, Asian-Americans save more of their wages and borrow less, preferring to keep large balances in conservative passbook accounts rather than investing their earnings. On the other hand, as one Asian-American advertising executive noted, "Prosperous Asians tend to be very status-conscious and will spend their money on premium brands, such as BMW and Mercedes-Benz, and the best French cognac and Scotch whiskey."[56] This group also is a good market for technically oriented products. They spend more than average on such products as VCRs, personal computers, and compact disc players.

Advertising that features Asian celebrities can be particularly effective. When Reebok used tennis star Michael Chang in one execution, shoe sales among Asian-Americans soared. Skating star Kristi Yamaguchi, shown here

Asian-American skating star Kristi Yamaguchi is the first athlete to grace the cover of Kellogg's Special K cereal. Courtesy of Kellogg Company. Kellogg's® and Special K® are registered trademarks of Kellogg Company.

on the Kellogg's Special K cereal box, has also been widely used for celebrity endorsements, despite some concerns that fears of anti-Japanese sentiment would prevent endorsement deals with many marketers.[57]

MARKETING BLUNDERS The problems encountered by American marketers when they first tried to reach the Hispanic market also occurred when targeting Asians and Asian-Americans. Some attempts to translate advertising messages and concepts into Asian media have backfired. Coca-Cola's slogan, "Coke Adds Life" was translated as "Coke brings your ancestors back from the dead" in Japanese. One company did attempt to run an ad in Chinese to wish the community a Happy New Year, but the characters were upside down.

Other advertisements have overlooked the complex differences among Asian subcultures (e.g., some advertisements targeted to Koreans have used Japanese models), and some have unknowingly been insensitive to cultural practices. Kentucky Fried Chicken, for example, ran into a problem when it described its chicken as finger-licking good to the Chinese, who don't lick their fingers in appreciation when food is good.[58] In another case, a footwear ad depicted Japanese women performing footbinding, a practice done exclusively in China.[59]

REACHING THE ASIAN-AMERICAN SEGMENT Many marketers are discouraged by the lack of media available to reach Asian-Americans.[60] Practitioners generally find that advertising in English works best for broadcast ads, while print ads are more effective when executed in Asian languages.[61] Filipinos are the only Asians who predominantly speak English among themselves; most Asians prefer media in their own languages.[62] The most frequently spoken languages among Asian-Americans are Mandarin Chinese, Korean, Japanese, and Vietnamese.[63] In an attempt to reach these groups, Pacific Bell produces its brochures in three of these languages, as shown in the photo here.

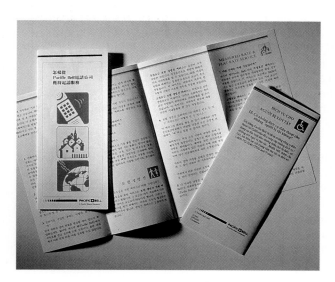

To counter the problem of overlooking differences among Asian-Americans, Pacific Bell produces its brochures in three languages: Korean (left), Vietnamese (center), and Chinese. © Pacific Bell 1993. Reprinted by permission of Pacific Bell. Photographer, David Dempster.

An example of Met Life's attempts to focus on family priorities is available as Transparency 38. The caption reads, "You protect your baby. Who protects you?"

One Success Story. One of the first companies to realize the potential of the Asian-American segment was Metropolitan Life Insurance Company. Since Asian-American consumers tend to be well educated and place a very high priority on the education and security of their children, they seemed ideal prospects for insurance products. Qualitative research showed marked differences among Asian subsegments in their attitudes toward insurance. These differences paralleled those between Cuban-Americans and Mexican-Americans, in that subsegments' degree of acculturation affect understanding and interest in products and services.

In general, Asians tend to be leery of buying insurance, superstitiously equating its purchase with old age and death. The company found that Chinese consumers emphasize family members' protection and education, so they were more likely to be interested in whole-life policies. On the other hand, Vietnamese consumers, many of whom were recent immigrants, tended to be unfamiliar with the concept of insurance. Still, this group is seen as having potential since they are very survival oriented.[64] Based on this research, a Chinese ad campaign stressed the role of insurance in protecting children. As a reward for its efforts, Met Life increased its premiums among Asian Americans by 22 percent in one year.[65]

Religious Subcultures

Heritage Village, a religiously oriented entertainment center in South Carolina, illustrates the relationship between religion and consumer behavior. Attendance at this 2300-acre complex is exceeded only by the Disney theme parks. It features a church, a passion play, and replicas of Old Jerusalem, along with a bustling shopping mall called Main Street USA. A central theme of the park is its idealized presentation of America's past and traditional values, the pristine vision of America desired by those who make the Heritage Village pilgrimage.[66]

Impact on Consumption

Religion *per se* has not been studied extensively in marketing, possibly because it is seen as a taboo subject.[67] However, the little evidence that has been accumulated indicates that religious affiliation has the potential to be a valuable predictor of consumer behavior.[68] Religious subcultures in particular may exert a significant impact on such consumer variables as personality, attitudes toward sexuality, birthrates and household formation, income, and political attitudes.

One study that examined this issue, for example, found marked differences among Catholic, Protestant, and Jewish college students in preferences for weekend entertainment activities, as well as the criteria used in making these decisions. For example, price was a relatively more important criterion for Protestants, while desire for companionship was highest for Jews. Catholics were most likely to designate dancing as a favored activity than were the other two groups, but much less likely to select sex.[69]

This controversial Benetton ad was rejected by some magazines because of what some perceived to be offensive religious symbolism. Photographer: O. Toscani for Benetton.

The Catholic Subculture

Catholic dogmas encompass virtually all of the individual's behavior. The Catholic Church is characterized by a rigid organizational structure, and personal interpretations of events are minimized. Some observers have inferred that Catholic consumers as a result tend to be fatalistic and are less likely to be innovators. The controversial Benetton ad shown here draws heavily on Catholic symbolism.

Catholics have more children than either Protestants or Jews. Sexuality is seen as instrumental, in the sense that it is performed for the purpose of procreation rather than recreation. There is some evidence that this attitude is changing: As far back as 1975, 50 percent of Catholics endorsed the idea that a husband and wife may engage in sex for pleasure alone, as compared to only 29 percent who said this in 1965.[70]

Members of this religious group traditionally have a lower socioeconomic status than Jews and Protestants. This deficit may stem from a variety of causes, including historical religious discrimination. Other factors include traditionalism, restricted knowledge seeking, and an emphasis on collective rather than individual initiative.

The Protestant Subculture

In contrast to Catholics, Protestant dogma stresses the faith of the individual. The bible is viewed more as descriptive than as evidence of divine control. This tradition encourages the acquisition of scientific knowledge. Protestants tend to be less authoritarian and to value work and personal hardship as an avenue toward upward social mobility.

While not all Protestants are wealthy, they appear in disproportionate numbers in the upper classes. Explanations for this relative affluence include the following.[71]

- An emphasis on industriousness and hard work.
- A low fertility rate that facilitates the upward mobility of children.
- A U.S. social structure in which Protestants were historically part of the *power-elite.*

Early colonists were overwhelmingly Protestant, which allowed this group to create the foundations of the American social system and thus create barriers-to-entry for other groups. The Protestant establishment still dominates leadership positions in the private sector and is also overrepresented in science, education, government, and the military.[72] It is only recently that Irish Catholics have reached economic parity with Protestants, while Conservative and Reform Jews have surpassed this level.[73]

The WASP Subculture: The Idealized American. The WASP (White Anglo-Saxon Protestant) subculture may be thought of as the one ethnic group not acknowledged to be an ethnic group. After all, no one has yet used the term WASP-American! Despite this ethnic invisibility, the WASP subculture has been a dominant force in the larger picture of American culture.[74] In fact, the WASP has been a symbol of the American ideal for some time. For many immigrants, the WASP still symbolizes the light at the end of the tunnel: If one desires to assimilate, to make it in America, the WASP is the goal.

As a result of this idealized view of the WASP, the formal eating rituals devised by WASPs and propagated by such etiquette guides as Emily Post are assumed to be the "proper" way to eat and entertain. The leisure activities associated with this subculture (e.g., golfing, yachting, squash) often are seen as socially correct.[75] Marketers have done more than their share to propagate this ideal. Idealized images of the WASP are frequently employed in advertising to epitomize the good life and the amenities associated with old money (see Chapter 12). In particular, the success of influential designer Ralph Lauren hinges on his ability to create images of an idealized WASP lifestyle.

The Jewish Subculture

Research Report: One study has examined the effect of including a kosher claim in a breakfast cereal ad on consumer information processing. See Michael A. Kamins and Lawrence J. Marks, "The Perception of Kosher as a Third Party Certification Claim in Advertising for Familiar and Unfamiliar Brands," *Journal of the Academy of Marketing Science* 19 (1991): 177–185.

Jewish ethnicity exerts an exceptionally strong influence, since it incorporates both cultural and religious dimensions. American Jews tend to be of relatively high socioeconomic status and average family size is relatively low (with the exception of some Orthodox groups).

Judaism reinforces individual responsibility for actions and self-education.[76] Jewish consumers have a personality structure characterized by high product innovation tendencies, need for achievement, anxiousness, emotionality, and individualism.[77] One study of Jewish versus gentile consumers indeed found that the Jewish respondents were more likely to have been exposed to educational materials in childhood, to use more sources in the process of information search, to be product innovators, and to transfer more consumption information to others.[78]

MARKETING AND THE JEWISH SUBCULTURE Some marketers have specifically employed Jewish symbolism in their advertising campaigns. The ads for Sun Maid and Delta Airlines shown here provide two examples of this strategy. The Bank Leumi Trust Company of New York, an Israel-based bank, capitalized on its ethnic ties to reach Jewish and gentile customers with ad copy such as the following used to promote Individual Retirement Accounts: "Some people need a little help getting to the Promised Land. If you dream of retiring to a land of milk and honey, you're going to need plenty of bread."[79]

Cross-Cultural Example: When Coors displayed the small U in a circle to indicate the product had obtained rabbinical certification that its beer complied with kosher dietary laws, sales increased by 15 percent in New York and a whopping 38 percent in Philadelphia. See Andrew Murr, "Move Over, Matzos," *Newsweek* (July 1, 1991): 45.

Some major companies, such as Sun Maid raisins and Delta Airlines, attempt to appeal to Jewish consumers by using symbolism and language understood by this consumer subculture. Courtesy of Sun-Diamond Growers of California and Delta Airlines.

One famous campaign for a bakery company used Chinese, blacks, and other spokesmen to tell consumers "You don't have to be Jewish to love Levy's real Jewish rye."[80]

MARKETING OPPORTUNITY

One of the most significant Jewish-related marketing developments is the increase in demand for kosher food. Each year, about 500 new kosher products appear on the market to satisfy this demand. This trend is being driven by two developments: The increased religious observance by young Jews, and the belief among many gentiles that kosher food is of higher quality. In addition to some Jews, Seventh-Day Adventists and Moslems have very similar dietary requirements and are good customers for kosher food.[81] It is estimated that less than a third of the 6 million consumers who buy kosher products are Jewish.[82]

The potential of the kosher market has prompted some of the nation's largest manufacturers to get involved. General Foods distributed 100,000 copies of a children's activity booklet called *Brachos* (Prayers) for Breakfast. Wise Potato Chips produces kosher chips, and Eagle Snacks also makes kosher snack foods. Of the 330 products made by Pepperidge Farm, Inc., 255 are now kosher.[83]

The Born-Again Subculture

Recent years have seen a dramatic increase in the number of consumers who profess to be born-again Christians, or evangelicals. A recent Gallup Poll indicates that one-third of American adults say they are born-again. While this movement has affected a variety of social classes and consumer types, it is strongest among women, older adults, and Southerners. It is also a relatively downscale phenomenon: The number of adults who describe themselves as being "born again" steadily decreases as education and income levels rise.[84] The born-again movement is exerting a significant impact on American marketing as well as on *demarketing*, which is the discouraging of demand for certain products and services. This community has been influential in altering the content of media programming and advertising that is seen to unduly emphasize sex and violence.

CONSUMPTION CHARACTERISTICS OF THE BORN-AGAIN SEGMENT The evidence is unclear as to whether the consumption behavior of born-again Christians is radically different from that of other subcultures. In general, highly religious Protestants are more likely to endorse traditional sex-role orientations, to be below-average users of credit, and to place relatively low emphasis on purchasing national brands. They also are not as likely as the general public to listen to rock-and-roll music (perhaps due to a perceived emphasis on sex and drugs), preferring gospel and contemporary Christian music. And, while there are no differences in terms of such activities as eating out or attending concerts, born-again Christians do attend movies less frequently than do other groups.[85]

MARKETING PITFALL

Some merchants who cater to the born-again segment have run into trouble for targeting these consumers *too* exclusively. A car dealer in Virginia is representative of attempts to service only true believers. He unveiled a Christian Members Buying Plan, which would allow some people to purchase their cars at rock-bottom prices. In addition, he proposed to donate part of the profit from every sale to the buyer's church. The American Civil Liberties Union and other groups quickly objected to the plan, arguing that it discriminates against non-Christians. The group had been involved in an earlier dispute, where a Florida gas station owner had posted a sign reading "For Christians Only: 10 percent discount on labor."[86]

Christian Media. Christian broadcast media have become a powerful cultural force for many consumers. Approximately 12 percent of all U.S. radio stations have a religious format. In addition, about 200 local television stations regularly feature religious programming, and television preachers have an estimated audience of over 15 million people. This number represents almost the combined membership of the United Methodist, Presbyterian, and Episcopal churches.[87]

Not surprisingly, some research indicates that born-agains subscribe to religious magazines at a much higher rate than do other Christians and that they are higher-than-average subscribers to home-oriented magazines. Also of no surprise is the finding that almost 15 percent of these consumers list a televised church service as one of their three favorite television programs.

The Christian publishing industry has also shown phenomenal growth. According to trade figures, 37 million people spend $1.4 billion annually at Christian bookstores. According to one industry official, consumers are now very selective about what they buy, so Christian merchants must adopt a commitment to excel as God's retailer.[88] Many Christian bookstores have expanded their product mix. In addition to the traditional assortment of inspirational books and records, most carry what one official termed "holy hardware." These stores stock items ranging from "I Am Blessed" jogging suits to watches with pictures of the twelve apostles. Grace, the pro-life doll, delivers this message when squeezed: "God knew me even before I was born

. . . . I used to be a little person inside my mother's tummy . . . . My mommy thinks I'm very special. She's so happy she had me." More than 20,000 of these dolls, priced from $40 to $50, were sold in a four-month period.[89]

Chapter Summary

- Consumers identify with many groups that share common characteristics and identities. These large groups that exist within a society are *subcultures*, and membership in them often gives marketers a clue about individuals' consumption decisions. A large component of a person's identity is often determined by his or her ethnic origins and religious background.

- Recently, several minority groups have caught the attention of marketers as their economic power has grown. Segmenting consumers by their *ethnicity* can be effective, but care must be taken not to rely on inaccurate (and sometimes offensive) ethnic stereotypes.

- African-Americans are a very important market segment. While in some respects the market expenditures of these consumers do not differ that much from whites, blacks are above average consumers in such categories as personal-care products. In the past, blacks were either ignored or portrayed negatively in mainstream advertising, but such depictions are changing as more blacks actually work on the development of campaigns and as specialized black media increase in importance.

- Hispanic-Americans and Asian-Americans are other ethnic subcultures that are beginning to be actively courted by marketers. The size of both groups is increasing rapidly and in the coming years will dominate some major markets. Asian-Americans on the whole are extremely well educated, and the socioeconomic status of Hispanics is increasing as well.

- Key issues for reaching the Hispanic market are consumers' degree of *acculturation* into mainstream American society and the recognition of important cultural differences among Hispanic subgroups (e.g., Puerto Ricans, Cubans, Mexicans).

- Both Asian-Americans and Hispanic-Americans tend to be extremely family-oriented and are receptive to advertising that understands their heritage and reinforces traditional family values.

- While the impact of religious identification on consumer behavior is not clear, some differences among religious subcultures do emerge. In particular, cultural characteristics of Protestants, Catholics, and Jews result in varied preferences for leisure activities and orientations toward consumption. Some of these factors are closely related to social class. White Anglo-Saxon Protestants (WASPs) in particular have played a dominant role in the formation of American cultural values largely due to their cultural emphasis on achievement and early domination of the American power structure.

- The market power of the growing numbers of born-again Christians is uncertain at this point, but opportunities exist to cater to the unique needs of this segment.

Key Terms

de-ethnicitization, p. 470   progressive learning   subculture, p. 468
ethnic subculture, p. 469   model, p. 483

Consumer Behavior Challenge

1. R.J. Reynolds' controversial plan to test-market a cigarette to black consumers raises numerous ethical issues about segmenting subcultures. As one observer noted, "The irony is that if R.J. Reynolds made shoes or shirts and specifically marketed to blacks, they would probably be regarded as progressive and socially positive."[90] Does a company have the right to exploit a subculture's special characteristics, especially to increase sales of a harmful product like cigarettes? What about the argument that virtually every business that follows the marketing concept designs a product to meet the needs and tastes of a preselected segment? For example, the chapter also notes that Maybelline developed a makeup line specifically for black women, yet this did not seem to bother anyone. What do you think?

2. The chapter notes that products can function as socialization agents for ethnic groups, citing the example of the air freshener product category. What other examples can you find that serve this important function? What special problems do these create for marketers?

3. Describe the progressive learning model and discuss why this phenomenon is important when marketing to subcultures.

4. Born-again Christian groups have been instrumental in organizing boycotts of products advertised on shows they find objectionable, especially those that, they feel, undermine family values. Do consumer groups have a right or a responsibility to dictate the advertising a network should carry?

5. An official with a Christian organization defended the Christian Members Buying Plan described in the chapter, arguing that "We are sick and tired of Christians and Christian values being expunged from every area of public life. This isn't separation of church and state; this is a private merchant."[91] Do you agree?

6. Can you locate any current examples of marketing stimuli that depend upon an ethnic stereotype to communicate a message? How effective are these appeals?

7. To understand the power of ethnic stereotypes, conduct your own poll. For a set of ethnic groups, ask people to anonymously provide attributes (including personality traits and products) most likely to characterize each group using the technique of free association. How much agreement do you obtain across people? Compare the associations for an ethnic group between actual members of that group and nonmembers.

CNN Connection

CNN A video segment is available to accompany this CNN connection.

Toy Diversity: More Than Child's Play?

In the 1950s, psychologists found that black girls were more likely to choose a white doll over a black one and cited this finding as evidence of the low self-esteem of minority children. The toys a child plays with can influence his or her identity and self-esteem. Perhaps that is why minority entrepreneurs are beginning to produce dolls that portray a broader spectrum of cultural backgrounds than are available through the major manufacturers. Although Mattel and other big companies do produce non-Caucasian versions of some of their dolls, they tend to be darker versions of dolls that still have Caucasian features. New dolls and superhero action figures are now being marketed that correspond more accurately to the physical features of non-white people. With the proportion of non-white children in the United States expected to exceed one-third by the year 2000, this trend is bound to intensify.

SIMMONS Connection: Data for this exercise is on the Simmons Data Disk inside the back cover of your Instructor's Annotated Edition.

SIMMONS Connection

Data File: Cultural Buying Patterns

Maria is a good example of an American consumer who is deeply immersed in a particular ethnic subculture. Although she herself may be a native-born American, her family and neighborhood have strong ties to their ethnic origins. And, she lives in a neighborhood that has managed to preserve at least some of the elements of Latino culture. In fact, her neighborhood may be very similar to neighborhoods in foreign countries such as Buenos Aires or Mexico City.

It is often easier for consumers to maintain their ethnic heritage if they are presented with the opportunity to do so. The concentrations of ethnic groups often found in larger American cities provide a "critical mass" that can support distinctive ethnic sub-cultures. This critical mass can provide greater availability of community or religious groups, or even the availability of specialty products such as foreign-language newspapers and specialty food items. So, geography may be an important variable in determining how readily an ethnic group can maintain a distinct identity.

Using the data from the Simmons file for this chapter, identify the group of products that are most distinctive for Latino consumers. How is this pattern different from that of African-American consumers? In what way does geographic location influence these patterns of behavior?

Notes

1. Michael Meyer, "Los Angeles 2010: A Latino Subcontinent," *Newsweek* (November 9, 1992): 32.
2. See Frederik Barth, *Ethnic Groups and Boundaries: The Social Organization of Culture Difference* (London: Allen and Unwin, 1969); Michel Laroche, Annamma Joy, Michael Hui, and Chankon Kim, "An Examination of Ethnicity Measures: Convergent Validity and Cross-Cultural Equivalence," in *Advances in Consumer Research* 18, ed. Rebecca H. Holman and Michael R. Solomon (Provo, Utah: Association for Consumer Research, 1991), 150–57; Melanie Wallendorf and Michael Reilly, "Ethnic Migration, Assimilation, and Consumption," *Journal of Consumer Research* 10 (December 1983): 292–302; Milton J. Yinger, Ethnicity, *Annual Review of Sociology* 11 (1985): 151–80.
3. Marty Westerman, "Death of the Frito Bandito," *American Demographics* (March 1989): 28.
4. Eils Lotozo, "The Jalapeno Bagel and Other Artifacts," *New York Times* (June 26, 1990): C1.
5. Quoted in Cara S. Trager, "Goya Foods Tests Mainstream Market's Waters," *Advertising Age* (February 9, 1987): S-20.
6. Wilbur Zelinsky, "You Are Where You Eat," *American Demographics* (July 1987): 6.
7. Molly O'Neill, "New Mainstream: Hot Dogs, Apple Pie and Salsa," *New York Times* (March 11, 1992): C1.
8. Quoted in Peter Schrag, *The Decline of the WASP* (New York: Simon and Schuster, 1971): 20.
9. Robert Pear, "New Look at the U.S. in 2050; Bigger, Older and Less White," *New York Times* (December 4, 1992): A1.
10. William O'Hare, "Blacks and Whites: One Market or Two?" *American Demographics* (March 1987): 44–48.
11. For recent studies on racial differences in consumption, see Robert E. Pitts, D. Joel Whalen, Robert O'Keefe, and Vernon Murray, "Black and White Response to Culturally Targeted Television Commercials: A Values-Based Approach," *Psychology & Marketing* 6 (Winter 1989): 311–28; Melvin T. Stith and Ronald E. Goldsmith, "Race, Sex, and Fashion Innovativeness: A Replication," *Psychology & Marketing* 6 (Winter 1989): 249–62.
12. Monroe Anderson, "Advertising's Black Magic Helping Corporate America Tap a Lucrative Market," *Newsweek* (February 10, 1986): 60.
13. Brad Edmonson, "Black Markets," *American Demographics* (November 1987): 20; O'Hare, "Blacks and Whites"; "Older Products Look to Blacks for Rejuvenated Sales Growth," *Wall Street Journal* (February 28, 1985): 1.
14. Nejet Delener, "Cosmetics & HBA's for Black Consumers: A Growing, Profitable But Ignored Market," *Marketing News* (March 15, 1985): 32.
15. Pat Sloan, "New Maybelline Line Targets Blacks," *Advertising Age* (December 17, 1990): 1.
16. Robert E. Wilkes and Humberto Valencia, "Hispanics and Blacks in Television Commercials," *Journal of Advertising* 18 (Winter 1989): 19.
17. Alvin P. Sanoff, "TV's Disappearing Color Line," *U.S. News & World Report* (July 13, 1987): 56.
18. W. Franklyn Joseph, "Blacks' Ambition Enters the Picture," *Advertising Age* (March 14, 1985): 26.
19. Marie Spadoni, "Marketing to Blacks How Media Segment the Target Audience," *Advertising Age* (November 19, 1984): 43.
20. Jeffery L. Kovach, "Minority Sell: Ads Target Blacks, Hispanics, but . . . ," *Industry Week* (November 11, 1985): 29.
21. "Plans for Testmarketing Cigarette Canceled," *Asbury Park Press* (January 1990): 20; Anthony Ramirez, "A Cigarette Campaign Under Fire," *New York Times* (January 12, 1990): D1.
22. Joseph, "Blacks' Ambition Enters the Picture."
23. Anderson, "Advertising's Black Magic: Helping Corporate America Tap a Lucrative Market."
24. Joseph, "Blacks' Ambition Enters the Picture."
25. "'Black Pride' Plays Role in Buying Goods," *Marketing News* (February 19, 1990): 10; Jerome D. Williams and William J. Qualls, "Middle-Class Black Consumers and Intensity of Ethnic Identification," *Psychology & Marketing* 6 (Winter 1989): 263–86.
26. Westerman, "Death of the Frito Bandito."
27. Michael Marriott, "I'm Bart, I'm Black, and What About It?" *New York Times* (September 19, 1990): C1.
28. Kim Foltz, "Mattel's Shift on Barbie Ads," *New York Times* (July 19, 1990): D17; Lora Sharpe, "Dolls in All the Colors of a Child's Dream," *Boston Globe* (February 22, 1991): 42.
29. Brad Edmondson, "Pepsi's Latin Fizz," *American Demographics* (September 1987): 22.
30. Joe Schwartz, "Hispanic Opportunities," *American Demographics* (May 1987): 56 59.
31. Schwartz, "Hispanic Opportunities."
32. Howard LaFranchi, "Media and Marketers Discover Hispanic Boom," *Christian Science Monitor* (April 20, 1988): 1.
33. Joe Schwartz, "Rising Status," *American Demographics* (Janaury 10, 1989).
34. Roberto Suro, "Switch by Hispanic Catholics Changes Face of U.S. Religion," *New York Times* (May 14, 1989): 1.

35. "'Cultural Sensitivity' Required When Advertising to Hispanics," *Marketing News* (March 19, 1982).

36. Westerman, "Death of the Frito Bandito."

37. Kristine Stiven, "Educational Approach Shines," *Advertising Age* (February 13, 1989): S-10.

38. "'Cultural Sensitivity' Required When Advertising to Hispanics": 45.

39. Richard Edel, "Future Seen in P&G's Well-Oiled Machine," *Advertising Age* (February 13, 1989): 5–14.

40. Schwartz, "Hispanic Opportunities."

41. "Dispel Myths Before Trying to Penetrate Hispanic Market," *Marketing News* (April 16, 1982): 1.

42. Schwartz, "Hispanic Opportunities."

43. Brad Edmondson, "Mexican Soap," *American Demographics* (January 1989): 18.

44. Sigfredo A. Hernandez and Carol J. Kaufman, "Marketing Research in Hispanic Barrios: A Guide to Survey Research," *Marketing Research* (March 1990): 11–27.

45. David J. Wallace, "How to Sell Yucas to YUCAs," *Advertising Age* (February 13, 1989): 5–6.

46. Marcy Magiera, "New Arrivals Find Warm Welcome as Consumers," *Advertising Age* (February 9, 1987): 5–14.

47. Melanie Wallendorf and Michael D. Reilly, "Ethnic Migration, Assimilation, and Consumption," *Journal of Consumer Research* 10 (December 1983): 292–302.

48. Ronald J. Faber, Thomas C. O'Guinn, and John A. McCarty, "Ethnicity, Acculturation and the Importance of Product Attributes," *Psychology & Marketing* 4, (Summer 1987): 121–34; Humberto Valencia, "Developing an Index to Measure Hispanicness," in *Advances in Consumer Research* 12, ed. Elizabeth C. Hirschman and Morris B. Holbrook (Provo, Utah: Association for Consumer Research, 1985), 118–21.

49. Rohit Deshpande, Wayne D. Hoyer, Naveen Donthu, "The Intensity of Ethnic Affiliation: A Study of the Sociology of Hispanic Consumption," *Journal of Consumer Research* 13 (September 1986): 214–20.

50. Schwartz, "Rising Status."

51. David J. Wallace, "How to Sell Yucas to YUCAs."

52. Fernando Gonzalez, "Study Finds Alcohol, Cigarette Makers Target Hispanics," *Boston Globe* (November 23, 1989): A11.

53. Richard Kern, "The Asian Market: Too Good to Be True?" *Sales & Marketing Management* (May 1988): 38.

54. Donald Dougherty, "The Orient Express," *The Marketer* (July/August 1990): 14; Cyndee Miller, "'Hot' Asian-American Market Not Starting Much of a Fire Yet," *Marketing News* (January 21, 1991): 12.

55. Kern, "The Asian Market."

56. Quoted in Dougherty, "The Orient Express."

57. Miller, "'Hot' Asian-Market Not starting Much of a Fire Yet."

58. Marty Westerman, "Fare East: Targeting the Asian-American Market," *Prepared Foods* (January 1989): 48-51.

59. Eleanor Yu, "Asian-American Market Often Misunderstood," *Marketing News* (December 4, 1989): 11.

60. Marianne Paskowski, "Trailblazing in Asian America," *Marketing and Media Decisions* (October 1986): 75–80.

61. Ellen Schultz, "Asians in the States," *Madison Avenue* (October 1985): 78.

62. Dougherty, "The Orient Express."

63. Westerman, "Fare East: Targeting the Asian-American Market."

64. Paskowski, "Trailblazing in Asian America."

65. John Schwartz and Dorothy Wang, "Tapping into a Blossoming Asian Market: The Pull of Ethnic Ties," *Newsweek* (September 7, 1987): 47.

66. Thomas C. O'Guinn and Russell W. Belk, "Heaven on Earth: Consumption at Heritage Village, USA," *Journal of Consumer Research* 16 (September 1989): 227–38.

67. Elizabeth C. Hirschman, "Religious Affiliation and Consumption Processes: An Initial Paradigm," *Research in Marketing* (Greenwich, Conn.: JAI Press, 1983), 131–70.

68. See, for example, Nejet Delener, "The Effects of Religious Factors on Perceived Risk in Durable Goods Purchase Decisions," *Journal of Consumer Marketing* 7 (Summer 1990): 27–38.

69. Hirschman, Religious Affiliation and Consumption Processes.

70. Andrew M. Greeley, *The American Catholic* (New York: Basic Books, 1977).

71. C. Wright Mills, *The Power Elite* (New York: Oxford University Press, 1956).

72. Kenneth R. Hardy, "Social Origins of American Scientists and Scholars," *Science* (September 9, 1975): 497–506; Hirschman, "Religious Affiliations and Consumption Processes"; Stanley Verba and Norman H. Nie, *Participation in America: Political Democracy and Social Equality* (New York: Harper & Row, 1972).

73. Wade Clark Roof, "Socioeconomic Differentials Among White Socioreligious Groups in the United States," *Social Forces* 58 (September 1979): 280–88.

74. Peter Schrag, *The Decline of the Wasp* (New York: Simon & Schuster, 1971), 14.

75. Elizabeth C. Hirschman, "Upper-Class WASPs as Consumers: A Humanist Inquiry," in *Research in*

Consumer Behavior, ed. Jagdish N. Sheth and Elizabeth C. Hirschman (Greenwich, Conn.: JAI Press, 1988), 115–48.

76. Elizabeth C. Hirschman, "American Jewish Ethnicity: Its Relationship to Some Selected Aspects of Consumer Behavior," *Journal of Marketing* 45 (Summer 1981): 102–10.

77. Hirschman, "Religious Affiliation and Consumption Processes."

78. Hirschman, "American Jewish Ethnicity."

79. Susan Chira, "Leumi Appeal Not Just Ethnic," *New York Times* (May 14, 1984): D1.

80. Westerman, "Death of the Frito Bandito."

81. Isadore Barmash, "The Drive to Promote Kosher Food," *New York Times* (April 11, 1989): D25.

82. Joan Delaney, "New Kosher Products, from Tacos to Tofu," *New York Times* (December 31, 1989): F13.

83. Delaney, "New Kosher Products, from Tacos to Tofu."

84. Brad Edmondson, "Bringing in the Sheaves," *American Demographics* (August 1988): 28.

85. Priscilla LaBarbera, "Consumer Behavior and Born Again Christianity," in *Research in Consumer Behavior*, ed. Sheth and Hirschman, 193–222.

86. "Auto Dealer's 'Christian Plan' Is Called Bias," *New York Times* (May 27, 1990): 23.

87. LaBarbera, "Consumer Behavior and Born Again Christianity"; Robert Ostling, "Power, Glory and Politics," *Time* (February 17, 1986): 62 69.

88. Quoted in Sandra Blakeslee, "Christian Publishing Industry Does a Hard Sell on Religion," *New York Times* (July 19, 1987).

89. Lenore Skenazy, "Grace Gives Pro-Life Message," *Advertising Age* (January 5, 1987).

90. "A Cigarette Campaign Under Fire," *New York Times* (January 12, 1990): D1.

91. "Auto Dealer's 'Christian Plan' Is Called Bias."

LONGEVITY MAGAZINE

A PRACTICAL GUIDE TO THE ART AND SCIENCE OF STAYING YOUNG

CHAPTER 15

Age and
Regional
Groups

Buying, Having, and Being: Selections 55–56 from *Buying, Having, and Being: The Washington Post Consumer Behavior Companion*, Second Edition, accompany this chapter.

It's the last week of summer vacation, and Bill's looking forward to going back to college. It's been a tough summer. He had trouble finding a summer job and seemed to be out of touch with his old friends—and with so much time on his hands just hanging around the house, he and his mother weren't getting along too well. As usual, Bill is plopped on the couch, watching the "Like We Care" show on MTV when his mother walks in, grabs the remote, and switches the channel to public television. Yet another retrospective is on about the Kent State shootings that she wants to see. When Bill protests, Mrs. Barke has the nerve to tell him, "Keep your cool. You might actually learn something about what it was like to be in college when it really meant something."

That's when Bill loses it. Even though he is a fairly decent student, he's tired of hearing about the "good old days" of Woodstock, Berkeley, and twenty other places he doesn't care about. Besides, most of his Mom's ex-hippie friends now work for the very corporations they used to protest about—who are they to preach to him about doing something meaningful with his life? Since they'd screwed up the economy so much, he'll be lucky to get a job as a bicycle messenger when he finally gets his degree next year.

In disgust, Bill storms into the room he's had since he was five years old, puts a Sonic Youth tape into his Walkman, and pulls the covers up over his head. So much for a constructive use of time. What's the difference, anyway—they'll probably all be dead from the "greenhouse effect" by the time he graduates . . . .

Age Cohorts

The era in which a consumer is born creates for that person a cultural bond with the millions of others born during the same time period. An **age cohort** consists of people of similar ages who have undergone similar experiences. They share many common memories about cultural heroes (e.g., John Wayne versus Clint Eastwood, or Frank Sinatra versus Bruce Springsteen), important historical events (e.g., the 1969 moon flight versus the 1986 Challenger disaster), and so on. Consumers tend to feel comfortable with others of their own age or background.

Bill's fight with his mother illustrated the growing chasm between "baby boomers," who were born between 1943 and 1960, and "baby busters," who were born between 1961 and 1981. The boomers are a formidable demographic group that has set the political and cultural agenda in America since the late 1960s. As they have aged, their collective will has been behind events as diverse as The Free Speech Movement and hippies in the 1960s to Reaganomics and yuppies in the 1980s.

The busters seem to be paying the price for the boomers' soul searching. They are a generation characterized by cynicism and are the first group of Americans that can't realistically expect to exceed their parent's standard of living. The inflation-adjusted income of adult men under age 35 has sunk by 20 percent since 1979. Twenty years ago, a 30-year-old male made 6 percent more than a typical 60-year-old male, while today he makes 14 percent *less*. While most teens expect to be earning $30,000 or more by age 30, the 1990 Census shows otherwise: For every American aged 25 to 29 making more than $30,000, there are eight who are making less than this income. Busters are finding it hard to get a good job and to establish an independent lifestyle the way their parents did. In fact, a buster with a high school degree has a 40 percent chance of moving back in with his or her parents at some point after graduation.

Busters are often cited as a symbol of America in decline. Busters, in turn, blame boomers for handing down the serious problems they now confront. They are cynical about adults who discuss problems but don't solve them. A recent *Fortune* survey asked busters if they would "like to be like" baby boomers, and 80 percent said no. Many busters resent what they see as boomers' arrogance; boomers tend to see themselves as the embodiment of moral wisdom, and their "new sobriety" (*The New York Times* went so far as to call them "grumpies," or grown-up mature professionals) is affecting the marketing of products from cigarettes to low-fat yogurt.[1] *Longevity* magazine, whose ad is shown at the beginning of this chapter, is one of many new media that have been developed to appeal to boomers who are youth conscious and concerned about aging.

This chapter considers marketing issues related to four age cohorts: teens, busters, boomers, and senior citizens. An important fifth group, children, is discussed in Chapter 8. In addition to spotlighting important age groups, some differences in consumption related to *where* a consumer lives (his/her regional identification) are also discussed in this chapter.

The Appeal of Nostalgia

Because consumers within an age group confront crucial life changes at roughly the same time, the values and symbolism used to appeal to them can evoke powerful feelings of nostalgia (see Chapter 4). Adults over thirty are particularly susceptible to this phenomenon.[2]

PRODUCTS EVOKE SHARED MEMORIES As noted in Chapter 4, product sales can be dramatically affected by linking the brand to vivid memories and experiences, especially for items that are associated with childhood or adolescence. As observed by the maker of a candy bar called the Big Hunk, which has been on the market since 1950, "Adults turn back into children when they bite into candy . . . . If you remember buying a Big Hunk every Saturday when you went to the movies, you're going to buy the memory every time you buy the product."[3]

Many advertising campaigns have played upon the collective memories of consumers by resuscitating old pop classics. Michelob's "The Night Belongs to Michelob" campaign sponsored such heroes of classic rock as Eric Clapton, Steve Winwood, and Roger Daltrey, and Ford Mercury commercials are pro-

Teaching Hint: Many boomers have not exactly prospered. Only the economic power of women and the rise in two-income households is keeping them ahead. One-quarter of all professional and managerial boomers are in fact "nebbies" (negative-equity boomers) teetering on the edge of personal bankruptcy. Still, unlike busters, they consider their careers, personal freedoms, and lives to be more meaningful than those of their parents. See Neil Howe and William Strauss, "The New Generation Gap," *The Atlantic Monthly* (December 1992)16: 67.

Teaching Hint: Bucking the trend toward micromarketing to specific age segments, the Avrett, Free & Ginsberg ad agency claims that age groups are converging— younger consumers are becoming more conservative as older people are becoming psychologically younger. The agency has endorsed the concept of "cross-genertional marketing" to appeal to both groups simultaneously. This perspective can be used to stimulate class discussion on age differences in worldview and how these have evolved over time. Are people (even those in their twenties) thinking and acting "older" as a whole? Instructors can also take this opportunity to trade "war stories" about the consumption experiences of college students in past decades versus today. See Stuart Elliott, "Mass-Marketing to a Nation That Thinks Middle-Aged," *New York Times* (June 11, 1992): D20; Jim Kirk, "Bud Tries to Bridge Generational Gap," *Adweek* (September 14, 1992): 4.

An extremely successful advertising campaign by the California Raisin Advisory Board used Motown music to appeal to baby boomers' memories of youth. Courtesy of the California Raisin Advisory Board.

duced against a background of classic songs. A campaign developed by The California Raisin Advisory Board featuring Marvin Gaye's "I Heard It Through the Grapevine" breathed new life into the flagging raisin industry. A clip from one popular commercial is shown here. *Memories* magazine, which was founded to exploit the nostalgia boom, goes so far as to offer advertisers discounts if they run old ads next to their current ones.

MARKETING OPPORTUNITY

A reunion is an event based on a shared age cohort. People who were not necessarily fond of each other in high school or college nonetheless get together to celebrate the common experience of being together at the same time and place. It is estimated that more than 50,000 reunions are held in the United States each year. In addition to the boon this nostalgia provides to caterers and professional reunion organizers, some marketers realize that the people who attend reunions often represent a valuable customer base. They are self-selected to be fairly successful, since the "failures" tend not to show up. Some companies are now using reunion-goers to test new products, and travel-related businesses interview attendees about their trips or provide special promotional packages for returning consumers.[4]

Common Musical Preferences: Glenn Miller Meets Bonjovi. An interesting demonstration of the power of a common age group to influence experiences throughout life concerns the relationship between age and musical

This ad for MTV emphasizes the social and cultural forces that have made it so appealing to teens. Courtesy of MTV Networks. Copyright © 1991. MTV Networks. The MTV: Music Television logo is a registered trademark of MTV Networks, a division of Viacom International Inc. Copyright © 1993. All rights reserved.

preferences. One study uncovered evidence that consumers tend to focus on the popular songs they enjoyed during the period in which they first reached maturity. Those same musical preferences carry forward into later life.[5]

This study found that the "imprinting" period for musical tastes peaks at around age 24 for most people—the songs that were popular at that age tend to be preferred in later years as well. Consumers who were 24 in, say, 1986, tended to prefer Peter Gabriel's "Sledgehammer," a chart topper in that year. Similar results were obtained for other hits, such as the Mills Brothers' "Smoke Rings" (1932) and "The Duke of Earl" by Gene Chandler (1962). Using a similar strategy, the Nickelodeon cable network programs its "Nick at Nite" segment, which features reruns, by selecting the shows that were highly rated when its major audience was 12 years old.[6]

The Teen Market: "Totally Rad"

As anyone who has been there knows, the process of puberty and adolescence can be both the best of times and the worst of times. Many exciting changes happen as individuals leave the role of child and prepare to assume the role of adult. These changes create a lot of uncertainty about the self, and the need to belong and to find one's unique identity as a person becomes extremely important. At this age, choices of activities, friends, and "looks" often are crucial to social acceptance. Teens actively search for cues from their peers and from advertising for the "right" way to look and behave. Advertising geared to teens is typically action oriented and depicts a group of "in" teens using the product. Teens use products to express their identities, to explore the world and their new-found freedoms in it, and also to rebel against the authority of their parents and other socializing agents. This desire to express defiance to authority is reflected in the MTV ad shown here.

Additional Example: Many advertisers who court teens have found that they have little patience for hype or pretentious ads. They prefer ads that talk to them in realistic ways and focus on their actual lifestyles. For example, Kodak is attempting to penetrate the teen market because company research showed that photos are especially important to teenage girls, who often adorn their bedroom mirrors with pictures of their friends. See Yankelovich Clancy Shulman, "Getting Hip to Free-Spending Teens," *Adweek* (June 15, 1992): 70.

Attractiveness of the Teen Market

Consumers in this age subculture have a number of needs, including experimentation, belonging, independence, responsibility, and approval from others. Product usage is a significant medium to express these needs. Because they are so interested in many different products and have the resources to obtain them, the teen market is avidly courted by many marketers. The average teen earns over $60 a week and has no bills to pay. Even younger teens can make $100 a month or more by mowing lawns, baby-sitting, or receiving an allowance. Much of this money goes toward "feel-good" products: cosmetics, posters, and fast food.

With discretionary income of over $50 billion, teens are the prime movers in many product categories, although this influence is waning as the number of consumers in this age group decreases relative to older groups. For example, people aged 15 to 25 are a major market for the movie industry, so movie producers pay close attention to the behavior of this segment. Most teens are preoccupied with their appearance and body image and are avid consumers of beauty products, clothing, and other appearance-related items.[7] The storyboard from the Mountain Dew commercial shown here is a typical appeal to an active, socially oriented teen lifestyle.

International Example: In recent years, the declining number of teens in Europe has altered the face of that market. The movie industry is releasing more "mature" films now than in the past to compensate for this demographic change. See Carol Terrizzi, "At the Movies," *American Demographics* (November 1987): 58–60

Research Report: A recent study found that 17 percent of the models in cigarette ads were perceived to be much younger than age 25, an apparent violation of the tobacco industry's voluntary guidelines. This finding can be used to instigate additional class discussion about the efforts of some marketers to entice younger consumers to engage in "inappropriate" forms of consumption. See Michael B. Mazis, Debra Jones Ringold, Elgin S. Perry, and Daniel W. Denman, "Perceived Age and Attractiveness of Models in Cigarette Advertisements," *Journal of Marketing* 56 (January 1992): 22–37.

BRAND LOYALTY Marketers view teens as "consumers-in-training," since brand loyalty often is developed during this age. A teenager who is committed to a brand may continue to purchase it for many years to come. Such loyalty creates a barrier-to-entry for other brands that were not chosen during these pivotal years. Thus, advertisers sometimes try to "lock in" consumers to certain brands so that in the future they will buy these brands more or less automatically. As one teen magazine ad director observed, "We . . . always say it's easier to start a habit than stop it."[8]

PURCHASE INFLUENCE Teens exert a big influence on the purchase decisions of their parents (see Chapter 8).[9] Sixty percent of teens, for instance, say they influence the vacation choices of their families.[10] In addition to providing "helpful" advice to parents, teens are increasingly *buying* products on behalf of the family. The majority of mothers are now employed outside the home and have less time to shop for the family. In fact, seven out of ten mothers of teens work, and five of those seven are employed full-time.[11]

This fundamental change in family structure has altered the way marketers must conceive of teenage consumers. Although teens still are a good market for discretionary items, in recent years their spending on such "basics" as groceries is even larger than for nonessentials. A market research firm specializing in this segment has gone so far as to label teens "skippies"—school kids with income and purchasing power.[12] One survey of 16- to 17-year-old girls found that over a three-month period a significant proportion of them had purchased such staple items as cereal, frozen meals, cheese, yogurt, and salad dressing.[13] Marketers are beginning to respond to these changes. The number of pages devoted to food advertising in *Seventeen* magazine increased by 31 percent in one year. A Campbell's Soup ad that ran on MTV reflected this change as well: It depicted a solitary teenager warming up soup in the kitchen.

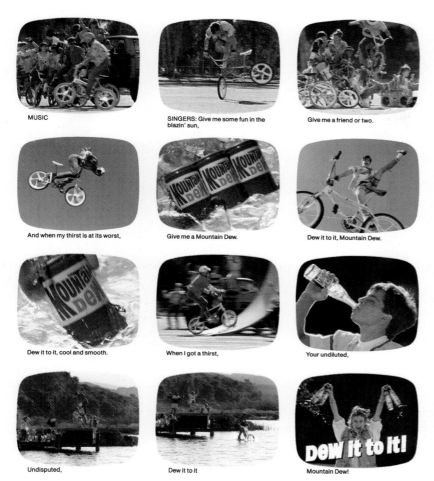

MUSIC

SINGERS: Give me some fun in the blazin' sun,

Give me a friend or two.

And when my thirst is at its worst,

Give me a Mountain Dew.

Dew it to it, Mountain Dew.

Dew it to it, cool and smooth.

When I got a thirst,

Your undiluted,

Undisputed,

Dew it to it

Mountain Dew!

This ad for Pepsi's Mountain Dew brand appeals to the teen market by showing attractive and popular young people in active settings. Courtesy of PEPSI-COLA COMPANY.

THE TWEENS SEGMENT "Tweens" are an emerging age segment now being targeted by some marketers. This term refers to kids aged 9 to 16, who are in that uneasy period between childhood and adolescence. They are seeking ways to mark their transition from childhood, often by mildly rebelling against parental control, as illustrated by the K-2 Snowboards ad shown on page 506. This group also tends to form brand preferences that differ from their parents'.

Because working parents have been giving kids in this age group increased responsibility for many purchases, some brand managers refer to tweens as "third parents," and a variety of companies are now trying to win their loyalty. Polaroid developed the "Cool Cam" for tweens, and Borden's research led to Spirals snacks. Focusing on the tween's potential role as influencer, an Acura dealer in California devised an ad showing three predriving age boys drooling over the car. The voice-over: "Number one in customer satisfaction, even among future consumers."

Jordache developed a controversial campaign for this segment when its research showed that customers for its jeans were more likely to be 12-year

Additional Examples: Since the National Dairy Board decided in 1987 to specifically target tweens in its advertising, milk consumption in this age group has been up 3 percent each year. Marvel Comics, a prime outlet for hard to reach male tweens, now carries ads for Sears, Warner-Lambert, and Milton Bradley. See Kate Fitzgerald, "Marketers Drawn to Comics," *Advertising Age* (September 14, 1992): 12; Laurie McLaughlin, "Tweens Blossom as Consumer Group," *Advertising Age* (October 14, 1991): 33.

Eat your vegetables.

Feed them to your dog.

K2 To talk to Dan and receive a snowboard brochure, call 1-800-842-3933. Or don't and be stupid.
an Anthony Industries company

This ad for K-2 Snowboards targets teens and "tweens" who are torn between the desire to obey authority figures and to rebel against them. Courtesy of K-2 Corporation.

olds than 25-year olds. The resulting ads, generated from focus groups with tweens, were eventually pulled, but not before they received a lot of media attention. Each ad had tweens talking about a sensitive subject. In one, a kid asked another, "Have you ever seen your parents naked?" while in another a girl complained, "I hate my mother. She's so much prettier than I am."[14]

MULTICULTURAL ⬤ DIMENSIONS

Japanese teens are big fans of global music and popular culture, and they're particularly fond of acquiring products associated with the American lifestyle. They love American fashions, particularly *Amekaji* (American casual). The California surfer look is also popular. In fact, the University of California at Los Angeles sells about $16 million worth of clothing with the UCLA logo to the Japanese per year. Surfer jackets and boards also sell well, as do skateboards and sailboards.[15] Some Japanese teenagers cruise down the main streets of Tokyo with surfboards on the roofs of their cars, even though they are not near the ocean. Like their Western peers, some of the favorite foods of Japanese teens are hamburgers, french fries, and ice cream.[16]

tional $8.9 billion in consumer expenditures.[27] For this reason, many marketers have turned to celebrities in this age group to endorse products. For example, tennis star Jimmy Connors, shown here in an ad for Nuprin, was 39 when the photo was shot.

The Baby Boomlet. In addition to the direct demand for products and services created by this age group, these consumers also are creating a new baby boom of their own to keep marketers busy in the future. Since fertility rates have dropped, this new boom is not as big as the one that created the baby boom generation; the new upsurge in the number of children born in comparison can best be described as a *baby boomlet*.

Many couples postponed getting married and having children because of the new emphasis on careers for women. These consumers now are beginning to hear the ticking of the biological "time clock." They are having babies in their late twenties and early thirties, resulting in fewer (but perhaps more pampered) children per family. Couples in the 25 to 34 age group account for 22 percent of all married couples, but for 35 percent of married couples with children. This new emphasis on children and the family has

This ad for Nuprin featuring Jimmy Connors at age 39 is among the many attempting to target aging baby boomers. Courtesy of J. Walter Thompson.

created opportunities for products such as cars (e.g., the success of the "mini-van" concept), services (e.g., the day-care industry, as exemplified by the Kinder-Care chain), and media (e.g., magazines such as *Working Mother* and localized magazines for parents that exist in more than 70 American cities).[28]

Segmenting Boomers: The "New Collars"

Although upscale consumers exert an influence on popular culture and marketing efforts far out of proportion to their size, they by no means speak for all baby boomers. An important baby boomer segment that is beginning to make its presence felt has been termed **new-collar workers**. These consumers occupy a gray area between professional and blue-collar jobs. Many of them hold service jobs vital to the functioning of our services-dominated economy, such as pharmacists, dental hygienists, and computer operators. They make approximately $15,000 to $30,000 a year, so they are neither affluent nor poor, despite the fact that many are college educated.

As a group, new-collars tend to be individualistic, pragmatic, and skeptical of institutions. These traits set them apart from older generations of gray- and pink-collar workers, who largely identified with the more traditional ideals of the working class. New-collars are a hybrid of traditional values and the liberalizing effects of their experiences growing up in the 1960s. They tend to exhibit a strong commitment to the family, but are more flexible—stylistically, sexually, and so on—than were their parents. These consumers tend to read such publications as *People* magazine and *TV Guide*, and music plays an important role in their lives as a bonding experience. Rock singer Bruce Springsteen can be thought of as the "poet laureate" of this segment.[29]

The Elderly Consumer: Marketing to the Gray Market

The old woman sits alone in her dark apartment, while the television blares out a soap opera. Once every couple of days, she slowly and painfully opens her triple-locked door with arthritic hands and ventures out to the corner store to buy essentials like tea, milk, and cereal, always being sure to pick the least expensive brand. Most of the time she sits in her rocking chair, thinking sadly of her dead husband and the good times she used to have.

Is this the image you have of a typical elderly consumer? Until recently, many marketers did. As a result, they largely neglected the elderly in their feverish pursuit of the baby boomer market. But as our population ages and people are living longer and healthier lives, the game is rapidly changing. A lot of businesses are beginning to replace the old stereotype of the poor recluse. The newer, more accurate image is of an elderly person who is active, interested in what life has to offer, and is an enthusiastic consumer with the means and willingness to buy many goods and services. The popularity of the television sitcom "The Golden Girls," starring four older women with full social lives, is indicative of the changing view of the elderly in American society.

Gray Power: Shattering Stereotypes

The elderly market consists of approximately 52 million people aged 55 and older, although for many purposes consumers are not classified as "elderly" until they reach the age of 65, when Social Security retirement benefits begin. The Bureau of Labor Statistics estimates that the mature market will grow by 62 percent between 1987 and 2015, compared to a 19 percent rate of growth for the overall U.S. population.[30] This increase makes the mature market the second fastest growing market segment in the United States, lagging only behind the babyboomers. Such dramatic growth can largely be explained by improved medical diagnoses and treatment, and the resulting increase in life expectancy.

SENIORS' ECONOMIC CLOUT   There is abundant evidence that the economic health of elderly consumers is good and getting better, a fact that is not lost on Cadillac dealers; as the ad shown here illustrates, they know that

It's not the amount of grey around the ears that distinguishes the Eldorado driver.

It's the amount of grey between them.

The 1992 Cadillac Eldorado is truly the thinking man's automobile.

Because not only does it possess a range of features too numerous

 to mention here, but it now also provides

instant gratification for the financially agile

mind: The $539 SmartLease. You'll want to

know all the details of course, so stop by your local Cadillac Dealer

of the South. It'll be an enlightening

as well as a rewarding experience.

BASED ON A 30 MONTH LEASE. FIRST MONTH'S LEASE PAYMENT OF $539, PLUS $575 REFUNDABLE SECURITY DEPOSIT FOR A TOTAL OF $1,114 DUE AT LEASE SIGNING. Tax, license, title fees and insurance extra. You must take retail delivery out of dealer stock by June 30, 1992. GMAC must approve lease. Example based on 1992 Eldorado: $34,527 MSRP, including destination charge. Monthly payment is based on a capitalized cost of $31,725. Total of monthly payments is $16,170. Payments may be slightly higher in Alabama, Arkansas, Hawaii, Texas and Virginia. Option to purchase at lease end for $18,990. Mileage charge of 10 cents per mile over 37,500. Lessee pays for excessive wear and use. See your participating dealer for qualification details.

CADILLAC® ELDORADO®

This ad for Cadillac dealers acknowledges that purchasers tend to be older but attempts to fight the "old fogey" image. *Courtesy of The Cadillac Dealers of the South and Fahlgren Martin.*

TABLE 15-1 Growth Opportunities in the Gray Market

Category	Trends	Growth Areas
The home	Emphasis on convenience and leisure time	Games, video, cooking, housekeeping aids
Health care	Need for nutritionally correct foods, health foods	Nursing homes, pharmaceuticals, exercise facilities
Travel and leisure	Leisure time, disposable income	Cruises, tourism
Education	Decline in number of college-aged students; more positive attitudes toward learning; self-help among older, better-educated consumers	Colleges, "how-to" books, and videos
Financial planning	Need for retirement planning, greater assets than in the past	Speculative investing, vacation homes
Health and fitness	Desire to recapture youth and retard aging	Cosmetic surgery, vitamins, skin treatments, bifocal contact lenses

Source: Adapted from Jeff Ostroff, "An Aging Market," *American Demographics* (May 1989): 26. Reprinted with permission, © *American Demographics.*

older consumers are the primary market for large luxury cars. In the period between 1979 and 1987, householders 65 and over showed an income gain of 16 percent, the largest increase of any age group. Some of the important areas that stand to benefit from the surging gray market are described in Table 15–1.

It is crucial to remember that income alone does not capture the spending power of this group. Elderly consumers are finished with many of the financial obligations that siphon off the income of younger consumers. Eighty percent of consumers past age 65 own their own homes, and 80 percent of those homes are mortgage free. In addition, child-rearing costs are over with. And, as evidenced by the popularity of the bumper sticker that proudly proclaims "We're Spending Our Children's Inheritance," many seniors now feel better about spending money on themselves rather than continuing to skimp for the sake of children and grandchildren.

MARKETING OPPORTUNITY

A few marketers are beginning to recognize the vast potential of the senior market and are designing products and services to cater to the specific needs of the elderly.

- One company has already targeted the elderly institutional market with a line of cookies, drinks, and puddings marketed under the Appleways logo.[31] These products offer extra calcium, nutrients, and fiber and are designed to alleviate some of the decline in sensory ability older people experience.

- Take Time, Inc., a health club chain, opened fitness centers for people over age 50.[32] In contrast to the "no pain, no gain" philosophy of some younger fitness enthusiasts, these centers emphasize the fun and social aspects of exercise. Instead of aerobics, older people do the Charleston to the accompaniment of big band music and then relax at a juice bar. The company has also developed a line of exercise clothing for this segment, and it released an exercise video starring singer Pat Boone.

- The Publix grocery chain in Florida, which has many elderly customers, puts benches in front of stores, makes restrooms easily available to patrons, and teaches employees how to make things easier for the stores' older clientele. For example, check-out clerks are instructed to give older customers two light bags to carry instead of one heavy bag.[33]

Self-Concept: You're Only as Old as You Feel

Market researchers who work with the elderly often comment that people think of themselves as being ten to fifteen years younger than they actually are. In fact, research confirms the popular wisdom that age is more a state of mind than of body. A person's mental outlook and activity level has a lot more to do with his or her longevity and quality of life than does *chronological age*, or the actual number of years lived.

PERCEIVED AGE A better yardstick to categorize the elderly is **perceived age**, or how old a person feels. Perceived age can be measured on several dimensions, including "feel-age" (i.e., how old a person feels) and "look-age" (i.e., how old a person looks).[34] The older the consumers get, the younger they feel relative to actual age. For this reason, many marketers emphasize product benefits rather than age-appropriateness in marketing campaigns, since many consumers will not relate to products targeted to their chronological age.[35] The ad for *Modern Maturity* magazine shown on page 516 echoes the idea that a person's perceived age is often 15 years younger than his or her chronological age.

Research Report: A study that polled advertising executives reported that the elderly are seen by this group to be most appropriate for advertising involving categories such as health and medicine, travel, and financial services. They are seen as least appropriate for shampoo, sporting goods, electronics, and automobiles, a rather curious sentiment given the increasing presence of elderly consumers in many of these categories. See Alan J. Greco, "The Elderly as Communicators: Perceptions of Advertising Practitioners," *Journal of Advertising Research* 28 (June–July 1988): 39.

M A R K E T I N G   P I T F A L L

Understanding the psychological needs of the elderly is especially acute in the housing industry.[36] Although developers frequently emphasize the term "retirement" in promotions for housing communities, in a Roper survey, only 5 percent of retirees said they would like to live only among people of their own age. The ads also tend to emphasize total leisure and older people's vulnerability, two points that are damaging to the elderly consumer's self-esteem. Promotions emphasizing an active, full life in a secure environment are more effective.

A major theme in this *Modern Maturity* ad is that consumers in the senior market segment think of themselves as ten to fifteen years younger than they actually are. Courtesy of *Modern Maturity Magazine*, a publication of AARP. © *Mature Americans*, The Daniel Yankelovich Group, 1987.

Additional Example: Affinity shampoo, developed specifically for older consumers, ran into problems because it reminded women that their hair needed extra care and that, by extension, they were getting older. Sales improved after the product's ad campaign was repositioned to emphasize the message that women of *any* age are sexy.

Repelling Messages. In fact, some marketing efforts targeted to the elderly have backfired because they reminded people of their age or presented their age group in an unflattering way. One of the more famous blunders was committed by Heinz. A company analyst found that many elderly people were buying baby food because of the small portions and easy chewing consistency, so it introduced a line of "Senior Foods" made especially for denture wearers. Needless to say, the product failed. Consumers did not want to admit that they required strained foods (even to the supermarket cashier). They preferred to purchase baby foods, which they could pretend they were buying for a grandchild.

MARKETING OPPORTUNITY

Old is beautiful: The aging of America is changing ideals of beauty. As the youth market declines, the standards we use to make judgments about beauty are evolv-

"Jockey For Her is the best fitting underwear I've ever worn. It's so comfortable. And now my favorite granddaughters wear Jockey For Girls®. Just Jockey."

Catherine Councell Moll
Grandmother/Banker
Sheboygan, Wisconsin

So Comfortable
JOCKEY
For Her

For Pantyhose That Fit . . . Wear Jockey For Her Pantyhose with Lycra®

Jockey Apparel is one of many advertisers that is increasingly featuring attractive older models in its ads. JOCKEY FOR HER, SO COMFORTABLE and JOCKEY Figure are trademarks of and used with permission of Jockey International, Inc.

ing (see Chapter 9). Slowly but surely, older models are beginning to redefine glamour and beauty. This appeal is exemplified in the Jockey underwear ad shown here. Several of the major modeling agencies have now established separate divisions for older women—what Ford Models, one of the largest agencies, terms "post-ingenue" talent.[37] *Lear's* magazine, launched in 1988, is designed "For the Woman Who Wasn't Born Yesterday." The magazine uses photographs of women aged 40 to 60, and does not retouch the pictures.

SEGMENTING SENIORS

The senior subculture represents an extremely large market: The number of Americans 65 and older exceeds the entire population of Canada.[38] Because

Teaching Hint: SRI International adapted the VALS system for a new project called LAVOA (Life-styles and Values of Older Americans). The VALS system was discussed in Chapter 13. See "Study Finds Lively 'Geromarket'," *Advertising Age* (May 18, 1987): 89.

this group is so large, it is helpful to think of the mature market as actually consisting of four subsegments: an "older" group (aged 55–64), an "elderly" group (aged 65–74), an "aged" group (aged 75–84), and finally a "very old" group (85 and up).[39]

The elderly market is well suited for segmentation. Older consumers are easy to identify by age and stage in the family life cycle. Most receive Social Security benefits, and many belong to organizations catering to the elderly. The American Association of Retired Persons has approximately 12 million dues-paying members. Its main publication, *Modern Maturity*, has the largest circulation of any American magazine.

CONFRONTING OLD AGE   Several segmentation approaches begin with the premise that a major determinant of elderly marketplace behavior is the way a person deals with being old.[40] Some people become depressed, withdrawn, and apathetic as they age, some are angry and resist the thought of aging, and some appear to accept the new challenges and opportunities this period of life has to offer. For example, one ad agency devised a segmentation scheme for American women over the age of 65 on two dimensions: self-sufficiency and perceived opinion leadership.[41] The study yielded many important differences among the groups. For example, the self-sufficient group was found to be more independent, cosmopolitan, and outgoing. They were more likely to read a book, attend concerts and sporting events, and dine out.

The Innovative Elderly.   This finding highlights the stereotype that elderly people are set in their ways, stubborn, and resistant to change. The implication is that mature consumers are exceptionally brand loyal and unwilling to try new products or services. This belief appears to be true only to the extent that the elderly are more experienced and skeptical of product claims and puffery. They don't appear to be as fickle as younger consumers, but will try new things if given a good reason for doing so.[42]

MARKETING OPPORTUNITY

Many consumer products will encounter a more sympathetic reception from the elderly if packages are redesigned to be sensitive to physical limitations. While aesthetically appealing, packages are often awkward and difficult to manage, especially for those who are frail or arthritic. Also, many serving sizes are not geared to smaller families, widows, and other people living alone, and coupons tend to be for family-sized products, rather than for single servings.

Seniors have difficulty with pull-tab cans and push-open milk cartons. Ziploc packages and clear plastic wrap also are difficult to handle. Packages need to be easier to read and should be made lighter and smaller. Finally, designers need to pay attention to contrasting colors. A slight yellowing of the lens as one ages makes it harder to see background colors on packages. Discerning between blues, greens, and violets becomes especially difficult. The closer identifying type colors are to the package's or advertisement's background color, the less visibility and attention they will command.

A few companies are beginning to confront these issues. Procter & Gamble is working on a snap-top lid for Tide detergent, and General Motors is redesigning some Oldsmobiles to include bigger buttons and clearer dashboard displays. A number of apparel manufacturers are replacing buttons with Velcro snaps.[43]

The Elderly and the Media

A number of specialty magazines have been introduced in recent years that focus on the active lifestyles of today's elderly. These include such publications as *Modern Maturity*, *50 Plus*, and *Lear's*. In addition, television is a very important medium, because the elderly often rely on it as a window onto society. The elderly watch 60 percent more television than average households and prefer programs that provide news and current events as a way to keep up. They also watch more golf, baseball, and bowling on television than the average consumer. The elderly tend to listen to radio news at all times of the day and are above the norm in readership of news magazines.

ADVERTISING TO THE ELDERLY   In one survey, one-third of consumers over age 55 reported that they deliberately did *not* buy a product because of the way an elderly person was stereotyped in the product's advertising.[44] Most contemporary advertising underrepresents the elderly, a situation that will have to change as the population ages. For example, more than one-third of Americans over the age of 50 are regular consumers of soft drinks, yet few older consumers are ever seen in soft drink advertising.

Some marketers, however, are beginning to glamorize older people, including DeBeers diamonds, Clairol hair-coloring products, and American Express. This strategy appears to be sound: In a Gallup Poll, 77 percent of respondents reported that they react positively to advertising featuring older people, and 63 percent believe that advertisers are overly obsessed with youth.[45] A longitudinal (i.e., historical) analysis indicated that the portrayal of the elderly in magazine advertising is in fact increasing and that the people in these ads tend to have prestigious positions.[46]

In general, the elderly have been shown to respond positively to ads that provide an abundance of information. Unlike other age groups, these consumers usually are not amused, or persuaded, by imagery-oriented advertising. A more successful strategy involves the construction of advertising that depicts the aged as well-integrated, contributing members of society, with emphasis on them expanding their horizons rather than clinging precariously to life.

Basic Guidelines.   Some basic guidelines have been suggested for effective advertising to the elderly. These include the following:[47]

- Keep language simple.
- Use clear, bright pictures.
- Use action to attract attention.
- Speak clearly, and keep the word count low.

- Use a single sales message, and emphasize brand extensions to tap consumers' familiarity.
- Avoid extraneous stimuli (i.e., excessive pictures and graphics can detract from the message).

Regional Groups: "Good Old Boys" and "Yankees"

If you have traveled to or lived in other parts of the country, you may have experienced the feeling of being slightly out of sync with your environment. The people may speak the same language, yet you may have difficulty understanding some things they say. Brands and store names may be confusing; some are familiar and some are not. And, some familiar items may masquerade under different names. One person's "hero" is another's "grinder" is another person's "submarine sandwich" is another person's "hoagie."

Citizens of the United States share the same national identity, yet the consumption patterns of different regions have been shaped by unique climates, cultural influences, and resources. This diversity is reflected in the ad shown here for Blair Television, which illustrates how dramatically one's lifestyle can be affected by place of residence. Such differences allow us to legitimately talk about "regional personalities" as well as a "national personality." In many cases it is efficient to divide the country up into geographic markets based upon definitions provided by the U.S. Census Bureau. These markets are called **Standard Metropolitan Statistical Areas (SMSAs)**, and are used as a reference by market researchers, manufacturers, and retailers.

Will It Play in Peoria? When choosing a geographical region or city for test marketing purposes, marketers typically try to locate a place that is the most representative of the country. They want a microcosm that will allow them to predict how the mass market will react to product designs or promotional ideas. The expression "Will it play in Peoria?" refers to the traditional designation of that city as most representative of the American heartland. More recently, Tulsa has replaced Peoria as the most typical city in America. It most closely matches the national average in terms of age distribution, racial mix, and housing prices. Other "typical cities" include Charleston, South Carolina; Midland, Texas; and Springfield, Illinois.[48]

Regional Consumption Differences

Research Report: The results of one study indicate that the top ten states with the highest tension levels are all in the West and South. Nevada is the most stressful state, while Nebraska boasts the lowest "tension level." "States of Stress," *American Demographics* (February 1987): 18

The lifestyles of people in each region differ in a variety of ways, some quite subtle and some quite noticeable, some easy to explain and some not so obvious. The fact that people in the Northeast are better customers for ski equipment than are those in the Southwest is fairly predictable. The reason that new mothers in the West are about 50 percent more likely to breastfeed their babies than their counterparts in the South may be a little harder to fathom.[49]

The beer industry has been particularly active in reinforcing regional identification. The Miller Brewing Company exhibited its own version of regional marketing when it developed a first—an entire campaign targeted only to one state. It seems that Texan consumers buy more Miller Lite than anyone else, so the company threw a beer party in six Texas cities that it billed as the biggest party in history.[50]

Heileman Distilleries is now fifth in sales in the United States largely because of its regional marketing efforts. The company operates ten breweries across the United States, and its position in each of its markets is backed up with sponsorship of major local events and other regional promotions. As the company's marketing vice president explained, "The primary objective of being a regional brand is to make the consumer think that 'this product is mine.' . . . People tend to think positively about their hometowns, and a product strongly identified with this aura is likely to strike a responsive chord . . . ."[51] Some of Heileman's successful regional brands include Old Style, Colt 45, Lone Star, Rainier, and Samuel Adams.

FOOD PREFERENCES Many national marketers regionalize their offerings to appeal to different tastes. Campbell's Soup puts a stronger dose of jalapeno pepper in its nacho cheese soup in the Southwest, and it sells

This trade ad for Blair Television reminds advertisers of the importance of lifestyle segmentation, especially for regional markets where spot television ads can be tailored to differences in lifestyles and tastes. Courtesy of Blair Television.

"ranch-style" beans only in Texas.[52] Similarly, some leading brands do significantly better in some parts of the country than others: While Kraft Miracle Whip is the nation's best seller in the mayonnaise category, it only turns in a third place performance in the Northeast.[53]

Denny's Restaurants, a national chain based in California, adapts its menu to the different regions it serves. For example, although chili is served in many outlets, this dish takes a variety of forms: In Texas, it contains no beans and is very spicy; in Cincinnati, "five-way" chili is served with chili sauce, cheese, raw onions, beans, and spaghetti; and on the West Coast, the same dish is served with a side order of salsa. Similarly, a Denny's customer can only order a bagel and cream cheese if he or she is in Hawaii, southern Florida, or the region north of Virginia and east of Harrisburg, Pennsylvania. Those customers, however, can't take advantage of the catfish special, which is only available in parts of the South and Midwest.[54]

Country America magazine is one of many media vehicles recently developed to appeal to readers' regional identification. Courtesy of *Country America Magazine.*

THE ARTS AND ENTERTAINMENT   The types of entertainment sought by consumers around the country differ markedly as well. A survey performed for the National Endowment for the Arts showed that jazz and classical music are the most popular in the West and Midwest, and that consumers in the West like museums and the theater more than other Americans.[55]

A Gallup Poll revealed that Easterners most prefer to watch television, read, and go to the movies, while those in the West most prefer eating out, dancing, and visiting with friends. Consumers in the Midwest were most likely to enjoy parlor games and cards. *Country America* magazine, illustrated in the ad shown here, is typical of the many magazines that have successfully carved out a regional niche by catering to the tastes of a specific part of the country.

The Nine Nations of North America

The U.S. Census Bureau divides the United States into regions, each of which encompasses a number of states. An alternate conceptualization of the country that specifically considered geographic subcultures was proposed by a journalist named Joel Garreau in 1981.[56] This scheme, called **The Nine Nations of North America**, postulates that "America" does not really exist at all. Garreau claimed that there actually are nine separate "nations" within the geographical boundaries of the United States and Canada, each with its own priorities and customs. This approach drew a lot of attention from marketers who were looking for new ways to divide their markets.

The map in Figure 15-3 provides more detail about the eight "nations" within the United States (excluding the "nation" of Quebec, which is centered in Canada), as adapted by the Ogilvy & Mather advertising agency for

FIGURE 15–3   **The Eight Nations of the United States** Source: Adapted from Joel Carreau, *The Ogily & Mather Listening Post* (New York: Ogilvy & Mather, 1983), p. 3.

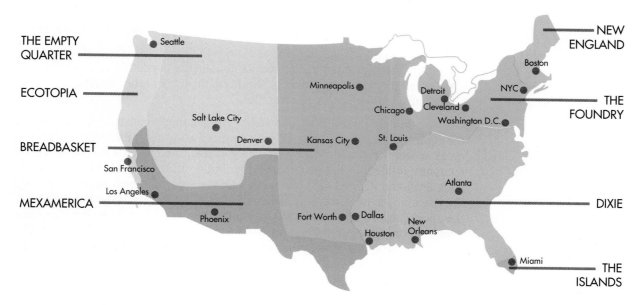

its own analyses. For example, the "Breadbasket" is home to "Middle America," where people are largely conservative and hard-working. "Ecotopia" in the Northwest United States is environmentally oriented and associated with "New Age" philosophy. "MexAmerica" in the Southwest is largely influenced by its Hispanic roots, and the culture of "The Islands" in southern Florida and the Caribbean also is heavily influenced by interactions with Latin America (including revenues from the illegal drug industry). Other nations include "Dixie" (or the "New South"), "The Foundry" (sometimes called "The Rust Belt"), "The Empty Quarter," and New England.

PROBLEMS WITH THE NINE NATIONS Garreau's insights were quite interesting, and many of his observations make intuitive sense. For example, subsequent work on this categorization scheme verifies that occupants of "Ecotopia" are more likely to be employed in executive or professional positions, are more likely to be college-educated and politically liberal, and tend to be highly inner directed. In contrast, "Dixie" residents are more likely to be blue collar, politically conservative, and outer directed.[57]

However, it is important to remember that the precise borders of The Nine Nations are largely based upon personal observations and guesses about how to divide up the country. Other researchers have noted that the "nations" themselves contain pockets that most likely better belong to other "nations" (e.g., ecologically minded Santa Monica, California, is in "MexAmerica," not "Ecotopia").

More systematic work that explicitly examined the values of people living in each "nation" has not provided overwhelming support for The Nine Nations typology *per se*.[58] Nonetheless, Garreau's observations were a valuable impetus to marketers to begin to think of the United States as a mosaic composed of many different regional groups.

Geodemography

When the Western Union Company wanted to improve the cost-effectiveness of its network of offices, it undertook a market evaluation with the following goals.[59]

- Analyze the number of Western Union agents needed in an area.
- Determine where new agents would be most profitably located.
- Identify new market opportunities.

This project involved several steps. The company constructed a profile of the typical customer for money wire services and then attempted to identify areas where these customers were likely to live. It engaged a market research company to identify the geographic distribution of these customers at the zip code level and defined areas as either unserved, partially served, or saturated. This search for new ways to segment markets more precisely, coupled with the increasing sophistication of data collection and analysis techniques, has enabled companies like Western Union to incorporate geographic variables into their marketing strategies. Marketers have looked at product movement since the 1930s, when A.C. Nielsen tracked changes in actual store inventories at the regional level.[60]

Modern **geodemographic** techniques allow companies to go well beyond broad regional differences. Many now segment markets down to the neighborhood block. The provision of this type of analysis to marketers has become a profitable niche for several market research companies. In addition, such information increasingly is being combined with other data to yield a more complete picture of the American consumer. Several marketing research ventures now employ **single-source data.** In these situations, all of the relevant information is collected on a matched basis, so that different aspects of consumption and demographic data can be combined for the same unit of analysis (e.g., a census tract). This comprehensive strategy was first implemented in the BehaviorScan project, begun in 1980 by Information Resources, Inc. The system combined UPC scanners, household panels, and television to track purchases. This type of total approach allows marketers to test the impact of changes in advertising, pricing, shelf placement, and promotions on consumer behavior patterns. Similar systems are now available or under development by other organizations, such as Nielsen and SAMI/Burke.[61]

APPLICATIONS OF GEODEMOGRAPHY Marketers have been successful at adapting sophisticated analytical techniques originally developed for other applications, such as the military and oil and gas exploration. These techniques, which can now employ data at the neighborhood or even household level, are being used in a variety of ways.

- A bank examined its penetration of accounts by customer zip codes.
- A utility company compared demographic data with billing patterns to fine-tune energy conservation campaigns.
- A chain of ice cream stores helped franchisees develop sales promotion programs for local markets by providing them with demographic profiles of actual users and information about the sales potential of untapped customer groups.

A basic assumption of geodemography is that "birds of a feather flock together"—that is, people who live near one another share similar characteristics. Some companies use U.S. Census data in a statistical technique known as *cluster analysis* to identify census tracts around the country that seem to share the same characteristics. Then, a marketer who wants to reach only those consumers in one or more of these clusters (say, a direct marketer who wants to mail expensive catalogs only to the most likely sales prospects) can target only certain zip codes in an area and ignore others.

ClusterPlus. One commercial system is ClusterPlus, distributed by Donnelly Marketing. This system assigns each of the country's census block groups into one of 47 clusters. The groupings range in affluence from the "established wealthy" (e.g., Greenwich, Connecticut) to "lowest income black female-headed families" (e.g., the Watts section of Los Angeles). One manufacturer of baking goods used the system to target consumers who bake from scratch by combining demographic information with Simmons consumption data. The top-ranking clusters for this activity were in older, rural, blue-collar areas in the South and Midwest. Commercials for this segment were placed on popular shows, such as "Rescue: 911," "America's Funniest Home Videos," and "Major Dad,"[62] that are widely watched in these areas.

Research Report: One group of market researchers used PRIZM to determine which groups are most and least receptive to being interviewed. They found that the clusters most responsive were in the South: "Tobacco Roads" (92% response rate) and "Share Croppers" (88% response rate). The least responsive were in wealthy metropolitan areas, including "Bohemian Mix" (56% response rate) and "Gray Power" (58% response rate). See Susan Krafft, "Who Slams the Door on Research?" *American Demographics* (September 1991): 14.

PRIZM: The "Real" Beverly Hills 90210 Another clustering technique is the PRIZM system developed by Claritas, Inc. This system classifies every U.S. zip code into one of forty categories, ranging from the most-affluent "Blue-Blood Estates" to the least well-off "Public Assistance."[63] A resident of Southern California might be classified as "Money & Brains" if he or she lives in Encino (zip code 91316), while someone living in Sherman Oaks (zip code 91423) would be a "Young Influential."[64]

Residents of different clusters display marked differences in their consumption of products from annuities to zip-lock bags. These groupings are also ranked in terms of income, home value, and occupation (i.e., a rough index of social class) on a ZQ (Zip Quality) scale. Table 15–2 provides an idea of how dramatically different the consumption patterns of two cluster can be. This table compares consumption data for "Furs & Station Wagons," the third-highest ranking cluster, with "Tobacco Roads," the third-lowest.

The PRIZM system is used to guide media buying and for direct mail targeting. Both *Time* and *Newsweek* sorted their mailing lists by cluster, sending special editions with ads for luxury products to residents of "Money & Brains" and "Blue Blood Estates." Colgate-Palmolive sent samples of a new detergent developed for young families to occupants of "Blue-Collar Nursery" cluster, which is largely occupied by new families.

TABLE 15–2   A Comparison of Two PRIZM Clusters

Furs & Station Wagons (ZQ3)		Tobacco Roads (ZQ38)	
New money, parents in 40s and 50s		Racially mixed farm towns in the South	
Newly built subdivisions with tennis courts, swimming pools, gardens		Small downtowns with thrift shops, diners, and laundromats; shanty-type homes without indoor plumbing	
Sample neighborhoods:		*Sample neighborhoods:*	
Plano, TX (75075)		Belzoni, MI (39038)	
Dunwoody, GA (30338)		Warrenton, NC (27589)	
Needham, MA (02192)		Gates, VA (27937)	
High Usage	*Low Usage*	*High Usage*	*Low Usage*
Country clubs	Motorcycles	Travel by bus	Knitting
Wine by the case	Laxatives	Asthma relief remedies	Live theater
Lawn furniture	Nonfilter cigarettes	Malt liquors	Smoke detectors
Gourmet	Chewing tobacco	*Grit*	*Ms.*
BMW 5 Series	*Hunting*	Pregnancy tests	Ferraris
Rye bread	Chevrolet Chevettes	Pontiac Bonnevilles	Whole-wheat bread
Natural cold cereal	Canned stews	Shortening	Mexican foods

Note: Usage rates as indexed to average consumption across all 40 clusters.

Source: "A Comparison of Two Prizm Clusters" from *The Clustering of America* by Michael J. Weiss. Copyright © 1988 by HarperCollins Publishers, Inc.

While some products may be purchased at an equivalent rate by consumers in two very different clusters, these similarities end when other purchases are taken into account. These differences highlight the importance of going beyond simple product category purchase data and demographics to really understand a market. For example, high-quality binoculars are bought by people in "Urban Gold Coast," "Money & Brains," and "Blue Blood Estates" communities, but also by consumers in the "Grain Belt," "New Homesteaders," and "Agri-Business" clusters. The difference is that the former groups use the binoculars to watch birds and other wildlife, while the latter use them to help line up the animals in their gun sights. And, while the bird watchers do a lot of foreign travel, listen to classical music, and host cocktail parties, the bird hunters travel by bus, like country music, and belong to veterans clubs.

Chapter Summary

- People have many things in common with others merely because they are about the same age or live in the same part of the country. Consumers who grew up at the same time share many cultural memories, so they may respond to marketers' *nostalgia* appeals that remind them of these experiences.

- Four important *age cohorts* are teens, college students, baby boomers, and the elderly. *Teenagers* are making a transition from childhood to adulthood, and their self-concepts tend to be unstable. They are receptive to products that help them to be accepted and enable them to assert their independence. Because many teens earn money but have few financial obligations, they are a particularly important segment for many nonessential or expressive products, ranging from chewing gum to clothing fashions and music. Because of changes in family structure, many teens also are taking more responsibility for their families' day-to-day shopping and routine purchase decisions. *College students* are an important, but hard to reach market. In many cases, they are living alone for the first time, so they are making important decisions about setting up a household.

- *Baby boomers* are the most powerful age segment because of their size and economic clout. As this group ages, its interests have changed and marketing priorities have changed as well. The needs and desires of baby boomers affect demands for housing, child care, automobiles, clothing, and so on. Only a small proportion of boomers fit into an affluent, materialistic category. Other emerging subsegments, such as *new-collar workers,* are probably more representative of future directions this age subculture will take.

- As the population ages, the needs of *elderly* consumers will also become increasingly influential. Many marketers traditionally ignored the elderly because of the stereotype that they are too inactive and spend too little. This stereotype is no longer accurate. Most of the elderly are healthy, vigorous, and interested in new products and experiences—and they have the income to purchase them. Marketing appeals to this age subculture should focus on consumers' self-concepts and perceived ages, which tend to be more youthful than their chronological ages. Marketers also should emphasize concrete benefits of products, since this group tends to be skeptical of vague, image-related promotions. Personalized service is of particular importance to this segment.

- Consumption preferences can differ dramatically depending on the *region* of the country. Tastes and traditions vary from East to West and North to South. Regional marketing rather than a uniform national strategy is beginning to be practiced by many companies, who are learning to tailor their products to local preferences. *Geodemographics,* sophisticated techniques that assume people who live together share important characteristics, are being developed to fine-tune advertising and direct-marketing efforts by identifying and targeting consumers with relevant demographics in common.

Key Terms

age cohort, p. 500
baby boomers, p. 509
geodemographics, p. 525

new-collar workers, p. 512
perceived age, p. 515
single-source data, p. 525

Standard Metropolitan, Statistical Areas (SMSAs), p. 520
The Nine Nations of North America, p. 523

Consumer Behavior Challenge

1. What are some possible marketing opportunities present at reunions? What effects might attending such an event have on consumers' self-esteem, body image, affect, and so on?
2. The chapter noted that college students are an especially good market for gifts and greeting cards. Why do you think this observation might be true?
3. Why have baby boomers had such an important impact on consumer culture in the second half of this century?
4. How has the baby boomlet changed attitudes toward child-rearing-practices and created demand for different products and services?
5. What are some marketing ramifications of the growth of the new-collar segment?
6. Is it practical to assume that people age 55 and older constitute one large consumer market? What are some approaches to further segmenting this age subculture?
7. What are some important variables to keep in mind when tailoring marketing strategies to the elderly?
8. Geodemographic techniques assume that people who live in the same neighborhood have other things in common as well. Why is this assumption made, and how accurate is it?
9. Single-source data systems give marketers access to a wide range of information about a consumer, just by knowing his or her address. Do

you believe this "knowledge power" presents any ethical problems with regard to consumers' privacy? Should access to such information be regulated by the government or other bodies? Should consumers have the right to limit access to these data?

10. Find good and bad examples of advertising targeted to elderly consumers. To what degree does advertising stereotype the elderly? What elements of ads or other promotions appear to determine their effectiveness in reaching and persuading this group?

11. Identify some regional differences in product preferences among members of your class. How might a marketing strategy for one of these products be tailored to each regional segment?

CNN Connection

CNN   A video segment is available to accompany this CNN connection.

The Aging of the Baby Boomers

Like Peter Pan, baby boomers refuse to grow up. They seem to want to have it both ways. On the one hand, this sizable and relatively affluent generation has successfully taken over the reins of American adult society—boomers control much of what happens in government, business, and the arts. On the other hand, many boomers seem to think they're still kids. Although their priorities and bodies are changing as they enter middle age, they do not respond well to marketing campaigns that remind them of this transition.

A boomer's psychological age is usually much younger than his or her chronological age, so marketing to this segment involves a delicate balance between providing products adapted to changing needs and advertising that informs boomers of these benefits. Levi Strauss' highly successful Dockers line of pants, for example, was designed to cater to boomers, but its advertising stresses male bonding rather than a roomier fit. Similarly, Pearle Vision tells viewers that its products help you enjoy life, not that it's time to surrender one's vanity and finally get glasses.

Many boomers do not intend to age gracefully—they plan to go out fighting the ravages of old age. Like Ponce de Leon, they search for the Fountain of Youth. This quest has fueled demand for anti-aging cosmetics. European consumers have long been devotees of skin creams and other products that supposedly retard aging, but this market is now growing in the United States as well. Although these applications cannot as yet actually reverse the aging process, companies such as Elizabeth Arden are spending millions on research in an effort to corner the market on a modern-day Fountain of Youth.

Notes

1. Neil Howe and William Strauss, "The New Generation Gap," *The Atlantic Monthly* (December 1992)16: 67.

2. Bickley Townsend, *"Ou sont les reiges d'antan? (Where are the snows of yesteryear?)" American Demographics* (October 1988): 2.

3. "Chuckles' Rebirth," *American Demographics* (May 1987): 23.

4. Jeffrey P. Rosenfeld, "Reliving It Up," *American Demographics* (June 1987): 48.

5. Morris B. Holbrook and Robert M. Schindler, "Some Exploratory Findings on the Development of Musical Tastes," *Journal of Consumer Research* 16 (June 1989): 119–24.

6. Randall Rothenberg, "The Past is Now the Latest Craze," *New York Times* (November 29, 1989): D1.

7. Selina S. Guber, "The Teenage Mind," *American Demographics* (August 1987): 42.

8. Ellen Goodman, "The Selling of Teenage Anxiety," *Washington Post* (November 24, 1979).

9. Ellen R. Foxman, Patriya S. Tansuhaj, and Karim M. Ekstrom, "Family Members' Perceptions of Adolescents' Influence in Family Decision Making," *Journal of Consumer Research* 15 (March 1989): 482–91.

10. Andrew Malcolm, "Teen-Age Shoppers: Desperately Seeking Spinach," *New York Times* (November 29, 1987): 10.

11. Malcolm, "Teen-Age Shoppers."

12. John Blades, "Tracking Skippies: TRU Researches Habits of Elusive Groups—Teens," *Asbury Park Press* (March 2, 1991): C1.

13. Malcolm, "Teen-Age Shoppers."

14. Alice Cueno, "Targeting 'Tweens': Madison Avenue's Call of the Child," *U.S. News and World Report* (March 20, 1989): 84; Carol Hall, "Tween Power," *Marketing and Media Decisions* 22 (October 1987): 56–62; Kit Mill, "Pre-Teen Buying Power," *Marketing and Media Decisions* (April 1989): 96–98.

15. Rose A. Horowitz, "California Beach Culture Rides Wave of Popularity in Japan," *Journal of Commerce* (August 3, 1989)2: 17; Elaine Lafferty, "American Casual Seizes Japan; Teenagers Go for N.F.L. Hats, Batman and the California Look," *Time* (November 13, 1989): 106.

16. Blayne Cutler, "Move Over, Miso," *American Demographics* (May 1988)2: 56.

17. Laura Zinn, "Move Over, Boomers," *Business Week* (December 14, 1992)7.

18. Quoted in Fannie Weinstein, "Time to Get Them in Your Franchise," *Advertising Age* (February 1, 1988): S-6.

19. Quoted in "Advertisers Target College Market," *Marketing News* (October 23, 1987).

20. Eben Shapiro, "New Marketing Specialists Tap College Consumers," *New York Times* (February 27, 1992): D16.

21. Beth Bogart, "Word of Mouth Travels Fastest," *Advertising Age* (February 6, 1989): S6; Janice Steinberg, "Media 101," *Advertising Age* (February 6, 1989): S-4.

22. Stuart Elliott, "Beyond Beer and Sun Oil: The Beach-Blanket Bazaar," *New York Times* (March 18, 1992): D17.

23. Liane McAllister, "Campus Clout," *Gifts & Decorative Accessories* (July 1987): 80.

24. Fabian Linden, "Middle-Aged Muscle," *American Demographics* (October 1987): 4.

25. Amy Dunkin, "Maxwell House Serves Up a Yuppie Brew," *Business Week* (March 2, 1987): 62.

26. Andrew Pollack, "Jeans Fade but Levi Strauss Glows," *New York Times* (June 26, 1989): D1.

27. Peter Francese, "A Symphony of Demographic Change," *Advertising Age* (November 9, 1988): 130.

28. Albert Scardino, "The New Baby Boom Spurs Local Magazines for Parents," *New York Times* (June 26, 1989): D1.

29. Kenneth I. Walsh and Sharon F. Golden, "The New-Collar Class," *U.S. News & World Report* (September 15, 1985): 59.

30. William Lazer and Eric H. Shaw, "How Older Americans Spend Their Money," *American Demographics* (September 1987): 36; see also Charles D. Schewe and Anne L. Balazs, "Role Transitions in Older Adults: A Marketing Opportunity," *Psychology & Marketing* 9 (March/April 1992): 85–99.

31. Charles D. Schewe, "Marketing to an Aging Population: Responding to Physiological Changes," *Journal of Consumer Marketing* (Summer 1988)5: 61–74.

32. Brad Edmondson, "Take Time for Exercise," *American Demographics* (January 1987): 22.

33. Paul B. Brown, "Last Year It Was Yuppies—This Year It's Their Parents," *Business Week* (March 10, 1986): 68–74.

34. Benny Barak and Leon G. Schiffman, "Cognitive Age: A Nonchronological Age Variable," in *Advances in Consumer Research* 8, ed. Kent B. Monroe (Provo, Utah: Association for Consumer Research, 1981)8, 602–06.

35. David B. Wolfe, "An Ageless Market," *American Demographics* (July 1987): 27–55.

36. Wolfe, "An Ageless Market."

37. Mary Martin Niepold, "Fabulous and 40-Plus," *Marketing Communications* (September 1988): 17–60; see also Karen Kaigler-Walker, "Social Comparison, Self-Esteem and Women's Satisfaction with Appearance: A Macro-Marketing Issue," *Pro-*

ceedings of the Academy of Marketing (1993).

38. Lenore Skenazy, "These Days, It's Hip to be Old," *Advertising Age* (February 15, 1988).

39. Lazer and Shaw, "How Older Americans Spend Their Money."

40. Ellen Day, Brian Davis, Rhonda Dove, and Warren A. French, "Reaching the Senior Citizen Market(s)," *Journal of Advertising Research* (December/January 1987/88): 23–30; Warren A. French and Richard Fox, "Segmenting the Senior Citizen Market," *Journal of Consumer Marketing* 2 (1985): 61–74; Jeffrey G. Towle and Claude R. Martin, Jr., "The Elderly Consumer: One Segment or Many?" in *Advances in Consumer Research* 3, ed. Beverlee B. Anderson (Provo, Utah: Association for Consumer Research, 1976), 463.

41. Day et al., "Reaching the Senior Citizen Market(s)."

42. Many studies have examined elderly consumers' shopping patterns and product choices, see J. Barry Mason and William O. Bearden, "Profiling the Shopping Behavior of Elderly Consumers," *The Gerontologist* 18 (1978)5: 454–61; James R. Lumpkin and Barnett A. Greenberg, "Apparel-Shopping Patterns of the Elderly Consumer," *Journal of Retailing* 58 (Winter 1982): 68–89; Mary C. LaForge, "Learned Helplessness as an Explanation of Elderly Consumer Complaint Behavior," *Journal of Business Ethics* 8 (May 1989): 359–66; Betsy D. Gelb, "Exploring the Gray Market Segment," *MSU Business Topics* 26 (Spring 1978): 41–46; Elaine Sherman, "The Senior Market: Opportunities Abound," *Direct Marketing* 50 (June 1987): 82; Valarie A. Zeithaml and Mary C. Gilly, "Characteristics Affecting the Acceptance of Retailing Technologies: A Comparison of Elderly and Nonelderly Consumers," *Journal of Retailing* 83 (Spring 1987): 49–68; Mary C. Gilly and Valarie A. Zeithaml, "The Elderly Consumer and Adoption of Technologies," *Journal of Consumer Research* 12 (December 1985): 353–57.

43. "Gray Expectations: A New Force in Design," *Business Week* (April 11, 1988): 108; Mary Bender, "Packaging for the Older Consumer," speech delivered at the Annual Winter Conference of the Gerontology Institute of New Jersey, Princeton, N.J., March 6, 1987.

44. Melinda Beck, "Going for the Gold," *Newsweek* (April 23, 1990): 74.

45. J. Ward, "Marketers Slow to Catch Age Wave," *Advertising Age* (May 22, 1989): S1.

46. Anthony C. Ursic, Michael L. Ursic, and Virginia L. Ursic, "A Longitudinal Study of the Use of the Elderly in Magazine Advertising," *Journal of Consumer Research* 13 (June 1986): 131–33.

47. Ward, "Marketers Slow to Catch Age Wave."

48. Steve Lohr, "Forget Peoria. It's Now: Will it Play in Tulsa?" *New York Times* (June 1, 1992)2: D1.

49. "States of Stress," *American Demographics* (February 18, 1987).

50. Dody Tsiantar and Annetta Miller, "Playing to the Home Crowd: 'Regional Advertising' Takes on a New Dimension," *Newsweek* (August 7, 1989): 45.

51. Quoted in George Rathwaite, "Heileman's National Impact with Local Brews," *Marketing Insights* (Premier Issue, 1989): 108.

52. Brad Edmondson, "From Dixie to Detroit," *American Demographics* (January 1987): 27.

53. Brad Edmondson, "America's Hot Spots," *American Demographics* (1988): 24–30.

54. Brad Edmondson, "Chili Recipes," *American Demographics* (April 1987): 22.

55. Edmondson, "From Dixie to Detroit."

56. Joel Garreau, *The Nine Nations of North America* (Boston, Mass.: Houghton Mifflin, 1981).

57. *Ogilvy & Mather Listening Post* (New York: Ogilvy & Mather, 1983).

58. Lynn R. Kahle, "The Nine Nations of North America and the Value Basis of Geographic Segmentation," *Journal of Marketing* 50 (April 1986): 37–47.

59. Thomas W. Osborn, "Analytic Techniques for Opportunity Marketing," *Marketing Communications* (September 1987): 49–63.

60. Osborn, "Analytic Techniques for Opportunity Marketing."

61. Osborn, "Analytic Techniques for Opportunity Marketing."

62. Jonathan Marks, "Clusters Plus Nielsen Equals Efficient Marketing," *American Demographics* (September 1991): 16.

63. Michael J. Weiss, *The Clustering of America* (New York: Harper & Row, 1988).

64. Bob Minzesheimer, "You Are What You Zip," *Los Angeles* (November 1984): 175.

V. The Consumer and Culture

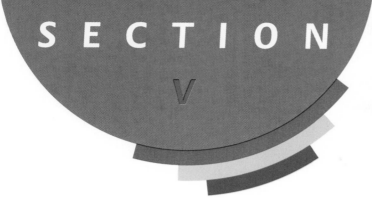

S E C T I O N

V

The Consumer

and Culture

The final section of this book considers consumers as members of a broad cultural system. Chapter 16 considers how consumer culture is created by marketers and how both aesthetic and functional products are adopted (or not adopted) by different types of consumers (the *diffusion process*). This chapter also looks at underlying cultural values that help to define a society, how these values are reflected in consumers' acceptance or rejection of products, and also at how these values differ across cultures.

Chapter 17 concludes with a focus on how our everyday lives as consumers are affected by our observance of cultural practices. It discusses how product usage is intricately connected with a society's myths and rituals and how these practices are changing in the evolving modern marketplace.

This chapter also takes a look at some harmful aspects of consumer behavior: This "dark side" of consumer behavior includes such issues as addiction, vandalism, and shoplifting. Finally, the chapter comes full circle as it further considers a central issue first raised in Chapter 1—that is, how marketers contribute to everyday consumer culture and how they even impact on our perceptions of what is "real" in important ways.

CHAPTER 16

The Creation and Diffusion of Consumer Culture

Buying, Having, and Being: Selections 57–59 from *Buying, Having, and Being: The Washington Post Consumer Behavior Companion*, Second Edition, accompany this chapter.

As Amanda is browsing through the racks at her local Limited store in Wichita, Kansas, her friend Alexandra yells to her from the accessories section: "Amanda, check this out! This chain is just what you need to go with your new outfit!" Alex is right. The oversized bright gold chain would go perfectly with her new gold baseball cap, and besides it looks just like the ones she has seen worn on MTV rap videos.

As Amanda takes the chain to the cash register, she's looking forward to wearing it to school the next day. All of her girlfriends in junior high compete with each other to dress just like the singers in Salt 'n Pepa and other groups—her friends just won't believe their eyes when they see her tomorrow. Maybe some of the younger kids in her school might even think she was fresh off the mean streets of New York City! Even though she has never been east of the Mississippi, Amanda just knows she would fit right in with all of the Bronx "sisters" she reads about in her magazines . . . .

Culture and Consumption

People often buy products because of what they *mean*, rather than for what they do. Consumption choices simply cannot be understood without considering the cultural context in which they are made: *Culture* is the "lens" through which people view products. Amanda's purchase of a gold chain reflects her desire to associate (with help from the media and marketers) with glamour, adventure, and trendiness. As a privileged member of "white bread" society, her display of this chain has a very different meaning in her suburban world than it would to street kids in New York City or LA. It might even be interpreted by them as a sign that this item is no longer in fashion, and it is time to move on to something else (which has in fact happened).

Amanda lives in a white middle-class area in the Midwest, but is able to "connect" symbolically with millions of other young consumers by wearing styles that originated far away—even though the original meanings of those styles have little relevance to her. The spread of hip-hop fashions and music is just one example of what happens when the meanings created by some members of a culture are interpreted and produced for mass consumption.

Outfits featuring gold vinyl skirts, huge gold chains, and bejeweled baseball caps that used to be seen only on the streets of impoverished urban areas are being adapted by *haute couture* fashion designers for the runways of New York and Paris. In addition, a high proportion of people who buy recordings of rap music are white. How did rap music and fashions, which began as forms of expression in the black urban subculture, make it to mainstream America? Here's a brief chronology.

- 1968: Hip-hop is invented in the Bronx by DJ Kool Herc.
- 1973–1978: Urban block parties feature break-dancing and graffiti.
- 1979: A small record company named Sugar Hill becomes the first rap label.

Additional Example: The Box is a new music television service that is already reaching 13 million viewers. A form of "interactive television," it allows viewers (for a $2–$3 charge that is added to their phone bills) to dial a 900 number and enter a three-digit code to select a video, which appears on the viewer's TV screen in about 20 minutes. The Box is being used in the industry to get a handle on people's musical preferences. One finding: Rap music videos account for one-third of all requests, and most of those who request this type are *white*. See John Maines, "The Box That's Challenging MTV," *American Demographics* (July 1992): 10.

- 1980: Graffiti artists are featured in Manhattan art galleries.
- 1981: Blondie's song "Rapture" hits #1 on the charts.
- 1985: Columbia Records buys the Def Jam label.
- 1988: MTV begins "Yo! MTV Raps," featuring Fab 5 Freddy.
- 1990: Hollywood gets into the act with the hip-hop film *House Party*; Ice-T's rap album is a big hit on college radio stations; amid controversy, white rapper Vanilla Ice hits the big time; NBC launches a new sitcom, "Fresh Prince of Bel Air."
- 1991: Mattel introduces its Hammer doll (a likeness of the rap star Hammer, formerly known as M.C. Hammer); designer Karl Lagerfeld shows shiny vinyl raincoats and chain belts in his Chanel collection; designer Charlotte Neuville sells gold vinyl suits with matching baseball caps for $800; Isaac Mizrahi features wide-brimmed caps and take-offs on African medallions (including an oversized gold Star of David); Bloomingdale's launches Anne Klein's rap-inspired clothing line by featuring a rap performance in its Manhattan store.
- 1992: Rappers start to abandon this look, turning to low-fitting baggy jeans, sometimes worn backwards; white rapper Marky Mark appears in a national campaign wearing Calvin Klein underwear, exposed above his hip-hugging pants; composer Quincy Jones launches a new magazine for people who are into hip-hop, and it gains a significant white readership.[1]
- 1993: Hip-hop fashions and slang continue to cross over into mainstream consumer culture. An outdoor ad for Coca-Cola proclaims, "Get Yours 24–7." The company is confident that many viewers in its target market will know that the phrase is urban slang for "always" (24 hours a day, 7 days a week).[2]

This chapter considers how the culture in which we live creates the meaning of everyday products and how these meanings move through a society to consumers. As Figure 16–1 shows, *meaning transfer* is largely

Additional Example: For students who are more into country music than rap, the popularity of singer Billy Ray Cyrus is a good example of how creative marketing tactics can propel an artist into the spotlight. To promote Cyrus' song, "Achy Breaky Heart," a dance called the "achy breaky" was invented. The singer's record company produced an instructional video targeted to dance teachers and began promoting dance contests at country bars. This strategy worked as the previously unknown Cyrus' album went to the top of the charts in 1992. See John Leland, "The Big Hunk of Country," *Newsweek* (June 22, 1992): 53.

Figure 16–1 is available as Transparency 42.

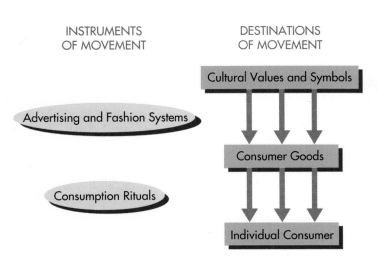

INSTRUMENTS OF MOVEMENT

DESTINATIONS OF MOVEMENT

Advertising and Fashion Systems

Consumption Rituals

Cultural Values and Symbols

Consumer Goods

Individual Consumer

FIGURE 16–1 The Movement of Meaning Source: Adapted from Grant McCracken, "Culture and Consumption: A Theoretical Account of the Structure and Movement of the Cultural Meaning of Consumer Goods," *Journal of Consumer Research* 13 (June 1986): 72. Reprinted with permission of The University of Chicago Press.

accomplished by such marketing vehicles as the advertising and fashion industries, which associate functional products with symbolic qualities. These goods, in turn, impart their meanings to consumers through different forms of ritual (these are discussed in Chapter 17).[3]

The first part of the chapter reviews what is meant by culture and how cultural priorities (or values) are identified and expressed. The second part considers how these meanings are created and how marketing affects the production of culture. The chapter then discusses how meanings move across consumer society: It considers how different people over time decide to try new products in a process called the *diffusion of innovations*, and it concludes by exploring the dynamics of the fashion system that are associated with the appearance of new styles and trends.

Understanding Culture

Culture, a concept crucial to the understanding of consumer behavior, may be thought of as a society's personality. It includes both abstract ideas, such as values and ethics, as well as the material objects and services, such as automobiles, clothing, food, art, and sports, that are produced or valued by a group of people. Culture is the accumulation of shared meanings, rituals, norms, and traditions among the members of an organization or society.

Ironically, the effects of culture on consumer behavior are so powerful and far-reaching that this importance is sometimes difficult to grasp or appreciate. Like a fish immersed in water, we do not always appreciate this power until we encounter a different culture. A consumer's culture determines the overall priorities he or she attaches to different activities and products. It also mandates the success or failure of specific products and services. A product that provides benefits consistent with those desired by members of a culture at any point in time has a much better chance of attaining acceptance in the marketplace.

For example, the U.S. culture started to emphasize the concept of thinness as an ideal of appearance in the mid-1970s. The premium placed on this goal, which stemmed from underlying values like mobility, wealth, and a focus on the self, greatly contributed to the success of Miller Lite beer at that time. However, when Gablinger introduced a lo-cal beer seven years earlier, in 1968, the product failed. This product was "ahead of its time," since American consumers were not interested in this benefit in the 1960s.

The relationship between marketing and culture is a two-way street. The study of new products and innovations in product design successfully produced by a culture at any point in time provides a window onto the dominant cultural ideals of that period. Consider, for example, some American products that reflect underlying cultural processes at the time they were introduced.

- The TV dinner, which hinted at changes in family structure.
- Cosmetics made of natural materials and not animal-tested, which reflected consumers' apprehensions about pollution, waste, and animal rights.
- Condoms marketed in pastel carrying cases for female buyers, which signaled changes in attitudes toward sexual responsibility and frankness.

Aspects of Culture

Culture is not static. It is continually evolving, synthesizing old ideas with new ones. A cultural system consists of three functional areas.[4]

1. *Ecology:* the way in which a system is adapted to its habitat. This area is shaped by the technology used to obtain and distribute resources (e.g., industrialized societies versus Third World countries). The Japanese, for example, greatly value products that are designed for efficient use of space because of the cramped conditions in that island nation.[5]
2. *Social structure:* the way in which orderly social life is maintained. This area includes the domestic and political groups that are dominant within the culture (e.g., the nuclear family versus the extended family).
3. *Ideology:* the mental characteristics of a people and the way in which they relate to their environment and social groups. This area revolves around the belief that members of a society possess a common **worldview**. They share certain ideas about principles of order and fairness. They also share an **ethos**, or a set of moral, aesthetic, and evaluative principles.

DIMENSIONS OF VARIABILITY Although every culture is different, four stable dimensions have been identified that appear to account for much of this variability.[6]

1. *Power distance:* the way in which interpersonal relationships form when differences in power are perceived. Some cultures emphasize strict, vertical relationships (e.g., Japan), while others, such as the United States, stress a greater degree of equality and informality. The AT&T ad shown on page 540 illustrates the Japanese emphasis on respect in its effort to promote long-distance calling.
2. *Uncertainty avoidance:* the degree to which people feel threatened by amibiguous situations and have beliefs and institutions that help them to avoid this uncertainty (e.g., organized religion).
3. *Masculinity/Feminity:* the degree to which sex roles are clearly delineated (see Chapter 7).
4. *Individualism:* the extent to which the welfare of the individual versus that of the group is valued (see Chapter 11). Cultures differ in their emphasis on **individualism** versus **collectivism**. In collectivist cultures, people subordinate their personal goals to those of a stable in-group. In contrast, consumers in individualist cultures attach more importance to personal goals, and people are more likely to change memberships when the demands of the group (e.g., workplace, church, etc.) become too costly. Whereas a collectivist society will stress such values as self-discipline and accepting one's position in life, people in individualist cultures emphasize personal enjoyment, excitement, equality, and freedom. Some strongly individualistic cultures include those of the United States, Australia, Great Britain, Canada, and the Netherlands. Venezuela, Pakistan, Taiwan, Thailand, Turkey, Greece, and Portugal are some examples of strongly collectivist cultures.[7]

BELIEFS AND PRACTICES Members of a culture share a system of meaning, which means that they have learned to accept a set of beliefs and prac-

Teaching Hint: Adherence to a worldview reduces anxiety arising from one's awareness of vulnerability and mortality. According to *terror management theory*, a culture provides security by reinforcing a conception of the world as a just place and by promising immortality (either in a theological sense or via contributions to the ongoing culture). See Abraham Rosenblatt, Jeff Greenberg, Sheldon Solomon, Tom Pyszczynski, and Deborah Lyon, "Evidence for Terror Management Theory: I. The Effects of Mortality Salience on Reactions to Those Who Violate or Uphold Cultural Values," *Journal of Personality and Social Psychology* 57 (1989)4: 681–90.

**Show your respect again.
Call Japan.**

She raised you from a little boy to a man of substance. Taught you loyalty, integrity, tradition. So when you left Tokyo, you took your mother's words of wisdom with you. Why not tell her how much they've meant to you?

With AT&T International Long Distance Service, it costs less than you'd think to stay close. So go ahead. **Reach out and touch someone?**

JAPAN, AUSTRALIA	Economy 3am–2pm	Discount 8pm–3am	Standard 2pm–8pm
AVERAGE COST PER MINUTE FOR A 10-MINUTE CALL*	$ .95	$1.20	$1.58

*Average cost per minute varies depending on the length of the call. First minute costs more; additional minutes cost less. All prices are for calls dialed direct from anywhere in the continental U.S. during the hours listed. Add 3% federal excise tax and applicable state surcharges. Call our toll-free number for further information or if you'd like to receive an AT&T International rates brochure 1 800 874-4000. © 1986 AT&T

AT&T
The right choice.

AT&T uses a cross-cultural appeal to generate more long-distance calling. Courtesy of AT&T INTERNATIONAL COMMUNICATIONS SERVICES.

International Example: As cultures become more complex and industrialized, they tend to become more individualistic as well. Japan is traditionally a collectivist society, but there are signs that this is changing among younger consumers. This new perspective is called *shinjinrui*, which translates as "new human race" or "new breed." The ethos of these consumers emphasizes individuality, a need for instant gratification, and a heightened concern with fashion. See Laurel Anderson and Marsha Wadkins, "The New Breed in Japan: Consumer Culture," unpublished manuscript, Arizona State University, Tucson, 1990.

tices governing their existence. These beliefs are taught to members of a culture by socialization agents, including parents, friends, and teachers. The process of learning the beliefs and behaviors endorsed by one' own culture is termed **enculturation**, while the learning of a new culture (usually a more difficult task) is **acculturation**.

Values. Every culture has a set of values that it imparts to its members. A value is an enduring belief that some state is preferable to its opposite.[8] For example, people in one culture might feel that being a unique individual is preferable to subordinating one's identity to the group, while another group may emphasize the opposite.

In many cases, values are universal. Who does not desire health, wisdom, or world peace? What sets cultures apart, though, is the *relative importance*, or ranking, of values. This set of rankings constitutes a culture's **value system**.[9] To illustrate a difference in value systems, consider the results of a study by the Dentsu advertising agency. Consumers in New York, Los Angeles, and Tokyo were asked to indicate their preferences regarding the goals an ideal society should aim for. Although the two American cities represent quite different regional subcultures (see Chapter 15), there was a high degree of consensus within the American sample. Both groups said their highest ideal is a "society in which people can live safely." In contrast, Tokyo residents ranked first the goal of a "society with a comprehensive welfare system." While about 45 percent of the Americans endorsed the idea of a "society which is very competitive, but in which everybody has an equal chance of success," only 25 percent of Tokyo residents echoed this sentiment.[10]

Norms. Values are very general ideas about good and bad goals. From these flow *norms,* or rules dictating what is right or wrong, acceptable or unacceptable. Some norms, called *enacted norms*, are explicitly decided upon, such as the rule that a green traffic light means "go" and a red one means "stop." Many norms, however, are much more subtle. These *crescive norms* are embedded in a culture and are only discovered through interaction with other members of that culture. Crescive norms include the following.[11]

- A *custom* is a norm handed down from the past that controls basic behaviors, such as division of labor in a household or the practice of particular ceremonies.

- A *more* is a custom with a strong moral overtone. A more often involves a taboo, or forbidden behavior, such as incest or cannibalism. Violation of a more often meets with strong punishment from other members of a society.

- *Conventions* are norms regarding the conduct of everyday life. These rules deal with the subtleties of consumer behavior, including the "correct" way to furnish one's house, wear one's clothes, host a dinner party, and so on.

All three types of crescive norms may operate to completely define a culturally appropriate behavior. For example, a more may tell us what kind of food is permissible to eat. Note that mores vary across cultures, so a meal of dog may be taboo in the United States, while Hindus would shun a steak, and Muslims would avoid pork products. A custom dictates the appropriate hour at which the meal should be served. Conventions tell us how to eat the meal, including such details as the utensils to be used, table etiquette, and even the appropriate apparel to be worn at dinnertime.

Again, we often take these conventions for granted, assuming that they are the "right" things to do. The belief in the superiority of one's own cultural practices and products is termed **ethnocentrism**. The degree to which consumers are ethnocentric can help to predict the likelihood they will accept foreign products.[12] American consumers who score high on a scale designed to measure this belief are more likely to prefer domestic brands to imports, and they also place more emphasis on choosing American-made products when weighing alternatives.

Myths

Every society possesses a set of myths that define that culture. A **myth** is a story containing symbolic elements that expresses the shared emotions and ideals of a culture. The story often features some kind of conflict between two opposing forces, and its outcome serves as a moral guide for people. In this way, a myth reduces anxiety because it provides consumers with guidelines about their world.

An understanding of cultural myths is important to marketers, who in some cases (most likely unconsciously) pattern their strategy along a mythic structure. Consider, for example, the way that a company like McDonald's takes on "mythical" qualities.[13] The "golden arches" are a universally recognized symbol, one that is virtually synonymous with American culture. They offer sanctuary to Americans around the world, who know exactly what to expect once they enter. Basic struggles involving good versus evil are played out in the fantasy world created by McDonald's advertising, as when Ronald McDonald confounds the Hamburglar. McDonald's even has a "seminary" (Hamburger University) where inductees go to learn appropriate behaviors.

Myths serve four interrelated functions in a culture.[14]

1. *Metaphysical:* They help to explain the origins of existence.
2. *Cosmological:* They emphasize that all components of the universe are part of a single picture.
3. *Sociological:* They maintain social order by authorizing a social code to be followed by members of a culture.
4. *Psychological:* They provide models for personal conduct.

THE STRUCTURE OF MYTHS: BINARY OPPOSITION   Myths can be analyzed by examining their underlying structures, a technique pioneered by the anthropologist Claude Levi-Strauss (no relation to the blue jeans company). Levi-Strauss noted that many stories involve *binary opposition* (e.g., nature versus technology). Characters, and in some cases, products, are often defined by what they are *not* rather than what they are (e.g., "This is *not* your father's Oldsmobile," "I can't believe it's *not* butter").

Mediating Characters.   The conflict between opposing forces is sometimes resolved by a mediating figure who can link the opposites by sharing characteristics of each. For example, many myths contain animals that have human abilities (e.g., a talking snake) to bridge the gap between culture and nature, just as cars (technology) are often given animal names (nature) like Cougar, Cobra, or Mustang. The Disney organization has used this principle quite effectively.[15] Its cartoon characters are often lovable, but possess exaggerated forms of human imperfections that make these flaws less threatening. Snow White's seven dwarfs, for example, can be viewed as a sanitized version of the "Seven Deadly Sins."

MODERN MYTHS   While we generally equate myths with the ancient Greeks or Romans, modern myths are embodied in many aspects of modern popular culture, including comic books, movies, holidays, and even commercials.

Pow! Wham! Comic Book Heroes.   Comic book superheroes demonstrate how a myth is communicated to consumers. Indeed, some of these figures represent a *monomyth*, a myth that is common to many cultures.[16] A hero emerges from the everyday world with supernatural powers and wins a decisive victory over evil forces. He then returns with the power to bestow good things on his fellow men. This basic theme can be seen in such stories as Lancelot, Hercules, and the Greek Odyssey.

古くなった広告、お取り替え致します。

クリエイティブが元気です。

マッキャンエリクソン博報堂
McCANN-ERICKSON HAKUHODO INC

This ad used in a corporate campaign for McCann-Erickson's Tokyo office plays off of the Superman myth by depicting a superhero with light beams radiating from his eyes. The headline reads: "We're ready to rejuvenate your advertising." Courtesy of McCann-Erickson Hakuhodo Inc.

These heroes are familiar to most consumers, and are often used to endorse products and sell merchandise. Indeed, they are often viewed as more credible and effective than celebrity endorsers. Not even counting movie spinoffs or licensing deals, comic books today are a $300 million a year industry. The American version of the monomyth is perhaps best epitomized by Superman, a Christ-like figure who renounces worldly temptations and restores harmony to his community. Heroes like Superman are sometimes used to blanket a product, store, or service with desirable attributes. The Japanese adaptation shown here illustrates how this monomyth has traveled across cultures.

Hollywood as Myth Machine. Many "blockbuster" movies draw directly on mythic themes. While dramatic special effects or attractive stars certainly don't hurt, a number of these movies perhaps also owe their success to their presentation of characters and plot structures that follow mythic patterns. Two examples of these mythic blockbusters follow.[17]

The extremely successful movie *E.T.* is based on a dominant cultural myth about Messianic visitation. Universal Shooting Star.

Additional Example: The television series "Star Trek" also relies on myths, such as the story of the New England Puritans exploring and conquering a new continent—"the final frontier." Encounters with the Klingons mirror skirmishes with American Indians. In addition, the quest for Paradise was a theme em-ployed in at least thirteen out of the 79 episodes filmed. See William Blake Tyrrell, "Star Trek as Myth and Television as Mythmaker," in *The Popular Culture Reader*, eds. Jack Nachbar, Deborah Weiser, and John L. Wright (Bowling Green, Ohio: Bowling Green University Press, 1978), 79–88.

- *Gone with the Wind.* Myths are often set in times of upheaval, such as warfare. In this story, the North (which represents technology and democracy) is pitted again the South (which represents nature and aristocracy). The movie depicts a romantic era (the antebellum South) where love and honor were virtues. This era is replaced by the newer forces of materialism and industrialization (i.e., modern consumer culture). The movie depicts a lost era where man and nature existed in harmony.

- *E.T.: The Extraterrestrial.* E.T., who is shown in one scene from the movie in the photo here, represents a familiar myth involving Messianic visitation. The gentle creature from another world visits Earth and performs miracles (e.g., reviving a dying flower). His "disciples" are neighborhood children, who help him combat the forces of modern technology and an unbelieving secular society. The metaphysical function of myth is served by teaching that the humans chosen by God are pure and unselfish.

HOLIDAY HEROES Most cultural holidays are based on a myth, and often a real (e.g., Miles Standish on Thanksgiving) or imaginary (e.g., Cupid on Valentine's Day) character is at the center of the story. These holidays persist because their basic elements appeal to consumers' deep-seated needs.[18]

The Santa Claus Myth. Perhaps the most important holiday myth involves Santa Claus. The Coca-Cola Company claims credit for inventing the modern image of Santa, which it distributed in its advertising in 1931. Until that time (the company claims), Santa was pictured as a cartoon-like elf.[19] More likely, the modern image of Santa Claus was shaped by the nineteenth-century cartoonist Thomas Nast, whose rendering of Santa was related to his other drawings of "fat cats" like Boss Tweed and the Robber Barons, greedy capitalists who exploited the poor and lived in useless luxury. One version is shown here.

Santa stands in opposition to Christ as a god of materialism. Perhaps it is no coincidence, then, that he appears in stores and shopping malls—*secular* temples of consumption. Whatever his origins, the Santa Claus myth serves the purpose of socializing children by teaching them to expect a reward when they are good and that members of society get what they deserve.

COMMERCIALS AS MYTHS Commercials can be analyzed in terms of the underlying cultural themes they represent. For example, commercials for

MERRY OLD SANTA CLAUS.

This Thomas Nast cartoon, published in 1881, provides some insights into the origins of the modern-day Santa Claus myth. This jolly figure is a caricature of a "fat cat" Robber Baron of the period who has accumulated an abundance of worldly possessions. Source: T. Nast, "Merry Old Santa Claus," in Russell W. Belk, *Journal of American Culture* (Spring 1987): 88. NorthWind Picture Archives.

Teaching Hint: Santa exhibits some interesting similarities and binary oppositions to Christ. He performs miracles (e.g., he can fly), his reindeer are like manger animals, letters to Santa resemble prayers, and the North Pole is a pure place resembling Heaven. In opposition, though, Santa is old and fat and wears rich furs. He comes through the cold snow rather than the hot desert, and he brings luxuries rather than necessities.
See Russell W. Belk, "A Child's Christmas in America: Santa Claus as Deity, Consumption as Religion," *Journal of American Culture* 10 (Spring 1987): 87–100.

Pepperidge Farm ask consumers to "remember" the mythical good old days when products were wholesome and natural. The mythical theme of the underdog prevailing over the stronger foe (i.e., David and Goliath) has been used by Chrysler and Avis.[20]

Global Marketing and Culture

Marketers contribute to culture by creating products and symbols that *signify* cultural ideals. Levi's jeans, Marlboro cigarettes, and Coca-Cola have been successfully linked with such abstract attributes as freedom and individuality and are viewed around the world as symbols of America. The Univision ad shown here displays some other uniquely American symbols.

Think Globally, Act Locally

As corporations increasingly find themselves competing in many markets around the world, the debate has intensified regarding the necessity of developing separate marketing plans for each culture. On one hand, it has been argued that many cultures, especially those of relatively industrialized countries, have become so homogenized that the same approach will work throughout the world. By standardizing marketing strategy, the company can benefit through economies of scale. There is little need to undergo the time and expense of developing a separate strategy for each culture.[21] This viewpoint represents an **etic perspective**, which focuses upon commonalities across cultures. An etic approach to a culture is objective and analytical; it reflects impressions of a culture as viewed by outsiders.

MULTICULTURAL DIMENSIONS

The etic approach has been chosen by many companies who have adopted a standardized strategy for marketing products in Europe. Although the unification of the European Economic Community has not happened as smoothly as many predicted, the prospect of many separate economies eventually being massed into one market of 325 million consumers has led many companies to begin to standardize their prices, brand names, and advertising.[22]

Many companies are responding to this dramatic change by consolidating the different brands sold in individual countries into common Eurobrands. In the United Kingdom and France, for example, the Marathon candy bar sold by Mars, Inc., is becoming the Snickers bar (a somewhat risky move, considering that the British refer to women's underwear as "knickers").[23]

Wella, the hair-care company, is aggressively developing a European strategy. In the next five years, 80 percent of its product line will be either introduced or relaunched as pan-European brands. Other companies that have "gone global" include Merrill Lynch, Xerox, and Chase Manhattan Bank. After testing four campaigns in seven countries, Seagram's Chivas Regal Scotch chose a series of 24 ads, each featuring a Chivas crest and the theme line: "There will always be a Chivas Regal."[24]

An additional example of globalization in a Citibank ad is available as Transparency 43.

AMONG THE SYMBOLS THAT MATTER MOST TO 20 MILLION AMERICANS IS A BRAND NEW ONE.

UNIVISION is Hispanic-America's television network. And we're introducing a brand new logo for the exciting new decade ahead.

UNIVISION

Univision, an Hispanic-American television network, attempts to associate its logo with some well-known symbols of America. COPYRIGHT UNIVISION, INC., created by Alan Stess & Associates.

NATIONAL CHARACTER On the other hand, many marketers endorse an **emic perspective**, which focuses on variations within a culture. They feel that each culture is unique, with its own value system, conventions, and regulations. This perspective argues that each country has a **national character**, a distinctive set of behavior and personality characteristics.[25] An effective strategy must be tailored to the sensibilities and needs of each specific culture. An emic approach to a culture is subjective and experiential; it attempts to explain a culture as it is experienced by *insiders*.

Taste and Stylistic Preferences. As opposed to Americans, Europeans favor dark chocolate over milk chocolate, which they regard as suitable only for children. Sara Lee sells its pound cake with chocolate chips in the United States, raisins in Australia, and coconut in Hong Kong. Whisky is considered a "classy" drink in France and Italy, but not in England. Crocodile bags are popular in Asia and Europe, but not in the United States. Americans' favorite tie colors are red and blue, while the Japanese prefer olive, brown, and bronze.[26]

Advertising Preferences and Regulations. Consumers in different countries are accustomed to different forms of advertising. In general, ads that focus on universal values, such as love of family, travel fairly well, while those with a specific focus on lifestyles do not. In some cases, advertising content is regulated. For example, pricing in Germany is controlled by the government, and special sales can be held only for a particular reason, such as going out of business or the end of the season. Advertising also focuses more on the provision of factual information rather than on the aggressive hard sell. Indeed, it is illegal to mention the names of competitors.[27] A similar emphasis on facts can be found in Spain and Denmark. In contrast, the British and the Japanese regard advertising as a form of entertainment. Compared to the United States, British television commercials contain less information,[28] and Japanese advertising is more likely to feature emotional appeals.[29] As in Germany, comparative advertising is rare in Japan, but for a different reason: The Japanese consider this practice impolite. They instead value commercial messages that contain a lot of references to nature and sensory experiences.

Superstitions and Cultural Sensitivities. Marketers must be aware of a culture's norms regarding such sensitive topics as taboos and sexuality. Opals signify bad luck to the British, while hunting dog or pig emblems are offensive to Muslims. The Japanese are superstitious about the number four. *Shi*, the word for four, is also the word for death. For this reason, Tiffany sells glassware and china in sets of five in Japan.

Modesty. Cultures vary sharply in the degree to which reference to sex and bodily functions is permitted. Many American consumers pride themselves on their sophistication. However, some would blush at much European advertising, where sexuality is more explicit. This dimension is particularly interesting in Japan, which is a culture of contradictions. On the one hand, the Japanese are publicly shy and polite. On the other hand, sexuality plays a significant role in this society. *Manga*, the extremely popular Japanese comic books that comprise a billion dollar industry, stress themes of sex and violence. Nudity is quite commonplace in Japanese advertising and general media.[30] Bare-breasted women are routinely featured in newspapers and on television.

The Japanese are also quite cavalier about bodily functions, largely due to the lack of privacy in their society. They often rely on earthy humor to sell products. One advertisement for a hemorrhoid preparation depicts a man sitting on the toilet, whining about his pain. Another spot featured a famous Japanese actress dressed as a tampon. The Fuji Latex Company, a large condom manufacturer, built a tower at its factory shaped like its product.[31]

On the other hand, a recent controversy in India illustrates differences in cultural norms about sexuality. The government-run television network rejected a spot for KamaSutra condoms that showed a couple sitting on a bed playing chess. As the woman sweeps the pieces off the board, she mouths the word "Check" while he mouths the word "Mate." The tagline reads, "For the pleasure of making love," which was considered unacceptable.[32]

DOES GLOBAL MARKETING WORK? Although the argument for a homogeneous world culture is appealing in principle, in practice it has met with mixed results. One reason for the failure of global marketing is that consumers in different countries have different conventions and customs, so they simply do not use products the same way. Kellogg, for example, discovered that in Brazil big breakfasts are not traditional—cereal is more commonly eaten as a dry snack. Procter & Gamble found that its ads for Camay soap in Japan did not work, because they featured men complimenting women on their appearance. This directness was very jarring to the Japanese, and the campaign had to be discontinued.[33]

Some large corporations, such as Coca-Cola, have been successful in crafting a single, international image. However, as noted earlier, it may be argued that they are really exporting a uniquely American image. Not many companies have such a strong franchise. Even Coca-Cola must make minor modifications to the way it presents itself in a culture. Although Coke commercials are largely standardized, local agencies are permitted to edit them to highlight close-ups of local faces.[34]

MARKETING PITFALL

The language barrier is one problem confronting marketers who wish to break into foreign markets. Chapter 14 noted some gaffes made by U.S. marketers when advertising to ethnic groups in their own country. Imagine how these mistakes are compounded outside of the United States! One technique that is used to avoid this problem is *back-translation*, where a translated ad is retranslated into the original language by a different interpreter to catch errors. Some specific translation obstacles that have been encountered around the world include the following.[35]

- Fresca (a soft drink) is Mexican slang for lesbian.
- When spelled phonetically, Esso means "stalled car" in Japan.
- Ford had several problems in Spanish markets. The company discovered that a truck model it called "Fiera" means ugly old woman in Spanish. Its Caliente model, sold in Mexico, is slang for a streetwalker. In Brazil, Pinto is a slang term meaning "small male appendage."
- When Rolls Royce introduced its "Silver Mist" model in Germany, it found that the word "mist" is translated as excrement. Similarly, Sunbeam's hair curling iron, called the "Mist-Stick," translated as *manure wand*.
- Vicks is German slang for sexual intercourse, so the company name had to be changed to Wicks in this market.

Identifying Cultural Values

Every culture is characterized by its members' endorsement of a value system. These end states may not be equally endorsed by everyone, and in some cases, values may even seem to contradict one another (e.g., Americans appear to value both conformity and individuality and seek to find some accommodation between the two). Nonetheless, it is possible to identify a general set of **core values** that seem to define a culture.

Such values as freedom, youthfulness, achievement, materialism, and activity have been claimed to characterize American culture, but even these basic beliefs are subject to change. For example, Americans' emphasis on youth is eroding as the population ages (see Chapter 15). Table 16–1 identifies the dominant values underlying a set of American print ads representing the period from 1900 to 1980. The prevalence of product effectiveness as an underlying advertising theme is obvious.

Despite their importance, values have not been widely applied to direct examinations of consumer behavior. One reason is that such broad-based concepts as freedom, security, or inner harmony are more likely to affect general purchasing patterns than to differentiate between brands within a product category. For this reason, some researchers have found it convenient to make distinctions among such broad-based *cultural values* as security or happiness, *consumption-specific values* as convenient shopping or prompt service, and such *product-specific values* such as ease of use or durability.[36]

Measuring Values

Since values drive much of consumer behavior (at least in a very general sense), it could be said that virtually all types of consumer research are ulti-

TABLE 16–1 Cultural Values Frequently Emphasized in American Advertising: 1900–1980

Overall Value	Themes Included	Proportion of Ads Using as Central Theme
Practical	Effective, durable, convenient	44
Family	Nurturance in family, happy home, getting married	17
New	Modern, improved	14
Cheap	Economical, bargain, good value	13
Healthy	Fitness, vigorous, athletic	12
Sexy/vain	Good appearance, glamorous, erotic	13
Wisdom	Knowledge, experience	11
Unique	Expensive, valuable, distinctive, rare	10

Source: Richard W. Pollay, "The Identification and Distribution of Values Manifest in Print Advertising 1900–1980." Adapted with the permission of Lexington Brooks, an imprint of Macmillan, Inc., from *Personal Values and Consumer Psychology* by Robert E. Pitts, Jr., and Arch G. Woodside, editors. Copyright © 1984 by Lexington books.

mately related to the identification and measurement of values. This process can take many forms, ranging from qualitative research techniques such as content analysis (which was used to obtain the data shown in Table 16–1) and ethnography to quantitative techniques such as laboratory experiments and large-scale surveys. An overview of these approaches is provided in Chapter 1. This section will describe some specific attempts by researchers to measure cultural values and apply this knowledge to marketing strategy.

THE ROKEACH VALUE SURVEY The psychologist Milton Rokeach identified a set of **terminal values**, or desired end states, that apply (to various degrees) to many different cultures. The *Rokeach Value Survey*, a scale used to measure these values, also includes a set of **instrumental values,** which are composed of actions needed to achieve these terminal values.[37] These two sets of values appear in Table 16–2.

THE LIST OF VALUES (LOV) Although some evidence indicates that differences on these global values do translate into product-specific preferences

Research Report: Some evidence indicates that the Rokeach Value Survey is culturally biased, because it does not sample a complete range of cultural values. Additional value dimensions that have been isolated in Asian samples include cultural inwardness versus social integration. See Michael Harris Bond, "Finding Universal Dimensions of Individual Variations in Multicultural Studies of Values: The Rokeach and Chinese Value Surveys," *Journal of Personality and Social Psychology* 55 (1988)6: 1009–15.

TABLE 16–2 Two Types of Values in the Rokeach Value Survey

Instrumental Values	Terminal Values
Ambitious	A comfortable life
Broadminded	An exciting life
Capable	A sense of accomplishment
Cheerful	A world at peace
Clean	A world of beauty
Courageous	Equality
Forgiving	Family security
Helpful	Freedom
Honest	Happiness
Imaginative	Inner harmony
Independent	Mature love
Intellectual	National security
Logical	Pleasure
Loving	Salvation
Obedient	Self-respect
Polite	Social recognition
Responsible	True friendship
Self-controlled	Wisdom

Source: Richard W. Pollay, "Measuring the Cultural Values Manifest in Advertising," *Current Issues and Research in Advertising* (1983): 71–92. Reptinted by permission of University of Michigan Division of Research.

International Example: In a study that tested linkages between scores on the LOV Scale and gift-giving behavior, both American and Asian participants in active social segments reported exerting greater effort and levels of gift-giving than did those in passive value segments. See Sharon E. Beatty, Lynn R. Kahle, and Pamela Homer, "Personal Values and Gift-Giving Behaviors: A Study Across Cultures," *Journal of Business Research* 22 (1991): 149–57.

and differences in media usage, the Rokeach Value Survey has not been widely applied to consumer behavior issues.[38] As an alternative, the *LOV (List of Values) Scale* was developed to isolate values with more direct marketing applications.

This instrument identifies nine consumer segments based on the values they endorse and relates each to differences in consumption behaviors. These segments include consumers who place a priority on such values as sense of belonging, excitement, warm relationships with others, and security. For example, people who endorse the value of sense of belonging are more likely to read *Reader's Digest* and *TV Guide*, drink and entertain more, prefer group activities, and be older than do people who do not endorse this value as highly. In contrast, those who endorse the value of excitement prefer *Rolling Stone* and are younger than those who do not.[39]

THE MEANS–END CHAIN MODEL Another research approach that incorporates values is termed a **means–end chain model**. This approach assumes that very specific product attributes are linked at levels of increasing abstraction to terminal values. The person has valued end states, and he or she chooses among alternative means to attain these goals. Products are thus valued as the means to an end. Through a technique called *laddering*, consumers' associations between specific attributes and general consequences are uncovered. Consumers are helped to climb up the "ladder" of abstraction that connects functional product attributes with desired end states.[40]

To understand how laddering works, consider a woman who expresses a liking for a flavored potato chip. Probing might reveal that this attribute is linked to a strong taste (another attribute). A consequence of a strong taste is that she eats fewer chips. As a result, she won't get fat, which in turn means that she will have a better figure. Finally, a better figure results in greater self-esteem, a terminal value for this person.[41]

MECCAs. The notion that products are consumed because they are instrumental to attaining more abstract values is central to one application of this technique, called the *Means–End Conceptualization of the Components of Advertising Strategy* (MECCAs). In this approach, researchers first generate a map depicting relationships between functional product or service attributes and terminal values. This information is then used to develop advertising strategy by identifying such elements as the following.[42]

- *Message elements:* the specific attributes or product features to be depicted.
- *Consumer benefit:* the positive consequences of using the product or service.
- *Executional framework:* the overall style and tone of the advertisement.
- *Leverage point:* the way the message will activate the terminal value by linking it with specific product features.
- *Driving force:* the end value upon which the advertising will focus.

This technique was used to develop advertising strategy for Federal Express. The researchers developed a "Hierarchical Value Map" for secretaries, an important group of decision makers in the category of overnight delivery services. As shown in Figure 16–2, concrete attributes of competitive services,

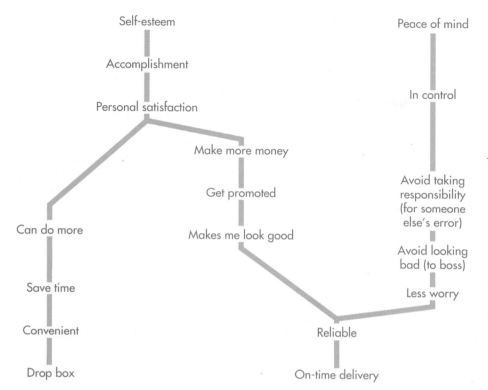

Self-esteem

Accomplishment

Personal satisfaction

Peace of mind

In control

Make more money

Get promoted

Can do more

Makes me look good

Avoid taking
responsibility
(for someone
else's error)

Avoid looking
bad (to boss)

Save time

Less worry

Convenient

Reliable

Drop box

On-time delivery

FIGURE 16–2 Secretaries' Hierarchical Value Map for Overnight Delivery Sevices Source: Adapted from Thomas J. Reynolds and Alyce Byrd Craddock, "The Application of the MECCAs Model to the Development and Assessment of Advertising Strategy: A Case Study," *Journal of Advertising Research* (April/May 1988): 43–54.

such as having a drop box or on-time delivery, were successively related to more abstract benefits, such as "makes me look good" or "save time." These intermediate levels were then linked, or laddered, to reveal their relationship to the terminal values of peace of mind and self-esteem.

Based on these results, an advertisement was created. Its message elements emphasized Federal Express' satellite communications network. The consumer benefit was the reliability of the service, which made work easier. The executional framework was a humorous one. A secretary is trying to track down an overnight delivery. She and her boss are interrupted and taken to view the Federal Express satellite system. As a result, the secretary sees the benefit of using the company. The leverage point is that using this service allows her to be in control, which in turn provides peace of mind, the driving force (terminal value).

SYNDICATED SURVEYS A number of companies track changes in values through large-scale surveys. The results of these studies are then sold to companies, who pay a fee to receive regular updates on changes and trends. These services, some of which are discussed in Chapter 13, include VALS 2, GlobalScan (Backer Spielvogel Bates), New Wave (Ogilvy & Mather), DDB Needham's Lifestyles Study, and the Lifestyle Monitor operated by Yankelovich Clancy Shulman.

Figure 16–2 is available as Transparency 44.

The Creation of Culture

The Rolling Stones. Miniskirts. Wide ties. Fast food. High-tech furniture. Post-modern architecture. Teenage Mutant Ninja Turtles. We inhabit a world brimming with different styles and possibilities. The food we eat, the cars we drive, the clothes we wear, the places we live and work, the music we listen to—all are influenced by the ebb and flow of popular culture and fashion.

Consumers may at times feel overwhelmed by the sheer number of choices in the marketplace. A person trying to decide on something as routine as a necktie has literally hundreds of alternatives to choose from. Despite this seeming abundance, however, the options available to consumers at any point in time actually represent only a small fraction of the total set of possibilities. The selection of certain alternatives over others—whether automobiles, dresses, computers, recording artists, political candidates, religions or even sci-

Figure 16–3 is available as Transparency 45.

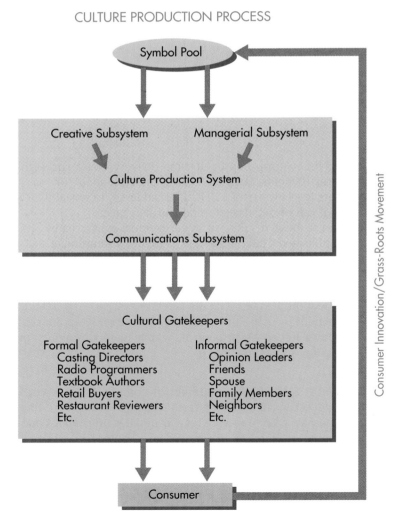

FIGURE 16–3 **The Culture Production Process** Source: Adapted from Michael R. Solomon, "Building Up and Breaking Down: The Impact of Cultural Sorting on Symbolic Consumption," in *Research in Consumer Behavior*, ed. J. Sheth and E. C. Hirschman (Greenwich, Conn.: JAI Press, 1988), 325–51.

entific methodologies—is the culmination of a complex filtration process resembling a funnel, as depicted in Figure 16–3. Many possibilities initially compete for adoption, and these are steadily winnowed down as they make their way down the path from conception to consumption.

Our tastes and product preferences are not formed in a vacuum. Choices are driven by the images presented to us in mass media, our observations of those around us, and even by our desires to live in the fantasy worlds created by marketers. These options are constantly evolving and changing. A clothing style or type of cuisine that is "hot" one year may be "out" the next, as the "obsolete" products in the AT&T ad shown here so painfully remind us.

Amanda's emulation of rap style illustrates some of the characteristics of fashion and popular culture.

- Styles are often rooted in and reflect deeper societal trends (e.g., politics and social conditions).

As this AT&T ad demonstrates, many product styles are doomed to become obsolete. Courtesy of AT&T INTERNATIONAL COMMUNICATIONS SERVICES.

Teaching Hint: The culture production system concept in some ways resembles that of a conventional distribution channel. However, the production of culture perspective does not necessarily focus upon manufacturer, wholesaler, and retailer functions, and it tends to deal with the spread of ideas or tastes rather than with physical product movement. See Elizabeth C. Hirschman and Michael R. Solomon, "Competition and Cooperation Among Culture Production Systems," in *Marketing Theory: Philosophy of Science Perspectives*, eds. Ronald F. Bush and Shelby D. Hunt (Chicago: American Marketing Association, 1982), 269–72.

Teaching Hint: Many judges or "tastemakers" influence the products that are eventually offered to consumers. These judges, who can be thought of as cultural gatekeepers, are responsible for filtering the overflow of information and materials intended for consumers. These agents include movie, restaurant, and car reviewers, interior designers, disc jockeys, retail buyers, magazine editors, and other consumer surrogates as discussed in Chapter 11. Collectively, this set of agents is known as the *through-put sector*. See Paul M. Hirsch, "Processing Fads and Fashions: An Organizational Set Analysis of Cultural Industry Systems," *American Journal of Sociology* 77 (1972)4: 639–59; Russell Lynes, *The Tastemakers* (New York: Harper and Brothers, 1954); Michael R. Solomon, "The Missing Link: Surrogate Consumers in the Marketing Chain," *Journal of Marketing* 50 (October 1986): 208–19.

- Styles usually originate as an interplay between the deliberate inventions of designers and business people and spontaneous actions by ordinary consumers. Designers, manufacturers, and merchandisers who can anticipate what consumers want will succeed in the marketplace. In the process, they also help to fuel the fire by encouraging mass distribution of the item.
- These trends can travel widely, often between countries and continents. Influential people in the media play a large role in deciding which of these trends will succeed.
- A style begins as a risky or unique statement by a relatively small group of people, then spreads as others increasingly become aware of the style and feel confident about trying it.
- Most styles eventually wear out, as people continually search for new ways to express themselves and marketers scramble to keep up with these desires.

Cultural Production Systems

No single designer, company, or advertising agency is totally responsible for creating popular culture. Every product, whether a hit record, a car, or a new clothing style, requires the input of many different participants. The set of individuals and organizations responsible for creating and marketing a cultural product is a **culture production system (CPS)**.[43]

The nature of these systems helps to determine the types of products that eventually emerge from them. Factors such as the number and diversity of competing systems and the amount of innovation versus conformity that is encouraged are important. For example, an analysis of the Country Western music industry has shown that the hit records it produces tend to be similar to one another during time periods when it is dominated by a few large companies, whereas there is more diversity when a greater number of producers are competing within the same market.[44]

The different members of a culture production system may not necessarily be aware of or appreciate the roles played by other members, yet many diverse agents work together to create popular culture.[45] Each member does his or her best to anticipate which particular images will be most attractive to a consumer market. Of course, those who are able to consistently forecast consumers' tastes most accurately will be successful over time. To illustrate these interrelationships, Table 16–3 highlights the many cultural specialists associated with the creation of a hit record.

Components of a CPS. A culture production system has three major subsystems: (1) a *creative subsystem* responsible for generating new symbols and/or products; (2) a *managerial subsystem* responsible for selecting, making tangible, mass producing, and managing the distribution of new symbols and/or products; and (3) a *communications subsystem* responsible for giving meaning to the new product and providing it with a symbolic set of attributes that are communicated to consumers. An example of the three components of a culture production system for a record would be (1) a singer (e.g., Madonna, a creative subsystem); (2) a company (e.g., Sire Records, which manufactures and distributes Madonna's records, a managerial sub-

TABLE 16-3 Cultural Specialists in the Music Industry

Specialist	Functions
Songwriter(s)	Compose music and lyrics; must reconcile artistic preferences with estimates of what will succeed in the marketplace.
Performer(s)	Interpret music and lyrics; may be formed spontaneously, or may be packaged by an agent to appeal to a predetermined market (e.g., The Monkees, Menudo, New Kids on the Block).
Teachers and Coaches	Develop and refine performers' talents.
Agent	Represents performers to record companies.
A&R (Artist & Repetoire) Executive	Acquire artists for the record label.
Publicists, Image Consultants, Designers, Stylists	Create an image for the group that is transmitted to the buying public.
Recording Technicians, Producers	Create a recording to be sold.
Marketing Executives	Make strategic decisions regarding performer's appearances, ticket pricing, promotional strategies, and so on.
Video Director	Interpret the song visually to create a music video that will help to promote the record.
Music Reviewers	Evaluate the merits of a recording for listeners.
Disc Jockeys, Radio Program Directors	Decide which records will be given airplay and/or placed in the radio stations' regular rotations.
Record Store Owner	Decide which of the many records produced will be stocked and/or promoted heavily in the retail environment.

system); and (3) the advertising and publicity agencies hired to promote the albums (a communications subsystem).

High Culture and Popular Culture

Do Beethoven and Ice-T have anything in common? While both the famous composer and the rap singer are associated with music, many would argue that the similarity stops here. Culture production systems create many diverse kinds of products, but some basic distinctions can be offered regarding their characteristics.

ARTS AND CRAFTS One distinction can be made between arts and crafts.[46] An **art product** is viewed primarily as an object of aesthetic contemplation without any functional value. A **craft product**, in contrast, is admired because of the beauty with which it performs some function (e.g., a ceramic ashtray or hand-carved fishing lures). A piece of art is original, subtle, and valuable, and is associated with the elite of society. A craft tends to follow a formula that permits rapid production. According to this framework, elite culture is produced in a purely aesthetic context and is judged by reference to recognized classics. It is high culture—"serious art."[47]

CULTURAL FORMULAE Mass culture, in contrast, churns out products specifically for a mass market. These products aim to please the average taste of an undifferentiated audience and are predictable because they follow certain patterns. As the *House & Garden* ad shown here illustrates, mass-produced products can alternate between being a functional object and a classic museum piece as its value fluctuates over time.

As illustrated in Table 16–4, many popular art forms, such as detective stories or science fiction, generally follow a **cultural formula,** where certain roles and props often occur consistently.[48] Romance novels are an extreme case of a cultural formula. Computer programs even allow users to "write" their own romances by systematically varying certain set elements of the story.

HIGH ART VERSUS LOW ART The distinction between high and low culture is not as clear as it may first appear. In addition to the possible class bias that drives such a distinction (i.e., we assume that the rich have culture while the poor do not), high and low culture are blending together in interesting

This *House & Garden* ad illustrates the life cycle of an Emerson radio to show how a mass-produced cultural product can change over time to become a classic and valuable collector's item. Reprinted by permission of *HG Magazine,* © 1989 CONDE NAST PUBLICATIONS, INC.

1940. 'The Patriot' by the Emerson Radio Corporation.

1946. No longer manufactured.

1947. Out of date.

1953. Garaged.

1980. Garage Sale.

1981. Flea Market.

1983. Antique Show.

1984. Madison Avenue Gallery.

1989. The Metropolitan Museum of Art.

Nothing endures but change.

HG HOUSE & GARDEN

TABLE 16–4 Cultural Formulae in Public Art Forms

Art Form/ Genre	Classic Western	Science Fiction	Hard-Boiled Detective	Family Sitcom
Time	1800s	Future	Present	Anytime
Location	Edge of civilization	Space	City	Suburbs
Protagonist	Cowboy (lone individual)	Astronaut	Detective	Father (figure)
Heroine	Schoolmarm	Spacegal	Damsel in distress	Mother (figure)
Villain	Outlaws, killers	Aliens	Killer	Boss, neighbor
Secondary characters	Townfolk, indians	Technicians in spacecraft	Cops, underworld	Kids, dogs
Plot	Restore law and order	Repel aliens	Find killer	Solve problem
Theme	Justice	Triumph of humanity	Pursuit and discovery	Chaos and confusion
Costume	Cowboy hat, boots, etc.	High-tech uniforms	Raincoat	Regular clothes
Locomotion	Horse	Spaceship	Beat-up car	Station wagon
Weaponry	Sixgun, rifle	Rayguns	Pistol, fists	Insults

Source: Arthur A. Berger, *Signs in Contemporary Culture: An Introduction to Semiotics* (New York: Longman, 1984), 86. Copyright © 1984. Reissued 1989 by Sheffield Publishing Company, Salem, Wisconsin. Reprinted with permission of the publisher.

ways. Popular culture reflects the world around us; these phenomena touch rich and poor.[49] In Europe, advertising is widely appreciated as an art form. Advertising executives are often public figures in Great Britain. For over ten years, Europeans have paid up to $30 to watch an all-night program in a movie theater consisting of nothing but television commercials.[50]

In a sense, all cultural products that are transmitted by mass media become a part of popular culture.[51] Classical recordings are marketed in much the same way as Top 40 albums, and museums use mass-marketing techniques to sell their wares. The Metropolitan Museum of Art even runs a satellite gift shop out of Macy's department store.

Art Sells. The arts are big business. Americans alone spend more than $2 billion per year to attend arts events.[52] Marketers often incorporate high art imagery to promote products, as illustrated in Colgate-Palmolive's adaptation of a Degas painting to sell bleach, as in the billboard ad shown on page 560. They may sponsor artistic events to build public goodwill or feature works of art on shopping bags.[53] When observers from Toyota watched customers in luxury car showrooms, the company found that these consumers tended to view a car as an art object. This theme was then used in an ad for the Lexus with the caption: "Until now, the only fine arts we supported were sculpture, painting, and music."[54]

Teaching Hint: Students will be amused and enlightened by a discussion of the Barbie doll (and her friends) as a cultural icon *and* as an art form. Barbie has been painted by Andy Warhol, and her likeness has been featured in museum shows and in movies. Students may be aware of a character in Rudy Rucker's cyberpunk novel *Wetware* called Kendoll, but they may not know that Barbie dolls have been exhibited at the Smithsonian Institution and the Victoria and Albert Museum in London. See Alice Kahn, "A One-time Bimbo Becomes a Muse," *New York Times* (September 29, 1991)3: H1.

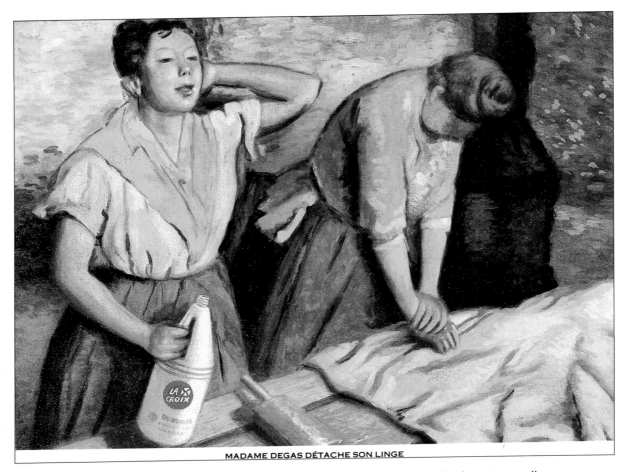

MADAME DEGAS DÉTACHE SON LINGE

This French billboard demonstrates the adaptation of famous paintings ("high art") to sell products ("low art"). In this version of Edgar Degas' "The Ironers," a brand of bleach (made by Colgate-Palmolive) replaces a bottle of wine. *Courtesy of Colgate Palmolive.*

AESTHETIC MARKET RESEARCH. Creators of aesthetic products are increasingly adapting conventional marketing methods to fine tune their mass-market offerings. Market research is used, for example, to test audience reactions to movie concepts. Although testing cannot account for such intangibles as acting quality or cinematography, it can determine if the basic themes of the movie strike a responsive chord in the target audience. This type of research is most appropriate for blockbuster movies, which usually follow one of the formulae described in Table 16–4.

The content of movies is sometimes influenced by consumer research. Typically, free invitations to pre-screenings are handed out in malls and movie theaters. Attendees are asked a few questions about the movie, then some are selected to participate in focus groups. Although groups' reactions usually result in only minor editing changes, occasionally more drastic effects result. When initial reaction to the ending of *Fatal Attraction* was negative, Paramount Pictures spent an additional $1.3 million to shoot a new one.[55]

MARKETING OPPORTUNITY

As the merchandising success of the lastest supermovie *Jurassic Park* illustrates, marketers increasingly are capitalizing on the public's enthusiasm for movies by developing numerous product tie-ins with blockbusters. The following listing provides some examples of major motion pictures of the recent past and the tie-ins they have spawned.

Movie	Number of Products	Notable Items
Aladdin	More than 100	Cave of Wonders Play Set
		Genie boxer shorts
		Children's slippers with curled-up toes
		Burger King "magic" cups (a genie appears when a beverage is poured in)
Bram Stoker's Dracula	About 100	$1500 bustier by special order from Macy's
		Red lace underpants with rosebud appliqué
		Bat, bug, and spider brooches ($500)
		Coffin lipstick holder with Vampire Red lipstick
Home Alone 2: Lost in New York	65–70	"Home Alone 2" backpack with scream ing burglar alarm
		Monster Sap Soap
		The Home Alone Survival Guide (safety tips for children)
Malcolm X	More than 100	"X" caps, T-shirts
		Malcolm X figurine with podium
		Automobile air fresheners

Source: Pat H. Broeske, "See the Movie, Buy the Automobile Air Freshener," *New York Times* (December 6, 1992): H12. Copyright © 1992, The New York Times Company. Reprinted by permission.

Additional Example: Robert Redford's film, "A River Runs Through It," is a touching story of two brothers' love for fly-fishing and for each other. Redford also distributes a Sundance Catalogue. Catalogue sales help to support his Sundance Institute, which supports the work of independent film makers and environmental causes. The catalogue features merchandise like a "River Runs Through It" T-shirt, a knife engraved with a fishing scene and the movie's title, a walking moose candlestick, a Sundance reindeer wall sconce, and so on. These tie-ins to "worthy causes" can generate interesting class discussion on whether the ends justify the means: Is commercial exploitation justified if done for the right reasons? See Caryn James, "Casting for Dollars," *New York Times* (December 6, 1992): H12.

The Diffusion of Innovations

New products and styles termed **innovations** constantly enter the market. If they are successful (most are not), they spread through the population. First they are bought and used by only a few people, and then more and more consumers decide to adopt them, until in some cases it seems that everyone has them. Of course, this saturation often is only temporary, as people get tired of products and/or new ones are introduced to take their place. **Diffusion** of innovations refers to the process whereby a new product, service, or idea spreads through a population.

Research Report: One study has provided a cross-national analysis of diffusion processes. See Hirokazu Takada and Dipak Jain, "Cross-National Analysis of Diffusion of Consumer Durable Goods in Pacific Rim Countries," *Journal of Marketing* 55 (April 1991): 48–54.

The issue of what exactly constitutes a "new" product is quite important to many businesses. It is said that "imitation is the sincerest form of flattery," and decisions regarding how much (if at all) one's product should resemble competitors are often a centerpiece of marketing strategy (e.g., packaging of "me-too" or look-alike products). On the other hand, the product cannot be a total duplicate; patent law is concerned with the precise definition of what is a new product and protecting that invention from illegal imitation.

A *knockoff* is a style that has deliberately been copied and modified, often with the intent to sell to a larger or different market. For example, *haute couture* clothing styles presented by top designers in Paris and elsewhere are commonly "knocked off" by other designers and sold to the mass market. It is difficult to legally protect a design (as opposed to a technological feature), but pressure is building in many industries to do just that. Manufacturers argue that, say, a distinctive curve on a car bumper is as important to the integrity of the car as is a mechanical innovation. Legislation is being considered to protect new designs with a ten-year copyright (clothing would be exempt).[56] This movement highlights the importance of the question: "What exactly is an innovation?"

Adopting Innovations

A consumer's decision to adopt an innovation resembles the sequence discussed in Chapter 7. The person moves through the stages of awareness, information search, evaluation, trial, and adoption, although the relative importance of each stage may differ depending upon how much is already known about a product, cultural factors, and so on.[57] However, not all people adopt an innovation at the same rate. Some do so quite rapidly, and others never do at all. Consumers can be placed into approximate categories based upon their likelihood of adopting an innovation. These categories can be related to phases of the product life-cycle concept used widely by marketing strategists.

As shown in Figure 16–4, the designation of a person as an innovator, an early adopter, part of the early or late majority, or as a laggard depends upon what stage of the life cycle a product is in when the person decides to use it. A laggard, for example, is quite slow to try something new; by the time he or she gets around to it, the product may well be on its last legs. The bell curve indicates the approximate percentage of consumers overall who fall under each category. The main point is that in many cases, roughly one-sixth of the population (innovators and early adopters) is very quick to adopt new products and one-sixth of the people are very slow. The other two-thirds are somewhere in the middle, and these majority adopters represent the mainstream public. These consumers are interested in new things, but they do not want them to be *too* new. In some cases, people deliberately wait to adopt an innovation because they assume that its technological qualities will be improved, or that the price will fall after it has been on the market awhile.[58]

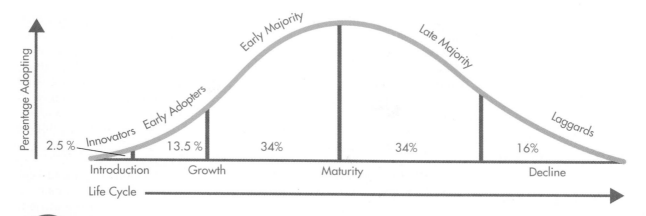

FIGURE 16–4 Types of Adopters

INNOVATORS Even though innovators represent only 2.5 percent of the population, marketers are always interested in identifying them. These are the brave souls who are always on the lookout for novel developments and will be the first to try a new offering. Just as generalized opinion leaders do not appear to exist (see Chapter 11), innovators tend to be category specific as well. A person who is an innovator in one area may even be a laggard in another. For example, a gentleman who prides himself as being on the cutting edge of fashion may have no conception of new developments in recording technology and may still stubbornly cling to his phonograph albums even while he searches for the latest *avant garde* clothing styles in obscure boutiques.

Despite this qualification, some generalizations can be offered regarding the profile of innovators.[59] Not surprisingly, for example, they tend to have more favorable attitudes toward taking risks. They also are likely to have higher educational and income levels and to be socially active.

EARLY ADOPTERS VERSUS INNOVATORS Early adopters share many of the same characteristics as innovators, but an important difference is their degree of concern for social acceptance, especially with regard to expressive products such as clothing, cosmetics, and so on. Generally speaking, an early adopter is receptive to new styles because he or she is involved in the product category and also places high value on being *in fashion*. What appears on the surface to be a fairly high-risk adoption (e.g., wearing a skirt 3 inches above the knee when most people are wearing them below the knee) is actually not *that* risky. The style change has already been "field-tested" by innovators, who truly took the fashion risk. Early adopters are likely to be found in "fashion-forward" stores featuring the latest "hot" designers. In contrast, true innovators are more likely to be found in small boutiques featuring as-yet unknown designers.

Types of Innovations

Innovations can occur on a symbolic level or a technological level. A *symbolic innovation* communicates a new social meaning (e.g., a new hairstyle or car design), while a *technological innovation* involves some functional change (e.g., central air conditioning or car airbags).[60] Whether symbolic or functional, new products, services, and ideas have characteristics that determine the degree to which they will probably diffuse. As a general rule, innovations that are more novel are *least* likely to diffuse, because things that are fairly similar to what is already available require fewer changes in behavior to use. On the other hand, an innovation that radically alters a person's lifestyle requires the person to modify his or her way of doing things, thus requiring more effort to adapt to the change.

BEHAVIORAL DEMANDS OF INNOVATIONS   Innovations can be categorized in terms of the degree to which they demand changes in behavior from adopters. Three major types of innovations have been identified, though these three categories are not absolutes. They refer in a *relative* sense to the amount of disruption or change they bring to people's lives.

A **continuous innovation** refers to a modification of an existing product, as when Cheerios introduces a Honey Nut version of its cereal or Levi's promotes shrink-to-fit jeans. This type of change may be used to set one brand apart from its competitors. Most product innovations are of this type. They are *evolutionary* rather than *revolutionary*. Small changes are made to position the product, add line extensions or merely to alleviate consumer boredom.

Consumers may be lured to the new product, but adoption represents only a minor change in consumption habits, perhaps adding to the product's convenience or to the range of choices available. A typewriter company, for example, many years ago modified the shape of its product to make it more "user friendly" to secretaries. One simple change was curving the tops of the keys, a convention that is carried over on today's computer keyboards. The reason: Secretaries complained that the flat surfaces were hard to use with long fingernails.

A **dynamically continuous innovation** is a more pronounced change in an existing product, as represented by self-focusing 35mm cameras or touch-tone telephones. These innovations will have a modest impact on the way people do things, creating some behavioral changes. The IBM Selectric typewriter, which uses a typing ball rather than individual keys, permitted secretaries to instantly change the typeface of manuscripts by replacing one Selectric ball with another.

A **discontinuous innovation** creates major changes in the way we live. Major inventions such as the airplane, the car, the computer, and television have radically changed modern lifestyles. The personal computer has in many cases supplanted the typewriter, and it has created the phenomenon of "telecommuters" by allowing many consumers to work out of their homes. Of course, the cycle continues, as new continuous innovations are constantly being made for computers (e.g., new versions of software), dynamically continuous innovations, such as the keyboard "mouse," compete for adoption, and discontinuous innovations like wrist-watch personal computers loom on the horizon.

PREREQUISITES FOR SUCCESSFUL ADOPTION   Regardless of how much behavioral change is demanded by an innovation, several factors are desirable for a new product to succeed.[61]

Compatibility. The innovation should be compatible with consumers' lifestyles. As one illustration, a manufacturer of personal-care products tried unsuccessfully several years ago to introduce a cream hair remover for men as a substitute for razors and shaving cream. This formulation was similar to that used widely by women to remove hair from their legs. Although the product was simple and convenient to use, it failed because men were not interested in a product they perceived to be too feminine and thus threatening to their masculine self-concepts.

Trialability. Since an unknown is accompanied by high perceived risk, people are more likely to adopt an innovation if they can experiment with it prior to making a commitment. To reduce this risk, companies often choose the expensive strategy of distributing free "trial-size" samples of new products.

Complexity. The product should be low in complexity. A product that is easier to understand and use will be chosen over a competitor. This strategy requires less effort from the consumer, and it also lowers perceived risk. Manufacturers of videocassette recorders, for example, have put a lot of effort into simplifying VCR usage (e.g., on-screen programming) to encourage adoption.

Observability. Innovations that are easily observable are more likely to spread, since this quality makes it more likely that other potential adopters will become aware of its existence. The rapid proliferation of "fanny packs" (pouches worn around the waist in lieu of wallets or purses) was due to their high visibility. It was easy for others to see the convenience offered by this alternative.

Relative Advantage. Most importantly, the product should offer relative advantage over other alternatives. The consumer must believe that its use will provide a benefit other products cannot offer. Two of the most popular new products introduced in 1992 demonstrated the importance of possessing a perceived relative advantage vis-a-vis existing products: Energizer Green Power Batteries were promoted as being better for the environment because they contain less mercury, and the Bugchaser is a wristband containing insect repellent. Mothers with young children liked it because it is nontoxic and nonstaining. In contrast, the Crazy Blue Air Freshener, which is added to windshield wiper fluid and emits a fragrance when the wipers are turned on, fizzled: People didn't see the need for the product, and felt there were simpler ways to freshen their cars if they cared to.[63]

The Fashion System

The **fashion system** consists of all those people and organizations involved in creating symbolic meanings and transferring these meanings to cultural goods. Although people tend to equate fashion with clothing, it is important to keep in mind that fashion processes affect all types of cultural phenomena, including music, art, architecture, and science (i.e., certain research topics and scientists are "hot" at any point in time). Even business practices are subject to the fashion process; they evolve and change depending on

Teaching Hint: It is important to emphasize that relative advantage does not just mean adding a product attribute, which may or may not be desired. One company offered a new type of deodorant made with Vitamin D and touted this addition as a relative advantage over other brands. Unfortunately, the company failed to convince consumers that spraying Vitamin D on their armpits was something to be desired, and the brand failed.

which management techniques are "in vogue," such as total quality management or just-in-time inventory control.

Fashion can be thought of as a *code*, or language, that helps us to decipher these meanings.[63] Unlike a language, however, fashion is context dependent. The same item can be interpreted differently by different consumers and in different situations.[64] The meaning of many products is *undercoded*—that is, there is no one precise meaning, but rather much room for interpretation among perceivers.

At the outset, it may be helpful to distinguish among some confusing terms. *Fashion* is the process of social diffusion by which a new style is adopted by some group(s) of consumers. A *fashion* (or style) refers to a particular combination of attributes. To be *in fashion* means that this combination is currently positively evaluated by some reference group. Thus, the term *Danish Modern* refers to particular characteristics of furniture design (i.e., a fashion in interior design); it does not necessarily imply that Danish Modern is a fashion that is currently desired by consumers.[65]

Cultural Categories

The meaning that does get imparted to products reflects underlying **cultural categories**, which reflect the basic ways we characterize the world.[66] Our culture makes distinctions between different times, between leisure and work, between genders, and so on. The fashion system provides us with products that signify these categories. For example, the apparel industry gives us clothing to denote certain times (e.g., evening wear, resort wear), it differentiates between leisure clothes and work clothes, and it promotes masculine and feminine styles. Some products that have represented the same cultural categories over time are displayed in the *House & Garden* ad shown here.

INTERDEPENDENCE AMONG PRODUCT MEANINGS These cultural categories affect many different products and styles. As a result, it is common to find that dominant aspects of a culture at any point in time tend to be reflected in the design and marketing of very different products. This concept is a bit hard to grasp, since on the surface a clothing style, say, has little in common with a piece of furniture or with a car. However, an overriding concern with a value such as achievement or environmentalism can determine the types of products likely to be accepted by consumers at any point in time. These underlying or *latent* themes then surface in various aspects of design. A few examples of this interdependence will help to demonstrate how a dominant fashion motif reverberates across industries.

- Costumes worn by political figures or movie and rock stars can affect the fortunes of the apparel and accessory industries. A movie appearance by actor Clark Gable without a T-shirt (unusual at that time) dealt a severe setback to the men's apparel industry, while Jackie Kennedy's famous "pillbox hat" prompted a rush for hats by women. Other cross-category effects include the craze for ripped sweatshirts instigated by the movie *Flashdance*, a boost for cowboy boots from the movie *Urban Cowboy*, and rock star Madonna's legitimation of lingerie as an acceptable outerwear clothing style.

1909 1958 1989

The Wedding Gift

Grandma's Silver Electric Percolator Cappuccino Machine

The Honeymoon

Atlantic City Havana, Cuba Hawaii

The Bed

Adirondack Bed Twin Beds Obelisk Bed

Nothing endures but change.

HG
HOUSE & GARDEN

This *House & Garden* ad demonstrates how different products represent the same cultural categories over time. Reprinted by permission of *HG Magazine* © 1989 CONDE NAST PUBLICATIONS, INC.

- The Louvre in Paris was recently remodeled to include a controversial glass pyramid at the entrance designed by the architect I.M. Pei. Shortly thereafter, several designers unveiled pyramid-shaped clothing at Paris fashion shows.[67]

- In the 1950s and 1960s, much of America was preoccupied with science and technology. This concern with "space-age" mastery was fueled by the Russians' launching of the Sputnik satellite, which prompted fears that America was falling behind in the technology race. The theme of technical mastery of nature and of futuristic design became a motif that cropped up in many aspects of American popular culture—from car designs with prominent tail-fins, as shown in the photo on page 568, to high-tech kitchen styles.

Collective Selection

Fashions tend to "sweep" the country; it seems that all of a sudden "everyone" is doing the same thing or wearing the same styles. Some sociologists view fashion as a form of *collective behavior,* or wave of social conformity. How do

A cultural emphasis on science in the late 1950s affected product designs, as seen in the design of automobiles with large tailfins (to resemble rockets). R. Gates/Frederic Lewis.

so many people get "tuned-in" to the same phenomenon at once, as happened with rap styles?

Remember that creative subsystems within a culture production system attempt to anticipate the tastes of the buying public. Despite their unique talents, members of this subsystem are also members of mass culture. As such, they are drawing from a common set of ideas and symbols and are influenced by the same cultural phenomena as the eventual consumers of their products. The process by which certain symbolic alternatives are chosen over others has been termed **collective selection**.[68] As with the creative subsystem, members of the managerial and communications subsystems also seem to develop a common frame of mind. Although products within each category must compete for acceptance in the marketplace, they can usually be characterized by their adherence to a dominant theme or motif—be it "The Western Look," "New Wave," "Danish Modern," or "Nouvelle Cuisine."

Behavioral Science Perspectives on Fashion

Fashion is a very complex process that operates on many levels. At one extreme, it is a macro, societal phenomenon affecting many people simultaneously. At the other, it exerts a very personal effect on individual behavior. A consumer's purchase decisions are often motivated by his or her desire to be in fashion. Fashion products also are aesthetic objects, and their origins are rooted in art and history. For this reason, there are many perspectives on the origin and diffusion of fashion. Although these cannot be described in detail here, some major approaches can be briefly summarized.[69]

PSYCHOLOGICAL MODELS OF FASHION Many psychological factors help to explain why people are motivated to be in fashion. These include conformity, variety-seeking, personal creativity, and sexual attraction. For example, many consumers seem to have a "need for uniqueness": They want to be different, but not *too* different.[70] For this reason, people often conform to the basic outlines of a fashion, but try to improvise and make a personal statement within these guidelines.

Fashion and Sexuality. One of the earliest theories of fashion proposed that "shifting erogenous zones" (sexually arousing areas of the body) accounted for fashion changes. Different parts of the female body are the focus of sexual interest, and clothing styles change to highlight or hide these parts. The different styles portrayed in the Maidenform ad shown here illustrate how various parts of the female form have been accentuated throughout history. For example, people in the Victorian era found shoulders exciting, a "well-turned ankle" was important in the beginning of this century, while the back was the center of attention in the 1930s. Some contemporary fashions suggest that the midriff is now an erogenous zone. (Note: Until very recently, the study of fashion focused almost exclusively on its impact on women. Hopefully, this concentration will broaden as scholars and practitioners begin to appreciate that men are affected by many of the same fashion influences.)

While these shifts may be due to boredom, some have speculated that there are deeper reasons for changes in focus; body areas symbolically

This ad for Maidenform illustrates that fashions have accentuated different parts of the female anatomy throughout history. Copyright © Maidenform, Inc. 1990.

reflect social values. In medieval times, for example, a rounded belly was desirable. This preference was most likely a reflection of the high mortality rate when virtually constant pregnancy was necessary to stabilize population growth. Interest in the female leg in the 1920s and 1930s coincided with women's new mobility and independence, while the exposure of breasts in the 1970s signaled a renewed interest in breast feeding.[71] Breasts were de-emphasized in the 1980s as women concentrated on careers, but a larger bust size is now more popular as women try to combine professional activity with child rearing (see Chapter 9).

ECONOMIC MODELS OF FASHION Economists approach fashion in terms of the model of supply and demand. Items that are in limited supply have high value, while those readily available are less desirable. Rare items command respect and prestige.

Conspicuous Consumption. Veblen's classic notion of *conspicuous consumption* proposed that the wealthy consume to display their prosperity, for example by wearing expensive (and at times impractical) clothing. As noted in Chapter 12, this approach is somewhat outdated, since upscale consumers often engage in *parody display*, where they deliberately adopt formerly low status or inexpensive products, such as jeeps or jeans. Other factors also influence the demand curve for fashion-related products. These include a *prestige-exclusivity effect*, where high prices still create high demand, and a *"snob" effect*, where lower prices reduce demand.[72]

SOCIOLOGICAL MODELS OF FASHION The collective selection model discussed previously is an example of a sociological approach to fashion. In addition, much attention has been focused on the relationship between product adoption and class structure.

The Trickle-Down Theory. The **trickle-down theory of fashion**, first proposed in 1904 by Georg Simmel, has been one of the most influential approaches to understanding fashion. It states that there are two conflicting forces that drive fashion change. Subordinate groups try to adopt the status symbols of the groups above them as they try to climb up the ladder of social mobility. Dominant styles thus originate with the upper classes and *trickle-down* to those below. Those people in the superordinate groups are constantly looking below them on the ladder to ensure that they are not imitated. They respond to imitation by adopting new fashions to differentiate them from those below. These two processes create a self-perpetuating cycle of change—the machine that drives fashion.[73]

Modifications to the Trickle-Down Theory. The trickle-down theory was quite useful for understanding the process of fashion changes when applied to a society with a stable class structure which permitted the easy identification of lower- versus upper-class consumers. This task is not so easy in modern times. In contemporary Western society, then, this approach must be modified to account for new developments in mass culture.[74]

- A perspective based on class structure cannot account for the wide range of styles that are simultaneously made available in our society. Modern consumers have a much greater degree of individualized choice than in the past because of advances in technology and distribution. Elite fashion has been largely replaced by mass fashion, since media exposure permits many groups to become aware of a style at the same time.

- Consumers tend to be more influenced by opinion leaders who are similar to them. As a result each social group has its own fashion innovators who determine fashion trends. It is often more accurate to speak of a *trickle-across* effect, where fashions diffuse horizontally among members of the same social group.[75]

- Finally, current fashions often originate with the lower classes and *trickle-up*. Grassroots innovators typically are people who lack prestige in the dominant culture (like urban youth). Since they are less concerned with maintaining the *status quo*, they are more free to innovate and take risks.[76]

Cycles of Fashion Adoption

In the early 1980s, Cabbage Patch dolls were all the rage among American children. Faced with a limited supply of the product, some retailers reported near-riots among adults as they tried desperately to buy the dolls for their children. A Milwaukee disc jockey jokingly announced that people should bring catcher's mitts to a local stadium because 2000 dolls were going to be dropped from an airplane. Listeners were instructed to hold up their American Express cards so their numbers could be aerially photographed. More than two dozen anxious parents apparently didn't get the joke; they showed up in subzero weather, mitts in hand.[77] Although the Cabbage Patch craze lasted for a couple of seasons, it eventually died out and consumers moved on to other things, such as Teenage Mutant Ninja Turtles, which grossed more than $600 million in 1989.[78] The fickleness of fashion cycles is the focus of the Jim Beam ad shown on page 572.

Although the longevity of a particular style can range from a month to a century, fashions tend to flow in a predictable sequence. The **fashion life cycle** is quite similar to the more familiar *product life cycle*. An item or idea progresses through basic stages from birth to death, as shown in Figure 16–5.

FIGURE 16–5 A Normal Fashion Cycle   Source: Reprinted with the permission of Macmillan College Publishing Company from *The Social Psychology of Clothing* by Susan Kaiser. Copyright ©1985 by Macmillan College Publishing Company, Inc.

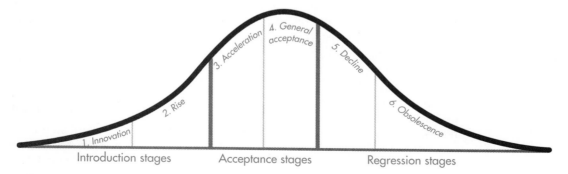

This Jim Beam ad illustrates the cyclical nature of fashion. Courtesy of Jim Beam Brand Co.

UP THE CHARTS WITH A BULLET: STAGES OF ACCEPTANCE The fashion acceptance cycle is evident in the Top 40 music industry. In the *introduction* stage, a song is listened to by a small number of music innovators. It may be played in clubs or on "cutting edge" college radio stations, which is exactly how "grunge rock" groups like Nirvana got their start. During the *acceptance* stage, the song enjoys increased social visibility and acceptance by large segments of the population. A record may get wide airplay on Top 40 stations, steadily rising up the charts "like a bullet."

In the *regression* stage, the item reaches a state of social saturation as it becomes overused, and eventually it sinks into decline and obsolescence as new songs rise to take its place. A hit record may be played once an hour on a Top 40 station for several weeks. At some point, though, people tend to get sick of it and focus their attention on newer releases. The former hit record eventually winds up in the discount rack at the local record store.

Figure 16–6 illustrates that fashions are characterized by slow acceptance at the beginning, which (if the fashion is to "make it") rapidly accelerates and then tapers off. Different classes of fashion can be identified by considering the relative *length* of the fashion acceptance cycle. While many fashions exhibit a moderate cycle, taking several years to work their way through the stages of acceptance and decline, others are extremely long-lived or short-lived. These two extreme forms of fashion are classics and fads.

Classics. A **classic** is a fashion with an extremely long acceptance cycle. It is in a sense "anti-fashion," since it guarantees stability and low risk to the purchaser for a long period of time. Keds sneakers, introduced in 1917, have been successful because they appeal to those who are turned off by the high fashion, trendy appeal of L.A. Gear, Reebok, and others. When consumers in focus groups were asked to project what kind of building Keds would be, a common response was a country house with a white picket fence. In other words, the shoes are seen as a stable, classic product. In contrast, Nikes were often described as steel-and-glass skyscrapers, reflecting their more modernistic image.[79]

Fads. A **fad** is a very short-lived fashion. Fads are usually adopted by relatively few people. Adopters may all belong to a common subculture, and the fad "trickles across" members but rarely breaks out of that specific group. Some successful fad products include hula hoops, snap bracelets, and "pet rocks." Streaking was a fad that hit college campuses in the mid-1970s. This term referred to students running naked through classrooms, cafeterias, and dorms. Although the practice quickly spread across many campuses, it was primarily restricted to college settings. Streaking highlights several important characteristics of fads.[80]

- The fad is non-utilitarian—that is, it does not perform any meaningful function.

Additional Example: Some fads can have dangerous consequences before they decline. In the mid-1980s, there was a brief craze in some urban areas for Cazals, eyeglass frames imported from West Germany which retailed for $85 to $200. At least four slayings were linked to youths desperate to obtain the frames. See William Robbins, "Fad for Eyeglass Frames Linked to 4 Slayings," *New York Times* (April 1, 1984): L23.

Figure 16–6 is available as Transparency 46.

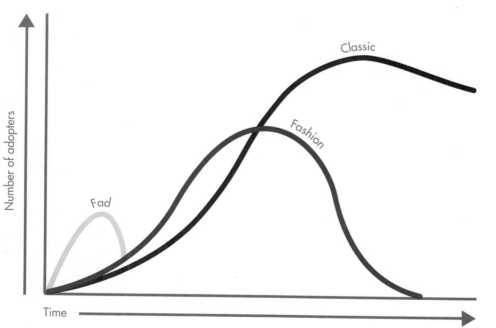

FIGURE 16–6 A Comparison of the Acceptance Cycles of Fads, Fashions, and Classics Source: Reprinted with the permission of Macmillan College Publishing Company from *The Social Psychology of Clothing* by Susan Kaiser. Copyright ©1985 by Macmillan College Publishing Company, Inc.

- The fad is often adopted on impulse; people do not undergo stages of rational decision-making before joining in.
- The fad diffuses rapidly, gains quick acceptance, and is short-lived.

• • • • • • • • • • • • • *Chapter Summary*

- A society's *culture* includes its values, ethics, and the material objects produced by its people. It is the accumulation of shared meanings and traditions among members of a society. A culture can be described in terms of ecology (the way people adapt to their habitat), its social structure, and its ideology (including people's moral and aesthetic principles). This chapter describes some aspects of culture and focuses on how cultural meanings are created and transmitted across members of a society.

- Members of a culture share a system of beliefs and practices, including *values*, or sets of enduring beliefs. The process of learning the values of one's culture is called *enculturation*, while learning those of another culture is *acculturation*. The belief in the superiority of one's own cultural practices and products is termed *ethnocentrism.*

- *Myths* are stories containing symbolic elements that express the shared ideals of a culture. Many myths involve some binary opposition, where values are defined in terms of what they are and what they are not (e.g., nature versus technology). Modern myths are transmitted through advertising, movies, and other media.

- The issue of whether marketing strategies developed for consumers in one culture can be adapted to other cultures is still subject to debate. Marketers who adopt an *etic perspective*, which focuses on finding commonalities across cultures, advocate standardized marketing efforts. Those who adopt an *emic perspective*, which focuses on the unique nature of each culture, are in favor of adapting themes and symbolism for each different market. In either case, marketers who venture into other countries must be sensitive to other cultures' norms, superstitions, and preferences.

- Each culture can be described by a set of core values. American culture has been characterized by such values as freedom, youthfulness, achievement, and materialism. *Values* can be identified by several methods, though it is often difficult to apply these results directly to marketing campaigns due to their generality.

- The styles prevalent in a culture at any point in time often reflect underlying political and social conditions. The set of agents responsible for creating stylistic alternatives is termed a *culture production system.* Factors such as the types of people involved in this system and the amount of competition by alternative product forms influence the choices that eventually make their way to the marketplace for consideration by end consumers.

- Culture is often described in terms of high (or elite) forms and low (or popular) forms. Products of popular culture tend to follow a cultural formula and contain predictable components. On the other hand, these distinctions are blurring in modern society as imagery from "high art" is increasingly being incorporated into marketing efforts.

- The *diffusion* of innovations refers to the process where a new product, service, or idea spreads through a population. A consumers' decision to adopt a new item depends on his or her personal characteristics (i.e., if he or she is inclined to try new things) and on characteristics of the item. Products stand a better chance of being adopted if they demand relatively little change in behavior from consumers and are compatible with current practices. They are also more likely to diffuse if they can be tried prior to purchase, if they not complex, if their use is visible to others, and most importantly, if they provide a relative advantage vis-a-vis existing products.

- The *fashion system* includes everyone involved in the creation and transference of symbolic meanings. Meanings that express common cultural categories (e.g., gender distinctions) are conveyed by many different products. New styles tend to be adopted by many people simultaneously in a process known as *collective selection*. Perspectives on motivations for adopting new styles include psychological, economic, and sociological models of fashion.

- Fashions tend to follow cycles that resemble the product life cycle. The two extremes of fashion adoption, *classics* and *fads*, can be distinguished in terms of the length of this cycle.

Key Terms

acculturation, p. 540

art product, p. 557

classic, p. 573

collective selection, p. 568

collectivism, p. 539

continuous innovation, p. 564

core values, p. 550

craft product, p. 557

cultural formula, p. 558

cultural categories, p. 566

culture, p. 538

culture production system (CPS), p. 556

diffusion, p. 561

discontinuous innovation, p. 564

dynamically continuous innovation, p. 564

emic perspective, p. 547

enculturation, p. 540

ethnocentrism, p. 541

ethos, p. 539

etic perspective, p. 546

fad, p. 573

fashion life cycle, p. 572

fashion system, p. 565

individualism, p. 539

innovation, p. 561

instrumental values, p. 551

means–end chain model, p. 552

myth, p. 541

national character, p. 547

trickle-down theory of fashion, p. 570

value system, p. 540

worldview, p. 539

Consumer Behavior Challenge

1. Culture can be thought of as a society's personality. If your culture were a person, could you describe its personality traits?
2. Marlboro, Coca-Cola, and Levi's are mentioned as brands that have become cultural symbols of America. Can you name some brands that perform the same function for other cultures? What are the strategic advantages of developing such a product?
3. What is the difference between an enacted norm and a crescive norm? Identify the set of crescive norms operating when a man and woman in

your culture go out for dinner on a first date. What products and services are affected by these norms?

4. At a library or newsstand, collect a set of advertisements for a product that is sold in many different countries. Analyze the cultural symbolism and values employed in these ads. How similar are the ads to each other? Is the company using a standardized marketing strategy or a localized one?

5. Perform a cultural analysis for a country other than the one you live in. Describe the culture in terms of its ecology, social structure, and ideology. If possible, consult members of this culture to determine its dominant values, as well as some specific norms regarding product consumption. How do these norms differ from your own culture? What adaptations would you have to make to market a snack food or personal care product to this culture?

6. What is the difference between an etic and an emic approach to the study of culture? How would adherence to one or the other perspective influence the development of a marketing plan for a foreign culture?

7. Construct a hypothetical means–end chain model for the purchase of a bouquet of roses. How might a florist use this approach to construct a promotional strategy?

8. Some people have raised objections to the commercial exploitation of cultural figures. For example, many consumers deplore the profits that filmmakers and business people have made off of films like *Malcolm X* (e.g., by selling a "Malcolm X" air freshener). Others argue that this commercialization merely helps to educate consumers about what such people stood for, and is inevitable in our society. What do you think?

9. Construct a "biography" of a product, tracing its progress from the time it was introduced. How long did it take to diffuse to the mass market? Do the same consumers use the product now as did those who first adopted it? What are its future prospects—is it destined for obsolescence? Would you characterize the product as either a classic or a fad?

10. Innovators are a small minority of consumers, yet marketers are very interested in identifying and reaching them. Why? How might you go about locating innovators?

11. Provide an example of a discontinuous innovation currently vying for adoption. What are the factors working for and against its eventual success in the marketplace?

12. Some consumers complain that they are "at the mercy" of designers: They are forced to buy whatever styles are in fashion, because nothing else is available. Do you agree that there is such a thing as a "designer conspiracy?"

13. What is the basic difference between a fad, a fashion, and a classic? Provide examples of each.

14. What is the difference between an art and a craft? Where would you characterize advertising within this framework?

15. The chapter mentions some instances where market research findings influenced artistic decisions, as when a movie ending was reshot to accommodate consumers' preferences. Many people would most likely oppose this use of consumer research, claiming that books, movies, records, or other artistic endeavors should not be designed to merely conform to what people want to read, see, or hear. What do you think?

CNN Connection

CNN A video segment is available to accompany this CNN connection.

The Fad Fair

Can life be complete without a Pet Rock? There seems to be no limit to what people will buy. As defined in the chapter, a fad is a very short-lived phenomenon. It serves no real function and is usually purchased on impulse. That description seems to fit the products exhibited at the annual Fad Fair held in New York City. This event is organized by Ken Hakuta, otherwise known as Dr. Fad. Mr. Hakuta made almost $20 million when he bought the rights to a toy he saw on a trip to Japan. He created the fad of the Wally Wallwalker, a little rubber octopus that climbs down walls. Now, Dr. Fad helps other enterprising fadmeisters get exposure for such "essentials" as the Dismembear, a teddy bear whose head and limbs can be pulled off as an outlet for frustration. Or, who could live without the Dobermask, a ferocious dog mask that fits over the head of a small dog to frighten off intruders? Other potential fads exhibited at the Fad Fair include the Everbrown, a dead tree that needs no water or care and a glow-in-the dark toilet seat to come to the aid of women everywhere whose husbands refuse to put the seat down!

Notes

1. Nina Darnton, "Where the Homegirls Are," *Newsweek* (June 17, 1991): 60; "The Idea Chain," *Newsweek* (October 5, 1992): 32.
2. Cyndee Miller, "X Marks the Lucrative Spot, But Some Advertisers Can't Hit Target," *Marketing News* (August 2, 1993); 1.
3. Grant McCracken, "Culture and Consumption: A Theoretical Account of the Structure and Movement of the Cultural Meaning of Consumer Goods," *Journal of Consumer Research* 13 (June 1986): 71–84.
4. Clifford Geertz, *The Interpretation of Cultures* (New York: Basic Books, 1973); Marvin Harris, *Culture, People and Nature* (New York: Crowell, 1971); John F. Sherry, Jr., "The Cultural Perspective in Consumer Research," in *Advances in Consumer Research* 13, ed. Richard J. Lutz (Provo, Utah: Association for Consumer Research, 1985), 573–75.
5. William Lazer, Shoji Murata, and Hiroshi Kosaka, "Japanese Marketing: Towards a Better Understanding," *Journal of Marketing* 49 (Spring 1985): 69–81.
6. Geert Hofstede, *Culture's Consequences* (Beverly Hills, Calif.: Sage, 1980); see also Laura M. Milner, Dale Fodness, and Mark W. Speece, "Hofstede's Research on Cross-Cultural Work-Related Values: Implications for Consumer Behavior," in *Proceedings of the 1992 ACR Summer Conference* (Amsterdam: Association for Consumer Research, 1992).
7. Daniel Goleman, "The Group and the Self: New Focus on a Cultural Rift," *New York Times* (December 25, 1990): 37; Harry C. Triandis, "The Self and Social Behavior in Differing Cultural Contexts," *Psychological Review* 96 (July 1989): 506; Harry C. Triandis, Robert Bontempo, Marcelo J. Villareal, Masaaki Asai, and Nydia Lucca, "Individualism and Collectivism: Cross-Cultural Perspectives on Self-Ingroup Relationships," *Journal of Personality and Social Psychology* 54 (February 1988): 323.
8. Richard W. Pollay, "Measuring the Cultural Values Manifest in Advertising," *Current Issues and Research in Advertising* (1983): 71–92.
9. Milton Rokeach, *The Nature of Human Values* (New York: Free Press, 1973).
10. *A New Partnership: New Values and Attitudes of the New Middle Generation in Japan and the U.S.A.* (Tokyo: Dentsu Institute for Human Studies, 1989).
11. George J. McCall and J.L. Simmons, *Social Psychology: A Sociological Approach* (New York: The Free Press, 1982).

12. Terence A. Shimp and Subhash Sharma, "Consumer Ethnocentrism: Construction and Validation of the CETSCALE," *Journal of Marketing Research* 24 (August 1987): 280–90.

13. Conrad Phillip Kottak, "Anthropological Analysis of Mass Enculturation," in *Researching American Culture*, ed. Conrad P. Kottak (Ann Arbor, Mich.: University of Michigan Press, 1982): 40–74.

14. Joseph Campbell, *Myths, Dreams, and Religion* (New York: E.P. Dutton, 1970).

15. Kottak, "Anthropological Analysis of Mass Enculturation."

16. Jeffrey S. Lang and Patrick Trimble, "Whatever Happened to the Man of Tomorrow? An Examination of the American Monomyth and the Comic Book Superhero," *Journal of Popular Culture* 22 (Winter 1988): 157.

17. Elizabeth C. Hirschman, "Movies as Myths: An Interpretation of Motion Picture Mythology," in *Marketing and Semiotics: New Directions in the Study of Signs for Sale*, ed. Jean Umiker-Sebeok (Berlin: Mouton de Guyter, 1987): 335–74.

18. Bruno Bettelheim, *The Uses of Enchantment: The Meaning and Importance of Fairy Tales* (New York: Alfred A. Knopf, 1976).

19. Jerry Schwartz, "At Age 104, Coke Congratulates Itself," *New York Times* (August 11, 1990): C3.

20. Bernie Whalen, "Semiotics: An Art or Powerful Marketing Research Tool?" *Marketing News* (May 13, 1983): 8.

21. Theodore Levitt, *The Marketing Imagination* (New York: The Free Press, 1983).

22. Kevin Cote, "The New Shape of Europe," *Advertising Age* (November 9, 1988): 98.

23. Steven Prokesch, "Selling in Europe: Borders Fade," *New York Times* (May 31, 1990): D1.

24. Gary Levin, "Ads Going Global," *Advertising Age* (July 22, 1991): 4; Dagmar Mussey and Anika Michalowska, "Wella Unifies Image," *Advertising Age* (March 11, 1991): 22.

25. Terry Clark, "International Marketing and National Character: A Review and Proposal for an Integrative Theory," *Journal of Marketing* 54 (October 1990): 66–79.

26. Julie Skur Hill and Joseph M. Winski, "Goodby Global Ads: Global Village is Fantasy Land for Marketers," *Advertising Age* (November 16, 1987): 22.

27. Matthias D. Kindler, Ellen Day, and Mary R. Zimmer, "A Cross-Cultural Comparison of Magazine Advertising in West Germany and the U.S.," unpublished manuscript, The University of Georgia, Athens, 1990.

28. Marc G. Weinberger and Harlan E. Spotts, "A Situational View of Information Content in TV Advertising in the U.S. and U.K.," *Journal of Marketing* 53 (January 1989): 89–94; see also Abhilasha Mehta, "Global Markets and Standardized Advertising: Is It Happening? An Analysis of Common Brands in USA and UK," in *Proceedings of the 1992 Conference of the American Academy of Advertising* (1992), 170.

29. Jae W. Hong, Aydin Muderrisoglu, and George M. Zinkhan, "Cultural Differences and Advertising Expression: A Comparative Content Analysis of Japanese and U.S. Magazine Advertising," *Journal of Advertising* 16 (1987): 68.

30. Laurel Anderson Hudson and Marsha Wadkins, "Japanese Popular Art as Text: Advertising's Clues to Understanding the Consumer," *International Journal of Research in Marketing* 4 (1988): 259–72.

31. Damon Darlin, "Myth and Marketing in Japan," *Wall Street Journal* (April 6, 1989): B1.

32. David Alexander, "Condom Controversy: Suggestive KamaSutra Ads Arouse India," *Advertising Age International* (April 27, 1992): I-12.

33. Hill and Winski, "Goodbye Global Ads."

34. Hill and Winski, "Goodbye Global Ads."

35. David A. Ricks, "Products That Crashed Into the Language Barrier," *Business and Society Review* (Spring 1983): 46–50.

36. Donald E. Vinson, Jerome E. Scott, and Lawrence R. Lamont, "The Role of Personal Values in Marketing and Consumer Behavior," *Journal of Marketing* 41 (April 1977): 44–50.

37. Milton Rokeach, *Understanding Human Values* (New York: The Free Press, 1979); see also J. Michael Munson and Edward McQuarrie, "Shortening the Rokeach Value Survey for Use in Consumer Research," in *Advances in Consumer Research* 15, ed. Michael J. Houston (Provo, Utah: Association for Consumer Research, 1988), 381–86.

38. B.W. Becker and P.E. Conner, "Personal Values of the Heavy User of Mass Media," *Journal of Advertising Research* 21 (1981): 37–43; Vinson, Scott, and Lamont, "The Role of Personal Values in Marketing and Consumer Behavior."

39. Sharon E. Beatty, Lynn R. Kahle, Pamela Homer, and Shekhar Misra, "Alternative Measurement Approaches to Consumer Values: The List of Values and the Rokeach Value Survey," *Psychology & Marketing* 2 (1985): 181–200; Lynn R. Kahle and Patricia Kennedy, "Using the List of Values (LOV) to Understand Consumers," *Journal of Consumer Marketing* 2 (Fall 1988): 49–56; Lynn Kahle, Basil Poulos, and Ajay Sukhdial, "Changes in Social Values in the United States During the Past Decade," *Journal of Advertising Research* 28 (February/March 1988): 35–41; see also Wagner A.

Kamakura and Jose Alfonso Mazzon, "Value Segmentation: A Model for the Measurement of Values and Value Systems," *Journal of Consumer Research* 18 (September 1991): 28.

40. Thomas J. Reynolds and Jonathan Gutman, "Laddering Theory, Method, Analysis, and Interpretation," *Journal of Advertising Research* 28 (February/March 1988): 11–34; Beth Walker, Richard Celsi, and Jerry Olson, "Exploring the Structural Characteristics of Consumers' Knowledge," in *Advances in Consumer Research* 14, eds. Melanie Wallendorf and Paul Anderson (Provo, Utah: Association for Consumer Research, 1986), 17–21.

41. Reynolds and Gutman, "Laddering Theory, Method, Analysis, and Interpretation."

42. Thomas J. Reynolds and Alyce Byrd Craddock, "The Application of the MECCAS Model to the Development and Assessment of Advertising Strategy: A Case Study," *Journal of Advertising Research* (April/May 1988): 43–54.

43. Richard A. Peterson, "The Production of Culture: A Prolegomenon," in *The Production of Culture*, Sage Contemporary Social Science Issues, ed. Richard A. Peterson (Beverly Hills: Sage, 1976)33, 7–22.

44. Richard A. Peterson and D.G. Berger, "Entrepreneurship in Organizations: Evidence from the Popular Music Industry," *Administrative Science Quarterly* 16 (1971): 97–107.

45. Elizabeth C. Hirschman, "Resource Exchange in the Production and Distribution of a Motion Picture," *Empirical Studies of the Arts* 8 (1990)1: 31–51; Michael R. Solomon, "Building Up and Breaking Down: The Impact of Cultural Sorting on Symbolic Consumption," in *Research in Consumer Behavior*, eds. J. Sheth and E.C. Hirschman (Greenwich, Conn.: JAI Press, 1988), 325–51.

46. Howard S. Becker, "Arts and Crafts," *American Journal of Sociology* 83 (January 1987): 862–89.

47. Herbert J. Gans, "Popular Culture in America: Social Problem in a Mass Society or Social Asset in a Pluralist Society?" in *Social Problems : A Modern Approach*, ed. Howard S. Becker (New York: Wiley, 1966).

48. Arthur A. Berger, *Signs in Contemporary Culture: An Introduction to Semiotics* (New York: Longman, 1984).

49. Ray B. Browne, "Popular Culture: The World Around Us," in *The Popular Culture Reader*, eds. Jack Nachbar, Deborah Weiser, and John L. Wright (Bowling Green, Ohio: Bowling Green University Popular Press, 1978), 12–17.

50. Peter S. Green, "Moviegoers Devour Ads," *Advertising Age* (June 26, 1989): 36.

51. Michael R. Real, *Mass-Mediated Culture* (Englewood Cliffs, N.J.: Prentice-Hall, 1977).

52. John P. Robinson, "The Arts in America," *American Demographics* (September 1987): 42.

53. Annetta Miller, "Shopping Bags Imitate Art: Seen the Sacks? Now Visit the Museum Exhibit," *Newsweek* (January 23, 1989): 44.

54. Kim Foltz, "New Species for Study: Consumers in Action," *New York Times* (December 18, 1989): A1.

55. Helene Diamond, "Lights, Camera . . . Research!" *Marketing News* (September 11, 1989): 10.

56. Edmund L. Andrews, "When Imitation Isn't the Sincerest Form of Flattery," *New York Times* (August 9, 1990): 20.

57. Eric J. Arnould, "Toward a Broadened Theory of Preference Formation and the Diffusion of Innovations: Cases from Zinder Province, Niger Republic," *Journal of Consumer Research* 16 (September 1989): 239–67; Susan B. Kaiser, *The Social Psychology of Clothing* (New York: Macmillan, 1985); Thomas S. Robertson, *Innovative Behavior and Communication* (New York: Holt, Rinehart and Winston, 1971); Everett M. Rogers, *Diffusion of Innovations*, 3rd ed. (New York: The Free Press, 1983).

58. Susan L. Holak, Donald R. Lehmann, and Fareena Sultan, "The Role of Expectations in the Adoption of Innovative Consumer Durables: Some Preliminary Evidence," *Journal of Retailing* 63 (Fall 1987): 243–59.

59. Hubert Gatignon and Thomas S. Robertson, "A Propositional Inventory for New Diffusion Research," *Journal of Consumer Research* 11 (March 1985): 849–67.

60. Elizabeth C. Hirschman, "Symbolism and Technology as Sources of the Generation of Innovations," in *Advances in Consumer Behavior* 9, ed. Andrew Mitchell (Provo, Utah: Association for Consumer Research, 1981), 537–41.

61. Rogers, *Diffusion of Innovations*.

62. Trish Hall, "Telling the 'Yeas' from the 'Nays' in New Products," *New York Times* (December 9, 1992)2: C1.

63. Umberto Eco, *A Theory of Semiotics* (Bloomington, Ind.: Indiana University Press, 1979).

64. Fred Davis, "Clothing and Fashion as Communication," in *The Psychology of Fashion*, ed. Michael R. Solomon (Lexington, Mass.: Lexington Books, 1985), 15–28.

65. Melanie Wallendorf, "The Formation of Aesthetic Criteria Through Social Structures and Social Institutions," in *Advances in Consumer Research* 7, ed. Jerry C. Olson (Ann Arbor, Mich.: Association for Consumer Research, 1980), 3–6.

66. Grant McCracken, "Culture and Consumption: A Theoretical Account of the Structure and Movement of the Cultural Meaning of Consumer Goods," *Journal of Consumer Research* 13 (June 1986): 71–84.

67. "The Eternal Triangle," *Art in America* (February 1989): 23.

68. Herbert Blumer, *Symbolic Interactionism: Perspective and Method* (Englewood Cliffs, N.J.: Prentice Hall, 1969); Howard S. Becker, "Art as Collective Action," *American Sociological Review* 39 (December 1973); Richard A. Peterson, "Revitalizing the Culture Concept," *Annual Review of Sociology* 5 (1979): 137–66.

69. For more details, see Kaiser, *The Social Psychology of Clothing*; George B. Sproles, "Behavioral Science Theories of Fashion," in *The Psychology of Fashion*, ed. Michael R. Solomon (Lexington, Mass.: Lexington Books, 1985), 55–70.

70. C.R. Snyder and Howard L. Fromkin, *Uniqueness: The Human Pursuit of Difference* (New York: Plenum Press, 1980).

71. Alison Lurie, *The Language of Clothes* (New York: Random House, 1981).

72. Harvey Leibenstein, *Beyond Economic Man: A New Foundation for Microeconomics* (Cambridge, Mass.: Harvard University Press, 1976).

73. Georg Simmel, "Fashion," *International Quarterly* 10 (1904): 130–55.

74. Grant D. McCracken, "The Trickle-Down Theory Rehabilitated," in *The Psychology of Fashion*, ed. Michael R. Solomon (Lexington, Mass.: Lexington Books, 1985), 39–54.

75. Charles W. King, "Fashion Adoption: A Rebuttal to the 'Trickle-Down' Theory," in *Toward Scientific Marketing*, ed. Stephen A. Greyser (Chicago: American Marketing Association, 1963), 108–25.

76. Alf H. Walle, "Grassroots Innovation," *Marketing Insights* (Summer 1990): 44–51.

77. "Cabbage-Hatched Plot Sucks in 24 Doll Fans," *New York Daily News* (December 1, 1983).

78. "Turtlemania," *The Economist* (April 21, 1990): 32.

79. Anthony Ramirez, "The Pedestrian Sneaker Makes a Comeback," *New York Times* (October 14, 1990): F17.

80. B.E. Aguirre, E.L. Quarantelli, and Jorge L. Mendoza, "The Collective Behavior of Fads: The Characteristics, Effects, and Career of Streaking," *American Sociological Review* (August 1989): 569.

CHAPTER 17

Consumer Behavior and Cultural Processes: Emerging Issues

Buying, Having, and Being: Selections 60–65 from *Buying, Having, and Being: The Washington Post Consumer Behavior Companion*, Second Edition, accompany this chapter.

F inally feeling settled in their new apartment, Robert and Bridget are looking over their wedding pictures. They recall the months of frantic preparation: the search for the perfect rings, the selection of the gowns and tuxedos, the rehearsals, conferences with the wedding coordinator about such weighty matters as hors d'oeuvres, floral arrangements, the cake. They had been so weary when the big day finally came! And now it all seemed like a long-ago dream even though only a few months had passed.

Turning to the pictures of their honeymoon trip, they smile and reminisce about how perfect it had been. Right after the reception, the new couple had jetted off to Disney World. Where else to commemorate their sacred union but in The Magic Kingdom? Robert and Bridget frolicked on the manmade beach with visitors from all over the world, shopped in Japan, China, Germany, and Mexico (without ever leaving EPCOT), experienced "terror" as King Kong ravaged the streets of Manhattan, and even got the autographs of two Teenage Mutant Ninja Turtles.

Robert finally flips to the photo he's been waiting to see. A high point of the trip for him was his encounter with his fantasy heart throb, Marilyn Monroe, at the Disney/MGM Studios. Even though he knew deep down that the woman he was standing next to was just a look-alike, he could swear that Marilyn's presence was somehow there. Bridget had not been too pleased with Robert's infatuation, but he made it up to her by buying her an authentic Mickey Mouse watch—it's amazing how a thoughtful gift can smooth ruffled feathers . . . .

The Future of Consumer Behavior

The Disney organization has succeeded in blurring the distinction between fantasy and reality for many, and it has exported its version of American culture to Europe and Japan, where visitors are welcomed by Minnie and Mickey dressed in traditional Japanese kimonos. As in most cultures, a wedding, the purchase of a gift (and its symbolic ability to cement or heal relationships), a trip to Disney World, and even celebrity worship are consumer activities whose significance goes beyond the simple act of buying a product. These phenomena can be better understood by adapting concepts from anthropology, sociology, and other social sciences to place our behavior as consumers in the context of other cultural events. Marketing researchers are beginning to make these connections, as they come to appreciate that even "ordinary" consumer activities are rich in deeper meanings.

As modern life becomes more complex, the convergence between marketing activities and the way we conduct our everyday lives grows. Chapter 1 noted that the marketplace is evolving as people adjust to the demands of a postmodern, information-based society. Important lifestyle and demographic changes (some of which were discussed in Chapters 13 through 15) are forcing marketers to rethink their role in society. Among these developments are the following.

- The growing influence of diverse ethnic and racial groups makes marketers more sensitive to cross-cultural variations in tastes and preferences and also fuels consumers' desires to experience the products of cultures other than their own. The downside of the globalization of culture is what some view as cultural imperialism, as American and European products and services penetrate other cultures and obliterate the unique customs and goods of non-Western cultures.

- Changes are taking place in the sex roles of men and women as ideals regarding marriages, homosexuality, child rearing, and career choices evolve. As uncertainty about the proper roles of men and women in our culture increases, consumers will continue to be influenced by how notions of masculinity and femininity are translated into product concepts and advertising practices by marketers.

- An increasing emphasis on the value of time as a commodity is motivating consumers to look for new ways to acquire experiences and products in more convenient and accessible forms. Advances in technology make possible more home-centered activities, whether for entertainment (e.g., the proliferation of cable stations) or for work (e.g., the trend toward "telecommuting" as more people use their personal computers and FAXes to establish offices at home).

- Increasing concern about the effect of consumption on the environment and "green marketing," whether in terms of the use of valuable resources to create products, health-related issues, or on problems

This ad for Palmolive dishwashing liquid, like those of many marketers, stresses environmental benefits of the product. Courtesy of Colgate Palmolive Company.

related to product disposal. The Palmolive ad shown here is one of many new attempts to position everyday products as "green."

- Changing priorities regarding exercise, nutrition, and self-indulgence, coupled with a premium placed on "anti-stress" services ranging from aroma therapy to personal trainers, are being sought as people try to cope with the numerous demands of their roles as parents and workers. The personal demands placed on us by modern society also affect the "dark side" of consumer behavior, as we grapple with such problems as addiction, prostitution, compulsive shopping, theft, and vandalism.

- Disenchantment with the accumulation of status goods has led many consumers to focus on the acquisition of experiences, whether from travel, high-quality music reproduction, or virtual reality games. The central role of marketers in creating and distributing experiences has led to the blurring of boundaries between commercial activities and popular culture. A campaign by Absolut Vodka featuring the work of popular artists illustrates how the two paths often cross. Two of the ads in this campaign are shown here.

These Absolut ads featuring popular artists help to blur the boundaries between marketing activities and popular culture. Absolut Vodka logo and bottle design are trademarks owned by V&S VIN & SPIRIT AB, Imported by Carillon Importers LTD., Teaneck, N.J.

This chapter considers some of the emerging issues that will be of increasing importance for understanding consumer behavior in the complex marketplace of the 1990s and beyond. The first section explores the parallels between consumer behavior and other "sacred" human activities: Our observance of holidays, our reverence for celebrities, our celebration of such rituals as weddings and graduations, and even such innocent acts as preening in front of a mirror are not as simple as they may seem. The second part of the chapter discusses some of the more negative aspects of consumer experience that many marketers are reluctant to acknowledge: the "dark side" of consumer behavior as manifested in excessive materialism, addiction, and other social problems. The chapter concludes with a discussion of the complex relationship between marketing activities and consumers' everyday experiences: To what degree does popular culture shape marketing decisions and vice-versa?

Sacred and Profane Consumption

Many types of consumer activity involve the demarcation, or binary opposition, of boundaries, such as good versus bad, male versus female, even regular versus lo-cal. One of the most important of these sets of boundaries is the distinction between the sacred and the profane. **Sacred consumption** involves objects and events that are "set apart" from normal and treated with some degree of respect or awe. They may or may not be associated with religion, but most religious items and events tend to be regarded as sacred. **Profane consumption** involves consumer objects and events that are ordinary, everyday objects and events that do not share the "specialness" of sacred ones. (Note that profane does not mean vulgar or obscene in this context.)

Due to social and cultural change in recent times, many consumer activities have moved from one sphere to the other. Some things that were formerly regarded as sacred have now become *desacralized* and profane, and other, everyday phenomena now are regarded as sacred.[1]

Desacralization

Desacralization occurs when a sacred item or symbol is removed from its special place or is duplicated in mass quantities becoming profane as a result. For example, souvenir reproductions of sacred monuments such as the Washington Monument or the Eiffel Tower, such artworks as *The Mona Lisa*, or adaptations of important symbols such as the American flag by clothing designers, eliminate their special aspects by turning them into unauthentic commodities, produced mechanically with relatively little value.[2]

IS RELIGION STILL SACRED?   Religion has to some extent been desacralized. Religious symbols, such as stylized crosses or New Age crystals, have moved into the mainstream of fashion jewelry.[3] Religious holidays, particularly Christmas, are regarded by many (and criticized by some) as having been transformed into secular, materialistic occasions devoid of their original sacred significance.

Cross-Cultural Example: Societies often devise ways to ensure that sacred things are kept separate. Legislation in Great Britain, for example, was passed to prevent advertising (a profane commodity) from appearing two minutes before or after the telecast of any royal occasion (a sacred event).   See Russell W. Belk, Melanie Wallendorf, and John F. Sherry, Jr., "The Sacred and the Profane in Consumer Behavior: Theodicy on the Odyssey," *Journal of Consumer Research* 16 (June 1989): 1–38.

Additional Example: Money is not necessarily profane. It is invested with good powers (as when a person saves up a nest egg or makes a donation) as well as bad (as when used as a ransom or for "blood money"). It can be used to buy "immortality" (as in philanthropy, when a building is named after a donor), life (as when children are adopted or a surrogate mother is hired), or even death (e.g., contract murders or abortion).   See Russell W. Belk and Melanie Wallendorf, "The Sacred Meanings of Money," *Journal of Economic Psychology* 11 (1990): 35–67.

For fast, fast, fast relief take two tablets.

In the Episcopal Church, we believe that some of the oldest ideas are still the best.
Like the regular worship of God. Come join us as we celebrate this Sunday.
The Episcopal Church

This ad for a Minneapolis church to help recruit worshipers is typical of the trend toward secular marketing practices being practiced by many organized religions. Courtesy of Church Ad Project, 1021 Diffley, Eagan, MN 55123.

Even the clergy are increasingly adopting secular marketing techniques. Televangelists rely upon the power of television, a secular medium, to convey their messages. The Catholic Church generated a major controversy after it hired a prominent public relations firm to promote its anti-abortion campaign.[4] Nonetheless, many religious groups have taken the secular route. The Mormons sponsored a $12 million campaign in *Readers Digest*, while *Newsweek: On Campus* featured the comedian Father Guido Sarducci in a humorous ad designed to recruit college students as padres.[5] An ad run by the Episcopal Church, as shown here, reflects this trend.

Sacralization

The **sacralization** process occurs when ordinary objects, events, and even people, take on sacred meaning to a culture or to specific groups within a culture. For example, events like the Super Bowl and people like Elvis Presley have become sacralized to some consumers.

Elvis Presley, who has taken on sacred status for many people, has also spawned his own (posthumous) souvenir industry at Graceland, where devoted fans find a vast array of Elvis "collectibles." Photo by Melloul–Racinan/Sygma.

OBJECTIFICATION   Sacredness is often concretized in objects. The *objectification* process means that profane products of various kinds take on sacred qualities. One way that this process can occur is through *contamination*, where objects associated with sacred events or people become sacred in their own right. This reason explains the desire by many fans for items belonging to, or even touched by, famous people. Even the Smithsonian Institution in Washington, D.C., maintains a display featuring such "sacred items" as the ruby slippers from *The Wizard of Oz*, a phaser from "Star Trek," and Archie Bunker's chair from the television show "All in the Family"—all reverently protected behind sturdy display glass.

Collections. In addition to museum exhibits displaying rare objects or those that have meaning to large numbers of people (such as Dorothy's ruby slippers), even mundane, inexpensive things may be set apart in *collections*, where they are transformed from profane items to sacred ones. An item is sacralized as soon as it enters a collection, and it takes on special significance to the collector that, in some cases, may be hard to comprehend by the outsider. The contents of collections range from movie memorabilia, rare books, and autographs to G.I. Joe dolls, Elvis memorabilia, and even junk mail.[6] As indicated in the photo shown here, Elvis souvenirs for sale at Graceland encompass a vast array of items that will ultimately make their way into the Elvis collections of the devoted fans who travel to this "shrine."

Transparency 47, showing a baseball aficionado, provides an additional illustration of the collection theme, in which extensive collections are displayed in personal "museums" in collectors' homes.

Domains of Sacred Consumption

Sacred consumption events permeate many aspects of consumers' experiences. We find ways to "set apart" a variety of places, people, and events.

Sacred Places

Sacred places have been "set apart" by a society because they have religious or mystical significance (e.g., Bethlehem, Mecca, Stonehenge) or because they commemorate some aspect of a country's heritage (e.g., the Kremlin, the Emperor's Palace in Tokyo, the Statue of Liberty). Remember that in many cases the sacredness of these places is due to the property of contamination—that is, something sacred happened on that spot, so the place itself takes on sacred qualities.

Still other places are created from the profane world and imbued with sacred qualities. Graumann's Chinese Theater in Hollywood, where movie stars leave their footprints in concrete for posterity, is one such place. Even the modern shopping mall can be regarded as a secular "cathedral of consumption," a special place where community members come to practice shopping rituals. Theme parks are a form of mass-produced fantasy that take on aspects of sacredness. In particular, Disney World and Disneyland (and their new outposts in Europe and Japan) are destinations for pilgrimages from consumers around the globe. Disney World displays many characteristics of more traditional sacred places. It is even regarded by some as having healing powers. A trip to the park is the most common "last wish" for terminally ill children.[7]

HOME SWEET HOME In many cultures, the home is a particularly sacred place. It represents a crucial distinction between the harsh, external world and consumers' "inner space." Americans spend more than $50 billion a year on interior decorators and home furnishings, and the home is a central part of consumers' identities.[8] Consumers all over the world go to great lengths to create a special environment that allows them to create the quality of "homeyness." This effect is created by personalizing the home as much as possible, using such devices as door wreaths, mantle arrangements, and a "memory wall" for family photos.[9]

The Modern Hex Sign. Various products have been used throughout history to protect the sacredness of the home. These items range from fear-inspiring markings, Amish hex signs, lamb's blood, and garlic (to keep away vampires) to homemade signs such as "If caught here tonight, you'll be found here in the morning."[10] In modern times, of course, the maintenance of this sacred space is the foundation of the home security industry, which provides both technical devices and ominous signs to ward off invaders.

Sacred People

As Robert's "worship" of Marilyn Monroe illustrates, people themselves can be sacred. They are idolized and set apart from the masses. Souvenirs, memorabilia, and even mundane items touched or used by sacred people become valuable.

> At $15.95 per head, about 700,000 people annually make the pilgrimage to Graceland, the home of Elvis Presley. True pilgrims surround themselves with Elvis artifacts. One such fan wears an Elvis watch and earrings, has furnished her home with Elvis plates, cups, clocks, statues, and rugs, and even named her daughter Lisa (after Presley's daughter). She claimed, "There can never be too much Elvis."[11]

Many businesses, including the U.S. Postal Service, thrive on consumers' desire for products associated with famous people, as exemplified by the Elvis postage stamp and the Marilyn chocolate shown here. As evidenced by the thriving market for celebrity autographs and artifacts, or objects once owned

Teaching Hint: Many believe that the "King" is actually still alive. Sightings in shopping malls or fast food restaurants are frequently reported in the tabloids. As one minister put it, "This has the makings of a new religion. Elvis is the god, and Graceland is the shrine . . . . And some even say he is rising again." Quoted in Richard Corliss, "The King is Dead—Or Is He? The Elvis Cult has the Makings of a New Religion," *Time* 10 (October 1988): 91.

Additional Example: Marilyn Monroe has been dead for over 30 years, but consumers and marketers have kept her spirit very much alive. She has inspired numerous books (over 70 at last count, including a 1992 work written by four psychics that claims to contain interviews with her spirit), plays, and television shows, and even a California wine bottle bears her likeness (the wine is called Marilyn Merlot). The Monroe estate makes over $1 million a year in licensing fees for the use of her name and likeness. At least 100 women make their living by impersonating Marilyn Monroe. See Pat H. Broeske, "Marketing Monroe: Still Big Box Office," *New York Times* (July 26, 1992): H16.

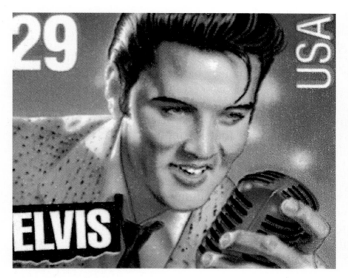

From Elvis postage stamps to Marilyn chocolates, products associated with celebrities are a source of big business for many entrepreneurs. Photo of Marilyn Monroe chocolate © M. Pelletier/Sygma.

by celebrities, are also extremely popular. One entrepreneur dug dirt from the lawns of Johnny Carson, Shirley MacLaine, Katharine Hepburn, and forty-three other stars. He sold 20,000 vials of celebrity dirt in three years, at $1.95 a vial. A store called "A Star is Worn" sells items donated by celebrities—a black bra autographed by Cher recently went for $575. As one observer commented about the store's patrons, "They want something that belonged to the stars, as if the stars have gone into sainthood and the people want their shrouds."[12]

Teaching Hint: The creation of celebrities by marketers may generate interesting class discussion. For a fascinating treatment of the subject, see Irving J. Rein, Philip Kotler, and Martin R. Stoller, *High Visibility* (New York: Dodd, Mead & Company, 1987).

MARKETING PITFALL

The public's fascination with the images of celebrities, living or dead, endures. The images of dead stars are frequently brought back to life to endorse products. James Dean hawks for Jack Purcells sneakers, and Babe Ruth sells Zenith products. Licensing fees for dead celebrities now average about $100 million per year.[13]

The sacredness of some celebrities has spawned a secondary industry—celebrity look-alikes and sound-alikes. The simulated voice of Louis Armstrong has appeared in ads for the Hershey Food Corporation, Canada Dry, and Milk Bones.[14] Elvis Presley has imitators around the world. By one estimate, about 100 women make their living impersonating Marilyn Monroe.[15] This type of advertising is so pervasive that several lawsuits have been brought by stars (e.g., Woody Allen) to prevent doubles from using their likenesses.[16] Nonetheless, look-alikes continue to be used, with disclaimer notices appearing in the ad.[17]

Sacred Events

Many consumers' activities also have taken on a special status. Public events in particular resemble sacred, religious ceremonies, as exemplified by the recitation of the "Pledge of Allegiance" before a game or the reverential lighting of matches at the end of a rock concert.[18]

SPORTS For many people, the world of sports is sacred and almost assumes the status of a religion. The roots of modern sports events can be found in ancient religious rites, such as fertility festivals (e.g., the original Olympics).[19] Indeed, it is not uncommon for teams to join in prayer prior to a game. The sports pages are like the Scriptures (and we describe ardent fans as reading them "religiously"), the stadium is a house of worship, and the fans are members of the congregation. Devotees engage in group activities, such as tailgate parties and the "Wave," where (resembling a revival meeting) participants on cue join the wave-like motion as it makes its way around the stadium.

Sports Heroes. The athletes that fans come to see are godlike; they are reputed to have almost superhuman powers (especially superstars like Michael Jordan, who is accorded the ability to fly in his Air Nikes). Athletes are central figures in a common cultural myth, the hero tale. Often the hero must prove him- or herself under strenuous circumstances (e.g., the starter is unexpectedly injured), and victory is achieved only through sheer force of will. One extremely popular Coke commercial, which featured the football player Mean Joe Greene and an admiring little boy, follows the same plot structure as the fairy tale of the Lion and the Mouse. The injured hero has his confidence restored by the humble mouse/boy, allowing his heroic persona to be rejuvenated. He then shows his gratitude to his benefactor.[20]

TOURISM Tourism is another example of a sacred, non-ordinary experience of extreme importance to marketers. When people travel on vacation, they occupy sacred time and space. The tourist is continually in search of "authentic" experiences that differ from his or her normal world.[21] The tourism experience involves binary oppositions between work and leisure and being "at home" versus "away." This theme is reflected in Club Med's motto, "The antidote to civilization."

Buying Memories. The desire to capture these sacred experiences in objects forms the bedrock of the souvenir industry. Whether a personalized matchbook from a wedding or New York City salt-and-pepper shakers, souvenirs represent a tangible piece of the consumer's sacred experience. The importance of these markers is obvious; U.S. gift shops alone sell 23 billion souvenirs a year. This product class provides a form of *tangibilized contamination*, where the sacredness of the experience "rubs off" onto the object.[22]

In addition to personal mementos, such as ticket stubs saved from a favorite concert, the following are other types of sacred souvenir icons:[23]

- Local products (e.g., wine from California)
- Pictorial images (e.g., post cards)

Teaching Hint: Virtually every sport has its own rituals. For example, members of bowling leagues go through the motions of drying their hands, powdering their fingers, acquiring their own personal ball, and sometimes even touching a high-scoring teammate for luck. Many individual athletes have also developed their own unique rituals and superstitions. The great hitter Honus Wagner, for example, always discarded a bat after getting 100 hits, because he believed there were no more hits left in it. See Linda Kay, "A Little Bit of Voodoo: Rituals Woman Athletes Use to Prepare for Competition," *Women's Sports and Fitness* (June 1986): 26.

Research Report: The role of the souvenir as a "marker" of sacred experiences can be so compelling that it can actually supersede the experience itself. One researcher observed that 30 percent of visitors arriving on buses at a Canadian museum visited *only* the gift shop. See Robert F. Kelly, "Culture as Commodity: The Marketing of Cultural Objects and Cultural Experiences," in *Advances in Consumer Research* 14, eds. Melanie Wallendorf and Paul Anderson (Provo, Utah: Association for Consumer Research, 1987), 347–51.

- "Piece of the rock" (e.g., seashells, pine cones)
- Symbolic shorthand in the form of literal representations of the site (e.g., a miniature Statue of Liberty)
- Markers (e.g., Hard Rock Cafe T-shirts)

Ritual

A **ritual** is a set of multiple, symbolic behaviors that occur in a fixed sequence and that tend to be repeated periodically.[24] Although bizarre tribal ceremonies, perhaps involving animal or virgin sacrifice, may come to mind when people think of rituals, in reality many contemporary consumer activities are ritualistic.

Rituals can occur at a variety of levels, as noted in Table 17–1. Some affirm broad cultural or religious values, while others occur in small groups or in isolation. Market researchers discovered, for example, that for many people the act of late-night ice cream eating has ritualistic overtones, often involving a favorite spoon and bowl.[25]

As in the case of Robert and Bridget's wedding, many businesses owe their livelihoods to their ability to supply **ritual artifacts,** or items used in the performance of rituals, to consumers. Birthday candles, diplomas, specialized foods and beverages (e.g., wedding cakes, ceremonial wine, or even hot dogs at the ball park), trophies and plaques, band costumes, greeting cards, and retirement watches are all used in consumer rituals. In addition, consumers often employ a *ritual script*, which identifies the artifacts, the sequence in which they are used, and who uses them. Examples include graduation programs, fraternity manuals, and etiquette books.

Additional Example: The dining room table, which often stands alone in a room, was traditionally a sacred, ceremonial place where the family came together for eating rituals. With the advent of the microwave oven, more relaxed eating rituals are being introduced, and with them the possibility that the warm stove, our last symbolic connection to the comfort of the primitive hearth fire, will also disappear.   Margaret Visser, "A Meditation on the Microwave," *Psychology Today* (December 1989): 38.

TABLE 17–1   Types of Ritual Experience

Primary Behavior Source	Ritual Type	Examples
Cosmology	Religious	Baptism, meditation, mass
Cultural values	Rites of passage	Graduation, marriage
	Cultural	Festivals, holidays (Valentine's Day), Super Bowl
Group learning	Civic	Parades, elections, trials
	Group	Fraternity initiation, business negotiations, office luncheons
	Family	Mealtimes, bedtimes, birthdays, Mother's Day, Christmas
Individual aims and emotions	Personal	Grooming, household rituals

Source: Dennis W. Rook, "The Ritual Dimension of Consumer Behavior," *Journal of Consumer Research* 12 (December 1985), 251–64. Reprinted with permission of The University of Chigago Press.

Grooming Rituals

Whether brushing one's hair 100 strokes a day or talking to oneself in the mirror, virtually all consumers undergo private grooming rituals. These are sequences of behaviors that aid in the transition from the private self to the public self or back again. These rituals serve various purposes, ranging from inspiring confidence before confronting the world to cleansing the body of dirt and other profane materials.

When consumers talk about their grooming rituals, some of the dominant themes that emerge from these stories reflect the almost mystical qualities attributed to grooming products and behaviors. Many people emphasize a before-and-after phenomenon, where the person feels magically transformed after using certain products (similar to the Cinderella myth).[26]

Two sets of binary oppositions that are expressed in personal rituals are private/public and work/leisure. Many beauty rituals, for instance, reflect a transformation from a natural state to the social world (as when a woman "puts on her face") or vice-versa. In these daily rituals, women reaffirm the value placed by their culture on personal beauty and the quest for eternal youth.[27] This focus is obvious in ads for Oil of Olay Beauty Cleanser, which proclaim ". . . And so your day begins. The Ritual of Oil of Olay." Similarly, the bath is viewed as a sacred, cleansing time, a way to wash away the sins of the profane world.[28]

Gift-Giving Rituals

The promotion of appropriate gifts for every conceivable holiday and occasion provides an excellent example of the influence consumer rituals can exert on marketing phenomena. In the **gift-giving ritual**, consumers procure the perfect object (artifact), meticulously remove the price tag (symbolically

The ritual of opening Christmas presents is one of the most familiar and beloved for many consumers. © Julie Marcotte/TWS-Click/ Chicago Ltd.

changing the item from a commodity to a unique good), carefully wrap it, and ritually deliver it to the recipient.[29] The familiar ritual of giving Christmas gifts is illustrated in the photo shown here.

Every culture prescribes certain occasions and ceremonies for giving gifts, whether for personal or professional reasons. The giving of birthday presents alone is a major undertaking. Americans on average buy about six birthday gifts a year—about one billion gifts in total.[30] Business gifts are an important component in defining professional relationships. Expenditures on business gifts exceed $1.5 billion per year, and great care is often taken to ensure that the appropriate gifts are purchased.

The importance of gift-giving rituals is underscored by considering Japanese customs, where the *wrapping* of a gift is as important (if not more so) than the gift itself. The economic value of a gift is secondary to its symbolic meaning.[31] Gifts are viewed as an important aspect of one's duty to others in one's social group. Giving is a moral imperative (known as *giri*). Each Japanese has a well-defined set of relatives and friends with which he or she shares reciprocal gift-giving obligations (*kosai*).[32] In keeping with the Japanese emphasis on saving face, presents are not opened in front of the giver, so that it will not be necessary to hide one's possible disappointment with the present.

THE GIFT-GIVING PROCESS The gift-giving ritual can be broken down into three distinct stages.[33] During *gestation*, the giver is motivated by an event to procure a gift. This event may be either *structural* (i.e., prescribed by the culture, as when people buy Christmas presents), or *emergent* (i.e., the decision is more personal and idiosyncratic). The second stage is *presentation*, or the process of gift exchange. The recipient responds to the gift (either appropriately or not), and the donor evaluates this response. In the third stage, known as *reformulation*, the bonds between the giver and receiver are adjusted (either looser or tighter) to reflect the new relationship that emerges after the exchange is complete. Negativity can arise if the recipient feels the gift is inappropriate or of inferior quality. The donor may feel the response to the gift was inadequate or insincere or a violation of the *reciprocity norm*, which obliges people to return the gesture of a gift with one of equal value.[34] Both participants may feel resentful for being "forced" to participate in the ritual.[35]

SELF-GIFTS People commonly find (or devise) reasons to give themselves something; they "treat" themselves. Consumers rely on the self-gifting process as a way to regulate their behavior—as a way of rewarding themselves for good deeds, consoling themselves after negative events, or motivating themselves to accomplish some goal.[36]

Figure 17–1 displays a projective stimulus similar to ones used in research on self-gifting. Consumers are asked to tell a story based on this picture, and their responses are analyzed to discover the reasons people view as legitimate for rewarding themselves with a **self-gift**. For example, one recurring story that might emerge would be that Mary, the woman in the figure, had a particularly grueling day at work and needs a "pick-me-up" in the form of a new fragrance. This theme (excitement) could then be incorporated into a promotional campaign for a perfume.

Cross-Cultural Example: The protocol attached to gift giving varies across cultures. One gift consultant related how she stepped in and salvaged a business relationship: An American executive was proud of the set of steak knives he planned to send to an Argentine colleague. Unfortunately, the giving of knives in Argentina symbolizes the cutting off of a relationship! See Joanne Levine, "It's Later Than You Think," *Sales & Marketing Management* 141 (August 1989): 55.

Teaching Hint: Not surprisingly, *gift wrapping* has been shown in one recent study to affect product attitudes. For a discussion of gift wrapping's ability to cue positive moods, see Daniel J. Howard, "Gift-Wrapping Effects on Product Attitudes: A Mood-Biasing Explanation," *Journal of Consumer Psychology* 1(1992)3: 197–223.

Teaching Hint: The likelihood of gift giving and the amount spent on gifts for those outside the family unit is related to family size, life-cycle stage, and education. It is also related to such variables as the number of female adults in the family, urbanization, ethnicity, and region. Gift giving is more likely to involve women, though men who have an egalitarian perspective on gender roles are more likely to participate. See Eileen Fischer and Stephen J. Arnold, "More Than a Labor of Love: Gender Roles and Christmas Gift Shopping," *Journal of Consumer Research* 17 (December 1990): 333; Thesia I. Garner and Janet Wagner, "Economic Dimensions of Household Gift Giving," *Journal of Consumer Research* 18 (December 1991): 368.

FIGURE 17–1 Projective Drawing to Study the Motivations Underlying the Giving of Self-Gifts Source: Based on David G. Mick, Michelle DeMoss, and Ronald J. Faber, "Latent Motivations and Meanings of Self-Gifts: Implications for Retail Management," Research Report, Center for Retailing Education and Research, University of Florida, 1990.

Figure 17–1 is available as Transparency 48.

Holiday Rituals

On holidays consumers step back from their everyday lives and perform ritualistic behaviors unique to those times.[37] Holiday occasions are filled with ritual artifacts and scripts and are increasingly cast as a time for giving gifts by enterprising marketers. Holidays also often mean big business to hotels, restaurants, travel agents, and so on. The marketing of Christmas products alone is worth about $37 billion a year.

MARKETING OPPORTUNITY

In addition to established holidays, new occasions are invented to capitalize on the need for cards and other ritual artifacts that will then have to be acquired. More than 120 million adults buy at least one greeting card in a year.[38] These cultural events often originate with the greeting card industry, which conveniently stimulates demand for more of its products. Some recently invented holidays include Secretaries' Day and Grandparents' Day.

VALENTINE'S DAY On Valentine's Day, standards regarding sex and love are relaxed or altered as people express feelings that may be hidden during the rest of the year. In addition to cards, a variety of gifts are exchanged, many of which are touted by marketers to represent aphrodisiacs or other sexually related symbols. For the "Valentine's couple who has everything," the Grand Hyatt in Washington, D.C., offers a Valentine's package that includes a night's stay in the hotel's best suite, round-the-clock chauffeured limo, bathrobes, a masseur, manicurist, hairstylist, makeup artist, two dozen roses, caviar, champagne, a gourmet breakfast-in-bed, and romantic message of the guests' choice towed through the sky by an airplane when the lucky couple checks in. Total cost: $10,000.[39]

HALLOWEEN Like Christmas, Halloween is a holiday that has been converted from a religious observance to a secular event. However, in contrast to Christmas, the rituals of Halloween (e.g., trick-or-treating and costume parties) primarily involve nonfamily members. Halloween is an unusual holiday, because its rituals are the *opposite* of many other cultural occasions. In contrast to Christmas, it celebrates evil instead of good and death rather than birth, and it encourages revelers to extort treats with veiled threats of "tricks" rather than rewarding only the good. Because of these oppositions, Halloween has been described as an *anti-festival*, where the symbols associated with other holidays are distorted. For example, the Halloween witch can be viewed as an inverted mother figure. The holiday also parodies the meaning of Easter by stressing the resurrection of ghosts and of Thanksgiving by transforming the wholesome symbolism of the pumpkin pie into the evil jack-o-lantern.[40]

Bring on the Baby BOOmers. Halloween observances among adults are booming, changing the character of this holiday. While adults bought only 10 percent of all Halloween costumes sold a decade ago, they now account for about 50 percent of all sales. Halloween is now the second most popular party night for adults (after New Year's Eve), and one in four grown-ups wear a costume. This transformation is reflected in the Hallmark ad shown on page 598, which parodies a baby boomer classic song by telling readers they are "*Bone* to be Wild."

The shift in the Halloween ritual has been attributed to adult fears aroused by stories of children receiving tampered candy containing poison, razor blades, and so on, which encouraged people to plan supervised parties rather than send their children out trick-or-treating.[41] Another factor accounting for the popularity of Halloween among adults is that, unlike other holidays, a family is not required to celebrate it, which thus permits single people to participate without feeling lonely or left out.[42]

Teaching Hint: Students can discuss whether Christmas is a secular or religious holiday in our society and what role marketing plays in their determination. A recent statement deploring the commercialization of Christmas was distributed by a prestigious group of Catholic, Protestant, and Unitarian clergy. The group claims that the "advertising lords" have "reduced Christmas to a carnival of mass marketing." The statement contends that "Consumption has taken on an almost religious quality. Malls have become the new shrines of worship. Massive and alluring advertising crusades have waged war on the essential meaning of the spiritual life, fostering the belief that the marketplace can fulfill our highest aspirations." Quoted in Ari L. Goldman, "A Christmas Plea on the 'Lords' of Commerce," *New York Times* (November 29, 1992): A29.

Cross-Cultural Example: In Japan, *only* men receive gifts of chocolate on Valentine's Day. This custom originated in the 1940s, when a chocolate company publicized February 14 as a day when women could express their love by giving chocolate to men they secretly fancied. See Keiko Kambara, "Valentine's Day in Japan: Ladies Don't Expect a Gift," *Christian Science Monitor* (February 13, 1989): 6.

M A R K E T I N G   P I T F A L L

Accompanying the new emphasis on Halloween as an adult holiday, the liquor industry has come under fire for attempting to reinforce the idea that Halloween is as much an occasion to drink as St. Patrick's Day or New Year's Eve.[43] The industry's goal is to boost sales during a normally slow period. Miller Brewing Company, Anheuser-Busch, Coors, and Jack Daniels are some companies that

This ad for Hallmark illustrates the growing trend of companies that promote Halloween as an adult holiday Courtesy of Leo Burnett U.S.A., Chicago.

have launched extensive Halloween promotions. A public advocacy group has complained that ". . . beer companies try to make drinking a part of every celebration . . . these types of promotions are clearly attractive to young consumers.[44] In many areas, the efforts of the liquor industry have been offset by school and community programs that promote "responsible partying."

Rites of Passage

What does a dance for recently divorced people have in common with a fraternity Hell Week? Both are examples of modern **rites of passage**, or special times marked by a change in social status. Every society, both primitive and modern, sets aside times where such changes occur. Some of these changes may occur as a natural part of consumers' life cycles (e.g., puberty or death), while others are more individual in nature (e.g., getting divorced and reentering the dating market).

Some marketers attempt to reach consumers on occasions in which their products can enhance a transition from one stage of life to another.[45] For example, a chain of fur stores ran a series of ads positioning a fur coat as a way to celebrate "all of life's moments." Suggested moments included a thirtieth birthday, a raise, a second marriage, and even a "divorce-is-final" fur coat": Shed the tears and slip into a fur," reads the ad.[46]

STAGES OF ROLE TRANSITION   Much like the metamorphosis of a caterpillar into a butterfly, consumers' rites of passage consist of three phases.[47] The first stage, *separation*, occurs when the individual is detached from his or her original group or status (e.g., the college freshman leaves home). *Liminality* is the middle stage, where the person is literally in-between statuses (e.g., the new arrival on campus tries to figure out what is happening during orientation week). The last stage, *aggregation*, takes place when the person reenters society after the rite of passage is complete (e.g., the student returns home for Christmas vacation as a college "veteran").

Rites of passage mark many consumer activities, as exemplified by fraternity pledges, recruits at boot camp, or novitiates becoming nuns. A similar transitional state can be observed when people are prepared for certain occupational roles. For examples, athletes and fashion models typically undergo a "seasoning" process. They are removed from their normal surroundings (e.g., athletes are taken to training camps, while young models often are moved to Paris), indoctrinated into a new subculture, and then returned to the real world in their new roles.

THE FINAL PASSAGE: MARKETING DEATH   The rites of passage associated with death support an entire industry. Survivors must make fairly expensive purchase decisions, often on short notice and driven by emotional and superstitious concerns. Funeral ceremonies help the living to organize their relationships with the deceased, and action tends to be tightly scripted, down to the costumes (e.g., the ritual black attire, black ribbons for mourners, the body in its best suit) and specific behaviors (e.g., sending condolence cards or holding a wake). Mourners "pay their last respects," and seating during the ceremony is usually dictated by mourners' closeness to the individual. Even the cortege (the funeral motorcade) is accorded special status by other motorists, who recognize its separate, sacred nature by not cutting in as it proceeds to the cemetery.[48]

The Dark Side of Consumer Behavior

Consumers are often depicted as rational decision makers calmly doing their best to obtain products and services that will maximize the health and well-being of themselves, their families, and their society. An expanded view of the consumer, as we have seen, also includes a person who often buys things on a whim or simply because they make him/her feel good or look good.

Even though this enlarged picture comes closer to an accurate portrayal, it still falls short of capturing some important aspects of consumer behaviors. These behaviors are not necessarily enlightened or constructive, and they can be quite negative. Other behaviors can stem from social pressures, such as excessive drinking or cigarette smoking, and the cultural value placed upon money can encourage such activities as shoplifting or insurance fraud. Exposure to unattainable media ideals of beauty and success can create dissatisfaction with the self.

Addictive Consumption

Consumer **addiction** is a physiological and/or psychological dependency on products or services. While most people equate addiction with drugs, virtually any product or service can be seen as relieving some problem or satisfying some need to the point where reliance on it becomes extreme. In some cases, it is fairly safe to say that the consumer, not unlike a drug addict, has little to no control over consumption. The products control the consumer, whether alcohol, cigarettes, chocolate, or diet colas. Even the act of shopping itself is an addicting experience for some consumers. Much negative or destructive consumer behavior can be characterized by three common elements.[49]

1. The behavior is not done by choice.
2. The gratification derived from the behavior is short-lived.
3. The person experiences strong feelings of regret or guilt afterwards.

GAMBLING Gambling is an example of a consumption addiction that touches every segment of consumer society. Whether it takes the form of casino gambling, playing the "slots," as shown here, betting on sports events with friends or through a bookie, or even buying lottery tickets, excessive gambling can be quite destructive, Taken to extremes, gambling results in lowered self-esteem, debt, divorce, neglected children, and so on. According to one psychologist, gamblers exhibit a classic addictive cycle of experiencing a "high" while in action and depression when stopped, which leads them back to the thrill of the action. Money, however, is the substance they abuse, not drugs.[50]

While gambling may be a now-and-again recreational activity for most consumers, it becomes a destructive behavior for consumers who become addicted to any form of gambling, whether it be casino gambling or wagering on sports events. ©Brad Bower/Picture Group.

COMPULSIVE CONSUMPTION For some consumers, the expression "born to shop" is taken quite literally. These consumers shop because they are compelled to do so, rather than because shopping is a pleasurable or functional task. **Compulsive consumption** is repetitive shopping, often excessive, as an antidote to tension, anxiety, depression, or boredom. "Shopaholics," as they are called, turn to shopping much the way addicted people turn to drugs or alcohol.[51]

Compulsive consumption is distinctly different from the impulse buying considered in Chapter 10. The impulse to buy a specific item is temporary and centers on a specific product at a particular moment. In contrast, compulsive buying is an enduring behavior that centers on the process of buying, not the purchases themselves. As one woman who spent $20,000 per year on clothing confessed, "I was possessed when I went into a store. I bought clothes that didn't fit, that I didn't like, and that I certainly didn't need.[52]

Consumed Consumers

People who are used or exploited, whether willingly or not, for commercial gain in the marketplace can be thought of as **consumed consumers**. The situations in which consumers themselves become commodities can range from traveling road shows that feature dwarfs and midgets to the selling of body parts and babies. Some examples of consumed consumers include the following.

- *Prostitutes:* Expenditures on prostitution in the United States alone are estimated at $20 billion annually. These revenues are equivalent to those in the domestic shoe industry.[53]
- *Organ, blood, and hair donors:* In the United States, over 11 million people per year sell their blood (not including voluntary donations).[54] A lively market also exists for organs (e.g., kidneys), and some women sell their hair to be made into wigs.
- *Babies for sale:* Several thousand surrogate mothers have been paid to be medically impregnated and carry babies to term for infertile couples.[55]

Illegal Activities

Many consumer behaviors are not only self-destructive or socially damaging, they are illegal as well. Crimes committed by consumers against businesses have been estimated at more than $40 billion per year. These include shoplifting, employee pilferage, arson, and insurance fraud. Arson alone causes $2 billion per year in damages and is growing by 25 percent annually.[56]

A retail theft is committed every five seconds. *Inventory shrinkage* due to shoplifting and employee theft is a massive problem for businesses that is passed onto consumers in the form of higher prices (about 40 percent of the losses can be attributed to employees rather than shoppers). A family of four spends about $300 extra per year because of markups to cover shrinkage.[57] The problem is not unique to the United States. For example, shrinkage losses in Great Britain are estimated at more than a million pounds per day.[58]

Shoplifting is America's fastest-growing crime; it increased by a third in a period of only four years. The large majority of shoplifting is not done by professional thieves or by people who genuinely need the stolen items.[59] About three-quarters of those caught are middle- or high-income people

Teaching Hint: Gamblers can be segmented by lifestyle and demographic variables. For example, slot and keno players are more likely to be Protestants who go to church regularly, while the craps table has a better chance of being patronized by non-observant Catholics (the religious group with the highest gambling frequency). Fundamentalists and atheists are the two religious groups least likely to gamble at all. Gambling is more popular in urban areas than rural ones and more widespread in the northern United States than in the South. See Brad Edmondson, "The Demographics of Gambling," *American Demographics* (July 1986): 38.

Cross-Cultural Example: It is common in many societies for a bride price to be paid by a husband to the woman's father in exchange for receiving this "property." Historically, women who were in some way "damaged" (e.g., by virtue of being widowed or raped) had no choice but to become prostitutes—their bodies were the only asset they had to sell. These women are often regarded as *profane commodities* and less than human. They are, in fact, often described in various animal terms, such as "chickens," "beavers," or just "meat." Not coincidentally, a group of women working for a pimp are referred to as his "stable." See Vern L. Bullough, *The Subordinate Sex* (Urbana, Ill.: University of Illinois Press, 1973); Elizabeth C. Hirschman, "Metaphor and Ideology in Profane Consumption: The Case of Prostitution and Pornography," unpublished manuscript, Rutgers University, New Brunswick, N.J., 1990.

FROM NOW ON, SHOPLIFTING IN THE U.S. IS A VERY, VERY DIRTY BUSINESS.

For the last four years, Colortag has significantly cut losses for European store owners.

The device is a plastic tag that doesn't beep, but sprays permanent ink on the garment when the thief breaks it open. A fifty dollar shirt becomes worthless. The motive to steal it is gone.

No false alarms. No big installations. No guards. No action needed from the store clerks. No expensive prosecutions.

And thefts are down by as much as 90%.

Cut your losses and increase your profits with Colortag. Because it's time shoplifting got even dirtier.

Call Don Barnett at our New York office for the full story. (212) 888-1629.

Colortag

Colortag, Inc., 3 West 57th Street, New York, NY. 10019.

This ad for the Colortag system promotes one technique that has been used in Europe and the United States to deter shoplifters: A plastic tag squirts ink on a garment when a thief breaks it open, rendering the item worthless. Courtesy of COLORTAG, INC.

who shoplift for the thrill of it or as a substitute for affection. The Colortag ad shown here promotes one technique to prevent shoplifting.

ANTICONSUMPTION One form of destructive consumer behavior can be thought of as **anticonsumption**, whereby products and services are deliberately defaced or mutilated. Anticonsumption can range from product tampering, where innocent consumers are hurt or killed, to graffiti on buildings and subways, as shown in the photo here. The following are some recent examples of such anticonsumption.

- In Detroit, sections of abandoned buildings literally disappear as bricks are hauled away by vandals, who then resell them at $50 per brick to dealers.[60]
- About one quarter of British Telecom's call boxes do not work because of vandalism. The company must cope with 500,000 attacks on its public phones in a year's time.[61]
- The Los Angeles bus system placed fifty ads featuring a provocative picture of Madonna in bus shelters to advertise *Interview* magazine. Fans

Graffiti on a New York subway is one form of anti-consumption. Gerd Ludwig/Woodfin Camp.

broke the glass panels in about 40 of the shelters to "liberate" the posters. The system also experienced the theft of 125 Batman posters.[62]

Motivations for anticonsumption can range from peer pressure to rage against some aspect of society. Whatever the cause, these varied behaviors result in large but unknown costs to society and reflect the overlooked importance of recognizing the dark side of consumer behavior.

Blurred Boundaries: Marketing, Popular Culture, and Reality

To what degree is the world of popular culture and even consumers' perception of reality shaped by the efforts of marketers? This book has stressed throughout the importance to consumer behavior of interactions between marketing activities and consumers' everyday lives. Consider the following examples of this blurring of boundaries between marketing and culture.[63]

- Pontiac sales rose when a black Trans Am was used by Burt Reynolds in the 1977 movie *Smokey and the Bandit.* Unfortunately, so did lawsuits as drivers were spurred on by the movie's chase scenes and later blamed the company for their highway zeal.

- When Nike used the Beatles song "Revolution" in 1987 to launch its line of Air shoes, purists were outraged. More currently, though, the company's use of John Lennon's "Instant Karma" has not caused a stir.

- After the Rodney King beating in Los Angeles (that eventually instigated the LA riots), Hyundai was forced to pull a commercial depicting a Hyundai Sonata as an unmarked police car chasing a BMW. The white BMW driver is stopped and frisked by a black policeman. King was driving a Hyundai Excel when he was stopped by the LAPD.

Many of the environments in which we find ourselves, whether shopping malls, sports stadiums, or theme parks, are composed at least partly of images and characters drawn from products or marketing campaigns. **Reality engineering** occurs as elements of popular culture are appropriated by marketers and converted to vehicles for promotional strategies.[64] These elements include sensory and spatial aspects of everyday existence, whether in the form of products appearing in movies, odors pumped into offices and stores, billboards, theme parks, video monitors attached to shopping carts, and so on.

The Pervasiveness of Marketing Symbols

Marketing sometimes seems to exert a "self-fulfilling prophecy" on popular culture. As commercial influences on popular culture increase, marketer-created symbols make their way into our daily lives to a greater degree. Historical analyses of Broadway plays, best-selling novels, and the lyrics of hit songs, for example, clearly show large increases in the use of brand names over time.[65]

PRODUCT PLACEMENT In many cases, **product placement**, or the appearance of specific products or the use of brand names in movie and TV scripts, is no accident. More than thirty companies in the United States specialize in product placement. Their job is to get exposure for a product by inserting it into a movie or a television show. This practice has become so common that 20 percent of consumers report they actively look for brands in movies.[66] Perhaps the greatest product placement success story was Reese's Pieces; sales jumped by 65 percent after the candy appeared in the film *E.T.*[67]

Some critics argue that the practice of product placement has gotten out of hand: Shows are created with the purpose of marketing products rather than for their entertainment value. Some children's shows have been berated for essentially being extended commercials for a toy. One major film company sent a letter to large consumer products companies to solicit product placements for an upcoming movie production and even provided a fee scale: $20,000 for the product to be seen in the movie, $40,000 for an actor to mention the product by name, and $60,000 for the actor to actually use the product.[68]

MULTICULTURAL DIMENSIONS

The melding of marketing activity with popular culture is also evident in other countries. A British coffee ad recently borrowed the words from the Beatles' song "A Day in the Life" and went so far as to include a shot of John Lennon's signature round glasses sitting on a table. The British Boy Scouts announced that they would begin accepting corporate sponsorships for merit badges. The Lost City, a new resort in South Africa, blurs the boundaries even further; it has created a "fake" Africa for affluent guests. The complex is drought-proof and disease-proof, and it features a three-story water slide, an "ocean" with a panic button that will stop the wave motion on command, and a nightly volcanic eruption complete with "non-allergenic" smoke.[69]

Types of Product Placement. There are two basic types of product placement. *On-set placement* is straightforward. The product is incorporated into the actual film set, as when specific brands of food are the focus in a kitchen scene.[70] *Creative placement* involves finding ways to insert the brand into filming, as when it "happens" to appear on outdoor advertising or in a real commercial playing on a television in the background. This strategy also includes the use of "plugs," where brand mentions are made in the context of news shows or other programming. The chart in Figure 17–2 provides further detail about where and when these plugs tend to occur.

Advertising Versus Editorial Content

The mass media play a large role in consumer socialization and decision making.[71] People often engage in *para-social interaction* with television, where they actively relate to television characters and vicariously experience and evaluate the different lifestyles portrayed.[72] Children in particular display a strong belief in the reality of contrived photographic images.[73] If anything, confusion between reality and advertising should accelerate as media programming and advertising come to resemble each other more and more. For example, marketers targeting youth have been strongly affected by the techniques used to make music videos, such as quick cuts and fast-paced musical accompaniment. As one MTV executive commented, "It's almost hard to tell one [video] from the other [commercials]."[74]

The blurring of marketing and reality is the issue behind current debates regarding distinctions between advertising and editorial content in print media. "Advertorials," advertisements that are composed in heavy type to look like articles, frequently appear in magazines and can account for up to 10 percent of a magazine's revenues.[75] The video version of this concept, known as an *infomercial*, was discussed in Chapter 6.

Additional Example: The cigarette industry is taking advantage of product placement strategies by planting plugs in new movies. The National Center on Television Violence reported that over 85 percent of movies contain smoking plugs. Philip Morris, Inc., paid $350,000 to place its Lark brand in the James Bond film *License to Kill*, where smoking is shown in 13 different scenes. See George W. Brown, "Subtle Cigarette Ads Abound in New Films," (September 1, 1991).

FIGURE 17–2 Product Plugs on TV   Source: Reprinted with permission from *Advertising Age* (January 29, 1990): 6.

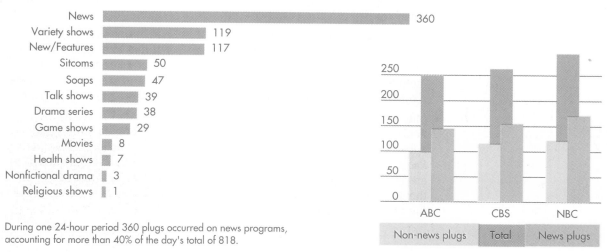

News	360
Variety shows	119
New/Features	117
Sitcoms	50
Soaps	47
Talk shows	39
Drama series	38
Game shows	29
Movies	8
Health shows	7
Nonfictional drama	3
Religious shows	1

During one 24-hour period 360 plugs occurred on news programs, accounting for more than 40% of the day's total of 818.

Non-news plugs   Total   News plugs

Some companies have even come under fire for designing highly visible cause-marketing campaigns. When the Quaker Oats Company announced plans to sponsor a series of public service announcements on behalf of the American Medical Association, some broadcasters refused to run the spots because the commercials featured company spokesman Wilford Brimley.[76]

THE CULTIVATION EFFECT   Media images appear to significantly influence consumers' perceptions of reality, affecting viewers' notions about such issues as dating behavior, racial stereotypes, and occupational status.[77] Studies of the **cultivation hypothesis**, which relates to media's ability to distort consumers' perceptions of reality, have shown that heavy television viewers tend to overestimate the degree of affluence in the country, and these effects also extend to such areas as perceptions of the amount of violence in one's culture.[78]

As consumers increasingly rely on mass-produced imagery as a window onto the "real world," they come to accept what they are seeing as real. As the boundaries between marketing and reality continue to blur, we hope future marketers will consider this phenomenon when they make their own contributions to this ubiquitous consumption imagery.

Chapter Summary

- Consumer activities can be divided into *sacred* and *profane domains*. Sacred phenomena are "set apart" from everyday activities or products. People, events, or objects can become sacralized. *Objectification* occurs when sacred qualities are ascribed to products or items owned by sacred people. Sacralization occurs when formerly sacred objects or activities become part of the everyday, as when "one-of-a-kind" works of art are reproduced in large quantities.

- A *ritual* is a set of multiple, symbolic behaviors that occurs in a fixed sequence. Modern rituals include grooming behaviors, rites of passage, and gift giving. Many rituals require the purchase and use of ritual artifacts, so they affect a variety of marketing domains.

- While textbooks often paint a picture of the consumer as a rational, informed decision maker, in reality many consumer activities are harmful to individuals or to society. The *dark side* of consumer behavior includes excessive materialism, addiction, the use of people as products (consumed consumers), and theft or vandalism (anticonsumption).

- Much of our daily lives is affected by the actions of marketers. As the boundaries blur between commercial activities and popular culture, a wider range of mundane events are influenced by the actions of marketers. *Reality engineering* refers to the process where aspects of our environment are modified to reflect commercial activities (e.g., product placement, theme parks, billboards). The *cultivation hypothesis* refers to the ability of the mass media to influence consumers' perceptions of reality.

Key Terms

addiction, p. 600

anticonsumption, p. 602

compulsive consumption, p. 601

consumed consumers, p. 601

cultivation hypothesis, p. 606

desacralization, p. 587

gift-giving ritual, p. 594

product placement, p. 604

profane consumption, p. 587

reality engineering, p. 604

rites of passage, p. 598

ritual, p. 593

ritual artifacts, p. 593

sacralization, p. 588

sacred consumption, p. 587

self-gifts, p. 595

Consumer Behavior Challenge

1. Discuss the distinction between sacred and profane consumption. What are some marketing implications of positioning a product as either sacred or profane?

2. How do the consumer decisions involved in gift giving differ from other purchase decisions?

3. The chapter argues that not all gift giving is positive. In what ways can this ritual be unpleasant or negative?

4. Observe people in the process of watching television. Can you find any evidence of para-social interaction?

5. Construct a ritual script for a wedding in your culture. How many artifacts can you list that are contained in this script?

6. What are some of the major motivations for the purchase of self-gifts? Discuss some marketing implications of these.

7. Everyday objects like cars, televisions, and money may be said to have sacred qualities. How do these objects become sacred? Do you agree with this contention?

8. Describe the three stages of the rite of passage associated with graduating from college.

9. Identify the ritualized aspects of football that are employed in advertising.

10. "People can be marketed just like any other product." Do you agree?

11. What do you personally feel are the three most significant social trends affecting consumer behavior in the 1990s? How might these developments affect your decisions as a marketer?

12. Should any limits be placed on topics, events, or places that are accessible to marketers (e.g., the commercialization of holidays, advertising in schools, promoting art)?

CNN Connection

 A video segment is available to accompany this CNN connection.

Compulsive Shopping

Is it healthy to "shop 'til you drop?" While shopping is merely a form of recreation for many, for others the mall is the devil's workshop. There is no such thing as a casual shopping trip for compulsive shoppers. The act of purchasing is a symptom of an underlying sickness, and the easy availability of products brings on the disease just as surely as a bottle of liquor tempts an alcoholic.

The urge to splurge is especially difficult to fight during the Christmas season, when so many environmental cues are exhorting consumers to spend, spend, spend. So, while the holidays are a time of joy for most, they merely intensify the guilt and anxiety experienced by compulsive shoppers, who may run up debts of $25,000 or even $100,000 for products they did not really want in the first place. Perhaps because of low self-esteem stemming from a troubled childhood, these people have learned that money buys happiness and friendship. They do not find pleasure in the things they buy, but rather are motivated by a need to buy still more. As a result, many "shopaholics" exhibit a pattern of "bulimic buying," where they engage in an endless cycle of buying, returning, and buying still more—not the most pleasant way to spend the holidays.

SIMMONS Connection

SIMMONS Connection: Data for this exercise is on the Simmons Data Disk inside the back cover of your Instructor's Annotated Edition.

Data File: High-Technology Buying Behavior

Robert and Bridget seem particularly enthralled by the sort of "engineered" entertainment environment that Disney is renowned for. Consumers seem to be more and more interested in becomming imersed in leisure (and even work) environments made possible by a host of new high-technology products. And, many of these products influence our perception of reality. As noted in the chapter, virtual reality systems may provide the amusement parks of the future, where all of the rides and attractions exist only in the "mind" of the computer and the mind of the user.

The marketing of high-technology products can be very lucrative. But, to be successful, it is critical that marketers target consumers who are not afraid of being on the "cutting edge." Some consumers shy away from new technologies—they prefer to wait until the new technology becomes "tried and true" and greatly simplified. Apple dealt with such concerns in its early Macintosh computer ads. These

ads emphasized the simplicity of using a Macintosh by showing that if you could roll a mouse and press a button, you could use the computer. But, how can we distinguish consumers who are willing to try products that embody new/emerging technologies from those who are not?

The Simmons file for this chapter breaks down the sample according to several psychographic variables. These are cross-tabulated with patterns of consumption for several high-technology product areas. On the basis of the index values for some of these products (for example, fax machines, digital audio tape recorders, or interactive computer services), generate a psychographic profile of the "innovator." Using the Reference Files for Self and Style data, generate a demographic profile that identifies this group. [Hint: Innovators can be defined by their joint use of a variety of high-technology products.]

Notes

1. Russell W. Belk, Melanie Wallendorf, and John F. Sherry, Jr., "The Sacred and the Profane in Consumer Behavior: Theodicy on the Odyssey," *Journal of Consumer Research* 16 (June 1989): 1–38.

2. Belk et al., "The Sacred and the Profane in Consumer Behavior."

3. Deborah Hofmann, "In Jewelry, Choices Sacred and Profane, Ancient and New," *New York Times* (May 7, 1989).

4. Quoted in "Public Relations Firm to Present Anti-Abortion Effort to Bishops," *New York Times* (August 14, 1990): A12.

5. Martin E. Marty, "Sunday Mass and the Media: There's a Fine Line in Religious Advertising Between Tasteful and Tacky," *Across the Board* 24 (May 1987): 55.

6. For an extensive bibliography on collecting, see Russell W. Belk, Melanie Wallendorf, John F. Sherry, Jr., and Morris B. Holbrook, "Collecting in a Consumer Culture," in *Highways and Buyways*, ed. Russell W. Belk (Provo, Utah: Association for Consumer Research, in press).

7. Conrad Phillip Kottak, "Anthropological Analysis of Mass Enculturation," in *Researching American Culture*, ed. Conrad P. Kottak (Ann Arbor, Mich.: University of Michigan Press, 1982), 40–74.

8. Joan Kron, *Home-Psych: The Social Psychology of Home and Decoration* (New York: Clarkson N. Potter, Inc., 1983); Gerry Pratt, "The House as an Expression of Social Worlds," in *Housing and Identity: Cross-Cultural Perspectives*, ed. James S. Duncan (London: Croom Helm, 1981), 135–79; Michael R. Solomon, "The Role of the Surrogate Consumer in Service Delivery," *The Service Industries Journal* 7 (July 1987): 292–307.

9. Grant McCracken, "'Homeyness': A Cultural Account of One Constellation of Goods and Meanings," in *Interpretive Consumer Research*, ed. Elizabeth C. Hirschman (Provo, Utah: Association for Consumer Research, 1989), 168–84.

10. Dennis W. Rook, "Modern Hex Signs and Symbols of Security," in *Marketing and Semiotics: New Directions in the Study of Signs for Sale*, ed. Jean Umiker-Sebeok (Berlin: Mouton de Guyter, 1987), 239–46.

11. Quoted in Peter Applebome, "New Stop for Elvis Fans Who Can't Get Enough," *New York Times* (August 7, 1989): A8.

12. James Hirsch, "Taking Celebrity Worship to New Depths," *New York Times* (November 9, 1988): C1.

13. Mindy Weinstein, "Dead Stars are In," *Advertising Age* (August 14, 1989): 44.

14. Judann Dagnoli, "Ads Trumpet Satchmo's Immortality," *Advertising Age* (April 30, 1990): 26.

15. Bob Greene, "Some Like It Hot," *Esquire* (October 1987): 59.

16. Fred Kirby, "Woody Allen Wins Lawsuit to Stymie National Video Lookalike," *Variety* (May 22, 1985): 84.

17. James P. Forkan, "Send in the Clones: Ads Must ID Celeb Doubles," *Advertising Age* (May 20, 1985): 2.

18. Emile Durkheim, *The Elementary Forms of the Religious Life* (New York: Free Press, 1915).

19. Susan Birrell, "Sports as Ritual: Interpretations from Durkheim to Goffman," *Social Forces* 60 (1981)2: 354–76; Daniel Q. Voigt, "American Sporting Rituals," in *Rites and Ceremonies in Popular Culture*, ed. Ray B. Browne (Bowling Green, Ohio: Bowling Green University Popular Press, 1980): 125–40.

20. Alf Walle, "The Epic Hero," *Marketing Insights* (Spring 1990): 63.

21. Dean MacCannell, *The Tourist: A New Theory of the Leisure Class* (New York: Shocken Books, 1976).

22. Belk et al., "The Sacred and the Profane in Consumer Behavior."

23. Beverly Gordon, "The Souvenir: Messenger of the Extraordinary," *Journal of Popular Culture* 20 (1986)3: 135–46.

24. See Dennis W. Rook, "The Ritual Dimension of Consumer Behavior," *Journal of Consumer Research* 12 (December 1985): 251–64; Mary A. Stansfield Tetreault and Robert E. Kleine III, "Ritual, Ritualized Behavior, and Habit: Refinements and Extensions of the Consumption Ritual Construct," in *Advances in Consumer Research* 17, eds. Marvin Goldberg, Gerald Gorn, and Richard W. Pollay (Provo, Utah: Association for Consumer Research, 1990), 31–38.

25. Kim Foltz, "New Species for Study: Consumers in Action," *New York Times* (December 18, 1989): A1.

26. Dennis W. Rook and Sidney J. Levy, "Psychosocial Themes in Consumer Grooming Rituals," in *Advances in Consumer Research* 10, eds. Richard P. Bagozzi and Alice M. Tybout (Provo, Utah: Association for Consumer Research, 1983), 329–33.

27. Diane Barthel, *Putting on Appearances: Gender and Attractiveness* (Philadelphia: Temple University Press, 1988).

28. Quoted in Barthel, *Putting on Appearances: Gender and Advertising* (Philadelphia: Temple University Press, 1988).

29. Belk et al., "The Sacred and the Profane in Consumer Behavior."

30. Monica Gonzales, "Before Mourning," *American Demographics* (April 1988): 19.

31. Colin Camerer, "Gifts as Economics Signals and Social Symbols," *American Journal of Sociology* 94 (Supplement 1988): 5180–214.

32. Robert T. Green and Dana L. Alden, "Functional

Equivalence in Cross-Cultural Consumer Behavior: Gift Giving in Japan and the United States," *Psychology & Marketing* 5 (Summer 1988): 155–68.

33. John F. Sherry, Jr., "Gift Giving in Anthropological Perspective," *Journal of Consumer Research* 10 (September 1983): 157–68.

34. Daniel Goleman, "What's Under the Tree? Clues to a Relationship," *New York Times* (December 19, 1989): C1.

35. John F. Sherry, Jr., Mary Ann McGrath, and Sidney J. Levy, "The Dark Side of the Gift," *Journal of Business Research* (1993).

36. David Glen Mick and Michelle DeMoss, "Self-Gifts: Phenomenological Insights from Four Contexts," *Journal of Consumer Research* 17 (December 1990): 327.

37. See, for example, Russell W. Belk, "Halloween: An Evolving American Consumption Ritual," in *Advances in Consumer Research* 17, eds. Richard Pollay, Jerry Gorn, and Marvin Goldberg, (Provo, Utah: Association for Consumer Research, 1990), 508–17; Melanie Wallendorf and Eric J. Arnould, "We Gather Together: The Consumption Rituals of Thanksgiving Day," *Journal of Consumer Research* 18 (June 1991): 13–31.

38. Rick Lyte, "Holidays, Ethnic Themes Provide Built-In F&B Festivals," *Hotel & Motel Management* (December 14, 1987): 56; Megan Rowe, "Holidays and Special Occasions: Restaurants are Fast Replacing 'Grandma's House' as the Site of Choice for Special Meals," *Restaurant Management* (November 1987): 69; Judith Waldrop, "Funny Valentines," *American Demographics* (February 1989): 7.

39. Lynn Asinof, "Valentine's Day Prompts Offbeat Promotions and Unusual Gifts," *Wall Street Journal* (February 8, 1990): A1.

40. Theodore Caplow, Howard M. Bahr, Bruce A. Chadwick, Reuben Hill, and Margaret M. Williams, *Middletown Families: Fifty Years of Change and Continuity* (Minneapolis, Minn.: University of Minnesota Press, 1982).

41. N.R. Kleinfeld, "The Weird, the Bad and the Scary," *New York Times* (October 15, 1989): 4.

42. Georgia Dullea, "It's the Year's No. 2 Night to Howl," *New York Times* (October 30, 1988): 20.

43. Paul Fahri, "Brewing Up More Spirits; Liquor Firms Promoting Halloween for Adults," *Washington Post* (October 31,1989): D1.

44. Quoted in Thomas R. King, "Brewers Hope for Treat from Promotion Tricks," *Wall Street Journal* (1989): B1.

45. Michael R. Solomon and Punam Anand, "Ritual Costumes and Status Transition: The Female Business Suit as Totemic Emblem," in *Advances in Consumer Research* 12, eds. Elizabeth C. Hirschman

and Morris Holbrook (Washington, D.C.: Association for Consumer Research, 1985), 315–18.

46. "Divorce Can be Furry," *American Demographics* (March 1987): 24.

47. Arnold Van Gennep, *The Rites of Passage*, trans. Maika B. Vizedom and Gabrielle L. Caffee (London: Routledge and Kegan Paul, 1960; orig. published 1908); Solomon and Anand, "Ritual Costumes and Status Transition."

48. Walter W. Whitaker III, "The Contemporary American Funeral Ritual," in *Rites and Ceremonies in Popular Culture*, ed. Ray B. Browne (Bowling Green, Ohio: Bowling Green University Popular Press, 1980), 316–25.

49. Georgia Witkin, "The Shopping Fix," *Health* (May 1988): 73; see also Arch G. Woodside and Randolph J. Tyrappey III, "Compulsive Consumption of a Consumer Service: An Exploratory Study of Chronic Horse Race Track Gambling Behavior," working Paper #90-MKTG-04, A.B. Freeman School of Business, Tulane University, 1990; see also Rajan Nataraajan and Brent G. Goff, "Manifestations of Compulsiveness in the Consumer-Marketplace Domain," *Psychology & Marketing* 9 (January 1992): 31–44.

50. James Barron, "Are We All Really Losers with Gambling, a Spreading Social Addiction?" *New York Times* (May 31, 1989): A18.

51. Thomas C. O'Guinn and Ronald J. Faber, "Compulsive Buying: A Phenomenological Explanation," *Journal of Consumer Research* 16 (September 1989): 154.

52. Quoted in Anastasia Toufexis, "365 Shopping Days Till Christmas," *Time* (December 26, 1988): 82; see also Ronald J. Faber and Thomas C. O'Guinn, "Compulsive Consumption and Credit Abuse," *Journal of Consumer Policy* 11 (1988): 109–21; Mary S. Butler, "Compulsive Buying—It's No Joke," *Consumer's Digest* (September 1986): 55.

53. Helen Reynolds, *The Economics of Prostitution* (Springfield, Ill.: Charles C. Thomas, 1986).

54. "Precious Drops," *The Economist* (October 14, 1989): 28.

55. Barbara Katz Rothman, "Cheap Labor: Sex, Class, Race and 'Surrogacy,'" *Society* 25 (March-April 1988): 21.

56. Paul Bernstein, "Cheating—The New National Pastime?" *Business* (October-December 1985): 24–33.

57. "Shoplifting: Bess Myerson's Arrest Highlights a Multibillion-Dollar Problem that Many Stores Won't Talk About," *Life* (August 1988): 32.

58. Roy Carter, "Whispering Sweet Nothings to the Shop Thief," *Retail & Distribution Management* (January/February 1986): 36.

59. Catherine A. Cole, "Deterrence and Consumer

Fraud," *Journal of Retailing* 65 (Spring 1989): 107–20; Stephen J. Grove, Scott J. Vitell, and David Strutton, "Non-Normative Consumer Behavior and the Techniques of Neutralization," in *Marketing Theory and Practice*, eds. Terry Childers, et al. (1989 AMA Winter Educators' Conference; Chicago: American Marketing Association, 1989), 131–35.

60. "Dismantling Detroit," *Time* (April 24, 1989): 25.
61. "Call Box Unobtainable," *Economist* (March 12, 1988): 57.
62. Bradley Johnson, "Madonna Scores in L.A. Bus Shelters," *Advertising Age* (June 18, 1990): 12.
63. "Goodbye Johnny, Hello Tic Tac," *Advertising Age* (May 25, 1992): 22; Cleveland Horton, "Hyundai Pulls Planned Ad in L.A. Beating Aftermath," *Advertising Age* (April 22, 1991): 2; Randall Rothenberg, "Does Integration Lead to Segregation?: The Ethical Problems of Integrated Marketing," in *Integrated Marketing Communications*, eds. Jeri Moore and Esther Thorson (Hillsdale, N.J.: Lawrence Erlbaum, 1992).
64. Michael R. Solomon and Basil G. Englis, "Reality Engineering: Blurring the Boundaries Between Marketing and Popular Culture," unpublished manuscript, Rutgers University, New Brunswick, N.J., 1992.
65. Monroe Friedman, "The Changing Language of a Consumer Society: Brand Name Usage in Popular American Novels in the Postwar Era," *Journal of Consumer Research* 11 (March 1985): 927–37; Monroe Friedman, "Commercial Influences in the Lyrics of Popular American Music of the Postwar Era," *Journal of Consumer Affairs* 20 (Winter 1986): 193.
66. Betty Sharkey, "Moviegoer Study Finds 20% Look for Brand Names," *Adweek's Marketing Week* (August 29, 1988): 27.
67. Benjamin M. Cole, "Products That Want to Be In Pictures," *Los Angeles Herald Examiner* (March 5, 1985): 36.
68. Randall Rothenberg, "Is it a Film? Is it an Ad? Harder to Tell?" *New York Times* (March 13, 1990): D23.
69. Bill Keller, "For Rich Tourists (and Not Too African)," *New York Times* (December 3, 1992)2: A1.
70. Brian Oliver, "The Latest Screen Stars," *Marketing* (March 1986): 12.

71. See Russell W. Belk and Richard Pollay, "Images of Ourselves: The Good Life in Twentieth Century Advertising," *Journal of Consumer Research* 11 (1985): 887–948; Irving Janis, "The Influence of Television on Personal Decision Making," in *Television and Social Behavior: Beyond Violence and Children*, eds. S. Whitney and R. Abels (Hillsdale: Lawrence Erlbaum, 1980), 161–89; Roy Moore and George Moschis, "The Effects of Family Communication and Mass Media Use on Adolescents' Consumer Learning," *Journal of Communication* 31 (1981): 42–51; Thomas C. O'Guinn and Ronald J. Faber, "Mass Mediated Consumer Socialization: Non-Utilitarian and Dysfunctional Outcomes," in *Advances in Consumer Research* 14, eds. Melanie Wallendorf and Paul Anderson (Ann Arbor, Mich.: Association for Consumer Research, 1987), 473–77.
72. Donald Horton and R. Richard Wohl, "Mass Communication and Para-Social Interaction," in *Drama in Life: The Uses of Communication in Society*, eds. J. Combs and M. Mansfield (New York: Hasting House, 1956), 212–78.
73. Paul Messaris and Larry Gross, "Interpretations of a Photographic Narrative by Viewers in Four Age Groups," *Studies in the Anthropology of Visual Communication* 4 (1974): 99–111.
74. Quoted in Jennifer Pendleton, "Chalk Up Another Victory for Trend-Setting Rock 'N' Roll," *Advertising Age* (November 9, 1988): 160.
75. Jonathan Alter, "The Era of the Big Blur," *Newsweek* (May 22, 1989): 73.
76. Julie Liesse, "Line Between Public Service, Paid Ads Blurs," *Advertising Age* (October 8, 1990): 28.
77. George Gerbner, Larry Gross, Nancy Signorielli, and Michael Morgan, "Aging with Television: Images on Television Drama and Conceptions of Social Reality," *Journal of Communication* 30 (1980): 37–47.
78. Stephen Fox and William Philber, "Television Viewing and the Perception of Affluence," *Sociological Quarterly* 19 (1978): 103–12; W. James Potter, "Three Strategies for Elaborating the Cultivation Hypothesis," *Journalism Quarterly* 65 (Winter 1988): 930–39; Gabriel Weimann, "Images of Life in America: The Impact of American T.V. in Israel," *International Journal of Intercultural Relations* 8 1984): 185–97.

Appendix I

Sources of Secondary Consumer Data

Many organizations in the government and private sector collect information on consumer buying patterns. The U.S. Government publishes a wide range of data, much of which is then used by private sources for their own purposes. The U.S. Bureau of the Census publishes separate censuses on specific industries (e.g., agriculture, construction, mining), as well as on housing, population, retail trade, transportation, and so on.

One of the major proprietary sources of information is the Simmons Market Research Bureau, a syndicated service that collects data on consumer purchases from a panel of over 20,000 American households. These data are used to help target products and advertisements to appropriate segments of the population. Through an exclusive agreement with Allyn and Bacon, Simmons Market Research Bureau has provided the data for the Simmons Connection Exercises at the ends of most chapters in the text; an accompanying Simmons Data Disk will be provided by your instructor. As you complete these exercises, you will be looking at the same types of secondary data that are used by many marketers.

The Simmons Study of Media & Markets is conducted annually and the results are tabulated into 34 separate volumes that are offered as Simmons products. Simmons also conducts studies of special groups such as computer professionals, teens between the ages of 12 and 19, and children younger than 12.

A selected list of other secondary data sources and indexes that are particularly useful to consumers researchers follows. Many of these sources are available in the reference section of your library.

- *ABI/Inform Ondisc.* Ann Arbor, Michigan: University Microfilms International—abstracts (on compact disk) of articles from business journals.

- *Aging America: Trends and Projections.* Washington, D.C., Government Printing Office: U.S. Senate Special Committee on Aging and the American Association of Retired Persons—data on demographic characteristics and growth projections of the elderly over the next 30 years.

- *American Marketing Association International Directory & Marketing Services Guide.* Chicago: American Marketing Association—complete directory of AMA members, including both individual and corporate listings; also includes a guide to marketing research firms, including areas of specialization (published annually).

- *BAR/LNA Multi-Media Service.* New York: Leading National Advertisers—listing of advertising expenditures for media and specific brands (updated quarterly).

- *Business Index.* Foster City, California: Information Access Company—index of business-related articles from the popular and legal press (microform).

- *Business Information Sources.* Berkeley: University of California Press—listing of sources of information about market research and statistical data.

- *Business Periodicals Index.* New York: H.W. Wilson Company—index of business periodicals (updated monthly).
- *Business Services and Information: The Guide to the Federal Government.* New York: Management Information Exchange—listing of U.S. Government publications, including addresses and phone numbers.
- *Communications Abstracts.* Beverly Hills, California: Sage Publications, Inc.—index of articles and books on topics related to advertising and marketing (published quarterly).
- *Data Sources for Business and Market Analysis.* Metuchen, New Jersey: Scarecrow Press—listing of sources of business information.
- *Directory of Online Databases.* Santa Monica, California: Cuadra Associates, Inc.—listing of databases that are accessible by computer.
- *Dissertation Abstracts International.* Ann Arbor, Michigan: University of Microfilms International—index of doctoral dissertations from major universities, including relevant studies in the Humanities and Social Sciences section (updated monthly).
- *Editor and Publisher Market Guide*—information about major metropolitan areas (published annually).
- *Encyclopedia of Information Systems and Services.* Detroit: Gale Research Company—information about producers of various databases.
- *FINDEX: The Directory of Market Research Reports, Studies, and Surveys.* Bethesda, Maryland: Cambridge Information Group—international guide to reports produced by research companies.
- *Guide to Consumer Markets.* New York: The Conference Board—data on consumer spending and income (published annually).
- *Marketing Information.* Atlanta: Business Publishing Division, Georgia State University—guide to marketing sources, including consultants, organizations, and government agencies.
- *Marketing Information Guide.* Washington, D.C.: U.S. Department of Commerce—information on assorted distribution and marketing statistics.
- *Rand McNally Commercial Atlas and Marketing Guide.* Chicago: Rand McNally Company—purchase data, demographic information, and maps for U.S. cities.
- *Social Sciences Citation Index.* Philadelphia: Institute for Scientific Information—index of articles in social science periodicals (updated three times a year).
- *Standard Directory of Advertisers.* Wilmette, Illinois: National Register Publishing Company—guide to companies whose advertising spending exceeds $75,000, including such information as their agencies, types of media used, and specific products advertised.
- *Statistical Abstract of the United States.* Washington, D.C.: U.S. Bureau of the Census—statistical profiles of demographic and social topics (updated annually).

Appendix II

Careers in Consumer Research

An understanding of consumers is of course essential in virtually every aspect of marketing. To prepare for a career in a consumer-related field, consider getting involved in relevant research that one of your professors may be doing. In addition to your Consumer Behavior course, be sure to take as many courses as possible in other aspects of marketing. Also try to achieve proficiency in statistics and computer skills. Courses in the social sciences, particularly psychology and sociology, are also helpful.

CAREER PATHS

The following list identifies aspects of marketing where knowledge of consumer behavior is particularly valuable.

- *Marketing research:* Researchers define problems and collect information needed to resolve them. They typically design projects, analyze data, present findings, and make recommendations to management. Researchers may be employed by corporations that maintain their own market research staff, or they may work for an independent market research firm, a trade organization, an advertising agency, the government, or a nonprofit organization.

- *Brand management:* Managers direct marketing efforts for a specific product or line of products. They oversee all aspects of product strategy, including research, packaging, sales, promotion, and forecasting.

- *Customer affairs:* A customer affairs representative acts as a liaison between the firm and its customers. He or she handles complaints and may act as an advocate for the customer within the company.

- *International marketing:* As firms globalize their operations, they need managers who understand the importance of cultural differences and who can adapt strategies to foreign markets.

- *Advertising copywriters:* Copywriters translate a brand's positioning strategy into concrete form by creating words and visual images that convey this imagery. They need to understand the target market in order to employ imagery that will create the desired response.

- *Advertising account executives:* An account exec supervises the development of a marketing plan and makes sure that the agency's clients understand and are happy with the plan. This job requires knowledge about all aspects of marketing, including an understanding of the target market.

- *Retail managers and merchandisers:* Department and store managers must make decisions about such factors as the store's sales force and how merchandise is displayed in the store. They must understand the factors that add to or subtract from the quality of the customer's experience while in the store.

- *Retail buyers:* Buyers purchase merchandise for a store. A good buyer is always "tuned in" in to upcoming trends and fashions and is sensitive to the wants and needs of the store's clientele.

- *Public relations:* Public relations specialists are responsible for maintaining positive public awareness of the firm and minimizing negative reactions to company activities. Knowledge of how people's perceptions are influenced by the media is integral to this job.

THE INDUSTRY ROUTE

Many entry-level jobs are available for a competent person with a bachelor's degree (though in some fields it is increasingly difficult to get hired without at least a master's degree). A typical starting position for a college graduate in a marketing research firm, for example, would be as an assistant project manager. This person assists in the design and administration of studies and ensures that they are enacted within the prescribed budget. The beginner may also be assigned to supervise field operations, overseeing the actual collection of data and perhaps coding and analyzing it.

Over time the person would move up to supervisory positions with increasing responsibility. Eventually, the person might attain the position of vice president of marketing research in a company, where he or she would be responsible for the entire company's marketing research efforts and be part of senior management. Chance of moving up tend to improve greatly if the individual received advanced training in statistics, experimental design, and other aspects of consumer psychology.

THE ACADEMIC ROUTE

Another alternative is to consider training to become a scholar in the field of consumer behavior. Many major business schools offer doctoral programs in Marketing, where it is possible to specialize in consumer behavior research. In addition, some psychology department offer doctoral programs in Consumer Psychology. The typical doctoral program involves from four to seven years of intensive study, where the student is trained in both theoretical and technical aspects of consumer research. Many doctoral students in business have already earned an M.B.A., though this is not always the case.

Most consumer behavior Ph.D.'s who did not obtain their degrees in Marketing were trained in Psychology. Other possible fields of study include Sociology, Anthropology, Economics, History, English, Human Ecology, and others—as the discipline's perspective continues to widen.

These individuals may take faculty positions in a business school, where they conduct research that is published in such academic journals as the *Journal of Consumer Research.* They may also work as consultants to corporations, advertising agencies, and the government. In addition, Ph.D.'s are in demand to work full-time in nonacademic positions, such as in consulting firms and "think tanks," or for ad agencies, manufacturers, trade groups (e.g., The Wool Bureau or The Conference Board), or government agencies (e.g., the Federal Trade Commission).

For further insight on these possibilities, consider asking your professor about his or her educational background and research activities.

FOR FURTHER INFORMATION

Selected Bibliography. The following publications and articles provide information on employment and career opportunities in marketing.

Advertising Career Directory: 1987. New York: Career Publishing, 1986.

American Marketing Association. *The Employment Kit: Your Career Advantage.* Chicago: American Marketing Association, 1992.

American Marketing Association International Directory & Marketing Services Guide. Chicago: American Marketing Association (published annually).

Barron's Guide to Graduate Business Schools, 6th ed. New York: Barron's Educational Series, Inc., 1989.

Fox, Marica R. *Put Your Degree to Work: The New Professional's Guide to Career Planning and Job Hunting,* 2nd ed. New York: W.W. Norton, 1988.

Fry, Ronald W., ed. *Marketing & Sales Career Directory,* 3rd ed. Hawthorne, N.J.: The Career Press, 1990.

Joby, John, and Mark Needel. "Entry-Level Marketing Research Recruits: What do Recruiters Need?" *Journal of Marketing Education* (Spring 1989): 68–73.

Kitaeff, Richard. "Market Research as a Career: What to Tell the Junior-Level Researcher." *Marketing Research A Magazine of Marketing Applications* (March 1992): 57–59.

Maresca, Carmela C. *Careers in Marketing: A Woman's Guide,* Englewood Cliffs, N.J.: Prentice-Hall, 1983.

Marketing Review. "Career Opportunities in Marketing Research." October 1990.

Nivens, Beatryce. *The Black Woman's Career Guide,* Garden City, N.Y.: Anchor Books, 1982.

U.S. Department of Labor, Bureau of Labor Statistics. *Occupational Outlook Handbook* (revised every two years).

Professional Organizations. The following organizations provide literature on careers and other relevant information.

American Association of Advertising Agencies, 666 Third Avenue, New York, NY 10017

American Advertising Federation, 1400 K Street NW, Suite 1000, Washington, DC 20005

American Management Association, 135 West 50th Street, New York, NY 10020

American Marketing Association, 250 South Wacker Drive, Chicago, IL 60606-5819

Association of National Advertisers, Inc., 155 East 44th Street, New York, NY 10017

Direct Marketing Association, 6 East 43rd Street, New York, NY 10017

Public Relations Society of America, Inc., 845 Third Avenue, New York, NY 10022

National Retail Merchants Association, 100 West 31st Street, New York, NY 10001

Glossary

Absolute threshold the minimum amount of stimulation that can be detected on a sensory channel (57)

Acculturation the process of learning the beliefs and behaviors endorsed by another culture (540)

Activation models of memory approaches to memory stressing different levels of processing that occur and activate some aspects of memory rather than others, depending upon the nature of the processing task (126)

Adaptation the process that occurs when a sensation becomes so familiar that it is no longer the focus of attention (64)

Addiction a physiological and/or psychological dependency on products or services (600)

Advertising clutter a condition that occurs when too many messages compete for consumers' attention in the same place or medium (62)

Affect the way a consumer feels about an attitude object (149)

Affinity marketing a strategy that allows a consumer to emphasize his or her identification with some organization, as, for example, when organizations issue credit cards with their names on them (372)

Age cohort a group of consumers of the same approximate age who have undergone similar experiences (500)

AIOs (Activities, Interests, and Opinions) the psychographic variables used by researchers in grouping consumers (448)

Androgyny the possession of both masculine and feminine traits (303)

Anticonsumption the actions taken by consumers that involve the deliberate defacement or mutilation of products (602)

Art product a creation viewed primarily as an object of aesthetic contemplation without any functional value (557)

Atmospherics the use of space and physical features in store design to evoke certain effects in buyers (340)

Attention the assignment of cognitive capacity to selected stimuli (64)

Attitude a lasting, general evaluation of people (including oneself), objects, or issues (148)

Attitude object (A_o) anything toward which one has an attitude (148)

Attitude toward the act of buying (A_{act}) the perceived consequences of a purchase (169)

Attitude toward the advertisement (A_{ad}) a predisposition to respond favorably or unfavorably to a particular advertising stimulus during a particular exposure occasion (153)

Autocratic decisions those purchase decisions that are made almost exclusively by one or the other spouse (262)

Baby boomers a large cohort of people born between the years of 1946 and 1964 who are the source of many important cultural and economic changes (509)

Balance theory a theory that considers relations among elements a person might perceive as belonging together, and people's tendency to change relations among elements in order to make them consistent or "balanced" (159)

Behavior a consumer's actions with regard to an attitude object (149)

Behavioral economics the study of the behavioral determinants of economic decisions (404)

Behavioral influence perspective the view that consumer decisions are learned responses to environmental cues (218)

Behavioral learning theories the perspectives on learning that assume that learning takes place as the result of responses to external events (111)

Body cathexis a person's feelings about aspects of his or her body (309)

Body image a consumer's subjective evaluation of his or her physical self (309)

Brand loyalty a pattern of repeat product purchases, accompanied by an underlying positive attitude toward the brand (240)

Classic a fashion with an extremely long acceptance cycle (573)

Classical conditioning the learning that occurs when a stimulus eliciting a response is paired with another stimulus that initially does not elicit a response on its own, but will cause a similar response over time because of its association with the first stimulus (112)

Closure the gestalt principle that describes a person's tendency to supply missing information in order to perceive a holistic image (69)

Cognition the beliefs a consumer has about an attitude object (149)

Cognitive development the ability to comprehend concepts of increasing complexity as a person ages (271)

Cognitive dissonance a state of tension that is created when beliefs or behaviors conflict with one another; people are motivated to reduce this inconsistency (or dissonance) and thus eliminate unpleasant tension (91)

Cognitive learning the learning that occurs as a result of internal mental processes; people actively use information from the world around them to master their environment and solve problems (116)

Cognitive structure the set of factual knowledge, or beliefs about a product, and the say these beliefs are organized 231

Collective selection the process by which certain symbolic alternatives tend to be jointly chosen over others by members of a society (568)

Collectivism a cultural orientation that encourages people to subordinate their personal goals to those of a stable in-group; values such as self-discipline and group accomplishment are stressed (539)

Communications model a framework specifying that a number of elements are necessary for communication to be achieved, including a source, message, medium, receivers, and feedback (182)

Comparative advertising a strategy in which a message compares two or more specifically named or recognizably presented brands and makes a comparison of them in terms of one or more specific attributes (193)

Comparative influence the process whereby a reference group influences decisions about specific brands or activities (367)

Compensatory decision rules a set of rules that allow information about attributes of competing products to be averaged in some way; poor standing on one attribute can potentially be offset by good standing on another (237)

Compulsive consumption the process of repetitive, often excessive, shopping used to relieve tension, anxiety, depression, or boredom (601)

Conclusive research a type of consumer research specifically designed to test a hypothesis that has been formulated in advance about a consumer issue; usually the findings are used as input to decision making (23)

Congruity theory a consistency theory that specifically addresses how attitudes are affected when a person is linked to an object (162)

Conspicuous consumption the purchase and prominent display of luxury goods to provide evidence of a consumer's ability to afford them (426)

Consumed consumers those people who are used or exploited, whether willingly or not, for commercial gain in the marketplace (601)

Consumer behavior the processes involved when individuals or groups select, purchase, use, or dispose of products, services, ideas, or experiences to satisfy needs and desires (7)

Consumer confidence the state of mind of consumers relative to their optimism or pessimism about economic conditions; people tend to make more discretionary purchases when their confidence in the economy is high (404)

Consumer satisfaction or dissatisfaction (CS/D) the overall attitude a person has about a product after it has been purchased (346)

Consumer socialization the process by which people acquire skills that enable them to function in the marketplace (268)

Consumption constellations a set of products and activities used by consumers to define, communicate, and perform social roles (441)

Continuous innovation a product change or new product that requires relatively little adaptation by the adopter (564)

Core values a set of important values that seem to define a specific culture (550)

Craft product a creation valued because of the beauty with which it performs some function; this type of product tends to follow a formula that permits rapid production, and it is easier to understand than an art product (557)

Cultivation hypothesis a perspective emphasizing media's ability to distort consumers' perceptions of reality (606)

Cultivation theory the perspective that the media teaches people about a culture's values and myths; the more a consumer is exposed to mass media, the more he or she will accept the images depicted there as accurate portrayals of the real world (269)

Cultural categories the grouping of ideas and values that reflect the basic ways members of a society characterize the world (566)

Cultural formula a sequence of media events where certain roles and props tend to occur consistently (558)

Culture the values, ethics, rituals, traditions, material objects, and services produced or valued by the members of a society (538)

Culture production system (CPS) the set of individuals and organizations responsible for creating and marketing a cultural product (556)

Decay the process whereby structural changes in the brain produced by learning begin to decrease, resulting in loss of memory (132)

De-ethnicitization the process whereby a product formerly associated with a specific ethnic group is detached from its roots and marketed to other subcultures (470)

Decision polarization the process whereby individuals' choices tend to become more extreme (polarized), in either a conservative or risky direction, following group discussion of alternatives (379)

Deindividuation the process whereby individual identities get submerged within a group, reducing inhibitions against socially inappropriate behavior (378)

Demographics the observable measurements of a population's characteristics, such as birth rate, age distribution, income (253)

Desacralization the process that occurs when a sacred item or symbol is removed from its special place, or is duplicated in mass quantities, and becomes profane as a result (587)

Determinant attributes those product features that significantly influence the consumer's choices among alternatives (10)

Differential threshold the ability of a sensory system to detect changes or differences among stimuli (57)

Diffusion the process whereby a new product, service, or idea spreads through a population (561)

Discontinuous innovation a product change or new product that requires a significant amount of adaptation by the adopter (564)

Drive the desire to satisfy a biological need in order to reduce physiological arousal (81)

Dynamically continuous innovation a product change or new product that requires a moderate amount of adaptation by the adopter (564)

Ego the system that mediates between the id and the superego (95)

Ego involvement the important of a product to a consumer's self-concept (86)

Elaboration likelihood model (ELM) the approach that one of two routes to persuasion (central versus peripheral) will be followed, depending upon the personal relevance of a message; the route taken determines the relative importance of message contents versus other character-istics, such as source attractiveness (202)

Embeds tiny figures inserted into magazine advertising by use of high-speed photography or airbrushing; these hidden figures, usually of a sexual nature, supposedly exert strong but unconscious influences on innocent readers (59)

Emic perspective an approach to studying cultures that stresses the unique aspects of each culture (547)

Encoding the process in which information from short-term memory is entered into long-term memory in a recognizable form (124)

Enculturation the process of learning the beliefs and behaviors endorsed by one's native culture (540)

Ethnic subculture a self-perpetuating group of consumers held together by common cultural ties (469)

Ethnocentrism the belief in the superiority of one's own cultural practices and products (541)

Ethnography an in-depth study of a group's behaviors, social rules, and beliefs, as performed in its natural environment (30)

Ethos a set of moral, aesthetic, and evaluative principles (539)

Etic perspective an approach to studying cultures that stresses commonalities across cultures (546)

Evaluative criteria the dimensions used by consumers to compare competing product alternatives (234)

Evoked set those products already in memory plus those prominent in the retail environment that are actively considered during a consumer's choice process (127, 230)

Exchange the process whereby two or more organizations or people give and receive something of value (7)

Exchange theory the perspective that every interaction involves an exchange of value (345)

Expectancy disconfirmation model the perspective that consumers form beliefs about product performance based upon prior experience with the product and/or communications about the product that imply a certain level of quality; their actual satisfaction depends on the degree to which performance is consistent with these expectations (348)

Expectancy theory the perspective that behavior is largely "pulled" by expectations of achieving desirable outcomes, or positive incentives, rather than "pushed" from within (83)

Experience the perception of stimuli that causes changes in attitudes or behavior (62)

Experiential perspective an approach stressing the gestalt or totality of the product or service experience, focusing on consumers' affective responses in the marketplace (219)

Exploratory research a type of consumer research performed to learn more about a consumer issue; usually the researcher does not have a prediction in advance, but is collecting data in order to help design future research (23)

Exposure an initial stage of perception where some sensations come within range of consumers' sensory receptors (62)

Extended Family traditional family structure where several generations live together (253)

Extended problem solving an elaborate decision-making process, often initiated by a motive that is fairly central to the self-concept and accompanied by perceived risk; the consumer tries to collect as much information as possible, and carefully weighs product alternatives (219)

Extended self the definition of self created by the external objects with which one surrounds oneself (299)

Extinction the process whereby a learned connection between a stimulus and response is eroded so that the response is no longer reinforced (115)

Fad a very short-lived fashion (573)

Family household a housing unit containing at least two people who are related by blood or marriage (253)

Family life cycle a classification scheme that segments consumers in terms of changes in income and family composition and the changes in demands placed upon this income (260)

Fantasy a self-induced shift in consciousness, often focusing on some unattainable or improbable goal; sometimes fantasy is a way of compensating for a lack of external stimulation or for dissatisfaction with the actual self (292)

Fashion life cycle the "career" or stages in the life of a fashion as it progress from introduction to obsolescence (572)

Fashion system those people and organizations involved in creating symbolic meanings and transferring these meanings to cultural goods (565)

Fear appeal an attempt to change attitudes or behavior through the use of threats or by the highlighting of negative consequences of noncompliance with the request (198)

Figure–ground relationship the gestalt principle whereby one part of a stimulus configuration dominates a situation while other aspects recede into the background (70)

Focus groups a qualitative research technique that gathers information from group interaction that is focused on a series of topics introduced by a discussion leader or moderator (24)

Fraudulent symbols the symbols, once associated with a specific social class, that diffuse through society and lose their original meaning and value (428)

Functional theory of attitudes a pragmatic approach that focuses on how attitudes facilitate social behavior; attitudes exist because they serve some function for the person (148)

Geodemographics techniques that combine consumer demographic information with geographic consumption patterns to permit precise targeting of consumers with specific characteristics (525)

Gestalt psychology a school of thought that maintains people derive meaning from the totality of a set of stimuli, rather than from any individual stimulus (67)

Gift-giving ritual the events involved in the presentation and acceptance of a gift (594)

Goal a consumer's desired end state (81)

Habitual decision making the consumption choices that are made out of habit, without additional information search or deliberation among products (219)

Heuristics the mental rules of thumb that lead to a speedy decision (237)

Hierarchy of effects a fixed sequence of steps that occurs during attitude formation; this sequence varies depending upon such factors as the consumer's level of involvement with the attitude object (149)

Homeostasis the state of being where the body is in physiological balance; goal-oriented behavior attempts to reduce or eliminate an unpleasant motivational state and return to a balanced one (82)

Hyperreality a phenomenon associated with modern advertising in which what is initially simulation or hype becomes real (71)

Id the system oriented toward immediate gratification (95)

Ideal of beauty a model, or exemplar, of appearance valued by a culture (310)

Impulse buying a process that occurs when the consumer experiences a sudden urge to purchase an item that he or she cannot resist (341)

Individualism a cultural orientation that encourages people to attach more importance to personal goals than to group goals; values such as personal enjoyment and freedom are stressed (539)

Inertia the process whereby purchase decisions are made out of habit because the consumer lacks the motivation to consider alternatives (83, 240)

Information search the process whereby a consumer searches for appropriate information to make a reasonable decision (223)

Informational social influence the conformity that occurs because the group's behavior is taken as evidence about reality (376)

Innovation a product or style that is perceived as new by consumers (561)

Instrumental values those goals that are endorsed because they are needed to achieve desired end states, or terminal values (551)

Interference a process whereby additional learned information displaces the earlier information, resulting in memory loss for the item learned previously (132)

Interpretation the process whereby meanings are assigned to stimuli (67)

Interpretivism a research perspective that produces a "thick description" of consumers' subjective experiences and stresses the importance of the individual's social construction of reality (21)

Involvement the motivation to process product-related information (83)

JND (Just Noticeable Difference) the minimum change in a stimulus that can be detected by a perceiver (58)

Lateral cycling a process where already-purchased objects are old to others or exchanged for other items (350)

Learning a relatively permanent change in a behavior caused by experience (110)

Lifestyle a set of shared values or tastes exhibited by a group of consumers, especially as these are reflected in consumption patterns (438)

Likert scale a numerical scale used to measure attitudes; the respondent indicates the extent to which he or she agrees or disagrees with a statement about some attitude object (33)

Limited problem solving a problem-solving process in which consumers are not motivated to search for information or to rigorously evaluate each alternative; they instead use simple decision rules to arrive at a purchase decision (219)

Long-term memory the system that allows us to retain information for a long period of time (126)

Market beliefs the specific beliefs or decision rules pertaining to marketplace phenomena (238)

Market maven a person who often serves as a source of information about marketplace activities (386)

Marketing mix the combination of variables over which marketers have control; these factors are often known as the "Four P's": product, place, price, and promotion (10)

Materialism the importance consumers attach to worldly possessions (442)

Means–end chain model an approach to studying values in which very specific product attributes are assumed to be linked at levels of increasing abstraction to terminal values (552)

Memory a process of acquiring information and storing it over-time so that it will be available when needed (124)

Metaphor the use of an explicit comparison ("A" is "B") between a product and some other person, place, or thing (200)

Motivation an internal state that activates goal-oriented behavior (81)

Motivational research a qualitative research approach, based on

psychoanalytic (Freudian) interpretations, with a heavy emphasis on unconscious motives for consumption (97)

Multi-attribute attitude models those models that assume that a consumer's attitude (evaluation) of an attitude object depends on the beliefs he or she has about several or many attributes of the object; the use of a multi-attribute model implies that an attitude toward a product or brand can be predicted by identifying these specific beliefs and combining them to derive a measure of the consumer's overall attitude (165)

Myth a story containing symbolic elements that expresses the shared emotions and ideals of a culture (541)

National character a distinctive set of behavior and personality characteristics that describe a country's people or culture (547)

Negative reinforcement the process whereby the environment weakens responses to stimuli so that inappropriate behavior is avoided (114)

New-collar workers a segment of consumers, primarily twenty-one to forty years old, who occupy a gray area between professional and blue collar jobs; these people tend to hold many traditional values but are also receptive to new values and lifestyles (512)

Noncompensatory decision rules a set of simple rules used to evaluate competing alternatives; a brand with a low standing on one relevant attribute is eliminated from the consumer's choice set (235)

Normative influence the process in which a reference group helps to set and enforce fundamental standards of conduct (367)

Normative social influence the conformity that occurs when a person alters his or her behavior to meet the expectations of a person or group (376)

Norms the informal rules that govern what is right or wrong (374)

Nostalgia a bittersweet emotion where the past is viewed with sadness and longing; many "classic" products appeal to consumers' memories of their younger days (133)

Nuclear family a contemporary living arrangement composed of a married couple and their children (253)

Observational learning the process in which people learn by watching the actions of others and noting the reinforcements they receive for their behaviors (117)

Operant conditioning the process by which the individual learns to perform behaviors that produce positive outcomes and to avoid those that yield negative outcomes (114)

Opinion leaders those people who are knowledgeable about products and who are frequently able to influence others' attitudes or behaviors with regard to a product category (385)

Paradigm a widely-accepted view or model of phenomena being studied; the perspective that regards people as rational information processors is currently the dominant paradigm, though this approach is now being challenged by a new wave of research that emphasizes the frequently subjective nature of consumer decision making (21)

Parental yielding the process that occurs when a parental decision maker is influenced by a child's product request (266)

Parody display the deliberate avoidance of widely used status symbols, whereby the person seeks status by mocking it (429)

Perceived age how old a person feels rather than his or her true chronological age (515)

Perceived risk the belief that use of a product has potentially negative consequences, either physical or social (228)

Perception the process by which stimuli are selected, organized, and interpreted (49)

Personality a person's unique psychological makeup, which consistently influences the way the person responds to his or her environment (289)

Persuasion an active attempt to change attitudes (181)

Pleasure principle the belief that behavior is guided by the desire to maximize pleasure and avoid pain (95)

Point of purchase stimuli (POP) the promotional materials that are deployed in stores or other outlets to influence consumers' decisions at the time products are purchased (342)

Positive reinforcement the process whereby rewards provided by the environment strengthen responses to stimuli (114)

Positivism a research perspective that relies on principles of the "scientific method" and assumes that a single reality exists; events in the world can be objectively measured, and the causes of behavior can be identified, manipulated, and predicted (21)

Principle of cognitive consistency the belief that consumers value harmony among their thoughts, feelings, and behaviors and that they are motivated to maintain uniformity among these elements (156)

Principle of similarity the Gestalt principle that describes how consumers tend to group objects that share similar physical characteristics (70)

Problem recognition the process that occurs whenever the consumer sees a significant difference between his or her current state of affairs and some desired or ideal state; this recognition initiates the decision-making process (220)

Product complementarity the view that products in different functional categories have symbolic meanings that are related to one another (441)

Product placement the process of obtaining exposure for a product by arranging for it to be inserted into a movie, television show, or some other medium (604)

Profane consumption the process of consuming objects and events that are ordinary or of the everyday world (587)

Progressive learning model the perspective that people gradually learn a new culture as they increasingly come in contact with it; consumers assimilate into a new culture, mixing practices from their old and new environments to create a hybrid culture (483)

Projective techniques the presentation of an ambiguous, unstructured object, activity, or person to which the consumer responds in some way (explaining the object, telling a story about it, drawing a picture of it, etc.); projectives are used when it is believed that a consumer will not or cannot respond meaningfully to direct questioning (25)

Psychographics the use of psychological, sociological, and anthropological factors to construct market segments (447)

Psychophysics the science that focuses on how the physical environment is integrated into the consumer's subjective experience (57)

Punishment the learning that occurs when a response is followed by unpleasant events (114)

Rank-order scale a measuring device that asks respondents to rank a set of products or stores in terms of their order of preference on some criterion (33)

Rational perspective a view of the consumer as a careful, analytical decision maker who tries to maximize utility in purchase decisions (217)

Reactance a "boomerang effect" that sometimes occurs when consumers are threatened with a loss of freedom of choice; they respond by doing the opposite of the behavior advocated in a persuasive message (380)

Reality engineering the process whereby elements of popular culture are appropriated by marketers and become integrated into marketing strategies; examples of this phenomenon include infomercials and product placement (604)

Reality principle the ego seeks ways to gratify the id that will be acceptable to society (95)

Reference group an actual or imaginary individual or group that has a significant effect upon an individuals' evaluations, aspirations, or behavior (365)

Relationship marketing the strategic perspective that stresses the long-term, human side of buyer/seller interactions (346)

Resonance a literary device, frequently used in advertising, that uses a play on words (a double meaning) to communicate a product benefit (200)

Retrieval the process whereby desired information is accessed from long-term memory (124)

Rites of passage sacred times marked by a change in social status (598)

Ritual a set of multiple, symbolic behaviors that occurs in a fixed sequence and that tend to be repeated periodically (593)

Ritual artifacts items (consumer goods) used in the performance of rituals (593)

Sacralization a process that occurs when ordinary objects, events, or people take on sacred meaning to a culture or to specific groups within a culture (588)

Sacred consumption the process of consuming objects and events that are set apart from normal life and treated with some degree of respect or awe (587)

Schema an organized collection of beliefs and feelings represented in a cognitive category (50)

Self-concept the attitude a person holds toward him- or herself (289)

Self-gifts the products or services bought by consumers for their own use as a reward or consolation (595)

Self-image congruence models the approaches based on the prediction that products will be chosen when their attributes match some aspect of the self (298)

Self-perception theory an alternative explanation of dissonance effects; it assumes that people use observations of their own behavior to infer their attitudes toward some object (158)

Semantic-differential scale a numerical scale that presents respondents with a set of bipolar (opposing) adjectives; a concept or product is then rated in terms of its standing on the dimension (33)

Semiotics a field of study that examines the correspondence between a sign and the meaning or meanings it conveys (72)

Sensation the immediate response of sensory receptors (eyes, ears, nose, mouth, fingers) to such basic stimuli as light, color, and sound (49)

Sensory memory the temporary storage of information received from the senses (125)

Sex-typed traits characteristics that are stereotypically associated with one sex or the other (302)

Shopping orientation a consumer's general attitudes and motivations regarding the act of shopping (336)

Short-term memory the system that allows us to retain information for a short period of time (125)

Single-source data a compilation of information that includes different aspects of consumption and demographic data for a common consumer segment (525)

Sleeper effect the process whereby differences in attitude change between positive and negative sources seem to diminish over time (189)

Social class the overall rank of people in a society; people who are grouped within the same social class are approximately equal in terms of their social standing, occupations, and lifestyles (407)

Social comparison theory the perspective that people compare their outcomes with others' as a way to increase the stability of their own self-evaluation, especially when physical evidence is unavailable (377)

Social judgment theory the perspective that people assimilate new information about attitude objects in light of what they already know or feel; the initial attitude acts as a frame of reference, and new information is categorized in terms of this standard (158)

Social marketing the promotion of causes and ideas (social products), such as energy conservation, charities, and population control (146)

Social mobility the movement of individuals from one social class to another (410)

Social power the capacity of one person to alter the actions or outcome of another (371)

Social stratification the process in a social system by which scarce and valuable resources are distributed unequally to status positions that become more or less permanently ranked in terms of the share of valuable resources each receives (409)

Social Trends the broad directions in which a society is moving (455)

Sociometric methods the techniques for measuring group dynamics that involve the tracing of communication patterns in and among groups (390)

Source attractiveness the dimensions of a communicator that increase his or her persuasiveness; these include expertise and attractiveness (184)

Source credibility a communications source's perceived expertise, objectivity, or trustworthiness (183)

Standard Metropolitan Statistical Area (SMSA) a major market area as defined by the U.S. Census Bureau, used as a reference by market researchers, manufacturers, and retailers (520)

Status crystallization the extent to which different indicators of a person's status (income, ethnicity, occupation) are consistent with one another (414)

Status hierarchy a ranking of social desirability in terms of consumers' access to such resources as money, education, and luxury goods (409)

Status symbols products that are purchased and displayed to signal membership in a desirable social class (425)

Stimulus ambiguity a condition occurring when the meanings conveyed by an ad are unclear; ambiguous stimuli will usually be interpreted in a way that is consistent with the consumer's own set of needs and motives (67)

Stimulus discrimination the process that occurs when behavior caused by two stimuli is different, as when consumers learn to differentiate a brand from its competitors (114)

Stimulus generalization the process that occurs when the behavior caused by a reaction to one stimulus occurs in the presence of other, similar stimuli (113)

Storage the process that occurs when knowledge entered in long-term memory is integrated with what is already in memory and "warehoused" until needed (124)

Store image a store's "personality," composed of such attributes as location, merchandise suitability, and the knowledge and congeniality of the sales staff (340)

Subculture a group whose members share beliefs and common experiences that set them apart from other members of a culture (468)

Subliminal perception the processing of information presented below the level of the consumer's awareness (59)

Superego the system that internalizes society's rules and that works to prevent the id from seeking selfish gratification (95)

Surrogate consumer a professional who is retained to evaluate and/or make purchases on behalf of a consumer (388)

Symbolic interactionism a sociological approach stressing that relationships with other people play a large part in forming the self; people live in a symbolic environment, and the meaning attached to any situation or object is determined by a person's interpretation of these symbols (295)

Symbolic self-completion theory the perspective that people who have an incomplete self-definition in some context will compensate by acquiring symbols associated with a desired social identity (297)

Syncratic decisions those purchase decisions that are made jointly by both spouses (263)

Synoptic ideal a model of spousal decision making where the husband and wife take a common view and act as joint decision makers, assigning each other well-defined roles and making mutually beneficial decisions to maximize the couple's joint utility (265)

Targeted marketing strategy an approach that defines both a market and the tactics used by the organization to satisfy that market (10)

Taste cultures a group of consumers who share aesthetic and intellectual preferences (417)

Terminal values end states desired by members of a culture (551)

The Nine Nations of North America a geographical classification scheme that divides America into separate "nations" within the geographical boundaries of the United States and Canada, each with its own priorities, customs, and consumption patterns (523)

Theory of reasoned action an updated version of the Fishbein multi-attribute attitude theory that considers such factors as social pressure and A_{act} (the attitude toward the act of buying a product), rather than attitudes toward just the product itself (168)

Trait the identifiable characteristics that define a person (290)

Trickle-down theory of fashion the perspective that fashions spread as the result of status symbols associated with the upper classes "trickling down" to other social classes as these consumers try to emulate those with greater status (570)

20/80 rule a rule-of-thumb in volume segmentation that says that about 20% of consumers in a product category (the heavy users) account for about 80% of sales (448)

Two-factor theory the perspective that two separate psychological processes are operating when a person is repeatedly exposed to an ad; repetition increases familiarity and thus reduces uncertainty about the product but over time boredom increases with each exposure, and at some point the amount of boredom incurred begins to exceed the amount of uncertainty reduced, resulting in wearout (191)

Value system a culture's ranking of the relative importance of values (540)

Values and Lifestyles (VALS) a psychographic segmentation system used to categorize consumers into clusters, or "VALS Types" (451)

Want the particular form of consumption chosen to satisfy a need (81)

Weber's Law the principle that the stronger the initial stimulus, the greater its change must be for it to be noticed (58)

Word-of-mouth communication (WOM) the information transmitted by individual consumers on an informal basis (381)

Worldview the ideas shared by members of a culture about principles of order and fairness (539)

Author Index

Heiman, M., 299
Heistand, M., 546
Hennessey, J. E., 198
Hernandez, S. A., 483
Herr, P. M., 171, 233
Hill, J. S., 445
Hill, R. P., 351, 410
Hirsch, P. M., 556
Hirschman, E. C., 556, 601
Hoch, S. J., 83, 220, 265
Hofacker, C. F., 290
Homer, P. M., 551
Hopper, J. S., 266
Hornik, J., 349
Houston, M. J., 131
Howard, D. R., 267, 595
Howe, N., 501
Hoyer, W. D., 128
Huber, J., 229
Hudson, L. A., 21
Hui, M., 469
Hume, S., 240
Hutchinson, J. W., 230, 231
Hutton, D. G., 288
Hwang, S. L., 240

Insko, C. A., 191

Jacoby, J., 128, 227
Jain, D., 561
James, C., 561
James, W., 295
Janiszewski, C., 114
John, D. R., 231
Johnson, B., 260
Johnson, R. D., 129
Jolibert, A., 345
Joy, A., 469

Kahle, L. R., 551
Kahn, A., 559
Kaiser, S. B., 297
Kambara, K., 597
Kamins, M. A., 488
Kanner, B., 52
Kaplan, G. M., 314
Kardes, F. R., 205
Kassarjian, H. H., 25, 26
Kaufman, C. F., 483
Kay, L., 592
Kelly, R. F., 592
Kesler, L., 260
Key, W. B., 60

Heider, F., 177
Heisley, D. D., 43
Heitmeyer, J. R., 398
Hendon, D. W., 434
Henry, W. A., 142, 143
Hernandez, S. A., 496
Herr, P. M., 142
Herrington, J. D., 355
Heslin, R., 209
Heslop, L. A., 249
Heyn, D., 322
Higie, R. A., 211, 398
Hill, J. S., 320, 578
Hill, R., 105, 210, 434, 610
Hine, T., 282
Hines, M. deCourcy, 284
Hirsch, J., 609
Hirschman, E. C., 8, 76, 106, 142, 209, 247,
    321, 435, 496, 497, 579
Hjorth-Andersen, Chr., 248
Hochswender, W., 76, 281
Hofacker, C. F., 319
Hofmann, D., 609
Hofstede, G., 577
Holak, S. L., 579
Holbrook, M. B., 42, 76, 106, 175, 176, 177,
    319, 357, 358, 435, 530, 609
Hollie, P. G., 209
Hollingshead, A. B., 434
Holman, R. H., 281, 354
Holsey, M., 435
Homans, G. C., 356
Homer, P. M., 208, 578
Hong, J. W., 320, 578
Hong, Sung-Tai, 249
Hook, S., 355
Hornik, J., 76, 354
Horowitz, R. A., 464, 530
Horsley, K., 283
Horton, C., 611
Horton, D., 611
House, J. S., 419, 435
Houston, M. J., 42, 105, 142, 143, 209
Hovland, C. I., 176, 208, 209
Howe, N., 530
Hoyer, W. D., 42, 247, 248, 356, 496
Huber, J., 247
Hudson, L. A., 22, 578
Huey, J., 463
Huffman, D. E., 434
Hui, M., 495
Hull, J. G., 319
Hunnicutt, G. G., 284
Hunt, J. B., 211
Hunt, S., 357
Hupp, G., 321
Hutchinson, J. W., 246, 247, 354
Hutton, D. G., 319

Iacobucci, D., 358
Ibrahim, Y. M., 281
Inkster, J. A., 176
Innis, D. E., 357
Insko, C. A., 141, 176, 248, 397
Isherwood, Baron C., 463
Isler, L., 282
Itoi, K., 282
Iyer, E., 321
Iyer, E. S., 303, 356

Jackson, A., 357
Jackson, D. N., 397
Jacobson, R., 357
Jacoby, J., 42, 177, 248, 319, 350, 358
Jaffe, F., 282
Jaffe, L. J., 321
Jagis, M. B., 247
Jain, S. C., 435
Janis, I., 611
Jaworski, B. J., 106
Jayanti, R., 357
Jhally, S., 107, 463
Joachimsthaler, E. A., 319, 464
Johansson, J. K., 249
Johar, J. S., 175
John, D. R., 141, 142, 248, 357. *See also*
    Roedder, D. L.
Johnson, B., 611
Johnson, D. L., 397
Johnson, E. J., 142, 143, 246
Johnson, K. A., 321
Johnson, M. D., 247
Jones, R. A., 397
Joseph, W. B., 208
Joseph, W. F., 495
Joy, A., 464, 495
Jung, Mary, 322

Kahl, J., 434
Kahle, L. R., 176, 208, 465, 531, 578
Kahn, B. E., 246
Kahneman, D., 248
Kaigler-Walker, K., 530
Kaiser, S. B., 283, 571, 573, 579
Kakkar, P., 354
Kalyanaram, G., 142
Kamakura, W. A., 579
Kamen, J. M., 208
Kamins, M. A., 208, 209
Kangun, N., 210
Kanner, B., 42, 141, 356
Kanter, R. M., 463
Kapferer, J.-N., 87, 106
Kardes, F. R., 142, 210
Kassarjian, H. H., 106, 319, 354
Katona, G., 404, 434
Katosh, J. P., 177
Katz, D., 75, 148
Katz, E., 398
Kaufman, C. F., 333, 354, 496
Kavas, A., 177
Kazuo, K., 282
Keenan, W., Jr., 356
Kegerreis, R. J., 398
Keitner, V., 435
Kellaris, J. J., 141
Keller, Bill, 611
Keller, K. L., 141, 142
Kelley, H. H., 396, 397
Kelman, H. C., 176, 208, 209
Kern, R., 496
Kernan, J. B., 77, 320, 399
Kiel, G. C., 247
Kilburn, D., 76
Kiley, D., 43
Kim, C., 495
Kindel, S., 282
Kindler, M. D., 578
King, C. W., 389, 398, 580

Mackenzie, S. B., 202
Macklin, M. C., 275
Madansky, M., 349
Madrigal, R., 267
Maines, J., 536
Marks, L. J., 488
Markus, H., 368
Matter, W., 368
Meadow, H. L., 290
Meyer, Marianne, 336
Meyer, T. P., 481
Meyers-Levy, J., 86
Michaels, J., 148
Miller, A., 163, 268, 470
Miller, C., 50
Miniard, P. W., 170
Mitchell, A. A., 190
Moore, T. E., 59
Morris, C., 53
Moschis, G. P., 268
Mowen, J. C., 158
Murr, A., 489
Murray, J. B., 22

Narayna, C., 349
Nedungadi, P., 152
Newman, J. W., 348

McIntyre, S. H., 356
Mackenzie, S. B., 176, 209
McKeogh, K. L., 396
Mackie, D. M., 321
McKinney, R. E., 434
Macklin, M. C., 284
McNeal, J. U., 106
McQuarrie, E. F., 106, 177, 201, 211, 578
McQueen, J., 211
McSweeney, F. K., 141
Madden, C. S., 208
Madden, T. J., 141, 210
Magiera, M., 496
Magrath, A. J., 358
Maheswaran, D., 321
Maister, D. H., 354
Malafarina, K., 175
Malcolm, A., 530
Malhotra, N. K., 42, 321
Mander, Jerry, 107
Manrai, L. A., 354
Maples, M. G., 322
Marin, R., 208
Markee, N. L., 322
Markham, W., 283
Marks, J., 531
Marks, L. J., 192, 209
Markus, H., 319, 396
Marlowe, J., 247
Marmorstein, H., 248
Marquardt, D., 322
Marriott, M., 495
Marshall, D. P., 141
Martilla, J. A., 398
Martin, C. R., Jr., 176, 531
Martin, I., 358
Martineau, P., 106
Marty, M. E., 609
Marx, Karl, 407
Maslow, A., 93, 106
Mason, J. B., 531
Mayer, J. D., 335, 355
Mayer, R. N., 283
Mazis, M. B., 176
Mazursky, D., 177, 209
Mazzon, J. A., 579
Mead, G. H., 42, 320
Mehta, A., 578
Meier, B., 2089
Menasco, M. B., 283
Mendoza, J. L., 580
Menzel, H., 398
Merikle, P. M., 76
Merton, R., 398
Messaris, P., 611
Messick, S., 397
Meyer, Marianne, 356
Meyer, Michael, 495
Meyer, R. J., 246
Meyers-Levy, J., 143, 248, 321
Michalowska, A., 578
Michman, R. D., 464
Mick, D. G., 77, 201, 211, 596, 610
Midgley, D. F., 247
Milbank, C. R., 435
Mill, K., 530
Millar, M., 397

Miller, A., 28, 42, 43, 177, 531, 579
Miller, C., 42, 208, 356, 434, 496, 577
Miller, G. A., 142
Miller, K. E., 354
Miller, L. C., 319
Miller, N., 397
Mills, C. W., 496
Mills, J., 208
Milner, L. M., 577
Minardi, D., 322
Miniard, P. W., 355
Minzesheimer, Bob, 531
Mischel, W., 319
Misra, S., 578
Mitchell, A. A., 105, 177, 191, 209, 211
Mitchell, Arnold, 451
Mittal, B., 175, 356
Molloy, J. T., 435
Monroe, K. B., 248, 357
Montgomery, D., 435
Moore, D. L., 876
Moore, J., 397
Moore, R., 611
Moore, T. E., 76
Moore, W. L., 247
Moorman, C., 106
Morgan, M., 611
Morganosky, M. A., 249
Morrell, R. W., 142
Morris, C., 76
Moschis, G. P., 283, 397, 611
Mowen, J. C., 246
Muderrisoglu, A., 578
Muehling, D. D., 176, 210
Munson, J. M., 106, 434, 578
Murata, S., 577
Murphy, P. E., 42
Murray, H., 92
Murray, V., 495
Murrow, D., 396
Murry, J. P., Jr., 176, 464
Mussey, D., 578
Myers, J. H., 398
Myers, P. N., Jr., 319

Nader, R., 18
Naruyama, G., 397
Nasar, J. L., 320
Nast, T., 545
Nataraajan, R., 610
Netemeyer, R. G., 356, 396
Newcomb, P., 187
Nicosia, F. M., 357
Nie, N. H., 496
Niepold, M. M., 530
Noble, B. P., 172, 177
Notarantonio, E. M., 176

Oakes, W. F., 141
Obermiller, C., 211
O'Connor, P. J., 282
O'Guinn, T. C., 496, 610, 611
Oh, Sejo, 357
O'Hare, W., 495
Okabe, M., 209
O'Keefe, R., 495
Oliver, B., 611
Olshavsky, R. W., 246
Olson, J. C., 105, 209, 211, 579

Subject Index

consumer satisfaction or dissatisfaction (CS/D), 348
consumption
   conspicuous, 426
   high-risk, 80
   sacred vs. profane, 587
contralateral conduction, 114
coupons, 342
credit cards, affinity cards, 439
critical theory, 22
cultural categories, 566, 568
cultural context
   attention-getting devices and, 65
   bilingual films and, 479
   ethnic foods and, 479, 489
   ethnic marketing and, 479, 480
   export of Western culture and, 443, 445, 446
   family decision making and, 266
   minority shoppers and, 473
   sex roles and, 305, 307
   television in Europe and, 269
   time and, 331
   women as property and, 601

individual vs. aggregate, 19–20
people in the marketplace and, 4–8
purchase and postpurchase activities, 326–52
purchase environment and, 336–46
situational effects on, 328–36
wheel of, 36–37
consumer behavior (field), 7, 18–22, 38, 620. See also consumer research
   career opportunities in, 18, 615–16
   consumers defined for, 8
   consumption process and, 7
   demographic developments and, 584–87
   interdisciplinary influences in, 18–20, 38
   lifestyle developments and, 584–87
   micro vs. macro levels of analysis and, 19–20
   professional organizations in, 616
   pyramid of consumer behavior and, 19–20
   resources on, 616–17
   strategic focus and, 20–21
Consumer Behavior Odyssey, 30
consumer boycotts, 384
consumer confidence, 404–5, 620
consumer education, brand loyalty and, 243
consumer group, 440
consumerism
   age of, 17–18
   public policy and, 16–18
consumer research. See also consumer behavior (field); motivational research; psychographics
   aesthetic, 560
   children and, 273
   classification of human needs and, 92–93
   conclusive, 23, 30–33
   consumer welfare and, 18
   exploratory, 23–30
   exploratory compared with conclusive, 23, 24, 38
   Freud and, 95–96, 97
   measurement of involvement and, 86–88
   methods in, 22–30
   positivist vs. interpretivist approach in, 21–22, 38
   primary data in, 33–35, 38
   quantitative surveys and, 447
   research design and, 22–23
   secondary data in, 35–36, 38, 613–14
   trait theory in, 290–91
   types of data in, 33–36
consumers, 8, 38, 620
   as "black boxes," in behavioral learning theories, 111
   as commodities, 601
   control over exposure to commercials, 63–64
   fanatic, 80
   impact of marketing on, 14–18
   impact on marketing strategy, 8–13
   marketing ethics and, 15–16
   misuse of products by, 18, 586, 599–603
   opinion leaders vs. other consumer types, 386–88
   planners vs. impulse purchasers, 341, 342
   as problem solvers, 216–20
   as role players, 8, 38
   sensation-seeking, 105
   shopping orientation and, 336
   surrogate, 388
   "typical," 11, 12

consumer satisfaction or dissatisfaction (CS/D), 346–49, 620
   consumer action on, 348–49
   expectations and, 348
   perceptions of quality and, 346–49
   product failures and, 348
consumer socialization, 268–69, 620
Consumers Union, 276
consumer welfare, 17, 18
consumption. See also sacred consumption
   addictive, 600–601
   advertising and, 103
   anticonsumption and, 602–3
   black/white differences in, 473
   conspicuous, 426–27
   culture and, 536–38
   effects of family structure on, 260–62
   environmental effects of, 585–86
   as goal (see materialism)
   hedonic, 51
   motives for, 98
   nonconsumption as lifestyle and, 459
   patterns of, 103, 462–63, 486
   process of, 7
   regional groups and, 520–23
   religious subcultures and, 486, 490–91
   sacred vs. profane, 587–89
   self-concept and, 296–99
consumption constellations, 441–42, 620
contamination, 589, 592
continuous innovation, 564, 620
contrast, creation of, 66
contrast effect, 159
convention (cultural), 541
co-oriented peer, 377
core values, 550, 620
cosmetic surgery, 314–15
Council of Better Business Bureaus, Inc., 275
counterarguments, 203
country-of-origin information, 243
coupons, 341
covariation, 238
CPS. See culture production system (CPS)
CR. See conditioned response
craft product, 557, 620
creative placement, 605
credentialing, 374
credibility
   attitude change and, 183–84
   celebrity endorsements, 188, 199
   enhancement of, 183–84
   knowledge bias and, 184
   source biases and, 184
credit cards
   affinity cards, 372
   buying styles and, 140
   classical conditioning and, 113
crescive norms, 541
cross-sectional research design, 31
CS. See conditioned stimulus
CS/D. See consumer satisfaction or dissatisfaction (CS/D)
cue check, 50
cues, perceptual, 6
cultivation effect, 606, 620
cultivation hypothesis, 269, 620
cultivation theory, 269, 620
cultural categories, 566, 620
   interdependence among product meanings and, 566–67

cultural context. *See also* **ethnic subculture;** international marketing; multicultural dimensions
  conformity and, 376
  consumer behavior and, 41
  consumer involvement and, 88
  consumer needs and, 102
  dimensions of variability and, 539
  export of Western culture and, 442–47
  gift-giving ritual and, 595
  Maslow hierarchy and, 94
  negotiations and, 345
  psychogenic needs and, 90
  stimulus discrimination and, 113
  symbolism in marketing and, 71
  television in Europe and, 275–76
  time and, 332, 333
cultural formula, 558, 620
cultural integration, 481–83
cultural values, 5
culture, 538, 620. *See also* popular culture
  consumption and, 536–38
  creation of, 554–61
  effects of, 538
  functional areas of, 539
  global marketing and, 546–49
  high vs. low art and, 557–59
  marketing and, 538–39
  myths and, 541–46
  variability among cultures and, 539
culture production system (CPS), 556–557, 620
custom, 541
customer affairs representatives, 615

death industry, 599
decay, 132, 620
decision making
  evaluation of alternatives, 229–43
  in the family, 252–53, 262–68, 504
  by groups, 378–79
  household decision roles, 267–68
  individual, 216–46, 252
  information search and, 223–29
  in-store, 340–46
  perspectives on, 217–19
  problem recognition and, 220–23
  social class and, 416–29
  stages in, 217
  types of decisions made by families, 267
  types of decisions made by individuals, 219–20
decision polarization, 379, 620
decision rules, 220, 234–37
  compensatory, 237
  noncompensatory, 235–36
de-ethnicitization, 470, 620
deindividuation, 379
  defined, 378, 621
demarketing, 490
demographics, 5, 253, 447, 621. *See also* **geodemographics; psychographics**
  distinguished from psychographics, 448
  privacy issues for data bases, 36
  segmentation variables and, 13, 38
dependent variables, 31
depth interviews, and motivational research, 97–98
desacralization, 587, 621
descriptive research, 31
determinant attributes, 10, 234, 621
dieting

body image and, 312–13
  cultural effects and, 538
  trend away from, 458–59, 586
differential fertility, 410
differential threshold, 57–59
  defined, 57, 621
diffusion, 538, 561–65, 621
directed learning, 224
Direct Marketing Association, 617
disabled consumers, 310
  as market segment, 14
discontinuous innovation, 564, 621
discounts, market beliefs about, 238
discretionary spending, 403, 404, 507
discrimination, stimulus, 64
displays, 342–44
dissociative cue hypothesis, 189
dissonance, 156
distraction, 198
door-in-the-face technique, 378
downward mobility, 410
drama, 202
dramaturgical perspective, 294
drive, 81, 621
  biological vs. learned needs and, 82–83
dual component model, 190
duration, stimulus, 64
dynamically continuous innovation, 564, 621

early adopters, vs. innovators, 563
eating disorders, 313–14
ecology, cultural, 539
economic consumer, 336
economic psychology. *See* **behavioral economics**
economics of information, 102, 226
ego, 95, 621
ego-defensive function of attitudes, 148–49
ego involvement, 86, 621
The Eight Nations of the United States, 523–24
elaboration, 83
elaboration likelihood model (ELM), 202–5, 621
  research support for, 204–5
elaborative rehearsal, 126
elderly consumers, 512–20
  ideals of beauty and, 516–17
  marketing opportunities and, 514–15
  media and, 518, 519–20
  packaging and, 518–19
  subsegments, 517–18
elimination-by-aspects rule, 236
ELM. *See* **elaboration likelihood model**
embeds, 59–60, 621
emic perspective, 547, 621
emotions. *See also* **affect**
  advertising recall and, 137
  appeals to, in advertising, 194–96
  dimensions of emotional states, 335
  elicited by advertising, 153–55
  forms of message presentation and, 202
  purchase decisions and, 334–35
enacted norms, 541
encoding, 124–26, 621
enculturation, 540, 621
endorsements, by celebrities, 89, 160–61, 188–89
enduring involvement, 86
England, 408

cultural gatekeepers, 556
culture, and marketing, 537
culture production system (CPS), 556
  decision making
    in the family, 349
    stages in, 217
deconstructionism, 21
dieting
  anti-diet rebellion, 313
  body image and, 312
direct marketing, 121
"discount-for-data" system, 338
distraction, 203
door-in-the-face technique, 158

elaboration likelihood model (ELM), 205
elderly consumers, 515, 516
embeds, 60
emergent design, 22
emotions
  dimensions of emotional states, 335
  prediction of behavior and, 170
England, 409

frame of reference, 158
framing, 190
France, Americanization and, 446, 462
fraudulent symbols, 428–29, 622
freedom, need for, 380–81
free will, concept of, 100–101
frequency marketing, 122
Freudian theory, hidden motives and, 95–96, 97
FTC. *See* Federal Trade Commission
functional theory of attitudes, 148–49, 622
fur industry, 180–81

gambling, 600
garbology, 35
gatekeeper, 267
gay consumers, 309
gender identity
    purchasing decisions and, 280–81
    sex role socialization and, 269–70
generalized opinion leader, 385
Generation X. *See* baby busters
geodemographics
    applications of, 525–27, 622
    ClusterPlus system, 525
    PRIZM system, 526–27
geographic segmentation variables, 13. *See also* international marketing; regional groups
gestalt, 67
    perceptual principles based on, 69–70
    of store, 340
Gestalt psychology, 67–69, 622
Get Set, 424–25
gift-giving
    college students and, 508–9
    as ritual, 594–95
gift-giving ritual, 594, 622
gift wrapping, 595
global marketing. *See* international marketing
goal, 81, 622
    distance between present state and, 82
    valence and, 90
goodwill, 240
green marketing, 174–75, 585–86
green movement, 456
grooming rituals, 594
group conformity. *See* conformity
group size, and conformity, 376–77

habitual decision making, 218–220, 622
habituation, 191
hair, sale of, 601
Halloween, 597–98
halo effect, 185
haute couture fashion design, 536, 562
hedonic consumption, 51
hedonic needs, 81, 88–89
heuristics, 237, 265, 622
    brand names as, 239–42
    consumer mood and, 335
    market beliefs as, 238–39
    price as, 239
    product signals as, 237–38
hierarchical processing model, 126
hierarchy of effects, 149–52, 622
Hispanic-Americans, 478–83
    demographic characteristics, 478–80
    marketing strategy and, 480–83
    market segmentation and, 483
historical effects, and attitudes, 172
historic imagery, 51

hitonami consciousness, 454
holiday rituals, 594, 596–98
home, as sacred place, 590
homeostasis, 82, 622
home security industry, 590
homophily, 385
hotel industry, fantasy appeals and, 294
household. *See also* family, the
    family, 253–56
    head of, 255
    nontraditional, 256
humor, in advertising, 197–98
hyperreality, 71, 622

ice cubes, messages in, 60
icon. *see* product icon
id, 95, 622
ideal of beauty, 310, 622
    body decoration and mutilation and, 315–16
    cosmetic surgery and, 314–15
    elderly consumers and, 516–17
    fattism and, 312–14
    historical change in, 310–12
    unrealistic standards and, 312–13
ideal self, 292, 370
identification
    attitudes and, 155
    reference group and, 368–69
identity campaign, 58
identity negotiation, 345
ideology, and culture, 539
illegal activities, 601
immigrant groups, 471–72
importance weights, 165
impulse buying, 341–342, 622
incentives, 83
incidental learning, 110
income, as segmentation variable, 13. *See also* **social class**; wealth
independence hypothesis, 153
independence vs. anticonformity, 380–81
independent variables, 31
index, sign as, 72, 73, 74
indices of class standing, 412–14, 432
individualism, 539, 622
individuality, 288–89, 376
inept set, 230
inertia, 83, 240, 622
    degrees of involvement and, 83–84
inert set, 230
influencer, 8
    as household decision role, 267
    likelihood of compliance and, 377
    teen as, 504
Influentials, 424–25
infomercials, 184, 606
information
    beauty as source of, 185
    economics of, 102, 226
    organization of, 132
    retrieval of, in memory, 128–34
    storage of, in memory, 126–28
informational influence, and reference group, 365, 366
informational social influence, 377–79, 622
information power, 371
information processing
    as approach to memory, 124–26
    capability for, and cognitive development, 271

framing, 131
frequency marketing, 122
"frequent shopper" programs, 338

gambling, 601
gestalt, 68
gift-giving, 551
gift wrapping, 595
green marketing, 349
greeting card industry, 328
grounded theory, 22

heuristics, 237
hierarchy of effects, 150
history (discipline), 31
humor, 197, 198
hyperreality, 71

IDB. *See* Information Display Board (IDB)
ideal of beauty, 312, 313
illness, and cultural differences, 548
imagined ugliness, 312
immigrant groups, 471
indices of class standing, 412
individuality, 288
Influentials, 390
information
    high status consumers and, 417
    omitted, 129
Information Display Board (IDB), 227
information processing, 83
    knowledge structures and, 128
    schemas and, 86

information search, 224, 227
   advertising as prompt to, 220
innovativeness, 290
international marketing, 547
   attention-getting devices
      and, 65
   color associations and, 52, 53
   cosmetic surgery and, 315
   reference groups and, 371
   toys and, 268
Interpretivism (postmodernism), 21, 22
involvement
   controversial advertising
      and, 89
   high-risk consumption and, 80
   political marketing and, 86
   strategies to increase, 85

Japan
   individualism in, 540
   sex roles in, 305
   status craze in, 425
   time poverty in, 331
   Western culture and, 445

knowledge function of
   attitudes, 149
knowledge structures, 128
kosher food, 488, 489

laddering (means-end chain
   model), 128
LAVOA (Life-styles and Values
   of Older Americans)
   project, 518
leisure time, 548
letter carriers, 9
Lifestages typology, 262
lifestyle
   gamblers and, 601
   marketing strategies and, 439

consumer involvement and, 83–84, 204–5
consumer mood and, 334–35
information search, 223–29, 622
   deliberate vs. accidental, 224–25
   determinants of, 226–29
   economics of information and, 226
   framework for, 224
   internal vs. external, 224
   product knowledge and, 227–28
   role of print media in, 225
   types of, 223–25
initiator, as household decision role, 267
inner- vs. outer-directed people, 451, 454
innovation, 561, 622
   adoption of, 562–63
   behavioral demands of, 564
   continuous, 564
   diffusion of, 538, 561–65
   prerequisites for success of, 564–65
   trickle-up effect and, 571
   types of, 563–64
innovative communicators, 386–87
innovativeness
   mature consumers and, 518
   opinion leaders and, 386–87, 518
   as trait, 290
innovators, 563
instinct, 82
instrumental learning. *See* **operant conditioning**
instrumental values, 551, 622
insurance industry, 486
intensity, of stimulus, 57–58, 64
interaction style, 346
interest, stimulation of
   country-of-origin information and, 243
   product categorization and, 233
interference, 132, 622
internalization, and attitudes, 155–56
international marketing. *See also* cultural
   context; multicultural dimensions
   career opportunities in, 615
   consumer involvement and, 88
   consumer needs and, 102
   counterfeit goods and, 113
   cultural differences and, 546–49
   effectiveness of, 549
   export of Western culture and, 442–47
   forms of advertising and, 548
   lifestyle segmentation and, 453–54
   reference groups and, 367
   rumors and, 384
interpersonal need, and family decisions, 267
interpretant, in marketing message, 70
interpretation, 67–73, 622
interpretive studies, 29–30
Interpretivism (postmodernism), 21, 22,
   38, 622
interviews
   depth, and motivational research, 97–98
   personal, 34, 273
inventory shrinkage, 601
involvement, 83, 87–88, 622
   consumer, 83–89
   cultural context and, 88
   defined, 83, 622
   ego, 86
   elaboration-likelihood model and, 204–5
   enduring, 86
   forms of, 85–86
   measurement of, 86–88

message-response, 85–86, 204–5
   product, and family decisions, 268
   purchase, 85
   segmentation of levels of, 88
   strategies to increase, 88–89
involvement profile, 87–88
Japan
   celebrity endorsements and, 187
   family decision-making and, 264
   gift-giving in, 595
   modesty and, 548
   psychographic segmentation in, 454
   status craze in, 425
   vending machines and, 344
   Western culture and, 462, 506
Jewish subculture, 488–90
JND (Just Noticeable Difference), 58, 623
Journal of Consumer Research, 18–19
The Jungle (Sinclair), 17

kin-network system, 265
knockoff, 562
knowledge
   evoked set and, 230
   information search and, 227–28
   levels of, 128
knowledge function of attitudes, 149
knowledge structures, 126–27, 131
kosher food, 490

laddering *See* **means-end chain model**, 552,
   623
language
   fashion system and, 566
   marketing pitfalls and, 481, 549
   "Laskerville," 30
latchkey children, 255
lateral cycling, 350, 623
lattitudes of acceptance and rejection,
   158–59
learning, 110, 623
   behavioral theories, 111–16
   cognitive theory, 116–18
   concept of, 110–11
   consumer socialization of children
      and, 269
   directed, 224
   incidental, 110, 224–25
   instrumental (*see* **operant conditioning**)
   marketing applications of principles of,
      118–23
   observational, 117–18
   procedural, 234
   role of memory in, 123–37
   television and, 269
   vicarious, 110
lecture, 202
legitimate power, 372–73
leisure class, 426–27
lesbian consumers, 309
leveling, 383
lexicographic rule, 236
licensing of brand names, 121
life, stage of. *See also* **age cohort**
   attitude tracking and, 172
   rites of passage and, 598–99
   as segmentation variable, 13
lifestyle, 438–46, 623
   dimensions of, 449
   marketing strategies and, 439
   materialism and, 442, 443
   product complementarity and, 441–42

message, consumer misunderstanding of, 128
Mexico, 443
milk marketing, 26
mood-management theory, 152
motivation, components of
process of, 81
mountain climbing, 80
multiplicative rule, 160
museum exhibit popularity, 35
myth, modern, 543, 544

"natural" products, 54
"nebbies," 501
new ethnic groups, 472
norms, 385
nostalgia, 132, 133

objective self-awareness (OSA)
theory, 289

types of, 124–25
visual vs. verbal, 131
memory trace, 127
men
exercise addiction and, 314
ideal figure for, 314
sex roles and, 307–9
single, 255
mere exposure effect, 191, 368
message
argument construction in, 192–94
as art form, 200–202
characteristics of, and attitude change,
189–202
drama vs. lecture distinction and, 202
impact of, compared with source, 202–5
meaning components in, 70
positive and negative effects in, 189
repetition of, 190–91
rhythm of, 130
source and, 182
symbolism in, 70–71
types of appeals in, 194–200
viewing environment of, and recall,
128–29
vividness of, 190–91
words vs. pictures and, 190
message-response involvement, 85–86,
204–5
metaphor, 200–202, 623
military personnel, as market segment, 14
mindlessness, 116
modeling, 117–18
modernism. *See* **positivism**
monomorphic experts, 385
monomyth, 542
mood, and purchase decisions, 334–35
mood congruence effect, 129–30
more (cultural), 541
motivationl, 81–82, 623
to comply with beliefs, 169
direction of, 89–94
hidden motives and, 94–99
message-processing involvement and,
204–5
for shopping, 335–36
strength of, 82–89
types of conflicts of, 90–91
motivational research, 97–99, 447, 623
movie industry, 504
consumer research and, 560
myths and, 543–44
product tie-ins, 561
multi-attribute attitude models, 165–68,
623
combination of elements in, 166
Fishbein model and, 165–66
strategic applications of, 166–68
weighted additive rule and, 237
multicultural dimensions. *See also* cultural
context; **ethnic subculture**; international marketing
brand image and, 6
celebrity endorsements and, 187
cultural boundaries and, 604
etic approach and, 546
evoked set and, 230
family decision making and, 264
fragrances and, 53
psychographic segmentation and, 450
reference group and, 367

sex roles and, 305
social class and, 408
theory of reasoned action and, 170
time and, 332
vending machines and, 344
multiple-item attitude measurement scales,
163–65
multiple selves, 294–96
music, 54
age cohorts and, 502–3
music industry, cultural specialists in, 557
mystery ads, 130
myth, 541, 623
commercials as, 546
cultural functions of, 541–42
defined,
holiday heroes and, 544–45
modern, 542–44
structure of, 542

national character, 547–49, 623
National Retail Merchants Association, 617
needs
for achievement, 92
for affiliation, 93
biogenic, 89
biological vs. learned, 82–83
classification of, 92–94
creation of artificial, 100–103
hedonic, 81, 88–89, 90, 101
for power, 93
psychogenic, 89
recognition of, 221
types of, 89–90
for uniqueness, 93
utilitarian, 81, 90
vs. wants, 89
negative reinforcement, 114–15, 623
neo-traditionalism, 455
network analysis, 391
new-collar workers, 512, 623
New Grown-Ups, 424–25
The Nine Nations of North America,
523–24, 626
noncompensatory decision rules, 235–36,
623
nonconformists, 380–81
nonconsumption, 459
nonmonotonic relationship, 198
non-store shopping, 337–38
normative beliefs, 169
normative influence, 367–68, 623
normative social influence, 376, 623
norms, 374, 541, 623
conformity and, 374–75
nostalgia, 133–34, 623
age cohort marketing and, 501–3
memory marketing and, 140
nouveau riches, 411, 423–24
novelty, 89, 130. *See also* **innovation**
nuclear family, 253, 623

object, in marketing message, 70
object-attitude linkages, 165
objectification, 589
observational learning, 117, 623
observational research, 34–35
occupation, 13, 411
old money, 421–23
omission, and memory mearsures, 137
ongoing search, 224
on-set product placement, 605

self-gifts, 596
self-image congruence
    models, 299
sensory thresholds, 59
sex
    addiction to, 600
    subliminal perception and, 59
sex roles
    product function and, 303
    stereotypes and, 270, 306
signal detection theory, 137
simulation of environments, 50
smell, and memory, 54, 130
social causes, linking of products
    with, 89
social class, 410
    codes and, 421
    color preference and, 52
    in England, 409
    influence of background
        and, 406
    wealth and, 409
social marketing, 147
softdrinks, 57
source credibility, 188
source effects, 184
souvenirs, 592
sports, 592
spousal influence, 265, 266
status symbols, 429
stimulus generalization, 121
stolen goods, and product dis-
    posal, 351
stuttering, 61

real vs. ideal selves and, 292–94
self-esteem advertising, 291–92
self-fulfilling prophecy, 296, 604
self-fulfillment, emphasis on, 456–57
self-gifts, 595, 596, 625
self-image, situational, 328
self-image congruence models, 298, 625.
    See also congruity theory
    problems with, 298–99
self-monitoring, 291
self-perception theory, 158, 625
self-sufficiency, among the elderly, 518
semantic-differential scale, 33, 625
    attitude measurement and, 164–65
semantic meaning, 124–25
semiotics, 70, 72–73, 74, 625
    social class and, 419–20
sensation, 49, 625
    perception and, 49–50
    sensory systems and, 51–57
sensory advertising, 75
sensory inputs, 51
sensory memory, 125, 625
sensory systems, 51–57
    smell, 53–54
    vision, 52–53
sensory thresholds, 57–59
    absolute, 57
    differential, 57–59
sentence completion technique, 28
sentiment relation, 159
serial reproduction, 383
service scripts, 128
sex
    cultural sensitivities about, 548–49
    embeds and, 59–60
    fashion and, 569–70
    fear appeals and, 198
    in Maslow hierarchy, 94
    product symbolism and, 96
    as segmentation variable, 13
sex appeals, 196
sex roles
    conformity and, 375, 377
    female, 304–7
    gender vs. sexual identity and, 301–9
    male, 307–9
    self-concept and, 300–309
    societal role of marketers and, 585
    variability of cultures and, 539
sex-role socialization
    of children, 269–70
    gender differences in, 300–301
sex-role stereotypes
    advertising and, 280–81
    family decision-making and, 264–65
sex-typed products, 302–3
sex-typed traits, 302–3, 625
sexual dimorphic markers, 312
sharpening, 383
shoplifting, 601–2
shopping
    compulsive, 608
    group influences and, 378
    home shopping parties, 379
    spontaneous, 341
shopping experience, 338–40
shopping motives, 335–36
shopping orientation, 336, 625
short-term memory (STM), 125–26, 625
sign

as component of marketing message, 70
    meaning and, 72–73, 74
signal, product, 237–38
signature goods, 429
sign value, 86
Silent Spring (Carson), 18
similarity, principle of, 70
    social comparison and, 377
SIMMONS Connection
    on consumers' self-concept, 318
    on consumption patterns, 462–63
    on credit card users, 140
    on cultural buying patterns, 494
    on gender-based purchasing decisions,
        280–81
    on green marketing, 174–75
    on high-tech buying behavior, 608
    on Index of Social Position, 432–33
    on magazine readers, 41
    on motorcycle ownership, 395
    on politically sensitive products, 207
simple additive rule, 237
simple processing, 83
simplicity, voluntary, 456
single adult consumers, 255
single-item attitude measurement scales, 163
single-source data, 525, 625
situational effects, 328–35
situational segmentation, 329, 330
situational self-image, 328
slackers. See baby busters
sleeper effect, 188–89, 625
SMSAs. See Standard Metropolitan Statisti-
    cal Areas (SMSAs)
SN. See subjective norm
"snob" effect, 570
social adaptation perspective, 185
social class, 407, 625
    anonymity and, 414
    codes and, 419–20
    components of, 411
    conspicious consumption and, 426–27
    in England, 408
    family decision making and, 264
    family structure and, 414
    fashion and, 570–71
    measurement of, 412–16
    occupational prestige and, 411
    problems with segmentation by, 426
    purchase decisions and, 416–29
    as segmentation variable, 13, 420–25
    taste cultures and, 417–19
    wealth and, 411, 415, 421–23
    women and, 415–16
    worldview and, 416–17
social comparison, 288
social comparison theory, 377–79, 625
social context, and purchase decisions,
    329–30, 331
social influence. See also conformity
    types of, 375–77
socialization of children
    consumer, 268–69
    sex-role, 269–70
    undesirable, 277
social judgment theory, 158–59, 625
social loafing, 378
social marketing, 146–47, 625
    psychographics and, 450–51
social mobility, 410, 625
social power, 371, 625